COMPUTER GRAPHICS

Volume 21 • Number 4 • July 1987
A publication of ACM SIGGRAPH
Production Editor Richard J. Beach

SIGGRAPH '87 Conference Proceedings
July 27-31, 1987, Anaheim, California
Edited by Maureen C. Stone

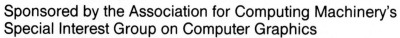

Sponsored by the Association for Computing Machinery's
Special Interest Group on Computer Graphics

The Association for Computing Machinery, Inc.
11 West 42nd Street
New York, New York 10036

ISBN 0-89791-227-6

SIGGRAPH '87 is sponsored by the Association for Computing Machinery's Special Interest Group on Computer Graphics in cooperation with the IEEE Technical Committee on Computer Graphics.

Additional copies may be ordered prepaid from:
ACM Order Department
P.O. Box 64145
Baltimore, MD 21264
ACM Order Number: 428870
ACM Toll Free Number: (800) 342-6626

Price:
Members: $30.00
All Others: $40.00

Manufactured By Promotion Graphics, NY

Printed in the U.S.A.

Contents

Technical Program, Thursday, 30 July 1987

Technical Program, Friday, 31 July 1987

Panel Sessions, Wednesday, 29 July 1987

Panel Sessions, Thursday, 30 July 1987

Panel Sessions, Friday, 31 July 1987

Preface

Welcome to SIGGRAPH '87, the 14th annual ACM Conference on Computer Graphics and Interactive Techniques. These proceedings publish the papers presented in the three days of the Technical Program at the conference and appear as a special issue of *Computer Graphics*. From the 140 submitted papers, 33 have been selected to represent the current state-of-the art in computer graphics research. We are also pleased to publish our first SIGGRAPH parody paper, "Ray-Tracing JELL-O® Brand Gelatin" by Paul Heckbert. The committee agreed unanimously to include it as part of the conference, both for its style and its conciseness.

It is traditional in this preface to discuss how the chosen papers where selected. The process begins when the call for participation is published and distributed at the previous year's SIGGRAPH conference (be sure and pick up the SIGGRAPH '88 call this year). The information in the call is also published in the October issue of *Computer Graphics*. The deadline for paper submission is typically in early January; this year, on January 13th. Nearly all the papers arrive within 2 days of the deadline, either by courier or hand-delivered in the dead of the night by bleary-eyed authors. For two days the technical program chair and her assistant sort, number, and acknowledge papers.

Next, the papers are distributed to the members of the Technical Program Committee, who act as senior reviewers for the papers. Every effort is made to be sure the papers and the reviewers are well matched. I would like to thank Frank Crow and Ed Catmull for their assistance in this very important step of the reviewing process.

Once the papers are assigned, three copies of each paper, including videotapes when available, plus a complete set of instructions and review forms, are sent to the designated senior reviewers as quickly as possible to ensure the maximum amount of time for review (about 6 weeks). Upon receiving the papers, each senior reviewer then distributes them to at least two other qualified reviewers, representing at least two unrelated views. Some fine-tuning of the distribution of papers to senior reviewers usually occurs at this point. Some senior reviewers even volunteer to read additional papers (thank you, Rob Pike).

One week before the Technical Program Committee meets to discuss the papers, summaries of the reviews are due back to the program chair. Around 90% of these come in on time. (Thank you 90%, the rest of you know who you are.) Once all the summaries are received, the papers are ranked and organized and we're ready for the Technical Program Committee Meeting.

The Technical Program Committee meets for two days. These days are spent reviewing the reviews, discussing the papers, arguing, eating, and drinking. During this process, papers may be read by other senior reviewers, groups may meet to compare similar papers, and the program chair may pound on the table. By the end of the two days, the group's opinions have jelled and we are convinced we have the best possible selection for the conference. This process is only as good as the Technical Program Committee and I think this year's committee was excellent. Thank you all very much for your time and energy.

Once the authors have been notified of the results, the list of accepted authors is handed to the SIGGRAPH Editor-in-Chief, who is responsible for producing the final camera-ready copy for the proceedings. This year, the job of Editor-in-Chief has passed from John Beatty to Rick Beach, who has an office conveniently next door to mine. Rick's job includes not only maintaining quality control on 34 authors, but also producing the table of contents, list of reviewers, award announcements, and the other random bits of information needed to make this a complete journal issue. Thank you, Rick, for making us all look so good in print.

I want to conclude with special thanks to Subhana Menis, who has worked as both Rick's and my assistant on SIGGRAPH '87. Subhana is organized, efficient, reliable and a joy to work with. Not only could we not have succeeded without her expert help, but the quality of the result can be directly attributed to her skill and desire for perfection. Thank you, Subhana, you've done a marvellous job.

Rick, Subhana and I would all like to thank our manager, Bob Ritchie, and the Xerox Corporation for supporting us in this grand endeavor. It was a lot of fun.

Maureen Stone
SIGGRAPH '87 Technical Program Chair

Preface to the Panel Summaries

As a part of the technical program, we are excited to offer thirteen panels covering a wide variety of topics and applications in computer graphics. This year, we're especially pleased to publish expanded descriptions of these panels in the SIGGRAPH '87 proceedings. We hope that these write-ups will provide a useful summary of the content of the panel discussions as a well as an archival pointer to issues and references on the panel topics.

Like the paper selection process, panel proposals are solicited in the call for participation. The call is available at the previous year's SIGGRAPH conference and in the fall issue of *Computer Graphics*. Information in the call describes the technical areas for the conference, suggested panel formats, information to be included in submitting a panel proposal and the deadline for submission.

Thirty-one panel proposals were received. Each panel committee member was asked to read all proposals and to formally review a selected subset of them. Each panel proposal was reviewed by at least three members of the panel committee, and review forms were returned to panel proposers.

After review forms were collected and summarized, the panel committee met to determine the final selection of panels for SIGGRAPH '87. The review forms and discussion focused on selecting panels that would appeal to a broad audience of computer graphics professionals, that would offer new insights or raise new questions, and that would provide an effective format for presenting information. The selection process is never easy and we thank all panel proposers for an interesting range of topics and issues.

The panel committee asked two of the panel chairs to include discussants in their panels. A panel discussant is a computer graphics professional who is not a direct part of the panel itself but rather acts as an unbiased "observer" to the panel presentation and discussion. As part of the panel session, the discussant summarizes, and possibly critiques, the panel content as a means of providing the audience with another view of the overall issues brought forth in the panel presentation.

Although much of the panel content comes from the interaction of the panelists with each other and with the audience at the conference, we hope to capture as much of the basis for the discussions in writing as possible. Each panel chair for the selected panels was asked to provide a summary of the panel content which now appears in these proceedings. Because this is the first year we've included panel descriptions in the proceedings, special thanks to the panel chairs for their efforts to make this happen. The descriptions were typed, edited and formatted at Xerox PARC with much help from my assistant Janice Heiler, the *Computer Graphics* editor Rick Beach, and Rick's assistant Subhana Menis. I thank them very much.

Each panel committee member chose to act as a liason with one or two panels following the selection process until the panel presentations at the conference. These liasons could support the panel chairs in a number of ways: by providing an additional contact, by helping with panel structure (such as finding appropriate discussants), and by early editing of the panel summaries for the proceedings. Liasons may also meet with panel members before the presentations at the conference.

Many thanks to the panel committee members for their work in support of the panel sessions. Special thanks to Janice Heiler for her exceptional administrative support of the panels in all phases of the process. I also thank my manager, Robert Flegal, and Xerox Corporation for their support of this work.

Sara Bly
SIGGRAPH '87 Panels Chair

Conference Committee

CONFERENCE CO-CHAIRS

James J. Thomas
(Battelle Pacific Northwest Laboratories)
Robert J. Young
(CAD/CAM Management Consultants)

CONFERENCE COMMITTEE CHAIRS

Maureen C. Stone, *Technical Program*
(Xerox PARC)
Sara A. Bly, *Panel Sessions*
(Xerox PARC)
Michael J. Bailey, *Courses*
(Megatek Corporation)
Richard L. Phillips, *Fundamentals Seminar*
(Los Alamos National Laboratory)
Gerry MacDonald, *Exhibits*
(Megatek Corporation)
Joan Collins, *Chair, Film and Video Show*
(Joan Collins & Associates)
Frank Foster, *Technical Director, Film and Video Show*
(Hybrid Arts, Inc.)
Joanne P. Culver, *Art Show*
(LAZERUS)
K. O. Beckman, *Audio/Visual*
(Sirius Communications Group)
Katherine Ann Talbert, *Conference Materials*
(ITT Gilfillan)
Bruce Eric Brown, *Slide Sets*
(The Quail Group, Inc.)
E. Jan Hurst Villano, *Conference Editor*
(Independent)
John E. French, Jr., *Special Interest Groups*
(GeoQuest Systems, Inc.)
Ernest Sasaki, *Treasurer*
(California Institute of Technology)
Brian Herzog, *Registration*
(AT&T Conversant Systems)
B. J. Anderson, *Chair, Public Relations*
(The Anderson Report)
Alan DiNoble, *Advisor, Public Relations*
(Abel Image Research)
Michael H. Bigbee, *Speaker Slides*
(Computer Associates/ISSCO)
Patricia A. Wenner, *Chair, Volunteer Coordinator*
(Bucknell University)
James A. Banister , *Assistant, Volunteer Coordinator*
(TRW)

CONFERENCE PLANNING COMMITTEE

Robert A. Ellis, *Chair* (Sun Microsystems, Inc.)
Pat Cole (Hewlett-Packard)
Raymond L. Elliott (Los Alamos National Laboratory)
Andrew C. Goodrich (University of Michigan)
Ellen Gore (Concept Productions)
Adele Newton (University of Waterloo)
James J. Thomas (Battelle Pacific Northwest Laboratories)
Robert J. Young (CAD/CAM Management Consultants)

TECHNICAL PROGRAM COMMITTEE

Richard J. Beach (Xerox PARC)
John C. Beatty (University of Waterloo)
R. Daniel Bergeron (University of New Hampshire)
James F. Blinn (Jet Propulsion Laboratory)
Edwin E. Catmull (PIXAR)
Elaine Cohen (University of Utah)
Robert L. Cook (PIXAR)
Franklin C. Crow (Xerox PARC)
Tony DeRose (University of Washington)
John C. Dill (Microtel Pacific Research)
Nick England (Trancept Systems, Inc.)
A. Robin Forrest (University of East Anglia)
Henry Fuchs (University of North Carolina at Chapel Hill)
Donald P. Greenberg (Cornell University)
James T. Kajiya (California Institute of Technology)
Martin E. Newell (CIMLINC)
Rob Pike (AT&T Bell Laboratories)
David F. Rogers (United States Naval Academy)
Maureen Stone, *Chair* (Xerox PARC)
Turner Whitted (Numerical Design, Ltd.)

PANELS COMMITTEE

Michael J. Bailey (Megatek Corporation)
Sara Bly, *Chair* (Xerox PARC)
Susan E. Brennan (Stanford University)
Glenn Entis (Pacific Data Images)
Lansing Hatfield (Lawrence Livermore National Laboratory)
Zsuzsanna Molnar (Silicon Graphics, Inc.)
Jean Shuler (Lawrence Livermore National Laboratory)

TECHNICAL PROGRAM REVIEWERS

Greg Abram
Debra Adams
Dan Asimov
Peter Atherton
John Austin
Norman Badler
Alan Barr
Brian A. Barsky
Richard H. Bartels
Eric Bier
Charles Bigelow
Gary Bishop
Ricki Blau
Frank Bliss
Sandra Bloomberg
Jules Bloomenthal
Adrian Bowyer
Ian Braid
Rob Bruce
Peter Burt
Tom Calvert
Rikk Carey
Loren Carpenter
Indranil Chakravarty
Richard Chuang
Jim Clark
Elizabeth Cobb
Ephraim Cohen
Michael Cohen
William B. Cowan
Joe Cychosz
Andy Day
Mark Dippé
David P. Dobkin
Tom Duff
David Em
John Eyles
Steve Feiner
Alain Fournier
Wm. Randolph Franklin
Don Fussell
Steve Gabriel
Darcy Gerbarg
Mike Gigante
Michael Girard
Andrew Glassner
Jack Goldfeather
Ronald N. Goldman
TNT Goodman
Cindy Goral
Charles Grant
Mark Green
Ned Greene
Trey Greer

(TECHNICAL PROGRAM REVIEWERS, continued)

Alan Greyer
John R. Gross
Charles Gunn
Satish Gupta
Karl Gutag
Paul Haeberli
Eric Haines
Roy Hall
Pat Hanrahan
Paul Heckbert
Scott Hemphill
Christoph M. Hoffmann
Klaus Hollig
Gary Hooper
Lincoln Hu
Dave Immel
James Jackson
George Joblove
Pierre Jolicoeur
Kenneth Joy
Michael Kaplan
Timothy Kay
James King
Fred Kitson
Doris Kochanek
William Kovacs
Jeff Lane
John Lasseter
Mark Leather
Mark Levoy
Richard J. Littlefield
Jon Luskin
Tom Lyche
Jock Mackinlay
Nelson Max
Charles McMath
Gary Meyer
Alan Middleditch
Jim Miller
Don P. Mitchell
Chuck Mosher
Eric Mueller
Brad Myers
Bruce Naylor
Alan V. Norton
Dan R. Olsen, Jr.
Eben Ostby
Fred Parke
Bill Paxton
Hans-Otto Peitgen
Alex Pentland
Ken Perlin
Tom Porter
Michael Potmesil
John Poulton
Hartmut Prautzsch
Jean Prevost
Peter Quarendon
Bill Reeves
Henry Rich
Richard Riesenfeld
Randi J. Rost
Holly Rushmeier
Malcolm Sabin
David Salesin
Hanan Samet
Ramon Sarraga
John Sederberg
Mark Shephard
Ken Shoemake
John Sibert
Kenneth Sloan, Jr.
Bob Sproull
Frank Stenger
Rodney Stock
Roger Swanson
Peter Tanner
Spencer Thomas
Robert Tilove
John G. Torborg
Kenneth Torrance
Herman Towles
Ken Turkowski
Jay Udupa
Samuel Uselton
Tim Van Hook
Michael Vannier
Herb Voelcker
Brian Von Herzen
John Wallace
John Warnock
Robert E. Webber
Kevin Weiler
Lee Westover
Mary Whitton
Tom Wright

PROFESSIONAL SUPPORT

ACM SIGGRAPH '87 Conference Coordinator
Molly S. Morgan

ACM SIGGRAPH Conference Coordinator
Betsy Johnsmiller

Administrative Assistants
Catherine Eby, *Treasurer*
Janice Heiler, *Panels*
Crimson Indigo, *Art Show*
Subhana Menis, *Technical Program*
Martha J. Schlegel, *Courses*

Audio/Visual Management
(Audio Visual Headquarters Corporation)
(A Samuelson Group Company)
Jim Bartolomucci
Alan Dwan
David Elliott
Doug Hunt
Kevin Ward

Conference Management / National Public Relations
(Smith Bucklin and Associates, Inc.)
Susan Argenti
Leona Caffey
Ellen Frisbie
Sheila Hoffmeyer
Joy Lee
Cynthia Stark

Conference Travel Agency
(Elegant Travel, Inc.)
Robert C. Kaitschuk

Decorator/Drayage
(Andrews-Bartlett and Associates, Inc.)
Bob Borsz
Betty Fuller
Ken Gallagher
Barby Patronski
John Patronski

Exhibition Management
(Robert T. Kenworthy, Inc.)
Robert T. Kenworthy
Hank Cronan
Barbara Voss

Graphic Design
(Nichol Graphics)
Lorraine Nichols

Exhibitors

Abekas Video Systems, Inc.
Academic Press, Inc.
ACS International, Inc.
ADAGE, Inc.
Addison-Wesley Publishing Company Inc.
Advanced Micro Devices
Advanced Technology Center
AED, Inc.
Alias Research Inc.
AMAP/CIRAD
American Association for the Advancement of Science (Science Magazine)
American Video Communications, Inc.
AMF Logic Sciences
Animatique Comparetti
Apollo Computer Inc.
Artronics
AST Research, Inc.
AT&T, Electronic Photography & Imaging Center
AV Video/Montage Publishing
AZTEK Incorporated
Barco Electronics Inc.
Barco-Industries, Inc.
Benson, Inc.
Robert Bosch Corporation
Bruning Computer Graphics
Cahners Publishing Company
CalComp
CAPTION
CELCO
Chief Manufacturing Inc.
CH Products
Chromatics
ColorGraphics Systems Inc.
Computer-Aided Engineering Magazine
Computer Friends, Inc.
Computer Graphics and Applications
Computer Graphics Laboratories, Inc.
Computer Graphics Today
Computer Graphics World
Computer Pictures Magazine
Computer Systems News (CMP Publications, Inc.)
Computerworld
Conrac Division, Conrac Corporation
Control Data Corporation
Convex Computer Corporation
Cray Research, Inc.
Crosfield Electronics Ltd.
Cubicomp Corporation
DAIKIRI
DALIM
Data Translation, Inc.
DEC Professional
DICOMED Corporation
Digital Arts Company
Digital Equipment Corporation
Digital Review
Dotronix, Inc.
Dubner Computer Systems, Inc.
Dunn Instruments
DYNAIR Electronics, Inc.
Eastman Kodak Company
EDN Magazine
EIKONIX Corporation
Electrohome Limited
Electronic Business
Electronic News
Electronic Systems Products Inc.
Elographics, Inc.
Equitable Life Leasing Corporation
Evans & Sutherland Computer Corporation
Fairlight Instruments, Inc.
Flamingo Graphics
Floating Point Systems, Inc.
French Expositions in the U.S., Inc.
General Electric - PDPO
General Electric - Silicon Systems Technology Department
General Parametrics Corporation
Genigraphics Corporation
Getris Images
Gigatek Limited
Gould Imaging & Graphics Division
GRACE
Grafpoint
Graftel, Inc.
Graphic Controls
GraphOn Corporation
Greyhawk Systems Inc.
GTCO Corporation
Karl Gutmann Incorporated
Hewlett-Packard Company
Hitachi America, Ltd.
hi-tech Marketing Corporation
Houston Instrument a Division of Ametek
Human Designed Systems, Inc.
IEEE Computer Society
Ikegami Electronics (USA), Inc.
Image Innovation Ltd.
Imagraph Corporation
I.N.A.
Inmos Corporation
Integra America
Intel Corporation
Intelligent Light Inc.
Interactive Machines Incorporated
International Imaging Materials, Inc.
Ioline Corporation
IO Research Ltd.
I.S.G. Technologies Inc.
Island Graphics
JVC Company of America
King Concept Corporation
Kitagawa Joho Kiki Company Ltd.
KMS Advanced Products, Inc.
KMW Systems Corporation/Auscom
Koh-I-Noor Rapidograph, Inc.
Kurta Corporation
LAZERUS

Lenco Computer Graphics Products Group
Lundy Electronics & Systems, Inc.
Lyon Lamb VAS Inc.
Mangum Sickles Industries, Inc.
MASSCOMP
Matrix Instruments
Matrox Electronic Systems Ltd.
Measurement Systems Inc.
Media Cybernetics, Inc.
Megascan Technology, Inc.
Megatek Corporation
Meiko Incorporated
Meret, Inc.
Metheus Corporation
Microfield Graphics, Inc.
Micro Magic
Mini-Micro Systems
Minolta Corporation
Mitsui & Company (USA) Inc.
Mitsubishi Electronics America, Inc.
Mitsubishi International Corporation
Moniterm Corporation
Monitronix Corporation
Morgan Kaufmann Publishers
Motorola
Multiwire Division, Kollmorgen Corporation
National Computer Graphics Association
National Semiconductor Corporation
National Technical Information Services
NEC Home
Neo-Visuals, Inc.
NISE, Inc.
Nova Graphics International Corporation
Number Nine Computer Corporation
Numonics Corporation
Omnicomp Graphics Corporation
Optical Computer Incorporated
Oxberry
Panasonic Industrial Company
Panasonic Industrial Company/PIC Communications Division
Pansophic Systems, Inc.
Parallax Graphics, Inc.
PC Week
Photo Research SpectraMetrics/Optronic Laboratories, Inc.
PictureWare, Inc.
PIXAR
Polaroid Corporation
Polhemus Navigation Sciences
Precision Image Corporation
Prime Computer
Productivity Products International
QMS, Inc.
Quantel
Quantum Data Inc.
Ramtek Corporation
Raster Technologies
Renaissance Graphics Inc.
Sampo Corporation of America
Seiko Instruments USA, Inc.
Shima Seiki USA, Inc.
Silicon Graphics
Sky Computers, Inc.
SlideTek Inc.
SOGITEC
Spaceward Microsystems, Ltd.
Springer-Verlag New York, Inc.
StereoGraphics Corporation
Storage Concepts, Inc.
Studio Systems Journal
Summagraphics Corporation
Sun Microsystems, Inc.
Symbolics Graphics Division
Talaris Systems Inc.
TDI (Thomson Digital Image)
Tech-Source Inc.
TELMAT
Test & Measurement Systems Inc.
Texas Instruments
Texas Memory Systems, Inc.
Texnai Inc.
Time Arts, Inc.
Toshiba America Inc.
Trancept Systems, Inc.
Uniras, Inc.
UNIX/World Magazine
Vectrix Corporation
Vermont Microsystems, Inc.
VersaCAD
Versatec, A Xerox Company
Versicolor Corporation (JCC)
Verticom Inc.
Vertigo Systems International Inc.
Video Monitors Inc.
Video Seven Inc.
Wasatch Computer Technology
Wavefront Technologies
West End Film Inc.
The Winsted Corporation
Xerox Corporation
Xicon Systems Inc.
Zenith Electronics Corporation
Zenographics, Inc.
Ziff-Davis Publishing Company
Ziff-Davis Technical Information Company

1987 ACM SIGGRAPH Awards

Steven A. Coons Award for Outstanding Creative Contributions to Computer Graphics

Prof. Donald P. Greenberg

This year ACM SIGGRAPH has selected Professor Donald P. Greenberg to receive the *Steven A. Coons Award for Outstanding Creative Contributions to Computer Graphics.* Professor Greenberg is both a pioneer of original ideas and a teacher of these ideas to numerous students, including this year's recipient of the *Computer Graphics Achievement Award.*

Greenberg began his professional life in the field of architecture. He then migrated to structural engineering for which he was educated at Cornell University and Columbia University, receiving his PhD in 1968. From 1960 to 1965 he served as a consulting engineer with Severud Associates, and was involved with the design of numerous outstanding building projects including the St. Louis Arch, New York State Theater of the Dance at Lincoln Center and Madison Square Garden. He, as is the case with many computer graphics workers, brought his previous experience to bear upon the exciting prospect of applying computers to architecture and engineering. Greenberg became involved in computer graphics in the mid-1960's. When equipment was not available at the university he "took his students" to the Visual Simulation Laboratory at the General Electric Company in Syracuse, New York. There he produced a sophisticated computer graphics movie, "Cornell in Perspective," as early as 1971.

During the last fifteen years, his research efforts have concentrated on establishing the scientific principles necessary for realistic image synthesis. Many publications on color science, light reflection models, image rendering techniques and global illumination algorithms, including both ray-tracing and radiosity, have emanated from the Cornell laboratory. More than one hundred articles have been published in these areas, including three in this year's SIGGRAPH conference proceedings.

Perhaps Greenberg's most important contribution has been the education of graduate students in computer graphics and computer-aided design. More than seventy students have received graduate degrees from the Program of Computer Graphics and he has advised more than forty students in computer graphics. Many of these graduates are now playing significant roles in teaching, research and computer graphics software development.

His energies are not just devoted to research but also to innovation within the educational environment and to service to the profession. As the Jacob Gould Shurman Professor of Computer Graphics at Cornell University he teaches computer graphics courses in the Department of Computer Sciences. He also is the director of the Program of Computer Graphics and was the director of the Computer Aided Design Instructional Facility, which he established. Now he is developing the future interactive graphics environment associated with Cornell's supercomputer facility. He serves his profession by participation on the editorial boards of *Computers and Graphics*, *Computer-Aided Design*, and *Transactions on Graphics* and by lecturing at other universities and various conferences including the SIGGRAPH short courses.

Previous award winners:

1985: Dr. Pierre Bézier
1983: Dr. Ivan E. Sutherland

1987 ACM SIGGRAPH Awards

Computer Graphics Achievement Award

Robert L. Cook

Robert Cook has been selected for his contributions to algorithms for realistic rendering of images.

In 1979, Cook entered the Program of Computer Graphics at Cornell University with a Sage Scholarship. There he coauthored the SIGGRAPH'80 paper "Synthetic Texturing Using Digital Filters," which includes an antialiasing algorithm he developed for using analytic weighted filters. His master's research at Cornell was described in a SIGGRAPH'81 paper entitled "A Reflectance Model for Computer Graphics," which presented a shading model that could simulate metals and other materials. This paper also explained why many previous models had given computer generated images a plastic look.

In 1981, Cook joined the computer research group at Lucasfilm. His first research result there was a general method for describing surface properties, presented in the SIGGRAPH'84 paper entitled "Shade Trees." He then worked with Loren Carpenter, the 1985 SIGGRAPH Computer Graphics Achievement Award recipient, to develop a new approach to image synthesis that would be suitable for specialized hardware. Cook developed a rendering system, described in the SIGGRAPH'87 paper, "The Reyes Image Rendering Architecture," that incorporated the algorithms proposed in his research. This system was used to render a number of animated films including *The Adventures of André and Wally B.*, *Luxo Jr.*, *Red's Dream* and the stained-glass man sequence in *Young Sherlock Holmes.*

As part of this research, Cook developed stochastic sampling, a method that avoids aliasing in point-sampling rendering algorithms and was published in *Transactions on Graphics* in 1986. He extended the algorithm from point sampling to distributed ray tracing in a paper presented at SIGGRAPH'84. The distributed ray tracing algorithm provided a solution for several problems in image synthesis including motion blur, depth of field, penumbrae, blurry reflection and translucency.

Cook was the film and video chair for SIGGRAPH'85 and has chaired and taught a number of SIGGRAPH courses.

A graduate from Duke University with a BS in Physics in 1974, Cook worked for a year writing medical software in the Neurosurgical Intensive Care Unit of the Hospital of the University of Pennsylvania. After that, he worked at Digital Equipment Corporation, where he wrote software for the IEEE-488 instrument bus and a user manual that won the National Society of Technical Writers award for the best technical training manual of 1978.

Previous award winners

1986: Dr. Turner Whitted
1985: Dr. Loren Carpenter
1984: Dr. James H. Clark
1983: Dr. James F. Blinn

A Muscle Model for Animating Three-Dimensional Facial Expression

Keith Waters †

Animation Research and Development
National Centre for Computer Aided Art and Design
Middlesex Polytechnic
England

Abstract

The development of a parameterized facial muscle process, that incorporates the use of a model to create realistic facial animation is described.

Existing methods of facial parameterization have the inherent problem of hard-wiring performable actions. The development of a muscle process that is controllable by a limited number of parameters and is non-specific to facial topology allows a richer vocabulary and a more general approach to the modelling of the primary facial expressions.

A brief discussion of facial structure is given, from which a method for a simple modelling of a muscle process that is suitable for the animation of a number of divergent facial types is described.

Cr Categories and Subject Descriptors:I.3.7 [Computer Graphics]: Three dimensional Graphics and Realism-Animation I.3.5[Computer Graphics]:Computational Geometry and Object modelling - Curve, surface, solid and object representations. I.6.4 [Computer Graphics]:Simulation and Modelling-Model Validation and Analysis

General Terms: Animation, Facial Expression.
Additional Keywords and Phrases: Minimum Set System, Digitization.

----

† Middlesex Polytechnic Cat Hill Barnet Herts England 01 440 5181

1. Introduction

There are two fundamental approaches to three-dimensional facial animation: key framing and parameterization [4][7]. Each has been exploited with varying degrees of success, but both have drawbacks. Key framing requires the complete specification of the model at each extreme, or at least the storage of the differences between facial positions [15]. Additionally, any unique subtle movement of the face must be constructed as a complete model, with the result that key framing is data-intensive and lacks specific manipulation. Parameterization avoids this problem of rigidity by grouping vertices together to preform specified tasks. However, generality is lost as soon as the process is applied to a new facial topology. Only by maintaining the same topological mesh will the parameterization hold true. Investigation by Parke [4] on the conformation of faces deals with the problem of utilizing these constraints, but it is doubtful whether the generality of such a topology will hold true over a wider range of facial types.

Facial parameterization techniques have dealt principally with the surface characteristics of the skin and have not been concerned with the motivators of the dynamics. Investigations by Badler [1] into the structural bases for the upper face dealt with the elastic nature of muscle and skin. The process is iterative in nature and deals adequately with the motivators of the actions. However, the complexities of the lower face jaw rotations render the processes unperformable. It is evident from such investigations that the motivators of the dynamic characteristics are complex, and that a simple and more general approach needs to be taken if muscle parameterization is to succeed.

This present research is concerned with the development of a more general and flexible muscle model for parameterization that will allow facial control without the requirement for hard-wiring the performable actions.

2. Motivation

The diversity of facial forms in terms of sex, age and race is enormous. It is these forms that allow us to recognize individuals and send complex non-verbal signals to one another. For the deaf and hard-of-hearing the face is a vital mode of communication, with the majority of attention placed on the observation of the lips [16][11]. As a result, a variety of models have been developed to imitate the actions of the lips [13].

Evidence from reasearch by Quentin Summerfield [17] for the deaf and hard-of-hearing has shown that real people speaking are unsatisfactory subjects for experiments into visual speech perception, because real people cannot produce specific and graded articulatory gestures. Furthermore it is evident that bi- or multi-modal emphasis in teaching the deaf lip reading should not be undervalued, as we are predisposed to relate what we hear to what we see.

Computer pre-operative surgical techniques need to determine the mobility remaining in the face after surgery. Surgical reconstruction of faces [20] uses a number of techniques to collect three-dimensional data: Moire patterning, lofting of CAT or EMR scans and lasers. The resultant data can vary enormously from one face to another, and so any resultant parameterization would, at best, be tedious to implement.

The facial muscle process described in this paper avoids direct hard-wiring of performable actions to the data structure, and offers a simple method to determine the motional bounds of the key facial nodes.

3. Developing parameter sets for the face

Parameterization is the most desirable method of generating and controlling complex articulated models. Isolating the appropriate parameters to use for the face is perplexing but fundamental.

Inanimate objects, such as the geometric primitives, "cube, cone, sphere", can be described in terms of width, length, height, diameter, colour, weight and material, that represent basic parameters. The advantage of this approach allows concise criteria to encapsulate every member of that group or class.

Few living forms can be determined by such precise parameters. Trees [3] and other recursively generated forms seem to be the only objects belonging to such bounded sets, and consequently they can be created from a small kernel of data that is easy to produce. Unfortunately the inherent nature of the face does not allow the formation of such discrete criteria, where the terminating description of an unbounded class becomes vague and is usually discerned by the resulting visual image. The Minimum Set System [19] accepts the complexities of the unbounded class and describes the smallest number of parameters required to preform definable facial expression.

It remains very difficult to extract the necessary facial parameters from real faces. The individual facial muscles beneath the skin (and the deeper layered muscle) have not been accurately measured. Work by the nineteeth century physiologist Duchenne, applied electrical currents to freshly guillotined heads to observe the facial contortions. Later he applied the same techniques to old inmates of alms houses to create artificial expressions. In 1906 Sir Charles Bell, the anatomist, illustrated the mechanisms of the major expressions in his book *Anatomy and Physiology of Expression*, and, as he explained, a multitude of processes coalesce to produce what we instinctively recognize as an expression.

This being the case, it is still open to question as to whether there are techniques to extract the necessary facial parameters from actual faces. Investigations by Quentin Summerfield [17] into the perception of visible articulatory movements measured the face using video tape techniques. Three major problems were encountered. Firstly, an axis frame must be defined to which the measured movements may be referred. Secondly, movements of the primary articulators such as the lips and jaw must be separated from the effects of global movements. Thirdly, the measurements must be sensitive since, relative to the size of the head, significant articulatory excursions are small and seldom exceed about 25mm. Despite these inherent problems, reasonable results were obtained that describe the surface displacements of the skin.

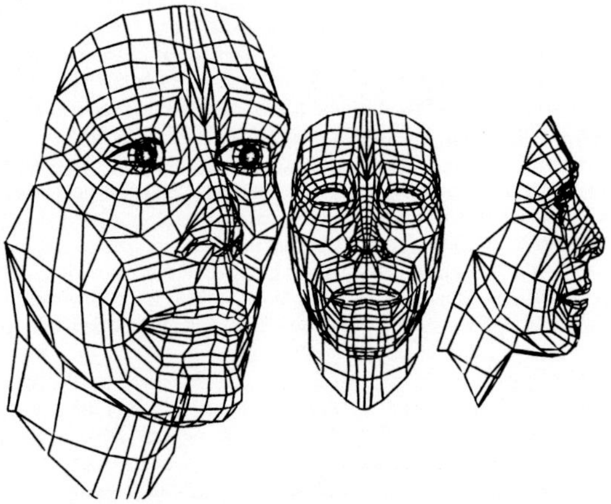

Figure 1
The Action Unit AU1 activates the inner brow raiser pulling the inner frontalis muscle. This action, with the combination of wide eyelids, pupils dilated, jaw rotated and the angular depressor pulled, displays the appearance of fear.

Significant work by Paul Ekman and Wallice Friesden, psychologists of non-verbal communication, created The Facial Action Coding System (FACS) [10], which is a notational-based environment that determines emotional states from the visible facial distortion. Individual muscles, or small groups of muscles, are described as Action Units (AU) that distort the skin tissue. This appears to be the best technique for the extraction of facial parameters useful for computer synthesis.

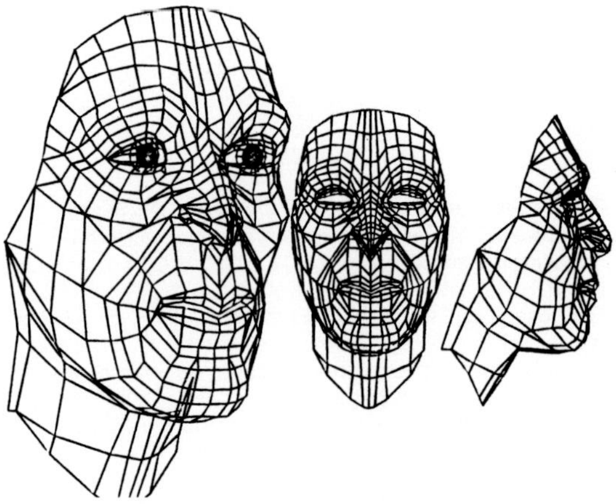

Figure 2
The Action Unit AU9 activates the Levator labii superioris alaque nasi muscle that runs from the zygomatic process to the upper lip. When it is activated the skin around the nose is pulled up dilating the nostrils and sometimes raising the upper lip.

The fifty independent facial actions can give rise to to several thousands of muscle combinations. The facial muscles can be trained, but activating them alone is not visually communicative. Six categories are described by Ekman [9]: Anger, Fear, Suprise, Disgust, Happiness and Sadness. Each of these uses multiple combinations of the Action Units. For example, one activity of the upper face in Fig 1 operates AU1, the inner brow raiser by contracting the inner frontalis muscle. In fig 2 AU9 is used, known as the 'nose wrinkler', this activates the levator labii superioris alaque nasi causing the nostrils to dilate, pulling the skin around the base of the nose up and sometimes raising the upper lip.

My own research ascribes, to individual muscles, or groups of muscles, particular parameters that remain consistant between one face and the next, in the same way that FACS is universal across a spectrum of facial types. Importantly, any contradiction between FACS and the computer parameters can easily be compared and corrected using this principle of Action Units. The goal is to model the basic facial expressions described by Ekman using FACS to validate the results.

4. The muscle and bone of the face

The cranium consists of fourteen major bones of which the manible is the only jointed structure. The mandible rotates horizontally about an axis near the ear. Inserted into the manible are the lower teeth, and the upper teeth are embeded into the maxilla process. From the front view, the teeth are the only visible bone structure, and should not be underestimated in the modelling of speech segments.

The muscles of facial expression, are subcutaneous voluntary muscles. In general they arise from the bone or facia of the head, and insert into the skin as in Fig 3. The muscle can be defined according to the orientation of the fasciculi (the individual fibres of the muscle) that may be parallel/linear, oblique or spiralized relative to the direction of pull at their attachment. There are a variety of these muscle types apparent on the face and they can be broadly divided into the upper and lower face. In the lower face there are five major groupings:

• Uppers and downers, that move the face upwards towards the brow and conversely towards the chin.

• Those that contract horizontally towards the ears and conversely towards the center line of the face.

• Oblique muscles that contract in an angular direction from the lips, upwards and outwards to the cheek bones.

• The orbitals that are circular or elliptical in nature, and run round the eyes and mouth.

• Sheet muscle, that carries out miscellaneous actions, particularly over the temporal zones, and the platysma muscle which extends downwards into the neck close beneath the skin.

The upper facial muscles are responsible for the changing appearance of the eyebrows, forehead and the upper and lower lids of the eyes (Fig 1). The muscles contract isotonically towards the static insertion into the cranium, consequently the surface tissue bunches and wrinkles perpendicularly to the direction of the muscle.

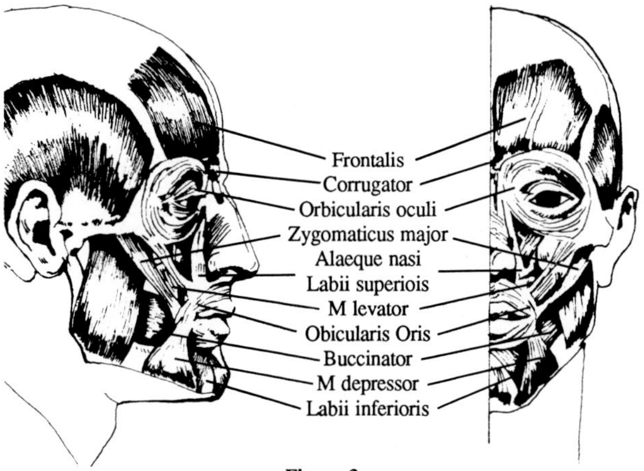

Figure 3
The major muscles of the face.

The muscles of the mouth have the most complex musclar interaction. The primary muscle being the Obicularis Oris which is a sphincter muscle with no bony attachment. Additionally the deep Buccinator muscle fibres decussate into the upper and lower lip and continue round the face to the opposite point of attachment. Three primary muscles, M Levator, Labii Superioris and Alaeque Nasi, join from above. The deeper muscles M Buccinator joins at the modiolus (the major node of the mouth) and contracts horizontally. From below, the M Depressor, Anguli Oris, M Depressor Labii Inferioris and Mentalis, all contract obliquely and vertically.

5. Factors determining the modelling of muscles

It is evident that the skin, being supported by bone and multiple layers of muscle, produces literally thousands of movement combinations. What is required is not the exact simulation of neurons, muscles and joints, but a model with a few dynamic parameters that emulate the primary characteristics. These parameters are relatively abstract, and do not attempt to model the biomechanical or neurophysiological mechanisms. Since the muscles themselves are grouped together to perform specific tasks, two broad types of muscles are considered: linear/parallel muscles that pull and sphincter muscles that squeeze. Defining the surface skin as a mesh determines that each node has a finite degree of mobility (DOM). The primary factors determining the nodal mobility are:

- Tensile strength of the muscle and skin
- Proximity to the muscle node of attachment
- Depth of tissue at the node and the proximity to the bone
- The elastic bounds of the relaxed tissue, and the interaction of other muscles.

The physical displacements of the facial nodes, especially around the mouth, have been measured by Summerfield [14] and his results indicate that displacements rarely exceed 25mm during the articulation of a/b/a sounds. Therefore assuming the node of bony attachment is static, a relationship for any intermediate node is required.

The structural-based representation suggested by Badler [1] simulates points on the skin which is distorted around an ovoid. Arcs connect points with their neighbours, so that one skin movement affects the position of its neighbour in much the same way as a network of springs. When a force F is applied to a node p the change in location is computed by:

$$p' = F/k$$

where k = sum of the spring constants at that point.

The iteration continues until a force is propagated out from the initiating point across the face. Badler's simulation is effective, but it does require specified facial models to operate upon, with tie points for the fixing of muscles to the bone and skin. This in turn requires information about length and elasticity to be determined before the iteration can begin.

With all the muscle forms it is evident that they have a highly complex three-dimensional structure endowed with viscous, elastic and other mechanical properties that result in the displacement of the skin. The simulation of such interactions would be formidible, and is not the object of this paper, however some basic issues can be established. Only a proportion of the force is effective along the line of contraction, especially as the fibres become more oblique in relation to the node of attachment. This can be determined from the length of the muscle fibre x cosine of the angle of attachment of the muscle fibres to the tendon or surface tissue [18]. This gives a general indication of the displacement of the remaining tissue. The elasticity of the skin varies with age. Young skin has a higher elasticity than older flesh and this factor too should be accommodated in the muscle model.

In addition to the static surface displacement features of the skin there are the motional characteristics. Here the requirement is to discern suitable motional criteria. Investigations by Kelso [14] into reiterant speech production outlined the dynamic properties during articulatory movement. For this process LED's were placed on the subject and monitored on an oscilloscope. Despite the inherent multi-dimensional process involved with speech, evidence showed that the system displayed near sinusoidal uniform motions, as if generated by a simple non-dissipative mass-spring system. This supports the early work of Parke [4] who produced convincing results utilizing the principle of cosine acceleration and deceleration. Subsequently this principal has been adopted as a first order approximation for this research, since the facial displacements are small and the rate at which the motions occur is extremely fast.

6. The Computer Model of muscles for the face

The research presented in this paper represents the action of muscles using the primary motivators on a non-specific deformable topology of the face. The muscle actions themselves are tested against FACS which employs action units directly to one muscle or a small group of muscles. Any differences found between real action units and those performed on the computer model are easily corrected by changing the parameters for the muscles, until reasonable results were obtained.

The muscle model was designed to be as 'naturalistic' as possible, in the representation. Two types of muscles were created: linear/parallel muscles that pull and sphincter muscles that squeeze. The key nodes of muscle attachment were measured on a number of faces, to establish the extremes of displacement and the maximum and minimum zone of influence. At best this proved to be difficult, as only the surface points could be measured, and the range of surface characteristics varies a great deal from face to face. However, it was confirmed that nodal displacements rarely exceed 25mm, the largest displacements originating from the mouth groups. The zone of influence depended upon the degree of contraction and, using FACS as a basis, it was established that the angle varied from 15 to 160 degrees, creating a convex zone. Additionally, using data from Summerfield [17], it was possible to establish degrees of freedom (DOF) for nodes around the mouth.

The fundamentals of most facial muscles determine that one end of a linear muscle has a bony attachment that remains static, while the other end is embedded in the soft tissue of the skin. When the muscle is operated, it contracts isotonically.

Looking at the concept of muscle vectors, the zone of influence in the simplest form can be viewed as circular, and the fall-off is along the radius as illustrated in Fig 4 on the three-dimensional grid. Muscle vectors can be described with direction and magnitude, both in two and three-dimensions. The direction is towards the point of attachment, and the magnitude that is zero at the point of attachment and increases to maximum at the other point of insertion into the skin.

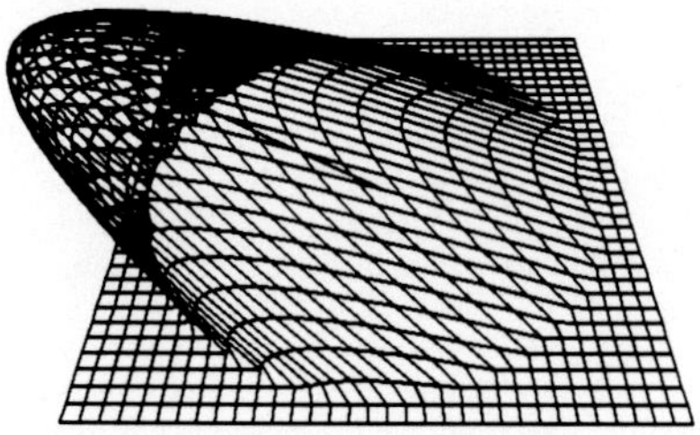

Figure 4
A muscle vector displacing a three dimensional grid with a circular cosine falloff.

The next problem is to describe how the adjacent tissue, such as the node p (Fig 5) is affected by this muscle vector contraction. At the point of attachment to the skin we can assume maximum displacement, and at the point of bony attachment zero displacement. A fall-off of the displacement is dissipated through the adjoining tissue, both across the sector Pm,Pn and V1, Ps. Using a non-linear interpolant, it is possible to represent the simple action of a muscle such as in Fig 6. Fig 5 describes the muscle vector in two dimensions. By applying the same principles to the third dimension, point p (x,y,z) is displaced p' (x',y',z').

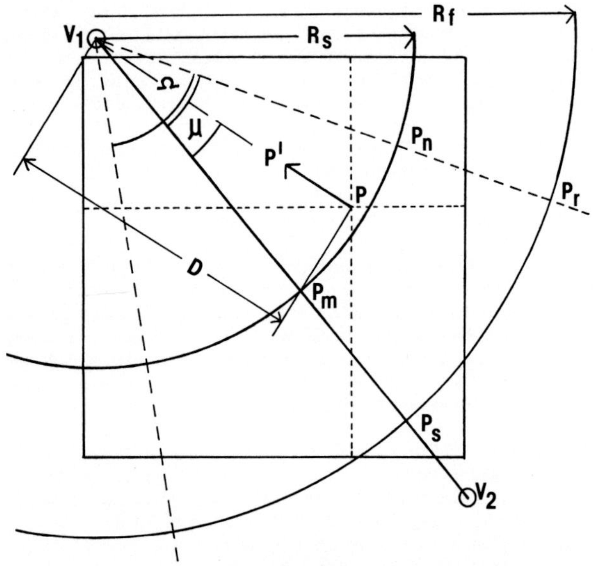

Figure 5
The muscle vector model influencing the sector V1 Pr Ps. Rs and Rf represent the fallstart fall finish of the muscle pull along the vector V1 V2.

Fig 5 V1 and V2 are two points located in two-dimensional space. Rs represents the fall-off radius start, as a real distance from V1.
Rf represents the falloff radius finish, as a real distance from V1.

Given any point P(x,y) located at a mesh node, within the zone V1 Pr Ps is displaced towards V1 along the vector P V1, this creates P' (x',y') where:

$$x' \propto f(K.A.R.x)$$
$$y' \propto f(K.A.R.y)$$

where:

K is the muscle spring constant
Ω is the maximum zone of influence
D is the vector V1 P distance

The angular displacement factor A is defined as:

$$A = \cos(\mu/\pi \,.\, \pi/2)$$

where μ is the angle between V1 V2 and V1 P
The radial displacement factor R is defined as:

$$R = \cos((1 - D/Rs)\, \pi/2)$$

for P inside V1 Pn Pm, and

$$R = \cos((D - Rs) / (Rf - Rs)\, \pi/2)$$

for P inside Pn Pr Ps Pm

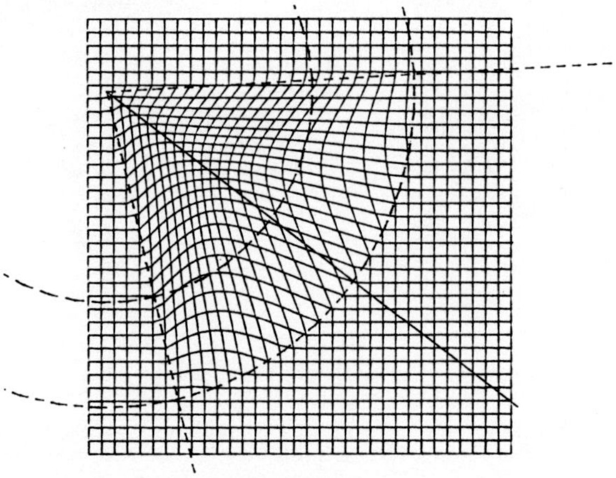

Figure 6
A three dimensional muscle vector laying in the x y plane. Zone of influence 35.0, fallstart 7.0, fallfin 14.0, muscle spring constant 0.75, elasticity 1.0.

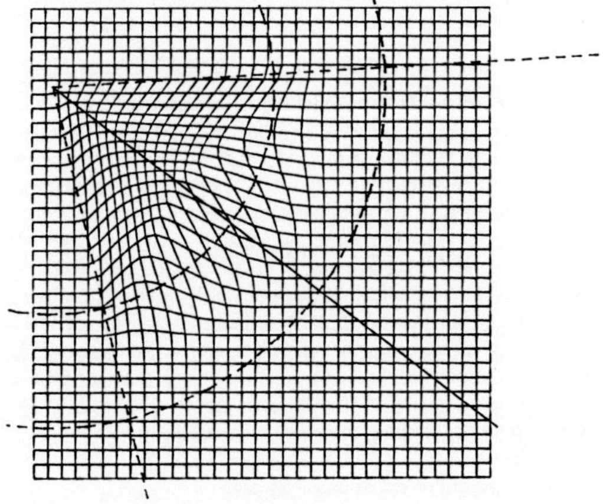

Figure 7
The same muscle vector parameters as in figure 6 but with the elasticity raised to a power 10.0.

Fig 6 illustrates the cosine interpolant, while Fig 7 shows the cosine raised to a power to decrease the elasticity of the mesh.

The sphincter muscle that squeezes the skin tissue can be described from a single point around which the surface contracts as if drawn together like a string bag. This can be described as occurring uniformly around the point of contraction, therefore the angular displacement is no longer required:

$$x' \propto f(K.R.x)$$
$$y' \propto f(K.R.y)$$

This results in the following activity in Fig 8.

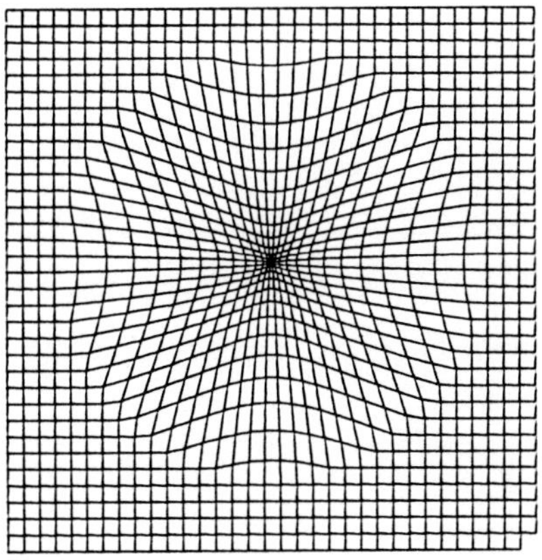

Figure 8
Sphincter muscle

Obviously muscles do not behave in such a regular fashion, therefore elliptical shapes are created that represents the shape of the oris by the addition of a longitudinal and vertical axis (Fig 9).

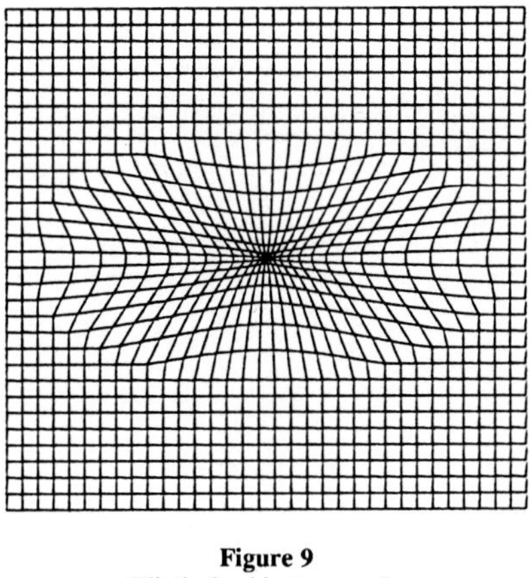

Figure 9
Eliptical sphincter muscle

The limits of a muscle action can be determined by the spring constant K, which represents the maximum displacement of the muscle. The problem associated with this model is that each muscle action is independent, and the actual nodal displacement is determined by a succession of muscle actions. This is more extreme when the contractions become isometric and nodes are shifted out of the zone of influence of adjoining muscle vectors. In this way there is a danger of exceeding the degree of freedom (DOF) of any node. The nodal structure of the face determines that each vertex has a finite DOF. By positioning the facial muscles, both feasible and impossible, and then preprocessing the structure, the DOF of each node can be determined. In this manner the order of the muscle contractions will not become isometric, as each node will store information about its common attractors (Fig 10).

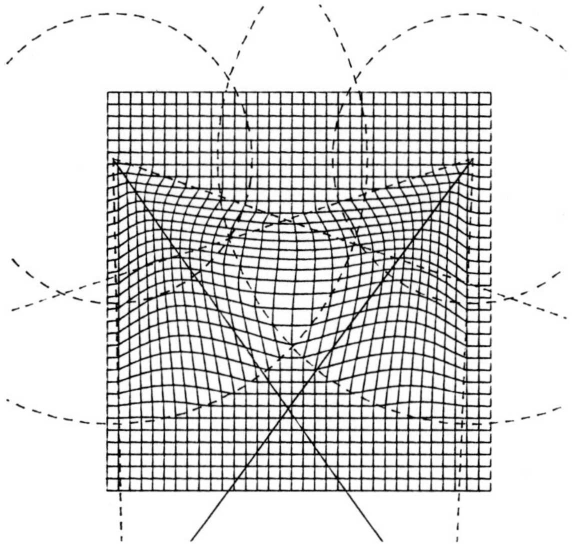

Figure 10
The confluence of two muscles

The modelling of the visco-elastic nature of skin as discussed has many variables and the cosine model is one possible solution to establishing a non-linear interpolant. Provided that the point of attachment is static and the muscle insertion into the skin has maximum displacement, any 'ramp' can be described to control the interpolant. The following examples Fig 11, where Fig 12 relates to (a), Fig 13 relates to (b), Fig 14 relates to (c). Illustrate the displacement activity where f is a function of (K.A.R.x). This allows a more flexible approach to the modelling of the elastic nature of skin.

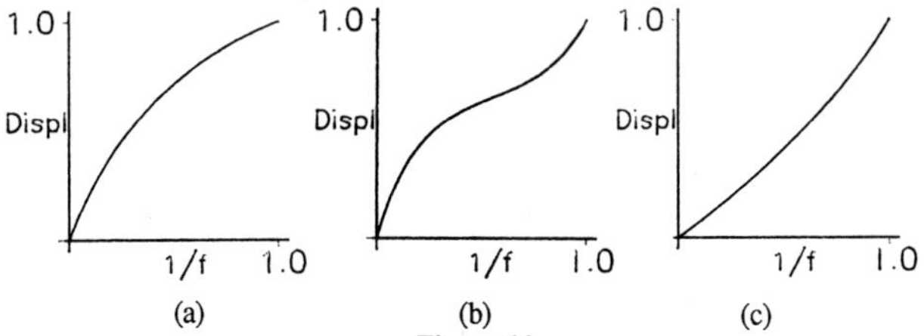

Figure 11

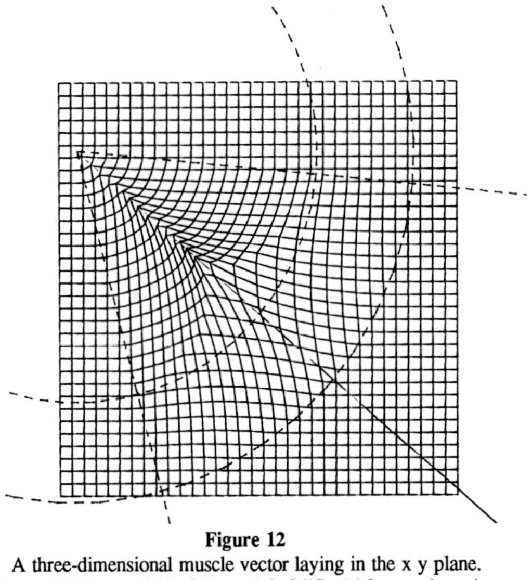

Figure 12
A three-dimensional muscle vector laying in the x y plane.
Zone of influence 35.0, fallstart 7.0, fallfin 14.0, muscle spring constant 0.3 relating to (a)

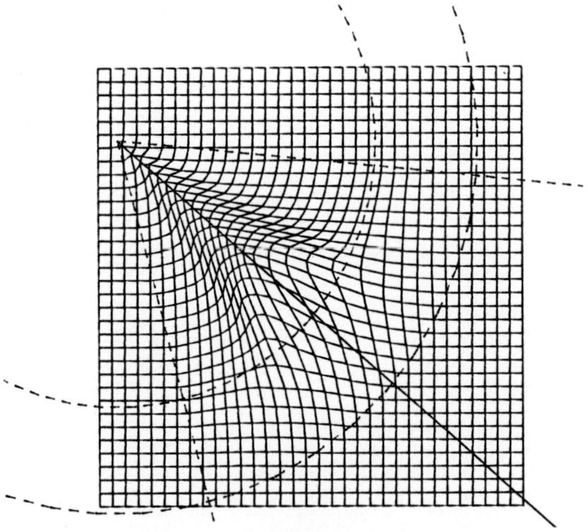

Figure 13
Same parameters as in figure 12 relating to (b)

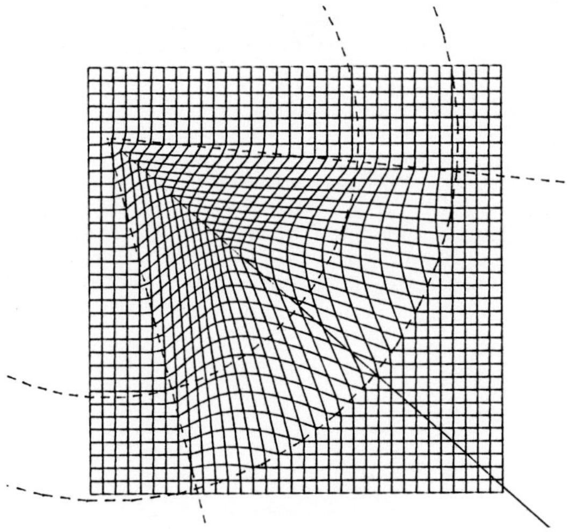

Figure 14
Same parameters as in figure 12 relating to (c)

7. The image synthesis and model operation

Polygonal data structures have been shown to be an acceptable mode of modelling facial topologies [5][7], and were adopted in this research for ease of use. The nature of the muscle model described above allows a free range in polygonal construction. This has proved to be important in the modelling of real people's faces that require specific topologies for recognition purposes Fig 15. However it remains important to maintain a mesh that is as regular as possible, to avoid polygonal intersections and 'facet popping' when the model is articulated. This can be remedied by increasing the density of polygonal detail where the curvature is higher. Additionally, all the facets need to be triangulated to maintain planer polygons for the renderer.

The heads shown Fig 15- 22 were modelled using photographic techniques [6] and mirrored about the meridian of the face. Although neither real faces nor the motional dynamics are symmetrical these are not problems as the muscles can operate independently on both sides of the face. For the simplicity of use, the faces illustrated were assumed to be symetrical in order to reduce the time-consuming effort of data duplication.

The eyelids were constructed from the existing vertices of the face to create fivc curves, three for the upper lid and two for the lower. The upper lids rotate about a horizontal axis to close the eyelids. Swept revolutions of profiles created the eyeballs that have controls for the dilation of the pupil and the focusing of the eyes. Highlights were important in giving a realistic effect and this was achieved either by using the Phong renderer or by extracting facets and shading them white. The teeth were simply formed from sets of Bezier curves that were set back into the mouth cavity. The lower teeth are rotated with the jaw. The positioning of the muscles was achieved by identifying key nodes on the face [18] and relating them to the computer model in three-dimensional space for the location of the muscle vector head and tail.

The model is implemented as a program that is parameter driven. The parameters are created in data files that control all the muscles, jaw rotations, eye focusing and the eyelids. The program generates polygonal or vector descriptions that can be rendered as desired. Ten muscles were implanted into the facial topology, representing those that are the required action units (AU) for FACS. Each linear muscle has parameters for:

• Zone of influence	half angle in degrees	Ω
• Fallstart	real radial distance	Fs
• Fallfin	real radial distance	Ff
• Muscle spring constant	$0<K<1$	
• Elasticity	$E >= 1$	

For the sphincter muscle:

• Tension	$0<T<1$
• Lx Ly	longitude and latitude real distances

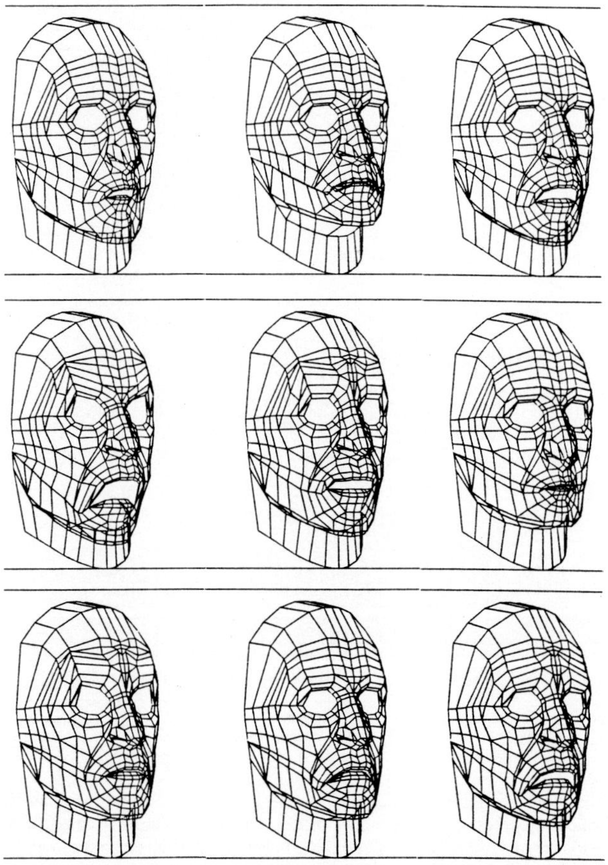

Figure 15

Illustrated are nine different facial expressions in both the upper and lower face on an alternative facial topology. Seven muscles (linear/parallel and sphincter muscles) were utilized with the jaw rotation to represent some of the actions from the Facial Action Coding System

8. Future Developments

- To increase the realism of the muscle model, the addition of creasing and buckling of the flesh as the muscle contracts would be advantageous. Most buckling occurs at right angles to the direction of contraction. By calculating the contraction length of the muscle vector and comparing it to the elasticity of the flesh convincing results could be produced.

- The flow of skin over the bone identified by Badler [1] could be solved by creating muscle vectors that curve round the underlying structure, in much the same way as real muscle, This however relies on the creation of an accurate model of the cranium and mandible.

- A more fundamental approach to the construction of the face needs to be taken that could encapsulate the widest range of facial types. Utilizing indices that are relevant to cranial form [18], the underlying structure of faces could be created according to sex, age and race groupings. More importantly, this underlying structure would indicate the precise position of the facial muscles. Additionally the mandible while being the only jointed bone, is not articulated by the muscle model. By ascribing those muscles responsible for the motion of the jaw more complex articulations could be achieved, of the lateral movement of the jaw during mastication.

- For speech, many of the problems associated with lip synchronization occur because of the co-articulation of phonemes. A simple parser that looked at the current, previous and next phonemes could establish what mouth shapes need to be created.

- The Phong renderer displays 'plastic' faces in a uniform manner, and texture-mapping real faces onto the polygon mesh would greatly enhance the realism, for example local texturing, such as stubble round the chin. Likewise hair could be grown in a particle fashion or texture-mapped.

- Finally, as the number of controlling parameters increases, it is evident that motional characteristics of the six primary emotions [9] could be grouped together to perform specified tasks. The development of a task-level system [21] would allow the global control over the complex motions of the face, while maintaining explicit controls over the facial details.

9. Conclusions

What has been presented here is a model for the muscles of the face that can be extended to any non rigid object and is not dependent on specific topology or network. A combination of parameterized techniques with the muscle model has been designed to perform complex articulations in reference to a notational-based system.

10. Acknowledgements

Thanks to Dr J A Vince my PhD supervisor for encouragment and support over the past two years, to Dr R Armes for his patience with the written material, and to Paul Brown at the National Centre and also Paul Hughes and Mark Hurry for valuable discussions.

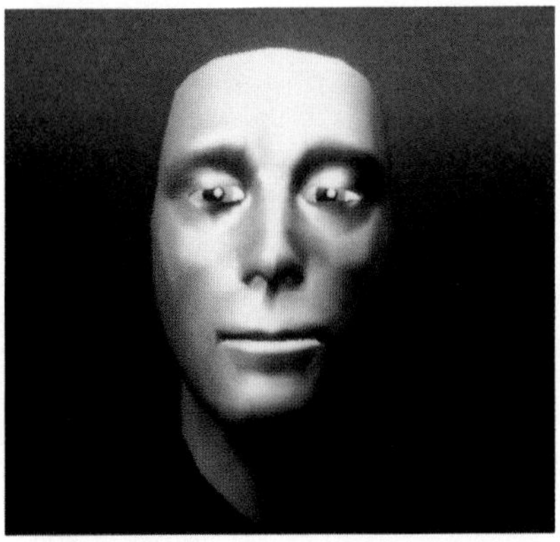

11. References

[1] Badler N I "Animating Facial Expression" *Proceedings Computer Graphics* 1981 Vol 15 No 3 245-252

[2] Boston D W "Synthetic Facial Communication" *British Journal of Audiology* 1973 Vol 7 95-101

[3] Oppenheimer P E "Real Time Design and Animation of Fractal Plants and Trees" *Proceedings Computer Graphics* 1986 Vol 20 No 4 55-64

[4] Parke F I "A Parameterized Model for Facial Animation" *IEEE Computer Graphics and Applications* 1982 Nov

[5] Parke F I "A Parameteric Model for Human Faces" *Technical Report* UTEC-CSc75-047 University of Utah 1984

[6] Parke F I "Measuring Three-Dimensional Surfaces with a Two-Dimensional Data Tablet" *Computer and Graphics* 1975 Vol 1 5-7 Pergamon Press

[7] Bergeron P "Techniques for Animating Characters" *Advanced Computer Animation Course Notes Siggraph* 1985

[8] Duncan J P "Anatomical Definition and Modeling" *Engineering in Medicine* 1986 Vol 15 No 3

[9] Ekman P and Friesen W "Unmasking the Human Face" *Prentice Hall Inc* 1975

[10] Ekman P and Friesen W "Manual for the the Facial Action Coding System" *Consulting Psychologist* 1977 Press Palo Alto California

[11] Fromkin V Lip "Postions in English American Vowels" *Journal of Language and Speech* No 7 215-225 1964

[12] Gillension M L "The Interactive Generation of Facial Images on a CRT using a Heuristic Stratergy" *PhD Thesis Ohio State University* 1974

[13] Hight R L Lip Reader Trainer: "A Computer Programme for the Hearing Impaired" *Proc. John Hopkins, First National Search for Application of Computing to Aid the Handicapped. IEEE Computer Society* 1981 LA 4-5

[14] Kelso et al "A qualitative dynamic analysis of reiterant speech production: Phase portraits, kinematics and dynamic modelling" *Journal of Accoustical Society American* Vol 77 No1 1985

[15] Moore J "Towards an Integrated Computer Package for Speech Therapy Training", "Talking Heads". *Microtech Solutions Report Bradford College of Art and Design* 1986

[16] Summerfield Q "Roles of the Lips and Teeth in Lipreading Vowels" *Proceedings of the Institute of Acoustics* 1984

[17] Summerfield Q "Analysis, Synthesis and Perception of Visible Articulatory Movements", *Academic Press Inc* 1983

[18] Warwick R "Grey's Anatomy" *35th edition Longman* 1973

[19] Waters K "Expressive Three Dimensional Faces" *Procceedings Computer Graphics Online Wembley* 1986

[20] Wood P D "An Interactive Graphics System for Planning Reconstructive Surgery" *National Procceedings Computer Graphics Association* Chicago 130-135 1986

[21] Zelter D L "Representation and Control of Three-dimensional Computer Animated Figures" *PhD Thesis Ohio State University* 1984

Figure 16
Neutral face with the muscles relaxed

Figure 17
Happiness the corners of the lips are drawn back and raised obliquely by the zygomatic major muscle.

Figure 19
Fear the inner brows are raised by the inner frontalis muscle, the eyes are wide with pupils dilated. The jaw is rotated and the lips drawn back.

Figure 21
Anger the brows are lowered and the inner part drawn together. The jaw is not rotated and the lips are tight.

Figure 20
Disgust the alaeque nasi muscle raises the upper lip pulling the skin around the nose and causing the nostrils to dilate.

Figure 22
Surprise the brows are curved and high, the eyelids wide and the pupils dilated.

Flocks, Herds, and Schools: A Distributed Behavioral Model

Craig W. Reynolds
Symbolics Graphics Division

1401 Westwood Boulevard
Los Angeles, California 90024

(Electronic mail: cwr@Symbolics.COM)

Abstract

The aggregate motion of a flock of birds, a herd of land animals, or a school of fish is a beautiful and familiar part of the natural world. But this type of complex motion is rarely seen in computer animation. This paper explores an approach based on simulation as an alternative to scripting the paths of each bird individually. The simulated flock is an elaboration of a particle system, with the simulated birds being the particles. The aggregate motion of the simulated flock is created by a distributed behavioral model much like that at work in a natural flock; the birds choose their own course. Each simulated bird is implemented as an independent actor that navigates according to its local perception of the dynamic environment, the laws of simulated physics that rule its motion, and a set of behaviors programmed into it by the "animator." The aggregate motion of the simulated flock is the result of the dense interaction of the relatively simple behaviors of the individual simulated birds.

Categories and Subject Descriptors: I.2.10 [Artificial Intelligence]: Vision and Scene Understanding; I.3.5 [Computer Graphics]: Computational Geometry and Object Modeling; I.3.7 [Computer Graphics]: Three-Dimensional Graphics and Realism—*Animation*; I.6.3 [Simulation and Modeling]: Applications.

General Terms: Algorithms, design.

Additional Key Words, and Phrases: flock, herd, school, bird, fish, aggregate motion, particle system, actor, flight, behavioral animation, constraints, path planning.

Introduction

The motion of a flock of birds is one of nature's delights. Flocks and related synchronized group behaviors such as schools of fish or herds of land animals are both beautiful to watch and intriguing to contemplate. A flock* exhibits many contrasts. It is made up of discrete birds yet overall motion seems fluid; it is simple in concept yet is so visually complex, it seems randomly arrayed and yet is magnificently synchronized. Perhaps most puzzling is the strong impression of intentional, centralized control. Yet all evidence indicates that flock motion must be merely the aggregate result of the actions of individual animals, each acting solely on the basis of its own local perception of the world.

One area of interest within computer animation is the description and control of all types of motion. Computer animators seek both to invent wholly new types of abstract motion and to duplicate (or make variations on) the motions found in the real world. At first glance, producing an animated, computer graphic portrayal of a flock of birds presents significant difficulties. Scripting the path of a large number of individual objects using traditional computer animation techniques would be tedious. Given the complex paths that birds follow, it is doubtful this specification could be made without error. Even if a reasonable number of suitable paths could be described, it is unlikely that the constraints of flock motion could be maintained (for example, preventing collisions between all birds at each frame). Finally, a flock scripted in this manner would be hard to edit (for example, to alter the course of all birds for a portion of the animation). It is not impossible to script flock motion, but a better approach is needed for efficient, robust, and believable animation of flocks and related group motions.

This paper describes one such approach. This approach assumes a flock is simply the result of the interaction between the behaviors of individual birds. To simulate a flock we simulate the behavior of an individual bird (or at least that portion of the bird's behavior that allows it to participate in a flock). To support this behavioral "control structure," we must also simulate portions of the bird's perceptual mechanisms and aspects of the physics of aerodynamic flight. If this simulated bird model has the correct flock-member behavior, all that should be required to create a simulated flock is to create some instances of the simulated bird model and allow them to interact.**

Some experiments with this sort of simulated flock are described in more detail in the remainder of this paper. The suc-

*In this paper *flock* refers generically to a group of objects that exhibit this general class of *polarized, noncolliding, aggregate motion*. The term *polarization* is from zoology, meaning alignment of animal groups. English is rich with terms for groups of animals; for a charming and literate discussion of such words see *An Exultation of Larks*. [16]

**This paper refers to these simulated bird-like, "bird-oid" objects generically as "boids" even when they represent other sorts of creatures such as schooling fish.

cess and validity of these simulations is difficult to measure objectively. They do seem to agree well with certain criteria [25] and some statistical properties [23] of natural flocks and schools which have been reported by the zoological and behavioral sciences. Perhaps more significantly, many people who view these animated flocks immediately recognize them as a representation of a natural flock, and find them similarly delightful to watch.

Our Foreflocks

The computer graphics community has seen simulated bird flocks before. The Electronic Theater at SIGGRAPH '85 presented a piece labeled "motion studies for a work in progress entitled 'Eurythmy'" [4] by Susan Amkraut, Michael Girard, and George Karl from the Computer Graphics Research Group of Ohio State University. In the film, a flock of birds flies up out of a minaret and, passing between a series of columns, flies down into a lazy spiral around a courtyard. All the while the birds slowly flap their wings and avoid collision with their flockmates.

That animation was produced using a technique completely unlike the one described in this paper and apparently not specifically intended for flock modeling. But the underlying concept is useful and interesting in its own right. The following overview is based on unpublished communications [3]. The software is informally called "the force field animation system." Force fields are defined by a 3 x 3 matrix operator that transform from a point in space (where an object is located) to an acceleration vector; the birds trace paths along the "phase portrait" of the force field. There are "rejection forces" around each bird and around static objects. The force field associated with each object has a bounding box, so object interactions can be culled according to bounding box tests. An incremental, linear time algorithm finds bounding box intersections. The "animator" defines the space field(s) and sets the initial positions, orientations, and velocities of objects. The rest of the simulation is automatic.

Karl Sims of MIT's Media Lab has constructed some behaviorally controlled animation of groups of moving objects (spaceships, inchworms, and quadrupeds), but they are not organized as flocks [35]. Another author kept suggesting [28, 29, 30] implementing a flock simulation based on a distributed behavioral model.

Particle Systems

The simulated flock described here is closely related to *particle systems* [27], which are used to represent dynamic "fuzzy objects" having irregular and complex shapes. Particle systems have been used to model fire, smoke, clouds, and more recently, the spray and foam of ocean waves [27]. Particle systems are collections of large numbers of individual particles, each having its own behavior. Particles are created, age, and die off. During their life they have certain behaviors that can alter the particle's own state, which consists of *color*, *opacity*, *location*, and *velocity*.

Underlying the boid flock model is a slight generalization of particle systems. In what might be called a "subobject system," Reeves's dot-like particles are replaced by an entire geometrical object consisting of a full local coordinate system and a reference to a geometrical shape model. The use of shapes instead of dots is visually significant, but the more fundamental difference is that individual subobjects have a more complex geometrical state: they now have orientation.

Another difference between boid flocks and particle systems is not as well defined. The behavior of boids is generally more complex than the behaviors for particles as described in the literature. The present boid behavior model might be about one or two orders of magnitude more complex than typical particle behavior. However this is a difference of degree, not of kind. And neither simulated behavior is nearly as complex as that of a real bird.

Also, as presented, particles in particle systems do not interact with one another, although this is not ruled out by definition. But birds and hence boids must interact strongly in order to flock correctly. Boid behavior is dependent not only on *internal state* but also on *external state*.

Actors and Distributed Systems

The behavioral model that controls the boid's flight and flocking is complicated enough that rather than use an *ad hoc* approach, it is worthwhile to pursue the most appropriate formal computational model. The behaviors will be represented as rules or programs in some sense, and the internal state of each boid must be held in some sort of data structure. It is convenient to encapsulate these behaviors and state as an *object*, in the sense of object-oriented programming systems [10, 11, 21]. Each *instance* of these objects needs a computational *process* to apply the behavioral programs to the internal data. The computational abstraction that combines process, procedure, and state is called an *actor* [12, 26, 2]. An actor is essentially a virtual computer that communicates with other virtual computers by *passing messages*. The actor model has been proposed as a natural structure for animation control by several authors [28, 13, 29, 18]. It seems particularly apt for situations involving interacting characters and behavior simulation. In the literature of parallel and distributed computer systems, flocks and schools are given as examples of robust self-organizing distributed systems [15].

Behavioral Animation

Traditional hand-drawn cel animation was produced with a medium that was completely inert. Traditional computer animation uses an active medium (computers running graphics software), but most animation systems do not make much use of the computer's ability to automate motion design. Using different tools, contemporary computer animators work at almost the same low level of abstraction as do cel animators. They tell their story by directly describing the motion of their characters. Shortcuts exist in both media; it is common for computer animators and cel animators to use helpers to interpolate between specified keyframes. But little progress has been made in automating motion description; it is up to the animator to translate the nuances of emotion and characterization into the motions that the character performs. The animator cannot simply tell the character to "act happy" but must tediously specify the motion that conveys happiness.

Typical computer animation models only the shape and physical properties of the characters, whereas *behavioral* or *character-based* animation seeks to model the behavior of the character. The goal is for such simulated characters to handle many of the details of their actions, and hence their motions. These *behaviors* include a whole range of activities from simple path planning to complex "emotional" interactions between characters. The construction of behavioral animation characters has attracted many researchers [19, 21, 13, 14, 29,

30, 41, 40], but it is still a young field in which more work is needed.

Because of the detached nature of the control, the person who creates animation with character simulation might not strictly be an *animator*. Traditionally, the animator is directly responsible for all motion in animation production [40]. It might be more proper to call the person who directs animation via simulated characters a *meta-animator*, since the animator is less a designer of motion and more a designer of behavior. These behaviors, when acted out by the simulated characters, lead indirectly to the final action. Thus the animator's job becomes somewhat like that of a theatrical director: the character's performance is the indirect result of the director's instructions to the actor. One of the charming aspects of the work reported here is not knowing how a simulation is going to proceed from the specified behaviors and initial conditions; there are many unexpected, pleasant surprises. On the other hand, this charm starts to wear thin as deadlines approach and the unexpected annoyances pop up. This author has spent a lot of time recently trying to get uncooperative flocks to move as intended ("these darn boids seem to have a mind of their own!").

Geometric Flight

A fundamental part of the boid model is the geometric ability to *fly*. The motion of the members of a simulated school or herd can be considered a type of "flying" by glossing over the considerable intricacies of wing, fin, and leg motion (and in the case of herds, by restricting freedom of motion in the third dimension). In this paper the term *geometric flight* refers to a certain type of motion along a path: a dynamic, incremental, rigid geometrical transformation of an object, moving along and tangent to a 3D curve. While the motion is rigid, the object's underlying geometric model is free to articulate or change shape within this "flying coordinate system." Unlike more typical animated motion along predefined spline curves, the shape of a flight path is not specified in advance.

Geometric flight is based on incremental translations along the object's "forward direction," its local positive Z axis. These translations are intermixed with *steering*—rotations about the local X and Y axes (*pitch* and *yaw*), which realign the global orientation of the local Z axis. In real flight, turning and moving happen continuously and simultaneously. Incremental geometric flight is a discrete approximation of this; small linear motions model a continuous curved path. In animation the motion must increment at least once per frame. Running the simulation at a higher rate can reduce the discrete sampling error of the flight model and refine the shape of motion blur patterns.

Flight modeling makes extensive use of the object's own coordinate system. Local space represents the "boid's eye view;" it implies measuring things relative to the boid's own position and orientation. In Cartesian terms, the left/right axis is X, up/down is Y, and forward/back is Z. The conversion of geometric data between the local and global reference frames is handled by the geometric operators *localize* and *globalize*. It is convenient to use a local scale so that the unit of length of the coordinate system is one *body length*. Biologists routinely specify flock and school statistics in terms of body lengths.

Geometric flight models conservation of momentum. An object in flight tends to stay in flight. There is a simple model of viscous speed damping, so even if the boid continually accelerates in one direction, it will not exceed a certain *maximum speed*. A *minimum speed* can also be specified but defaults to zero. A *maximum acceleration*, expressed as a fraction of the maximum speed, is used to truncate over-anxious requests for acceleration, hence providing for smooth changes of speed and heading. This is a simple model of a creature with a finite amount of available energy.

Many physical forces are not supported in the current boid model. *Gravity* is modeled but used only to define banking behavior. It is defined procedurally to allow the construction of arbitrarily shaped fields. If each boid was accelerated by gravity each frame, it would tend to fall unless gravity was countered by *lift* or *buoyancy*. Buoyancy is aligned against gravity, but aerodynamic lift is aligned with the boid's local "up" direction and related to velocity. This level of modeling leads to effects like normally level flight, going faster when flying down (or slower up), and the "stall" maneuver. The speed limit parameter could be more realistically modeled as a frictional *drag*, a backward pointing force related to velocity. In the current model steering is done by directing the available *thrust* in the appropriate direction. It would be more realistic to separately model the *tangential* thrusting forces and the *lateral* steering forces, since they normally have different magnitudes.

Banking

Geometric flight relates translation, pitch, and yaw, but does not constrain *roll*, the rotation about the local Z axis. This degree of freedom is used for *banking*—rolling the object to align the local Y axis with the (local XY component of the total) acceleration acting upon it. Normally banking is based on the lateral component of the acceleration, but the tangential component can be used for certain applications. The lateral components are from steering and gravity. In straight flight there is no radial force, so the gravitational term dominates and banking aligns the object's -Y axis with "gravitational down" direction. When turning, the radial component grows larger and the "accelerational down" direction swings outward, like a pendulum hanging from the flying object. The magnitude of the turning acceleration varies directly with the object's velocity and with the curvature of its path (so inversely with the radius of its turn). The limiting case of infinite velocity resembles banking behavior in the absence of gravity. In these cases the local +Y (up) direction points directly at the center of curvature defined by the current turn.

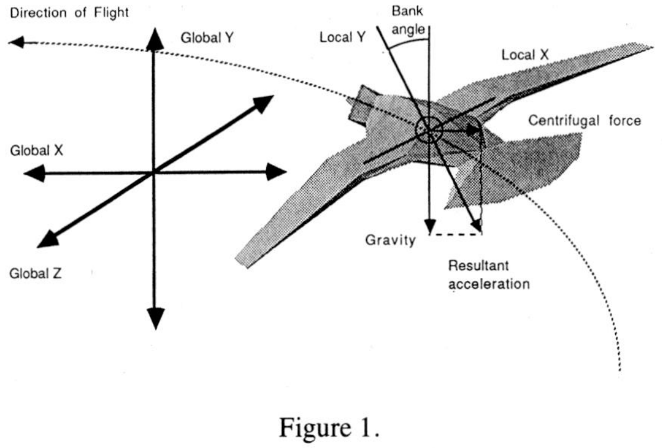

Figure 1.

With correct banking (what pilots call a *coordinated turn*) the object's local space remains aligned with the "perceptual" or "accelerational" coordinate system. This has several advantages: it simplifies the bird's (or pilot's) orientation task, it keeps the lift from the airfoils of the wings pointed in the most efficient direction ("accelerational up"), it keeps the passengers' coffee in their cups, and most importantly for animation, it makes the flying boid fit the viewer's expectation of how flying objects should move and orient themselves. On the other hand, realism is not always the goal in animation. By simply reversing the angle of bank we obtain a cartoony motion that looks like the object is being flung outward by the centrifugal force of the turn.

Boids and Turtles

The incremental mixing of forward translations and local rotations that underlies geometric flight is the basis of "turtle graphics" in the programming language *Logo* [5]. Logo was first used as an educational tool to allow children to learn experimentally about geometry, arithmetic, and programming [22]. The Logo *turtle* was originally a little mechanical robot that crawled around on large sheets of paper laid on the classroom floor, drawing graphic figures by dragging a felt tip marker along the paper as it moved. Abstract *turtle geometry* is a system based on the frame of reference of the turtle, an object that unites position and heading. Under program control the Logo turtle could move forward or back from its current position, turn left or right from its current heading, or put the pen up or down on the paper. The turtle geometry has been extended from the plane onto arbitrary manifolds and into 3D space [1]. These "3d turtles" and their paths are exactly equivalent to the boid objects and their flight paths.

Natural Flocks, Herds, and Schools

". . . and the thousands of fishes moved as a huge beast, piercing the water. They appeared united, inexorably bound to a common fate. How comes this unity?"

—Anonymous, 17th century (from Shaw)

For a bird to participate in a flock, it must have behaviors that allow it to coordinate its movements with those of its flockmates. These behaviors are not particularly unique; all creatures have them to some degree. Natural flocks seem to consist of two balanced, opposing behaviors: a desire to stay close to the flock and a desire to avoid collisions within the flock [34]. It is clear why an individual bird wants to avoid collisions with its flockmates. But why do birds seem to seek out the airborne equivalent of a nasty traffic jam? The basic urge to join a flock seems to be the result of evolutionary pressure from several factors: protection from predators, statistically improving survival of the (shared) gene pool from attacks from predators, profiting from a larger effective search pattern in the quest for food, and advantages for social and mating activities [33].

There is no evidence that the complexity of natural flocks is bounded in any way. Flocks do not become "full" or "overloaded" as new birds join. When herring migrate toward their spawning grounds, they run in schools extending as long as 17 miles and containing millions of fish [32]. Natural flocks seem to operate in exactly the same fashion over a huge range of flock populations. It does not seem that an individual bird can be paying much attention to each and every one of its flockmates. But in a huge flock spread over vast distances, an individual bird must have a localized and filtered perception of the rest of the flock. A bird might be aware of three categories: itself, its two or three nearest neighbors, and the rest of the flock [23].

These speculations about the "computational complexity" of flocking are meant to suggest that birds can flock with any number of flockmates because they are using what would be called in formal computer science a *constant time algorithm.* That is, the amount of "thinking" that a bird has to do in order to flock must be largely independent of the number of birds in the flock. Otherwise we would expect to see a sharp upper bound on the size of natural flocks when the individual birds became overloaded by the complexity of their navigation task. This has not been observed in nature.

Contrast the insensitivity to complexity of real flocks with the situation for the simulated flocks described below. The complexity of the flocking algorithm described is basically $O(N^2)$. That is, the work required to run the algorithm grows as the *square* of the flock's population. We definitely **do** see an upper bound on the size of simulated flocks implemented as described here. Some techniques to address this performance issue are discussed in the section Algorithmic Considerations.

Simulated Flocks

To build a simulated flock, we start with a boid model that supports geometric flight. We add behaviors that correspond to the opposing forces of collision avoidance and the urge to join the flock. Stated briefly as rules, and in order of decreasing precedence, the behaviors that lead to simulated flocking are:

1. Collision Avoidance: avoid collisions with nearby flockmates
2. Velocity Matching: attempt to match velocity with nearby flockmates
3. Flock Centering: attempt to stay close to nearby flockmates

Velocity is a vector quantity, referring to the combination of *heading* and *speed*. The manner in which the results from each of these behaviors is reconciled and combined is significant and is discussed in more detail later. Similarly, the meaning *nearby* in these rules is key to the flocking process. This is also discussed in more detail later, but generally one boid's awareness of another is based on the distance and direction of the offset vector between them.

Static *collision avoidance* and dynamic *velocity matching* are complementary. Together they ensure that the members of a simulated flock are free to fly within the crowded skies of the flock's interior without running into one another. Collision avoidance is the urge to steer away from an imminent impact. *Static* collision avoidance is based on the relative position of the flockmates and ignores their velocity. Conversely, velocity matching is based only on velocity and ignores position. It is a *predictive* version of collision avoidance: if the boid does a good job of matching velocity with its neighbors, it is unlikely that it will collide with any of them any time soon. With velocity matching, separations between boids remains *approximately invariant* with respect to ongoing geometric flight. Static collision avoidance serves to establish the minimum required separation distance; velocity matching tends to maintain it.

Flock centering makes a boid want to be near the center of the flock. Because each boid has a localized perception of the world, "center of the flock" actually means the center of the nearby flockmates. Flock centering causes the boid to fly in a direction that moves it closer to the centroid of the nearby boids. If a boid is deep inside a flock, the population density in its neighborhood is roughly homogeneous; the boid density is approximately the same in all directions. In this case, the centroid of the neighborhood boids is approximately at the center of the neighborhood, so the flock centering urge is small. But if a boid is on the boundary of the flock, its neighboring boids are on one side. The centroid of the neighborhood boids is displaced from the center of the neighborhood toward the body of the flock. Here the flock centering urge is stronger and the flight path will be deflected somewhat toward the local flock center.

Real flocks sometimes split apart to go around an obstacle. To be realistic, the simulated flock model must also have this ability. Flock centering correctly allows simulated flocks to bifurcate. As long as an individual boid can stay close to its nearby neighbors, it does not care if the rest of the flock turns away. More simplistic models proposed for flock organization (such as a *central force* model or a *follow the designated leader* model) do not allow splits.

The flock model presented here is actually a better model of a school or a herd than a flock. Fish in murky water (and land animals with their inability to see past their herdmates) have a limited, short-range perception of their environment. Birds, especially those on the outside of a flock, have excellent long-range "visual perception." Presumably this allows widely separated flocks to join together. If the flock centering urge was completely localized, when two flocks got a certain distance apart they would ignore each other. Long-range vision seems to play a part in the incredibly rapid propagation of a "maneuver wave" through a flock of birds. It has been shown that the speed of propagation of this wavefront reaches three times the speed implied by the measured startle reaction time of the individual birds. The explanation advanced by Wayne Potts is that the birds perceive the motion of the oncoming "maneuver wave" and time their own turn to match it [25]. Potts refers to this as the "chorus line" hypothesis.

Arbitrating Independent Behaviors

The three behavioral urges associated with flocking (and others to be discussed below) each produce an isolated suggestion about which way to steer the boid. These are expressed as *acceleration requests*. Each behavior says: "if **I** were in charge, **I** would accelerate in *that* direction." The acceleration request is in terms of a 3D vector that, by system convention, is truncated to unit magnitude or less. Each behavior has several parameters that control its function; one is a "strength," a fractional value between zero and one that can further attenuate the acceleration request. It is up to the *navigation module* of the boid brain to collect all relevant acceleration requests and then determine a single behaviorally desired acceleration. It must combine, prioritize, and arbitrate between potentially conflicting urges. The *pilot module* takes the acceleration desired by the navigation module and passes it to the *flight module*, which attempts to fly in that direction.

The easiest way to combine acceleration requests is to average them. Because of the included "strength" factors, this is actually a weighted average. The relative strength of one behavior to another can be defined this way, but it is a precarious interrelationship that is difficult to adjust. An early version of the boid model showed that navigation by simple weighted averaging of acceleration requests works "pretty well." A boid that chooses its course this way will fly a reasonable course under typical conditions. But in critical situations, such as potential collision with obstacles, conflicts must be resolved in a timely manner. During high-speed flight, hesitation or indecision is the wrong response to a brick wall dead ahead.

The main cause of indecision is that each behavior might be shouting advice about which way to turn to avoid disaster, but if those acceleration requests happen to lie in approximately opposite directions, they will largely cancel out under a simple weighted averaging scheme. The boid would make a very small turn and so continue in the same direction, perhaps to crash into the obstacle. Even when the urges do not cancel out, averaging leads to other problems. Consider flying over a gridwork of city streets between the skyscrapers; while "fly north" or "fly east" might be good ideas, it would be a bad idea to combine them as "fly northeast."

Techniques from artificial intelligence, such as expert systems, can be used to arbitrate conflicting opinions. However, a less complex approach is taken in the current implementation. *Prioritized acceleration allocation* is based on a strict priority ordering of all component behaviors, hence of the consideration of their acceleration requests. (This ordering can change to suit dynamic conditions.) The acceleration requests are considered in priority order and added into an accumulator. The *magnitude* of each request is measured and added into another accumulator. This process continues until the sum of the accumulated magnitudes gets larger than the *maximum acceleration* value, which is a parameter of each boid. The last acceleration request is trimmed back to compensate for the excess of accumulated magnitude. The point is that a fixed amount of acceleration is under the control of the navigation module; this acceleration is parceled out to satisfy the acceleration request of the various behaviors in order of priority. In an emergency the acceleration would be allocated to satisfy the most pressing needs first; if all available acceleration is "used up," the less pressing behaviors might be temporarily unsatisfied. For example, the flock centering urge could be correctly ignored temporarily in favor of a maneuver to avoid a static obstacle.

Simulated Perception

The boid model does not directly simulate the senses used by real animals during flocking (vision and hearing) or schooling (vision and fishes' unique "lateral line" structure that provides a certain amount of pressure imaging ability [23, 24]). Rather the perception model tries to make available to the behavior model approximately the same information that is available to a real animal as the end result of its perceptual and cognitive processes.

This is primarily a matter of filtering out the surplus information that is available to the software that implements the boid's behavior. Simulated boids have direct access to the geometric database that describes the exact position, orientation, and velocity of all objects in the environment. The real bird's information about the world is severely limited because it perceives through imperfect senses and because its nearby flockmates hide those farther away. This is even more pronounced in herding animals because they are all constrained to be in the same plane. In fish schools, visual perception of neighboring fish is further limited by the scattering and absorption of light by the sometimes murky water between them. These factors combine to strongly localize the information available to each animal.

Not only is it unrealistic to give each simulated boid perfect and complete information about the world, it is just plain wrong and leads to obvious failures of the behavior model. Before the current implementation of localized *flock centering* behavior was implemented, the flocks used a central force model. This leads to unusual effects such as causing all members of a widely scattered flock to simultaneously converge toward the flock's centroid. An interesting result of the experiments reported in this paper is that the aggregate motion that we intuitively recognize as "flocking" (or schooling or herding) **depends** upon a limited, localized view of the world.

The behaviors that make up the flocking model are stated in terms of "nearby flockmates." In the current implementation, the neighborhood is defined as a spherical zone of sensitivity centered at the boid's local origin. The magnitude of the sensitivity is defined as an inverse exponential of distance. Hence the neighborhood is defined by two parameters: a radius and exponent. There is reason to believe that this field of sensitivity should realistically be exaggerated in the forward direction and probably by an amount proportional to the boid's speed. Being in motion requires an increased awareness of what lies ahead, and this requirement increases with speed. A forward-weighted sensitivity zone would probably also improve the behavior in the current implementation of boids at the leading edge of a flock, who tend to get distracted by the flock behind them. Because of the way their heads and eyes are arranged, real birds have a wide field of view (about 300 degrees), but the zone of overlap from both eyes is small (10 to 15 degrees). Hence the bird has stereo depth perception only in a very small, forward-oriented cone. Research is currently under way on models of forward-weighted perception for boids.

In an early version of the flock model, the metrics of attraction and repulsion were weighted linearly by distance. This spring-like model produced a bouncy flock action, fine perhaps for a cartoony characterization, but not very realistic. The model was changed to use an inverse square of the distance. This more gravity-like model produced what appeared to be a more natural, better damped flock model. This correlated well with the carefully controlled quantitative studies that Brian Partridge made of the spatial relationships of schooling fish [23]; he found that "a fish is much more strongly influenced by its near neighbors than it is by the distant members of the school. The contribution of each fish to the [influence] is inversely proportional to the square or the cube of the distance." In previous work he and colleagues [23, 24] demonstrated that fishes school based on information from both their visual system and from their "lateral line" organ which senses pressure waves. The area of a perspective image of the silhouette of an object (its "visual angle") varies inversely with the square of its distance, and that pressure waves traveling through a 3D medium like water fall off inversely with the cube of the distance.

The boid perception model is quite *ad hoc* and avoids actually simulating vision. Artificial vision is an extremely complex problem [38] and is far beyond the scope of this work. But if boids could "see" their environment, they would be better at path planning than the current model. It is possible to construct simple maze-like shapes that would confuse the current boid model but would be easily solved by a boid with vision.

Impromptu Flocking

The flocking model described above gives boids an eagerness to participate in an acceptable approximation of flock-like motion. Boids released near one another begin to flock together, cavorting and jostling for position. The boids stay near one another (*flock centering*) but always maintain prudent separation from their neighbors (*collision avoidance*), and the flock quickly becomes "polarized"—its members heading in approximately the same direction at approximately the same speed (*velocity matching*); when they change direction they do it in synchronization. Solitary boids and smaller flocks join to become larger flocks, and in the presence of external obstacles (discussed below), larger flocks can split into smaller flocks.

For each simulation run, the initial position (within a specified ellipsoid), heading, velocity, and various other parameters of the boid model are initialized to values randomized within specified distributions. A restartable random-number generator is used to allow repeatability. This randomization is not required; the boids could just as well start out arranged in a regular pattern, all other aspects of the flock model are completely deterministic and repeatable.

When the simulation is run, the flock's first action is a reaction to the initial conditions. If the boids started out too closely crowded together, there is an initial "flash expansion" where the mutual desire to avoid collision drives the boids radially away from the site of the initial over-pressure. If released in a spherical shell with a radius smaller than the "neighborhood" radius, the boids contract toward the sphere's center; otherwise they begin to coalesce into small flockettes that might themselves begin to join together. If the boids are confined within a certain region, the smaller flocks eventually conglomerate into a single flock if left to wander long enough.

Scripted Flocking

The behaviors discussed so far provide for the ability of individual birds to fly and participate in happy aimless flocking. But to combine flock simulations with other animated action, we need more direct control over the flock. We would like to direct specific action at specific times (for example, "the flock enters from the left at :02.3 seconds into the sequence, turns to fly directly upward at :03.5, and is out of the frame at :04.0").

The current implementation of the boid model has several facilities to direct the motion and timing of the flock action. First, the simulations are run under the control of a general-purpose animation scripting system [36]. The details of that scripting system are not relevant here except that, in addition to the typical interactive motion control facilities, it provides the ability to schedule the invocation of user-supplied software (such as the flock model) on a frame-by-frame basis. This scripting facility is the basic tool used to describe the timing of various flock actions. It also allows flexible control over the time-varying values of parameters, which can be passed down to the simulation software. Finally the script is used to set up and animate all nonbehavioral aspects of the scene, such as backgrounds, lighting, camera motion, and other visible objects.

The primary tool for scripting the flock's path is the *migratory urge* built into the boid model. In the current model this urge is specified in terms of a global target, either as a global direction (as in "going Z for the winter") or as a global position—a target point toward which all birds fly. The model computes a bounded acceleration that incrementally turns the boid toward its migratory target.

With the scripting system, we can *animate* a dynamic parameter whose value is a global position vector or a global direction vector. This parameter can be passed to the flock, which can in turn pass it along to all boids, each of which sets its own "migratory goal register." Hence the global migratory behavior of all birds can be directly controlled from the script. (Of course, it is not necessary to alter all boids at the same time, for example, the delay could be a function of their present position in space. Real flocks do not change direction simultaneously [25], but rather the turn starts with a single bird and spreads quickly across the flock like a shock wave.)

We can lead the flock around by animating the goal point along the desired path, somewhat ahead of the flock. Even if the migratory goal point is changed abruptly the path of each boid still is relatively smooth because of the flight model's simulated conservation of momentum. This means that the boid's own flight dynamics implement a form of smoothing interpolation between "control points."

Avoiding Environmental Obstacles

The most interesting motion of a simulated flock comes from interaction with other objects in the environment. The isolated behavior of a flock tends to reach a steady state and becomes rather sterile. The flock can be seen as a *relaxation* solution to the constraints implied by its behaviors. For example, the conflicting urges of *flock centering* and *collision avoidance* do not lead to constant back and forth motion, but rather the boids eventually strike a balance between the two urges (the degree of damping controls how soon this balance is reached). Environmental obstacles and the boid's attempts to navigate around them increase the apparent complexity of the behavior of the flock. (In fact the complexity of real flocks might be due largely to the complexity of the natural environment.)

Environmental obstacles are also important from the standpoint of modeling the scene in which we wish to place the flock. If the flock is scripted to fly under a bridge and around a tree, we must be able to represent the geometric shape and dimension of these obstacles. The approach taken here is to independently model the "shape for rendering" and the "shape for collision avoidance." The types of shapes currently used for environmental obstacles are much less complicated than the models used for rendering of computer graphic models. The current work implements two types of shapes of environmental collision avoidance. One is based on the *force field* concept, which works in undemanding situations but has some shortcomings. The other model called *steer-to-avoid* is more robust and seems closer in spirit to the natural mechanism.

The force field model postulates a field of repulsion force emanating from the obstacle out into space; the boids are increasingly repulsed as they get closer to the obstacle. This scheme is easy to model; the geometry of the field is usually fairly simple and so an avoidance acceleration can be directly calculated from the field equation. These models can produce good results, such as in "Eurythmy" [4], but they also have drawbacks that are apparent on close examination. If a boid approaches an obstacle surrounded by a force field at an angle such that it is exactly opposite to the direction of the force field, the boid will not turn away. In this case the force field serves only to slow the boid by accelerating it backwards and provides no side thrust at all. The worst reaction to an impending collision is to fail to turn. Force fields also cause problems with "peripheral vision." The boid should notice and turn away from a wall as it flies toward it, but the wall should be ignored if the boid is flying alongside it. Finally, force fields tend to be too strong close up and too weak far away; avoiding an obstacle should involve long-range planning rather than panicky corrections at the last minute.

Steer-to-avoid is a better simulation of a natural bird guided by vision. The boid considers only obstacles directly in front of it. (It finds the intersection, if any, of its local Z axis with the obstacle.) Working in local perspective space, it finds the silhouette edge of the obstacle closest to the point of eventual impact. A radial vector is computed which will aim the boid at a point one body length beyond that silhouette edge (see figure 2). Currently steer-to-avoid has been implemented for several obstacle shapes: spheres, cylinders, planes, and boxes. Collision avoidance for arbitrary convex polyhedral obstacles is being developed.

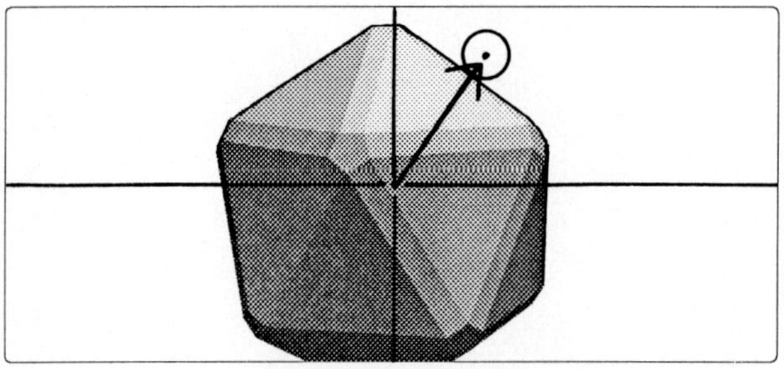

Figure 2.

Obstacles are not necessarily fixed in space; they can be animated around by the script during the animation. Or more interestingly, the obstacles can be behavioral characters. Sparrows might flock around a group of obstacles that is in fact a herd of elephants. Similarly, behavioral obstacles might not merely be in the way; they might be objects of fear such as predators. It has been noted [25] that natural flocking instincts seem to be sharpened by predators.

Other Applications of the Flock Model

The model of polarized noncolliding aggregate motion has many applications, visual simulation of bird flocks in computer animation being one. Certain modifications yield a fish school model. Further modifications, such as limitation to a 2D surface and the ability to follow the terrain, lead to a herd model. Imagine a herd of PODA-style legged creatures [9], using Karl Sims' techniques for locomotion over uneven, complex terrain [35]. Other applications are less obvious. Traffic patterns, such as the flow of cars on a freeway, is a flock-like motion. There are specialized behaviors, such as being constrained to drive within the lanes, but the basic principles that keep boids from colliding are just as applicable on the freeway. We could imagine creating crowds of "extras" (human or otherwise) for feature films. However the most fun are the offbeat combinations possible in computer graphics by mixing and matching: a herd of pogo sticks, a flock of Pegasus-like winged horses, or a traffic jam of spaceships on a 3D interplanetary highway.

One serious application would be to aid in the scientific investigation of flocks, herds, and schools. These scientists must work almost exclusively in the observational mode; experiments with natural flocks and schools are difficult to perform and are likely to disturb the behaviors under study. It might be possible, using a more carefully crafted model of the realistic behavior of a certain species of bird, to perform controlled and repeatable experiments with "simulated natural flocks." A theory of flock organization can be unambiguously tested by implementing a distributed behavioral model and simply comparing the aggregate motion of the simulated flock with the natural one.

Algorithmic Considerations

A naive implementation of the basic flocking algorithm would grow in complexity as the order of the square of the flock's population ("$O(N^2)$"). Basically this is because each boid must reason about each of the other boids, even if only to decide to ignore it. This does not say the algorithm is slow or fast, merely that as the size of the problem (total population of the flock) increases, the complexity increases even faster. Doubling the number of boids quadruples the amount of time taken.

However, as stated before, real birds are probably not as sensitive to the total flock population. This gives hope that the simulated boid could be taught to navigate independently of the total population. Certainly part of the problem is that we are trying to run the simulation of the whole flock on a single computer. The natural solution is to use distributed processing, as the real flock does. If we used a separate processor for each boid, then even the naive implementation of the flocking algorithm would be $O(N)$, or *linear* with respect to the population. But even that is not good enough. It still means that as more boids are added to the flock, the complexity of the problem increases.

What we desire is a *constant time algorithm*, one that is insensitive to the total population. Another way to say this is that an N^2 algorithm would be OK if there was an efficient way to keep N very small. Two approaches to this goal are currently under investigation. One is dynamic spatial partitioning of the flock; the boids are sorted into a lattice of "bins" based on their position in space. A boid trying to navigate inside the flock could get quick access to the flockmates that are physically nearby by examining the "bins" near its current position. Another approach is to do incremental collision detection ("nearness testing"). General collision detection is another N^2 algorithm, but if one does collision detection incrementally, based on a partial solution that described the situation just a moment before, then the algorithm need worry only about the changes and so can run much faster, assuming that the incremental changes are small. The incremental collision detection algorithm used in Girard's PODA system [9] apparently achieves constant time performance in the typical case.

Computing Environment

The boids software was written in Symbolics Common Lisp. The code and animation were produced on a Symbolics 3600 Lisp Machine, a high-performance personal computer. The flock software is implemented in Flavors, the object-oriented programming extensions to Symbolics Common Lisp. The geometric aspects of the system are layered upon S-Geometry, an interactive geometric modeler [37]. Boids are based on the flavor 3D:OBJECT, which provides their geometric abilities. The flock simulations are invoked from scripts created and animated with the S-Dynamics [36] animation system, which also provided the real-time playback facility used to view the motion tests. The availability of this graphical toolkit allowed the author to focus immediately on the issues unique to this project. One example of the value of this substrate is that the initial version of the flock model, including implementation, testing, debugging, and the production of seven short motion tests was accomplished in the ten days before the SIGGRAPH '86 conference.

The boid software has not been optimized for speed. But this report would be incomplete without a rough estimate of the actual performance of the system. With a flock of 80 boids, using the naive $O(N^2)$ algorithm (and so 6400 individual boid-to-boid comparisons), on a single Lisp Machine without any special hardware accelerators, the simulation ran for about 95 seconds per frame. A ten-second (300 frame) motion test took about eight hours of real time to produce.

Future Work

This paper has largely ignored the internal animation of the geometrical model that provides the visual representation of the boid. The original motion tests produced with these models all show flocks of little abstract rigid shapes that might be paper airplanes. There was no flapping of wings nor turning of heads, and there was certainly no character animation. These topics are all important and pertinent to believable animation of simulated flocks. But the underlying abstract nature of flocking as polarized, noncolliding aggregate motion is largely independent of these issues of internal shape change and articulation. This notion is supported by the fact that most viewers of these simulations identify the motion of these abstract objects as "flocking" even in the absence of any internal animation.

But doing a believable job of melding these two aspects of the motion is more than a matter of concatenating the action of an internal animation cycle for the character with the motion defined by geometrical flight. There are important issues of synchronization between the current state of the flight dynamics model, and the amplitude and frequency of the wing motion cycle. Topics of current development include internal animation, synchronization, and interfaces between the simulation-based flock model and other more traditional, interactive animation scripting systems. We would like to allow a skilled computer animator to design a bird character and define its "wing flap cycle" using standard interactive modeling and scripting techniques, and then be able to take this cyclic motion and "plug it in" to the flock simulation model causing the boids in the flock to fly according to the scripted cycle.

The behaviors that have been discussed in this paper are all simplistic, isolated behaviors of low complexity. The boids have a geometric and kinematic state, but they have no significant *mental state*. Real animals have more elaborate, abstract behaviors than a simple desire to avoid a painful collision; they have more complex motivations than a simple desire to fly to a certain point in space. More interesting behavior models would take into account hunger, finding food, fear of predators, a periodic need to sleep, and so on. Behavior models of this type have been created by other investigators [6, 19, 21], but they have not yet been implemented for the boid model described here.

Conclusion

This paper has presented a model of polarized, noncolliding aggregate motion, such as that of flocks, herds, and schools. The model is based on simulating the behavior of each bird independently. Working independently, the birds try both to stick together and avoid collisions with one another and with other objects in their environment. The animations showing simulated flocks built from this model seem to correspond to the observer's intuitive notion of what constitutes "flock-like motion." However it is difficult to objectively measure how valid these simulations are. By comparing behavioral aspects of the simulated flock with those of natural flocks, we are able improve and refine the model. But having approached a certain level of realism in the model, the parameters of the simulated flock can be altered at will by the animator to achieve many variations on flock-like behavior.

Acknowledgments

I would like to thank flocks, herds, and schools for existing; nature is the ultimate source of inspiration for computer graphics and animation. I would also like to acknowledge the contributions to this research provided by workers in a wonderfully diverse collection of pursuits:

To the natural sciences of behavior, evolution, and zoology: for doing the hard work, the Real Science, on which this computer graphics approximation is based. To the Logo group who invented the appropriate geometry, and so put us in the driver's seat. To the Actor semantics people who invented the appropriate control structure, and so gave the boid a brain. To the many developers of modern Lisp who invented the appropriate programming language. To my past and present colleagues at MIT, III, and Symbolics who have patiently listened to my speculations about flocks for years and years before I made my first boid fly. To the Graphics Division of Symbolics, Inc., who employ me, put up with my nasty disposition, provide me with fantastic computing and graphics facilities, and have generously supported the development of the work described here. And to the field of computer graphics, for giving professional respectability to advanced forms of play such as reported in this paper.

References

1. Abelson, H., and diSessa, A., "Maneuvering a Three Dimensional Turtle" in *Turtle Geometry: The Computer as a Medium for Exploring Mathematics*, The MIT Press, Cambridge, Massachusetts, 1981, pp. 140–159.

2. Agha, G., *Actors: A Model of Concurrent Computation in Distributed Systems*, The MIT Press, Cambridge, Massachusetts, 1986.

3. Amkraut, S., personal communication, January 8, 1987.

4. Amkraut, S., Girard, M., Karl, G., "motion studies for a work in progress entitled 'Eurythmy' " in *SIGGRAPH Video Review*, Issue 21 (second item, time code 3:58 to 7:35), 1985, produced at the Computer Graphics Research Group, Ohio State University, Columbus, Ohio.

5. Austin, H., "The Logo Primer," MIT A.I. Lab, Logo Working Paper 19, 1974.

6. Braitenberg, V., *Vehicles: Experiments in Synthetic Psychology*, The MIT Press, Cambridge, Massachusetts, 1984.

7. Burton, R., *Bird Behavior*, Alfred A. Knopf, Inc., 1985.

8. Davis, J. R., Kay, A., Marion, A., unpublished research on behavioral simulation and animation, Atari Research, 1983.

9. Girard, M., Maciejewski, A. A., "Computational Modeling for the Computer Animation of Legged Figures," in *Computer Graphics* V19 #3, 1985, (proceedings of acm SIGGRAPH '85), pp. 263–270.

10. Goldberg, A., Robson, D., *SMALLTALK-80, The Language and its Implementation*, Addison-Wesley Publishing Company, Reading Massachusetts, 1983.

11. Goldberg, A., Kay, A., *SMALLTALK-72 Instruction Manual*, Learning research group, Xerox Palo Alto Research Center, 1976.

12. Hewitt, C., Atkinson, R., "Parallelism and Synchronization in Actor Systems," *acm Symposium on Principles of Programming Languages 4*, January 1977, Los Angeles, California.

13. Kahn, K. M., *Creation of Computer Animation from Story Descriptions*, MIT Artificial Intelligence Laboratory, Technical Report 540 (doctoral dissertation), August 1979.

14. Kahn, K. M., Hewitt, C., *Dynamic Graphics using Quasi Parallelism*, May 1978, proceedings of ACM SIGGRAPH, 1978.

15. Kleinrock, L., "Distributed Systems," in *Communications of the ACM*, V28 #11, November 1985, pp. 1200–1213.

16. Lipton, J., *An Exaltation of Larks (or, The Venereal Game)*, Grossman Publishers, 1977. Reprinted by Penguin Books 1977, 1980, 1982, 1983, 1984, 1985.

17. Maciejewski, A. A., Klein, C.A., "Obstacle Avoidance for Kinematically Redundant Manipulators in Dynamically Varying Environments," to appear in *International Journal of Robotic Research*.

18. Magnenat-Thalmann, N., Thalmann, D., *Computer Animation: Theory and Practice*, Springer-Verlag, Toyko, 1985.

19. Marion, A., "Artificially Motivated Objects," [installation piece], ACM SIGGRAPH art show, 1985.

20. Moon, D. A., "Object-oriented Programming with Flavors," in *Proceedings of the First Annual Conference on Object-Oriented Programming Systems, Languages, and Applications*, ACM, 1986

21. Myers, R., Broadwell, P., Schaufler, R., "Plasm: Fish Sample," [installation piece], ACM SIGGRAPH art show, 1985.

22. Papert, S., "Teaching Children to be Mathematicians vs. Teaching Them About Mathematics," *International Journal of Mathematical Education and Sciences*, V3, pp. 249–262, 1972.

23. Partridge, B. L., "The Structure and Function of Fish Schools," *Scientific American*, June 1982, pp. 114–123.

24. Pitcher, T. J., Partridge, B. L., Wardle, C. S., "Blind Fish Can School," *Science* 194, #4268 (1976), p. 964.

25. Potts, W. K., "The Chorus-Line Hypothesis of Manoeuver Coordination in Avian Flocks," letter in *Nature*, Vol 309, May 24, 1984, pp. 344–345.

26. Pugh, J., "Actors—The Stage is Set," *acm SIGPLAN Notices*, V19 #3, March 1984, pp. 61–65.

27. Reeves, W., T., "Particle Systems—A Technique for Modeling a Class of Fuzzy Objects," *acm Transactions on Graphics*, V2 #2, April 1983, and reprinted in *Computer Graphics*, V17 #3, July 1983, (acm SIGGRAPH '83 Proceedings), pp. 359–376.

28. Reynolds, C. W., *Computer Animation in the World of Actors and Scripts*, SM thesis, MIT (the Architecture Machine Group), May 1978.

29. Reynolds, C. W., "Computer Animation with Scripts and Actors," *Computer Graphics*, V16 #3, July 1982, (acm SIGGRAPH '82 Proceedings), pp. 289–296.

30. Reynolds, C. W., "Description and Control of Time and Dynamics in Computer Animation" in the notes for the course on Advanced Computer Animation at acm SIGGRAPH '85, and reprinted for the notes of the same course in 1986.

31. Selous, E., *Thought-transference (or what?) in Birds*, Constable, London, 1931.

32. Scheffer, V. B., *Spires of Form: Glimpses of Evolution*, Harcourt Brace Jovanovich, San Diego, 1983 (reprinted 1985 by Harvest/HBJ), p. 64.

33. Shaw, E., "Schooling in Fishes: Critique and Review" in *Development and Evolution of Behavior*. W. H. Freeman and Company, San Francisco, 1970, pp. 452–480.

34. Shaw, E., "Fish in Schools," *Natural History* 84, no. 8 (1975), pp. 40–46.

35. Sims, K., *Locomotion of Jointed Figures Over Complex Terrain*, SM thesis, MIT Media Lab, currently in preparation, April 1987.

36. Symbolics Graphics Division, *S-Dynamics* (user's manual), Symbolics Inc., November 1986.

37. Symbolics Graphics Division, *S-Geometry* (user's manual), Symbolics Inc., October 1986.

38. Pinker, S. (editor), *Visual Cognition*, The MIT Press, Cambridge, Massachusetts, 1985.

39. Thomas, F., Johnson, O., *Disney Animation: The Illusion of Life*, Abbeville Press, New York, 1981, pp. 47–69.

40. Wilhelms, J., "Toward Automatic Motion Control," *IEEE Computer Graphics and Applications*, V7 #4, April 1987, pp. 11–22.

41. Zeltzer, D., "Toward an Integrated View of 3-D Computer Animation," *The Visual Computer*, V1 #4, 1985, pp. 249–259.

PRINCIPLES OF TRADITIONAL ANIMATION APPLIED TO 3D COMPUTER ANIMATION

John Lasseter
Pixar
San Rafael
California

"There is no particular mystery in animation... it's really very simple, and like anything that is simple, it is about the hardest thing in the world to do." Bill Tytla at the Walt Disney Studio, June 28, 1937. [14]

ABSTRACT

This paper describes the basic principles of traditional 2D hand drawn animation and their application to 3D computer animation. After describing how these principles evolved, the individual principles are detailed, addressing their meanings in 2D hand drawn animation and their application to 3D computer animation. This should demonstrate the importance of these principles to quality 3D computer animation.

CR Categories and Subject Descriptors:
I.3.6 *Computer Graphics* : Methodology and Techniques - Interaction techniques;
I.3.7 *Computer Graphics* : Three-dimensional Graphics and Realism - Animation;
J.5 *Computer Applications* : Arts and Humanities - Arts, fine and performing.

General Terms: Design, Human Factors.

Additional Keywords and Phrases: Animation Principles, Keyframe Animation, Squash and Stretch, Luxo Jr.

1. INTRODUCTION

Early research in computer animation developed 2D animation techniques based on traditional animation. [7] Techniques such as storyboarding [11], keyframe animation, [4,5] inbetweening, [16,22] scan/paint, and multiplane backgrounds [17] attempted to apply the cel animation process to the computer. As 3D computer animation research matured, more resources were devoted to image rendering than to animation. Because 3D computer animation uses 3D models instead of 2D drawings, fewer techniques from traditional animation were applied. Early 3D animation systems were script based [6], followed by a few spline-interpolated keyframe systems. [22] But these systems were developed by companies for internal use, and so very few traditionally trained animators found their way into 3D computer animation.

"Luxo" is a trademark of Jac Jacobsen Industries AS.

The last two years have seen the appearance of reliable, user friendly, keyframe animation systems from such companies as Wavefront Technologies Inc., [29] Alias Research Inc., [2] Abel Image Research (RIP), [1] Vertigo Systems Inc., [28] Symbolics Inc., [25] and others. These systems will enable people to produce more high quality computer animation. Unfortunately, these systems will also enable people to produce more **bad** computer animation.

Much of this bad animation will be due to unfamiliarity with the fundamental principles that have been used for hand drawn character animation for over 50 years. Understanding these principles of traditional animation is essential to producing good computer animation. Such an understanding should also be important to the designers of the systems used by these animators.

In this paper, I will explain the fundamental principles of traditional animation and how they apply to 3D keyframe computer animation.

2. PRINCIPLES OF ANIMATION

Between the late 1920's and the late 1930's animation grew from a novelty to an art form at the Walt Disney Studio. With every picture, actions became more convincing, and characters were emerging as true personalities. Audiences were enthusiastic and many of the animators were satisfied, however it was clear to Walt Disney that the level of animation and existing characters were not adequate to pursue new story lines-- characters were limited to certain types of action and, audience acceptance notwithstanding, they were not appealing to the eye. It was apparent to Walt Disney that no one could successfully animate a humanized figure or a life-like animal; a new drawing approach was necessary to improve the level of animation exemplified by the *Three Little Pigs* . [10]

FIGURE 1. Luxo Jr.'s hop with overlapping action on cord. Flip pages from last page of paper to front. The top figures are frames 1-5, the bottom are frames 6-10.

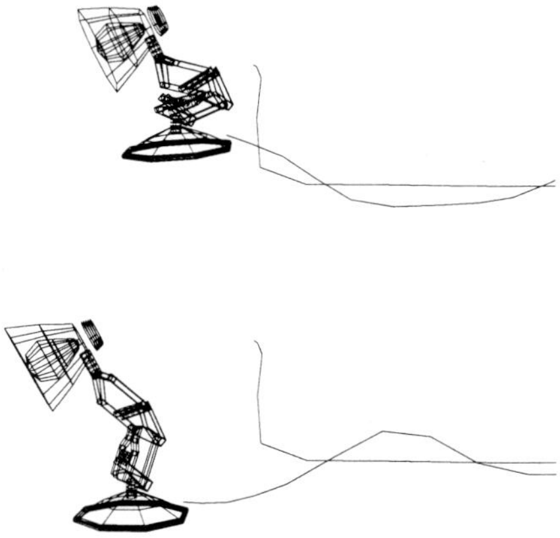

Disney set up drawing classes for his animators at the Chouinard Art Institute in Los Angeles under instructor Don Graham. When the classes were started, most of the animators were drawing using the old cartoon formula of standardized shapes, sizes, actions, and gestures, with little or no reference to nature. [12] Out of these classes grew a way of drawing moving human figures and animals. The students studied models in motion [20] as well as live action film, playing certain actions over and over. [13] The analysis of action became important to the development of animation.

Some of the animators began to apply the lessons of these classes to production animation, which became more sophisticated and realistic. The animators continually searched for better ways to communicate to one another the ideas learned from these lessons. Gradually, procedures were isolated and named, analyzed and perfected, and new artists were taught these practices as rules of the trade. [26] They became the fundamental principles of traditional animation:

1. *Squash and Stretch* -- Defining the rigidity and mass of an object by distorting its shape during an action.

2. *Timing* -- Spacing actions to define the weight and size of objects and the personality of characters.

3. *Anticipation* -- The preparation for an action.

4. *Staging* -- Presentating an idea so that it is unmistakably clear.

5. *Follow Through and Overlapping Action* -- The termination of an action and establishing its relationship to the next action.

6. *Straight Ahead Action and Pose-To-Pose Action* -- The two contrasting approaches to the creation of movement.

7. *Slow In and Out* -- The spacing of the inbetween frames to achieve subtlety of timing and movement.

8. *Arcs* -- The visual path of action for natural movement.

9. *Exaggeration* -- Accentuating the essence of an idea via the design and the action.

10. *Secondary Action* -- The action of an object resulting from another action.

11. *Appeal* -- Creating a design or an action that the audience enjoys watching.

The application of some of these principles mean the same regardless of the medium of animation. 2D hand drawn animation deals with a sequence of two dimensional drawings that simulate motion. 3D computer animation involves creating a three dimensional model in the computer. Motion is achieved by setting keyframe poses and having the computer generate the inbetween frames. Timing, anticipation, staging, follow through, overlap, exaggeration, and secondary action apply in the same way for both types of animation. While the meanings of squash and stretch, slow in and out, arcs, appeal, straight ahead action, and pose-to-pose action remain the same, their application changes due to the difference in medium.

2.1 SQUASH AND STRETCH

The most important principle is called *squash and stretch.* When an object is moved, the movement emphasizes any rigidity in the object. In real life, only the most rigid shapes (such as chairs, dishes and pans) remain so during motion. Anything composed of living flesh, no matter how bony, will show considerable movement in its shape during an action. For example, when a bent arm with swelling biceps straightens out, only the long sinews are apparent. A face, whether chewing, smiling, talking, or just showing a change of expression, is alive with changing shapes in the cheeks, the lips, and the eyes. [26]

The squashed position depicts the form either flattened out by an external pressure or constricted by its own power. The stretched position always shows the same form in a very extended condition. [26]

The most important rule to squash and stretch is that, no matter how squashed or stretched out a particular object gets, its volume remains constant. If an object squashed down without its sides stretching, it would appear to shrink; if it stretched up without its sides squeezing in it would appear to grow. Consider the shape and volume of a half filled flour sack: when dropped on the floor, it squashed out to its fullest shape. If picked up by the top corners, it stretched out to its longest shape. It never changes volume. [26]

The standard animation test for all beginners is drawing a bouncing ball. The assignment is to represent the ball by a simple circle, and then have it drop, hit the ground, and bounce back into the air. A simple test, but it teaches the basic mechanics of animating a scene, introducing timing as well as squash and stretch. If the bottom drawing is flattened, it gives the appearance of bouncing. Elongating the drawings before and after the bounce increases the sense of speed, makes it easier to follow and gives more snap to the action. [26,3] (figure 2)

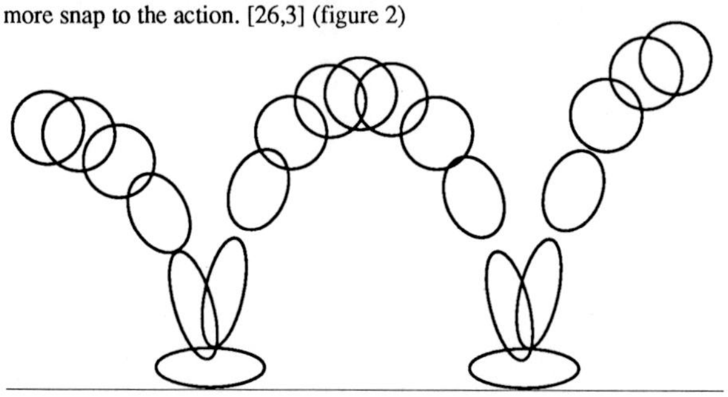

FIGURE 2. Squash & stretch in bouncing ball.

Squash and stretch also defines the rigidity of the material making up an object. When an object is squashed flat and stretches out drastically, it gives the sense that the object is made out of a soft, pliable material and vice versa. When the parts of an object are of different materials, they should respond differently: flexible parts should squash more and rigid parts less.

An object need not deform in order to squash and stretch. For instance, a hinged object like Luxo Jr. (from the film, *Luxo Jr.* [21]), squashes by folding over on itself, and stretches by extending out fully. (figure 3)

FIGURE 3. Squash & stretch in Luxo Jr.'s hop.

Squash and stretch is very important in facial animation, not only for showing the flexibility of the flesh and muscle, but also for showing the relationship of between the parts of the face. When a face smiles broadly, the corners of the mouth push up into the cheeks. The cheeks squash and push up into the eyes, making the eyes squint , which brings down the eyebrows and stretches the forehead. When the face adopts a surprised expression, the mouth opens, stretching down the cheeks. The wide open eyes push the eyebrows up, squashing and wrinkling the forehead.

Another use of squash and stretch is to help relieve the disturbing effect of strobing that happens with very fast motion because sequencial positions of an object become spaced far apart. When the action is slow enough, the object's positions overlap, and the eye smooths the motion out. (figure 4a) However, as the speed of the action increases, so does the distance between positions. When the distance becomes far enough that the object does not overlap from frame to frame, the eye then begins to perceive separate images. (figure 4b) Accurate motion blur is the most realistic solution to this problem of strobing, [8,9] but when motion blur is not available, squash and stretch is an alternative: the object should be stretched enough so that its positions **do** overlap from frame to frame (or nearly so), and the eye will smooth the action out again. (figure 4c)

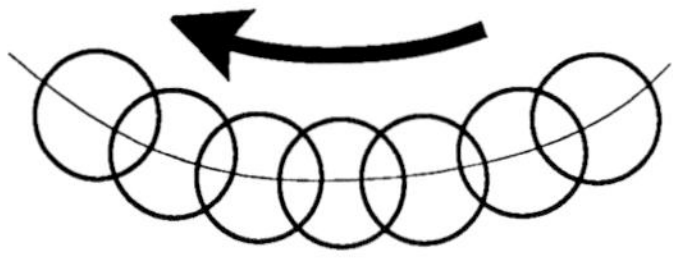

FIGURE 4a. In slow action, an object's position overlaps from frame to frame which gives the action a smooth appearance to the eye.

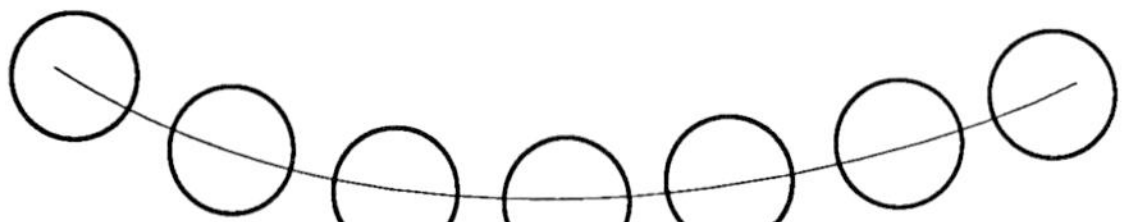

FIGURE 4b. Strobing occurs in a faster action when the object's positions do not overlap and the eye perceives seperate images.

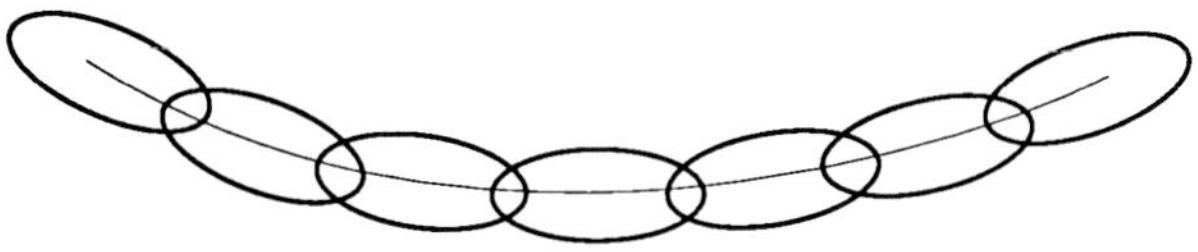

FIGURE 4c. Stretching the object so that it's positions overlap again will relieve the strobing effect.

In 3D keyframe computer animation, the scale transformation can be used for squash and stretch. When scaling up in Z, the object should be scaled down in X and Y to keep the volume the same. Since the direction of the stretch should be along the path of action, a rotational transformation may be required to align the object along an appropriate axis.

2.2 TIMING

Timing , or the speed of an action, is an important principle because it gives meaning to movement-- the speed of an action defines how well the idea behind the action will read to an audience. It reflects the weight and size of an object, and can even carry emotional meaning.

Proper timing is critical to making ideas readable. It is important to spend enough time (but no more) preparing the audience for: the anticipation of an action; the action itself; and the reaction to the action. If too much time is spent on any of these, the audience's attention will wander. If too little time is spent, the movement may be finished before the audience notices it, thus wasting the idea. [30]

The faster the movement, the more important it is to make sure the audience can follow what is happening. The action must not be so fast that the audience cannot read it and understand the meaning of it. [30]

More than any other principle, timing defines the weight of an object. Two objects, identical in size and shape, can appear to be two vastly different weights by manipulating timing alone. The heavier an object is, the greater its mass, and the more force is required to change its motion. A heavy body is slower to accelerate and decelerate than a light one. It takes a large force to get a cannonball moving, but once moving, it tends to keep moving at the same speed and requires some force to stop it. When dealing with heavy objects, one must allow plenty of time and force to start, stop or change their movements, in order to make their weight look convincing. [30]

Light objects have much less resistance to change of movement and so need much less time to start moving. The flick of a finger is enough to make a balloon accelerate quickly away. When moving, it has little momentum and even the friction of the air quickly slows it up. [30]

Timing can also contribute greatly to the feeling of size or scale of an object or character. A giant has much more weight, more mass, more inertia than a normal man; therefore he moves more slowly. Like the cannonball, he takes more time to get started and, once moving, takes more time to stop. Any changes of movement take place more slowly. Conversely, a tiny character has less inertia than normal, so his movements tend to be quicker. [30]

The way an object behaves on the screen, the effect of weight that it gives, depend entirely on the spacing of the poses and not on the poses themselves. No matter how well rendered a cannonball may be, it does not look like a cannonball if it does not behave like one when animated. The same applies to any object or character. [30]

The emotional state of a character can also be defined more by its movement than by its appearence, and the varying speed of those movements indicates whether the character is lethargic, excited, nervous or relaxed. Thomas and Johnston [26] describe how changing the timing of an action gives it new meaning:

Just two drawings of a head, the first showing it leaning toward the right shoulder and the second with it over on the left and its chin slightly raised, can be made to communicate a multitute of ideas, depending entirely on the Timing used. Each inbetween drawing added between these two "extremes" gives a new meaning to the action.

NO inbetweens........... The Character has been hit by a tremendous force. His head is nearly snapped off.

ONE inbetweens......... The Character has been hit by a brick, rolling pin, frying pan.

TWO inbetweens......... The Character has a nervous tic, a muscle spasm, an uncontrollable twitch.

THREE inbetweens..... The Character is dodging a brick, rolling pin, frying pan.

FOUR inbetweens........... The Character is giving a crisp order, "Get going!" "Move it!"

FIVE inbetweens........... The Character is more friendly, "Over here." "Come on-hurry!"

SIX inbetweens........... The Character sees a good looking girl, or the sports car he has always wanted.

SEVEN inbetweens........... The Character tries to get a better look at something.

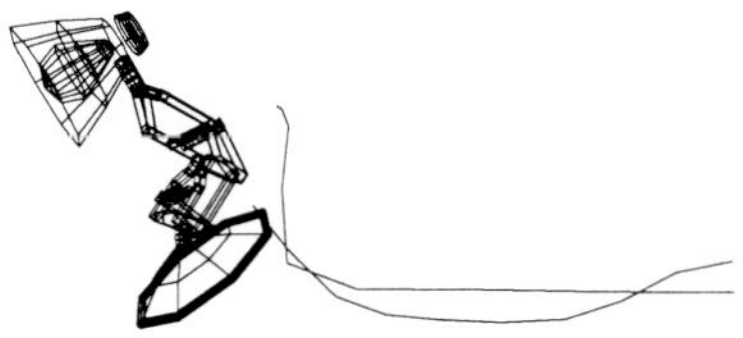

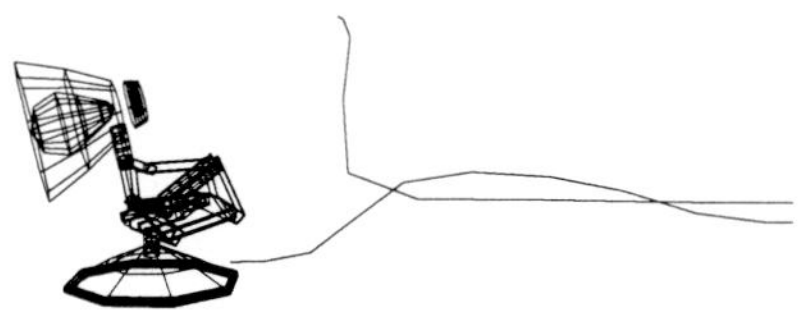

EIGHT inbetweens........... The Character searches for the peanut butter on the kitchen shelf.

NINE inbetweens...........The Character appraises, considering thoughtfully.

TEN inbetweens........... The Character stretches a sore muscle.

FIGURE 5. Wally B.'s zip off shows use of squash and stretch, anticipation, follow through, overlapping action, and secondary action.

2.3 ANTICIPATION

An action occurs in three parts: the preparation for the action, the action proper, and the termination of the action. *Anticipation* is the preparation for the action; the latter two are discussed in the next sections.

There are several facets to Anticipation. In one sense, it is the anatomical provision for an action. Since muscles in the body function through contraction, each must be first be extended before it can contract. A foot must be pulled back before it can be swung forward to kick a ball. [12] Without anticipation many actions are abrupt, stiff and unnatural.

Anticipation is also a device to catch the audience's eye, to prepare them for the next movement and lead them to expect it before it actually occurs. Anticipation is often used to explain what the following action is going to be. Before a character reaches to grab an object , he first raises his arms as he stares at the article, broadcasting the fact that he is going to do something with that particular object. The anticipatory moves may not show **why** he is doing something, but there is no question about **what** he is going to do next. [26]

Anticipation is also used to direct the attention of the audience to the right part of the screen at the right moment. This is essential for preventing the audience from missing some vital action. In the very beginning of *Luxo Jr.*, Dad is on screen alone looking offstage. He then reacts, anticipating something happening there. When Jr. does hop in, the audience is prepared for the action.

The amount of anticipation used considerably affects the speed of the action which follows it. If the audience expects something to happen, then it can be much faster without losing them. If they are not properly prepared for a very fast action, they may miss it completely; the anticipation must be made larger or the action slower. [30] In a slow action the anticipation is often minimized and the meaning carried in the action proper. [12] In one shot in*The Adventures of Andre and Wally B.* , Wally B. zips off to the right. The actual action of the zip off is only 3 or 4 frames long, but he anticipates the zip long enough for the audience to know exactly what is coming next. (figure 5)

Anticipation can also emphasize heavy weight, as for a character picking up an object that is very heavy. An exaggerated anticipation, like bending way down before picking up the object, helps the momentum of the character to lift the heavy weight. Likewise for a fat character standing up from a seated position: he will bend his upper body forward, with his hands on the armrests of the chair, before pushing up with his arms and using the momentum of his body. [31]

2.4 STAGING

Staging is the presentation of an idea so it is completely and unmistakably clear; this principle translates directly from 2-D hand drawn animation. An action is staged so that it is understood; a personality is staged so that it is recognizable; an expression so that it can be seen; a mood so that it will affect the audience. [26]

To stage an idea clearly, the audience's eye must be led to exactly where it needs to be at the right moment, so that they will not miss the idea. Staging, anticipation and timing are all integral to directing the eye. A well-timed anticipation will be wasted if it is not staged clearly.

It is important, when staging an action, that only one idea be seen by the audience at a time. If a lot of action is happening at once, the eye does not know where to look and the main idea of the action will be "upstaged" and overlooked. The object of interest should contrast from the rest of the scene. In a still scene, the eye will be attracted to movement. In a very busy scene, the eye will be attracted to something that is still. Each idea or action must be staged in the strongest and the simplest way before going on to the next idea or action. The animator is saying, in effect, "Look at this, now look at this, and now look at this." [26]

In *Luxo Jr.* , it was very important that the audience was looking in the right place at the right time, because the story, acting and emotion was being put across with movement alone, in pantomime, and sometimes the movement was very subtle. If the audience missed an action, an emotion would be missed, and the story would suffer. So the action had to be paced so that **only** Dad **or** Jr. was doing an important action at any one time, never both. In the beginning of the film, Dad is on screen alone your eye was on him. But as soon as Jr. hops on-screen, he is moving faster than Dad, therefore the audience's eyes immediately goes to him and stays there.

Most of the time Jr. was on-screen, Dad's actions were very subtle, so the attention of the audience was always on Jr. where most of the story was being told. If Dad's actions were important, Jr.'s actions were toned down and Dad's movements were emphasized and the attention of the audience would transfer to Dad. For example, when Jr. looks up to Dad after he's popped the ball and Dad shakes his head, all eyes are on him.

Another idea developed in the early days at Disney was the importance of staging an action in silhouette. In those days, all the characters were black and white, with no gray values to soften the contrast or delineate a form. Bodies, arms and hands were all black, so there was no way to stage an action clearly except in silhouette. A hand in front of a chest would simply disappear. Out of this limitation, the animators realized that it is always better to show an action in silhouette. Charlie Chaplin maintained that if an actor knew his emotion thoroughly, he could show it silhouette. [26]

In *The Adventures of Andre and Wally B.,* Andre awakes and sits up, then scratches his side. If he were to scratch his stomach instead of his side, the action would happen in front of his body and would be unclear what was happening. (figure 6)

FIGURE 6. Andre's scratch was staged to the side (in "silhouette") for clarity and because that is where his itch was.

In *Luxo Jr.*, all the action was animated with silhouette in mind. When Dad and Jr. come face to face for the first time, it is easy to see what is happening because it is staged to the side. If Jr. was in front of Dad looking up at him, it would be difficult to read. (figure 7) Jr. hopping on the ball would be confusing if the action was to happen with Jr. facing the camera. Viewed from the side it is perfectly clear. (figure 8)

2.5 FOLLOW THROUGH AND OVERLAPPING ACTION

Just as the anticipation is the preparation of an action, *follow through* is the termination of an action. Actions very rarely come to a sudden and complete stop, but are generally carried past their termination point. For example, a hand, after releasing a thrown ball, continues past the actual point of release.

In the movement of any object or figure, the actions of the parts are not simultaneous: some part must initiate the move, like the engine of a train. This is called the *lead*. In walking, the action starts with the hips. As the hip swings forward, it sets a leg in motion. The hip "leads", the leg

FIGURES 7-8. In *Luxo Jr.*, all action was staged to the side for clarity.

"follows." As the hip twists, the torso follows, then the shoulder, the arm, the wrist, and finally the fingers. Although most large body actions start in the hips, the wrist will lead the fingers in a hand gesture, and the eyes will usually lead the head in an action. [12]

Appendages or loose parts of a character or object will move at a slower speed and "drag" behind the leading part of the figure. Then as the leading part of the figure slows to a stop, these appendages will continue to move and will take longer to settle down. As with squash and stretch, the object's mass is shown in the way the object slows down. The degree that the appendages drag behind and the time it takes for them to stop is directly proportional to their weight. The heavier they are the farther behind they drag and the longer they take to settle to a stop. Conversely, if they are lighter, they will drag less and stop more quickly.

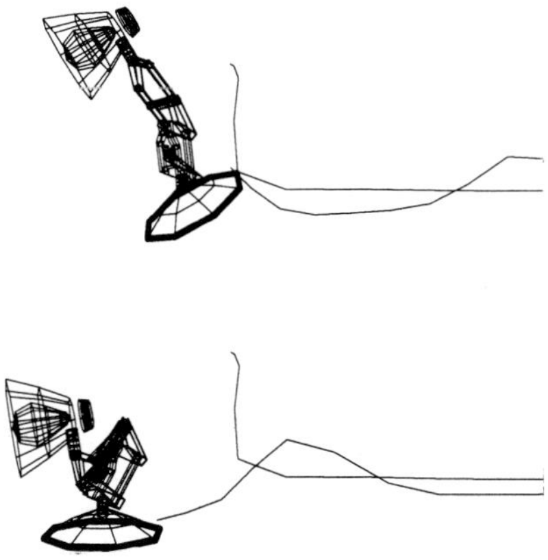

In *The Adventures of Andre and Wally B.*, this principle was used extensively on Wally B.'s feet, antennae and stinger. They all dragged behind his head and body, and continued to move well after the body had stopped. To convey that these loose appendages were made of different materials and different masses, the rate of the follow through was different for each type. His antennae were fairly light, so they dragged behind just slightly. His stinger was like stainless steel, so it dragged behind the action more than the antennae. And his feet were heavy and very flexible, as though they were water balloons; therefore, they always followed far behind the main action with a lot of squash and stretch. In the zip off illustrated above (figure 5), the action of Wally B.'s body was so fast and the feet weighed so much that they dragged far behind. They were even left on screen frames after the body had disappeared.

Often, slight variations are added to the timing and speed of the loose parts of objects. This *overlapping action* makes the object seem natural, the action more interesting. In Wally's zip off (figure 5), his feet zipped off, one after the other, about one or two frames apart. The action was so fast that it was difficult to see each foot going off separately, but It made the action as a whole more interesting.

Perhaps more important, overlapping is critical to conveying main ideas of the story. An action should never be brought to a complete stop before starting another action, and the second action should overlap the first. Overlapping maintains a continual flow and continuity between whole phrases of actions.

Walt Disney once explained overlapping this way, *"It is not necessary for an animator to take a character to one point, complete that action completely, and then turn to the following action as if he had never given it a thought until after completing the first action. When a character knows what his is going to do he doesn't have to stop before each individual action and think to do it. He has it planned in advance in his mind. For example, the mind thinks, ' I'll close the door - lock it - then I'm going to undress and go to bed.' Well, you walk over to the door - before the walk is finished you're reaching for the door - before the door is closed you reach for the key - before the door is locked you're turning away - while you're walking away you undo your tie - and before you reach the bureau you have your tie off. In other words, before you know it you're undressed - and you've done it in one thought, ' I'm going to bed.' "* [12]

2.6 STRAIGHT AHEAD ACTION AND POSE-TO-POSE ACTION (KEYFRAMES)

There are two main approaches to hand drawn animation. The first is known as *straight ahead action* because the animator literally works straight ahead from his first drawing in the scene. He knows where the scene fits in the story and the business it has to include. He does one drawing after another, getting new ideas as he goes along, until he reaches the end of the scene. This process usually produces drawings and action that have a fresh and slightly zany look, because the whole process was kept very creative. Straight ahead action is used for wild, scrambling actions where spontaneity is important.

The second approach is called *pose-to-pose*. Here the animator plans his actions, figures out just what drawings will be needed to animate the business, makes the drawings concentrating on the poses, relates them to each other in size and action, and then draws the inbetweens. Pose-to-pose is used for animation that requires good acting, where the poses and timing are all important.

The pose-to-pose technique applies to keyframe computer animation with timing and pose control of extremes and inbetweens. The difficulty in controlling the inbetweens makes it incorrect to approach keyframe computer animation exactly as one would pose-to-pose hand drawn animation. In working with a complex model, creating a complete pose at a time would make the inbetweens too unpredictable. The path of action will in general be incorrect and objects will intersect one another. The result is much time-consuming reworking of inbetweens.

There is a much better approach in the context of a hierarchical modelling system, which works "layer by layer" down the hierarchy. Instead of animating one complete pose to another, one transformation is animated at a time, starting with the trunk of the hierarchical tree structure, working transformation by transformation down the branches to the end. Fewer extremes are used. Not all translates, rotates and scales have extremes on the same frames; some have many extremes and others very few. With fewer extremes, the importance of the inbetweens increases. Tension and direction controls on the interpolating splines are helpful in controlling the spacing of the inbetween and to achieve slow in and out. [16] (See Slow In and Out)

This layer approach to animation shares many important elements with the pose-to-pose technique in hand drawn animation. Planning the animation out in advance, as in pose-to-pose, becomes even more important. The action must be well thought out, the timing and poses planned so that even in the early layers, the poses and actions are clear.

The Aventures of Andre and Wally B. and *Luxo Jr.* were both animated using a keyframe animation system called Md (Motion Doctor). [19] *Luxo Jr.* was animated using this layered approach to the keyframes. Jr.'s hop (figure 1) was animated by first setting the keyframes for his forward movement only: two keyframes were set for the X translation, the first where the hop starts and the second where he lands. This defined the timing of his hop. The height of his hop was then defined by setting a keyframe in the Z translation (Z being up in this case). The next step, animating the rotation of Jr.'s arms, was important because the arms define the anticipation, squash and stretch, and follow through of the action. Keyframes were set for just about every frame, rotating the arms together before the hop for the anticipation, then immediately far apart for the stretch of the jump. The arms were rotated together again at the top of the arc where the action slows slightly, then rotated far apart, stretching to anticipate the landing. To indicate the shock of the landing, the arms were rotated quickly together two frames after the base lands on the floor. This is the follow through of the action. His base and shade were animated in the next two steps. Like the arms, many keyframes were set to define the rotation of the base and shade because their movement was important for anticipation and follow through.

2.7 SLOW IN AND OUT

Slow in and slow out deals with the spacing of the inbetween drawings between the extreme poses. Mathematically, the term refers to second- and third-order continuity of motion.

In early animation, the action was limited to mainly fast and slow moves, the spacing from one drawing to the next fairly even. But when the poses of pose-to-pose animation became more expressive, animators wanted the audience to see them. They found that by grouping the inbetweens closer to each extreme, with only one fleeting drawing halfway between, they could achieve a very spirited result, with the character zipping from one attitude to another. "Slowing out" of one pose, then "slowing in" to the next pose simply refers to the timing of the inbetweens.

The animator indicates the placement of the inbetweens, the slow in or slow out, with a "timing chart" drawn on the side of the drawing. This tells himself, or his assistant who will be doing the inbetweens later, how he wanted the timing to be and where he wanted the inbetween drawings placed. (figure 9)

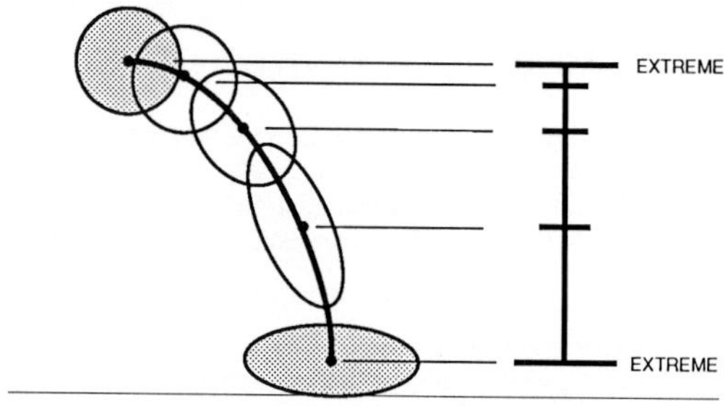

FIGURE 9. Timing chart for ball bounce.

In most 3D keyframe computer animation systems, the inbetweening is done automatically using spline interpolation. Slow in and slow out is achieved by adjusting the tension, direction or bias, and continuity of the splines. [16] This works well to give the affect of slow in and out, but a graphical representation of the spline is required to see the effect of tension, direction, and continuity have on its shape.

With this type of spline interpolation, a common problem is the spline overshooting at extremes when there is a large change in value between them, especially over a small number of frames. This also happens when the direction control of an extreme is adjusted. The danger is that, depending on the variable the spline controls (translate, rotate, or scale), the value will shoot in the wrong direction just before (or just after) the large change in value. Sometimes this effect works out well when it occurs just before a large movement, it may appear to be an anticipation. However, more often than not, it gives an undesirable effect.

In *Luxo Jr.* , there was an example of this problem of overshooting splines. Jr.'s base was very heavy and when he hopped, we wanted the base to start stationary, then pop up in the air from the momentum of his jump, arc over, then land with a thud, suddenly stationary again. For the up translation, there were three keyframes, the two stationary positions and the highest point of his jump. The spline software forced continuity, so that his base would move down under the surface of the floor just before and after the jump. (figure 10a) The solution was to put two new extremes, equal to the two stationary extremes, on the frames just before and just after the extremes. This "locked" down the spline, so that the up translation stayed the same value, popped up in the air, landed and then stayed the same value again. This gave the desired feeling of weight to his little base. (figure 10b)

The same solution can be achieved by breaking the spline using its continuity parameter [16] at the two stationary extremes. This solution requires a graphical display of the spline so that the correct shape can be achieved.

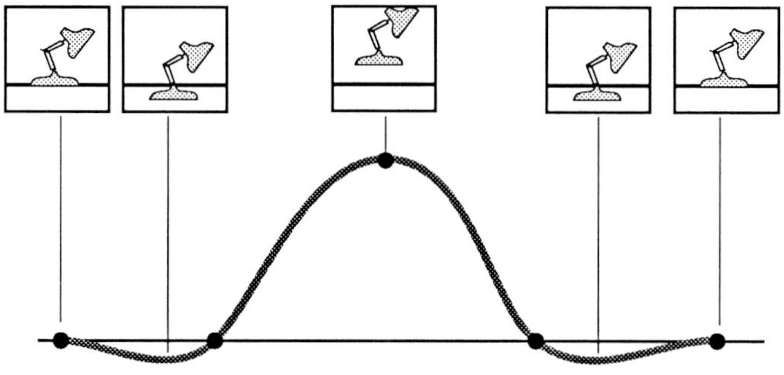

FIGURE 10a. This spline controls the Z (up) translation of Luxo Jr. Dips in the spline cause him to intersect the floor.

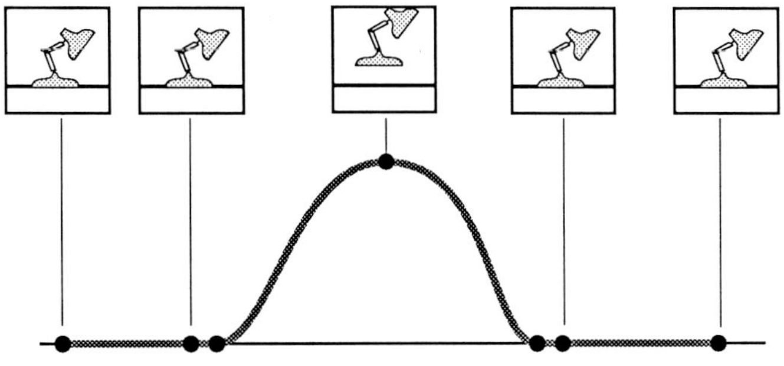

FIGURE 10b. Two extra extremes are added to the spline which removes the dips and prevents Jr. from going into the basement.

2.8 ARCS

The visual path of action from one extreme to another is always described by an *arc*. Arcs in nature are the most economical routes by which a form can move from one position to another. In animation, such arcs are used extensively, for they make animation much smoother and less stiff than a straight line for the path of action. In certain cases, an arc may resolve itself into a straight path, as for a falling object, but usually, even in a straight line action, the object rotates. [12]

In most 3D keyframe computer animation systems, the path of action from one extreme to another is controlled by the same spline that controls the timing (slow in and out) of the inbetween values. This may simplify computating the inbetweens but it has unfortunate effects. When a motion is slow, with many inbetweens, the arc of the path of action is curved, as desired. But when the action is fast, the arc flattens out: the faster the action, the flatter the arc. Sometimes this is desirable, but more often, the path of even a fast motion should be curved or arced. Straight inbetweens can completely kill the essence of an action.

The spline that defines the path of action should be separate from the spline that defines the timing or spacing of the inbetweens for several reasons: so that the arc of a fast action doesn't flatten out; so that you can adjust the timing of the inbetweens without effecting the path of action; so that you can use different splines to define the path of action (where a B-spline is appropriate for its smoothness) and the timing (a Catmull - Rom spline so you can adjust it's tension and direction controls to get slow in and out). This technique is not common, but research is being done in this area. [15]

2.9 EXAGGERATION

The meaning of exaggeration is, in general, obvious. However, the principle of *exaggeration* in animation does not mean arbitrarily distorting shapes or objects or making an action more violent or unrealistic. The animator must go to the heart of anything or any idea and develop its essence, understanding the reason for it , so that the audience will also understand it. If a character is sad, make him sadder; if he is bright, make him shine; worried, make him fret; wild, make him frantic.

A scene has many components to it: the design, the shape of the objects, the action, the emotion, the color, the sound. Exaggeration can work with any component, but not in isolation. The exaggeration of the various components should be balanced. If just one thing is exaggerated in an otherwise lifelike scene, it will stick out and seem unrealistic.

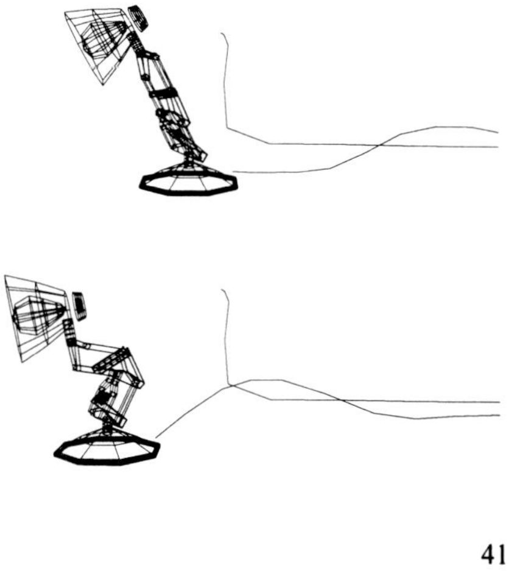

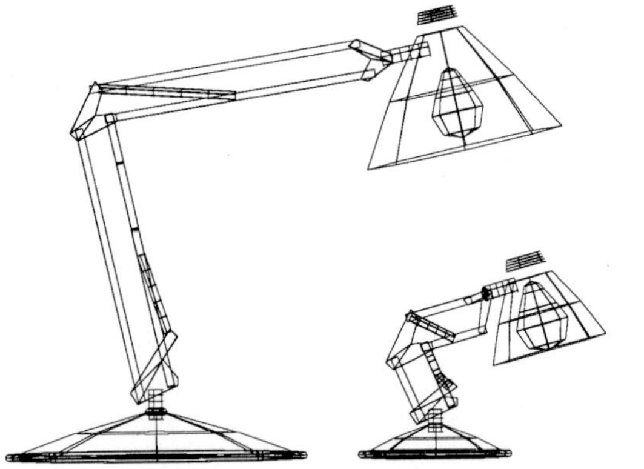

FIGURE 11. Varying the scale of different parts of Dad created the child-like proportions of Luxo Jr.

FIGURE 12. Andre's yawn was made more interesting by not duplicating the poses and the action from one side of his body to the other.

However, exaggerating everything in a scene can be equally unrealistic to an audience. Some elements must be based in nature, with others exaggerated unnaturally. If there is an element that the audience can recognize, something that seems natural to them, that becomes the ground for comparison of the exaggeration of the other elements, and the whole scene remains very realistic to them.

In *Luxo Jr.*, all the components of the scene, some naturalistic, some exaggerated, worked together to make it believable and realistic. The design of the lamps was based on the real Luxo lamp, but certain parts were exaggerated. Jr.'s proportions were exaggerated to give the feeling of a child (See Appeal).

The movement had the sense of natural physics, yet almost every motion and action was exaggerated to accentuate it: when Jr. he hit the ball, he really whacked it. When he jumped up for a hop, his whole body movement was exaggerated to give the feeling of realistic weight to his base. When he landed after a hop, the impact was shown in the exaggeration of his body movements. On the soundtrack, the lamp sounds were recorded from a real Luxo lamp, then exaggerated sounds were added to accent certain actions. [23] The ironic effect of all this exaggeration was to make the film more realistic, while making it entertaining.

2.10 SECONDARY ACTION

A *secondary action* is an action that results directly from another action. Secondary actions are important in heightening interest and adding a realistic complexity to the animation. A secondary actions is always kept subordinate to the primary action. If it conflicts, becomes more interesting, or dominates in any way, it is either the wrong choice or is staged improperly. [26]

Wally B.'s feet dragging behind the main action of his body is a secondary action because the movement of the feet is a direct result of the movement of the body. (figure 5) The rippling movement of Luxo Jr.'s cord results directly from the hopping action of his base. (figure 1)

The facial expression of a character will sometimes be a secondary action. When the main idea of an action is being told in the movement of the body, the facial expression become subordinate to the main idea. If this expression is going to animate or change, the danger is **not** that the expression will dominate the scene, but that it will never be seen. The change must come before, or after, the move. A change in the middle of a major move will go unnoticed, and value intended will be lost. It must also be staged to be obvious, though secondary. [26]

2.11 APPEAL

The word *appeal* is often misrepresented to suggest cuddly bunnies and soft kittens. It doesn't; it means anything that a person likes to see: a quality of charm, pleasing design, simplicity, communication, or magnetism. Your eye is drawn to the figure or object that has appeal, and, once there, it is held while you appreciate the object. A weak drawing or design lacks appeal. A design that is complicated or hard to read lacks appeal. Clumsy shapes and awkward moves all have low appeal. Where the live action actor has charisma, the animated character has appeal. [26]

The appeal in *Luxo Jr.* was achieved in different ways. In designing the characters, the feeling of a baby lamp and a grown up lamp was very important. The effect was achieved using exaggeration in proportion, in the same way a puppy is proportioned very differently than an adult dog, or a human baby is different from an adult. The light bulb is the same size on Jr., while the shade is smaller. The springs and support rods are the same diameter as Dad's, yet they are much shorter. (figure 11)

In creating an appealing pose for a character, one thing to avoid is called "twins", where both arms and both legs are in the same position, doing the same thing. This gives the pose a stiff, wooden, unappealling quality. If each part of the body varies in some way from its corresponding part, the character will look more natural and more appealing. Likewise one side of a face should never mirror the other.

In *The Aventures of Andre and Wally B.*, Andre wakes up and yawns. The yawn is more appealing because the poses and actions are not duplicated from one side of his body to the other. His feet rotate with a slight difference, the head rotates to one side, the upper part of his body rotates to the right and tilts, which raises his right arm higher than his left. When he stretches his arms, the right arm moves out first, followed by the left, and the actions overlap. (figure 12)

3. PERSONALITY

This final section discusses the underlying goal of all the principles discussed earlier. *Personality* in character animation is not a principle unto itself, but the intelligent application of all of the principles of animation.

When character animation is successful and the audience is thoroughly entertained, it is because the characters and the story have become more important and apparent than the technique that went into the animation. Whether drawn by hand or computer, the success of character animation lies in the **personality** of the characters

In character animation, all actions and movements of a character are the result of its thought processes. "The thinking animation character *becomes* a character." [12] Without a thought process, the actions of a character are just a series of unrelated motions. With a thought process to connect them, the actions bring a character to life.

In order to get a thought process into an animation, it is critical to have the personality of a character clearly in mind at the outset, so that it makes sense to ask at any moment, "What mood is the character in. How would he do this action?"

One character would not do a particular action the same way in two different emotional states. An example of this, in *Luxo Jr.*, is the action of Jr. hopping. When he is chasing the ball, he is very excited, happy, all his thoughts on the ball. His hops are fast, his head up looking at the ball, with very little time on the ground between hops because he can't wait to get to the ball. After he pops the ball, however, his hop changes drastically, reflecting his sadness that the object of all of his thoughts and energy just a moment ago is now dead. As he hops off, each hop is slower, with much more time on the ground between hops, his head down. Before, he had a direction and purpose to his hop. Now he is just hopping off to nowhere.

No two characters would do the same action in the same way. For example, in *Luxo Jr.*, both Dad and Jr. bat the ball with their heads. Yet Dad, who is larger and older, leans over the ball and uses only his shade to bat it. Jr., however, who is smaller, younger, and full of excited energy, whacks the ball with his shade, putting his whole body into it.

When defining the character, it is important to make the personality distinct, and at the same time have characteristics that are familiar to the audience. If the actions of a character ring true, the audience will be able to relate to the character, and he will be believable to them.

4. CONCLUSION

Whether it is generated by hand or by computer, the first goal of the animator is to entertain. The animator must have two things: a clear concept of exactly what will entertain the audience; and the tools and skills to put those ideas across clearly and unambiguously. Tools, in the sense of hardware and software, are simply not enough. The principles discussed in this paper, so useful in producing 50 years of rich entertainment, are tools as well... tools which are just as important as the computers we work with.

5. ACKNOWLEDGMENTS

The author would like to express sincere thanks to Bill Reeves and Eben Ostby for their unending support, education and creativity with the technical aspects of computer animation. Steve Upstill for making it sound like I know English. Nancy Tague for her ruthless editing even on my birthday. Kate Smith and Michael Shantzis for their assistance in editing this paper even when they could have been watching Willie Wonka on video tape. Craig Good for helping with the video tape portion of this paper. Joey Tague for being pals and for telling us what happened in Willie Wonka. And especially to Frank Thomas and Ollie Johnston for their instruction in animation when the author was at the Disney Studio, and for their continued inspiration with their book. [26]

6. REFERENCES

1. Abel Image Research, 953 N. Highland Ave., Los Angeles, CA 90038-2481

2. Alias Research Inc., 110 Richmond St. East, Suite 500, Toronto, Ontario, Canada m5c-1p1

3. Blair, Preston, *Animation* , Walter T. Foster, Santa Ana CA, 1949.

4. Burtnyk, Nester and Wein, Marceli, "Computer Generated Keyframe Animation," Journal of the SMPTE 80, pp.149-153, March 1971.

5. Burtnyk, Nester and Wein, Marceli, "Interactive Skeleton Techniques for Enhanced Motion Dynamics in Key Frame Animation," Communications of the ACM 19 (10), pp 564-569, October, 1976.

6. Catmull, Edwin, "A System for Computer Generated Movies," Proceedings ACM Annual Conference, pp. 422-431, August 1972.

7. Catmull, Edwin, "The problems of Computer- Assisted Animation," SIGGRAPH '78, Computer Graphics, Vol. 12, No. 3, pp. 348-353, August 1978.

8. Cook, Robert L., "Stochastic Sampling in Computer Graphics," ACM Transactions on Graphics, Vol. 5, No. 1, pp. 51-72, January 1986.

9. Cook, Robert L., Porter, Thomas, and Carpenter, Loren, "Distributed Ray Tracing," SIGGRAPH '84, Computer Graphics, Vol. 18, No. 3, pp.137-145, July, 1984.

10. Walt Disney Productions, *Three Little Pigs* , (film), 1933.

11. Gracer, F., and Blagen, M. W., "Karma: A System for Storyboard Animation," Proceeding Ninth Annual UAIDE Meeting, pp. 210-255, 1970.

12. Graham, Don, *The Art of Animation* , unpublished.

13. Graham, Don, transcripts of action analysis class at the Walt Disney Studio, June 21, 1937.

14. Graham, Don, transcripts of action analysis class with Bill Tytla at the Walt Disney Studio, June 28, 1937.

15. Hardtke, Ines, and Bartels, Richard, "Kinetics for Key-Frame Interpolation," unpublished.

16. Kochanek, Doris, and Bartels, Richard, "Interpolating Splines with Local Tension, Continuity, and Bias Control," SIGGRAPH '84, Computer Graphics, Vol. 18, No. 3, pp. 33-41, July, 1984.

17. Levoy, Marc, "A Color Animation System Based on the Multi-Plane Technique," SIGGRAPH '77, Computer Graphics, Vol. 11, No. 2, pp. 64-71, July, 1977.

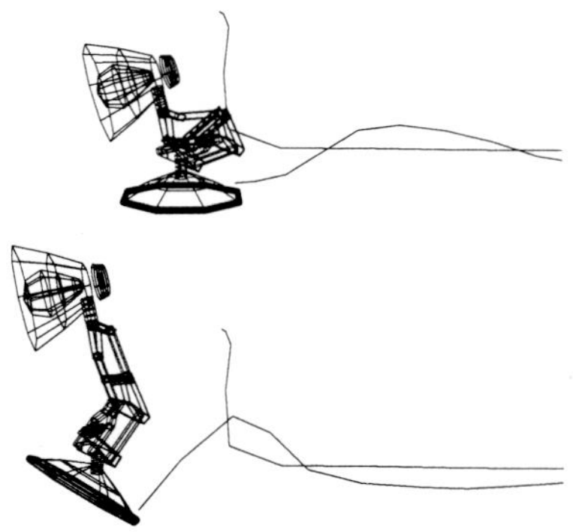

18. Lucasfilm Ltd. Computer Graphics Div., *The Adventures of Andre and Wally B.* , (film), 1984.

19. Ostby, Eben, Duff, Tom, and Reeves, William, Md (motion doctor), animation program, Lucasfilm Ltd., 1982-1986.

20. Perine, Robert, *Chouinard, An Art Vision Betrayed* , Artra Publishing, Encinitas CA, 1985.

21. Pixar, *Luxo Jr.* , (film), 1986.

22. Reeves, William, "Inbetweening for Computer Animation Utilizing Moving Point Constraints," SIGGRAPH '81, Computer Graphics, Vol. 15, No. 3, pp. 263-270, August 1981.

23. Rydstrom, Gary, Soundtrack for *Luxo Jr.* , Sprocket Systems Div., Lucasfilm Ltd., July, 1986.

24. Stern, Garland, "Bboop--A System for 3D Keyframe Figure Animation," Tutorial Notes: Introduction to Computer Animation , SIGGRAPH '83, July 1983.

25. Symbolics Inc., 1401 Westwood Blvd., Los Angeles, CA 90024

26. Thomas, Frank and Johnston, Ollie, *Disney Animation-- The Illusion of Life* , Abbeville Press, New York, 1981.

27. Thomas, Frank, "Can Classic Disney Animation Be Duplicated On The Computer?" Computer Pictures, Vol. 2, Issue 4, pp. 20-26, July/August 1984.

28. Vertigo Systems International Inc., 119 W. Pender St., Suite 221, Vancouver, BC, Canada v6b 1s5

29. Wavefront Technologies, 530 East Montecito, Santa Barbara, CA 93101

30. Whitaker, Harold and Halas, John, *Timing for Animation* , Focal Press, London, 1981.

31. White, Tony, *The Animator's Workbook* , Watson-Guptill, New York, 1986.

Principles and Applications of Pencil Tracing

Mikio Shinya Tokiichiro Takahashi
Seiichiro Naito
NTT Electrical Communications Laboratories
3-9-11, Midori-cho, Musashino-shi
Tokyo 180, Japan

Abstract

Pencil tracing, a new approach to ray tracing, is introduced for faster image synthesis with more physical fidelity. The paraxial approximation theory for efficiently tracing a pencil of rays is described and analysis of its errors is conducted to insure the accuracy required for pencil tracing. The paraxial approximation is formulated from a 4×4 matrix (a system matrix) that provides the basis for pencil tracing and a variety of ray tracing techniques, such as beam tracing, ray tracing with cones, ray-object intersection tolerance, and a lighting model for reflection and refraction. In the error analysis, functions that estimate approximation errors and determine a constraint on the spread angle of a pencil are given.

The theory results in the following fast ray tracing algorithms; ray tracing using a system matrix, ray interpolation, and extended 'beam tracing' using a 'generalized perspective transform'. Some experiments are described to show their advantages. A lighting model is also developed to calculate the illuminance for refracted and reflected light.

CR Categories and Subject Descriptors: I.3.3 [***Computer Graphics***]: Picture/Image Generation; I.3.7 [***Computer Graphics***]: Three-Dimensional Graphics and Realism
Additional Keywords and Phrases: Ray Tracing, Paraxial Theory

1 Introduction

The ray tracing algorithms [1] provide powerful tools for creating realistic images. However, from a practical viewpoint, there have been problems such as high computational cost and aliasing. Many attempts have been made to tackle those problems, and some of them have produced good results by tracing a *pencil* [1] (or bundle) of rays, instead of an individual ray. However, as the methods lack sufficient mathematical bases, they are limited to specific applications.

Heckbert proposed a method called 'beam tracing'[2] which works well for reflecting polygonal objects. His method uses a pencil to be traced by introducing affine transformations in an object space. Unfortunately, the method finds only limited applications because of the way in which it approximates refractions. Moreover, since an error estimation method has not been proposed for guaranteeing the image accuracy, the accuracy cannot be controlled.

Amanatides proposed a 'ray tracing with cones' technique for anti-aliasing, fuzzy shadows, and dull reflections[3], where a conic pencil is traced. However, it failed to present a general equation for characterizing the spread-angle change of a conic pencil through an optical system. Such an equation is also required for the calculation of ray-object intersections proposed by Barr[4], where the calculation tolerance is related to the pencil spread-angle. In a lighting model, the equation will also play an important role, because the illuminance distribution results from the calculation of how the light pencils converge and diverge according to reflections and refractions.

This paper describes the theory of pencil tracing and its applications to provide general mathematical tools for efficiently tracing a pencil and also for conducting error analysis to insure the image accuracy. In the theory, a linear approximation approach is taken, because, in general, the exact behavior of a pencil cannot be analytically obtained. The theory is based on the paraxial approximation theory[5,6], where a pencil transformation through an optical system is formulated from a 4×4 matrix (a system matrix). This formulation is well-known in optical design and electromagnetic analysis[6]. The error analysis provides functions that estimate approximation

[1] The rays that are near to a given axial ray are called paraxial and are said to form a pencil.

errors and determine a constraint on the spread angle of a pencil to insure the required accuracy of generated images.

Applications of the theory result in the following fast ray tracing algorithms: ray tracing using a system matrix, ray interpolation, and extended 'beam tracing' using a 'generalized perspective transform'. Some experiments are described to show their advantages. A lighting model from which to calculate the illuminance for refracted and reflected light is also developed.

2 Paraxial approximation theory

The paraxial approximation theory provides a linear approximation for ray changes due to refraction, reflection, and 'transfer', where 'transfer' means propagation in a homogeneous medium. A linear ray change can be represented by a matrix, and thus, paraxial ray tracing by a matrix product. Since the paraxial approximation theory seems little known in computer graphics today, it will be briefly reviewed here. For details, see [5],[6].

2.1 Definitions

Ray:

A *paraxial ray* is a ray extending along the vicinity of a given axial ray [2]. Thus, it is appropriate to represent a paraxial ray with respect to the axial ray. In the theory, a paraxial ray is represented by a four-dimensional vector (*ray vector*) in a coordinated system formed with respect to the axial ray (*ray coordinate system*).

Ray coordinate system In Figure 1, an orthogonal coordinate system $\hat{x}_1$-$\hat{x}_2$-$\hat{z}$, called a 'ray coordinate system', is used to represent a paraxial ray. The origin O is a point on the axial ray, and the $\hat{z}$-axis is the direction of the axial ray. The $\hat{x}_1$- and $\hat{x}_2$-axes can be arbitrarily chosen, and the $\hat{x}_1$-$\hat{x}_2$ plane is perpendicular to the $\hat{z}$-axis.

Ray vector for a paraxial ray Generally, a ray is uniquely specified by its direction and the position it passes. Thus, referring to $\hat{x}_1$ and $\hat{x}_2$, a paraxial ray can be represented by two kinds of vectors: the position vector $\boldsymbol{x} = (x_1 x_2)^t$ to represent the intersection of the paraxial ray with the $\hat{x}_1$-$\hat{x}_2$ plane relative to the origin O, and the direction vector $\boldsymbol{\xi} = (\xi_1 \xi_2)^t$ which is the projection of the normalized ray direction vector $\boldsymbol{s}$ of the paraxial ray onto the $\hat{x}_1$-$\hat{x}_2$ plane. Combining those two vectors, the paraxial ray is defined by a four-dimensional vector ψ at O by the equality

[2] An axial ray has nothing to do with the axes of optical systems having special physical or mathematical meanings in the systems, such as a lens axis. An adequate ray can be chosen as the axial ray for a pencil to trace, e.g., the center line of a cone in the case of a conic pencil.

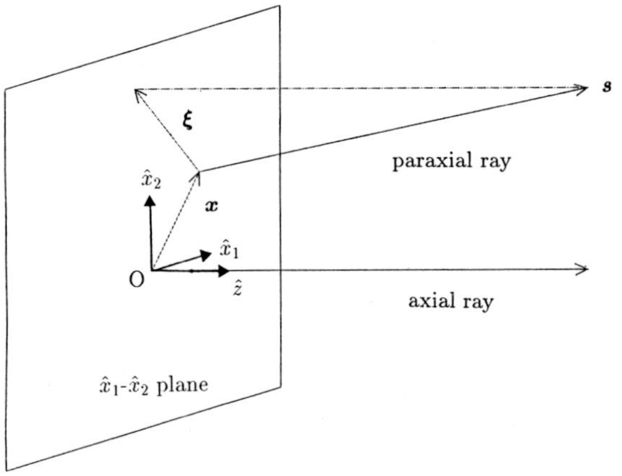

Figure 1 Definition of ray vector

$$\psi = \begin{pmatrix} \boldsymbol{x} \\ \boldsymbol{\xi} \end{pmatrix}.$$

The four-dimensional vector ψ is called a ray vector.

Pencil:

A pencil is made up of an axial ray and a bundle of paraxial rays around it represented by ray vectors. A pencil is mathematically represented by a domain in four-dimensional space, $\boldsymbol{x}$-$\boldsymbol{\xi}$, representing the deviations in positions and directions of its paraxial rays from its axial ray. In image synthesis, all rays to be traced usually start at a common point, or a pin hole. In this case, a pencil can be simply represented by its direction deviation from its axial ray at the pin hole, or the pencil spread angle.

System matrix:

When a ray goes through an optical system, the ray vector changes due to reflections, refractions and transfers. The deviation of a paraxial ray from the axial ray can be chosen small enough that the transformation representing a ray vector change is regarded as linear and can be represented by the matrix

$$\psi' = T\psi,$$

where ψ is the input ray vector and ψ' is the output vector. T is a 4×4 matrix called a system matrix. When a system consists of two sub-systems in cascade and their respective system matrices are known, the overall system matrix is simply the product of the two matrices.

2.2 System matrices

In computer graphics, optical systems usually consist of homogeneous regions separated by smooth surfaces, where any optical phenomenon can be represented by a reflection, a refraction or a transfer. Therefore, an overall system matrix for any system can easily be obtained, if system matrices are given for each *element system*, i.e., a transfer, a reflection, or a refraction. Surface smoothness is an essential condition for the system matrix approach; the surface in a system should have continuous second-order differentials. If discontinuities or edges exist in a system, it should be spatially divided into sub-systems so that no system contains an edge.

Element-system matrices are given analytically by using Snell's law and geometry. They are formulated as follows:

(1) Transfer:

In a homogeneous region, rays are straight. Thus, the propagation along the axial ray from $z = 0$ to z_0 shown in Figure 2 is represented by

$$T = \begin{pmatrix} 1 & z_0 \\ 0 & 1 \end{pmatrix}, \qquad (1)$$

where each element is a 2×2 matrix and 1 means a 2×2 identity matrix.

(2) Refraction:

Consider a refraction on the surface Σ in Figure 3. The optical indices of the two media are n and n'. At the origin O, the incident axial ray meets Σ. The orthogonal coordinate systems $\hat{x}_1$-$\hat{x}_2$ and $\hat{x}'_1$-$\hat{x}'_2$ are the incident ray coordinate system and the refracted ray coordinate system, respectively, and both coordinate planes are perpendicular to their respective axial rays. Another orthogonal coordinate system $\hat{u}_1$-$\hat{u}_2$ is perpendicular to the normal of Σ at O and is used to represent Σ. For simplicity, the coordinates are chosen such that $\hat{x}_2=\hat{u}_2=\hat{x}'_2$. The formulation of the system matrix for a refraction on Σ is performed by approximating Σ to a paraboloid; an approach somewhat similar to Barr's tangent plane approximation[4]. Thus, the transformation is analytically derived using Snell's law as

$$T = \begin{pmatrix} \Theta'\Theta^{-1} & 1 \\ (\Theta'^t)^{-1}hQ\Theta^{-1} & (n/n')(\Theta'^t)^{-1}\Theta^t \end{pmatrix}, \qquad (2)$$

where

$$\Theta = \begin{pmatrix} \hat{\boldsymbol{x}}_1\cdot\hat{\boldsymbol{u}}_1 & \hat{\boldsymbol{x}}_1\cdot\hat{\boldsymbol{u}}_2 \\ \hat{\boldsymbol{x}}_2\cdot\hat{\boldsymbol{u}}_1 & \hat{\boldsymbol{x}}_2\cdot\hat{\boldsymbol{u}}_2 \end{pmatrix}, \Theta' = \begin{pmatrix} \hat{\boldsymbol{x}}'_1\cdot\hat{\boldsymbol{u}}_1 & \hat{\boldsymbol{x}}'_1\cdot\hat{\boldsymbol{u}}_2 \\ \hat{\boldsymbol{x}}'_2\cdot\hat{\boldsymbol{u}}_1 & \hat{\boldsymbol{x}}'_2\cdot\hat{\boldsymbol{u}}_2 \end{pmatrix},$$

$$h = \cos\theta' - (n/n')\cos\theta,$$

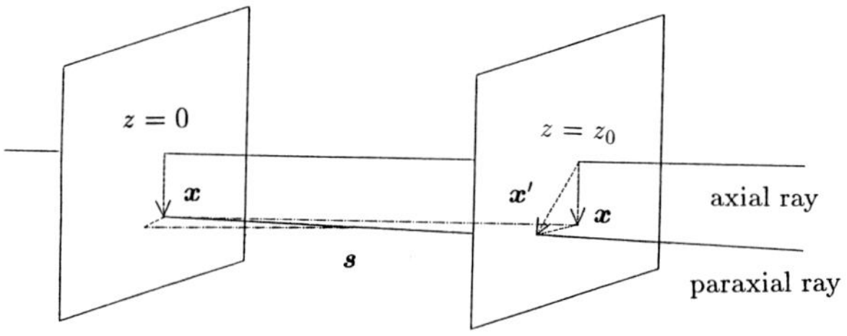

Figure 2 System matrix for transfer

and $\hat{\boldsymbol{x}}_1$ is a unit vector of the $\hat{x}_1$ axis direction. When the coordinate systems are chosen as in the figure, the matrices Θ and Θ' are diagonalized as

$$\Theta = \begin{pmatrix} \cos\theta & 0 \\ 0 & 1 \end{pmatrix}, \Theta' = \begin{pmatrix} \cos\theta' & 0 \\ 0 & 1 \end{pmatrix}.$$

The matrix Q is the curvature matrix of Σ in the $\hat{u}_1$-$\hat{u}_2$ coordinate. For example, when Σ is a sphere of radius r,

$$Q = \begin{pmatrix} 1/r & 0 \\ 0 & 1/r \end{pmatrix}.$$

(3) Reflection:

The system matrix for a reflection is derived mathematically as a special case of a refraction. It is obtained by simply replacing θ' with $(\pi-\theta)$ and n' with n in Eq.(2).

3 Tolerance and error analysis

In this section, pencil tracing approximation errors and tolerances for calculated ray-object intersections are discussed to show that they are given as functions of the system matrices. This leads to a discussion of how to determine a limit on the spread angle of a pencil in order to retain accuracy and fidelity in calculated images.

3.1 Tolerances

The criterion used here is similar to Barr's[4], which is based on pixel width and ray sampling interval. Since the sampling interval limits the resolution of a ray-traced image, an approximation error smaller than the interval has little effect on the resolution. Although Barr's tolerance equation is not applicable to refracted or reflected pencils, it can easily be extended by using a system matrix.

Consider the situation shown in Figure 4, where δ is a four-dimensional vector representing a ray interval, i.e., a sampling interval of position and direction, and

$$T = \begin{pmatrix} t_1 & t_2 \\ t_3 & t_4 \end{pmatrix}$$

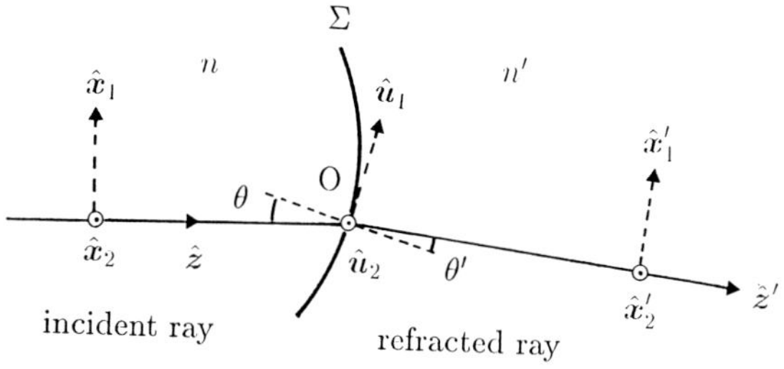

Figure 3
Refraction of a pencil. A circle with a dot denotes a vector emarging perpendicular to the page.

is an overall system matrix. The sampling interval of the intersection points on the $\hat{x}_1$-$\hat{x}_2$ plane becomes $\left(t_1 \ \ t_2 \right) \delta$, and the tolerance τ on the plane is given in terms of parameter ρ as

$$\tau = \rho \left| \left(t_1 \ \ t_2 \right) \delta \right|, \tag{3}$$

where ρ indicates the ratio of the tolerance to the interval, and it represents the image accuracy. When one-pixel-width resolution is required, ρ should be less than 1/2. Equation (3) is also applicable to Barr's intersection calculation method.

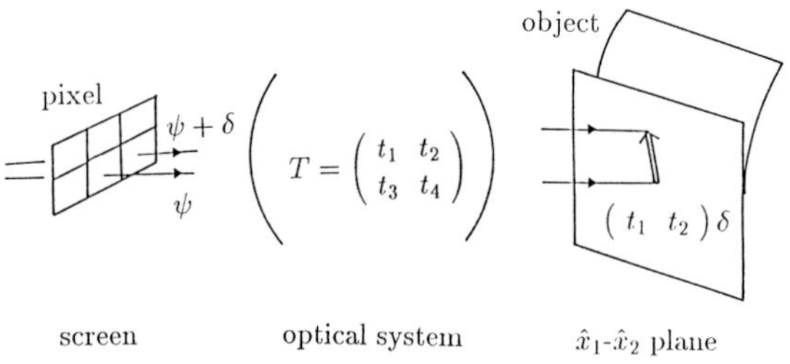

Figure 4 Sampling interval and tolerance

3.2 Error estimation function

When a paraxial ray ψ^{in} is changed into ψ^{out} through an optical system, ψ^{out} may be expressed in terms of a power series of ψ^{in}. The i-th component of the vector ψ^{out} is represented by

$$\begin{aligned}(\psi^{out})_i &= \sum_{j=1}^{4} t_{ij}^{(1)}(\psi^{in})_j + \sum_{j,k=1}^{4} t_{ijk}^{(2)}(\psi^{in})_j(\psi^{in})_k + \cdots \\ &= (\psi'^{out})_i + (\Delta\psi)_i + o((\psi^{in})_j^3),\end{aligned}$$

where $t_{ij}^{(1)}$ is an element of the system matrix, and

$$t_{ijk}^{(2)} = \partial^2(\psi^{out})_i / \partial(\psi^{in})_j \partial(\psi^{in})_k.$$

Since higher-order terms are considered to be negligible for small ψ^{in} value, the second-order term $\Delta\psi$ alone is enough to estimate the linear approximation error $(\psi^{out} - \psi'^{out})$.

The coefficients $t_{ijk}^{(2)}$ for each element system, e.g., refraction, can be derived analytically and they can be applied to general systems. However, a straightforward computation of $\Delta\psi$ is rather cumbersome because of the complicated forms of its elements. Furthermore, since the absolute values of error vectors, $\Delta\boldsymbol{x}$ and $\Delta\boldsymbol{\xi}$, are far more important than their directions in terms of error estimation, we introduce the more compact error estimation functions, e_x and e_ξ, to estimate the absolute values of errors. This results in the expressions

$$\begin{aligned} e_x(x_0, \xi_0) &= A x_0^2 + B x_0 \xi_0 + C \xi_0^2 \\ &\geq |\Delta\boldsymbol{x}| \end{aligned}$$

and

$$\begin{aligned} e_\xi(x_0, \xi_0) &= D x_0^2 + E x_0 \xi_0 + F \xi_0^2 \\ &\geq |\Delta\boldsymbol{\xi}|, \end{aligned} \tag{4}$$

where

$$\begin{pmatrix} \Delta\boldsymbol{x} \\ \Delta\boldsymbol{\xi} \end{pmatrix} = \Delta\psi$$

$$x_0 = |\boldsymbol{x}_0|, \ \xi_0 = |\boldsymbol{\xi}_0|$$

$$\begin{pmatrix} \boldsymbol{x}_0 \\ \boldsymbol{\xi}_0 \end{pmatrix} = \psi^{in}.$$

A - F are constants and depend on the system matrices, axial incident angles, optical indices, and so on. As the derivation is very complicated, the details are omitted here. The results are presented in the appendix.

Equations (3) and (4) provide the condition for pencil tracing with the required accuracy. If all paraxial rays in a pencil satisfy the inequality

$$e_x(x_0, \xi_0) \leq \tau, \tag{5}$$

the generated image is accurate enough.

In the case where a pencil emerges from a pin hole, x_0 is 0 and Eq. (5) is simplified as

$$C\xi_0^2 \leq \tau, \tag{6}$$

to provide the maximum pencil spread angle for the required accuracy.

4 Applications

Since the theory describes general pencil behaviors, it can be used in many places in computer graphics. In this section, three fast ray tracing methods are proposed, and a general illuminance formula for refracting and reflecting environments is introduced that demonstrates actual applications of the theory.

4.1 Pencil tracer as a fast ray tracer

(1) Ray tracing with system matrix:

This method is a straight-forward installation of the theory, and accelerates image systhesis of smooth refracting and reflecting objects by replacing conventional refraction and reflection calculations with matrix-vector manipulations.

Paraxial rays are traced by a system matrix, calculated by Eqs. (1) and (2). The pencil spread angle is controlled to satisfy tolerance condition (6). Since ray tracing with a system matrix is not applicable in the neighborhoods of object edges because of the smoothness requirement, individual rays in those regions are traced with a conventional ray tracer.

The procedure is as follows:

1) Divide the screen into $n \times m$ initial domains of a certain number of pixels[3]. Do the following process for each domain:
2) Set the axial ray at the center of a domain, and trace it with the conventional ray tracer. Calculate the system matrix.
3) Check the smoothness condition (to be discussed below). If an edge exists in the domain, trace all the rays with the conventional ray tracer.
4) If there is no edge, calculate the tolerance and the maximum pencil-spread angle by using Eqs. (4) and (6). Then, according to the maximum pencil-spread angle, do the following:
   a) Trace all paraxial rays in the domain with the system matrix if the maximum spread angle of the domain is smaller than that of the pencil.
   b) Trace all paraxial rays with the ray tracer, if the maximum pencil spans an area less than one pixel wide.
   c) Otherwise, divide the domain into sub-domains so that their maximum spread angles are less than that of the pencil. Repeat 2)- 4) for each sub-domain.

Anti-aliasing by subpixel sampling can be achieved in the same way by using the system matrix, except in the neighborhood of an edge.

In our preliminary implementation, the smoothness condition is roughly checked by comparing the ray trees among the neighboring domains, and the condition is assumed to be satisfied when no difference is detected among the ray trees. It is possible for an object smaller than the initial domain area to vanish from the image. This problem can be solved by estimating the distances between an axial ray and object surfaces, as in the case of ray tracing with cones [3]. Amanatides' method can deal with the estimation for simple objects such as spheres and polygons. It is considered that the bounding volume techniques([7] among others) will be effective for this estimation. However, further investigation is required to solve the problem.

(2) Ray interpolation:

In this method, the intersection point and the direction of an interior paraxial ray are linearly interpolated without a system matrix calculation in order to provide further computational saving.

Consider the situation shown in Figure 5, where two rays, ψ_0 and $\psi_0 + \delta$, are traced and x'_0 and x'_1 give their

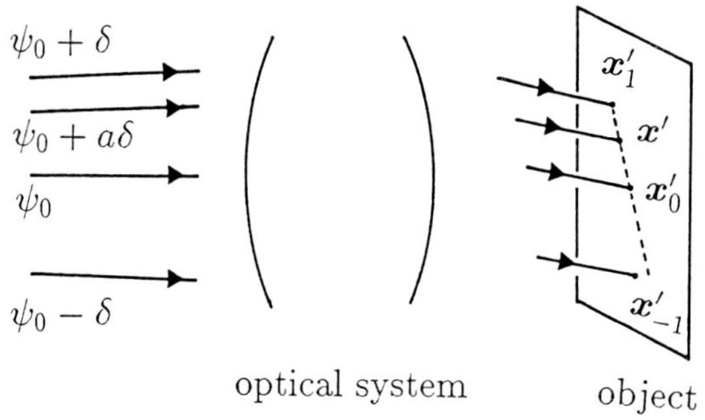

Figure 5 Ray interpolation

intersections with the object. A paraxial ray represented by $\psi' = \psi_0 + a\delta$ can be considered to intersect with the object at the point that can be linearly interpolated by the expression

$$x' = a x'_1 + (1 - a) x'_0.$$

The direction vector of the paraxial ray can also be interpolated in the same manner.

A precise analysis of the interpolation error is not an easy task. However, if a second order approximation is good enough to estimate the true x', the error can be estimated by evaluating first and second order interpolations. For this, one more intersection of another ray is necessary. For example, when the intersection x'_{-1} of the ray $\psi_0 - \delta$ is given, the error is estimated by

$$e_{int} = |(\text{second order interpolation})-(\text{liner interpolation})|,$$

where

$$(\text{second order interpolation}) = a(a-1)x'_{-1}/2 + (1-a)(1+a)x'_0 + a(1+a)x'_1/2$$

In case that the second-order approximation is not good, e_{int} simply checks the linearity of x with respect to a.

Comparing with the system matrix method, the ray interpolation has the advantage in computation speed, but a disadvantage in the precision of the error estimation. Thus, it is considered that the method is effective for tracing a thin pencil, e.g., in the case of subpixel sampling for anti-aliasing. This will be shown in the section 5.

Note that if linearity is assumed for brightness $I(x')$, the brightness can also be interpolated by

$$I(x') = aI(x'_1) + (1-a)I(x'_0).$$

(3) Generalized perspective transformation:

This method is a modification of Heckbert's beam tracing[2], and it is effective for refracting and reflecting polygonal environments. Although the beam tracing

[3]Larger initial domains do not necessarily lead to faster image synthesis. There is a certain point in a domain area (5×5 pixels in our experiment) beyond where the speed of image synthesis no longer improves.

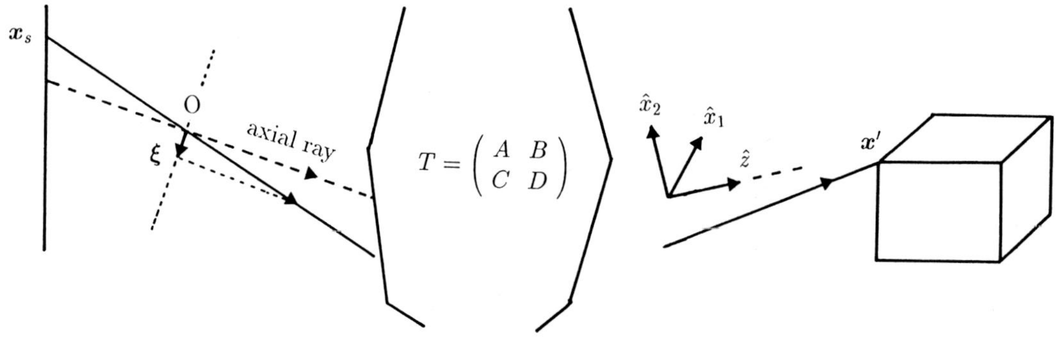

Figure 6 Generalized perspective transformation

method works well for reflections, it provides a rather poor approximation for refraction. It assumes either that incident rays are nearly perpendicular to a surface, or that all rays are parallel.

The system matrix provides a better approximation using local linearity. Consider the situation shown in Figure 6. The ray $\psi = (0, \boldsymbol{\xi})^t$ goes from the pin hole to the object point $\boldsymbol{x}'$ through the optical system, where $\boldsymbol{x}'$ is represented in the ray coordinate system. Using the system matrix, it is expressed as,

$$\boldsymbol{x}' = A\boldsymbol{\xi},$$

where A is a 2×2 sub-matrix of the system matrix. The screen point $\boldsymbol{x}_s$ is directly calculated by $\boldsymbol{\xi}$, wherein the linear approximation is represented by

$$\boldsymbol{x}_s = S\boldsymbol{\xi},$$

where S is a 2×2 matrix. Thus, the transformation from an object point to a screen point is given by

$$\boldsymbol{x}_s = SA^{-1}\boldsymbol{x}' = P\boldsymbol{x}'. \qquad (7)$$

Here, P is considered as a 'local' perspective transformation for refracting and reflecting systems. The transformation P coincides with the usual perspective transformation for a transfer, and with the ones of the beam tracing for a reflection and the perpendicular incident refraction.

The transformation can be implemented in almost the same way as the beam tracing: a pencil formed by a polygon boundary is approximated by a pyramidal pencil that is represented also by a polygon on the $\boldsymbol{\xi}$-plane or on the screen. The system matrix is calculated by Eqs. (1) and (2), and the polygons in the object space are mapped onto the screen by Eq. (7) to allow searching for visible polygons through a polygon clipping technique and a hidden surface technique by referring to z-values in the ray coordinate system.

Anti-aliasing can be performed by the techniques for the scan line algorithm. Errors can be estimated by using Eq. (4), and dividing the pencil can assure image accuracy though this has not been implemented yet. This method is free from the edge problem of the system matrix.

4.2 Illuminance formula

A light is converged or diverged by refractions, and reflections on curved surfaces. This makes a variety of shadow patterns caused by light concentration. Conventional illumination models fail to simulate this phenomena and they create unnatural sharp shadows for transparent objects. Kajiya succeeded in creating realistic shadows of transparent objects by using his powerful rendering equation and a Monte Carlo method[8]. However, there are two problems with his method. First, the equation he

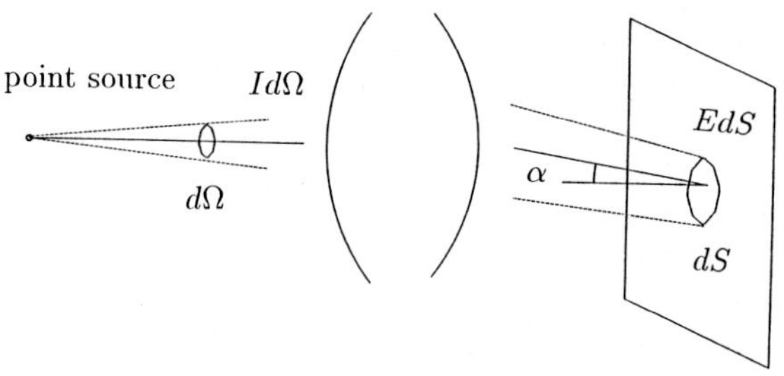

Figure 7 Light pencil emitted from a point source

used is based on the inverse square law of light intensity which is not valid for refracted or reflected light. Strictly speaking, the calculated illuminance is theoretically incorrect. Second, it requires a tremendous amount of computation time, even for a very simple situation.

It is easy to extend the intensity law by using a system matrix[6], and the illuminance is analytically calculated for point light sources and parallel light beams when using it. Consider a pencil emitted from a point source and passing through an optical system onto an object surface, as shown in Figure 7. For simplicity, assume that the same medium, e.g. air, surrounds both the source and the object. Let the luminous intensity of the source be I, the illuminance on the surface E, and the transmittance of the system t_r. Then, energy preservation is represented by

$$t_r I d\Omega = E dS,$$

where $d\Omega$ is the emitted pencil solid angle, and dS is the illuminated area on the surface. Using the system matrix and the ray coordinate systems gives

$$\begin{pmatrix} \boldsymbol{x}' \\ \boldsymbol{\xi}' \end{pmatrix} = \begin{pmatrix} A & B \\ C & D \end{pmatrix} \begin{pmatrix} \boldsymbol{x} \\ \boldsymbol{\xi} \end{pmatrix},$$

and

$$\boldsymbol{\xi} = \begin{pmatrix} \xi_1 \\ \xi_2 \end{pmatrix}, \boldsymbol{x}' = \begin{pmatrix} x_1' \\ x_2' \end{pmatrix},$$

and $d\Omega$ and dS are given by

$$d\Omega = |d\xi_1 d\xi_2|, \text{ and } dS = |dx_1 dx_2 / \cos\alpha|,$$

where α is the angle between the axial ray and the surface normal. Thus, the illuminance is given by

$$E = t_r I \cos\alpha |d\xi_1 d\xi_2 / dx_1' dx_2'| = t_r I \cos\alpha |1/det(B)|. \quad (8)$$

In the case of a transfer, $det(B)$ is z^2, where z is the distance between the source and the illuminated point, and thus, Eq. (8) represents the inverse square law. However, for a refracted light pencil, the inverse square law is not valid, because in general $det(B) \neq z^2$.

Likewise, for a parallel light source, it is derived that

$$E = t_r I \cos\alpha / |1/det(A)|. \quad (9)$$

Using Eq. (8) instead of the inverse square law, Kajiya's equation becomes perfectly correct. However, for a simple situation where point sources illuminate transparent objects, the pencil tracer traces light pencils from the sources, simulating caustics and shadows more efficiently. This becomes more distinctive in the case of the proposed generalized perspective transformation for polygonal objects, as will be shown in Section 5. Furthermore, the illuminance formula (8) and the generalized perspective transformation can be applied to Nishita and Nakamae's radiosity method[9] for simulating interreflection between both refracting and diffusive polyhedra.

5 Experimental Results

Figure 8 shows an image generated through ray tracing with a system matrix and anti-aliased by nine rays per pixel subpixel-sampling using the ray interpolation technique. The computation time is about 230 seconds on a VAX11/780 for 256×256 pixels, which is 7.6 times faster than our conventional ray tracing program. Since ray interpolation is a computationally inexpensive process, the improvement in speed becomes more significant as the subpixel sampling rate increases.

Figure 9 shows the ratio of the CPU time of the pencil tracer to the time of the conventional one, with respect to the number of ray samples per pixel. The time ratio decreases to less than 1/10 as the sampling ratio increases to 49. This suggests that the method is particularly efficient in creating 'high quality' anti-aliased images. The tolerance used here is one-half pixel width, or $\rho = 1/2$.

Figure 10 shows the error distribution of the image, where the error is measured by the distance between ray-object (checkerboard) intersections obtained by the pencil tracer and by the ray tracer normalized by one pixel-interval on the checkerboard. Errors are less than the specified tolerance, 1/2, in over 99.8% of the image area, and the largest error is only 0.66 pixel width. This suggests that errors are estimated strictly enough. Since the error estimation is a worst case estimation, the actual errors are considered to be much smaller than the tolerance in most areas, as shown in the figure.

Figure 11 shows an image of a transparent polyhedron consisting of 100 polygons generated by the generalized perspective transformation without error estimation and anti-aliasing. The illuminance on the three-colored rectangle is calculated by illuminance formula (8), simulating the light pencil concentration effect caused by refractions. The shadows and the image are created individually, and each computation time is about 200 seconds and 74 seconds, respectively, on a VAX11/780 for 512×512 pixels. The ray tracing program takes about 49 minutes and it creates only a non-shadowed image using a rectangular solid bounding volume. It is estimated that it would take several tens of times more to calculate precise shadows like in Fig. 11 by the ray tracer, because, from Kajiya's experiment[8] and our experiences, it is believed that several tens of rays per pixel sampling might be necessary for a good approximation.

6 Conclusion

In this paper, the theory and applications of pencil tracing have been described. In the theory, we introduced a system matrix approximation and analyzed the approximation errors. The system matrix describes general pencil behavior, and it provides the basis for pencil tracing. From approximation error analysis, we derived a parabolic error estimation function that enables pencil

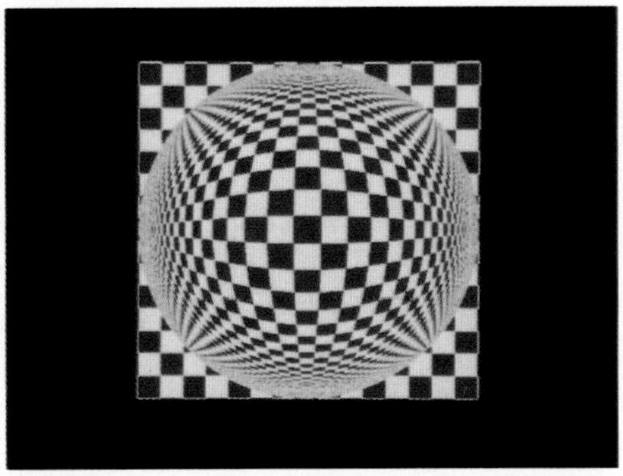

Figure 8
A transparent sphere generated by ray tracing with system matrix

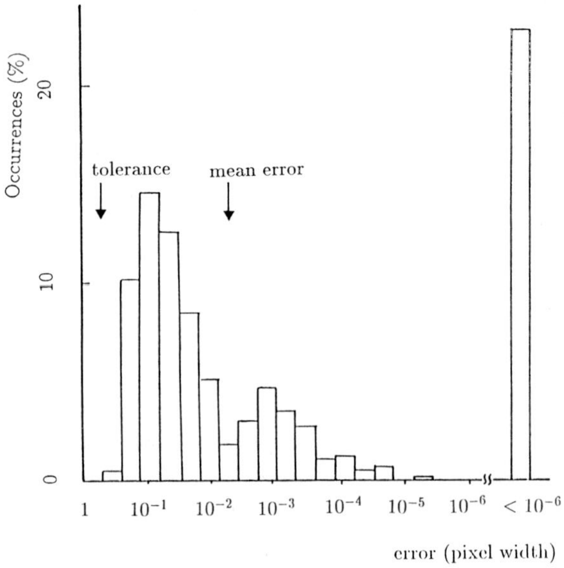

Figure 10 Error distribution of the image

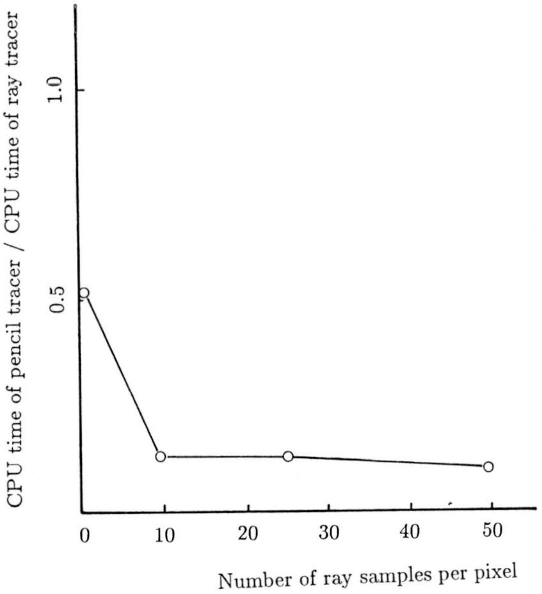

Figure 9
Ratio of CPU time of the pencil tracer to time of the ray tracer, with respect to the number of ray samples per pixel

Figure 11
Transparent polyhedron and its shadow using generalized perspective transformation and the illuminance formula (8).

tracers to assure a required image accuracy.

The theory solves a variety of ray tracing problems in the following ways:

- The system matrix provides a better approximation of refraction and error estimation tools for beam tracing[2].
- The system matrix provides a general calculation method to obtain a pencil-spread angle which is necessary for ray tracing with cones[3].
- The system matrix provides a general method for tolerance calculation which is essential for Barr's ray tracing method[4].
- The system matrix provides a general illuminance formula that describes the light concentration effect.
- The system matrix provides fast ray tracing and anti-aliasing methods for smooth refracting and reflecting objects. Image accuracy is assured due to the error estimation function.

As applications, we proposed three fast ray tracing algorithms, ray tracing with a system matrix, ray interpolation, and generalized perspective transformation. An illuminance formula that describes the intensity law for general situations is also presented. Using the formula, pencil tracers can analytically calculate illuminances for refracted and reflected light emitted by point sources. Experiments confirmed their efficiency in speed, accuracy and reality for smooth transparent objects. The edge problem still remains in ray tracing with the system matrix, and further research is required.

As the theory provides general tools for pencil tracing, it is considered that pencil tracing is applicable to many situations that require tracing many close rays. These situations include, for example, when creating a motion-blurred picture, demonstrating the dispersion effect of transparent objects, making many pictures from a continuously moving view point, and distributed ray tracing[10].

Acknowledgment

We would like to thank Dr. S. Shimada, for his continuous support. We would also like to thank Dr. K. Tsukamoto, Dr. I. Masuda, Mr. K. Ueno, Dr. T. Mashiko, Mr. T. Naruse, Mr. M. Yoshida, and Mr. H.Murase for their invaluable advice and encouragement. We are greatly indebted to Dr. N. Osumi for preparing the paper, and to the reviewers for their useful comments.

References

[1] T.Whitted, 'An improved illumination model for shaded display', Comm. ACM, ***23***, No.6, pp.343-349 (1980)

[2] P.S.Heckbert and P. Hanrahan, 'Beam tracing polygonal object', Computer Graphics, ***18***, No.3, pp.119-127 (1984)

[3] J.Amanatides, 'Ray tracing with cones', Computer Graphics, ***18***, No.3, pp.129-135 (1984)

[4] A.H.Barr, 'Ray tracing deformed surfaces', Computer Graphics, ***20***, No.4, pp.287-296 (1986)

[5] M.Born and E.Wolf, Principles of Optics, pp.190-196, New York: Pergamon, 1959

[6] G.A.Deschamps, 'Ray techniques in electromagnetics', Proceedings of the IEEE, ***60***, No.9, pp.1022-1035 (1972)

[7] S.M.Rubin and T.Whitted, 'A three dimensional representation for fast rendering of complex scenes', Computer Graphics, ***14***, No.3, pp.110-116 (1980)

[8] J.T.Kajiya, 'The rendering equation', Computer Graphics, ***20***, No.4, pp.143-150 (1986)

[9] T.Nishita and E.Nakamae, 'Continuous tone representation of three-dimensional objects taking account of shadows and interreflection', Computer Graphics, ***19***, No.3, pp.23-30 (1985)

[10] R.L.Cook, T.Porter, and L.Carpenter, 'Distributed ray tracing', Computer Graphics, ***18***, No.3, pp.137-145 (1984)

Appendix

Error estimation functions, e_x and e_ξ

(1) Transfer:

Since the second term of a ray change $\Delta\psi$ is zero, the error estimation function is equal to zero.

(2) Refraction or reflection:

$$\begin{aligned} e_x &= ax^2 + bx\xi + c\xi^2 \\ e_\xi &= dx^2 + ex\xi + f\xi^2 \end{aligned} \qquad \text{(A-1)}$$

where

$$\begin{aligned} a &= (\cos\theta'/2R\cos^2\theta)|\alpha + \beta\tan\theta'|, \\ b &= (|\alpha|/\gamma)(n/n'), \\ c &= 0, \\ d &= (|\beta|/\cos^2\theta)[(1/4R^3)\{\tan\theta + (2+|\beta|)\tan\theta'\} \\ &\quad + \sqrt{2}d_{3m}], \\ e &= |\gamma\tan\theta' - (1/\gamma)\tan\theta|/(R\cos\theta)(n/n'), \\ f &= (\gamma|\alpha|/2)(n/n'), \\ \alpha &= \tan\theta - \gamma\tan\theta', \\ \beta &= 1-\gamma, \\ \gamma &= n\cos\theta/n'\cos\theta' \end{aligned}$$

and R is the maximum curvature of the surface at the origin, θ and θ' are the incident and refracted axial ray angles, and d_{3m} is the maximum third differential value at the point, defined by

$$d_{3m} = \max_{i,j,k=1,3}(|\partial^3 f/\partial u_i \partial u_j \partial u_k|).$$

(3) General system

Consider a system composed of n element systems, wherein the system matrix is

$$T = T_n T_{n-1} \cdots T_1,$$

where T_i is the system matrix of an i element system. For simplicity, let the 4×4 matrices T_i^a and T_i^b be

$$\begin{aligned} T_i^a &= \begin{cases} T_n T_{n-1} \cdots T_{i+1} & \text{for } i = 1, 2, \cdots, n-1 \\ 1 & \text{for } i = n \end{cases} \\ &= \begin{pmatrix} A_{1i}^a & A_{2i}^a \\ A_{3i}^a & A_{4i}^a \end{pmatrix}, \\ T_i^b &= \begin{cases} 1 & \text{for } i = 1 \\ T_{i-1} T_{i-2} \cdots T_1 & \text{for } i = 2, 3, \cdots, n \end{cases} \\ &= \begin{pmatrix} A_{1i}^b & A_{2i}^b \\ A_{3i}^b & A_{4i}^b \end{pmatrix}, \end{aligned}$$

where A_{ji}^a and A_{ji}^b are 2×2 matrices. The error estimation functions are given by

$$e_x(\zeta) = \zeta^t \{ \sum_{i=1}^{n} M_i^t (\lambda_{1i} P_i + \lambda_{2i} Q_i) M_i \} \zeta,$$

and

$$e_\xi(\zeta) = \zeta^t \{ \sum_{i=1}^{n} M_i^t (\lambda_{3i} P_i + \lambda_{4i} Q_i) M_i \} \zeta,$$

where

$$\begin{aligned} \zeta &= \begin{pmatrix} x \\ \xi \end{pmatrix}, \\ M_i &= \begin{pmatrix} \mu_{i1} & \mu_{i2} \\ \mu_{i3} & \mu_{i4} \end{pmatrix}, \\ P_i &= \begin{pmatrix} a_i & b_i/2 \\ b_i/2 & c_i \end{pmatrix}, \\ Q_i &= \begin{pmatrix} d_i & e_i/2 \\ e_i/2 & f_i \end{pmatrix}. \end{aligned}$$

The values μ_{ij} and λ_{ij} are square roots of the larger eigen values of $A_{ij}^b (A_{ij}^b)^t$ and $A_{ij}^a (A_{ij}^a)^t$, respectively. The value a_i to f_i is a coefficient of the error estimation function for the i element system, given by Eq. (A-1).

Fast Ray Tracing by Ray Classification

James Arvo
David Kirk

Apollo Computer, Inc.
330 Billerica Road
Chelmsford, MA 01824

Abstract

We describe a new approach to ray tracing which drastically reduces the number of ray-object and ray-bounds intersection calculations by means of 5-dimensional space subdivision. Collections of rays originating from a common 3D rectangular volume and directed through a 2D solid angle are represented as hypercubes in 5-space. A 5D volume bounding the space of rays is dynamically subdivided into hypercubes, each linked to a set of objects which are candidates for intersection. Rays are classified into unique hypercubes and checked for intersection with the associated candidate object set. We compare several techniques for object extent testing, including boxes, spheres, plane-sets, and convex polyhedra. In addition, we examine optimizations made possible by the directional nature of the algorithm, such as sorting, caching and backface culling. Results indicate that this algorithm significantly outperforms previous ray tracing techniques, especially for complex environments.

CR Categories and Subject Descriptors:
I.3.3 [**Computer Graphics**]: Picture/Image Generation;
I.3.7 [**Computer Graphics**]: Three-Dimensional Graphics and Realism;

General Terms: Algorithms, Graphics

Additional Key Words and Phrases: Computer graphics, ray tracing, visible-surface algorithms, extent, bounding volume, hierarchy, traversal

1. Introduction

Our goal in studying algorithms which accelerate ray tracing is to produce high-quality images without paying the enormous time penalty traditionally associated with this method. Recent algorithms have focused on reducing the number of ray-object intersection tests performed since this is typically where most of the time is spent, especially for complex environments. This is achieved by using a simple-to-evaluate function to cull objects which are clearly not in the path of the ray.

1.1 Previous Work

Rubin and Whitted [14] developed one of the first schemes for improving ray tracing performance. They observed that "exhaustive search" could be greatly improved upon by checking for intersection with simple bounding volumes around each object before performing more complicated ray-object intersection checks. By creating a hierarchy of bounding volumes, Rubin and Whitted were able to reduce the number of bounding volume intersection checks as well. Weghorst, et. al. [17] studied the use of different types of bounding volumes in a hierarchy, and discussed how ease of intersection testing and "tightness" of fit determine the bounding volume's effectiveness in culling objects.

The object hierarchy of Rubin and Whitted made the crucial step away from the linear time complexity of exhaustive search but still did not achieve acceptable performance on complex environments. This was due in part to the top down search of the object hierarchy required for every ray. Another factor was the difficulty of obtaining a small bound on the number of ray-object intersection tests and ray-bounds comparisons required per ray since this depended strongly on the organization of the hierarchy.

Another class of algorithms employs 3D space subdivision to implement culling functions. The initial candidates for intersection are associated with a 3D volume containing the ray origin. Successive candidates are identified by regions which the ray intersects. Concurrently and independently, Glassner [4], and Fujimoto, et. al. [3] pursued this approach. Glassner investigated partitioning the object space using an octree data structure, while Fujimoto compared octrees to a rectangular linear grid of 3D voxels. Kaplan [7] proposed a similar scheme and observed that a binary space partitioning tree could be used to accomplish the space subdivision. A drawback common to all of these approaches is that a ray which misses everything must be checked against the contents of each of the regions or voxels which it intersects.

None of these algorithms made use of the coherence which exists between similar rays. Speer, et. al. [15] examined the concept of "tunnels" as a means of exploiting ray-tree coherence. Speer attempted to construct cylindrical "safety regions" within which a ray would miss all objects, but observed that despite considerable coherence, the cost of constructing and using the cylindrical tunnels negated the benefit of the culling they accomplished.

Kay and Kajiya [8] introduced a new type of bounding volume, plane-sets, and a hierarchy traversal algorithm which is able to check objects for intersection in a particular order, regardless of the locality of the bounding volume hierarchy. This algorithm had the key advantage over previous object hierarchy schemes that objects could be checked for intersection in approximately the order that they would be encountered along the ray length.

1.2 A New Approach

Our ray classification approach differs significantly from previous work in that it extends the idea of space subdivision to include ray direction. The result is an extremely powerful culling function that is, empirically, relatively insensitive to environment complexity.

A key feature of the algorithm is that a single evaluation of its culling function is capable of producing a small but complete set of candidate objects, even if the ray misses everything. This is accomplished by adaptively subdividing the space of all relevant rays into equivalence classes, $E_1, E_2, \ldots, E_m$, and constructing candidate object sets $C_1, C_2, \ldots, C_m$, such that C_i contains all objects which the rays in E_i can intersect. Evaluating the culling function reduces to classifying a given ray as a member of an equivalence class and retrieving the associated candidate set. The algorithm strives to keep $|C_i|$ small for all i, and several new techniques are employed which lessen the impact of those sets for which it fails to do so.

2. 5-Space and Ray Classification

In many ray tracing implementations, rays are represented by a 3D origin coupled with a 3D unit direction vector, a convenient form for intersection calculations. However, geometrically a ray has only five degrees of freedom, as evidenced by the fact that the same information can be conveyed by only five values: for instance, a 3D origin and two spherical angles. Consequently, we can identify rays in 3-space with points in 5-space, or, more precisely, with points in the 5-manifold $\mathbf{R}^3 \times \mathbf{S}^2$, where $\mathbf{S}^2$ is the unit sphere in $\mathbf{R}^3$. It follows that any neighborhood of rays, a collection of rays with similar origins and directions, can be parametrized by a subset of $\mathbf{R}^5$. We shall use such parametrizations in constructing a culling function which makes use of all five degrees of freedom of a ray.

The ray classification algorithm can be broken into five subtasks. All but the last operate at least partly in 5-space. These are:

[1] *5D Bounding Volume:*
Find a bounded subset, $E \subset \mathbf{R}^5$, which contains the 5D equivalent of every ray which can interact with the environment.

[2] *5D Space Subdivision*:
Select subsets $E_1, \ldots, E_m$ which partition $E \subset \mathbf{R}^5$ into disjoint volumes.

[3] *Candidate Set Creation*:
Given a set of rays represented by a 5D volume E_i, create a set of candidates, C_i, containing *every* object which is intersected by one of the rays.

[4] *Ray Classification*:
Given a ray corresponding to a point in E, find a set, E_i, of a partitioning, $E_1, \ldots, E_m$, which contains the point, and return the associated candidate set C_i.

[5] *Candidate Set Processing*:
Given a ray and a set of candidate objects, C_i, determine the closest ray-object intersection if one exists.

For each ray that is intersected with the environment, [4] is used to retrieve a set of candidate objects and [5] does the actual ray-object intersections using this set. As we shall see, [1] is carried out only once while [2] and [3] incrementally refine the partitioning and candidate sets in response to ray classification queries in [4]. Ideally we seek a partitioning in [2] such that corresponding candidate sets created in [3] contain fewer than some predetermined number of objects. These subtasks are described in detail in sections 3 through 7.

2.1 Beams as 5D Hypercubes

Because much of the algorithm involves 5D volumes it is important to choose volumes which have compact representations and permit efficient point-containment queries and subdivision. For these reasons we use 5D axis-aligned parallelepipeds, or hypercubes. These are stored as five ordered pairs representing intervals along the five mutually orthogonal coordinate axes which we label X, Y, Z, U, and V.

Each hypercube, representing a collection of rays, has a natural 3D manifestation which we call a *beam*. This is the unbounded 3D volume formed by the union of semi-infinite lines, or rays in the geometrical sense, defined by the points of the hypercube. Beams play a central role in candidate set creation since they comprise exactly those points in 3-space which are reachable by a set of rays. Given the importance of this role it is essential that hypercubes define beam volumes which are easily represented, such as convex polyhedra. This geometry is completely determined by the way we identify rays with 5D points.

2.2 Rays as 5D Points

In this section we describe the means of associating a unique point in $\mathbf{R}^5$ with each distinct ray in $\mathbf{R}^3$. As mentioned earlier, a ray can be mapped to a unique 5-tuple, (x,y,z,u,v), consisting of its origin followed by two spherical angles. Unfortunately the beams associated with hypercubes under this mapping are not generally polyhedra. To remedy this, we piece together several mappings which have the desired properties locally, and together account for the whole space of rays.

Consider the intersection of a ray with an axis-aligned cube of side two centered at its origin. Each distinct ray direction corresponds to a unique intersection point on this cube. A 2D coordinate system can be imposed on these points by normalizing the ray direction vector, **d**, with respect to the ∞-norm, as shown in Equation 1, and extracting (u,v) from the result, as shown in Equation 2.

$$\mathbf{w} = \frac{\mathbf{d}}{\|\mathbf{d}\|_\infty} = \frac{(d_x, d_y, d_z)}{\mathrm{MAX}(|d_x|, |d_y|, |d_z|)} \qquad [1]$$

$$(u, v) = \begin{cases} (w_y, w_z) \text{ if } w_x = \pm 1, \text{ or else} \\ (w_x, w_z) \text{ if } w_y = \pm 1, \text{ or else} \\ (w_x, w_y) \text{ if } w_z = \pm 1 \end{cases} \qquad [2]$$

This establishes a one-to-one correspondence between $[-1,1] \times [-1,1]$ and rays passing through a single face of the cube. By partitioning the rays into six dominant directions defined by the faces of the cube, and restricting the mapping to each of these domains, we obtain six bicontinuous one-to-one mappings. We associate each with a *dominant axis*, denoted +X, −X, +Y, −Y, +Z, or −Z. The inverse mappings, or parametrizations, define an atlas of $\mathbf{S}^2$, covering the set of ray directions with images of $[-1,1] \times [-1,1]$. This is trivially extended to $\mathbf{R}^3 \times \mathbf{S}^2$. In order to meet our requirement of a global one-to-one correspondence, however, we index into six "copies" of $[-1,1] \times [-1,1]$ using the dominant axis of a ray. For a given ray, this axis is determined by the axis and sign of its largest absolute direction component.

Intervals in U and V together define pyramidal solid angles through a single cube face while intervals in X, Y, and Z define rectangular 3D volumes. Hypercubes then define beams which are unbounded polyhedra with at most nine faces. This is shown in Figure 1b along with a 2D analogy as an aid to visualization in Figure 1a.

3. The 5D Bounding Volume

The first step of the ray classification algorithm is to find a bounded subset of $\mathbf{R}^5$ containing all rays which are relevant to the environment. We start by finding a 3D bounding box, B, which contains all the objects of the environment. Such a box is easily obtained from individual object extents. The desired bounding volume can then be built from six copies of the hypercube $B \times [-1,1] \times [-1,1]$, each corresponding to a unique dominant axis and accounting for directions covering one sixth of the unit sphere, $\mathbf{S}^2$.

The 3D bounding box, B, also serves another purpose. If the eye point is outside of B, then every first-generation ray must be checked for intersection with it. If there is no intersection, we know the ray hits nothing in the environment. Otherwise, the ray must be moved into the 5D bounding volume by resetting its origin to the point of intersection.

Other bounding volumes can be used in place of B for this second purpose. For instance, plane-sets [8] can produce a much tighter bound, thereby identifying more rays which miss all the objects in the environment. Another advantage lies in ray re-origining. By pushing the rays up to the boundary of the tighter volume, we reduce the space of rays, making the space subdivision task more efficient.

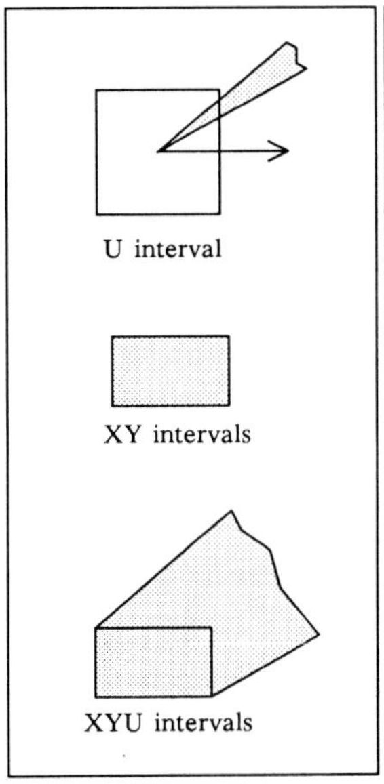

Figure 1a.
Beams in 2-Space.

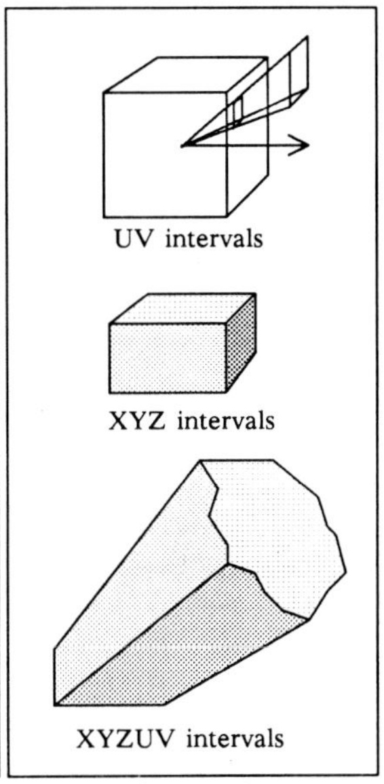

Figure 1b.
Beams in 3-Space.

4. 5D Space Subdivision

When intersecting a ray with the environment we need only consider the set of objects whose bounding volumes are intersected. The purpose of tasks 1 through 4 in section 2 is to produce a set of objects containing these, and few others, for any ray in the environment. This is done efficiently by exploiting scene coherence, which ensures that similar rays are likely to intersect similar sets of objects. Due to the continuity of our ray parametrizations, this implies that decreasing the diameter of a hypercube increases the likelihood that the rays of its beam behave similarly. The role of 5D space subdivision is to produce hypercubes which are sufficiently small that the rays of each corresponding beam intersect approximately the same objects. This allows us to share one set of candidate objects among all the rays of a beam.

We use binary space subdivision to create a hypercube hierarchy, dividing intervals exactly in half at each level, and repeatedly cycling through the five axes. Any ray can be contained in a hypercube of arbitrarily small diameter by this mechanism. Given that we use only a sparse subset of the potential rays, however, it is unnecessary to finely subdivide the entire 5D bounding volume. Instead, we confine subdivision to occur in those regions populated with rays generated during ray tracing. We subdivide only on demand, when the 5D coordinates of a ray are found to reside in a hypercube which is too large. Thus, beginning with the six bounding hypercubes, we construct the entire hierarchy by lazy evaluation.

When a ray causes new paths to be formed in the hypercube hierarchy, two heuristics determine when subdivision terminates. We stop if either the candidate set or the hypercube falls below a fixed size threshold. A small candidate set indicates that we have achieved the goal of making the associated rays inexpensive to intersect with the environment. The hypercube size constraint is imposed to allow the cost of creating a candidate set to be amortized over many rays.

5. Candidate Set Creation

Given a hypercube, the task of creating its candidate set consists of determining all the objects in the environment which its rays can intersect. This is done by comparing each object's bounding volume with the beam defined by the hypercube. If the volumes intersect, the object is *classified* as a candidate with respect to that hypercube and is added to the candidate set.

The six bounding hypercubes are assigned candidate sets containing all objects in the environment. As subdivision proceeds, candidate sets are efficiently created for the new hypercubes by making use of the hierarchy. Only those objects in an ancestor's candidate set need be reclassified.

For space efficiency, we need not create a candidate set for every intermediate hypercube in the hierarchy. When a hypercube is subdivided along one axis, the beams of the resulting hypercubes usually overlap substantially, and are quite similar to the parent beam. Consequently, a single subdivision eliminates few candidates. This suggests performing several subdivisions before creating a new candidate set. A strategy which we have found to be effective is to subdivide each of the five axes before creating a new candidate set. While this allows up to 2^5 hypercubes to derive their candidate sets from the same ancestor, the reduction in storage is significant. Also, due to lazy evaluation of the hierarchy, it is rare that all descendants are even created.

5.1 Object Classification

The object classification method used in candidate set creation is critical to the performance of the ray tracer. A very fast method may be too conservative, creating candidate sets which are much too large. This causes unnecessary overhead in both candidate set creation and processing. A classifying method which performs well in rejecting objects may be unacceptable if it is too costly. As with object extents used for avoiding unnecessary ray-object intersection checks, there must be a compromise between the cost of the method and its accuracy [17]. In the following subsections we discuss the tradeoffs of three object classification techniques which can be used independently or in combination.

5.1.1 Classifying Objects with LP

The first object classification method we describe employs linear programming to test for object-beam intersection, and requires objects to be enclosed by convex polyhedra. A polyhedral bounding volume is conveniently represented by its vertex list, or hull points, and can be made arbitrarily close to the convex hull of the object. Since the beam is itself a polyhedron, the object classification problem reduces to testing for intersection between two polyhedra. This is easily expressed as a linear program using the hull points [12] and then solved using the simplex method [13]. The result is an exact classification scheme for this type of bounding volume. That is, an object is classified as a candidate of a hypercube if and only if some ray of the beam intersects its bounding polyhedron.

Unfortunately, our experience has shown that the computation required to solve the linear program is prohibitively high, precluding its use as the primary object classification method. It is overly complex for handling the very frequent cases of objects which are either far from the beam or inside it. Nevertheless, it is a useful tool for testing and evaluating the effectiveness of approximate object-classification methods.

5.1.2 Classifying Objects with Planes

The linear programming approach rejects an object from the candidate set if and only if there exists a separating plane between the beam and the object's bounding polyhedron. This suggests a simpler approach which tests several planes directly, classifying an object as a candidate if none of the planes are separators.

For every beam there are several planes which are particularly appropriate to test, each with the entire beam in its positive half-space. Four of these planes are parallel to the faces of the UV pyramid, translated to the appropriate XYZ extrema of the hypercube. Up to three more are found "behind" the beam, containing faces of the XYZ hypercube extent. If all of the vertices of an object's bounding polyhedron are found to be in the negative half-space of one of these planes, the object is rejected. The half-space tests are greatly simplified by the nature of these planes, since all are parallel to at least one coordinate axis.

This method is fast and conservative, never rejecting an object which is actually intersected by the beam. It is also approximate, since objects will be erroneously classified as candidates when, for example, their bounding polyhedra intersect both a U and a V plane without intersecting the beam.

5.1.3 Classifying Objects with Cones

Another approach to object classification uses spheres to bound objects and cones to approximate beams. This is similar to previous uses of cones in ray tracing. Amanatides [1] described the use of cones as a method of area sampling, providing accurate and inexpensive anti-aliasing. Kirk [9] used cones as a tool to calculate proper texture filtering apertures, and to improve anti-aliasing of bump-mapped surfaces. In our context, cones prove to be very effective for classifying objects bounded by spherical extents.

To create a candidate set for a hypercube we begin by constructing a cone, specified by a unit axis vector, **W**, a spread angle, θ, and an apex, **P**, which completely contains the beam of the hypercube. If this cone does not intersect the spherical extent of an object, the object is omitted from the candidate set. The details of the cone-sphere intersection calculation are given in both [1] and [9]. We describe the construction of the cone below with the aid of function **F** in Equation 3, which defines inverse mappings of those described in section 2.2.

$$\mathbf{F}(u, v) = \begin{cases} (1, u, v) & \text{if } +X \text{ is dominant} \\ (-1, u, v) & \text{if } -X \text{ is dominant} \\ (u, 1, v) & \text{if } +Y \text{ is dominant} \\ (u, -1, v) & \text{if } -Y \text{ is dominant} \\ (u, v, 1) & \text{if } +Z \text{ is dominant} \\ (u, v, -1) & \text{if } -Z \text{ is dominant} \end{cases} \qquad [3]$$

The cone axis vector, **W**, depends only on the dominant axis of the hypercube and its U and V intervals, (umin,umax) and (vmin,vmax). It is constructed by bisecting the angle between the vectors **A** and **B**, which are given by Equations 4 and 5.

$$\mathbf{A} = \mathbf{F}(\text{umin}, \text{vmax}) \qquad [4]$$

$$\mathbf{B} = \mathbf{F}(\text{umax}, \text{vmin}) \qquad [5]$$

To find the cone spread angle we also construct vectors **C** and **D** using Equations 6 and 7. We then compute θ as shown in Equation 8.

$$\mathbf{C} = \mathbf{F}(\text{umin}, \text{vmin}) \qquad [6]$$

$$\mathbf{D} = \mathbf{F}(\text{umax}, \text{vmax}) \qquad [7]$$

$$\theta = \text{MAX}(\mathbf{A}\angle\mathbf{W}, \mathbf{B}\angle\mathbf{W}, \mathbf{C}\angle\mathbf{W}, \mathbf{D}\angle\mathbf{W}) \qquad [8]$$

Once the axis and spread angle are known, the apex of the cone, **P**, is determined by the 3D rectangular volume, R, defined by the XYZ intervals of the hypercube. The point **P** is located by displacing the centroid of R in the negative cone axis direction until the cone exactly contains the smallest sphere bounding R. The resulting expression for **P** is given in Equation 9, where $\mathbf{R}_0$ and $\mathbf{R}_1$ are the min and max extrema of R.

$$\mathbf{P} = \frac{\mathbf{R}_0 + \mathbf{R}_1}{2} - \mathbf{W}\frac{\| \mathbf{R}_0 - \mathbf{R}_1 \|_2}{2 \text{ SIN } \theta} \qquad [9]$$

The cone is used to classify all potential candidates of the hypercube and is constructed only once per hypercube. The comparison between the cone and the object's bounding sphere is fast, making the cost of a distant miss low. This reduces the penalty of infrequent candidate list creation, the space saving measure discussed in section 5.

A linear transformation, M, applied to an object can also be used to modify its bounding sphere. By transforming the center of the sphere by M and scaling its radius by $\| M \|_2$, we obtain a new sphere which is guaranteed to contain the transformed object. The matrix 2-norm is given by $\sqrt{\rho(M^T M)}$ [11], where ρ, the spectral radius, is the largest absolute eigenvalue of a matrix. If $M^T M$ is sparse, the eigenvalue calculation is quite simple. An iterative technique like the power method can be used for the remaining cases [5].

6. Ray Classification

Every ray-environment intersection calculation begins with ray classification, which locates the hypercube containing the 5D equivalent of the ray. This entails mapping the ray into a 5D point and traversing the hypercube hierarchy, beginning with the bounding hypercube indexed by the dominant axis of the ray, until we reach the leaf containing this point. Due to lazy evaluation of the hierarchy, this traversal may have the side effect of creating a new path terminating at a sufficiently small hypercube containing the ray if such a path has not already been built on behalf of another ray. If the candidate set associated with the leaf hypercube is empty, we are guaranteed that the ray intersects nothing. Otherwise, we process this set as described in the next section.

7. Candidate Set Processing

Once ray classification has produced a set of candidate objects for a given ray, this set must be processed to determine the object which results in the closest intersection, if one exists. To optimize this search we continue to make use of object bounding volumes for coarse intersection checks. We also reject objects whose bounding volumes intersect the ray beyond a known object intersection. This can further reduce the number of ray-object intersection calculations, but still requires that the ray be tested against all bounding volumes of the candidate set.

We can remove this latter requirement by taking advantage of the fact that all rays of a given beam share the same dominant axis. By sorting the objects of the candidate sets by their minimum extents along this axis, then processing them in ascending order, we can ignore the tail of the list if we reach a candidate whose entire extent lies beyond a known intersection. This is an enormous advantage because it can drastically reduce the number of bounding volume checks in cases where the ray intersects an object near the head of the list. For example, in Figure 2 only the first two objects are tested because all subsequent objects are guaranteed to lie beyond the known intersection. By sorting the candidate sets of the six bounding hypercubes along the associated dominant axes before 5D space subdivision begins, the correct ordering can be inherited by all subsequent candidate sets with no additional overhead. Object bounding boxes provide the six keys used in sorting these initial candidate sets.

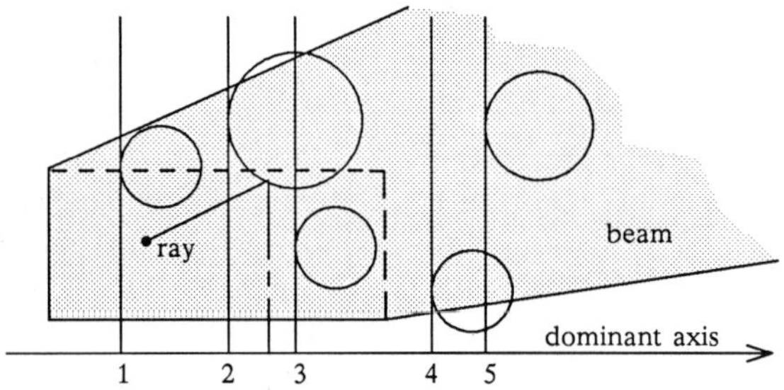

Figure 2. Sorted candidates.

8. Backface Culling

Though backface culling is a popular technique in the field of computer graphics [10], it has previously been of very limited use in ray tracing since polygons which are not in the direct line of sight can still affect the environment by means of shadows, reflections, and transparency. When creating the candidate set of a hypercube, however, it is appropriate to eliminate those polygons which are part of an opaque solid and are backfacing with respect to *every* ray of its beam. When classifying with cones, this latter criterion is met if Equation 10 is satisfied, where **N** is the front-facing normal of the polygon, **W** is the cone axis, and θ is the cone spread angle.

$$\mathbf{N} \bullet \mathbf{W} > \sin \theta \qquad [10]$$

Using this technique, rays headed in opposite directions through the same volume of space may be tested against totally disjoint sets of polygons. By eliminating nearly half the candidates of most hypercubes, backface culling greatly accelerates both the creation and processing of candidate sets.

9. Image Coherence and Caching

Due to image coherence, two neighboring samples in image space will tend to produce very similar ray trees. This implies that successive rays of a given generation will tend to be elements of the same beam. We use this fact to great advantage by caching the most recently referenced hypercubes of each generation and checking new rays first against this cache. If a ray is contained, it is a cache hit, and the previous candidate set is returned immediately, without re-traversing the hypercube hierarchy. Otherwise, we classify the ray by traversal and update the cache with the new hypercube and candidate set. Although hierarchy traversal is very efficient, verifying that a point lies within a hypercube requires only ten comparisons, a considerable shortcut.

A related caching technique is used exclusively for shadows. Rays used for sampling light sources are special because there is no need to compute the closest intersection. It suffices to determine the existence of an opaque object between the ray origin and the intersection with the light source. If a given point in 3-space is in shadow, nearby points are likely shadowed by the same object. The shadow cache simply records the last object casting a shadow with respect to each light source and checks that object first, as part of the next shadow calculation.

10. Candidate Set Truncation

Because we cannot decide when one object occludes another based on bounding volumes alone, a candidate set must contain all objects whose bounding volumes intersect the beam. Thus, even extremely narrow beams can produce candidate sets which are large. This poses no problem for candidate set processing because sorting insures that far-away occluded objects will never be tested. This does increase storage requirements, however, by increasing the number of candidate sets which contain a given object.

We can drop far-away objects from a candidate set at the expense of a slight penalty incurred by rays which are not blocked by the nearer objects. This is done by truncating a sorted candidate set at a point where the remaining objects are outside the XYZ extent of the hypercube and marking this point with a *truncation plane* orthogonal to the dominant axis. For example, in Figure 2 this could occur just before the fourth object. We process a truncated candidate set differently only when no object intersection is found in front of the truncation plane. See Figure 3. In this case we re-position the ray to the truncation plane, re-classify, and process the new candidate set. Though this is similar to previous 3D space subdivision techniques [3][4][7], we retain the distinct advantages of sorting and backface culling within the truncated candidate sets, as well as the ability to pass rays through unobstructed regions of space with virtually no work.

We reduce the cost of occasional re-classification steps by adding a cache dimension indicating the number of times a ray has been reclassified. This allows most re-classifications to be done without traversing the hypercube hierarchy. Moreover, re-reclassifying a ray often results in a net gain by narrowing the included volume as we proceed further away from the original ray origin. See Figure 4.

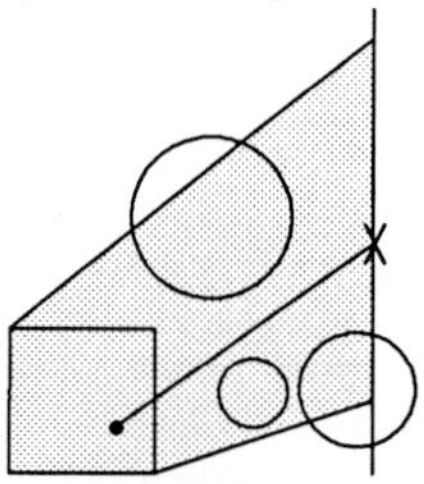

Figure 3.
Set truncation.

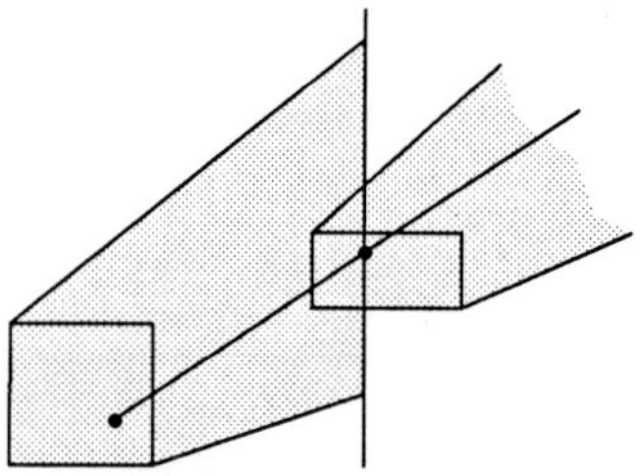

Figure 4.
Beam narrowing.

11. First-Generation Rays

First-generation rays have only two degrees of freedom, making them easy to characterize, and frequently outnumber all other rays, making them important to optimize. Many ray tracing implementations obviate the need for first-generation rays altogether by means of more conventional scan-line or depth-buffer algorithms. For extremely complex environments, however, the value of these methods diminishes, since they are forced to expend some effort on every object, even those which do not contribute to the final image. It is therefore worthwhile to examine ray tracing techniques which can perform superlinearly on these rays.

The ray classification algorithm benefits in a number of ways from the special nature of first-generation rays. Because they originate from a degenerate 3D volume, the eye point, first-generation rays can be classified using u and v alone. This increases the efficiency of ray classification by simplifying the traversal of the hypercube hierarchy, which becomes a hierarchy of 2D rectangles. Candidate set creation also benefits because the beams associated with the degenerate hypercubes are non-overlapping pyramids. Candidate sets are therefore cut in half, on average, with every subdivision. This makes it feasible to obtain smaller candidate sets, thereby speeding up candidate set processing as well. The result of these optimizations for first-generation rays is an image-space algorithm which closely resembles the 2D recursive subdivision approach introduced by Warnock [16].

12. Summary

We have described a method which accelerates ray tracing by drastically reducing the number of ray-object and ray-bounds intersection checks. This is accomplished by extending the notion of space subdivision to a 5D scheme which makes use of ray direction as well as ray origin. Rays are classified into 5D hypercubes in order to retrieve pre-sorted sets of candidate objects which are efficiently tested for intersection with each ray. The computational cost of intersecting a ray with the environment is very low because similar rays share the benefit of culling far-away objects, thereby exploiting coherence. This technique can be used to accelerate all applications which rely upon ray-environment intersections, including those which perform Monte Carlo integration [2][6]. Empirical evidence indicates that performance is closer to constant time than previous methods, especially for very complex environments.

13. Results

All test images were calculated at 512 by 512 pixel resolution with one sample per pixel for timing purposes. All of the images in the figures were calculated at 512 by 512 pixel resolution and anti-aliased using adaptive stochastic sampling with 5x5 subpixels and a cosine-squared filter kernel. Figures 5a and b are false color images of the recursive pyramid with four levels of recursion, from [8]. The hue of the false color indicates the number of ray-bounds checks which were performed in the course of computing each pixel. The scale proceeds from blue for 0 bounding volume checks to red for 50 or more. Figure 5a depicts the performance of the ray classification algorithm without the first-generation ray optimization, and Figure 5b shows how performance improves when this optimization is enabled.

The same basic model is instanced to ten levels of recursion in Figure 5c. This environment contains over four million triangles and was ray traced in 1 hour and 28 minutes (see table in Figure 6).

Figure 7 is a reflective teapot on a checkerboard, and Figure 8 shows the original five Platonic Solids and the newly discovered Teapotahedron.

Figure 9a shows the Caltech tree with leaves as they might appear rather late in the year. Figure 9b is a false color rendering with the same scale as described above. The fine yellow and red lines at the edge of the dark blue shadows in the false color image indicate shadow calculations which required processing a candidate set. The interior areas of the shadows are dark blue, indicating very few bounding volume checks, due to the shadow cache optimization.

The same tree is shown in Figure 10 rendered in false color without leaves. Even though there are fewer primitives, the number of ray-bounds checks is not much different from that of the tree with leaves. This is due to the difficulty of accurately classifying long arbitrarily oriented cylinders.

Figure 11a is a true color image of a grove of 64 instanced trees with leaves. This environment contains 477,121 objects and was ray traced in 4 hours and 53 minutes. Figure 11b is a false color rendering of the grove of trees.

We wish to compare the performance of our algorithm with that of previous methods. Due to the generosity of Tim Kay at Caltech, we were able to run benchmarks using the same databases used in [8]. Since we did not have access to a Vax 11/780 for our benchmarks, we chose an Apollo DN570, which has roughly the same level of performance. Kay and Kajiya compared the performance of their program on the recursive pyramid of Figure 9 with the performance reported by Glassner [4]. Glassner's program took approximately 8700 Vax 11/780 seconds to render the scene, while Kay's program took approximately 2706 seconds, which translates roughly to a factor of 2.6 improvement after accounting for differences in the scene. Our program took approximately 639 seconds on an Apollo DN570, representing a further factor of 4.2 improvement.

Acknowledgements

We would like to thank Rick Speer, both for organizing an informal ray tracing discussion group at the 86 SIGGRAPH conference, and for directing the discussion toward coherence and directional data structures. Pat Hanrahan deserves credit for supplying the insight that directional classification of rays need not be tied to objects. Thanks to Christian Bremser, John Francis, Olin Lathrop, Jim Michener, Semyon Nisenzon, Cary Scofield, and Douglas Voorhies for their diligent critical reading of early drafts of the paper. Special thanks to Olin Lathrop and John Francis for help in defining and implementing the "ray tracing kernel", the testbed used for this work, and to Jim Michener for his many helpful technical comments. Resounding applause to Tim Kay for making his pyramid and tree databases available. Last but by no means least, thanks to Apollo Computer and particularly to Christian Bremser and Douglas Voorhies for making time available to perform this work.

References

[1] Amanatides, John., "Ray Tracing with Cones," Computer Graphics, 18(3), July 1984, pp. 129–135.

[2] Cook, Robert L., Thomas Porter, and Loren Carpenter., "Distributed Ray Tracing," Computer Graphics 18(3), July 1984, pp. 137–145.

[3] Fujimoto, Akira,, and Kansei Iwata., "Accelerated Ray Tracing," Proceedings of Computer Graphics Tokyo '85, April 1985.

[4] Glassner, Andrew S., "Space Subdivision for Fast Ray Tracing," IEEE Computer Graphics and Applications, 4(10), October, 1984, pp. 15–22.

[5] Johnson, Lee W., and Riess, Dean R., "Numerical Analysis," Addison-Wesley, 1977.

[6] Kajiya, James T., "The Rendering Equation," Computer Graphics 20(4), August 1986, pp. 143–150.

[7] Kaplan, Michael R., "Space Tracing: A Constant Time Ray Tracer," ACM SIGGRAPH '85 Course Notes 11, July 22–26, 1985.

[8] Kay, Timothy L. and James Kajiya., "Ray Tracing Complex Scenes," Computer Graphics, 20(4), August 1986, pp. 269–278.

[9] Kirk, David B., "The Simulation of Natural Features using Cone Tracing," Advanced Computer Graphics (Proceedings of Computer Graphics Tokyo '86), April 1986, pp. 129–144.

[10] Newman, William M., and Robert F. Sproull., "Principles of Interactive Computer Graphics," 1st edition, McGraw-Hill, New York, 1973.

[11] Ortega, James M., "Numerical Analysis, A Second Course," Academic Press, New York, 1972.

[12] Preparata, Franco P., and Michael I. Shamos., "Computational Geometry, an Introduction," Springer-Verlag, New York, 1985.

[13] Press, William H., Brian P. Flannery, Saul A. Teukolsky, William T. Vetterling., "Numerical Recipes," Cambridge University Press, Cambridge, 1986.

[14] Rubin, Steve, and Turner Whitted., "A Three-Dimensional Representation for Fast Rendering of Complex Scenes," Computer Graphics 14(3), July 1980, pp. 110–116.

[15] Speer, L. Richard, Tony D. DeRose, and Brian A. Barsky., "A Theoretical and Empirical Analysis of Coherent Ray Tracing," Computer-Generated Images (Proceedings of Graphics Interface '85), May 27–31, 1985, pp. 11–25.

[16] Warnock, John E., "A Hidden-Surface Algorithm for Computer Generated Half-tone Pictures,", Ph.D. Dissertation, University of Utah, TR 4–15, 1969.

[17] Weghorst, Hank, Gary Hooper, and Donald Greenberg., "Improved Computational Methods for Ray Tracing," ACM Transactions on Graphics, 3(1), January 1984, pp. 52–69.

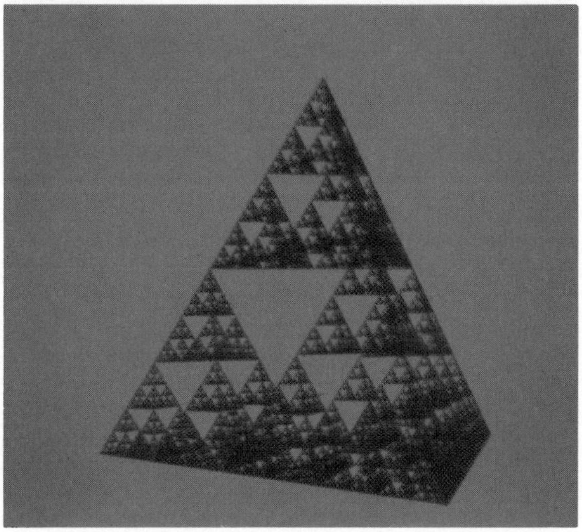

Figure 6: Run–time Statistics

All pixel, ray, and classify counts are in thousands

	Pyramid **4	Pyramid **10	Tree Branches	Tree Leaves	Grove 64 Trees	Teapot	Platonic Solids
Objects	1024	4.2E6	1272	7455	477,121	1824	1405
Pixels	262	262	262	262	262	262	262
Shading Rays	262	262	262	262	262	262	262
Shadow Rays	37	28	133	150	128	187	224
Total Rays	299	290	395	412	390	534	515
Rays that hit	43	30	149	191	213	206	240
Beam/Object Classifies	10.50	117.06	16.01	17.02	46.46	47.71	10.41
Object Intersections	188	288	989	716	1884	523	4896
CPU Time, DN570 sec.	639	5335	2194	3230	17607	3100	2474
(sec/ray)	0.002	0.018	0.006	0.008	0.045	0.006	0.008
(sec/ray that hit)	0.015	0.178	0.015	0.017	0.083	0.015	0.010

Figure 7. Reflective Teapot

Figure 8. Platonic Solids

Figure 9a. Autumn Tree

Figure 9b. False Color Tree with Leaves

Figure 10. Leafless Tree

Figure 11a. Grove of Trees

Figure 11b. False Color Grove of Trees

Generating Antialiased Images at Low Sampling Densities

Don P. Mitchell

AT&T Bell Laboratories
Murray Hill, New Jersey 07974

ABSTRACT

Ray tracing produces point samples of an image from a 3-D model. Constructing an antialiased digital picture from point samples is difficult without resorting to extremely high sampling densities. This paper describes a program that focuses on that problem. While it is impossible to eliminate aliasing totally, it has been shown that nonuniform sampling yields aliasing that is less conspicuous to the observer. An algorithm is presented for fast generation of nonuniform sampling patterns that are optimal in some sense. Some regions of an image may require extra sampling to avoid strong aliasing. Deciding where to do extra sampling can be guided by knowledge of how the eye perceives noise as a function of contrast and color. Finally, to generate the digital picture, the image must be reconstructed from the samples and resampled at the display pixel rate. The nonuniformity of the samples complicates this process, and a new nonuniform reconstruction filter is presented which solves this problem efficiently.

CR Categories and Subject Descriptions: I.3.3 [**Computer Graphics**]: Picture/Image Generation

General Terms: Algorithms

Additional Keywords and Phrases: Adaptive Sampling, Antialiasing, Filtering, Noise Perception, Nonuniform Sampling, Ray Tracing, Reconstruction

1. Introduction

While ray tracing is a straightforward technique for image synthesis, it has in some ways proven to be one of the most perverse. On the one hand, impressive effects of shading, reflection, and refraction can be simulated by ray tracing [WHI80], and it remains one of the simplest methods for evaluating constructive solid geometry models [ROT82]. On the other hand, ray tracing is expensive, and because it is based on point sampling it is especially prone to aliasing problems.

This paper describes a method that uses the point-sampling characteristics of ray tracing more effectively than alternative techniques. The ray tracer itself is viewed as a black box capable of supplying samples of a two-dimensional image signal (by casting rays into a scene). A separate *antialiasing module* decides where to take samples, how densely to sample each region of the image, and how to construct a digital picture from all the sample information. The only data passed from the ray tracer to the antialiasing module are sample values. This cleanly isolates the aliasing problem from ray-tracing issues, and allows a variety of ray tracers (and other sample-generating algorithms) to be used.

The antialiasing module is composed of three principal stages. First, the entire image is sampled at a relatively low density. Then, on the basis of these initial sample values, some regions of the image may be sampled further at a higher density to reduce noise. Finally, in the reconstruction phase, all of the samples of the image are used to generate the pixel values for a displayed image.

Of the many issues involved in optimizing ray tracing, this paper will focus on reducing sampling density while still producing an image of high quality. The approach has been to consider the perception of noise and operate near its threshold. While perception of noise is a complex subject, basic facts learned from work in color-television encoding and image noise measurement can be applied to this problem [LIM77, SAK77].

By varying position and density of the sampling, a more optimal sampling pattern can be obtained. For example, certain nonuniform sampling patterns have been shown to scatter aliasing into high-frequency random noise [YEL83]. Deciding where to concentrate sampling can be guided by estimation of the noise visibility as a function of contrast and color.

2. The Preliminary Sampling Pattern

The choice of sampling strategy is now known to be closely related to the aliasing problem. The history of this problem began with Crow's realization that the "jaggies" in synthetic pictures were an example of aliasing, a well-known phenomenon of signal processing [CRO77]. According to the Sampling Theorem [SHA49], aliasing can only be reduced by either filtering out the high-frequency components of the image (above the Nyquist frequency) or by increasing the sampling density to an appropriate level. Both of these techniques have been used to combat aliasing in ray tracers [AMA84, WHI80], but neither is completely satisfactory. Prefiltering has been done only approximately and for scenes built up from a restricted class of primitive objects. The alternative of increasing the sampling density means a corresponding increase in computing cost.

An entirely different approach to the problem is suggested by Yellott's work [YEL83]: when aliasing cannot be removed, it can still be made less conspicuous by sampling nonuniformly. Uniform sampling tends to produce highly visible forms of noise because regular structure in the image can "beat" with the sampling pattern producing Moiré patterns and "jaggies". With nonuniform sampling, aliasing noise can be random and structureless. Yellott realized this by studying the layout of photoreceptors in the retina of the eye. This concept was first applied to image synthesis by researchers at Lucasfilm and has since been explored by a number of others [COO84, KAJ84, ABR85, DIP85, LEE85, MIT85, COO86, KAJ86].

Unfortunately, nonuniform sampling of nonbandlimited signals is poorly understood. For the most part, only problems that are very remote to the image-synthesis problem have been studied by signal processing experts (e.g., the extraction of statistics from nonbandlimited stationary noise [SHA69]). In the application to graphics, several important questions remain unanswered. In particular, the quality of images produced by nonuniform sampling has been questioned [ABR85], and systems which definitely do produce high-quality images [COO84, LEE85] use rather high lower bounds on sampling densities (16 and 8 samples per pixel, respectively).

For fixed-density (i.e., nonadaptive) sampling, two common forms of nonuniform sampling have been discussed. Yellott [YEL83] recommends using the distribution he observed in retinal cells, a *Poisson-disk* distribution (a Poisson distribution with a minimum-distance constraint between points). Except for a few experimental pictures [DIP85], I know of no rendering system that uses this pattern. Instead, the more easily generated *jitter* pattern is commonly used [COO86]. A jitter pattern is formed by randomly perturbing the points of a uniform sampling pattern.

Theoretical evidence in favor of the Poisson-disk sampling pattern was presented by Yellott [YEL83]. He proposed that the least-conspicuous form of aliasing would be produced if the spectrum of the sampling pattern had two properties. First, the spectrum should be noisy and lack any concentrated spikes of energy. If present, such spikes could yield coherent aliasing in the same way that uniform sampling can. Secondly, the spectrum should have a deficiency of low-frequency energy. This causes aliasing noise to be concentrated in higher, less conspicuous frequencies. These conditions will be referred to as the *blue-noise criteria*. Figure 1 shows an instance of such a sampling pattern (generated by the dart-throwing algorithm described below) and its Fourier transform.

Studies have shown that the eye is most sensitive to noise in intermediate frequencies [SAK77]. While frequencies up to 60 cycles per degree can be visible, the maximum response to noise is at about 4.5 cycles per degree. Taking advantage of this response is also how ordered dither improves the quality of halftoned images [LIM69]. By adding high-frequency noise to an image before quantizing, Limb discovered that annoying contour effects were masked. Although more noise was added to the image, the results were far more pleasing when viewed at a reasonable distance.

Figure 2 shows the pattern and spectrum of a jitter process. The sampling pattern is clumpier, or more "granular", and the spectrum shows a smaller noise-free region around the origin. This implies that noise with lower frequencies (i.e., larger features) would be generated by this type of sampling.

Figures 3 through 5 give a more direct visual demonstration of uniform, jitter, and Poisson-disk sampling, respectively. For these figures, a test pattern has been designed specifically to generate aliasing. It is given by the following simple formula:

$$\left\lfloor \frac{100x}{x+y} \right\rfloor \bmod 2 \tag{1}$$

Images of this test pattern were originally 160 by 160 pixels, and in figures 3 to 5, an average of one sample per pixel was made. The images were then enlarged by digital resampling to 512 by 512 to magnify the details of aliasing. As expected, uniform sampling (Figure 3) yields large Moiré patterns, which are visible even at a distance. Comparing Figures 4 and 5, both lack Moiré patterns, but jitter sampling (Figure 4) has introduced significantly more "grain noise" into the picture. The pits and bumps along edges are much less severe when Poisson-disk sampling (Figure 5) is used.

What has made jitter sampling attractive is undoubtedly its simplicity. Poisson-disk sampling is somewhat more complicated. Several point processes could be referred to as "Poisson-disk" [RIP77], but by strict definition, a true Poisson-disk process is realized by generating complete patterns with Poisson statistics until one is found that meets the minimum-distance constraint.

A more practical point distribution is realized by a "dart-throwing" algorithm [MIT85, COO86], in which points are generated randomly with uniform distribution over the area being filled (this by itself closely approximates a Poisson distribution). Each new point is rejected if it falls within a certain distance of any previously chosen points, otherwise it is added to the pattern, and the process continues. This process is repeated until no new points can be added to the pattern This is an expensive algorithm (several hours of VAX 780 time to generate 1024-point pattern), which is only practical for precomputing a small pattern with periodic boundary conditions to be permanently stored and replicated over the entire picture. As mentioned above, this pattern satisfies the blue-noise criteria.

I have found that Poisson-disk samples can be generated cheaply on the fly by an algorithm inspired by the Floyd-Steinberg halftoning algorithm [FLO75]. To generate a pattern with an average of one sample per pixel, the algorithm selects points from a uniform two-dimensional grid four times finer than the display pixel lattice (i.e., there are 16 grid points per pixel area). A small amount of random jitter can be added to these sample positions to dislocate them from the grid.

As the algorithm proceeds, the grid points are operated on in a scan-line order. Each point on the grid is associated with a diffusion value D_{ij}, which is computed from previously computed diffusion values and a noise source R:

$$T = \frac{4D_{i-1,j} + D_{i-1,j-1} + 2D_{i,j-1} + D_{i+1,j-1}}{8} + R \tag{2}$$

The noise source R is a uniform random value in a range of 1/16 - 1/64 to 1/16 + 1/64. This will ensure that about one out of 16 grid points will be selected as a sampling point and provides enough fluctuation to prevent orderly structures from appearing in the pattern. The diffusion values (defined below) correspond to the diffusing quantization error in the Floyd-Steinberg algorithm.

The temporary value T is used to decide whether to select a grid point as a sampling position:

$$\text{SELECT} = \begin{cases} 0 & \text{if } T < 0.5 \\ 1 & \text{Otherwise} \end{cases} \tag{3}$$

If SELECT is 1, the grid point is a sampling position. Finally, a local diffusion value is computed as:

$$D_{i,j} = T - SELECT \tag{4}$$

Only two scan lines of D values must be stored to execute this algorithm. Equation 2 assumes a scanning from left to right. A more isotropic pattern is produced if scanning sweeps back and forth. Figure 6 shows the pattern and spectrum produced by this algorithm. The error-diffusion weights in (2) have been chosen experimentally to produce a sampling pattern that satisfies the blue-noise criteria. In addition, these weights do not require any multiplications in an efficient implementation. This method of generating Poisson-disk patterns is called the *point-diffusion algorithm.*

3. Adaptive Sampling

Nonuniform sampling by itself does not eliminate aliasing; it merely changes the characteristics of aliasing to make it less noticeable. However, when a region of an image contains an edge or some other type of high-frequency pattern, the sampling density must be increased to get a genuine reduction of aliasing noise.

Adaptive sampling is not a new idea. Whitted describes an adaptive sampling algorithm based around uniform sampling [WHI80]. Two basic types of adaptive nonuniform sampling have been described in the literature. One approach allows sampling density to vary as a function of local image variance [LEE85, KAJ86]. An example of another approach is in [COO86] where two levels of sampling density are used, a regular pattern for most areas and a higher-density pattern for troublesome spots. For low densities, a two-level strategy is appealing because it allows the optimal blue-noise pattern to be used easily. In the prototype antialiasing module, the entire image is sampled in a *base pattern* with an average of one sample per pixel. Additional local supersampling is typically done at a density of 4 to 9 samples per pixel. At 4 samples per pixel, aliasing noise is barely visible, and at 9 samples per pixel, the image looks perfect. Much higher supersampling densities may be required if "distributed ray tracing" is being done.

Having chosen to use two levels of sampling, where should the high density sampling be invoked? For this purpose, the image is divided into small square *supersampling cells* each containing eight or nine of the low-density samples. The samples within each cell (or withing some neighborhood of the cell) are tested to determine whether the entire cell should be supersampled.

Theoretically, it is not possible to detect infallibly the presence of high frequency regions in an image by sampling at such a low rate. The success of this algorithm depends on additional assumptions about the structure of typical images. For example, this method is likely to detect edges, and it is known that edges are a common type of region that needs high-density sampling. On the other hand, coarse base sampling can miss minute isolated features; special action would have to be taken to ensure that they will be sampled. Objects which are going to appear small in the scene could be surrounded by a larger invisible bounding surface [WHI80], but this cannot be applied to small features resulting from shadows, reflections or highlights.

Given the set of eight or nine samples in a supersampling cell, some quantitative measure of variation in signal is needed to decide whether supersampling should be done. The variance of the sample values can be used to indicate high frequency [LEE85]; however, variance is a poor measure of visual perception of local variation. The nonlinear response of the eye to rapid variations in light intensity is more closely modeled by contrast [CAE81]:

$$C = \frac{I_{\max} - I_{\min}}{I_{\max} + I_{\min}} \tag{5}$$

Each sample value actually consists of three separate intensities for red, green, and blue. These could be combined into a luminance value before contrasts are computed, but a safer method is to compute three separate contrasts for red, green, and blue. These three contrasts are each tested against separate thresholds, and supersampling is done if any one is higher than threshold. In a prototype system, red, green, and blue thresholds are set to 0.4, 0.3, and 0.6 respectively.

This test is most sensitive to green in accordance with the human eye's known response to noise as a function of color. Because green-sensitive cone cells are far more common in the human retina (and thus green is sampled more densely), sensitivity to green-colored noise is twice as great as to red-colored noise and four times greater than to blue-colored noise. This knowledge has been used in the encoding of color television transmission to make the most economical use of bandwidth [LIM77].

Figure 7 shows an image generated by a prototype antialiasing module combined with a basic ray tracer. Figure 8 indicates with white where supersampling had been selected. In the thin shadow of the tripod's leg (seen between the footpads) a couple of small gaps can be seen. This is a failure of the high-frequency detection (as discussed above), but overall detection is remarkably good for such coarse sampling (one base sample per pixel). This small flaw can be removed by doubling the density of the base sampling, and thus doubling the cost of the picture; a typical dilemma when rendering is entrenched in point sampling.

4. Reconstruction from Nonuniform Samples

A digital picture is a uniform array of pixel values. These must be computed from the nonuniform sample values obtained by the methods described above. Ideally, this is done by constructing a surface that interpolates the sample values and can be *resampled* at the uniform pixel locations. At the same time, this surface must be bandlimited so that the resampling process does not itself introduce aliasing. This bandlimited interpolation is known as *reconstruction* in the signal-processing domain.

Little practical information exists for dealing with nonuniform samples. Yen discusses the reconstruction problem and presents solutions for several one-dimensional cases [YEN56]. Unfortunately, these formulas—as Yen points out—are too unstable to be of real use. Many *ad hoc* algorithms exist for "smooth" interpolation of nonuniform data (Franke gives a good review of this subject. [FRA82]), but none of these algorithms are suited for the problem at hand. In general, they are not meant to deal with such a large number of points (on the order of a million samples must be processed in a typical digital color picture), and they are not designed with any digital filtering characteristics in mind.

If the samples had been made uniformly, the problem would be quite a bit simpler. Reconstruction can then be done by convolving the samples with an appropriate filter k. In one dimension, this is:

$$f(x) = G \sum_{n=-\infty}^{\infty} f(x_n) k(x - x_n) \tag{6}$$

where $f(x_n)$ are the sample values. It is important to note that a constant factor G is needed for normalization. This is inversely proportional to sampling density. The summation is infinite, but in practice, filter kernels are zero beyond some finite width.

If any filter could be used in the reconstruction, its design would be a complex problem. In addition to well-understood quantitative criteria such as bandpass and leakage characteristics, filters for images must deal with poorly understood subjective criteria. Ringing and blurring effects must be traded off [BRO69], and because the filter is two-dimensional, there are conflicts between isotropy and interpolation [PET62].

High-frequency leakage is a particularly important filter characteristic because aliasing can result *during resampling* if the reconstruction from the nonuniform samples is not properly bandlimited. Figures 9 and 10 demonstrate this fact. Each of these figures has been sampled nonuniformly 100 times per pixel. Figure 9 is reconstructed with a box filter, and some faint aliasing can be seen near the origin. This aliasing is reduced in Figure 10 where a better filter has been used (a sinc filter with a Hamming window).

When samples are nonuniform, there are many added complications, and the convolution in (6) is no longer valid. If samples clump together in a small region, (6) would make that area too bright; and similarly, regions where the samples were sparse would be too dark. This unwanted effect of sample-density fluctuation is called *grain noise.*

If the sampling pattern is not too clumpy, grain noise can easily be handled by turning the filter in (6) into a *weighted-average filter.* In one dimension this would be:

$$f(x) = \frac{\sum_{n=-\infty}^{\infty} k(x - x_n) f(x_n)}{\sum_{n=-\infty}^{\infty} k(x - x_n)} \tag{7}$$

This filter has been used in a number of implementations of nonuniform sampling [COO86, DIP85], but unfortunately, it does not handle extreme variation in local sampling density. An example of this failure can be seen in Figure 11. In this 3D plot, height represents the gray level in a 2D image. This figure has been generated by sampling a step function nonuniformly. In a narrow region about the step, sampling is 16 times more dense than in the rest, simulating the effects of adaptive sampling. The surface shown is a weighted-average reconstruction from those samples.

A simple weighted average fails because it allows dense clumps of supersamples to overwhelm the influence of near-by base samples, as demonstrated by a simple thought experiment: Imagine a white circle being rendered against a black background with simple box filtering (i.e. area averaging). In one pixel, the edge of the circle may barely graze a corner. However, that tiny corner may be covered with many supersamples, while only one base sample at the opposite corner of the pixel lies on the black background. If all the samples in the pixel are averaged, the whole pixel will be nearly white, possibly creating a visible bump on the edge.

A practical solution, used in the prototype antialiasing module, is a *multi-stage filter*. Weighted-average filters are repeatedly applied with ever-narrowing low-pass cutoff until the proper bandwidth for the display is reached (i.e. until frequencies above the Nyquist frequency for the display are eliminated). This filter operates on a discrete two-dimensional grid much finer than the display pixels; 16 grid points per pixel area. For efficiency, each individual stage is a box filter.

Figure 12 shows the result of applying the first stage of this filter. For each grid square, all samples lying within it are added up and the result divided by the number of samples. This is equivalent to filtering with a weighted-average box filter one grid square in width (one fourth the width of a display pixel).

Figure 13 shows the second stage after applying a box filter twice as wide (i.e. with half the frequency bandwidth) as the first. This half-pixel filter is applied twice in the prototype antialiasing module to improve the filter characteristics.

Figure 14 shows the result of applying the final stage of the filter. A weighted-average box filter one full pixel wide has been applied to complete a smooth surface.

There are three relevant properties of this filter that make it successful. First, it is quite simple and efficient. The evaluation of the multi-stage filter dominates the computing cost of the antialiasing module, but because it is made up of box filters and because fixed-point arithmetic is used in the filter evaluation, only about two minutes of CPU time (on a VAX 8650) are used for a 640-by-480 picture. That time is more or less constant for all pictures, and it is almost always dwarfed by the time spent in the ray tracer computing sample values for a picture (which is typically 30 minutes to several hours).

Secondly, the multistage filter deals well with highly variable sampling density. This filter is a generalization of the reconstruction used by Whitted [WHI80] in his adaptive sampling scheme. Dense clusters of supersamples are averaged and normalized locally before being combined with nearby base-sample values.

Finally, the low-pass filter characteristics are adequate. The stages of the filter can be described by the convolution of four box filters:

$$k(x) = box(x) * box(2x) * box(2x) * box(4x) \tag{8}$$

This results in a piece-wise cubic filter. As shown below, the multi-stage filter has much less leakage of signal above the low-pass cutoff than a simple box filter. The following figures have been scaled to set the cutoff frequency to 1.

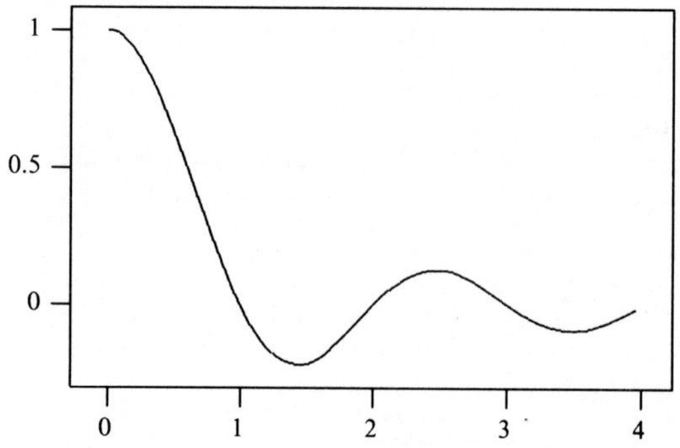

Box Filter Spectrum

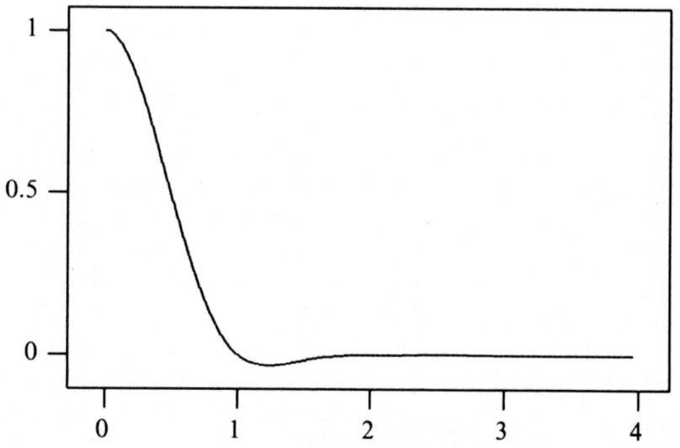

Multi-Stage Filter Spectrum

This filter fits into a general scheme for nonuniform reconstruction proposed by Netravali [NET86]. He suggests that the interpolation and bandwidth properties of the reconstruction be separated. First, the nonuniform samples can be interpolated with any simple algorithm that does not attenuate too much signal below the display bandwidth. In a second stage, the surface resulting from the first step is then filtered in a more sophisticated manner to remove frequencies above the display bandwidth. The multi-stage filter accomplishes this, but in a sequence of gradual steps.

5. Conclusions

Constructing a digital picture from a point-sampling function (e.g., a ray tracer) is complicated by the problem of aliasing. Nonuniform sampling is now recognized as a method for making aliasing noise less conspicuous to the viewer. Experiments with test patterns indicate that sampling patterns that meet the blue-noise criteria of Yellott produce results that are superior to those produced by sampling at the same density with jitter. The point-diffusion algorithm for generating such blue-noise sampling patterns is presented.

Some regions of an image may contain a large high-frequency component and require local supersampling to reduce the intensity of aliasing noise. Rather than sample many times in one pixel area, a larger neighborhood of low-density base samples are used to detect high frequency, and this entire neighborhood is supersampled if necessary. This allows a lower overall sampling density to be used at the expense of less-precise targeting of supersampling.

Ideally, the decision of whether or not to supersample should be based on whether or not aliasing would be visible if supersampling were not done. A step in that direction is to measure local variation in sample intensity by a function reflecting the eye's non-linear response to contrast. In color images, red, green, and blue contrasts are calculated and compared against three separate thresholds. The red, green, and blue thresholds can be adjusted to account for the eye's highly variable sensitivity to noise as a function of color.

Having gathered all samples, the final step in producing a digital picture is to reconstruct and resample at the display pixel rate. The nonuniformity of the samples and the sudden changes in sampling density (on the boarders of supersampled regions) make reconstruction difficult. A multi-stage filtering algorithm is presented that solves these problems efficiently.

6. Acknowledgements

I would like to thank Jim Kaiser, Henry Landau, John Limb, and Arun Netravali for many educational discussions about image and signal processing. Tom Duff wrote the program which produced figures 11 though 14.

7. References

[ABR85] Abram, Greg, Lee Westover, Turner Whitted, "Efficient Alias-free Rendering using Bit-masks and Look-up Tables", *Computer Graphics,* Vol. 19, No. 3, July 1985, p. 57.

[AMA84] Amanatides, John, "Ray Tracing with Cones", *Computer Graphics,* Vol. 18, No. 3, July 1984, pp. 129-135.

[BRO69] Brown, Earl F., "Television: The Subjective Effects of Filter Ringing Transients", *Journal of the SMPTE,* Vol. 78, No 4, April 1969, pp. 249-255.

[CAE81] Caelli, Terry, *Visual Perception: Theory and Practice,* Pergamon Press, Oxford (1981).

[COO84] Cook, Robert L, Thomas Porter, Loren Carpenter, "Distributed Ray Tracing", *Computer Graphics,* Vol. 18, No. 3, July 1984, pp. 137-145.

[COO86] Cook, Robert L, "Stochastic Sampling in Computer Graphics", *ACM Trans. Graphics,* Vol. 5, No. 1, January 1986.

[CRO77] Crow, Franklin C., "The Aliasing Problem in Computer-Generated Shaded Images", *Comm. ACM,* Vol. 20, No. 11, November 1977, pp 799-805.

[DIP85] Dippe, Mark A. Z. and Erling Henry Wold, "Antialiasing Through Stochastic Sampling", *Computer Graphics,* Vol. 19, No. 3, July 1985, pp. 69-78.

[FLO75] Floyd, R. and L. Steinberg, "An Adaptive Algorithm for Spatial Grey Scale", *SID Digest,* 1975, 36-37.

[FRA82] Franke, Richard, "Scattered Data Interpolation: Tests of Some Methods", *Mathematics of Computation,* Vol. 38, No. 157, January 1982.

[KAJ84] Kajiya, James T., *Engineering and Science,* Vol 48, No. 2, California Institute of Technology: November 1984.

[KAJ86] Kajiya, James T., "The Rendering Equation", *Computer Graphics,* Vol. 20, No. 4, July 1986, pp. 143-150.

[LEE85] Lee, Mark, Richard A. Redner, Samuel P. Uselton, "Statistically Optimized Sampling for Distributed Ray Tracing", *Computer Graphics,* Vol. 19, No. 3, July 1985, pp. 61-67.

[LIM69] Limb, J. O., "Design of Dither Waveforms for Quantized Visual Signals", *Bell System Tech. J.,* Vol 48, pp. 2555-2582, 1969.

[LIM77] Limb, John O., "Digital Coding of Color Video Signals--A Review", *IEEE Trans. Comm.,* Vol. COMM-25, No. 11, November 1977, pp. 1349-1382.

[MIT85] Mitchell, Don P., "Antialiased Ray Tracing By Nonuniform Sampling", unpublished Bell Labs report, April 1985.

[NET86] Netravali, Arun, *Personal Communication.*

[PET62] Petersen, Daniel P., David Middleton, "Sampling and Reconstruction of Wave-Number-Limited Functions in N-Dimensional Euclidean Spaces", *Information and Control,* Vol. 5, 1962, pp. 279-323.

[RIP77] Ripley, B. D., "Modeling Spatial Patterns", *J. Roy. Statist. Soc. B,* Vol. 39, 1977, pp. 172-212.

[ROT82] Roth, S. D., "Ray Casting for Modeling Solids", *Computer Graphics and Image Processing,* Vol. 18, 1982, pp. 109-144.

[SAK77] Sakrison, David J., "On the Role of the Observer and a Distortion Measure in Image Transmission.", *IEEE Trans. Comm.,* Vol. COM-25, No. 11, November 1977, pp 1251-1267.

[SHA49] Shannon, C.E., "Communication in the presence of noise.", *Proc. IRE* Vol. 37, 1949, pp. 10-21.

[SHA60] Shapiro, Harold S. and Richard A. Silverman, "Alias-Free Sampling of Random Noise", *J. SIAM,* Vol. 8, No. 2, June 1960, pp. 225-248.

[WHI80] Whitted, Turner, "An Improved Illumination Model for Shaded Display", *Comm. ACM,* Vol. 23, No. 6, June 1980, pp. 343-349.

[YEL83] Yellott, John I. Jr., "Spectral Consequences of Photoreceptor Sampling in the Rhesus Retina", *Science,* Vol. 221, 1983, pp. 382-385.

[YEN56] Yen, J. L., "On Nonuniform Sampling of Bandwidth-Limited Signals", *IRE Trans. Circuit Theory,* Vol. 3, Dec. 1 1956, pp. 251-257.

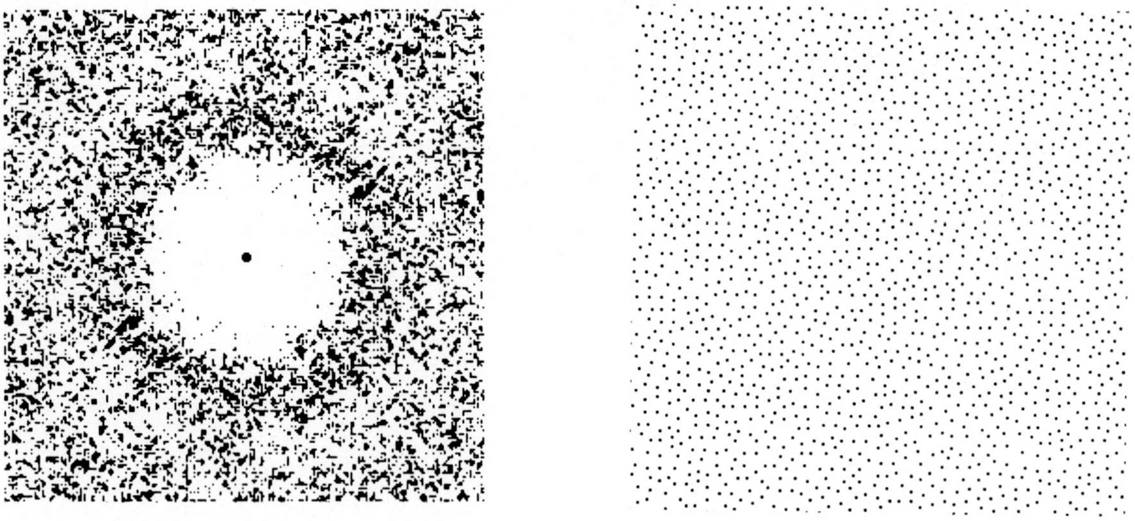

Figure 1.

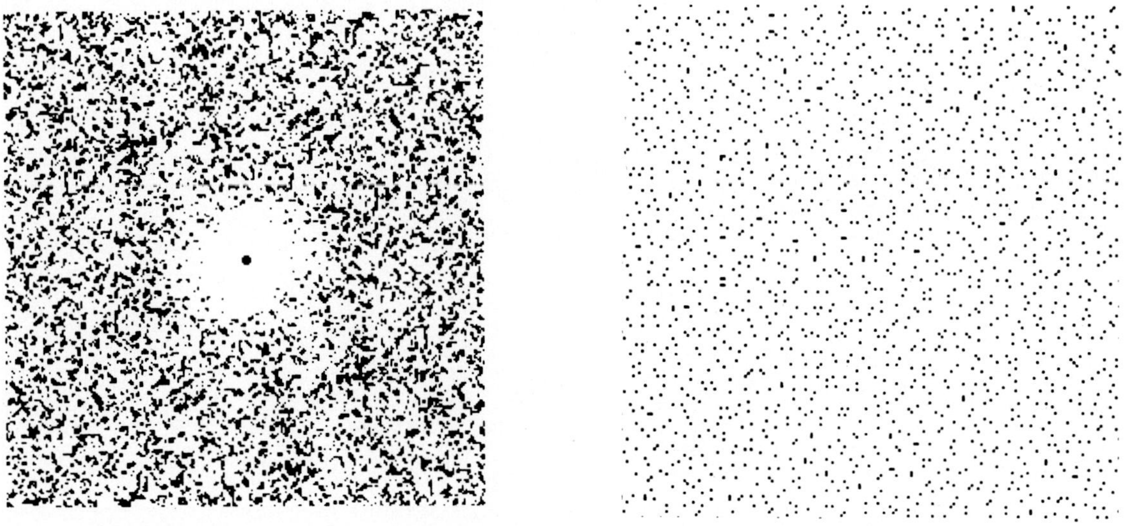

Figure 2.

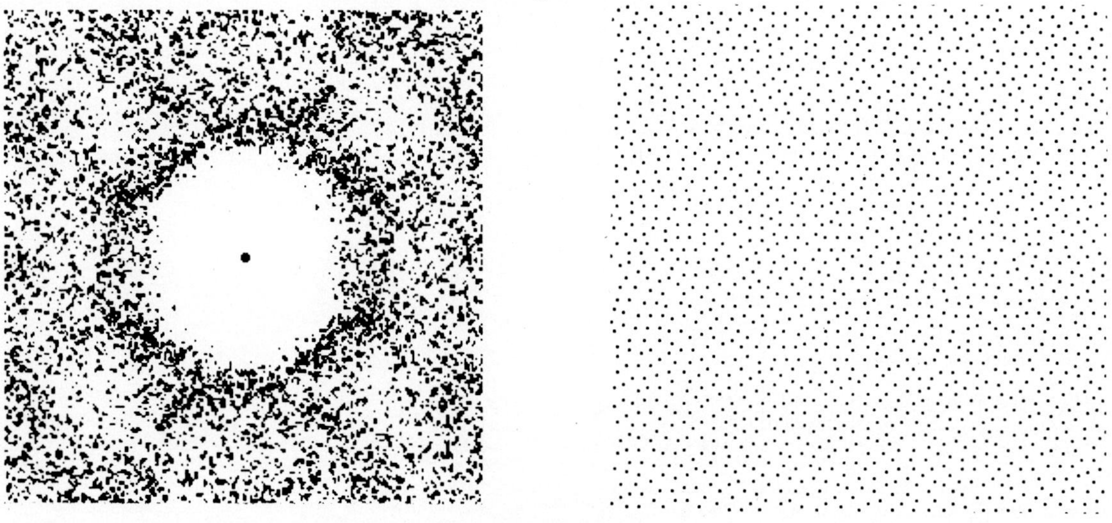

Figure 6.

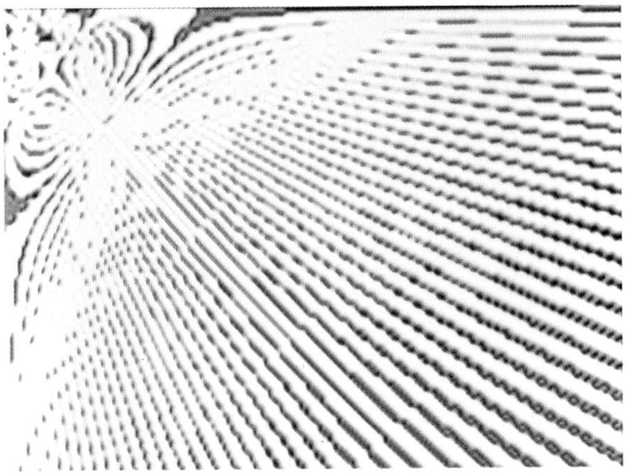

Figure 3.

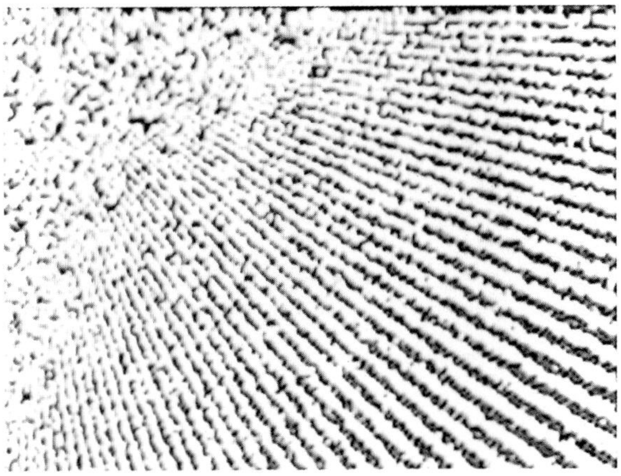

Figure 4.

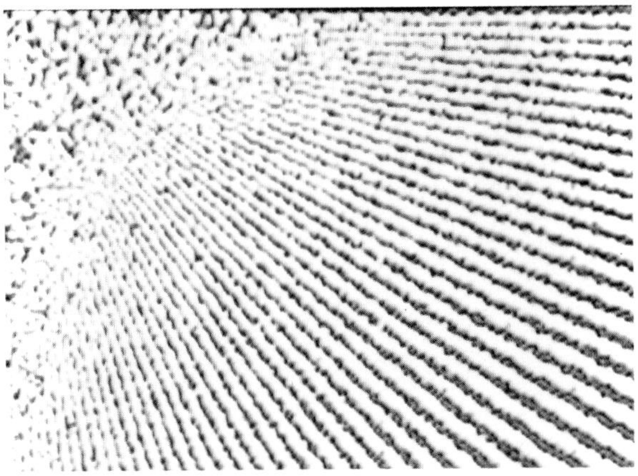

Figure 5.

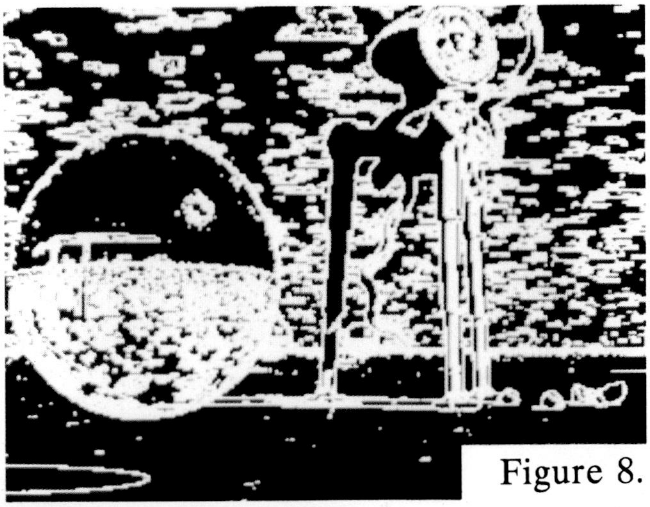

Figure 8.

Figure 7.

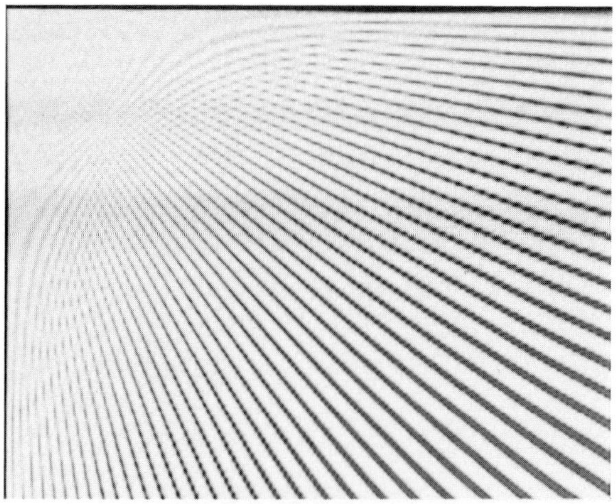

Figure 9.

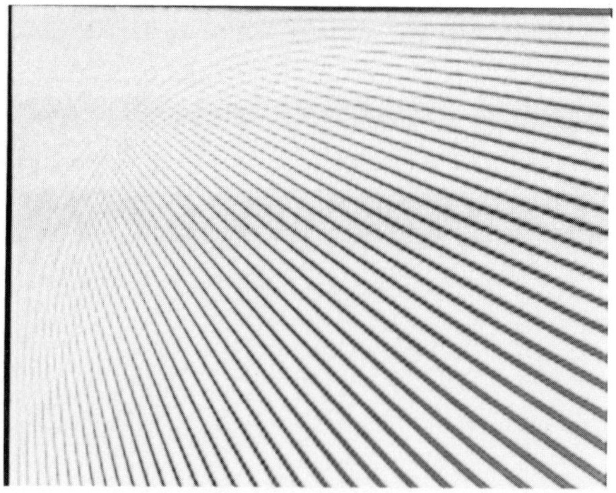

Figure 10.

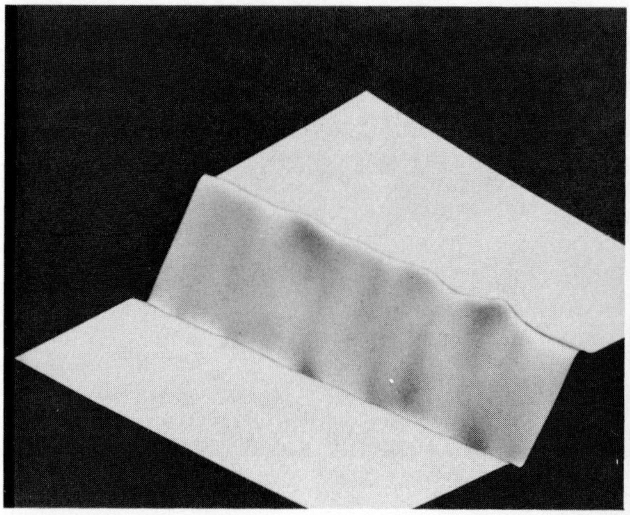

Figure 11.

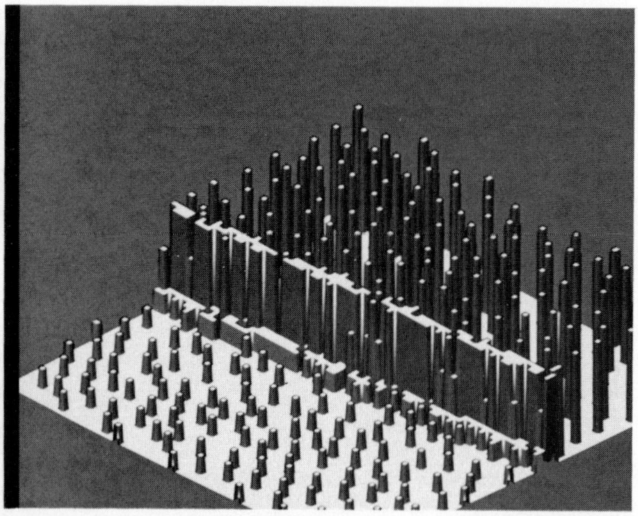

Figure 12.

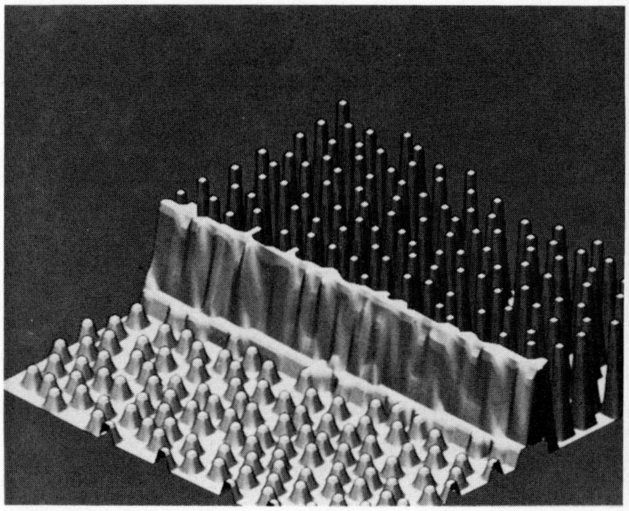

Figure 13.

Figure 14.

Ray Tracing JELL-O® Brand Gelatin

Paul S. Heckbert
Dessert Foods Division
Pixar
San Rafael, CA

ABSTRACT

Ray tracing has established itself in recent years as the most general image synthesis algorithm. Researchers have investigated ray-surface intersection calculations for a number of surface primitives, including checkerboards, glass balls, green fractal hills, mandrills, abstract blue surfaces, more glass balls, robot arms, pool balls, low-resolution clouds, morphine molecules, aquatic blobby things making strange noises, fantastic cities, and running skeletons. Unfortunately, *nobody has ray traced any food.* The *Dessert Realism Project* here at Pixar is addressing this problem. This paper presents new technology for ray tracing Jell-O® brand gelatin. We believe the method may have application to other brands of gelatin and perhaps pudding as well.

CR Categories: C.1 **[Processor Architectures]**: Multiprocessors – *Array and vector processors;* I.3.7 **[Computer Graphics]**: Three-Dimensional Graphics and Realism – *color, shading, shadowing, and texture;* J.3 **[Life and Medical Sciences]**: Health.

General Terms: algorithms, theory, food.

Additional Key Words and Phrases: ray tracing, lattice algorithm, Jell-O®, gelatin.

Introduction

Ray tracing has established itself in recent years as the most general image synthesis algorithm [Whitted, 1980]. Ray tracing food has remained an open problem, however. So far the most realistic foods were Blinn's classic orange and strawberry images, but these were created with a scanline algorithm [Blinn, 1978]. This paper presents new technology for ray tracing a restricted class of dessert foods, in particular Jell-O®† brand gelatin.

Our paper is divided into three parts: methods for modeling static Jell-O®, simulation of Jell-O® motion using impressive mathematics, and ray-Jell-O® intersection calculations.

Jell-O® Shape

To model static Jell-O® we employ a new synthesis technique wherein attributes are added one at a time using abstract object-oriented classes we call *ingredients. Ingredient* attributes are combined during a preprocessing pass to accumulate the desired set of material properties (consistency, taste, torsional strength, flame resistance, refractive index, etc.). We use the RLS orthogonal basis (raspberry, lime, and strawberry), from which any type of Jell-O® can be synthesized [Weller, 1985].

Ingredients are propagated through a large 3-D lattice using vectorized pipeline SIMD parallel processing in a systolic array architecture which we call the *Jell-O® Engine.* Furthermore, we can compute several lattice points simultaneously. Boundary conditions are imposed along free-form surfaces to control the Jell-O® shape, and the *ingredients* are mixed using *relaxation* and *annealing* lattice algorithms until the matrix is chilled and *ready-to-eat.*

Jell-O® Dynamics

Previous researchers have observed that, under certain conditions, Jell-O® *wiggles* [Sales, 1966]. We have been able to simulate these unique and complex Jell-O® dynamics using spatial deformations [Barr, 1986] and other hairy mathematics. From previous research with rendering systems we have learned that a good dose of gratuitous partial differential equations is needed to meet the paper quota for impressive formulas.

Therefore, we solve the Schrödinger wave equation for the Jell-O® field **J**:

$$\nabla^2 \mathbf{J} + \frac{2m}{\hbar}(E - V)\mathbf{J} = 0$$

Transforming to a spherical coordinate system [Plastock, 1986]:

$$\nabla \mathbf{J} = \xi_x \frac{\partial \mathbf{J}}{\partial r} + \xi_y \frac{1}{r}\frac{\partial \mathbf{J}}{\partial \theta} + \xi_z \frac{1}{r\sin\theta}\frac{\partial \mathbf{J}}{\partial \phi}$$

$$\nabla^2 \mathbf{J} = \frac{1}{r^2}\frac{\partial}{\partial r}\left[r^2 \frac{\partial \mathbf{J}}{\partial r} \right] + \frac{1}{r^2 \sin\theta}\frac{\partial}{\partial \theta}\left[\sin\theta \frac{\partial \mathbf{J}}{\partial \theta} \right] + \frac{1}{r^2\sin^2\theta}\frac{\partial^2 \mathbf{J}}{\partial \phi^2}$$

Fuller has given a concise and lucid explanation of the derivation from here [Fuller, 1975]:

> *The "begetted" eightness as the system-limit number of the nuclear uniqueness of self-regenerative symmetrical growth may well account for the fundamental octave of unique interpermutative integer effects identified as plus one, plus two, plus three, plus four, as the interpermuted effects of the integers one, two, three, and four, respectively; and as minus four, minus three, minus two, minus one, characterizing the integers five, six, seven, and eight, respectively.*

In other words, to a first approximation:

$$\mathbf{J} = 0$$

The Jell-O® Equation

Ray-Jell-O® Intersection Calculation

The ray-Jell-O® intersection calculations fortunately require the solution of integral equations and the simulation of Markov chains [Kajiya, 1986], so they cannot be computed efficiently. In fact, we have proven that their solution is linear-time reducible to the traveling salesman problem, where n is the number of Jell-O® molecules, so we can be sure that ray tracing Jell-O® will be practical only on a supercomputer [Haeberli, 1872].

Implementation

A preliminary implementation has been completed on a VAX 11/780 running the UNIX‡ operating system. To create a picture using the full Jell-O® Engine simulation, we estimate that 1 cpu-eon of CRAY time and a lot of hard work would be required. We made several simplifying approximations, however, since the paper is due today. As a first approximation we have modeled a gelatin cube governed by the first order Jell-O® Equation with judiciously selected surface properties, i.e. color=(0,255,0). Figure 1 was created with this model.

Work is underway on a complete Jell-O® Engine implementation in lisp *flavors*. We will shortly begin computing a 100x100 image of a bowl of lime Jell-O® using a roomful of Amigas [Graham, 1987]. The picture should be ready in time for SIGGRAPH with hours to spare.

† Jell-O® is a trademark of General Foods. ‡ UNIX is a trademark of Bell Laboratories.

Conclusions

Jell-O® goes well with a number of other familiar objects, including mandrills, glass balls, and teapots. The composition and animation possibilities are limited only by your imagination [Williams, 1980]. The Dessert Foods Division is generalizing the methods described here to other brands of gelatin. Future research areas include the development of algorithms for ray tracing puddings and other dessert foods. Another outstanding problem is the suspension of fruit in Jell-O®, in particular fresh pineapple and kiwi fruit.

Acknowledgements

Thanks to Paul Haeberli for tipping back a few with me on this research and to H.B. Siegel for key observations. The SIGGRAPH technical committee also deserves thanks for recognizing that *There's always room for Jell-O* ®.

References

[Barr, 1986] Barr, Alan H., "Ray Tracing Deformed Surfaces", *SIGGRAPH '86 Proceedings,* 20(4), Aug. 1986, pp. 287-296.

[Blinn, 1978] Blinn, James F., "Computer Display of Curved Surfaces", PhD thesis, CS Dept., U. of Utah, 1978.

[Fuller, 1975] Fuller, R. Buckminster, *Synergetics,* MacMillan Publishing Co., 1975, p. 125.

[Graham, 1987] Graham, Eric, "Graphic Scene Simulations", *Amiga World,* May/June 1987, pp. 18-95.

[Haeberli, 1872] Haeberli, Paul, and Paul Heckbert, "A Jell-O® Calculus", *ACM Transactions on Graphics,* special issue on ray tracing moist surfaces, 1872, to appear.

[Kajiya, 1986] Kajiya, James T., "The Rendering Equation", *SIGGRAPH '86 Proceedings,* 20(4), Aug. 1986, pp. 143-150.

[Plastock, 1986] Plastock, Roy A., and Gordon Kalley, *Schaum's Outline of Computer Graphics,* McGraw-Hill, New York, 1986.

[Sales, 1966] Sales, Soupy, *The Soupy Sales Show,* 1966.

[Weller, 1985] Weller, Tom, *Science Made Stupid,* Houghton Mifflin Co., Boston, 1985.

[Whitted, 1980] Whitted, Turner, "An Improved Illumination Model for Shaded Display", *Communications of the ACM,* 23(6), June 1980, pp. 343-349.

[Williams, 1980] Williams, Lance, personal communication, 1980.

fig. 1: lime Jell-O®

GRAPE: An Environment to Build Display Processes

Tom Nadas†
Alain Fournier‡

Computer Systems Research Institute
University of Toronto
Toronto, Ontario M5S 1A4
{tom|alain}@csri.toronto.edu

Abstract

New modelling primitives and new rendering techniques are appearing at a rapid rate. To be able to implement and evaluate them easily, we need a very flexible display environment. We describe an environment which allows experimenting both with the basic modelling and rendering operations and with the process structure of the display system.

The desired operations are implemented in *nodes*, coded in a traditional programming language, which can then be structured into arbitrary directed acyclic graphs. These nodes are all "plug compatible", and pass streams of *appels*, which are generalized pixels, that is data structures containing information necessary for pixel evaluation. In addition, synchronization parameters are used to allow the expansion or the reduction of the stream of appels.

This approach allows the assembly of new display systems from existing modules without coding, making it easy to experiment with different architectures and display processes. Algorithm designers are also able to test an algorithm at any point of the display process with a minimum of new coding.

We describe an implementation of the scheme with a library of nodes written in C and the assembly of the graphs made through the use of the directory manipulation tools provided under UNIX™. We give examples of the uses of the implementation to build basic nodes, variations in compositing and texture mapping and special-purpose display systems.

CR Categories: I.3.2 [**Computer Graphics**]: Graphics Systems; I.3.3 [**Computer Graphics**]: Picture/Image Generation — *display algorithms*; I.3.4 [**Computer Graphics**]: Graphics Utilities; I.3.7 [**Computer Graphics**]: Three-Dimensional Graphics and Realism, — *Color, shading, shadowing and textures*.

General Terms: display systems.

Additional Keywords and Phrases: data flow.

† Address until September 1987: Departement de la Recherche Prospective, INA, 4 Avenue de l'Europe, Bry-sur-Marne, 94360, France

‡ Address until September 1987 CSL, Xerox PARC, 3333 Coyote Hill Road, Palo Alto, CA, 94304 ARPAnet: fournier.pa@XEROX.COM

™ UNIX is a registered trademark of AT&T Bell Laboratories.

1. Introduction

Systems to produce raster images from three-dimensional models are not as simple as they used to be (if they ever were). The past few years have seen a large increase in the number of modelling primitives, illumination models, filtering techniques, manipulations on raster images, and even a few new geometric operations. The simple pipeline described in Figure 1a, with a single flow of information between the modelling, geometric and display operations, is still useful for a global description of a generic display system, but is not representative of what most real systems are doing.

At the very least current systems deal with many types of modelling primitives, which are kept in separate parallel streams until they are merged into a common stream of geometric primitives (Figure 1b). Generally, these geometric primitives are polygons, and adding a new modelling primitive is relatively simple if one knows a reasonable way to break it down into polygons. In the class of rendering techniques which includes ray-tracing and ray-casting, the flow of information is different, but the topology of the display system is very much the same (Figure 1c). In this case, a single geometric primitive, the ray, fans out to multiple modelling primitives. Adding a modelling primitive again simply reduces to being able to compute its intersection with a ray. In spite of their different process flows, many operations in these systems, such as shading, can be the same, and should not need to be rewritten.

In most existing systems any internal change to the display process is a serious job that only brave souls dare undertake. Remarks by Porter and Duff in [PoDu84] about Reyes, and by Greene and Heckbert [GrHe86] about the NYIT display system are indicative of how hard modifications can be.

2. Previous Work

Of course we are not the first ones to perceive these problems and needs, and many solutions, some of them very effective, have been proposed and/or implemented. It is interesting to note that most of the earlier work was to achieve more flexibility at the level of the structure of the process, while most of the recent work bore on the functional level.

2.1. General Environments

Several workers addressed the problems by designing flexible testing environments. Whitted and Weimer [WhWe82] designed a testbed whose structure is diagramed in Figure 2a. The various flows from the various modelling primitives eventually converge into common *span buffers*. While certainly a useful system, especially to experiment with new modelling primitives and fully integrate them quickly with the rest of the display process, it does not have much flexibility either at the global or at the local level. Crow [Crow82] discusses a system which is notable in this context mainly for the attempt to decouple the *scene analysis* from the rendering operations. The scene analysis step is intended to facilitate the processing of objects in parallel, as long as they are determined not to interfere with each other's visibility. The resulting images are merged on the screen according to the priorities determined during the scene analysis. The rendering processes themselves are specified by the objects, and therefore considerable flexibility is gained in mixing different modelling primitives. In addition one of the goals was to allow for more flexibility in the assignment of the various processes to the available processors.

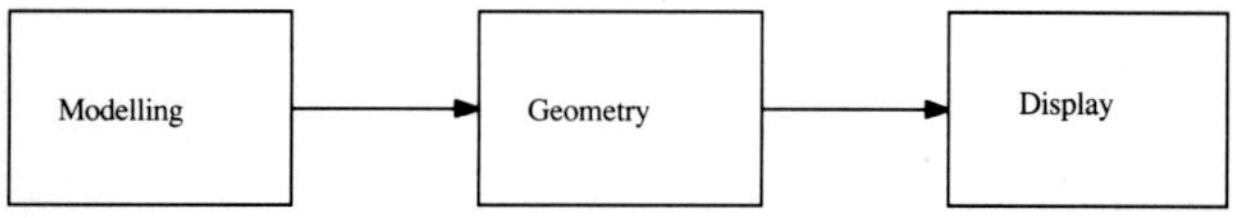

Simplified view of the display pipeline

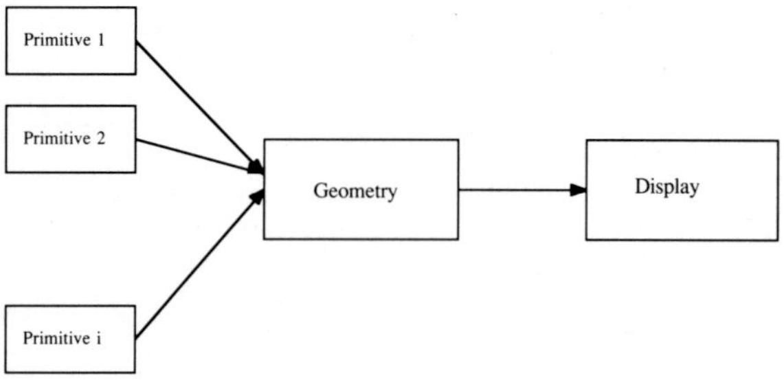

Structure of many current display systems

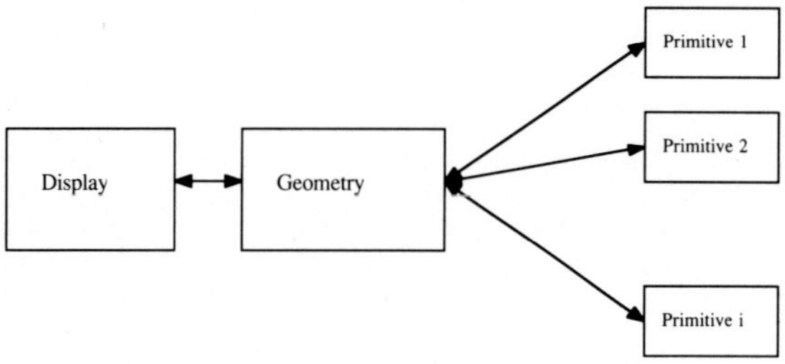

Structure of conventional raytracing

Figure 1. Various display structures

Hall and Greenberg [HaGr84] describe another testbed, this one oriented more towards ray-tracing. Within our context, the interesting point is that the structure resembles the one diagramed in Figure 2b. The new factor is that there is an additional fanout at the end of the system into several rendering processes. The other main characteristic is that the communication between the various modules of the system is through files. This has the advantage of simplicity and flexibility, but the distinct disadvantage (besides inefficiency, which might not be of prime concern in testing) is that there is no guaranteed common interface between modules. The structure of the information contained in the files has to be known by each module which uses them.

2.1.1. Reyes

Reyes is the rendering system designed and implemented at Pixar and described in [CoCC87]. The overall structure of Reyes is similar to the one diagramed in Figure 1b, with many modelling primitives reduced to a common geometric primitive, in this case *micro-polygons*. Reyes represents probably the best implementation for that type of structure. In particular it achieves additional flexibility by the use of *shade trees* (see below) for shade computations, and by the introduction of many "hooks" to extend its capabilities [ReSC87].

In summary these types of general environment indeed facilitate experiments with new modelling primitives and sometimes make it easier to replace modules, but do not allow experiments with the very structure of the display system.

2.1.2. Data Flow Systems

Much closer to the present work are systems based on *data flow*. Hedelman [Hedel84] describes a data flow approach to modelling, which also includes functions for display. He clearly shows the advantages of a data flow approach for modelling and rendering. Haeberli [Haeb86] describes a data flow manager implemented under UNIX. The processes communicate through files, and the data exchanged are typed messages. The emphasis is on interactive control of the processes, and the system has an excellent user interface for that purpose. Similar work has been conducted in the area of sound processing. *Virtual Patch-Cords* [BKGS86] is an example of a system which creates standard interfaces to facilitate the connection of a library of modules.

2.2. Compositing Environments

Compositing in essence merges the output of several independent display pipelines at the latest stage of the process (see Figure 3).

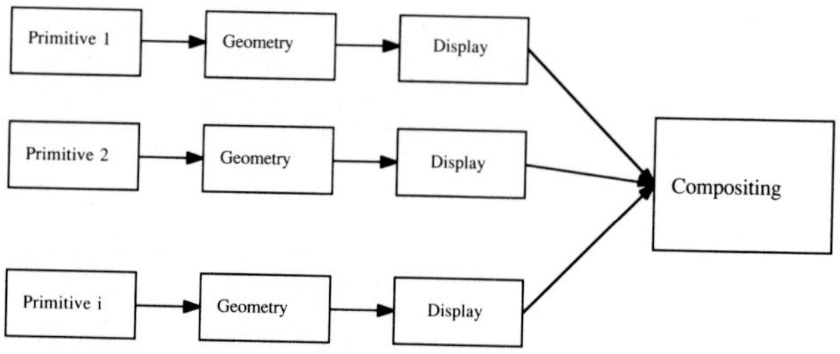

Figure 3. The process structure in compositing

The variations in compositing are about what kind of information and/or operation is used to compute the final image as a function of the original ones. In one early such environment [Duff80], each of several specialized renderers used the depth-buffer left by the preceding ones. The obvious advantage of such a system is the ease with which specialized renderers may be added since the only restriction is that they adhere to the depth-buffer format.

To solve the aliasing problem this might cause, one can add information about the amount of coverage (often called the *opacity*) to each pixel value [PoDu84]. This also allows one to define many interesting operations based on the opacity values. One can of course get better results by combining the two techniques [Duff85].

Compositing is a very powerful and useful technique, especially in the form described in [PoDu84] and [Duff85]. It is relatively easy to implement, and allows one to merge pictures from very different systems. It is both a strength and a drawback of compositing that it is not concerned with the structures of the display processes which generated the pictures on which it operates. As a result, many global effects such as shadows and reflections are out of reach. It also offers no help in building the display processes themselves.

2.3. Pixel Evaluators

In many ways, the compositing operations are too late in the display process, and an environment which aids in the creation of *pixel evaluators* would prove to be an invaluable tool. A pixel evaluator may be defined as a specialized process that converts a list of parameters associated with a single pixel (such as normals, surface characteristics, depth) into a pixel colour. Note that in this context we use the word pixel in its generic sense of picture element, rather than as one entry in an array of raster values.

2.3.1. Shade Trees

The first notable attempt at providing an environment in which pixel evaluators could be created stemmed from the need to provide a more flexible shading module in a traditional rendering system [Cook84]. It was recognized that the shading process could be broken down into a number of basic operations which could then be organized in a tree-like structure. Hence, these particular pixel evaluators have been dubbed *shade trees*.

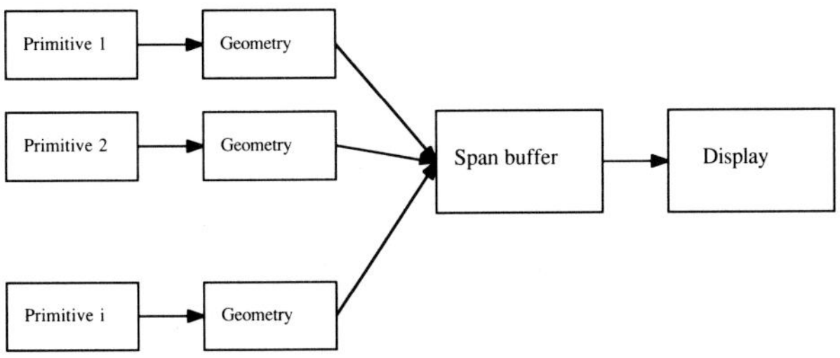

a) Structure of testbed described in [WhWe82]

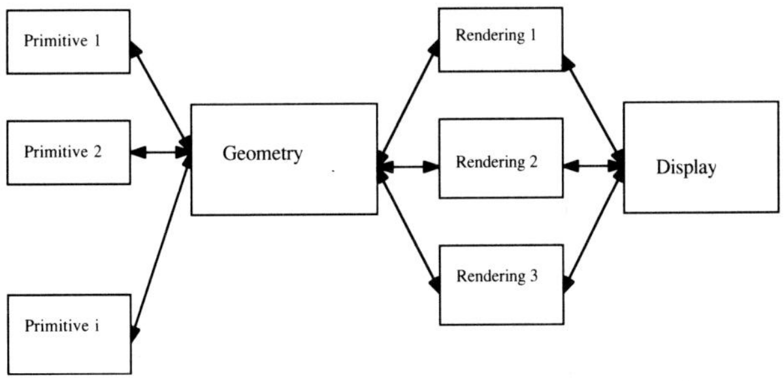

b) Structure of testbed described in [HaGe83]

Figure 2. The structure of two testbeds.

In the implementation described in [Cook84], the tree nodes are basically function calls, and the writing of a node is equivalent to writing a C function. Each 'node' interface is therefore unique and, as with any function, the user must ensure that it is called with appropriate values and that it is used properly. As a result, the user must be an experienced programmer, since the tree description is an actual *program*. Shade trees are driven by a traditional general rendering program that calls the appropriate shade trees for each pixel (even though shade trees are object specific, in the Reyes implementation they are called at the micropolygon level, which is at the sub-pixel level). The program passes a standard list of parameters to the shade tree, and expects a final colour and opacity value to be returned.

2.3.2. Pixel Stream Editors

A pixel stream editor is a pixel evaluator which is used to edit or manipulate a pixel stream [Perl85]. A pixel stream is simply a list of an arbitrary number of pixels, where a pixel, in this context, is any combination of appearance parameters. The pixel evaluator edits one pixel at a time and either alters one or more appearance parameters or converts the pixel format by adding and/or removing appearance parameters. Although the ultimate goal is to provide a pixel stream whose pixel format is a colour, any individual pixel stream editor may output a stream of any type of format. In fact, there is not even a requirement that the number of pixels in the incoming and outgoing streams be the same.

A single pixel stream editor may be as simple or as complex as desired, and is therefore analogous to a sub-tree in the shade tree environment. However, a complex combination of pixel stream editors may suffer from the same problem as the shade tree program, in that it may become a seemingly unrelated list of commands. Some advantages have been lost from the shade trees; in a shade tree, a node or sub-tree only inputs the required appearance parameters and only outputs those which it alters or generates. In contrast, any single pixel stream editor may input and output other seemingly redundant appearance parameters to be used by other pixel stream editors later on.

2.4. Pipe-Based Systems

Since UNIX pipes constitute a very convenient tool for linking processes it is natural to use them to link the modules of a display system.

This approach to build a flexible tool for image manipulation has been proposed by Paeth and Booth [PaBo86]. Their *Image Manipulator* is essentially a set of modules inputing a stream of pixels and outputting same, and communicating through pipes. This yields a system which is powerful, easy to use and easy to add on to. In its method of communication between modules, it is similar to the system described in [HaGr84]. Their system has the additional benefit of a flexible pixel representation, so that each module can determine the information which is passed to it. In this respect, their pixel files are very similar to the streams of *appels* we will define later. Its main weakness is to be limited to what amounts to single operand operations on stream of pixels. The topology of the system is restricted by the use of pipes to a single-flow pipeline.

Potmesil and Hoffert [PoHo87] have, in their system named FRAMES, developed a set of software tools which are linked through pipes. Their modules are meant to implement all the operations of a rendering system. There is no standardization as to what type of data flows through the pipes. Their system offers much flexibility in the rearrangement of the modules, and in the distribution of their execution to multiple processors. The main drawback is again that the overall system is constrained to a pipeline structure.

It is interesting to note that a linear flow of information is not as much a restriction in building display systems as it may appear at first. Because it is always possible to embed a partial order into a linear order by *topological sorting*, any directed graph corresponding to a partial order can be "squeezed" into a pipeline. The drawback of course is that the true relationships between modules are lost, and that potentially large amounts of data are passed around needlessly.

3. GRAPE

3.1. Goals of GRAPE

We designed and implemented a system called a *General Rendering Applications Programming Environment*, or GRAPE, to facilitate experiments with the structure and basic algorithms of a display system. It was not intended as a production system or as a demonstration of any particular algorithm (more details about the implementation of GRAPE can be found in [Nada86]). The main goals were:

- to permit flexibility in the rendering environment. In particular we did not want the system to be biased toward any particular rendering solution. A look at all the systems described above shows that most have at least a "conceptual bottleneck", where all the data has to be converted to the same primitives. We wanted to avoid this phenomenon, which limits experimentation and inhibits new solutions.
- to provide the reusability of the software components. Even if we create different systems with different structures, it is very likely that they will share some of the basic components. We wanted to make it easy to reuse these without reprogramming.
- to facilitate standardization of the software tools. At first glance this seems in contradiction with the goal of flexibility. But in fact the standardization is not in the content of the tools, but in their interface with each other.
- to allow experimentation with the basic operations. This is the kind of flexibility which is normally achieved in a well designed modular software system. We did not want to lose it.
- to allow experimentation with the flow of processes. This is the most powerful aspect of shade trees and pixel stream editors. We also wanted to allow these experiments to be conducted with very little or no code writing.

To meet these goals, we created a programming environment on two levels. At the *micro* level, it is very much like a traditional programming environment, in which code is written in a conventional language (C in our current implementation), to create *nodes* implementing basic algorithms which can be placed in a library. At the *macro* level, the user puts together these nodes into graphs which belong to the class of *directed acyclic graphs*, or *dags*. That is the most general class of data flow graphs without cycles. To work at either level one does not have to know or worry about the other level. At the micro level, GRAPE will automatically create the standard interface to ensure interconnectivity of the nodes. At the macro level, the user only has to know the functionality of the nodes to be able to use them, and GRAPE will connect them together in the manner described through a *dag compiler*. The distinction between the levels is not merely one of functionality, but also signifies a difference between the skills required of the users at each level. At the micro level, users are algorithm designers and programmers. At the macro level, users work more like system designers. If the environment created is really successful and complete, then the users of the macro level can be picture and animation designers. That is to say they can build without coding a display system specifically for a given picture, a given effect or a given animation sequence.

3.2. Appels

Basically, GRAPE is an environment to build dataflow systems. That is, once designed and compiled, the working rendering system obtained is a data flow system [AgAr82]. But since our targets are specifically display processes, all the nodes communicate through a common data element which we call *appels*, a contraction of *appearance elements*. Appels are the common datatypes on which the nodes operate. They were designed for rather conflicting roles: they have to be general enough to contain any information any node in the rendering system would operate on, and they have to be the "standard format" through which all nodes communicate. The way to meet both of these goals was to have an appel be made of any number of *appel slices*, that is specific appearance elements (such as colour, transparency, normal, shading parameters), and each collection of similar appels is preceded by an *appel core* which identifies their content. Obviously, in most applications, an appel core will be followed by a large stream of appels, so there is very little overhead introduced by the appel core. It is important to note that there is no prescribed correspondence between *pixels* and *appels*. As the process gets closer to the final image, appels will look more and more like pixels, but farther "upstream", appels can be polygons, parametric surfaces, spans, etc.

Appels play their roles as standard connectors in the following simple way. The only data the nodes input and output are appels identified by an appel core. Therefore the nodes can be connected in any way after they have been written, with the only requirement being that the appel core for the input of a node is a subset of the union of the appel cores output by the nodes connected to its input. The system verifies this automatically when the dag is compiled.

As an example we show below an appel core used as the header of a file full of appels. The first two lines give the name of the core and the resolution. The rest is the appel core proper. Notice that the appel core allows the specification of both the semantics and the data type of the slices. This makes it easy to use "foreign" files as input to GRAPE, since most of the time the only thing to do is to insert the appropriate header.

```
span
512 by 512
masterName as string
instanceName as string
identNum as 1byte
screenPos as 2int
colour as 3byte
dcolour as 3float
normal as 3float
dnormy as 3float
depth as 1float
devicePos as 3float
eyepos as 3float
worldpos as 3float
objectpos as 3float
dobjectY as 3float
texturepos as 2float
dtextureY as 2float
```

4. The Micro Environment

The micro environment is a fairly traditional programming environment, where the user codes the nodes in the C programming language. The purpose of the environment is to ensure that the nodes created conform to the standard format so that they can be used and linked freely in the macro environment. The nodes implement operations on streams of appels, and appels are their only input and output. Ideally these operations should be rather specific, and affect only a small number of appel slices. For example, typically, a node would perform a shading operation and therefore output only a colour. This is how the user can obtain maximum reusability of the nodes. Figure 4 gives the diagram of such a shading node. But this is only a guideline; the only rule is "appels in, appels out". As a consequence the nodes are guaranteed to have no side effect. The fact that each node and node writer does not have to know or care where the appel slices it needs come from means not only that nodes are easy to use, but can be used in ways that were totally unpredicted when they were written.

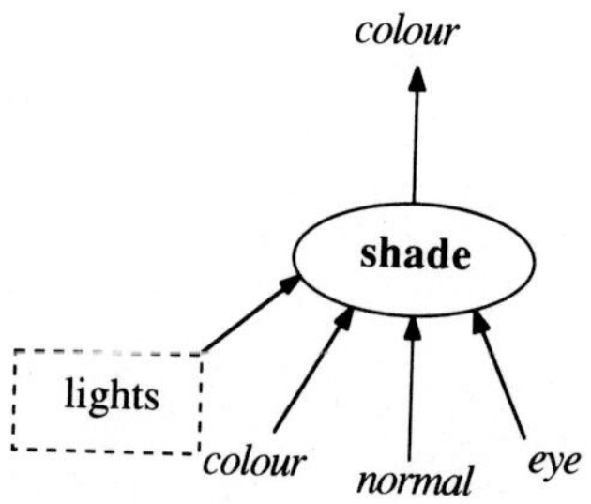

Figure 4. A simple case of a GRAPE shade node

4.1. Gofors and Servers

To ensure proper communication with the other nodes, each node is surrounded by two functions, a *gofor* to deal with its input and a *server* to deal with its output. The gofors and servers standardize the nodes by forcing all the communications through them, and for the rest of the world (the macro environment) the nodes are only gofor and server functions (see Figure 5).

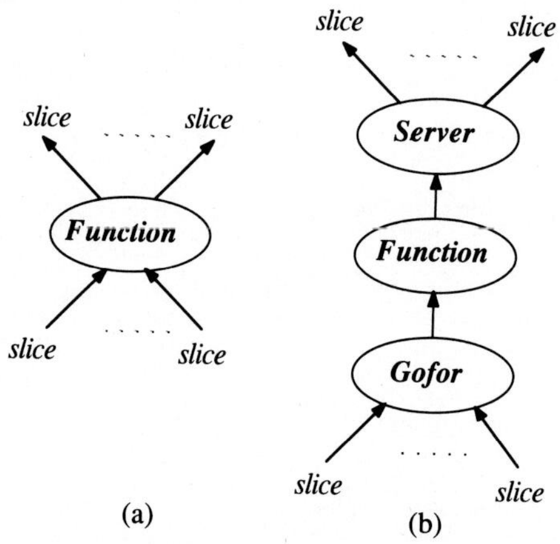

Figure 5. A GRAPE node, as indicated functionally (a), and as it exists in the micro environment (b). Note that the actual node function has only one input and one output branch, regardless of the number of links in the graph.

Every time a node needs an appel slice, it calls its gofor indicating the slice required, and the gofor calls the appropriate server. Note that which server is appropriate is only dependent on the particular graph in which the node is used, and therefore the linkage has to be made by the dag compiler at the macro level (more in the next section).

The server has several roles. The simplest one is to pass the appel slices its client node produces to the gofor(s) to which it is connected. Its crucial role is to make sure that its client is only called when necessary. For that purpose it *buffers* the appels produced by the node, supplies them to the gofors, and only actually calls its node when the buffer is empty. Most nodes need specific information which is not and should not be in the appels, such as constants, light position for a shade node, etc. This is provided through *static parameters*, and it is also the role of the server to provide these to its client node. For that purpose, the server calls an initialization routine the first time it is called, to read in the static parameters. Those parameters can be read from a file, or computed by the initialization routine. They are then stored by the server, and provided to the client node with each call.

In our current implementation, each node is placed in its own UNIX subdirectory, which contains the source code, the header definition containing the code for the gofor and server, files for the static parameters, and files which list the input and output slices the node uses, for the benefit of the macro environment (see Figure 6).

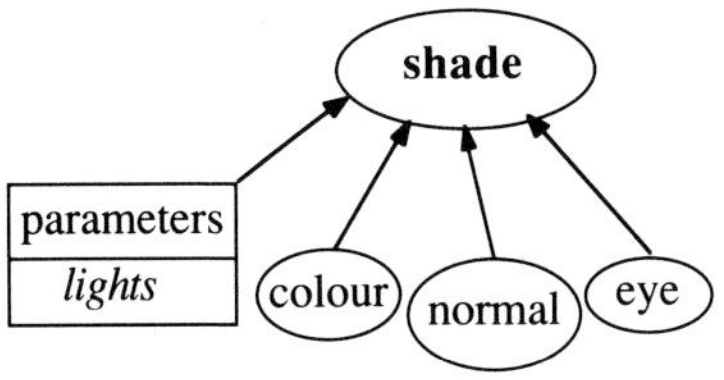

Figure 6. The directories corresponding to the shade node. Names of directories are in ellipses, names of files in rectangles.

A node *mold* is provided as a template to help in writing nodes. Of course, the programmer does not write the gofors and servers, this is part of the role of the dag compiler.

5. The Macro Environment

The role of the macro environment is to help the user put together the available nodes into display systems. The system to be built is described by its graph, that is, for each node in the graph, the user indicates the nodes to which it is to be connected, and the appel slices to be passed at each connection. The dag compiler then creates the gofors and servers for that graph and invokes the UNIX linker to link the code. During execution, each gofor is called with the name of the slice which is required so it can call the appropriate server. This assumes that at compile time those servers exist, and therefore the compilation of the dag is done in a bottom-up fashion.

A mechanism is included in the compiled dag to synchronize the flow of appels. For each node that initiates an output request, there is a *dag driver* function that calls the node server with an input request and generates a synchronization value which is then propagated down the dag by all servers, nodes and gofors. Each server can then determine whether it is necessary to call its client node.

As mentioned before, each node is given a directory, and the corresponding gofor and server are stored in this directory. This was chosen to take advantage of the existing UNIX directory tools to list, navigate through and display graphically the directory structure. A node can output to more than one other node, which is why the graphs are dags, not trees. To allow this in the UNIX directory structure, *symbolic links* have to be used. Figure 7 shows a typical GRAPE graph.

Each graph has one or more roots, that is nodes without any output, and one or more leaves, which generate the initial streams of appels. The usual root node is a *WriteFile* node, which simply writes the appels to a file. A slight variant of the *WriteFile* node is one which writes directly to a frame buffer. The typical leaf node is a *ReadFile* node, which does the obvious. Clearly these nodes can be connected to any appel producing or appel consuming process instead of files. In the UNIX environment, this is trivial thanks to the availability of pipes. In this manner entire external display systems can be virtual leaf nodes for a GRAPE graph, and in turn a GRAPE graph can provide appels to any external system, including other GRAPE graphs.

Once a given GRAPE graph as been made, tested and found useful, it can be stored and subsequently used as a node for other systems. The only requirement is that it has one designated root, which will be given a server when it is used as a node.

6. Examples

The goal of GRAPE is to limit as little as possible the variety of nodes and topology of the display systems that can be easily built. Consequently we can here present only a small sample of what can be done. We will limit ourselves to variations on familiar themes.

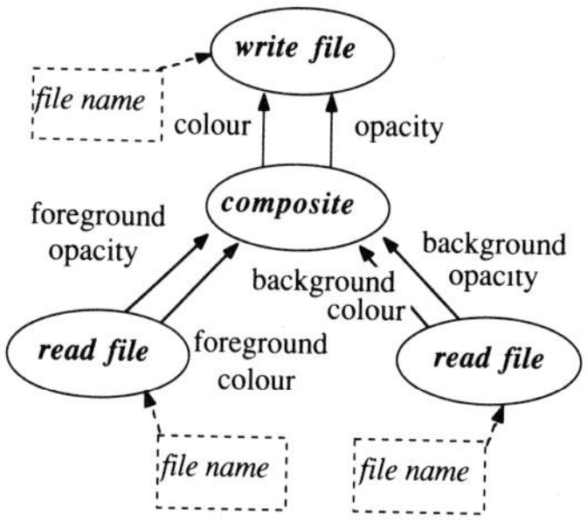

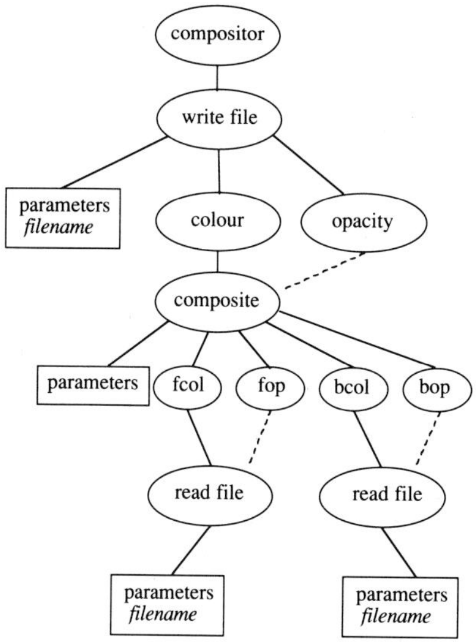

Figure 7. A simple GRAPE graph and its corresponding directory structure. Symbolic links are indicated by dashed lines.

6.1. Node Examples

6.1.1. A Composite Node

This example of a *Composite* node inputs two appel-streams in pixel format, the foreground and background images, and outputs a single pixel-format appel-stream, the composited image. This node is examined since it contains an assortment of process and control flows typically found in a number of other nodes, while the actual algorithm involved is rather simple.

The composite node can perform a variety of composite-related Boolean operations as described in [PoDu84], but for simplicity, it is presented here with the standard foreground *OVER* background operation. In the following pseudo-code description, it should be noted that the constant and static parameter definitions are those that would appear in the ''.h'' file, and the initializations would be done in the associated initialization procedure.

```
/********************************/
/*   Composite description   */
/********************************/

/* constant definitions */
   FOREGROUND_COLOUR
   FOREGROUND_OPACITY
   BACKGROUND_COLOUR
   BACKGROUND_OPACITY
/* static parameters */
   int operation;    /* to indicate the compositing operation */
/* Initialization */
   OpenFile (parameters);
```

```
  GetParam (operation);
/* The Basic Node procedure */
Composite:
  /* local variables */
  Colour foreCol, backCol;        /* foreground and background colours */
  Opacity foreOp, backOp;         /* foreground and background opacities*/
  float foreWeight, backWeight;   /* foreground and background weights */
  /* get opacities */
  gofor (FOREGROUND_OPACITY, &foreOp, sync);
  if (gofor (BACKGROUND_OPACITY, &backOp, sync) == INACTIVE)
    backOp = 1.0;
  /* calculate colour factors */
  switch (operation) {
    case OVER:
      /* basic composite operation */
      foreWeight = foreOp;
      backWeight = backOp * (1-foreOp);
      break;
      .
      .
      .
   as described in [PoDu84]}
  /* get colours only if needed */
  if (foreWeight != 0.0)
    gofor (FOREGROUND_COLOUR, &foreCol, sync);
  if (backWeight != 0.0)
    gofor (BACKGROUND_COLOUR, &backCol, sync);
  result->colour = foreWeight*foreCol + backWeight*backCol;
end Composite.
```

The above code illustrates a number of functions commonly found in other nodes. Note how the constant definitions of input branch alias are set up and used, how the *parameters* file is initially used to set the desired composite operation, and how the result is returned by a simple assignment.

The composite node also illustrates a number of ways in which the input slices may be obtained. The most common is the way the foreground opacity is retrieved, by a straightforward gofor call. When the background opacity is requested, a check is made to see if the slice actually exists in the input. If not, the gofor returns the value *INACTIVE* and a default value of 1.0 is set. In this way, the background opacity branch in the graph is optional.

Finally, since the factors used to weight the colours upon a composite may be zero, the foreground and background colours are retrieved only if they are required. This is a way of incorporating *lazy evaluation* into a GRAPE graph, where sub-graphs are executed only when necessary. In this particular case, if the background weight is zero (when the foreground completely occludes it), the background colour is not requested. If the sub-graph linked to the corresponding branch is complex (possibly containing a number of texturing nodes, for example), then the run time savings could be quite substantial. It should be noted, however, that this assumes a forward random access to the input stream (as provided by the ReadFile node previously described).

6.1.2. The SpanToAppel Node

The *SpanToAppel* node converts a span stream into a general appel stream. Each span is expanded into a stream of pixels that make up the span. The values of the span ends are linearly interpolated to derive the individual pixel values. Note that the resulting stream is indeed an appel stream and not a pixel stream since only those pixels contained within a span will be present in the stream.

The SpanToAppel node is typical of nodes that control the input and output flow rate independently. It acts as a leaf node for the sub-graph above it, and as a root node for the sub-graph below it. This means that for every call it returns the next appel in the output stream, but it only requests appels from the input stream when required. The following is a pseudo-code version of the SpanToAppel node:

```
/********************************/
/*   SpanToAppel description */
/********************************/

/* static parameters */
  Appel nextValue;   /* The next call's output appel        */
  Appel increment;   /* The pixel increment across the span */
  int pixelsLeft;    /* Number of pixels left in the span   */
  int inputSync;     /* The input stream sync value         */
/* Initialization */
  pixelsLeft = -1;   /* To get the first span */
  sync = -1;         /* To start at the beginning of the stream */
/* The Basic Node procedure */
SpanToAppel:
  /* local variables */
  Appel spanLeft, spanRight;  /* the span-end appels  */
  if (pixelsLeft < 0) {
    /* get next span */
    inputSync++;
    gofor (APPEL, &spanLeft, inputSync);
    inputSync++;
    gofor (APPEL, &spanRight, inputSync);
    /* reset static parameters */
    nextValue = spanLeft;
    pixelsLeft = spanRight.screenPos.x - spanLeft.screenPos.x;
    increment = (spanRight - spanLeft) / pixelsLeft;
  }
  /* assign resultant output appel and setup for next call */
  resultAppel = nextValue;
  nextValue += increment;
  pixelsLeft--;
end SpanToAppel.
```

Note how the information is retained for one span at a time and a new span is retrieved only when required. The input synchronization value is always incremented immediately before each input appel request, which is the typical method used by nodes that control flow.

6.2. Building Applications

Designing and writing nodes is again very similar to designing and writing programs in an ordinary programming language (in fact any C programmer can do it). The power of GRAPE really comes from the ability to assemble the existing nodes in various dags of different functionality.

As a straightforward example of the use of nodes within GRAPE graphs, consider a 'basic' compositing operation. In its simplest form it may be used to composite a foreground onto a background as expected. A minor variation of this graph can take advantage of the fact that each appel slice is provided as a separate input branch. Instead of taking the foreground opacity from the same node as the colour, it may be taken from a completely independent one (Figure 8). The result is a mask provided by the opacity channel applied to the foreground as before; however in this case they are totally unrelated. This technique (texture mapping under mask) is extensively used in flight simulators [RoZi84]

Another example illustrates something that a user would probably not do in a different environment. The difference between *Gouraud* and *Phong* shading interpolation is well known. In GRAPE, to implement one rather than the other consists merely of exchanging the order of the shading and the span expansion node. One could muse about whether the same trick could be used for texture mapping. That is, the texture mapping would be done before the scan conversion rather than after. Again, in GRAPE, to test this idea, one merely exchanges the order of some nodes. As shown in Figure 9, in one dag the order of the nodes is *scan polygon*, *texture map* and *shade* and in the other one, the same nodes are ordered as *texture map*, *shade* and *scan polygon*. The first order is the traditional order, while the second could be dubbed "Gouraud texture mapping". In the system used, this part of the graph took 8.5 minutes for the first sub-graph and about 0.5 minute for the second. So one can, at only the cost of a GRAPE graph compile, judge the look of pictures produced with the second approach, compare the costs and assess the worth of the technique. It is clear that while the second picture is not good enough for a final picture, it might be sufficient for quick previews while still having an indication of the effect of the textures.

As a final example, the picture of Figure 10 was generated by several GRAPE dags implemented specifically for this purpose. The rock, walls and floors were rendered together. The rock is made of parametric surfaces which have been "bump-mapped". A special node created the floor by separating the tiles into three categories: pink marble, dark green marble (both solid textures *a la* Perlin) and nothing. The clouds and the shadow of the rock on the clouds were generated as another picture. Clouds are again a solid texture on a plane. The shadow was computed as a perspective view of the rock on the cloud plane, which was then defocused by a gaussian filter and composited with the clouds. The result was then composited with the rest of the scene. All the nodes already existed in some form, except for the node to categorize the floor tiles and the node to blur, which were written for the occasion. Note that in this example we did not compile the whole GRAPE graph, but used several sub-graphs to better examine the intermediary results.

7. Evaluation

The actual implementation described is not an ideal one. Nevertheless, it has been shown to be the powerful tool we expected, and it clearly illustrates that the concepts within GRAPE are sound and easily applied. We will review some of the problems with the implementation, and explore some further applications and extensions of GRAPE.

7.1. The Macro Environment

Most of the drawbacks of the current implementation stem from the dependence on the UNIX directory structure. Since this structure cannot support the true multiple parent nodes required by the GRAPE dag structure, symbolic links are used instead. This results in the macro users having the extra responsibility of differentiating true directories from symbolic links. Also, these symbolic links may be easily corrupted whenever the associated directory is moved. In fact, entire GRAPE dags are susceptible to corruptions since the macro environment has no control over the UNIX utilities that may alter the dag format.

This is only one aspect of the issue of the GRAPE user interface in general. So far there had been no serious attempt at providing the current implementation with a proper user interface, since its only purpose was to illustrate the principles behind GRAPE. The work of Haeberli [Haeb86], who built an excellent user interface to control the flow of processes, is a good pointer to the possibilities for an activity very similar to the design of GRAPE graphs.

7.2. The Micro Environment

The current micro environment does not suffer from as serious problems as the macro environment, even though it is also UNIX dependent. The main reason is that both UNIX and the micro environment are meant to be programming environments. The only potential problem of the micro environment is that there is nothing to guard against users not obeying the standard format rules. However, it is assumed that micro users are competent enough programmers so that this problem is not significant.

7.3. Making GRAPE More Efficient

The main use of GRAPE is as a development environment. However, GRAPE is equally useful for the design of specialized renderers. Such applications often require execution times to be minimized, since small time savings per pixel result in many hours of savings per frame or per second of animation. In addition, GRAPE may be used to develop more general rendering tools, such as compositors and image processors. In these cases, since the resulting appel-stream editors are used as utilities, it would also be desirable for them to be time and space efficient as well.

Space can be wasted because each node allocates space for a complete output appel, even though it may only use a single slice. This may be cured by having the server only allocate memory for the individual output slices which are recorded in the output file in the master node library.

There are basically two major causes of time inefficiency in GRAPE. The most obvious is the increased number of functions calls, and the other is due to unnecessary type conversions. For example in general the composite operations may be just as easily performed using colour in byte format as opposed to the internal float format. As another example, a *copy* dag, which simply reads and copies GRAPE format file, uses about two minutes of CPU time (VAX 11/780) for a 512 by 512 pixel stream of colour slices recorded as three bytes. Most of this time is due to the type conversions from bytes to floats and back.

It is easy to conceive of a simple optimizing compiler that would connect master node functions together directly, without the use of gofors and servers. In this case each node instance would be an almost identical copy of the master node. The resulting nodes would differ from the present nodes in a few minor ways. The function call would include an appel slice request, and the function would return the requested appel. Also, each gofor call could be replaced by a direct call to another master function. In addition, the optimizing compiler could hard-code all static parameter initializations not provided by the parameter server. In this way, the resulting program can be completely stand-alone. More comprehensive optimizing compilers, that reduce type conversions for example, would require more specific information about each particular case, and this would result in a more complicated set of rules for the micro environment.

7.4. Multiprocessing and parallel processing

In its present format GRAPE is biased towards a single processor system. However, the data flow approach used in GRAPE greatly facilitates both the prototyping and the implementation of distributed processing. In a parallel multi-processing environment, each processor may execute a particular sub-graph. However, care must be taken in making such assignments in order to even the load. In a pipeline multi-processing environment, each processor may execute a level or set of levels of the graph. This requires that appel streams be globally passed between levels much like in the pixel-stream-editor environment. Finally, in an array-processor environment individual appels from the stream may be processed in parallel on separate processors.

The main point here is that GRAPE facilitates the exploration of the issues of multiprocessing and of the characteristics of different structures and different assignments to processors. All that is needed to determine the load distribution is to profile the GRAPE graphs once built, and to assign weights to the different nodes according to the processors to which they would be assigned.

8. Conclusions

The General Rendering Applications Programming Environment described here helps solve some of the problems associated with traditional graphics systems, by providing a flexible environment that may be used by people with various degrees of expertise. It permits graphics programmers to implement and test algorithms that may be easily and quickly integrated into existing systems. It also allows one to develop specialized rendering systems without new coding by piecing together a number of standard library operations. The lack of bias toward any particular rendering solution should let new ideas bloom, both good and bad. Quick and easy implementation will help us decide which are which.

9. Acknowledgements

The authors benefited from much useful advice in Toronto from John Amanatides, Dave Blythe, Ed Chillack, Eugene Fiume, Ralph Hill and Colin Hui. John in particular contributed much code which formed the core of GRAPE nodes. This work was partially sponsored by Canada NSERC and by the CAE Ltd. Avi Naiman provided macros, critical review, and considerable help in the preparation of the camera-ready version of this paper. The first author thanks Thomson Digital Image in general, and Alain Nicolas and Herve Loizeau in particular, for help in producing the illustrations. Credits for the picture in Figure 10 go to Herve Loizeau and Alain Nicolas, in addition to the two of us. The second author also thanks the Imaging group at Xerox PARC for providing a very congenial environment while this paper was written and Hewlett Packard Co for the use of their typesetting facilities. And finally, we thank the Siggraph referees and the *ad hoc* committee led by Rick Beach for many suggestions which considerably improved the readability of this paper.

10. References

AgAr82 Agerwala, T. and Arvind, "Data Flow Systems", *Computer*, Volume 15, Number 2, February 1982, pp. 10-13.

BKGS86 Blythe, D., Kitamura, J., Galloway, D. and Snelgrove, M., "Virtual Patch-Cords for the Katosizer", *Proceedings of the 1986 International Computer Music Conference*, October 1986, pp. 359-364.

CoCC87 Cook, R. L., Carpenter, L. and Catmull, E., "The Reyes Image Rendering Architecture", *These Proceedings*.

Cook84 Cook, R. L., "Shade Trees," *Computer Graphics,* Volume 18, Number 3, July 1984, pp. 223-231.

Crow82 Crow, F. C., "A More Flexible Image Generation Environment," *Computer Graphics,* Volume 16, Number 3, July 1982, pp. 9-18.

Duff80 Duff, T., *The Soid and Roid Manual,* NYIT Computer Graphics Laboratory internal memorandum, 1980.

Duff85 Duff, T., "Compositing 3-D Rendered Images," *Computer Graphics,* Volume 19, Number 3, July 1985, pp. 41-44.

Gour71 Gouraud, H., "Continuous Shading of Curved Surfaces," *IEEE Transactions on Computers,* Volume 20, Number 6, June 1971, pp. 623-629.

GrHe86 Greene, N. and Heckbert, P. S., "Creating Raster Omnimax Images from Multiple Perspective Views Using Elliptical Weighted Average Filter," *IEEE Computer Graphics and Applications,* Volume 6, Number 6, June 1986, pp. 21-27.

Haeb86 Haeberli, P. "A Data Flow Manager for an Interactive Programming Environment", *Proceedings of USENIX Summer Conference*, Atlanta, GA, 1986.

HaGr83 Hall, R. A. and D. P. Greenberg, "A Testbed for Realistic Image Synthesis," *IEEE Computer Graphics and Applications*, Volume 3, Number 11, November 1983, pp. 10-20.

Hedel84 Hedelman, H., "A Data Flow Approach to Procedural Modeling", *IEEE Computer Graphics and Applications*, Volume 4, Number 1, January 1984, pp. 16-26.

Nada86 Nadas, T. P., *The Computation of Appearance Elements*, M. Sc. Thesis, Department of Electrical Engineering, University of Toronto, 1986.

PaBo86 Paeth, A. W. and K. S. Booth, "Design and Experience with a Generalized Raster Toolkit," *Graphics Interface 1986 Proceedings*, May 1986, pp. 91-97.

Perl85 Perlin, K., "An Image Synthesizer," *Computer Graphics*, Volume 19, Number 3, July 1985, pp. 287-296.

Phon75 Bui-Tuong Phong, "Illumination for Computer Generated Pictures," *Communications of the ACM*, Volume 18, Number 6, June 1975, pp. 311-317.

PoDu84 Porter, T. and T. Duff, "Compositing Digital Images," *Computer Graphics*, Volume 18, Number 3, July 1984, pp. 253-259.

PoHo87 Potmesil, M. and Hoffert, E. M., "FRAMES: Software Tools for Modeling, Rendering and Animation of 3D Scenes", *These Proceedings*.

RoZi84 Robinson, J. and S. Zimmerman, "Exploiting Texture in an Integrated Training Environment", *CIG Technical Report*, Evans & Sutherland, 1984.

ReSC87 Reeves, W. T., Salesin, D. H. and Cook, R. L., "Shadowing with Texture Maps", *These Proceedings*.

WhWe82 Whitted, T. and D. M. Weimer, "A Software Testbed for the Development of 3D Raster Graphics Systems," *ACM Transactions on Graphics*, Volume 1, Number 1, January 1982, pp. 43-58.

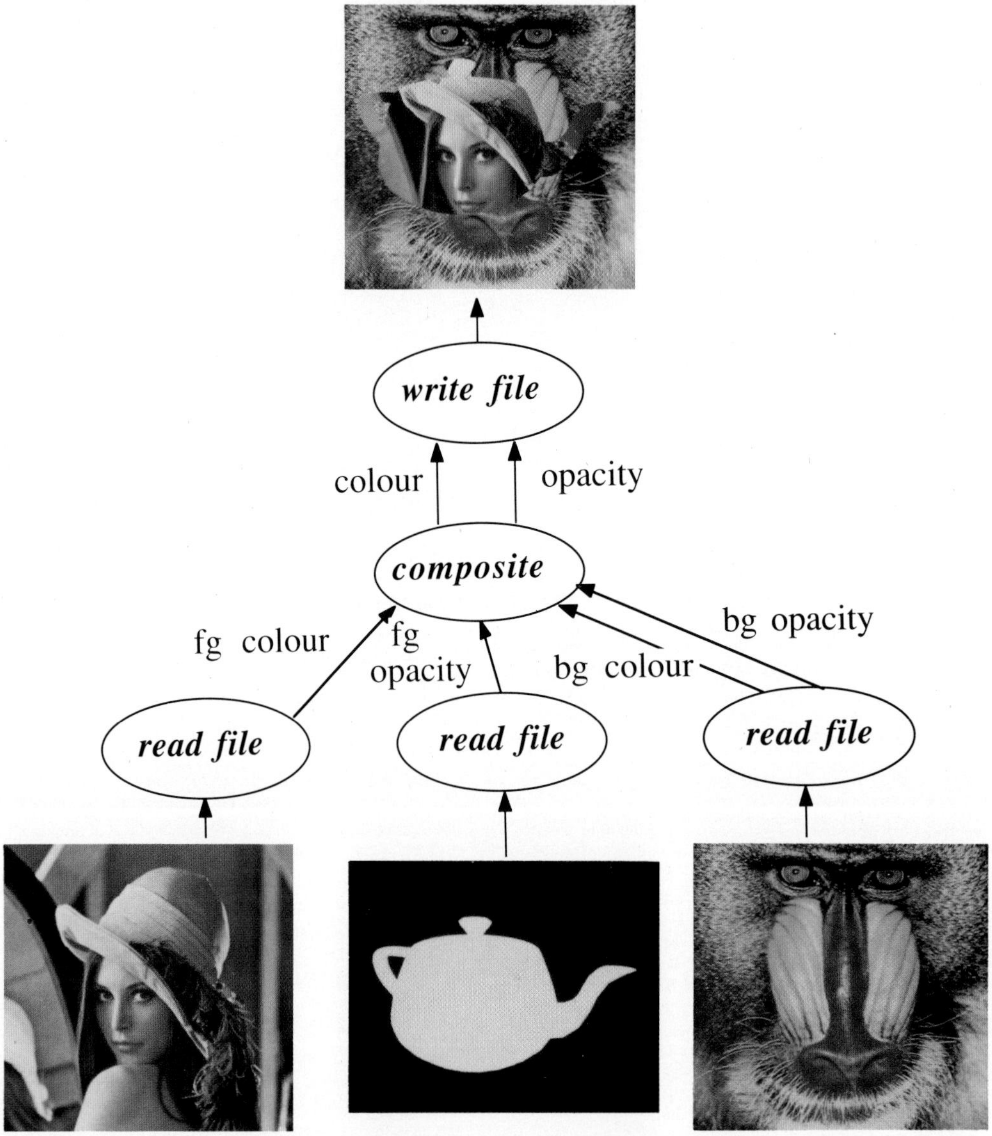

Figure 8. A variation on the basic composite tree.

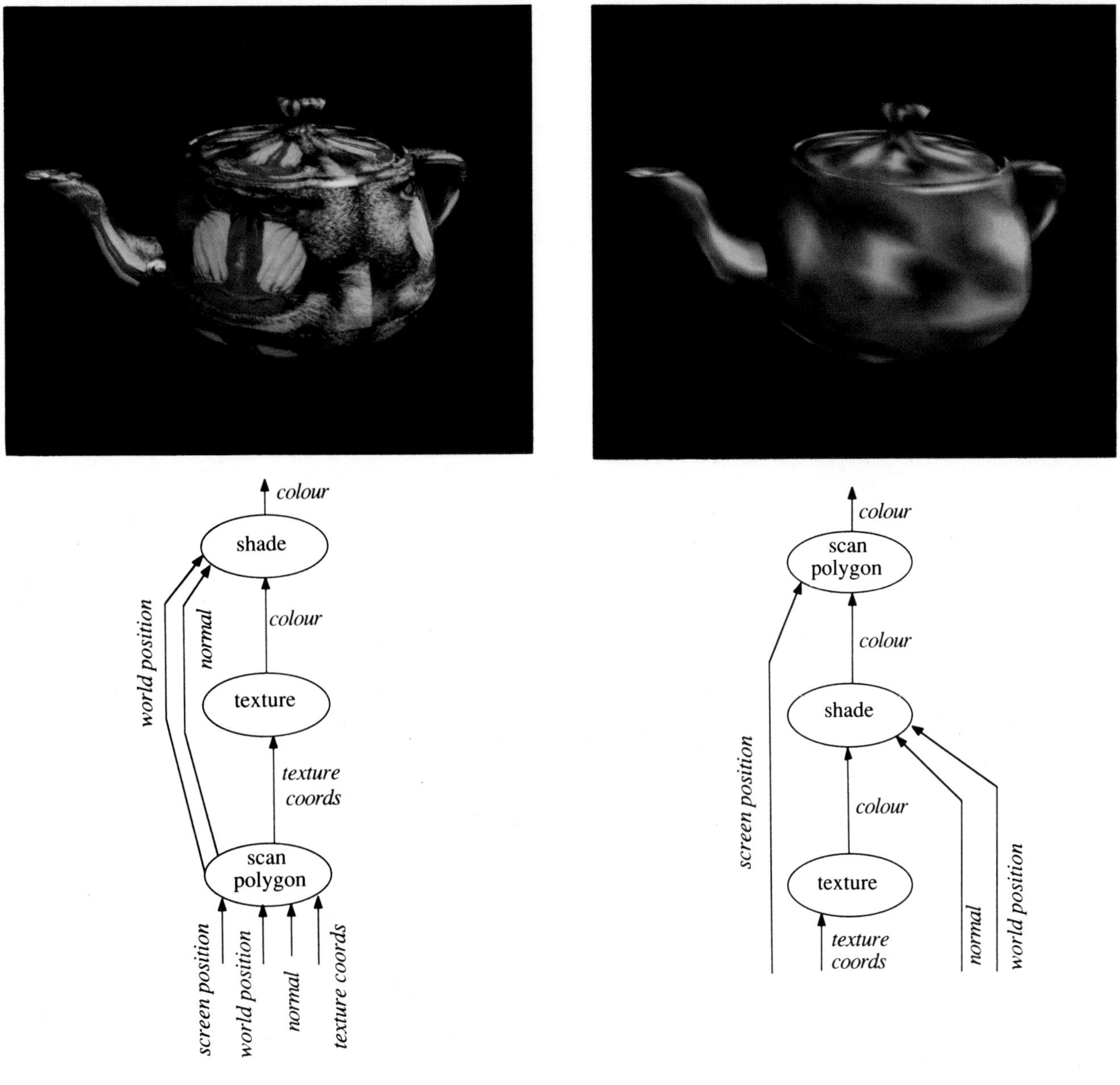

Figure 9. Traditional texture mapping and "Gouraud" texture mapping.

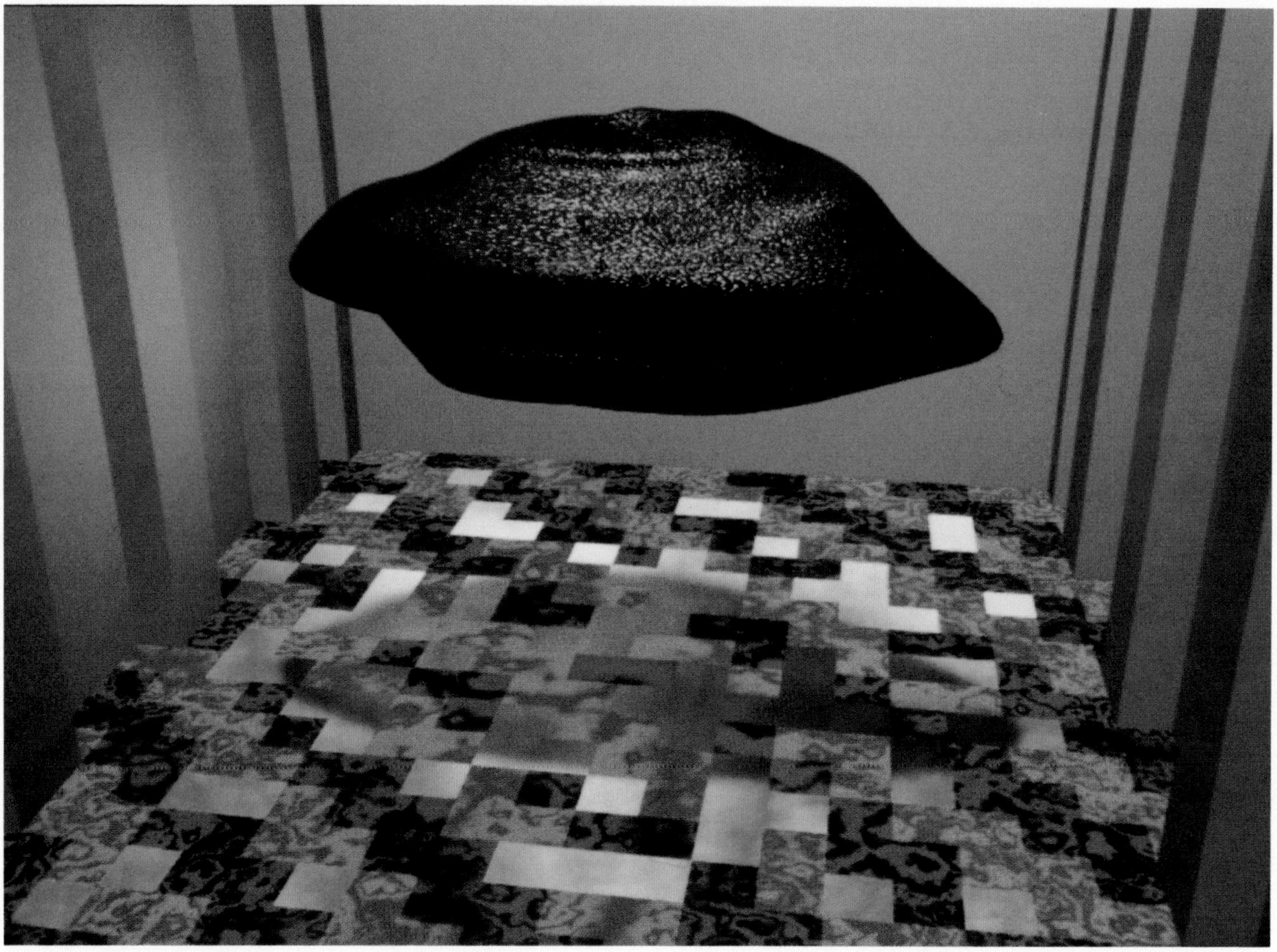

Figure 10. This is not a grape.

FRAMES: Software Tools for Modeling, Rendering and Animation of 3D Scenes

Michael Potmesil
Eric M. Hoffert

AT&T Bell Laboratories
Holmdel, NJ 07733

ABSTRACT

FRAMES is a set of flexible software tools, developed for the UNIX* programming environment, that can be used to generate images and animation of 3D scenes. In FRAMES, each stage of the image-rendering pipeline is assigned to a UNIX System filter. The following is a typical FRAMES pipe sequence where each filter performs a task implied by its name:

```
cat scene.frm | euclid | mover | shade | camera | abuf
```

FRAMES was designed to be easy to use, to permit flexible experimentation with new ideas in image rendering and geometric modeling, to allow distribution of different parts of the rendering pipeline to different processors, and to specify images in a common format for display on a variety of devices.

The user communicates with FRAMES via a command language. This language is extended whenever a software developer needs to incorporate a new idea into the system by adding new commands. Data flowing through the pipeline is modified by a collection of filter programs and passed through the pipe in text or binary format.

The modular and pipe-based nature of FRAMES allows for multi/parallel processor implementations and device independence. FRAMES has generated images on a local-area network of minicomputers (each filter runs on a different processor) and on a 64-processor hypercube machine (one filter runs on 64 processors). Applications of FRAMES have ranged from reconstruction of neurons from serial sections to rendering of antialiased octree objects with subpixel detail.

CR Categories and Subject Descriptors: I.3.2 **[Computer Graphics]:** Graphics Systems—Distributed/network graphics; I.3.3 **[Computer Graphics]:** Picture/Image Generation—Display algorithms—Viewing algorithms; I.3.5 **[Computer Graphics]:** Computational Geometry and Object Modeling—Curve, surface, solid and object representations; I.3.7 **[Computer Graphics]:** Three Dimensional Graphics and Realism—Animation—Visible line/surface algorithms.

General Terms: algorithms, computer graphics systems.

Additional Key Words and Phrases: UNIX System; pipeline; filter; a-buffer; parallel image rendering.

* Registered trademark of AT&T.

1. Introduction

FRAMES (Flexible Rendering, Animation and Modeling Experimentation System) is a set of tools that can be used to model, render, and animate 3D objects in the UNIX programming environment. FRAMES was designed to fulfill the following major objectives:

- To be a tool for experimenting with the process of image rendering, i.e., to try out new shaders, visible-surface algorithms, or texturing techniques.
- To function as a canned system, one that can be used in its current state by novice users to generate still images and animation.
- To manage growth in a controlled and flexible manner, so that programs written for any particular application become part of the system rather than be discarded.
- To experiment with distribution of image rendering tasks over local-area networks and parallel processors.
- To allow generation of images specified in a common format on diverse output devices, so that only a high-level filter needs to be written for each device.

FRAMES consists of a number of UNIX System filters linked together by a common interpreter which controls the flow of data through each filter. Flexibility arises from adding, removing, or modifying filters in the modeling, rendering, and animation pipeline. A user can specify input commands describing a 3D scene (Figure 1) and produce a high-quality image (Figure 2) by invoking a pipeline of basic FRAMES tools, as in:

```
cat salt.frm | molecule | euclid | shade | camera | abuf
```

where `salt.frm` is a text file containing all of the FRAMES commands relevant to making an image called `salt.img`. The filter `molecule` generates molecular models as sphere and cylinder object descriptions, `euclid` converts these descriptions into polygons, and `shade` computes surface illumination at vertices of the polygons. Filter `camera` transforms, clips, and projects these polygons into screen coordinates. Finally, `abuf` performs scan conversion, visible-surface determination, pixel shading and antialiasing. The computed image `salt.img` in Figure 2 shows a lattice structure of a simple cubic molecule—one half of a salt molecule. This example illustrates the basic capabilities of the system.

2. Raster Testbed Revisited

In addition to the design goals for FRAMES mentioned above, it was desired to address many of the shortcomings found in the experimental image-rendering systems described in the literature. The following is a brief look at some of these 3D graphics systems and their features and drawbacks.

Whitted and Weimer built a 3D raster testbed [18]. Their system was designed to allow for the rendering of different object types, such as bicubic surface patches, quadric surfaces, and polygon meshes by using a common data structure called a *span buffer*. However, the raster testbed contains too cumbersome a data structure for someone writing

```
//
//    a salt molecule scene ....
//
.Initialize
.SetFrame 0 512 0 512
.ClearFrame 50 50 50
.PerspProjection 50.0 1.0 50.0 2000.0
.LookAtView 700 550 750 0 70 70 120
.PointLightSource 700 0 800 200 200 200
.PointLightSource -300 0 700 200 200 200
.ComputeVertexNormals
.SpecularReflection 0.45 11
.SimpleCubic 4 4 4 10 20 6 8 250 Sepia Sepia
.OpenEncodedImage 'salt.img'
.WriteImage
.Exit
```

Figure 1 Sample FRAMES input file `salt.frm` of a simple-cubic molecular lattice.

Figure 2 Sample FRAMES image `salt.img` generated by the commands listed in Figure 1.

an application program or for a novice user. A large amount of data associated with each polygon is required, such as pointers to adjacent vertices and edges, and list pointers. In addition, their system had no command-language interpreter or a high-level method of expressing what to do.

Crow [5] describes his image-rendering system, which consists of a supervisory process controlling heterogeneous subprocesses. It resolves the scene complexity a priori and then renders each object type independently in the correct depth order. Crow's approach facilitates experimentation with rendering algorithms. Usage of a command language makes it easy to define scenes and objects.

Reynolds [14] discusses ASAS, a *lisp*-based programming language used to describe 3D animation. The user creates a script with procedural definitions of the objects and events in an animation and modifies it until the animation is perfected. ASAS is the type of language that can serve as a high-level preprocessor for an image-rendering system such as FRAMES.

Blinn, in a discussion of a system developed to simulate graphically the Voyager spacecraft's fly-by of Saturn and the formation of DNA [2], advocates the use of *loose coupling*, the ability to join easily different pieces of a complex graphics system, but disparages anything which is *totally integrated*, i.e., conforms to one set of rules. We feel that loose coupling and total integration are not mutually exclusive. In fact, FRAMES is rigidly consistent in the general way it processes data, but at the same time, is designed to have additional filters built, which can be both connected to and interchanged with existing filters.

Duff [7, 8] describes a common representation for compositing images. He uses a command language interpreter to piece together scenes and speaks of a *call to arms* for modularity in graphical programming. This is in reaction against the monolithic nature of the Lucasfilm's REYES system [4, 7], which consists of one very large program that very few people understand. Duff claims that the *rgbα* representation is efficient in that it makes image creation modular by allowing one to work on different pieces of a picture and then combine them when they are perfected.

Sequin, et al [16, 17] developed pipeline-based modeling and rendering tools called UNIGRAFIX. FRAMES and UNIGRAFIX have much in common with respect to the use of pipes and filters in a UNIX System environment. However, the UNIGRAFIX system was geared towards offering only a wide range of tools for geometric modeling, a collection of UNIX modules to create and operate on a diverse collection of 3D and 4D objects. Little mention is made of offering flexibility in other areas, such as solid modeling, shading models, cameras, and visible-surface algorithms.

Some prominent problems with these systems are the lack of a facility for modifying or adding new features, and a tendency for the rendering code to grow very large and unstable. FRAMES makes adding new features simple by allowing the user to specify new functions in a high-level structure, and stays manageable by breaking down the rendering process into a number of small pieces.

3. Pipelined 3D Modeling, Image Rendering, and Animation

We have divided the tasks that FRAMES should perform into three major steps:

- **Image rendering**—generation and display of images of 3D scenes.
- **Geometric modeling**—design of 3D models.
- **Animation**—generation of sequences of images.

In this paper, we concentrate on the task of image rendering. Generating computer images is a well-known pipeline process [18] that converts a description of a picture to an array of *rgb* intensity values (pixels). The stages of this pipeline are:

- **Geometric transformations**—scaling, translation, rotation and other modifications to an object's shape, location and orientation, and transformation into an eye coordinate system.
- **Clipping**—elimination of parts of objects outside the viewing pyramid bounded by six clipping planes: the four edges of the screen and near (hither) and far (yon) planes.
- **Back-face removal**—optional removal of faces of solid opaque objects facing away from the screen.
- **Triangulation**—conversion of concave and convex polygons into triangles to allow spatially invariant shading.
- **Shading**—determination of intensity at discrete points (e.g., polygon vertices) on the surface of an object based on orientation relative to light sources.
- **Projection**—mapping of object data from a 3D eye coordinate space to a 3D screen (image) coordinate space.
- **Raster-scan conversion, visible-surface determination, and antialiasing**—conversion of the projected data to pixels, determination of surface visibility, evaluation of intensity of visible pixels, and elimination of sampling effects by antialiasing.

4. FRAMES System Overview

We wanted to mirror the pipeline processes, described above, in the UNIX System by assigning each stage of the graphical pipeline to a UNIX System filter. This filter is a program that reads some input, performs a transformation on it, and writes some output [11].

The use of filters and pipes in the UNIX System provides a powerful method for modeling pipeline processes in software. We wanted to exploit the flexibility inherent in the use of these filters and pipes, but in the context of 3D computer graphics. Each stage of the 3D modeling and image rendering pipeline is a separate filter in FRAMES.

The use of a pipeline of filters in conjunction with an interpretive mechanism common to every filter are the basic components of FRAMES. The command language interpreter selectively focuses on those parts of the data stream that each filter needs to do its processing. All other parts of the data stream are passed on to the next filter for processing in the pipeline sequence. The command language and pipeline structure are discussed briefly in the following sections.

4.1 Command Language Format

Input to FRAMES consists of `*.frm` files containing all commands relevant to executing a pipeline of filters. Commands as well as other messages are passed through a pipeline and interpreted by filters. There are three types of messages that can be sent through a pipeline: command messages, comment messages, and error messages. Command messages are specified in either text (ascii) format or in binary format. In text format, a command name is prefixed with the '.' symbol and followed by a list of parameters. A binary command message is prefixed with the '%' symbol followed by an opcode, parameter size and parameters, all specified in the internal representation of the computer being used. Most error signals generated by the UNIX System are detected by FRAMES and produce error messages in the FRAMES format. These error messages can be interpreted by other filters downstream in a pipeline.

4.2 Command Language Extensions

FRAMES was designed for maximum ease-of-use. A novice user can perform new tasks by arranging existing filters into pipelines; a sophisticated user can easily extend the command language and add functionality to the system by writing a new FRAMES filter.

FRAMES is built on a library of C functions that handles all input/output data stream processing and on a list of graphical data types (command parameters) shared by all filters. To write a new FRAMES filter, a developer writes the C functions that perform the graphics processing; declares all the commands that will be read by the filter from the data stream and the commands that will be written by the filter to the data stream; and, if necessary, defines new commands that will be processed by the filter. Once written and compiled, the filter is linked with the FRAMES library, which services all requests for data stream input/output and formats the data for the current mode (binary or text). The complexity of a graphics task performed by a command ranges from flipping the sign of a normal vector to constructing a detailed geometric model.

4.3 Pipeline Structure

The execution time of a pipeline is always constrained by the slowest element in the pipeline. If one filter is significantly slower than any of the other ones, then either more effort should be devoted to optimizing the slow filter (for a single processor pipeline) or the filter should be broken down into a number of smaller filters (for a multi-processor pipeline). Ideally, the computational load should be distributed equally among all of the filters in a pipeline. In practice, however, this can be difficult to achieve.

Pipes cost more to use than function calls. Timing profiles of typical FRAMES filters reveal that about one-third of the total CPU time can be spent performing text input/output of command messages. However, the input/output overhead can be reduced to only one-tenth of the total CPU time by using binary input/output mode. Commands in binary format reduce the amount of data sent through a pipe and eliminate the time required to encode and decode command parameters. When comparing only the time spent reading and writing command messages, binary mode is five times faster than text mode.

We feel that the extra cost of using pipes is justified by the power gained from the filter and pipeline design. With pipes, the interface between filters can be loosely defined; with function calls, the interface between subroutines must be explicitly defined. Pipes are useful for debugging because they permit examination of the data stream at the interface between any two filters. In addition, filter pipelines can be reconfigured in more than one way to perform different tasks, whereas a large program cannot be reconfigured for a new task without being rewritten and recompiled.

4.4 Pipeline Constraints

When reconfiguring filters to perform a new task, it is important to understand that certain filters are limited to the number of tasks they can perform. For example, some filters are capable of only one myopic function, while others can be used for a broad variety of applications; some filters can be used at a number of different points in the pipeline (i.e., triangulation can occur in object space, eye space, and screen space), while others can be used at only one point in the pipeline. Therefore, to utilize the FRAMES system, the user must understand the constraints on the capabilities of individual FRAMES filters.

The pipelines described in this paper are all linear pipes, with the data flowing in only one direction. We hope to add a FRAMES *shell* to control the execution of a pipeline and allow filter configurations other than linear pipes. This should include the capability to have a filter performing input/output on more than one data stream at a time.

5. FRAMES Software Tools

The following sections illustrate the flexibility in image rendering afforded by the pipeline implementation of 3D graphics. These sections are presented according to the stages of the image-rendering pipeline. The description of each filter includes both a general overview and methods that exploit its flexibility.

5.1 Geometric Modeling [`euclid`, ...]

Geometric modeling in FRAMES is performed by two types of filters—filters that generate 3D objects and filters that operate on the representations of the objects. Examples of the object generators are filters that create Euclidean solids, parametric and implicitly defined surfaces, and octree objects. Examples of object operators are filters that perform Boolean operations and global or local deformations of shape.

FRAMES offers a number of object generators, such as `euclid`, `patch`, `tube`, and `genoct`. The `euclid` filter creates object descriptions of spheres, cylinders, hemi-spheres, hemi-cylinders, topless and bottomless cylinders, superquadric ellipsoids, and objects of revolution. The `tube` filter generates generalized cylinders by dragging a template 2D curve along a 3D space curve, such as Hermite or Bezier, defined in turn by the `spline` filter. The `genoct` filter generates octree objects, described by finite-state tables [10] and outputs leaf nodes (voxels) tessellated into polygonal faces. The `patch` filter generates a number of different types of bicubic patches. An image containing all of these objects can be generated by:

```
cat assorted.frm | euclid | tube | genoct | patch | ...
```

Figure 3 shows an image of a chair model generated by the `tube` and `euclid` filters.

FRAMES allows easy construction of hierarchical and high-level objects. These objects are created by stringing together a number of filters that sequentially decompose a high-level description of an object into its most primitive elements. A simple example is the use of the `molecule` filter, which takes as input high-level descriptions of molecular structures and outputs appropriate sphere and cylinder locations, sizes, colors, and other model properties. The `euclid` filter

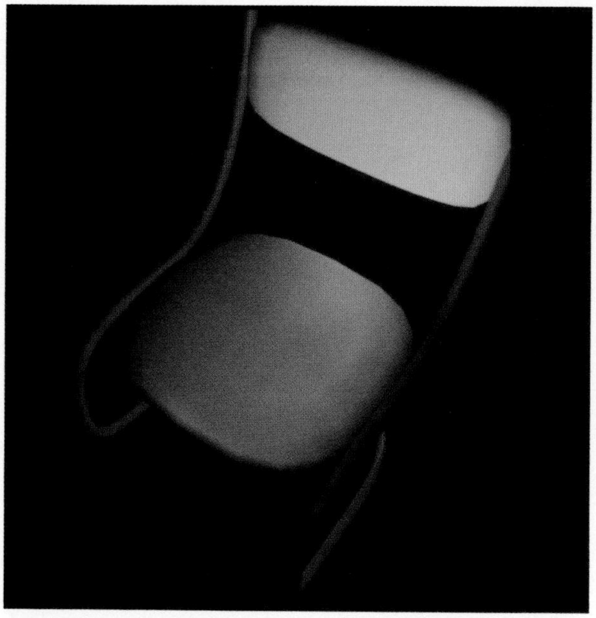

Figure 3 A chair model generated by the pipeline:

```
cat chair.frm | spline -t | tube | euclid | ...
```

where filter `spline` computed a 3D cubic spline trajectory from input data (option `-t` outputs the tangent vectors along the curve), `tube` computed the polygonal mesh of a generalized cylinder and `euclid` generated two superquadric ellipsoids.

then accepts such ball-and-stick models and outputs the surfaces tesselated into polygons:

```
cat body_centered_cubic.frm | molecule | euclid | ...
```

Figure 4 shows an image, generated by the above sequence, of the interior view of a body-centered-cubic molecular space lattice. Another example of this approach to object generation is filter `office_maker` illustrated in Figure 5.

In addition to object generators, FRAMES offers a number of filters that operate on various representations of 3D objects (object operators). Object operators are used for geometric modeling tasks or for converting data from one geometric representation to another. The geometric modeling filters (i.e., `twist`, `shear`, and `slice`) can be concatenated to form powerful *sculpting* pipelines.

This aspect of FRAMES—having a large collection of small filters that both generate and operate on 3D geometric objects—is most similar to UNIGRAFIX. The similarity, however, ends here. As described in the following sections, flexibility in lighting models, visible-surface algorithms, and other rendering functions (*not just geometric modeling*) are of paramount importance.

5.2 Transformations [`mover`]

The filter `mover` transforms all 3D geometric data, such as polygons, normal vectors, and light sources, from one object coordinate system to another. It can be used, for example, to convert a hierarchical object description, where each object is defined in a relative object space, into a leveled object description in an absolute object space. This filter constructs its transformations from standard translation, rotation, and scaling commands or accepts transformations prepared by other filters. It maintains a stack of transformation matrices **T** which map the source coordinate system to the destination one. Surface-normal vectors are transformed using transposed inverse matrices $(\mathbf{T}^{-1})^t$.

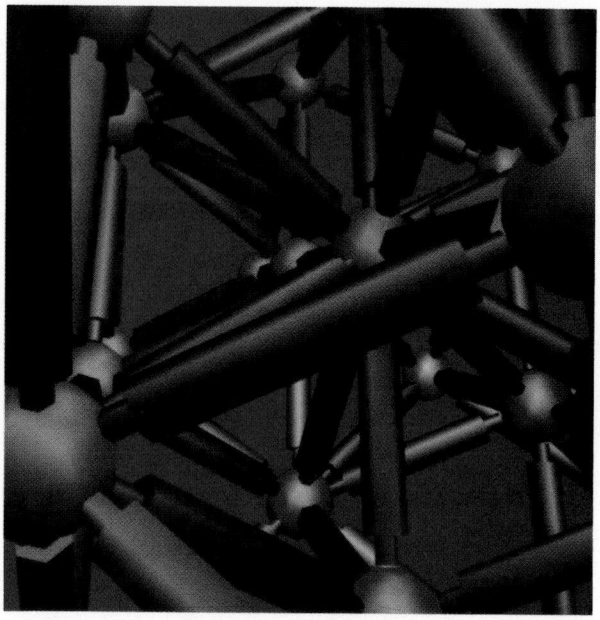

Figure 4 A body-centered cubic lattice generated by the pipeline:

```
cat bcc.frm | /kiwi/molecule | /avocado/euclid | ...
        ... | /pixel/shade | ... | /apricot/abuf
```

This image was generated using distributed processing. Each filter in the pipeline was run on a different processor in a local-area network. The processor name precedes each filter name. Running FRAMES in this mode decreases execution time of the pipeline. The *bottleneck* filters were run on the fastest processors (in this case, `shade` on `pixel` and `abuf` on `apricot`).

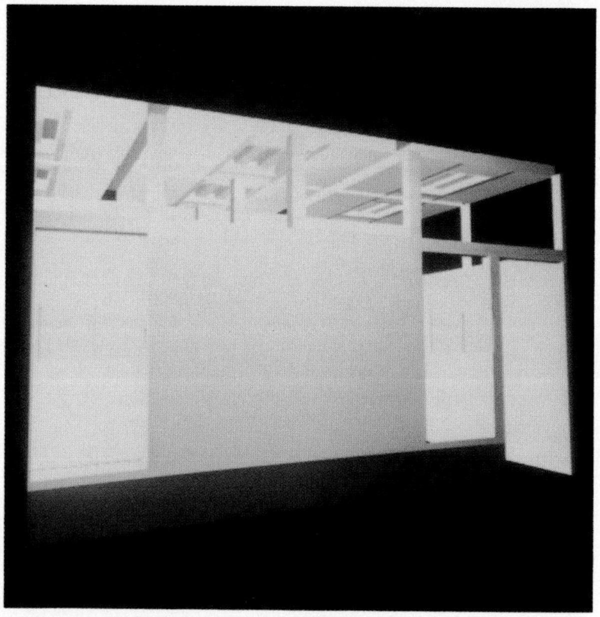

Figure 5 An aisle of offices generated by the pipeline:

```
cat holmdel.frm | office_maker | poly | ...
```

where filter `office_maker` generates models of office buildings. In this case, the offices are without windows or carpets.

Geometric objects are placed into their absolute locations, orientations, and sizes in the object coordinate system by specifying the `-obj` option:

```
cat hierarchy.frm | euclid | mover -obj > flat.frm
```

The filter can also place geometric objects into an eye coordinate system when the `-eye` option is specified:

```
cat zztop.frm | euclid | mover -eye | ... | shade | ...
```

In this context, the filter can be used to prepare objects for shading with the view point at the origin of the eye space and the view vector in the z direction.

5.3 Shading [shade]

Following the placement of all geometric entities into their absolute locations in the object or eye coordinate system, we are ready to perform shading computations. The `shade` filter starts the user off with a few well-known shading models. A simple Lambertian reflection model (diffuse shader only) and Gouraud shading (diffuse and specular) are included:

```
cat shaded_picture.frm | mover | shade | camera | ...
```

We assume that each scan-conversion program can evaluate flat, Gouraud and Phong interpolations on a per-pixel basis.

Shading is a complex issue in computer image synthesis. Typically, a user will want to have a variety of shading models to choose from, as well as a variety of options for the specification of light sources. The distribution of these shaders over the objects in a scene is not uniform. A scene may have a diffuse shader for most objects, a specular model for one object, a textured shader for another, and a Torrance-Sparrow model for yet another. FRAMES allows the user to attach easily different shaders to individual objects or groups of objects. The current shader specified in the input file is active until another is specified.

As new shaders evolve, `shade` can be updated, replaced entirely, or augmented with a number of small specialized shading filters.

5.4 Cameras [camera]

The `camera` filter performs geometric transformations, clipping, and projections of points, lines, and polygons from a 3D object or eye coordinate system into a 3D screen coordinate system. Also, other geometric data, such as surface-normal vectors and light source locations and orientations, can be transformed by `camera` but not clipped or projected. Commands interpreted by `camera` can be divided into the following categories:

- **Modeling transformations**—specify translations, rotations, and scale factors applied to 3D data in matrix **M**.
- **Viewing transformations**—specify the location and orientation of camera in matrix **V**.
- **Projection transformations**—specify projection type (perspective or orthographic) and projection parameters (locations of the six clipping planes) in matrix **P**.
- **Viewport**—specify the size and location of a rectangular viewport in screen (image) coordinates.
- **Transformation control**—specify control of a stack of transformation matrices **T = MVP**.
- **Viewport control**—specify control of a stack of viewport parameters.
- **Geometric data**—define points, lines, polygons, their colors, surface-normal vectors and other attributes, and positions, orientations and colors of light sources.

The clipping algorithm in the `camera` filter clips all points, lines, and polygons to the inside of a viewing pyramid and to the near (hither) and far (yon) clipping planes. Any data associated with a clipped line or edge, such as normal vectors, texture parameters or colors, are also properly clipped (interpolated). The filter maintains a stack of transformation matrices, **T**, and an independent stack of viewport parameters. Transposed inverse versions of transformation matrices are again used for the transformation of surface-normal vectors. This filter is normally used to transform, clip, and project geometric data into a screen viewport.

The `camera` filter can also transform all geometric data to an eye coordinate system, in a manner similar to `mover`, using the `-eye` option. The major difference is that unlike `mover -eye`, `camera -eye` performs clipping. A second option `-screen` is then used to perform projection of the eye space coordinates to an image viewport in screen coordinates. A shading filter can be inserted between these two uses of `camera` to perform shading on clipped polygons in the eye coordinate system before they are distorted by projection:

```
... | camera -eye | fphong | camera -screen | ...
```

In this context, `camera -eye` outputs the x, y, z, w homogeneous coordinates of clipped points, lines, and polygons. Light sources are also transformed into this space, but they are not clipped. Next, `fphong` computes the coefficients of shading interpolation [1] from the eye space coordinates of polygons. Finally, `camera -screen` projects the eye space coordinates into the X, Y, Z screen space coordinates. The Z value represents the distance (depth) from the screen.

5.5 Visible Surfaces, Scan Conversion, and Antialiasing [abuf, zbuf, ...]

The final steps in the image-rendering pipeline are scan conversion, determination of visibility, pixel shading, and antialiasing. We have implemented an *a−buffer* filter, `abuf`, which performs all these steps.

The original a-buffer [3], as well as many other visible-surface algorithms, is *scan-line order* based. We felt that scan-line order was not necessary for the a-buffer. This requirement adds an extra sorting step to the image-rendering pipeline (use of the a-buffer already includes sorting in depth) and, therefore, more complexity. In addition, process sizes are getting larger under the UNIX System and memory prices continue to drop, making scan-line algorithms less of a requirement. Instead, FRAMES uses a fully active image-sized a-buffer, rasterizing on-the-fly and writing into any part of the screen image at any time. When `abuf` runs out of fragment memory, it has to compact all fragment lists into pixels and release the fragments' memory for future reuse. Because we maintain a full image-sized a-buffer, triangles can be sent to `abuf` in arbitrary order without any prior sorting. Antialiasing is accomplished with an exact-area box filter [9].

The approach using a fully active image-sized a-buffer simplifies the pipeline and allows for a novel type of 3D digital compositing. Objects or parts of scenes can be computed as separate a-buffer images. Each image has its a-buffer data written as a binary file. When the elements are composited, each input a-buffer binary file is read in, and the individual a-buffers are merged. The complete image is the result of *compacting* the merged a-buffers. A-buffers contain pixels that are *empty* (contain no object), *full* (z and *rgb*, as in a z-buffer), or *partial* (fragment list with detailed subpixel data). A data compression format, similar to run-length encoding, was developed for a-buffers to decrease disk storage and input/output time.

It is often desirable to use different hidden-surface techniques for different purposes when producing an image. For example, if one needs high-quality images for film recording or slides, an a-buffer would be most appropriate. A scene is processed using the a-buffer as:

```
cat pretty_picture.frm | ... | camera | abuf
```

However, at times, only a quick look at a dirty (jagged) image may be necessary. In this context, a z-buffer without antialiasing would be more appropriate. FRAMES supplies a simple *z−buffer* algorithm, `zbuf`, as well:

```
cat ugly_picture.frm | ... | camera | zbuf
```

A promising approach to the problem of scan conversion, which we consider to be the bottleneck of the rendering processes, is the use of *parallel processing.* We have been experimenting with a parallel z-buffer algorithm [13] implemented on a 64-processor (node) hypercube machine [6]. The parallel z-buffer filter, `pzbuf`, is used similarly to the other visible-surface filters:

```
cat tabby.frm | ... | camera | pzbuf
```

The nodes of the hypercube machine are assigned to image pixels in an interleaved pattern. Typically, a node will process every eighth pixel in every eighth scan line. Scan conversion, *z* depth, and pixel shading are performed by incrementally evaluating an expression in the form $ax + by + c$ for each edge, depth, and color of a triangle. Preliminary results indicate that this algorithm is 10 to 20 times faster than `zbuf` running on a super minicomputer. Currently, we are planning the addition of a parallel a-buffer algorithm, `pabuf`, which will evolve from `pzbuf` and probably use the antialiasing bit-mask technique described in [9].

Our experience with the a-buffer leads us to conclude that it is only a temporary solution to the long-standing problem of visible-surface determination. Although it is capable of good to excellent quality images, it is, unfortunately, difficult to implement, inefficient, and prone to errors. Therefore, when the next generation hidden-surface technique is perfected, the use of `newbuf` is recommended. A user unenchanted with buffer-type, visible-surface algorithms could always implement something different and use it at the end of the pipeline.

We have also found that `abuf` is a bottleneck in the rendering pipeline. Therefore, our next step is to look at ways to break up `abuf` into two or three smaller filters that can be distributed over a network of computers. We are considering a filter that performs scan conversion and fragment generation, a filter that creates and maintains fragment lists for an a-buffer image array, and a filter that, given a fragment list, computes a pixel color.

We would also like to add a ray-tracing filter to FRAMES that can be used in place of all the image-rendering filters to process objects directly from geometric modeling filters. A typical pipeline sequence might be:

```
cat tango.frm | patch | euclid | poly | ... | rays
```

5.6 Back-Face Removal [`noback`]

The most popular method of back-face removal is culling those polygons that have either back facing polygon-normal vectors or *all* back facing vertex-normal vectors. We developed a filter, called `noback`, that removes back faces of opaque *solid* objects and leaves back faces of transparent objects untouched. Optionally, the filter can also remove all transparent faces and front-facing faces. We felt that back-face removal was not something that should be *hard-wired* into FRAMES, again, for the sake of flexibility. For example, an object clipped by a hither clipping plane may show some of its back-facing polygons while only its front-facing faces are visible before hither clipping. If back-face removal is active, the back faces will not be rendered and the object will appear incorrect. For this case, back-face removal is counter-productive. To sum up, if back-face removal is desired, we recommend the use of `noback` when polygons are in the *eye* coordinate system:

```
cat food.frm | ... | mover -eye | noback | ... | zbuf
```

Back-face removal can also be performed on a per-object basis. This is done by turning the back-face removal command on and off for selected objects in an input file. Back-face removal is an example of a graphics function that can be controlled on an individual basis in the data stream or globally over the data stream by just invoking the filter.

5.7 Diversity of Devices [`irview, plotview`]

Our graphical-device environment is typical of that found in many graphics laboratories. We have a number of devices, each with its own unique commands to draw lines and curves, write and read pixels, etc. There is no commonality between any two devices. In addition, some devices perform part of the image-rendering pipeline, such as geometric transformations in hardware, while others do not; some devices are raster-based and some are vector-based. Given these facts, we wanted a system capable of specifying pictures using only one description method and displaying them on all of the available devices without having to exert much programming effort. By modularizing the graphical process, it becomes trivial to use different devices in this manner.

To deal with device independence for batch-type image creation, the last stage of the rendering pipeline (`abuf` or other) writes a device independent *rgb* image file (run-length encoded or dumped). For devices of a more interactive or (closer to) real-time nature (typically for our purposes, the former are frame buffers and the latter are vector displays), FRAMES is structured so that the last stage of the pipeline is a filter that outputs rendering/drawing commands unique to that device. The following are two examples of using FRAMES to obtain output on our display devices.

The Silicon Graphics IRIS terminal performs 3D geometric transformations, clipping, and perspective projection in hardware. We can exploit this hardware feature by piping 3D objects, generated by FRAMES, into an IRIS system without using the FRAMES filters `camera` and `mover`. This is possible because all `camera` and `mover` operations can be performed by the IRIS hardware, thereby saving host CPU time. We also do not need to use `shade`, `abuf`, and other filters since we are only generating vector-drawings, as in:

```
cat chair.frm | chair_maker | ... | irview -2D
```

where `chair.frm` is an input file for a chair picture, `chair_maker` generates 3D models of designer chairs and `irview` with the `-2D` option draws a wire-frame image. If the option `-3D` is invoked, `irview` loads the 3D scene into a display list. The 3D model can then be previewed interactively on the screen.

The AT&T Teletype* 5620 terminal, formerly known as the *blit* terminal, has bit-mapped graphics with the *bitblt* operations [12] in multiple overlapping windows. This terminal is a good candidate to preview scenes for animation or to design models of objects, especially if an IRIS system is not readily available and particularly if not remotely near a civilization† [19]. Unlike the IRIS system, there is no hardware performing transformations, clipping, and projections in the Teletype 5620 terminal. Hence, the `camera` filter must be used here.

An advantage of FRAMES is its ability to easily convert geometric data from one representation to another by filtering it. This advantage has been exploited to interface FRAMES to the standard UNIX System `plot` utilities. A filter called `plotview` converts FRAMES commands to the UNIX System `plot` language. By piping the output of `plotview` into any one of the UNIX System `plot` filters, one can view FRAMES pictures on a variety of devices. For example, the following sequence outputs bicubic patches in wire-frame representation to the Teletype 5620 terminal:

```
cat blit.frm | patch | camera | plotview | t5620
```

where `t5620` takes `plot` language as input and displays the input data as lines on the Teletype 5620 terminal in the window from which the command was executed. Figure 6 illustrates the use of `plotview` in a multi-window environment. It is also possible to output to hard-copy printers with the `plot` tools. For example, the following sequence will output some 2D splines using the FRAMES `spline` filter:

```
cat imagen.frm | spline -l | plotview | plot -printer
```

where `-printer` selects a laser printer for output. The interface to `plot` is useful for hard-copy output and fast terminal previewing of 2D and 3D objects.

* Registered trademark of AT&T.

† Recent work has yielded a portable Teletype 5620 terminal with a hand-held viewer—3D graphics work in Death Valley, CA is now not far off.

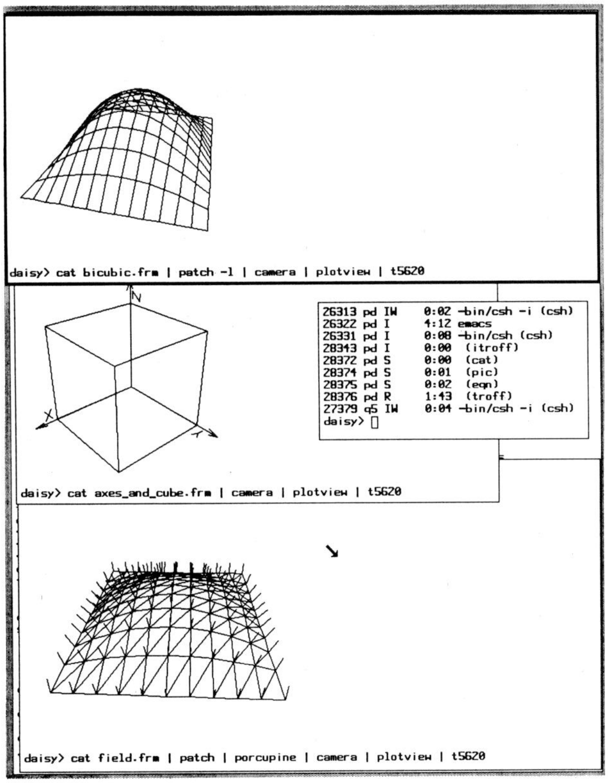

Figure 6 Previewing 3D objects on diverse devices. This figure shows three windows of a Teletype 5620 terminal. Each window shows a FRAMES pipeline and the picture it generated. The top window shows a bicubic patch generated by `patch` (option `-l` outputs lines, default is to output triangles), the middle window shows an object contained entirely in the input file `axes_and_cube.frm`, and the bottom window shows the usage of the `porcupine` filter which displays normal vectors to illustrate surface curvature.

6. Distributed Rendering

The distribution of graphical and modeling tasks among multiple filters allows for flexibility in multiprocessing. A primary objective of modularity was to study the computing requirements of each rendering module and, subsequently, to tailor specialized hardware to each module. For example, the `camera` and `mover` filters should be supported by an array or digital-signal processor and the renderers, `abuf` and `zbuf`, would be optimized by distributing their tasks on a parallel processor.

By using FRAMES extensively and analyzing how and where CPU time is spent in each filter, we hope to improve our understanding of the best method for distributing FRAMES over various classes of hardware.

We have experienced significant speed improvements when using FRAMES with the Remote File System (RFS)—a public-domain transparent file-sharing system, analogous to the Sun Microsystems' Network File System—running on an Ethernet* local-area network of VAX† minicomputers. By running each stage of the FRAMES pipeline on a different VAX machine and piping from one VAX to another, we obtain the benefits of distributed processing without special hardware. Distributing the filters in a pipeline over (comparable) machines in a network decreases the *real time* elapsed for pipeline execution, while the CPU time consumed by all filters in the pipeline remains constant.

Each filter is run on a separate machine by invoking the remote shell command (rsh) for each filter. The following is a typical example of each filter running on a distinct VAX computer called `daisy`, `dixie`, and `pixie`:

```
cat morris.frm | /daisy/tube -b | ...
        ... | /dixie/camera -b | /pixie/abuf
```

To run the parallel z-buffer on a hypercube machine attached to a Sun Workstation‡ named `cube`, with all other filters again on VAX computers, we enter:

```
cat morris.frm | /daisy/tube -b | ...
        ... | /dixie/camera -a | /cube/pzbuf
```

Note that the pipe between the last VAX (`dixie`) and the Sun (`cube`) must be done in text (ascii) format, by specifying the `-a` option, rather than in binary format because the two systems have incompatible internal integer and floating-point representations.

7. Further Examples

FRAMES was tested on a few guinea-pig projects. The first application was the reconstruction of neurons from serial sections [15]. Figure 7 shows an image of four serial cross sections of neurons in the crustacean *Daphnia*. This image was generated by converting each original section image into an array of 3D polygons (squares) with `rdimg`. Figure 8 shows two 3D neurons (the front neuron branches), modeled by polygons, reconstructed from 22 such serial sections.

FRAMES was used to display 3D fractal volumes modeled by octrees [10]. Figure 9 shows two images of the *Menger sponge*, which has a sponge property that its volume approaches *zero*, while its surface area approaches *infinity* as the number of recursion levels increases. Each sponge object in Figure 9 has three levels of recursion. The sponge in Figure 9(b) was generated by inverting the octree representation of the sponge in Figure 9(a).

We have also been using FRAMES as a testbed for simulating image-rendering algorithms on various parallel computer architectures. Figure 10 shows a bicubic patch rendered with depth-cued aliased and antialiased lines. This image was generated by filter `dc`, which performs depth-cueing of lines, and filter `psim`, which simulates an $m \times n$ array of rendering processors where each processor accesses only every mth pixel on every nth scan line. We have also been experimenting with various texturing techniques. In Figure 11, the walls and columns are solid-textured (clouds and marble, respectively) and the gallery picture is a summed-area table texture map.

8. Conclusions and Summary

We have described a flexible system for 3D modeling and image synthesis. The system is made of relatively small and simple UNIX System filter programs that can be flexibly configured into pipes to perform more complex tasks.

We feel that we have developed the basic image-rendering tools and now need to start developing front-end geometric modeling and animation tools with higher-level commands and constructs. Analogous to the UNIX typesetting tools, we have developed the equivalents of `troff`, `tbl`, and `eqn` and now should continue by developing the equivalents of `pic` and `grap`.

The notions of both loose coupling and combining a number of small not-so-powerful programs to form a more powerful whole allow usage of a system in ways not intended *a priori*. They also permit gradual evolution of the system as image-rendering techniques advance.

---

* Trademark of Xerox Corp.

† Trademark of Digital Equipment Corp.

‡ Registered trademark of Sun Microsystems, Inc.

Currently, AT&T Pixel Machines is developing a parallel image computer that embodies some of the ideas of the FRAMES software environment in hardware. The computer consists of pipelines of *transformation nodes* and an array of parallel *pixel nodes* that access a distributed frame buffer. The system is completely programmable and software configurable.

9. Acknowledgements

We would like to thank Kicha Ganapathy for hints on how to generate solid space curve geometries, Dave Weimer for his help on constructing a data compression format for binary a-buffer files, Peter Selfridge for use of his neurons, the many SIGGRAPH reviewers for their detailed comments, and especially Bill Ninke for his support.

10. References

[1] Bishop, G., and Weimer, D., "Fast Phong Shading," *ACM Computer Graphics 20*, 3 (August 1986), 103-106.

[2] Blinn, J., "System Aspects of Computer Image Synthesis and Computer Animation," *SIGGRAPH 1984 Advanced Image Synthesis Course Notes* (July 1984).

[3] Carpenter, L., "The A-buffer, An Antialiased Hidden Surface Method," *ACM Computer Graphics 18*, 3 (July 1984), 103-108.

[4] Cook, R., "Shade Trees," *ACM Computer Graphics 18*, 3 (July 1984), 223-231.

[5] Crow, F. C., "A More Flexible Image Generation Environment," *ACM Computer Graphics 16*, 3 (July 1982), 9-18.

[6] DeBenedictis, E., *The Bell Labs Hypercube Machine*, personal communication (April 1986).

[7] Duff, T., and Porter, T., "Compositing Digital Images," *ACM Computer Graphics 18*, 3 (July 1984), 253-259.

[8] Duff, T., "Compositing 3D Rendered Images," *ACM Computer Graphics 19*, 3 (July 1985), 41-44.

[9] Hoffert, E. M., and Bishop, G., "Exact and Efficient Area Sampling Techniques for Spatial Antialiasing," Technical Memorandum, AT&T Bell Laboratories (December 1985).

[10] Hoffert, E. M., and Potmesil, M., "Generation and Display of Self-Similar and Volume-Diminishing Cubes in 3D," accepted for presentation at *Eurographics '87*, Amsterdam, Holland (August 1987).

[11] Kernighan, B., and Pike, R., *The UNIX Programming Environment*, Englewood Cliffs, NJ: Prentice Hall, 1984.

[12] Pike, R., "Graphics in Overlapping Bitmap Layers," *ACM Transactions on Graphics 2*, 2 (April 1983), 135-160.

[13] Potmesil, M., "A Parallel Z-Buffer Implementation on a 64-Processor Hypercube Machine," Technical Memorandum, AT&T Bell Laboratories, [in preparation].

[14] Reynolds, C. W., "Computer Animation with Scripts and Actors," *ACM Computer Graphics 16*, 3 (July 1982), 289-296.

[15] Selfridge, P., "Using a Simple Shape Measure to Improve Automatic 3D Reconstruction," *Pattern Recognition Letters 5*, 5 (May 1987).

[16] Sequin, C., et. al., "More ... Creative Geometric Modeling," Technical Report UCB/CSD 86/278, Berkeley, University of California (December 1985).

[17] Sequin, C., "The Berkeley UNIGRAFIX Tools, Version 2.5," Technical Report UCB/CSD 86/281, Berkeley, University of California (December 1985).

[18] Whitted, T., and Weimer, D., "A Software Testbed for the Development of 3D Raster Graphics Systems," *ACM Transactions on Graphics 1*, 1 (January 1982), 43-77.

[19] Zimmer, C., "A Portable 5620 Terminal with a Hand Held Viewer," Technical Memorandum, AT&T Bell Laboratories (October 1985).

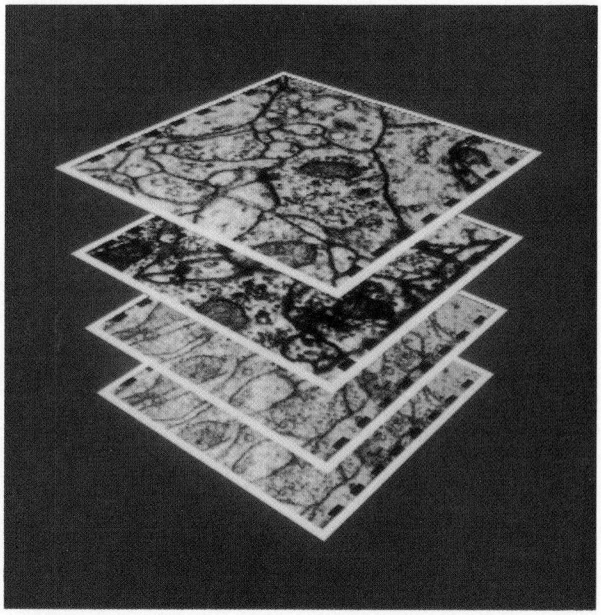

Figure 7 Four slices of neuronal tissue converted by filter `rdimg` from 2D pixels to 3D polygons in the pipeline:

`cat neuron.frm | rdimg | camera | abuf`

The intensities of the original grey-scale images are used here, therefore, `shade` is not necessary in the pipeline. The use of `abuf` insures that the contents of the four projected images will be properly resampled and antialiased.

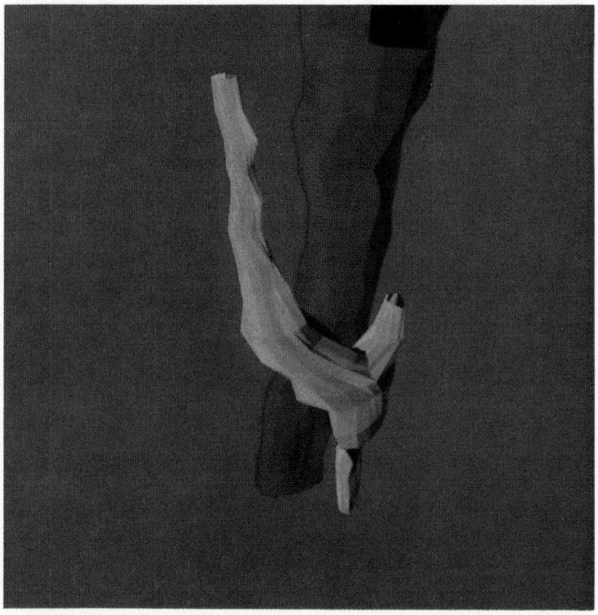

Figure 8 Two neurons reconstructed from 22 slices of neuronal tissue and generated by the pipeline:

`cat cross_sections.frm | contour | polynorm | ...`

where filter `contour` outputs a polygonal mesh by connecting adjacent contours and filter `polynorm` computes polygon normals for each polygon (assuming a consistent polygonal orientation). Flat shading was performed by `shade` here.

(a)

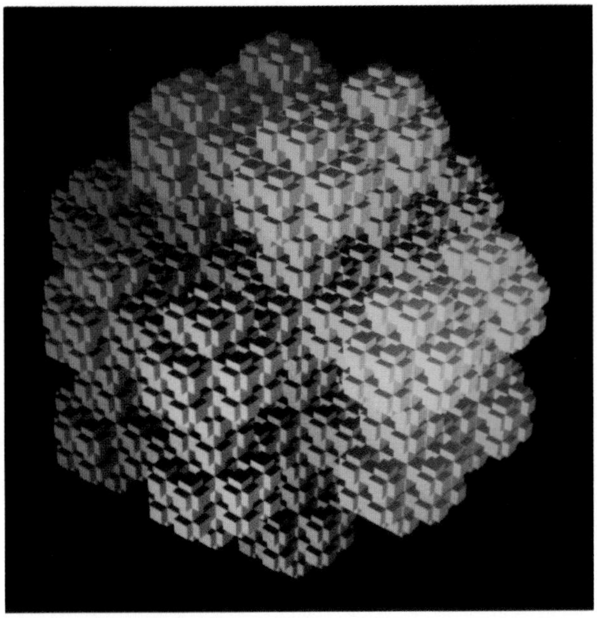

(b)

Figure 9 A fractal Menger sponge modeled by octree representation and generated by the pipeline:

```
cat sponge.frm | genoct | camera | abuf
```

This object has a sponge property that its volume approaches *zero* while its surface area approaches *infinity* as the number of recursion levels increases. The sponge in image (a) is tesselated with 169,728 faces. The sponge in image (b) was generated by inverting the representation of the sponge in image (a) and contains 112,896 faces. The colors for this object were generated by interpolating the *rgb* values at each corner of the cube (this was done by `genoct`). No other shading was desired, therefore, the filter `shade` was not used here.

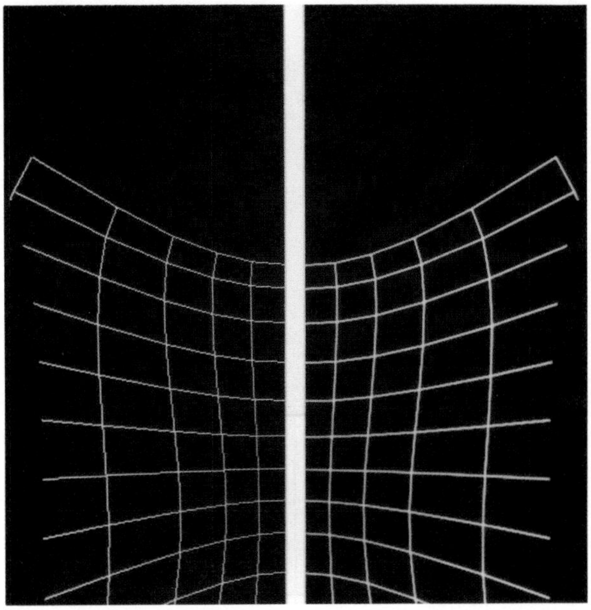

(a) (b)

Figure 10 Simulation of aliased and antialiased parallel line-drawing algorithms by the pipeline:

```
cat symmetric.frm | ... | camera | dc | psim -p 4 4
```

where filter `dc` computes depth-cued colors of lines and filter `psim` simulates a parallel architecture of drawing processors. In this case, the processors were arranged into a 4×4 interleaved pattern with each processor accessing every fourth pixel in every fourth scan line of the raster image. Image (a) shows 1-pixel wide aliased lines; image (b) shows 1½-pixel wide antialiased lines.

Figure 11 A textured room with a view generated by the pipeline:

```
cat cloudy_room.frm | ... | zbuf
```

where filter `zbuf` served as a testbed for experimenting with texturing techniques. In this case, summed-area tables and solid texture functions were employed.

The Reyes Image Rendering Architecture

Robert L. Cook
Loren Carpenter
Edwin Catmull

Pixar
P. O. Box 13719
San Rafael, CA 94913

An architecture is presented for fast high-quality rendering of complex images. All objects are reduced to common world-space geometric entities called micropolygons, and all of the shading and visibility calculations operate on these micropolygons. Each type of calculation is performed in a coordinate system that is natural for that type of calculation. Micropolygons are created and textured in the local coordinate system of the object, with the result that texture filtering is simplified and improved. Visibility is calculated in screen space using stochastic point sampling with a z buffer. There are no clipping or inverse perspective calculations. Geometric and texture locality are exploited to minimize paging and to support models that contain arbitrarily many primitives.

CR CATEGORIES AND SUBJECT DESCRIPTORS: I.3.7 [**Computer Graphics**]: Three-Dimensional Graphics and Realism;

ADDITIONAL KEY WORDS AND PHRASES: image rendering, computer image synthesis, texturing, hidden surface algorithms, z buffer, stochastic sampling

1. Introduction

Reyes is an image rendering system developed at Lucasfilm Ltd. and currently in use at Pixar. In designing Reyes, our goal was an architecture optimized for fast high-quality rendering of complex animated scenes. By fast we mean being able to compute a feature-length film in approximately a year; high-quality means virtually indistinguishable from live action motion picture photography; and complex means as visually rich as real scenes.

This goal was intended to be ambitious enough to force us to completely rethink the entire rendering process. We actively looked for new approaches to image synthesis and consciously tried to avoid limiting ourselves to thinking in terms of traditional solutions or particular computing environments. In the process, we combined some old methods with some new ideas.

Some of the algorithms that were developed for the Reyes architecture have already been discussed elsewhere; these include stochastic sampling [12], distributed ray tracing [10, 13], shade trees [11], and an antialiased depth map shadow algorithm [32]. This paper includes short descriptions of these algorithms as necessary, but the emphasis in this paper is on the overall architecture.

Many of our design decisions are based on some specific assumptions about the types of complex scenes that we want to render and what makes those scenes complex. Since this architecture is optimized for these types of scenes, we begin by examining our assumptions and goals.

- **Model complexity.** We are interested in making images that are visually rich, far more complex than any pictures rendered to date. This goal comes from noticing that even the most complex rendered images look simple when compared to real scenes and that most of the complexity in real scenes comes from rich shapes and textures. We expect that reaching this level of richness will require scenes with hundreds of thousands of geometric primitives, each one of which can be complex.
- **Model diversity.** We want to support a large variety of geometric primitives, especially data amplification primitives such as procedural models, fractals [18], graftals [35], and particle systems [30, 31].
- **Shading complexity.** Because surface reflection characteristics are extremely varied and complex, we consider a programmable shader a necessity. Our experience with such a shader [11] is that realistic surfaces frequently require complex shading and a large number of textures. Textures can store many different types of data, including surface color [8], reflections (environment maps) [3], normal perturbation (bump maps) [4], geometry perturbation (displacement maps) [11], shadows [32], and refraction [25].
- **Minimal ray tracing.** Many non-local lighting effects can be approximated with texture maps. Few objects in natural scenes would seem to require ray tracing. Accordingly, we consider it more important to optimize the architecture for complex geometries and large models than for the non-local lighting effects accounted for by ray tracing or radiosity.
- **Speed.** We are interested in making animated images, and animation introduces severe demands on rendering speed. Assuming 24 frames per second, rendering a 2 hour movie in a year would require a rendering speed of about 3 minutes per frame. Achieving this speed is especially challenging for complex images.
- **Image Quality.** We eschew aliasing and faceting artifacts, such as jagged edges, Moiré patterns in textures, temporal strobing, and highlight aliasing.
- **Flexibility.** Many new image rendering techniques will undoubtedly be discovered in the coming years. The architecture should be flexible enough to incorporate many of these new techniques.

2. Design Principles

These assumptions led us to a set of architectural design principles. Some of these principles are illustrated in the overview in Figure 1.

1. **Natural coordinates.** Each calculation should be done in a coordinate system that is natural for that calculation. For example, texturing is most naturally done in the coordinate system of the local surface geometry (e.g., *uv* space for patches), while the visible surface calculations are most naturally done in pixel coordinates (screen space).
2. **Vectorization.** The architecture should be able to exploit vectorization, parallelism and pipelining. Calculations that are similar should be done together. For example, since the shading calculations are usually similar at all points on a surface, an entire surface should be shaded at the same time.
3. **Common representation.** Most of the algorithm should work with a single type of basic geometric object. We turn every geometric primitive into *micropolygons*, which are flat-shaded subpixel-sized quadrilaterals. All of the shading and visibility calculations are performed exclusively on micropolygons.
4. **Locality.** Paging and data thrashing should be minimized.
   a. **Geometric locality.** Calculations for a geometric primitive should be performed without reference to other geometric primitives. Procedural models should be computed only once and should not be kept in their expanded form any longer than necessary.
   b. **Texture locality.** Only the textures currently needed should be in memory, and textures should be read off the disk only once.
5. **Linearity.** The rendering time should grow linearly with the size of the model.
6. **Large models.** There should be no limit to the number of geometric primitives in a model.
7. **Back door.** There should be a back door in the architecture so that other programs can be used to render some of the objects. This give us a very general way to incorporate any new technique (though not necessarily efficiently).
8. **Texture maps.** Texture map access should be efficient, as we expect to use several textures on every surface. Textures are a powerful tool for defining complex shading characteristics, and displacement maps [11] can be used for model complexity.

We now discuss some of these principles in detail.

2.1. Geometric Locality.

When ray tracing arbitrary surfaces that reflect or refract, a ray in any pixel on the screen might generate a secondary ray to any object in the model. The object hit by the secondary ray can be determined quickly [20,21,34], but that object must then be accessed from the database. As models become more complex, the ability to access any part of the model at any time becomes more expensive; model and texture paging can dominate the rendering time. For this reason, we consider ray tracing algorithms poorly suited for rendering extremely complex environments.

In many instances, though, texture maps can be used to approximate non-local calculations. A common example of this is the use of environment maps [3] for reflection, a good approximation in many cases. Textures have also been used for refractions [25] and shadows [32,36]. Each of these uses of texture maps represents some non-local calculations that we can avoid (principles 4a and 8).

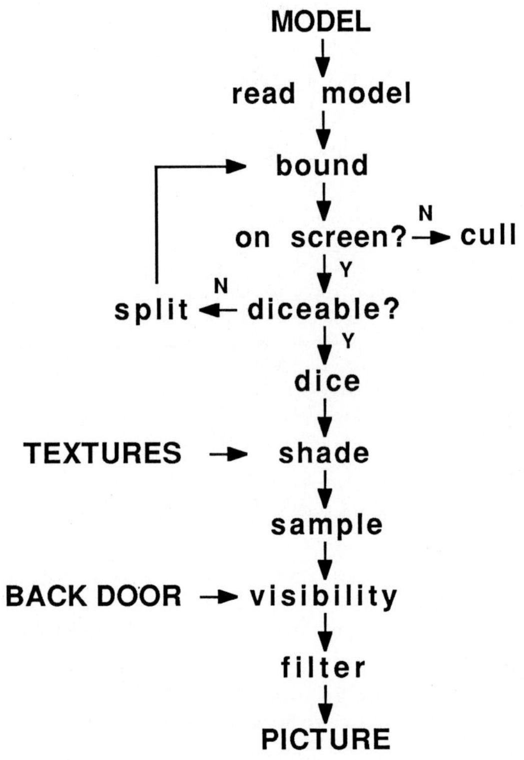

Figure 1. Overview of the algorithm.

2.2. Point sampling.

Point sampling algorithms have many advantages; they are simple, powerful, and work easily with many different types of primitives. But unfortunately, they have been plagued by aliasing artifacts that would make them incompatible with our image quality requirements. Our solution to this problem is a Monte Carlo method called *stochastic sampling*, which is described in detail elsewhere [12]. With stochastic sampling, aliasing is replaced with noise, a less objectionable artifact.

We use a type of stochastic sampling called *jittering* [12]. Pixels are divided into a number of subpixels (typically 16). Each subpixel has exactly one sample point, and the exact location of that sample point within the subpixel is determined by jittering, or adding a random displacement to the location of the center of the subpixel. This jittered location is used to sample micropolygons that overlap the subpixel. The current visibility information for each sample point on the screen is kept in a z buffer [8].

The z buffer is important for two reasons. First, it permits objects to be sent through the rest of the system one at a time (principles 2, 4, 5 and 6). Second, it provides a back door (principle 7); the z buffer can combine point samples from this algorithm with point samples from other algorithms that have capabilities such as ray tracing and radiosity. This is a form of 3-D compositing; it differs from Duff's method [15] in that the compositing is done before filtering the visible samples.

Glossary

CAT	a coherent access texture, in which *s* is a linear function of *u* and *t* is a linear function of *v*.
CSG	constructive solid geometry. Defines objects as the union, intersection, or difference of other objects.
depth complexity	the average number of surfaces (visible or not) at each sample point
dicing	the process of turning geometric primitives into grids of micropolygons.
displacement maps	texture maps used to change the location of points in a grid.
ε plane	a plane parallel to the hither plane that is slightly in front of the eye. The perspective calculation may be unreliable for points not beyond this plane.
eye space	the world space coordinate system rotated and translated so that the eye is at the origin looking down the $+z$ axis. $+x$ is to the right, $+y$ is down.
grid	a two-dimensional array of micropolygons.
geometric locality	the principle that all of the calculations for a geometric primitive should be performed without reference to other geometric primitives.
hither plane	the z=min plane that is the front of the viewing frustum.
jitter	the random perturbation of regularly spaced points for stochastic sampling
micropolygon	the basic geometric object for most of the algorithm, a flat-shaded quadrilateral with an area of about ¼ pixel.
RAT	a random access texture. Any texture that is not a CAT.
s* and *t	parameters used to index a texture map.
screen space	the perspective space in which the x and y values correspond to pixel locations.
shade tree	a method for describing shading calculations [11].
splitting	the process of turning a geometric primitive into one or more new geometric primitives.
stochastic sampling	a Monte Carlo point-sampling method used for antialiasing [12].
texture locality	the principle that each texture should be read off the disk only once.
u* and *v	coordinates of a parametric representation of a surface.
world space	the global right-handed nonperspective coordinate system.
yon plane	the z=max plane that is the back of the viewing frustum.

2.3. Micropolygons.

Micropolygons are the common basic geometric unit of the algorithm (principle 3). They are flat-shaded quadrilaterals that are approximately ½ pixel on a side. Since half a pixel is the Nyquist limit for an image [6, 26], surface shading can be adequately represented with a single color per micropolygon.

Turning a geometric primitive into micropolygons is called *dicing*. Every primitive is diced along boundaries that are in the natural coordinate system of the primitive (principle 1). For example, in the case of patches, micropolygon boundaries are parallel to u and v. The result of dicing is a two-dimensional array of micropolygons called a *grid* (principle 2). Micropolygons require less storage in grid form because vertices shared by adjacent micropolygons are represented only once.

Dicing is done in eye space, with no knowledge of screen space except for an estimate of the primitive's size on the screen. This estimate is used to determine how finely to dice, i.e., how many micropolygons to create. Primitives are diced so that micropolygons are approximately half a pixel on a side in screen space. This adaptive approach is similar to the Lane-Carpenter patch algorithm [22].

The details of dicing depend on the type of primitive. For the example of bicubic patches, screen-space parametric derivatives can be used to determine how finely to dice, and forward differencing techniques can be used for the actual dicing.

All of the micropolygons in a grid are shaded together. Because this shading occurs before the visible surface calculation, at a minimum every piece of every forward-facing on-screen object must be shaded. Thus many shading calculations are performed that are never used. The extra work we do is related to the *depth complexity* of the scene, which is the average number of surfaces at each sample point. We expect pathological cases to be unusual, however, because of the effort required to model a scene. Computer graphics models are like movie sets in that usually only the parts that will be seen are actually built.

There are advantages that offset the cost of this extra shading; the tradeoff depends on the particular scene being rendered. These are some of the advantages to using micropolygons and to shading them before determining visibility:

- **Vectorizable shading.** If an entire surface is shaded at once, and the shading calculations for each point on the surface are similar, the shading operations can be vectorized (principle 2).
- **Texture locality.** Texture requests can be made for large, contiguous blocks of texture that are accessed sequentially. Because shading can be done in object order, the texture map thrashing that occurs in many other algorithms is avoided (principle 4b). This thrashing occurs when texture requests come in small pieces and alternate between several different texture maps. For extremely complex models with lots of textures, this can quickly make a renderer unusable.
- **Texture filtering.** Many of the texture requests are for rectilinear regions of the texture map (principle 1). This is discussed in detail in the next section.
- **Subdivision coherence.** Since an entire surface can be subdivided at once, we can take advantage of efficient techniques such as forward differencing for patch subdivision (principles 1 and 2).
- **Clipping.** Objects never need to be clipped along pixel boundaries, as required by some algorithms.
- **Displacement maps** [11]. Displacement maps are like bump maps [4] except that the location of a surface can be changed as well as its normal, making texture maps a means of modeling surfaces or storing the results of modeling programs. Because displacement maps can change the surface location, they must be computed before the hidden surface calculation. We have no experience with the effects of large displacements on dicing.
- **No perspective.** Because micropolygons are small, there is no need to correct for the perspective distortion of interpolation [24]. Because shading occurs before the perspective transformation, no inverse perspective transformations are required.

2.4. Texture Locality.

For rich, complex images, textures are an important source of information for shading calculations [3, 8]. Textures are usually indexed using two parameters called *u* and *v*. Because *u* and *v* are also used for patch parameters, we will call the texture parameters *s* and *t* to avoid confusion. Surfaces other than patches may also have a natural coordinate system; we will use *u* and *v* for those surface coordinates too.

For many textures, *s* and *t* depend only on the *u* and *v* of the patch and can be determined without knowing the details of the shading calculations. Other textures are accessed with an *s* and *t* that are determined by some more complex calculation. For example, the *s* and *t* for an environment map depend on the normal to the surface (though that normal might in turn depend on a bump map that is indexed by *u* and *v*).

We accordingly divide textures into two classes: *coherent access textures* (CATs) and *random access textures* (RATs). CATs are textures for which s=**a**u+**b** and t=**c**v+**d**, where **a**, **b**, **c**, and **d** are constants. All other textures are RATs. Many CATs have $s=u$ and $t=v$, but we have generalized this relationship to allow for single textures that stretch over more than one patch or repeat multiple times over one patch.

We make this distinction because CATs can be handled much more easily and often significantly faster than RATs. Because *st* order is the same as *uv* order for CATs, we can access the texture map sequentially if we do our shading calculations in *uv* order (principles 1 and 4b). Furthermore, if micropolygons are created so that their vertices have *s* and *t* values that are integer multiples of powers of ½, and if the textures are prefiltered and prescaled and stored as resolution pyramids [36], then no filtering calculations are required at run time, since the pixels in the texture line up exactly with the micropolygons in the grid (principle 1). Figure 2 shows a primitive diced into a 4x4 grid and the corresponding texture map; notice how the marked micropolygon corresponds exactly to the marked texture region because we are dicing along *u* and *v*, the texture's natural coordinate system.

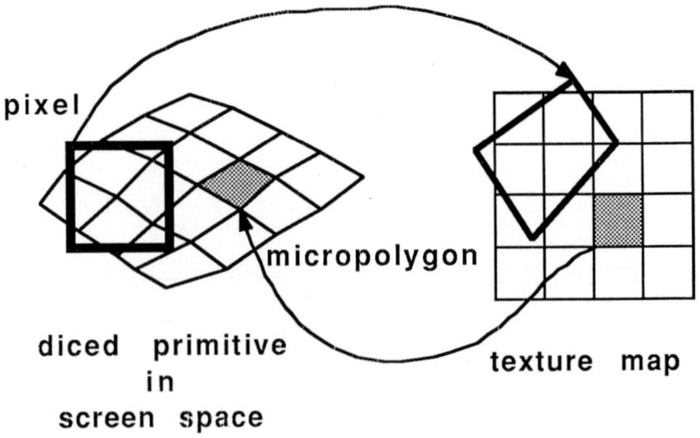

Figure 2. With CATs, micropolygons map exactly to texture map pixels. With the inverse pixel method, pixels map to quadrilateral areas of texture that require filtering.

By contrast, in the more traditional pixel texture access, the pixel boundary is mapped to texture space, where filtering is required. Filtering without a resolution pyramid gives good results but can be expensive [17]. Using a resolution pyramid requires interpolating between two levels of the pyramid, and the filtering is poor [19]. Summed area tables [14] give somewhat better filtering but can have paging problems.

RATs are more general than CATs, but RAT access is slower. RATs can significantly reduce the need for ray tracing. For example, reflections and refractions can frequently be textured onto a surface with environment maps. Environment maps are RATs because they are indexed according to the reflection direction. Another example of a RAT is a decal [2], which is a world-space parallel projection of a texture onto a surface, so that *s* and *t* depend on *x*, *y* and *z* instead of on *u* and *v*.

```
Initialize the z buffer.
For each geometric primitive in the model,
    Read the primitive from the model file
    If the primitive can be bounded,
        Bound the primitive in eye space.
        If the primitive is completely outside of the hither-yon z range, cull it.
        If the primitive spans the ε plane and can be split,
            Mark the primitive undiceable.
        Else
            Convert the bounds to screen space.
            If the bounds are completely outside the viewing frustum, cull the primitive.
    If the primitive can be diced,
        Dice the primitive into a grid of micropolygons.
        Compute normals and tangent vectors for the micropolygons in the grid.
        Shade the micropolygons in the grid.
        Break the grid into micropolygons.
        For each micropolygon,
            Bound the micropolygon in eye space.
            If the micropolygon is outside the hither-yon range, cull it.
            Convert the micropolygon to screen space.
            Bound the micropolygon in screen space.
            For each sample point inside the screen space bound,
                If the sample point is inside the micropolygon,
                    Calculate the z of the micropolygon at the sample point by interpolation.
                    If the z at the sample point is less than the z in the buffer,
                        Replace the sample in the buffer with this sample.
    Else
        Split the primitive into other geometric primitives.
        Put the new primitives at the head of the unread portion of the model file.
Filter the visible sample hits to produce pixels.
Output the pixels.
```

Figure 3. Summary of the algorithm.

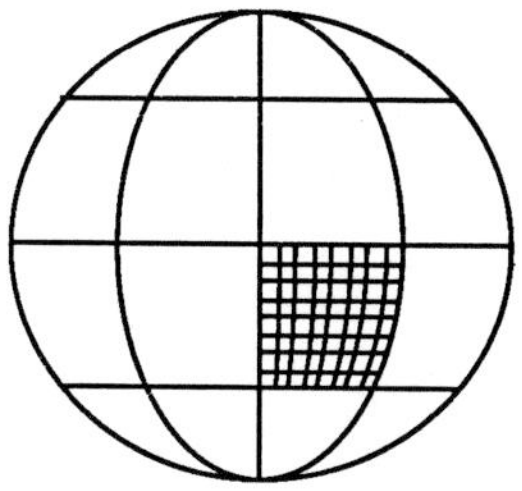

Figure 4a. A sphere is split into patches, and one of the patches is diced into a 8×8 grid of micropolygons.

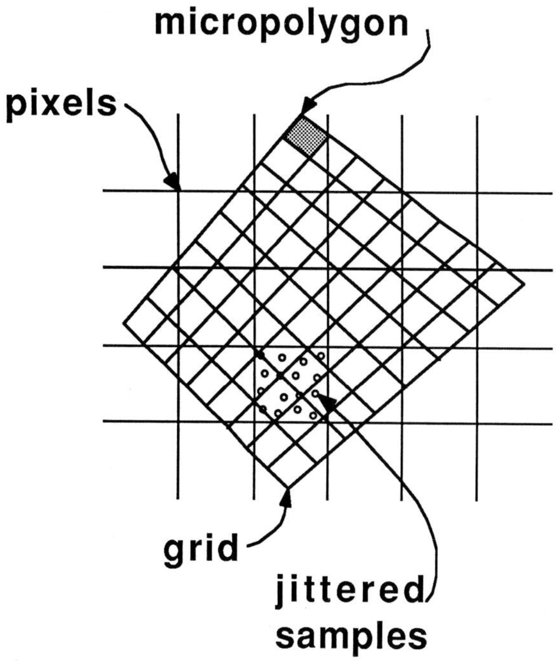

Figure 4b. The micropolygons in the grid are transformed to screen space, where they are stochastically sampled.

3. Description of the Algorithm

The algorithm is summarized in Figure 3. In order to emphasize the basic structure, this description does not include transparency, constructive solid geometry, motion blur, or depth of field. These topics are discussed later.

Each object is turned into micropolygons as it is read in. These micropolygons are shaded, sampled, and compared against the values currently in the *z* buffer. Since only one object is processed at a time, the amount of data needed at any one time is limited and the model can contain arbitrarily many objects.

Primitives are subdivided only in *uv* space, never in screen space. The first part of the algorithm is done in *uv* space and world space, and the second half is done in screen space. After the transformation to screen space, there is never any need to go back to world space or *uv* space, so there are no inverse transformations.

Each type of geometric primitive has the following routines:

- **Bound.** The primitive computes its eye-space bound; its screen-space bound is computed from the eye-space bound. A primitive must be guaranteed to lie inside its bound, and any primitives it is split into must have bounds that also lie inside its bound. The bound does not have to be tight, however. For example, a fractal surface can be bounded if the maximum value of its random number table is known [7, 18]. The fractal will be guaranteed to lie within this bound, but the bound probably will not be very tight. The effect of displacement maps must be considered in the calculation of the bound.
- **Dice.** Not all types of primitives need to be diceable. The only requirement is that each primitive be able to split itself into other primitives, and that this splitting eventually leads to primitives that can all be diced.
- **Split.** A primitive may split itself into one or more primitives of the same type or of different types.
- **Diceable test.** This test determines whether the primitive should be diced or split and returns "diceable" or "not diceable" accordingly. Primitives should be considered not diceable if dicing them would produce a grid with too many micropolygons or a large range of micropolygon sizes.

The bound, split, and dice routines are optional. If the diceable routine ever returns "diceable", the dice routine must exist; if the diceable routine ever returns "not diceable", the split routine must exist. If the bound routine exists, it is used for culling and for determining how finely a primitive should be diced in order to produce micropolygons of the correct size on the screen.

For example, consider one possible set of routines for a sphere. The sphere diceable routine returns "diceable" for small spheres and "not diceable" for large spheres. The sphere dice routine turns a sphere directly into micropolygons. The sphere split routine turns the sphere into 32 patches [16]. The patch dice routine creates a rectangular grid of micropolygons so that the vertices differ in *u* and *v* by integer multiples of powers of ½. This is done to obviate CAT filtering, but in this case it is also necessary for the prevention of patch cracks [9]. Figure 4a shows a sphere being split into patches and one of those patches being diced into an 8x8 grid of micropolygons. Figure 4b shows this grid in screen space with jittered sample locations in one of the pixels.

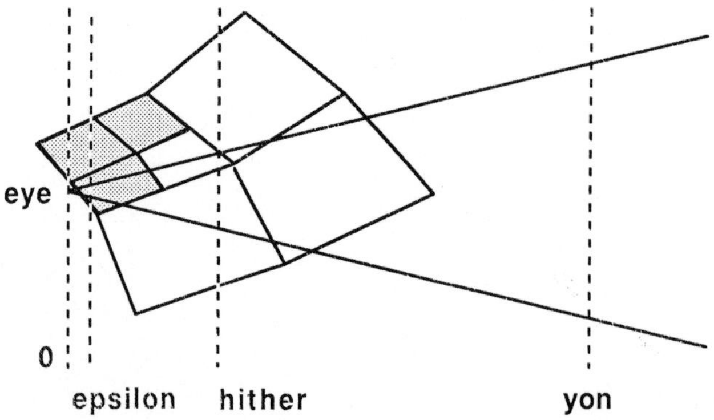

Figure 5. A geometric primitive that spans the ε and hither planes is split until its pieces can be culled or processed. The culled pieces are marked.

This algorithm does not require clipping. The viewing frustum consists of a screen space *xy* range and an eye space hither-yon *z* range. Objects that are known to be completely outside of this region are culled. Objects that are partly inside the frustum and partly outside are kept, shaded and sampled. Regions of these objects that are outside of the viewing frustum in the *x* or *y* directions are never sampled. Regions that are in front of or behind the viewing frustum may be sampled, but their hits are rejected if the sampled surface point lies outside the hither-yon *z* range. Note that if the filter that is used to sample the *z* buffer to produce pixels is wider than a pixel, the viewing frustum must be expanded accordingly because objects that are just off screen can affect pixels on the screen.

Sometimes an object extends from behind the eye to inside the viewing frustum, so that part of the object has an invalid perspective calculation and another part is visible. This situation is traditionally handled by clipping to the hither plane. To avoid clipping, we introduce the *ε plane*, a plane of constant *z* that lies slightly in front of the eye as shown in Figure 5. Points on the $z<\varepsilon$ side of this plane can have an invalid perspective calculation or an unmanageably large screen space *x* and *y* because of the perspective divide. If a primitive spans both the ε plane and the hither plane, it is considered "not diceable" and is split. The resulting pieces are culled if they are entirely outside of the viewing frustum, diced if they lie completely on the $z>\varepsilon$ side of the ε plane, and split again if they span both the ε plane and the hither plane. As long as every primitive can be split, and the splits eventually result in primitives with smaller bounds, then this procedure is guaranteed to terminate successfully. This split-until-cullable procedure obviates clipping. Objects that cannot be bounded can still be protected against bad perspective situations, since micropolygons are created in eye space. Their micropolygons can be culled or be run through a split-until-cullable procedure.

4. Extensions

Since this algorithm was first developed, we have found it easy to add a number of features that were not specifically considered in the original design. These features include motion blur, depth of field, CSG (constructive solid geometry) [1, 33], shadows [32] and a variety of new types of models. The main modification for transparency and CSG calculations is that each sample location in the *z* buffer stores multiple hits. The hits at each sample point are sorted in *z* for the transparency and CSG calculations. Motion blur and depth of field are discussed elsewhere in detail [10, 12, 13]. In the case of motion blur, micropolygons are moved for each sample point to a jittered time associated with that sample. For depth of field, they are moved in *x* and *y* according to a jittered lens location. Both motion blur and depth of field affect the bound calculations; the details are described elsewhere [13].

5. Implementation

We had to make some compromises to implement this algorithm on a general purpose computer, since the algorithm as described so far can require a considerable amount of *z* buffer memory. The screen is divided into rectangular buckets, which may be kept in memory or on disk. In an initial pass, each primitive is bounded and put into the bucket corresponding to the upper left corner of its screen space bound. For the rest of the calculations, the buckets are processed in order, left-to-right and top-to-bottom. First all of the primitives in the bucket are either split or diced; as primitives are diced, their micropolygons are shaded and put into every bucket they overlap. After all of the primitives in a bucket have been split or diced, the micropolygons in that bucket are sampled. Once a bucket is empty, it remains empty, so we only need enough *z* buffer memory for one bucket. The number of micropolygons in memory at any one time can be kept manageable by setting a maximum grid size and forcing primitives to be considered "not diceable" if dicing them would produce too large a grid.

We have implemented this revised version of the algorithm in C and have used it to make a number of animated films, including *The Adventures of André and Wally B.* [27], the stained glass man sequence in *Young Sherlock Holmes* [25], *Luxo Jr.* [28], and *Red's Dream* [29]. The implementation performs reasonably well, considering that the algorithm was designed as a testbed, without any requirement that it would run efficiently in C. For a given shading complexity, the rendering time is proportional to the number of micropolygons (and thus to screen size and to the number of objects).

An example of a image rendered with this program is shown in Figure 6. It is motion blurred, with environment maps for the reflections and shadow depth maps for the shadows [32]. The picture is by John Lasseter and Eben Ostby. It was rendered at 1024x614 pixels, contains 6.8 million micropolygons, has 4 light sources, uses 15 channels of texture, and took about 8 hours of CPU time to compute. Frames in *André* were 512x488 pixels and took less than ½ hour per frame. *Sherlock* frames were 1024x614 and took an hour per frame; *Luxo* frames were 724x434 and took 1½ hours per frame. Statistics on *Red's Dream* frames are not available yet. All of these CPU times are for a CCI 6/32, which is 4-6 times faster than a VAX 11/780.

Figure 6. 1986 Pixar Christmas Card by John Lasseter and Eben Ostby.

6. Discussion

This approach has certain disadvantages. Because shading occurs before sampling, the shading cannot be calculated for the specific time of each sample and thus cannot be motion blurred correctly. Shading after sampling would have advantages if the coherency features could be retained; this is an area of future research. Although any primitive that can be scan-converted can be turned into micropolygons, this process is more difficult for some primitives, such as blobs [5]. The bucket-sort version requires bounds on the primitives to perform well, and some primitives such as particle systems are difficult to bound. No attempt is made to take advantage of coherence for large simply-shaded surfaces; every object is turned into micropolygons. Polygons in general do not have a natural coordinate system for dicing. This is fine in our case, because bicubic patches are our most common primitive, and we hardly ever use polygons.

On the other hand, our approach also has a number of advantages. Much of the calculation in traditional approaches goes away completely. There are no inversion calculations, such as projecting pixel corners onto a patch to find normals and texture values. There are no clipping calculations. Many of the calculations can be vectorized, such as the the shading and surface normal calculations. Texture thrashing is avoided, and in many instances textures require no run time filtering. Most of the calculations are done on a simple common representation (micropolygons).

This architecture is designed for rendering exceedingly complex models, and the disadvantages and advantages listed above reflect the tradeoffs made with this goal in mind.

Acknowledgements

Thanks to Bill Reeves, Eben Ostby, David Salesin, and Sam Leffler, all of whom contributed to the C implementation of this algorithm. Conversations with Mark Leather, Adam Levinthal, Jeff Mock, and Lane Molpus were very productive. Charlie Gunn implemented a version of this algorithm in *chas*, the assembly language for the Pixar Chap SIMD processor [23]. Paul Heckbert helped analyze the texture quality, and Ricki Blau studied the performance of the C implementation.

References

1. ATHERTON, PETER R., "A Scanline Hidden Surface Removal Procedure for Constructive Solid Geometry," *Computer Graphics (SIGGRAPH '83 Proceedings)* **17**(3), pp. 73-82 (July 1983).
2. BARR, ALAN H., "Decal Projections," in *SIGGRAPH '84 Developments in Ray Tracing course notes* (July 1984).
3. BLINN, JAMES F. AND MARTIN E. NEWELL, "Texture and Reflection in Computer Generated Images," *Communications of the ACM* **19**(10), pp. 542-547 (October 1976).
4. BLINN, JAMES F., "Simulation of Wrinkled Surfaces," *Computer Graphics (SIGGRAPH '78 Proceedings)* **12**(3), pp. 286-292 (August 1978).
5. BLINN, JAMES F., "A Generalization of Algebraic Surface Drawing," *ACM Transactions on Graphics* **1**(3), pp. 235-256 (July 1982).
6. BRACEWELL, RONALD N., *The Fourier Transform and Its Applications,* McGraw-Hill, New York (1978).
7. CARPENTER, LOREN, "Computer Rendering of Fractal Curves and Surfaces," *Computer Graphics (SIGGRAPH '80 Proceedings)* **14**(3), pp. 9-15, Special Issue (July 1980).
8. CATMULL, EDWIN E., "A Subdivision Algorithm for Computer Display of Curved Surfaces," Phd dissertation, University of Utah, Salt Lake City (December 1974).
9. CLARK, JAMES H., "A Fast Algorithm for Rendering Parametric Surfaces," *Computer Graphics (SIGGRAPH '79 Proceedings)* **13**(2), pp. 7-12, Special Issue (August 1979).
10. COOK, ROBERT L., THOMAS PORTER, AND LOREN CARPENTER, "Distributed Ray Tracing," *Computer Graphics (SIGGRAPH '84 Proceedings)* **18**(3), pp. 137-145 (July 1984).
11. COOK, ROBERT L., "Shade Trees," *Computer Graphics (SIGGRAPH '84 Proceedings)* **18**(3), pp. 223-231 (July 1984).
12. COOK, ROBERT L., "Stochastic Sampling in Computer Graphics," *ACM Transactions on Graphics* **5**(1), pp. 51-72 (January 1986).

13. COOK, ROBERT L., "Practical Aspects of Distributed Ray Tracing," in *SIGGRAPH '86 Developments in Ray Tracing course notes* (August 1986).

14. CROW, FRANKLIN C., "Summed-Area Tables for Texture Mapping," *Computer Graphics (SIGGRAPH '84 Proceedings)* **18**(3), pp. 207-212 (July 1984).

15. DUFF, TOM, "Compositing 3-D Rendered Images," *Computer Graphics (SIGGRAPH '85 Proceedings)* **19**(3), pp. 41-44 (July 1985).

16. FAUX, I. D. AND M. J. PRATT, *Computational Geometry for Design and Manufacture,* Ellis Horwood Ltd., Chichester, England (1979).

17. FEIBUSH, ELIOT, MARC LEVOY, AND ROBERT L. COOK, "Synthetic Texturing Using Digital Filtering," *Computer Graphics* **14**(3), pp. 294-301 (July 1980).

18. FOURNIER, ALAIN, DON FUSSELL, AND LOREN CARPENTER, "Computer Rendering of Stochastic Models," *Communications of the ACM* **25**(6), pp. 371-384 (June 1982).

19. HECKBERT, PAUL S., "Survey of Texture Mapping," *IEEE Computer Graphics and Applications* (November 1986).

20. KAPLAN, MICHAEL R., "Space-Tracing, A Constant Time Ray-Tracer," in *SIGGRAPH '85 State of the Art in Image Synthesis seminar notes* (July 1985).

21. KAY, TIMOTHY L. AND JAMES T. KAJIYA, "Ray Tracing Complex Scenes," *Computer Graphics (SIGGRAPH '86 Proceedings)* **20**(4), pp. 269-278 (Aug. 1986).

22. LANE, JEFFREY M., LOREN C. CARPENTER, TURNER WHITTED, AND JAMES F. BLINN, "Scan Line Methods for Displaying Parametrically Defined Surfaces," *Communications of the ACM* **23**(1), pp. 23-34 (January 1980).

23. LEVINTHAL, ADAM AND THOMAS PORTER, "Chap - A SIMD Graphics Processor," *Computer Graphics (SIGGRAPH '84 Proceedings)* **18**(3), pp. 77-82 (July 1984).

24. NEWMAN, WILLIAM M. AND ROBERT F. SPROULL, *Principles of Interactive Computer Graphics (2nd ed.),* McGraw-Hill, New York (1979). pp. 361-363

25. PARAMOUNT PICTURES CORPORATION, *Young Sherlock Holmes,* Stained glass man sequence by Pixar and Lucasfilm Ltd. 1985.

26. PEARSON, D. E., *Transmission and Display of Pictorial Information,* Pentech Press, London (1975).

27. PIXAR, *The Adventures of André and Wally B.*, July 1984.

28. PIXAR, *Luxo Jr.*, July 1986.

29. PIXAR, *Red's Dream,* July 1987.

30. REEVES, WILLIAM T., "Particle Systems – A Technique for Modeling a Class of Fuzzy Objects," *ACM Transactions on Graphics* **2**(2), pp. 91-108 (April 1983).

31. REEVES, WILLIAM T. AND RICKI BLAU, "Approximate and Probabilistic Algorithms for Shading and Rendering Structured Particle Systems," *Computer Graphics (SIGGRAPH '85 Proceedings)* **19**(3), pp. 313-322 (July 1985).

32. REEVES, WILLIAM T., DAVID H. SALESIN, AND ROBERT L. COOK, "Shadowing with Texture Maps," *Computer Graphics (SIGGRAPH '87 Proceedings)* **21** (July 1987).

33. ROTH, S. D., "Ray Casting for Modeling Solids," *Computer Graphics and Image Processing*(18), pp. 109-144 (1982).

34. RUBIN, STEVEN M. AND TURNER WHITTED, "A 3-Dimensional Representation for Fast Rendering of Complex Scenes," *Computer Graphics (SIGGRAPH '80 Proceedings)* **14**(3), pp. 110-116 (July 1980).

35. SMITH, ALVY RAY, "Plants, Fractals, and Formal Languages," *Computer Graphics (SIGGRAPH '84 Proceedings)* **18**(3), pp. 1-10 (July 1984).

36. WILLIAMS, LANCE, "Pyramidal Parametrics," *Computer Graphics (SIGGRAPH '83 Proceedings)* **17**(3), pp. 1-11 (July 1983).

Accurate Triangulations of Deformed, Intersecting Surfaces

Brian Von Herzen
Alan H. Barr
California Institute of Technology
Pasadena, CA 91125

Abstract

A quadtree algorithm is developed to triangulate deformed, intersecting parametric surfaces. The biggest problem with adaptive sampling is to guarantee that the triangulation is accurate within a given tolerance. A new method guarantees the accuracy of the triangulation, given a "Lipschitz" condition on the surface definition. The method constructs a hierarchical set of bounding volumes for the surface, useful for ray tracing and solid modeling operations. The task of adaptively sampling a surface is broken into two parts: a subdivision mechanism for recursively subdividing a surface, and a set of subdivision criteria for controlling the subdivision process.

An adaptive sampling technique is said to be robust if it accurately represents the surface being sampled. A new type of quadtree, called a *restricted quadtree*, is more robust than the traditional unrestricted quadtree at adaptive sampling of parametric surfaces. Each sub-region in the quadtree is half the width of the previous region. The restricted quadtree requires that adjacent regions be the same width within a factor of two, while the traditional quadtree makes no restriction on neighbor width. Restricted surface quadtrees are effective at recursively sampling a parametric surface. Quadtree samples are concentrated in regions of high curvature, and along intersection boundaries, using several subdivision criteria. Silhouette subdivision improves the accuracy of the silhouette boundary when a viewing transformation is available at sampling time. The adaptive sampling method is more robust than uniform sampling, and can be more efficient at rendering deformed, intersecting parametric surfaces.

Categories and Subject Descriptors: I.3.5 [Computer Graphics]: Computational Geometry and Object Modeling- curve, surface, solid, and object representations; geometric algorithms, languages and systems; J.6 [Computer Applications]: Computer-Aided Engineering- computer-aided manufacturing (CAM).

General Terms: Algorithms

Additional Key Words and Phrases: Restricted quadtrees, adaptive sampling of parametric surfaces.

Introduction

Motivation for Studying Surface Sampling Techniques

Interesting mathematical formulations for deformed surfaces have recently been developed [BARR84], [SEDERBERG86]. Robust and efficient algorithms for rendering these surfaces, however, do not currently exist. We need to correctly render highly curved regions on deformed surfaces. In addition, we must accurately render such critical areas as silhouette boundaries and surface intersections.

The simplest sampling algorithm covers a surface with a parametrically uniform grid of samples, and divides the surface into small polygons that are easy to render. Frequently, aliasing occurs in highly curved regions, due to the constant sampling rate. Regions of low curvature are oversampled, wasting polygons.

An alternative approach is to concentrate samples where they are needed the most. A quadtree subdivision technique is presented here that concentrates samples in regions of high curvature and in other critical regions. The technique is more robust than uniform sampling of parametric surfaces, and is more efficient for the examples given here.

With uniform sampling, a trade-off must be made between image quality and number of polygons in representing parametric surfaces. Adaptive sampling can produce better images with fewer polygons than the uniform sampling approach. The uniform chain in Figure 1 shows an image that took 53 minutes on an IBM 4341 using uniform sampling, because most of the time was spent on small regions of the image. The nearest link is not sampled adequately, as compared with the quadtree image of the same object, which took 45 minutes to compute, as shown in Figure 2. The CPU times represent the time required to sample complex bending and twisting deformation functions of parametric primitives for nearly 100,000 sample points.

Background

Quadtree algorithms have been developed for screen space and parametric space applications. Quadtrees have been used to rasterize polygons [WARNOCK69]. Quadtree subdivision in screen space has been used as an antialiasing technique in ray tracing [WHITTED80]. Bicubic patches have been rendered using recursive subdivision techniques in the parametric space of the surface [CATMULL75], [CARLSON82], [SCHWEITZER82]. Lane and Riesenfeld [LANE80] describe a method for the display and intersection of piecewise polynomial surfaces. Lane and Carpenter [LANE79] describe a recursive technique for sampling parametric surfaces using a curvature subdivision criterion. Scan-line techniques have been used to render a variety of parametric surfaces [BLINN78]. Adaptive subdivision has been used for fitting surfaces to sampled data [SCHMITT86].

It is often attractive when ray-tracing complex surfaces to break them into triangles before rendering [BARR86], [KAY86], [SNYDER87]. The memory required for such a decomposition varies directly with the number of triangles. Adaptive subdivision greatly reduces the number of triangles needed to accurately describe a surface. In addition, a new application of

Figure 1: Uniform chain, 60,000 polygons, sampling time 53 minutes.

Figure 2: Quadtree chain, 50,000 polygons, sampling time 45 minutes.

the Lipschitz condition to parametric surfaces can guarantee the accuracy of polygonal approximations.

A new type of quadtree, the *restricted quadtree,* is described here for subdividing a surface. Restricted quadtrees differ from unrestricted quadtrees in that neighboring squares may differ in width by at most a factor of two. While the unrestricted quadtree does not reliably follow features such as the local maximum of the curve in Figure 3, the restricted quadtree is much more robust at adequately sampling curves and surfaces. An efficient set of subdivision criteria control the sampling process for rendering deformed, intersecting surfaces. Several subdivision criteria are examined, including curvature subdivision, intersection subdivision, and potential intersection subdivision. A view-dependent subdivision criterion causes subdivision at the silhouette boundary from a given viewpoint. Each region is subdivided if any of the subdivision criteria are not met. Regions of low curvature are represented with a few relatively large polygons, while regions of high curvature are represented with many little polygons.

Bounding Volumes for Parametric Surfaces

Given a continuous parametric surface, we will show how to construct bounding volumes that contain the surface. Bounding volumes are useful for intersection operations, for collision detection, for ray tracing parametric surfaces, and for triangulating a parametric surface accurately.

The ideal method guarantees that each part of the surface remains within its bounding volume. The task is impossible, however, if we are given a completely arbitrary parametric surface and no additional information. We know what the function values are, wherever we have sampled the surface. There is no way to guarantee what the function is doing where we haven't sampled, if the samples are the only information available to us. With a single additional value, however, called a Lipschitz constant, we can bound the surface.

The Lipschitz Condition for a Parametric Curve

First we define the Lipschitz condition for a parametric curve $\mathbf{F}(u)$ over a domain $0 \le u \le 1$ (Figure 4) [LIN74]. The Lipschitz condition states that

$$| \mathbf{F}(u_1) - \mathbf{F}(u_0) | \le K | u_1 - u_0 | ,$$

where K is the Lipschitz constant, and u_0 and u_1 are in the interval $0 \le u_i \le 1$. The Lipschitz constant bounds the maximum parametric derivative of the function $\mathbf{F}(u)$: $|d\mathbf{F}/du| \le K$. Consider a value u_2 between u=0 and u=1. We have

$$| \mathbf{F}(u_2) - \mathbf{F}(u{=}0) | \le K | u_2 - (u{=}0) |, \quad \text{and}$$
$$| \mathbf{F}(u{=}1) - \mathbf{F}(u_2) | \le K | (u{=}1) - u_2 |.$$

Adding the equations,

$$| \mathbf{F}(u_2) - \mathbf{F}(u{=}0) | + | \mathbf{F}(u{=}1) - \mathbf{F}(u_2) | \le Ku_2 + K(1 - u_2) = K.$$

We take the limiting case:

$$d_1 + d_2 = K, \qquad d1 = | \mathbf{F}(u_2) - \mathbf{F}(u{=}0) |, \qquad d2 = | \mathbf{F}(u{=}1) - \mathbf{F}(u_2) |.$$

The solution of the equation is an ellipsoid with foci $\mathbf{F}(u{=}0)$ and $\mathbf{F}(u{=}1)$ such that the sum of the distances from the foci to any point on the ellipsoid is equal to K. We basically have a string of fixed length, tied at both ends to the points $\mathbf{F}(u{=}0)$ and $\mathbf{F}(u{=}1)$.

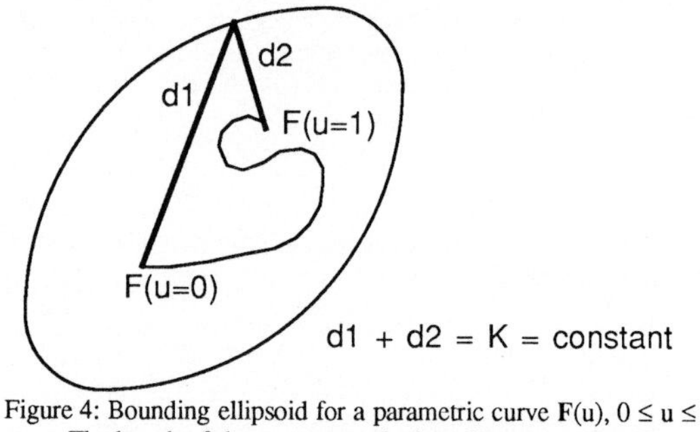

Figure 4: Bounding ellipsoid for a parametric curve $\mathbf{F}(u)$, $0 \le u \le 1$. The length of the curve must be less than or equal to K.

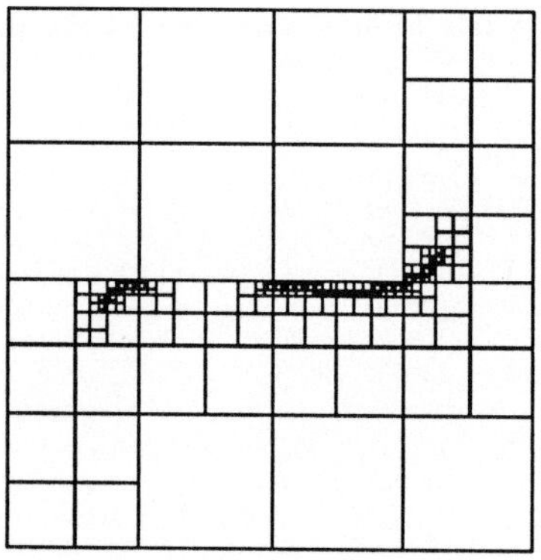

Figure 3a: An unrestricted quadtree omits the local maximum in a curve.

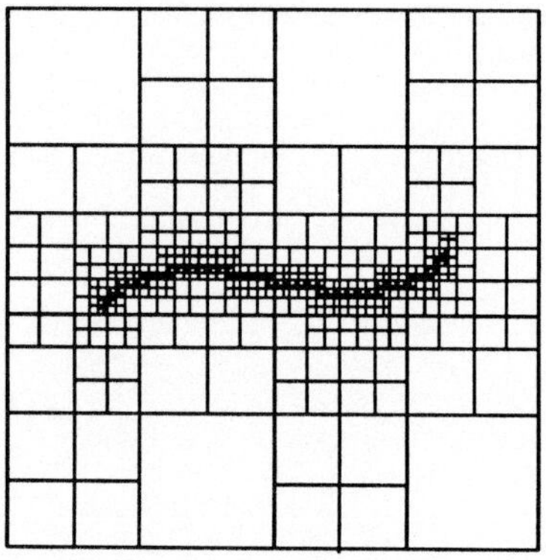

Figure 3b: A *restricted quadtree* adequately samples the same cubic curve.

The Lipschitz Condition for a Parametric Surface
Now we extend the result to parametric surfaces of two variables, **F**(u, v). The Lipschitz condition on a parametric surface **F(P)** over a domain **P**=(u,v) is defined by:

$$| \mathbf{F}(\mathbf{P}_1) - \mathbf{F}(\mathbf{P}_0) | \le K | \mathbf{P}_1 - \mathbf{P}_0 |,$$

where $\mathbf{P}_0$ and $\mathbf{P}_1$ are any two points in the parametric space of the surface, and K is the Lipschitz constant. The constant K determines a maximum distance between two points in modeling space, given the distance of the two points in parameter space. We use the L_2 norm for the Lipschitz equation: $\|\Delta V\|_2 = (\Delta x^2 + \Delta y^2 + \Delta z^2)^{1/2}$.

$$\| \mathbf{F}(\mathbf{P}_1) - \mathbf{F}(\mathbf{P}_0) \|_2 \le K \| \mathbf{P}_1 - \mathbf{P}_0 \|_2.$$

The L_2 norm represents the Euclidean distance between any two point in the plane or in three-space. In contrast, the L_1 norm represents the sum of perpendicular distances between any points in the plane or in three-space. The L_1 norm is given by $\|\Delta V\|_1 = |\Delta x| + |\Delta y| + |\Delta z|$, and we always have $\|\Delta V\|_2 \le \|\Delta V\|_1$, since the shortest distance between any two points falls along a straight line. Therefore we can use the L2 norm in modeling space and the L1 norm in parametric space:

$$\| \mathbf{F}(\mathbf{P}_1) - \mathbf{F}(\mathbf{P}_0) \|_2 \le K \| \mathbf{P}_1 - \mathbf{P}_0 \|_2 \le K \| \mathbf{P}_1 - \mathbf{P}_0 \|_1.$$

The L_1 norm is attractive because the distance from $\mathbf{P}_0$ to $\mathbf{P}_1$ via **P** is independent of **P** (Fig. 5).

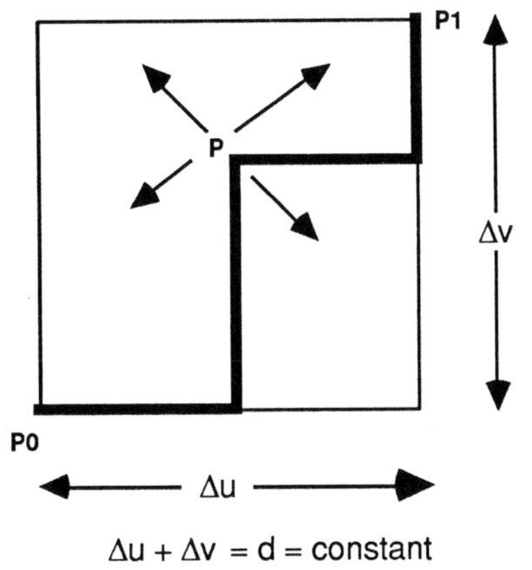

Figure 5: L_1 distance from $\mathbf{P}_0$ to $\mathbf{P}_1$ via **P**. The L_1 distance **d** is independent of **P**.

We evaluate the Lipschitz condition from $\mathbf{P}_0$ to **P** and from **P** to $\mathbf{P}_1$, where **P** is anywhere in the rectangle formed by opposite corners $\mathbf{P}_0$ and $\mathbf{P}_1$:

$$\| \mathbf{F}(\mathbf{P}) - \mathbf{F}(\mathbf{P}_0) \|_2 \le K \| \mathbf{P} - \mathbf{P}_0 \|_1,$$
$$\| \mathbf{F}(\mathbf{P}_1) - \mathbf{F}(\mathbf{P}) \|_2 \le K \| \mathbf{P}_1 - \mathbf{P} \|_1.$$

Adding the two equations,

$$\|\mathbf{F}(\mathbf{P}) - \mathbf{F}(\mathbf{P}_0)\|_2 + \|\mathbf{F}(\mathbf{P}_1) - \mathbf{F}(\mathbf{P})\|_2 \le K \|\mathbf{P} - \mathbf{P}_0\|_1 + K \|\mathbf{P}_1 - \mathbf{P}\|_1.$$

Taking the limiting case,

$$d_1 + d_2 = K((u-u_0) + (v-v_0)) + K((u_1 - u) + (v_1 - v)) = C,$$
$$d_1 + d_2 = C,$$

where $d_1 = \|\mathbf{F}(\mathbf{P}) - \mathbf{F}(\mathbf{P}_0)\|_2$, $d_2 = \|\mathbf{F}(\mathbf{P}_1) - \mathbf{F}(\mathbf{P})\|_2$, and $C = K((u_1 - u_0) + (v_1 - v_0))$.

The solution of the equation is an ellipsoid with foci $F(\mathbf{P}_0)$ and $F(\mathbf{P}_1)$ such that the sum of the distances from the foci to any point on the ellipsoid is equal to C. We again have a string of fixed length, tied at both ends to the points $\mathbf{F}(\mathbf{P}_0)$ and $\mathbf{F}(\mathbf{P}_1)$ (Figure 6).

We now have a mechanism for enclosing any region or subregion of the parametric surface in a bounding ellipsoid. Given a quadtree that spans the parametric domain of a surface (a *surface quadtree*), every region of the quadtree has a bounding ellipsoid that encloses it. The same hierarchy used in the quadtree may be used to construct a hierarchy of bounding volumes

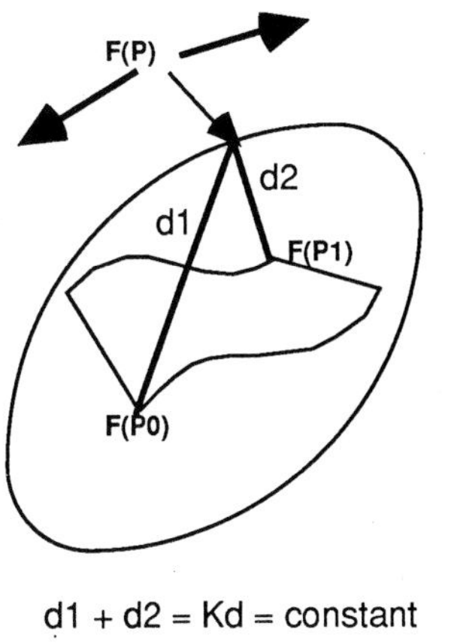

Figure 6: Bounding ellipsoid for the parametric surface **F**(**P**).

[KAY86]. The hierarchy of bounding volumes is useful for ray tracing, for collision detection, and for guaranteeing the accuracy of a triangulation. Each region in a surface quadtree has a maximum error based on its bounding ellipsoid. Given a desired error tolerance, we can subdivide the regions until the tolerance is reached. We obtain an arbitrarily accurate sampling of the surface.

Determining the Lipschitz Constant
The Lipschitz constant may be derived directly from the parametric equation, by taking the global maximum of the parametric derivatives of the surface. If the surface is differentiable, we can use the parametric derivatives to obtain the Lipschitz constant K:

$$K \ge \max\left[\left|\frac{\partial F(u,v)}{\partial u}\right| + \left|\frac{\partial F(u,v)}{\partial v}\right| \right], \quad 0 \le u \le 1, \quad 0 \le v \le 1.$$

The technique is feasible for surfaces such as bicubics, superquadrics, and low order polynomials, because local maxima are easy to find in the parametric derivatives of these functions. If the surface is piecewise differentiable, then the maximum derivative of each of the pieces may be used. If the user does not require a guarantee about the bounding volume, then the Lipschitz constant may be estimated from samples and path lengths.

A Recursive Subdivision Mechanism

The problem of rendering deformed, intersecting surfaces is split into two subproblems: 1) the *subdivision mechanism*, determining how to subdivide a surface into simple elements; 2) the *subdivision criteria*, determining where additional sampling is necessary. Here we examine the recursive subdivision mechanism for adaptively sampling a set of surfaces.

An ideal recursive subdivision mechanism should smoothly adjust the sampling frequency over the parametric surface, adapting to variable sampling requirements. A quadtree technique is one approach for a subdivision mechanism. The parametric (u, v) space of a surface is broken into a set of regions. Whenever more accuracy is needed in the surface quadtree, a region is divided into four smaller regions. Samples are obtained at the corners of each region.

Figure 7: Uniformly sampled sphere.

Figure 9: Quadtree sphere.

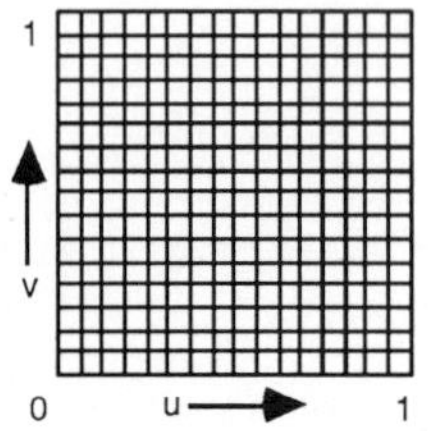

Figure 8: Parametric space of the uniform sphere.

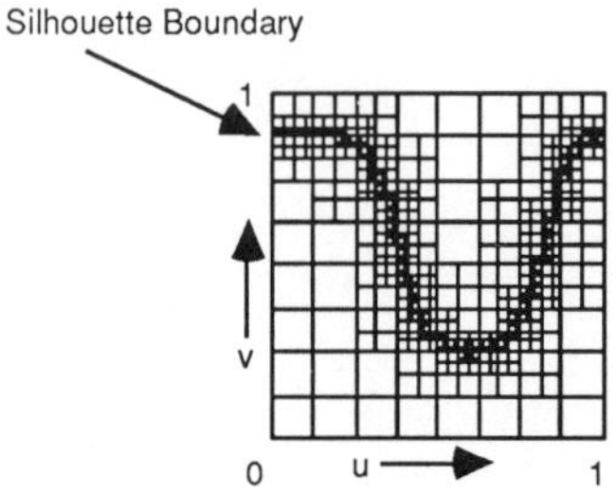

Figure 10: Parametric space of the quadtree sphere.

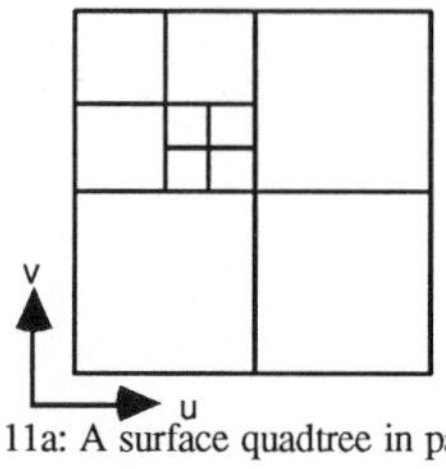

Figure 11a: A surface quadtree in parametric space.

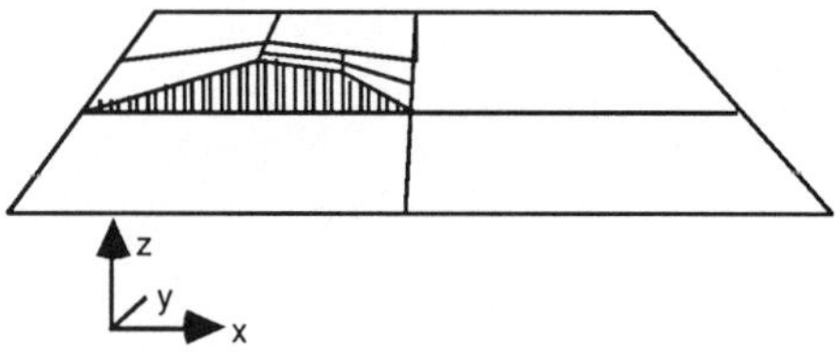

Figure 11b: Cracks in the surface quadtree in modeling space.

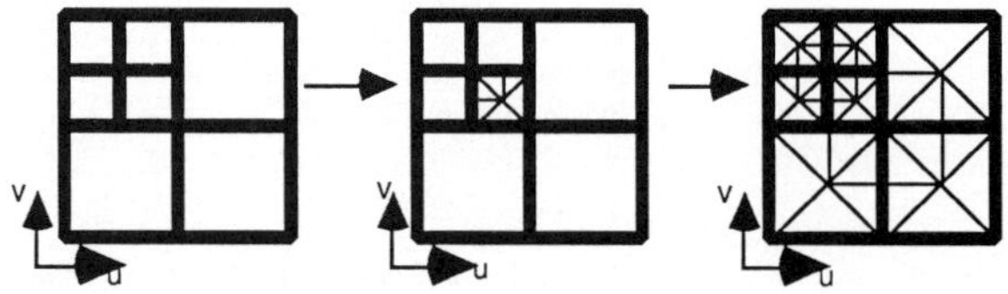

Figure 12: Transforming a restricted quadtree into a triangular subdivision.

Basic Approach

The subdivision technique uses the following steps:

1. The surface is sampled on a uniform parametric grid at some initial resolution.
2. Each region is evaluated using several acceptance criteria.
3. If the region isn't acceptable, then it is split into four smaller regions.
4. Steps 2. and 3. are repeated until the entire surface is sampled adequately.
5. The regions are broken into triangles.
6. The triangles are clipped at the intersection with other surfaces, forming a smooth boundary.
7. The triangles are rendered.

Figure 7 shows a uniformly sampled sphere. Lines are drawn on the surface of the sphere to show how it has been broken into polygons. The surface has been sampled at the corner of each square. The north pole has more samples than necessary. Figure 8 shows the parametric space (u, v) of the sphere.

Figure 9 shows a sphere sampled using the quadtree technique. Squares have been concentrated along the boundary of the sphere as seen from the point of view in Figure 9, and reduced in the middle and on the back side of the sphere. Figure 10 shows the parametric space of the sphere. The sinusoidal line of small squares represents the silhouette boundary of the sphere, where more samples are needed to reduce visual artifacts of the sampling process. The north pole of the sphere has fewer samples than with uniform subdivision.

Data Structure for Quadtrees

The quadtree consists of pointers to regions arranged in a hierarchy that tessellate the parametric space of the surface. Samet describes basic data structures and access procedures for quadtrees [SAMET82], [SAMET84]. We attach a parametric sample to the standard quadtree data structure at the corner of each quadtree region. Several regions access the same corner sample, so the samples are stored in a two-dimensional bucket array for easy access.

Quadrilaterals vs. Triangles

Care must be taken in creating a polygon mesh from a quadtree. Adjacent squares in a quadtree frequently vary in size. Since the corners of these adjacent squares do not always match up, cracks appear in the surface wherever small squares adjoin larger squares (see Figure 11: Cracks in a surface quadtree). To eliminate cracks, it is necessary to construct a *planar subdivision* of the parametric space [KIRKPATRICK83]. A planar subdivision is a collection of line segments that intersect only at segment endpoints. A *triangular subdivision* (see Figure 12) is a planar subdivision containing only triangles. Although a quadtree is not a planar subdivision, since corners touch edges, a triangular subdivision may be constructed from the quadtree, as shown in the next section.

Restricted Quadtrees

The adaptive sampling process relies on the limited sampling information available to decide whether to obtain additional samples. One indication to subdivide is that the neighboring regions have subdivided for some reason.

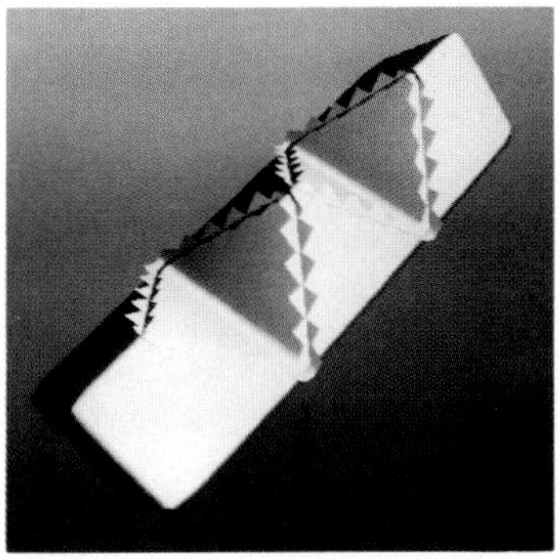

Figure 13: Uniform sampling without triangle clipping.

Figure 14: Quadtree sampling with triangle clipping.

A new type of quadtree, called a *restricted quadtree*, propagates the subdivision information to neighbors.

The rule about restricted quadtrees is that neighboring regions must be within one level of each other in the quadtree hierarchy (Figure 3). Regions that share an edge are considered neighbors. Regions that only share a corner are not considered neighbors. The rule prevents sudden changes in the sampling rate over a surface. Artifacts associated with the change in sampling rate are minimized. Restricted quadtrees concentrate samples near important features, making the algorithm more robust. The robustness of curve-finding algorithms is improved as well.

Figure 3 shows the difference between an unrestricted quadtree and a restricted quadtree sampling near a cubic curve. The squares subdivide only if their corners span the cubic curve. The unrestricted quadtree misses a large portion of the curve, but the restricted quadtree is much more robust at exploring the complete curve.

A square in a restricted quadtree is decomposed into triangles using a simple rule. Every square is broken into eight triangles, or two triangles per edge, unless the edge borders a larger square. In that case a single triangle is formed along the edge (see Figure 12).

Neighbor-Finding Algorithm
An efficient technique exists for finding neighbors in a quadtree [SAMET82]. The algorithm finds the nearest common ancestor between a square and its neighbor, and requires an average of four node traversals of the quadtree, for quadtrees of arbitrary size. The algorithm is used to maintain the restricted quadtree, and to triangulate the quadtree. Alternatively, the neighbors may be explicitly stored with pointers at each square, which requires additional memory.

Parametric Space Wrap-Around
For closed parametric surfaces such as a sphere, the east boundary must match the west boundary exactly. Otherwise cracks may appear at the "date line." The neighbor-finding algorithm may be extended at parametric boundaries. We define squares on the west edge of the quadtree to be neighbors of squares on the east edge of the quadtree. For toroids, the squares on the north edge of the quadtree are neighbors of squares on the south edge of the quadtree. The seam at the parametric boundary is eliminated by forming a triangular subdivision across the boundary.

Triangle Clipping
After the squares of the quadtree are broken into triangles, the triangles are tested against inside-outside functions of other surfaces, and are clipped at the intersection boundary. The clipping removes the ragged appearance that otherwise occurs (Figure 13: Uniform sampling of a puzzle piece without triangle clipping). Figure 14 shows the effects of clipping boundary triangles and quadtree sampling. The technique dramatically improves the quality of the images.

Recursive Subdivision Criteria

A set of recursive subdivision criteria is needed to determine where subdivision should occur. The philosophy of the method is to mathematically measure the visible "badness" of each part of the surface, and subdivide until a prescribed tolerance is reached. The criteria should include a method to detect surface curvature, and to locate silhouette and surface intersection boundaries.

We use three coordinate systems here: (u, v) parametric space, (x, y, z) modeling space, and (X, Y) screen space. Parametric space spans the domain of the parametric surface. The surface is embedded in three-dimensional modeling space. Screen space uses a viewing transformation to project modeling space coordinates onto the image plane. Screen space is useful for determining the visual size of a feature when a model is resampled each frame of an animation [BARR86].

The recursive sampling process is started with a coarse initial grid of samples. The grid provides basic information about the surface to make decisions about further subdivision. The following criteria control the subdivision process:

"Curvature" Subdivision
Curvature subdivision estimates the local curvature of an object. Where the curvature is high, a region is subdivided. The subdivision process terminates when a region becomes sufficiently planar. Curvature estimation may be performed in several ways. Lane and Carpenter[LANE79] measure the distance from a surface to its planar approximation. Alternatively, normal vectors may be computed approximately or analytically from the equation for the surface. Normal vectors are used here, since they are computed anyway for shading computations. A simple vector equation of these normals provides a curvature subdivision criterion. Every adjacent pair of normal vectors ($\mathbf{N}_1$, $\mathbf{N}_2$) of a region must satisfy $(1 - \mathbf{N}_1 . \mathbf{N}_2) < \varepsilon$, where ε is determined empirically by adjusting ε until the image quality is satisfactory. The normal vectors are normalized to unit length. Subdivision stops if the region is smaller than a pixel. The actual curvature κ is given by $\kappa = (d\theta/dx)$, where θ is an angle and x is a distance. The normal vector estimation $(1 - \mathbf{N}_1 . \mathbf{N}_2)$ computes a term proportional to $(\Delta\theta)^2$, where $\Delta\theta$ is the change in θ across the region.

Tangent vectors must pass the same curvature test, $(1 - \mathbf{T}_1 . \mathbf{T}_2) < \varepsilon$. It is possible for all of the normal vectors to point in the same direction, but the tangent vectors may point in different directions. Distorting a rectangle into a U-shape is a good example (Figure 15). The sheet stays in the plane, but its tangent vectors are not parallel. Such highly curved regions must be sampled finely. Tangent curvature subdivision eliminates the problem (Figure 16: Drain with tangent curvature subdivision), improving the robustness of the curvature subdivision criterion.

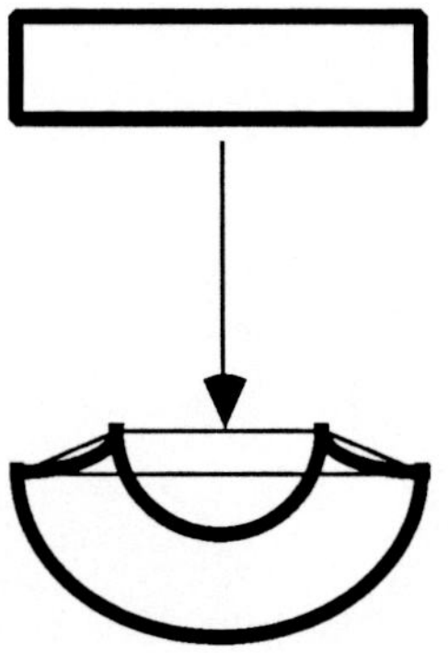

Figure 15: Bending a rectangle in the plane into a horseshoe shape. The quadrilateral is a very poor approximation to the bent shape.

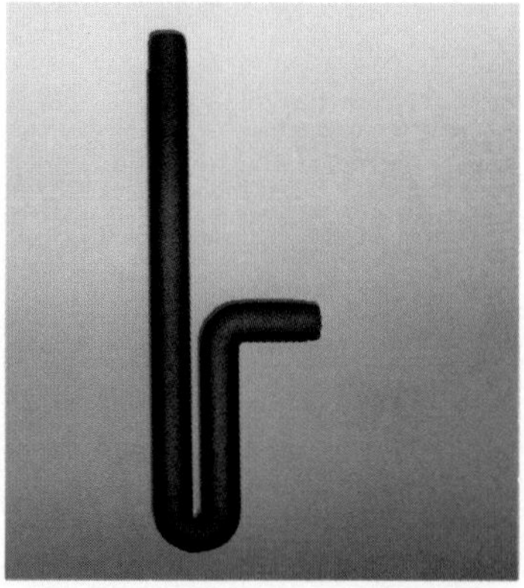

Figure 16: Drain with tangent curvature subdivision.

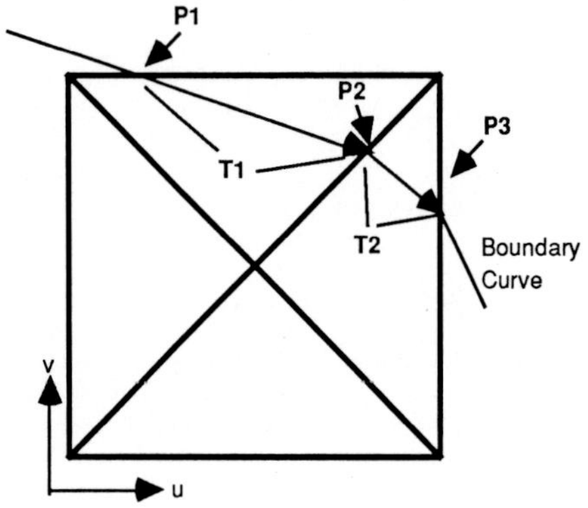

Figure 17: Geometry for boundary subdivision.

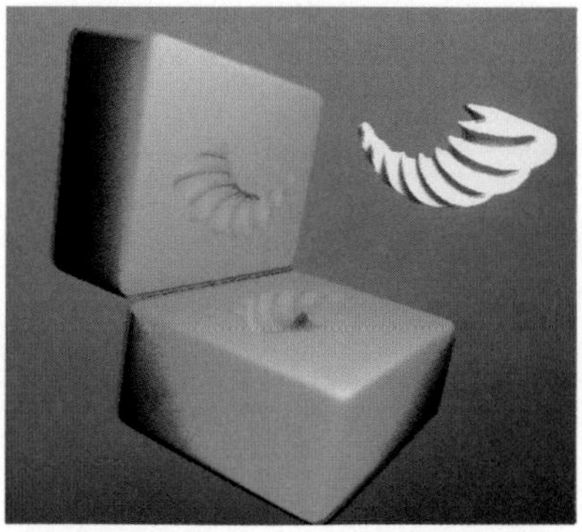

Figure 18: Subtraction of a deformed surface.

Intersection Subdivision

A sharp boundary is created where surfaces intersect. The boundaries should be finely sampled to avoid aliasing artifacts. One approach is to subdivide boundary regions until they are smaller than a pixel. The technique is robust, but expensive, in computing the boundary of the surface. An alternative technique is explored here, which measures the straightness of the boundary. Subdivision occurs until the boundary is straight in modeling (x, y, z) space. In regions where the boundary forms a sharp corner, subdivision stops if the region is smaller than a pixel. Where the boundary is straight, larger triangles can be used. Triangle clipping at the boundary produces an accurate boundary if the boundary is straight.

The test for straightness of a boundary curve across a region is computed using approximate tangent vectors of the boundary curve. Figure 17 shows a square with four corner vertices connected to a center vertex. Note that any straight line crossing the square must intersect the lines of the square in at least three places, $\mathbf{P}_1$, $\mathbf{P}_2$, $\mathbf{P}_3$. The intersection points are found by interpolating between corner samples and a center sample on the square until a boundary point is obtained. A variation of the *regula falsi* iteration method is effective [RAO84]. We approximate the boundary by the line segments $\mathbf{T}_1 = \mathbf{P}_2 - \mathbf{P}_1$, and $\mathbf{T}_2 = \mathbf{P}_3 - \mathbf{P}_2$. $\mathbf{T}_1$ and $\mathbf{T}_2$ are approximate tangent vectors to the boundary curve. The two tangent vectors are normalized and tested with the condition $(1 - \mathbf{T}_1 . \mathbf{T}_2) < \varepsilon$. The region is subdivided until the condition is met, unless the region is smaller than a pixel in screen space. Triangle clipping smooths the edges created.

Samples may be classified as internal or external to an intersecting object in a couple of ways. A hierarchical set of bounding volumes determines the proximity of the sample to the intersecting surface. Alternatively, an inside-outside, or implicit, formulation for the surface classifies the sample point [BARR83], [SEDERBERG86]. Figure 18 shows an example of a deformed surface subtracted from a mold.

Silhouette Boundaries

Given a camera viewpoint, silhouette subdivision concentrates samples along the silhouette boundary to minimize artifacts at the silhouette. The eye is quick to pick up slight irregularities at the sharp border of an object, which has high spatial frequencies. Polygonal artifacts are easier to see near the silhouette boundary of a surface than on the interior. The silhouette criterion is evaluated in a similar manner to the intersection subdivision criterion. The sphere in Figures 9 and 10 demonstrates the silhouette subdivision process.

The dot product between the surface normal **N** and the view vector **V** determines whether a sample is front-facing ($\mathbf{N.V} < 0$), back-facing ($\mathbf{N.V} > 0$), or on the silhouette boundary ($\mathbf{N.V} = 0$). Subdivision continues until the curvature of the silhouette boundary in screen space is less than a threshold value, or when the region is smaller than a pixel. The second termination condition prevents sharp corners from causing infinite recursion.

Proximity Subdivision

Proximity subdivision searches for intersection points between surfaces. It is a precursor to the intersection criterion, which finds the entire intersection boundary given an intersection point. A surface is subdivided until either an intersection is found or a local minimum is found in the inside-outside functions of the other surfaces. If an implicit inside-outside function is not available, bounding volumes or surface regions may be used to determine the need for additional subdivision.

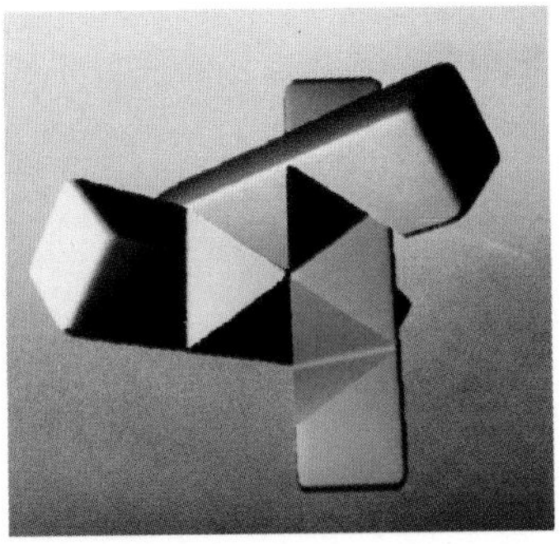

Figure 19: Triple cluster.

Figure 20: Hex Puzzle.

Figure 21: Bicycle chainwheel.

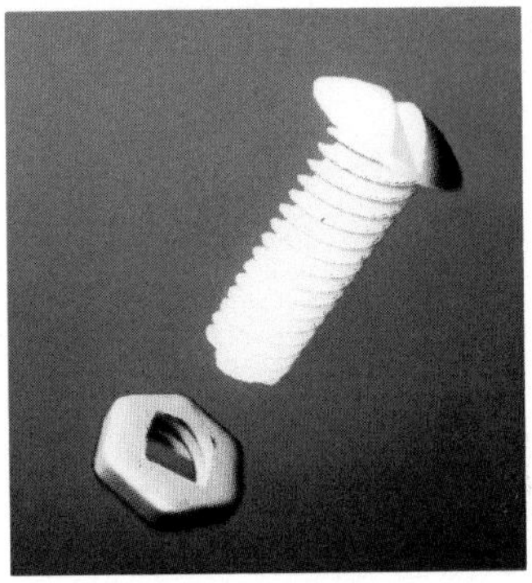

Figure 22: Nut and bolt.

Efficient Combination of Subdivision Criteria

Each of the subdivision criteria described above are computed for each region. Sometimes it is possible to determine that a region requires further subdivision without computing all the criteria. In this case it makes sense to compute the inexpensive criteria first, and possibly avoid unneccessary computation. Once the region passes all subdivision criteria once (or is culled from further consideration), a flag is set to indicate that the region should not be reexamined during the next pass through the quadtree. Some of the criteria use view-dependent tests, since a viewing transformation may be available at sampling time. In addition to the criteria mentioned here, the region may be forced to subdivide due to the constraint of restricted quadtrees that neighboring regions remain the same width within a factor of two. The following tests are ordered roughly according to increasing computational cost:

1. If the square is bigger than the initial sampling grid, then subdivide.
2. Else if the square is facing away from the viewer, then **end**.
3. Else if the square is smaller than a pixel, then **end**.
4. Else if the proximity test reveals a potential intersection, then subdivide.
5. Else if the square is culled by a surface intersection, then **end**.
6. Else if the square fails the flatness test, then subdivide.
7. Else if the square contains curved intersection boundaries, subdivide.
8. Else if the square contains curved silhouette boundaries, subdivide.
9. **end**.

Imaging Results

The following illustrations show the variety of deformed, intersecting parametric surfaces that may be rendered using the adaptive sampling techniques described.

Puzzle

The puzzle is modeled with six identical pieces that fill the volume of the interior of the puzzle. An individual piece is formed by taking a superquadric block, and subtracting two similar blocks to cut wedges in the piece (Figure 14). Three pieces may be assembled to form the cluster shown in Figure 19: Triple Cluster. The completed puzzle is formed with a left-handed triple cluster and a right-handed triple cluster (Figure 20: Hex Puzzle).

Bicycle Chainwheel

The chainwheel uses the boolean subtraction operation extensively (Figure 21). Fifty-two cylinders are subtracted from a disk to form the teeth for the gear. The proximity subdivision criterion helps to locate the position of the teeth. Deformed cylinders cut holes in the gear to make it lighter. Superquadric cranks and pedals are added after the cutting process.

Nut and Bolt

A type of screw thread may be formed by taking a superquadric with a square profile and twisting it for several revolutions (Figure 22). The thread is subtracted from the nut, and merged with the bolt head, to form the nut and bolt combination.

Conclusions

Surface quadtrees are an effective way to triangulate deformed, intersecting parametric surfaces. The adaptive sampling problem may be decomposed into two subproblems: the mechanism for subdivision, and the subdivision criteria. Images of these parametric surfaces have been created using a robust subdivision mechanism, and a small set of subdivision criteria.

Restricted quadtrees are more robust than unrestricted quadtrees in the triangulation of parametric surfaces. Curvature, intersection, proximity and silhouette subdivision techniques provide a robust set of criteria for the recursive sampling of parametric surfaces. These techniques are found to be more efficient than uniform subdivision at producing triangulations of deformed, intersecting surfaces.

References

Barr, Alan H., "Geometric Modeling and Fluid Dynamic Analysis of Swimming Spermatozoa," Ph.D. Thesis, Rensselaer Polytechnic Institute, 1983.

Barr, Alan H. Local and Global Deformations of Solid Primitives. Proceedings of SIGGRAPH'84 (Minneapolis, Minnesota, July 23-27, 1984). In *Computer Graphics 18*, 3 (July 1984), 21-30.

Barr, Alan H. Ray Tracing Deformed Surfaces. Proceedings of SIGGRAPH'86 (Dallas, Texas, August 18-22, 1986). In *Computer Graphics 20*, 4 (August 1986), 287-296.

Blinn, Jim, "Computer Display of Curved Surfaces," Ph.D. Thesis, University of Utah, 1978.

Carlson, Wayne E. An algorithm and data structure for 3D Object Synthesis using Surface Patch Intersections. Proceedings of SIGGRAPH'82 (Boston, Massachusetts, July 26-30, 1982). In *Computer Graphics 16*, 3 (July, 1982), 255.

Catmull, Ed, "Computer Display of Curved Surfaces," *IEEE Conference Proceedings on Computer Graphics, Pattern Recognition and Data Structures*, May 1975, p. 11.

Kay, Tim and Jim Kajiya. Ray Tracing Complex Scenes. Proceedings of SIGGRAPH'86 (Dallas, Texas, August 18-22, 1986). In *Computer Graphics 20*, 4 (August 1986), 269.

Kirkpatrick, David, "Optimal Search in Planar Subdivisions," *SIAM J. Comput.*, Volume 12, Number 1, February 1983, p. 28.

Lane, Jeff and Loren Carpenter, "A Generalized Scan Line Algorithm for the Computer Display of Parametrically Defined Surfaces," *Computer Graphics and Image Processing*, Volume 11, 1979, p. 290.

Lane, Jeff and Richard F. Riesenfeld, "A Theoretical Development for the Computer Generation and Display of Piecewise Polynomial Surfaces," *IEEE Transactions on Pattern Analysis and Machine Intelligence,* Volume PAMI-2, Number 1, January 1980, pp. 35-46.

Lin C. C., and L. A. Segel, *Mathematics Applied to Deterministic Problems in the Natural Sciences.* Macmillan Publishing Co., Inc., New York, 1974, pp. 56-57.

Rao, S. S., "Optimization Theory and Applications," Wiley Eastern Limited, New Delhi, India, 1984, pp. 248-249.

Samet, Hanan "Neighbor Finding Techniques for Images Represented by Quadtrees," *Computer Graphics and Image Processing*, Volume 18, 1982, p. 37.

Samet, Hanan "The Quadtree and Related Hierarchical Data Structures," *Computing Surveys 16,* 2 (June 1984), 187-260.

Schmitt, Francis, Brian Barsky, Wen-Hui Du. An Adaptive Subdivision Method for Surface-Fitting from Sampled Data. Proceedings of SIGGRAPH'86 (Dallas, Texas, August 18-22, 1986). In *Computer Graphics 20*, 4 (August 1986), 179-188.

Schweitzer, D., and E. S. Cobb. Scanline Rendering of Parametric Surfaces. Proceedings of SIGGRAPH'82 (Boston, Massachusetts, July 26-30, 1982). In *Computer Graphics 16*, 3 (July, 1982), 265.

Sederberg, Tom and Scott Parry. Free-Form Deformation of Solid Geometric Models. Proceedings of SIGGRAPH'86 (Dallas, Texas, August 18-22, 1986). In *Computer Graphics 20*, 4 (August 1986), 151-160.

Snyder, John M. and Al Barr, "Ray Tracing Complex Models Containing Surface Tessellations," Proceedings of SIGGRAPH'87 (Anaheim, California, July 27-31, 1987). In *Computer Graphics 21*, 3 (July 1987),.

Warnock, J.E., "A Hidden-Line Algorithm for Halftone Picture Representation," Ph.D. thesis, University of Utah, 1969.

Whitted, Turner, "An Improved Illumination Model for Shaded Display," *Communications ACM,* Volume 23, Number 6, June 1980, p. 343.

Adaptive Forward Differencing for Rendering Curves and Surfaces

Sheue-Ling Lien, Michael Shantz and Vaughan Pratt

Sun Microsystems, Inc.
2500 Garcia Avenue
Mountain View, CA 94043

Abstract

An adaptive forward differencing algorithm is presented for rapid rendering of cubic curves and bicubic surfaces. This method adjusts the forward difference step size so that approximately one pixel is generated along an ordinary or rational cubic curve for each forward difference step. The adjustment involves a simple linear transformation on the coefficients of the curve which can be accomplished with shifts and adds. This technique combines the advantages of traditional forward differencing and adaptive subdivision. A hardware implementation approach is described including the adaptive control of a forward difference engine. Surfaces are rendered by drawing many curves spaced closely enough together so that no pixels are left unpainted. A simple curve anti-aliasing algorithm is also presented in this paper. Anti-aliasing cubic curves is supported via tangent vector output at each forward difference step. The adaptive forward differencing algorithm is also suitable for software implementation.

CR Categories and Subject Descriptors: I.3.5 [**Computer Graphics**]: Computational Geometry and Object Modelling - Curve, surface, solid, and object representations; Geometric algorithms, and systems; I.3.3 [**Computer Graphics**]: Picture/Image Generation - Display algorithms; I.3.7 [**Computer Graphics**]: Three-dimensional Graphics and Realism - Color, shading, shadowing, and texture.

Additional Key Words and Phrases: image synthesis, adaptive forward differencing, parametric curves and surfaces.

Introduction

Parametric curves and curved surfaces are a common form of surface and object representation. In particular, non-uniform rational b-splines have gained popularity for mechanical CAD applications. Since high speed hardware capable of rendering vectors and polygons is widely available, high speed curve and surface rendering is usually done by subdividing and rendering them as straight lines or planar polygons. For conics, non-parametric, incremental solutions of the implicit equations[7, 8, 3, 1] are well known and a few hardware curve generators have been built. Less progress has been made on hardware techniques for rendering higher order curves and surfaces. Research has focused largely on subdivision methods for rendering and modelling.[2, 6] Recursive subdivision for curve and surface rendering is expensive to implement in hardware due to the high speed stack memory requirements and the fact that frame buffer memory access is easier to optimize if the pixels are being written to adjacent addresses.

Lane and others[5] developed scan line methods for rendering bicubic patches. They used Newton iteration to compute the intersections of the patch with the plane of the scanline. These approaches were not intended for, nor are they simple enough for hardware implementation.

Our adaptive forward difference (AFD) technique is an extension of well known[4] ordinary forward differencing and is related to the adaptive subdivision methods in that it adjusts the step size to the next pixel by transforming the equation of the curve to an identical curve with different parameterization. AFD differs from recursive subdivision or traditional forward differencing by generating points sequentially along the curve while adjusting the parameterization to give pixel sized steps. AFD allows a surprisingly simple hardware implementation, and is compatible with frame buffer memory interleaving for high performance.

This paper develops the theory of adaptive forward differencing and covers several related aspects and problem areas.

1) Reparameterization of cubic or rational cubic curves
2) Drawing surfaces by spacing curves δs apart
3) Generating anti-aliased curves
4) Trimming and image mapping on patches

With special purpose hardware for rendering these curves and surfaces directly, the usual subdivision overhead is reduced, and the appearance of the rendered objects is more accurate. The method lends itself to hardware fast shading techniques by functional approximations of the unit normal function over a patch.[9]

Principles

The method of adaptive forward differencing unifies the processes of recursive subdivision and forward differencing. In this section we present the principles underlying the method. The key insights are that these processes are both instances of linear substitution, and that efficiency is optimized by a choice of basis appropriate to the mix of substitutions.

We consider curves and surfaces in a space S, taken for the sake of illustration to be R^4 (homogeneous coordinates x,y,z,w). A *parametric object* in S is a function $f:X \rightarrow S$ where X is a set constituting the *parameter space*. The object is a *curve*, *segment*, *surface*, or *patch* when X is respectively the set R of reals, the real interval $[0,1]$, the real plane R^2, or the unit square $[0,1]^2$. We take s and t for the parameters, making f either $f(t)$ or $f(s,t)$.

A *linear substitution* transforms $f(t)$ into $f(at+b)$ and $f(s,t)$ into $f(as+b,ct+d)$, expressible as the composition of f with a linear or bilinear function respectively. The geometric effect of linear substitution is to translate and scale a segment or patch within the curve or surface containing it. Any segment of a curve can be mapped to any other segment of the same curve by some linear substitution, and likewise for patches.

Let us denote by L the linear substitution $t/2$ and by R the linear substitution $(t+1)/2$. Then L and R act on a segment C to yield the "left" and "right" halves LC and RC of C. These are the transformations associated with recursive subdivision; they may be applied recursively to subdivide a curve segment into quarters LLC, LRC, RLC, RRC (Figure 1(a)), eighths, etc.

Let us denote by E the linear substitution $t+1$. Then E acts on a segment C to yield its "right neighbor" EC. One use for E is as the forward difference operator. To render a long segment C, start with a very small initial segment D of C (e.g. $D = LL \cdots LC$) and generate the remaining (also small) segments of C by $ED, EED, EEED, \cdots$. This process is usually called forward differencing.

Another use for E is as a substitute for R in recursive subdivision: we may represent R as EL, as illustrated by the top half of Figure 1(b). However, rather than computing LC and RC separately we can compute LC once and then apply E to LC to get the right half, allowing us to discard C after applying L to it and so avoiding a "stack pop" when the time comes to apply R. The lower half of Figure 1(b) shows that this can be extended down another layer of recursion: we can get to RLC, LRC, and RRC by starting from LLC and repeatedly applying E, thanks to the additional identity $ER = LE$ (i.e. $EEL = LE$) which allows E to make the jump from RLC to LRC. This ability of E to run across the whole tree holds at any depth. At sufficient depth the method turns into ordinary forward differencing as per the previous paragraph.

A disadvantage of forward differencing is that it may not traverse C with uniform velocity. Recursive subdivision

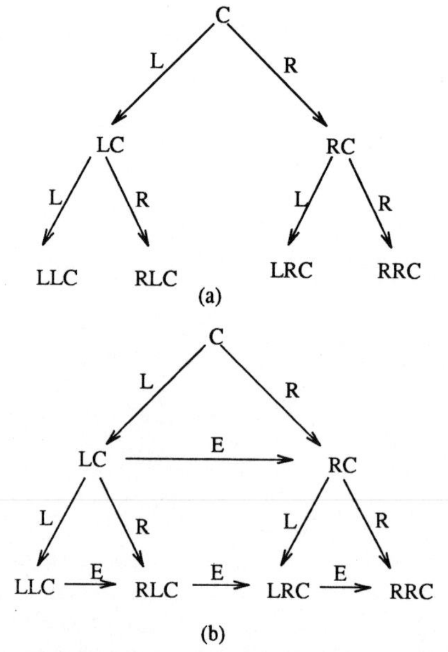

Figure 1. Relationship of linear substitutions L, R, and E.

avoids this difficulty by stopping at different depths in different parts of the recursion tree. We may transfer this advantage of recursive subdivision to forward differencing by inserting an occasional L or L^{-1} (the substitution $2t$) into the stream of E's whenever the velocity is too great or too small respectively. This has the effect of changing our level in the recursion tree as we forward-difference across it. We call this technique *adaptive forward differencing*.

In order to implement the above we require concrete representations for C, L, E, etc. We do this in the usual way: independently for each dimension of S take C to be a polynomial in t (and s), regard the polynomial as a point in a vector space of dimension one more than its degree, regard linear substitutions as a particular kind of linear transformation of this space, and perform the transformations in an appropriate basis for the space. One key property of linear substitution is that it does not increase polynomial degree, the other is that its action on a polynomial viewed as a vector is indeed that of a linear transformation.

While any basis will do, certain bases favor certain transformations. For example the total number of 1's in the binary representation of a particular transformation may be quite small in a particular basis, permitting the transformation to be carried out with just a few shifts and adds. Catmull [2] gives a basis for which L and R can be cheaply computed with only three adds and four shifts.

$$L_c = \begin{bmatrix} 1 & 0 & 0 & 0 \\ 0 & 1/4 & 0 & 0 \\ 1/2 & -1/8 & 1/2 & -1/8 \\ 0 & 1/8 & 0 & 1/8 \end{bmatrix}$$

$$R_c = \begin{bmatrix} 1/2 & -1/8 & 1/2 & -1/8 \\ 0 & 1/8 & 0 & 1/8 \\ 0 & 0 & 1 & 0 \\ 0 & 0 & 0 & 1/4 \end{bmatrix}$$

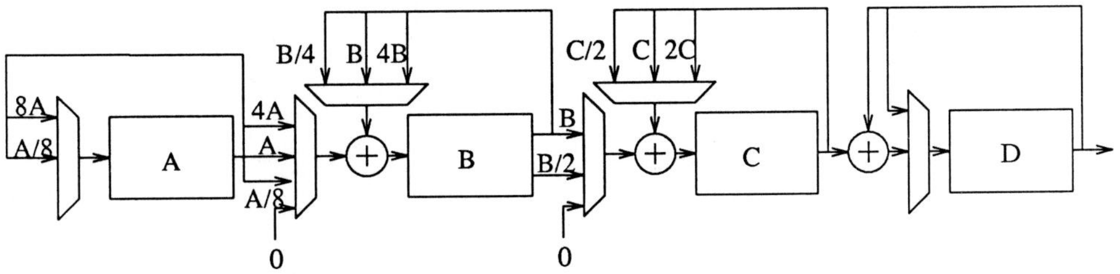

Figure 2. Block diagram of an AFD unit.

However, for forward differencing neither Catmull's basis for L and R nor any of the other bases usually considered for recursive subdivision are particularly well suited to the matrix representation of E. The best basis for E is the forward difference basis which allows parallel additions suitable for a pipeline implementation.

Adaptive Forward Difference Algorithm

For adaptive forward differencing we require a basis that works well with L and L^{-1}, especially with E, on the ground that E occurs significantly more often than L in practice. The following set is the forward difference basis which is considered to be the most appropriate.

$$B_3 = \frac{1}{6}(t^3-3t^2+2t) = \frac{1}{6}t(t-1)(t-2)$$

$$B_2 = \frac{1}{2}(t^2-t) = \frac{1}{2}t(t-1)$$

$$B_1 = t$$

$$B_0 = 1$$

The E matrix of this basis requires only three adds which can be done in parallel.

$$E = \begin{bmatrix} 1 & 1 & 0 & 0 \\ 0 & 1 & 1 & 0 \\ 0 & 0 & 1 & 1 \\ 0 & 0 & 0 & 1 \end{bmatrix}$$

The L and L^{-1} matrices can be implemented with simple shifts and adds.

$$L = \begin{bmatrix} 1 & 0 & 0 & 0 \\ 0 & 1/2 & -1/8 & 1/16 \\ 0 & 0 & 1/4 & -1/8 \\ 0 & 0 & 0 & 1/8 \end{bmatrix} \quad L^{-1} = \begin{bmatrix} 1 & 0 & 0 & 0 \\ 0 & 2 & 1 & 0 \\ 0 & 0 & 4 & 4 \\ 0 & 0 & 0 & 8 \end{bmatrix}$$

This algorithm is implemented in hardware called an AFD unit. An AFD unit is a third order digital differential analyzer which implements an adaptive forward difference solution to a parametric cubic function of t. The parameter t varies from 0 to 1 along the curve. The dt step size for t is adaptively adjusted so that the curve steps along in approximately one pixel steps in screen coordinates. Figure 2 shows a block diagram of an AFD unit. †

† Sun Microsystems, Inc. is pursuing patent protection in the United States and abroad on the technology described in this paper.

Four AFDUs can be used to generate the x,y,z,w values of the pixels along a cubic curve. Figure 3 shows the 4 required AFDUs and the divide by w circuit necessary for rendering rational curves. The filter unit is the controller for the adaptive step size, and performs other functions.

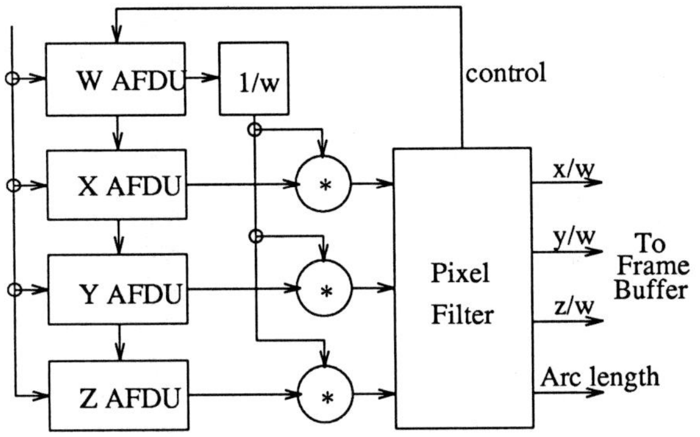

Figure 3. Block diagram of the AFD hardware. Each AFDU computes a 3rd order parametric function.

1. Reparameterization

A parametric cubic function f(t) can be represented in forward difference basis as

$$f = aB_3(t)+bB_2(t)+cB_1(t)+dB_0(t)$$

A cubic curve is defined by four cubic functions x(t), y(t), z(t), and w(t), each implemented by a separate AFD unit.

$$x(t) = a_xB_3+b_xB_2+c_xB_1+d_xB_0$$

$$y(t) = a_yB_3+b_yB_2+c_yB_1+d_yB_0$$

$$z(t) = a_zB_3+b_zB_2+c_zB_1+d_zB_0$$

$$w(t) = a_wB_3+b_wB_2+c_wB_1+d_wB_0$$

The coefficients a, b, c, and d are loaded into the 4 coefficient registers of each AFD unit. At each clock event the parameter t increases by dt and the four AFDUs generate the coordinates of one pixel.

If the x,y address step, corresponding to the dt step, is more than one pixel, dt is divided by two (adjusted down) so that each clock generates approximately one pixel along the curve. If the x,y address step is less than 1/2 pixel then dt is doubled (adjusted up) to increase the change in x,y coordinates.

To reduce dt by half, we transform the cubic functions x(t), y(t), z(t), w(t) by applying the L matrix:

$$x'(t) = x(\frac{t}{2}) = a'_x B_3 + b'_x B_2 + c'_x B_1 + d'_x B_0$$

$$y'(t) = y(\frac{t}{2}) = a'_y B_3 + b'_y B_2 + c'_y B_1 + d'_y B_0$$

$$z'(t) = z(\frac{t}{2})$$

$$w'(t) = w(\frac{t}{2})$$

The coefficients of the two sets of cubic functions are related by

$$a' = \frac{1}{8}a$$

$$b' = \frac{1}{4}b - \frac{1}{8}a$$

$$c' = \frac{1}{2}c - \frac{1}{8}b + \frac{1}{16}a$$

$$d' = d$$

To double dt, we transform the cubic functions by applying the L^{-1} matrix:

$$x'(t) = x(2t)$$

$$y'(t) = y(2t)$$

$$z'(t) = z(2t)$$

$$w'(t) = w(2t)$$

Here the coefficient transformation is

$$a' = 8a$$

$$b' = 4b + 4a$$

$$c' = 2c + b$$

$$d' = d$$

If the step size is correct then we apply the E matrix.

$$x'(t) = x(t+1)$$

$$y'(t) = y(t+1)$$

$$z'(t) = z(t+1)$$

$$w'(t) = w(t+1)$$

The AFD units in this case generate a new pixel and advance to the next pixel with the corresponding coefficients transformed by

$$a' = a$$

$$b' = b + a$$

$$c' = c + b$$

$$d' = d + c$$

The adaptive forward differencing mechanism is illustrated below.

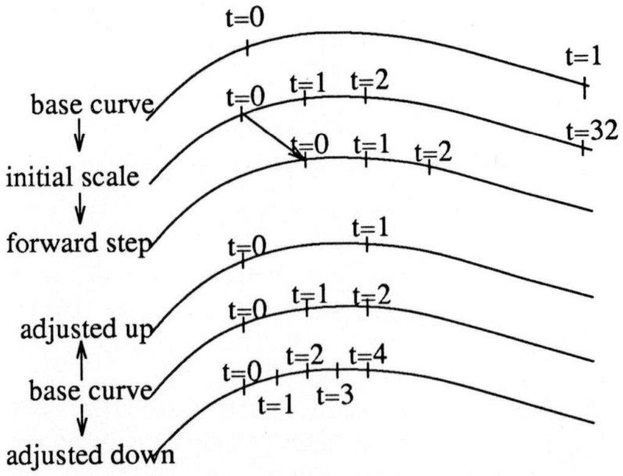

Figure 4 Operations of "adjust up", "adjust down", and "forward step".

We have measured the percentage of steps requiring an adjust up or adjust down using the Utah teapot at various scale factors. Drawing the cubic curves comprising a wire mesh on the bicubic patches making up the surface involved 73,000 forward steps, and 600 adjustment steps. The overhead for the adaptive nature of the forward difference scheme is therefore quite small. It increases when the curves being drawn have large accelerations.

2. Initial Setup

To render a cubic curve C we first convert to the forward difference basis. We then start with a small initial segment D of the curve by applying $L^n = L.L.......L$ to the curve C. The initial scale down is not really required. However, if not done, the adaptive mechanism may adjust down many times until the pixel step size is approximately one pixel before it starts rendering. In practice the parameterization is scaled down before loading into the AFD units to be within the hardware register precision. The AFDUs adjust from there.

3. Pixel filtering

The pixel filter performs five functions. 1) It compares the current pixel coordinates with the previous pixel coordinates generated by the AFD units and tells the AFD units whether they should adjust up, adjust down, or step forward to the next pixel. 2) The pixel filter also detects and replaces "elbow" sequences of the form x,y to x,y+1 to x+1,y+1 with a diagonal move x,y to x+1,y+1. This is done to improve the appearance of generated curves. 3) It also generates arc length along the curve generated by the AFD units. It adds 1 to the arc length if the curve steps either horizontally or vertically and adds 1.414 if the curve steps diagonally. The output arc length is used to address the pattern memory for mapping texture along curves. 4) The filter unit performs clipping on t, x, y, and z. t is clipped between a tmin register and a tmax register to assist in rendering trimmed patches. x, y, and z are clipped to their respective min and max register values. 5) The filter generates the instantaneous tangent and normal vectors for the purpose of anti-aliasing curves.

The pixel filter thus acts as the controller for the AFD units and also computes arc length, and antialias weights.

4. Rendering conics and rational cubics

One of the AFD units generates the homogeneous coordinate w as a parametric cubic function of t. For rational cubic curves x, y, and z must be divided by w at each point. This is accomplished by using a reciprocal unit which computes a truncated Taylor series approximation of 1/w.

The reciprocal 1/w is computed as follows which can be easily implemented with look-up tables, adders and mutipliers.

$$\frac{1}{w} = \frac{1}{w_0} - \frac{\delta}{w_0^2}$$

The following example shows how to set up AFDUs to draw an ellipse with radius r_x, r_y centered at $<x_0, y_0>$ and rotated by an angle θ. A half ellipse with radius r_x, r_y can be defined in parametric form as

$$x_1(t) = r_x \frac{t(1-t)}{t^2-t+0.5}$$

$$y_1(t) = r_y \frac{0.5-t}{t^2-t+0.5}$$

We can get the other half of the ellipse by mirroring the image. By rotating the ellipse by an angle θ and then translating it to $<x_0, y_0>$, we get a set of cubic functions which describe an ellipse with radius r_x, r_y centered at x_0, y_0 and rotated by an angle θ:

$$x(t) = r_x t(1-t)\cos\theta + r_y(0.5-t)\sin\theta + x_0(t^2-t+0.5)$$

$$= (x_0 - r_x\cos\theta)t^2 + (r_x\cos\theta - r_y\sin\theta - x_0)t$$

$$+ 0.5(r_y\sin\theta + x_0)$$

$$y(t) = -r_x t(1-t)\sin\theta + r_y(0.5-t)\cos\theta + y_0(t^2-t+0.5)$$

$$= (y_0 + r_x\sin\theta)t^2 - (r_x\sin\theta + r_y\cos\theta + y_0)t$$

$$+ 0.5(r_y\cos\theta + y_0)$$

$$w(t) = t^2 - t + 0.5$$

By converting the above cubic functions to DDA basis, we get a set of coefficients

$$a_x = 0$$

$$b_x = 2(x_0 - r_x\cos\theta)$$

$$c_x = (x_0 - r_x\cos\theta) + (r_x\cos\theta - r_y\sin\theta - x_0)$$

$$d_x = 0.5(r_y\sin\theta + x_0)$$

$$a_y = 0$$

$$b_y = 2(y_0 + r_x\sin\theta)$$

$$c_y = (y_0 + r_x\sin\theta) - (r_x\sin\theta + r_y\cos\theta + y_0)$$

$$d_y = 0.5(r_y\cos\theta + y_0)$$

$$a_w = 0.0$$

$$b_w = 2.0$$

$$c_w = 0.0$$

$$d_w = 0.5$$

We can set up the AFD units with the above coefficients for drawing the ellipse (see Figure 6).

5. Anti-aliasing cubic curves

AFD gives a simple means of generating the instantaneous tangent vector $<t_x, t_y>$ along the curve by simply subtracting the last point from the previous one. The instantaneous tangent vector gives an indication of whether the current pixel is in an x_major ($t_x > t_y$) or y_major ($t_x < t_y$) slope. An approximate distance of the current pixel away from the center curve is computed from this tangent and the fractional portion of the pixel addresses as follows. Here α is the ratio of variation of intensity, and α is used to blend the curve color and the background color. This is a rather crude approximation but gives surprisingly improved curve appearance. Figure 5 shows the result of this curve anti-aliasing method drawn with the software simulation.

If the tangent vector indicates x_major, we compute

$$\alpha = (f_y - 0.5) + \frac{t_y}{t_x}(f_x - 0.5)$$

where $<t_x, t_y>$ is the tangent and f_x and f_y are the fractional portion of the pixel x and y address. If α is positive, then the intensity of pixel <x,y> is blended by (1.0−α), and pixel <x,y+1> by α. In case of a negative α, pixel <x,y> is blended by (1.0+α), and pixel <x,y-1> by −α. For y_major, α is

$$\alpha = (f_x - 0.5) + \frac{t_x}{t_y}(f_y - 0.5)$$

In this case, pixel <x,y> is blended by (1.0−α), and pixel <x+1,y> by α if α is positive; otherwise pixel <x,y> by (1.0+α) and pixel <x-1,y> by −α.

One advantage of this anti-aliasing scheme is that it applies as well to both nonrational and rational curves. Figure 6 shows a set of anti-aliased rational curves rendered with this scheme.

Shading Bicubic Patches

The AFD technique can be used to render shaded, curved, trimmed patches, generate anti-aliased curves, and map texture and imagery onto curves and surfaces as a function of either arc-length or parameter.

Shading and image mapping onto bicubic or rational bicubic surface patches is performed by drawing many curves very close to each other. Each curve is a cubic in t formed by setting s at a constant $s=s_i$. We therefore need to find the spacing δs from one curve to the next so that no pixel gaps exist in between them. To compute the spacing δs in between the current curve $f(s=s_i, t)$ and the next curve, we run a series of testing curves in the orthogonal direction (i.e. s direction) at $t = (0.0, 0.125, ..., 1.0)$ and examine the step size used by those curves at the positions $s=s_i$. The minimum size used is then chosen as the spacing for the next curve $f(s_i+\delta s, t)$. When the δs gets smaller, it indicates that the next curve should be filled in closer to the current one; when δs increases, the next curve can be a little less close.

We explain next how AFD is used to adaptively adjust the spacing in between curves. For a bicubic patch $F(s,t)$ represented in forward difference basis,

$$F(s,t) = < f_x(s,t), f_y(s,t), f_z(s,t), f_w(s,t) >$$

each $f(s,t)$ is a bicubic function of s and t. For example the x component

$$f_x(s,t)=\begin{bmatrix} B_0(t), B_1(t), B_2(t), B_3(t) \end{bmatrix} \begin{bmatrix} x_{00} & x_{01} & x_{02} & x_{03} \\ x_{10} & x_{11} & x_{12} & x_{13} \\ x_{20} & x_{21} & x_{22} & x_{23} \\ x_{30} & x_{31} & x_{32} & x_{33} \end{bmatrix} \begin{bmatrix} B_0(s) \\ B_1(s) \\ B_2(s) \\ B_3(s) \end{bmatrix}$$

where $x_{i,j}$ are the x coordinates of the control points of the patch. A curve at a constant s, $f(s=s_i,t)$, is a cubic function represented in forward difference basis as

$$f(s=s_i,t)=dB_0(t)+cB_1(t)+bB_2(t)+aB_3(t)$$

where the four coefficients a,b,c,d are cubic functions of s in forward difference basis:

$$d(s)=x_{00}B_0(s)+x_{01}B_1(s)+x_{02}B_2(s)+x_{03}B_3(s)$$

$$c(s)=x_{10}B_0(s)+x_{11}B_1(s)+x_{12}B_2(s)+x_{13}B_3(s)$$

$$b(s)=x_{20}B_0(s)+x_{21}B_1(s)+x_{22}B_2(s)+x_{23}B_3(s)$$

$$a(s)=x_{30}B_0(s)+x_{31}B_1(s)+x_{32}B_2(s)+x_{33}B_3(s)$$

We apply AFD to these four cubic functions to generate the value of coefficients for the next curve. When the spacing δs for the next curve is the same as the previous one, the E matrix is applied. If the spacing for the next curve doubles, L^{-1} and then the E matrix are applied to double the spacing. If the spacing halves, we apply L and then the E matrix to reduce it. We are still examining methods for minimizing this redundancy through subdivision and tuning of the adjustment criterion.

Figure 7 shows a Phong shaded Utah teapot rendered on a 1152 x 900 screen with 80 patches using the AFD technique, for comparison with the equivalent polygon shaded version in Figure 8 containing 4060 triangles.

Trimmed patches are rendered by scan converting the trimming region in s,t space using the δs scanline width. (Here a scanline in s,t space is different from a scanline in the screen space.) This produces a "scanline" curve segment at each constant s_i bounded by one or more tmin, tmax pairs. These curve segments are rendered with clipping to the appropriate tmin and tmax. Figure 9 shows a shaded, image mapped, bicubic patch trimmed with a SUN logo.

Discussion

In rendering curves we set the threshhold of adjustment to be 0.5 and 1.0, i.e. we adjust up if x and y step by less than .5 pixel and we adjust down if x or y step by greater than 1 pixel. Using this threshhold we do not overpaint too many pixels, and neither do we leave gaps between pixels. Patches are rendered by filling many curves very close together. However, using the 0.5 and 1.0 threshhold in rendering a patch we tend to get missing pixels in the patch. This problem is solved by reducing the pixel adjustment threshold down to 0.35 and 0.7, instead of by reducing the spacing in between adjacent curves. We are currently trying to establish the optimal adjustment criterion for ensuring no pixel gaps.

For performance comparison purposes, we used the following three schemes to render a wireframe mesh of curves for a piece of teapot handle on a 512 x 512 screen with ten curves in each direction: (1) ordinary forward differencing, (2) adaptive subdivision, and (3) adaptive forward differencing. In this test, the ordinary forward differencing technique took 8192 forward steps, the adaptive subdivision technique took 3887 subdivisions, and AFD took 49 adjust_up's, 36 adjust_down's and 3910 forward steps. It is obvious that the ordinary forward differencing technique usually requires more forward steps than our technique because it uses the smallest step required for no gaps and cannot adjust to a longer step when appropriate. Each forward operation takes three adds, each adjust_up or adjust_down takes 3 adds and 2 multiplies. The first scheme required a total of 24516 adds. Our technique required 11900 adds and 255 multiplies. The subdivision technique took a total of 11661 adds and 15548 multiplies, where a single subdivision requires 3 adds and 4 multiplies.

We used the adaptive subdivision technique and our patch rendering technique to compare the patch rendering performance on rendering a piece of teapot body and a piece of teapot handle on a 512 x 512 screen. The termination condition we used in the subdivision technique was to constrain the minimum bounding box of the control points of a Bezier patch within 1.0 by 1.0. The subdivision technique on the teapot body required 86380 subdivisions to fill the entire patch. Since a subdivision takes 36 adds and 48 multiplies, it requires approximately 3 million adds and 4 million multiplies. Our technique required 708 adjust up, 513 adjust down, and 218513 forward step operations. Thus AFD used approximately 0.66 million adds and 3700 multiplies. Our method has a curve set up overhead of 12 adds per curve - a total of 6000 adds in this test case, which is negligible. In the case of the teapot handle, it took 143379 subdivisions with adaptive subdivision, whereas the new method performed 537 adjust up, 727 adjust down, and 187386 forward step operations, i.e., 5.16 million adds and 6.88 million multiplies against 0.56 million adds and 2528 multiplies.

Clearly, both subdivision and AFD can be implemented with integer arithmetic given sufficient precision. In both methods the above multiplies can be performed using simple shifts. The shifts required for the L and L^{-1} matrices can be implemented with "wires" in hardware since all elements are integer powers of 2. A complete error analysis of a fixed point integer implementation of AFD is currently being conducted.

The relatively poor performance of adaptive subdivision is due to the fact that a subdivision operation takes significantly more computation than a forward difference operation. This new method has the advantage of producing picture quality equivalent to adaptive subdivision without the memory stack management overhead of recursive subdivision and is thus more suitable for hardware implementation. AFD also makes patch rendering performance competitive with polygon rendering. When doing image mapping and patch trimming, our technique operates in s,t space but polygon methods operate in the screen scanline order, therefore, our method does not require a transformation from screen space to image coordinates as the polygon method does.

Acknowledgements

The following people contributed greatly to the ideas, simulations, and design of these algorithms: Jerry Evans, David Elrod, Nola Donato, Bob Rocchetti, Sue Carrie, Serdar Ergene, Jim Van Loo, Paul Tien, and Mark Moyer.

References

1. Jerry Van Aken and Mark Novak, "Curve-Drawing Algorithms for Raster Displays," *ACM Transactions on Graphics*, vol. 4, no. 2, pp. 147-169, April 1985.
2. Edwin Catmull, *A Subdivision Algorithm for Computer Display of Curved Surfaces,* Thesis in Computer Science, University of Utah, UTEC-CSc-74-133, 1974.
3. George M. Chaikin, "An Algorithm for High Speed Curve Generation," *Computer Graphics and Image Processing*, vol. 3, pp. 346-349, 1974.
4. Steven A. Coons, *Surfaces for Computer-Aided Design of Space Forms,* Project MAC, MIT, MAC-TR-41, June 1967.
5. Jeffrey Lane, Loren Carpenter, Turner Whitted, and James Blinn, "Scan Line Methods for Displaying Parametrically Defined Surfaces," *CACM*, vol. 23, no. 1, January 1980.
6. Jeffrey M. Lane and Richard F. Riesenfeld, "A Theoretical Development for the Computer Generation of Piecewise Polynomial Surfaces," *IEEE Transactions on Pattern Analysis and Machine Intelligence*, vol. PAMI-2, no. 1, pp. 35-46, January 1980.
7. M. L. V. Pitteway, "Algorithm for drawing ellipses or hyperbolae with a digital plotter," *Computer Journal*, vol. 10, no. 3, pp. 282-289, Nov. 1967.
8. Vaughan Pratt, "Techniques for Conic Splines," *Computer Graphics*, vol. 19, no. 3, July 1985.
9. Michael Shantz and Sheue-Ling Lien, "Shading Bicubic Patches," *Computer Graphics*, vol. 21, no. 4, July 1987.

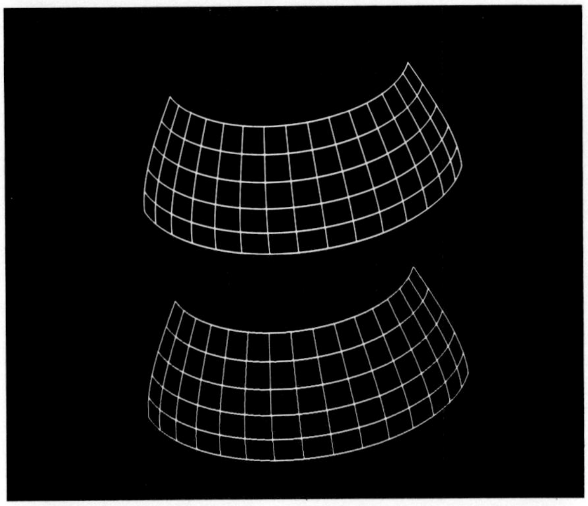

Figure 5. Comparison of antialiased and ordinary non_rational cubic curves rendered with adaptive forward difference scheme.

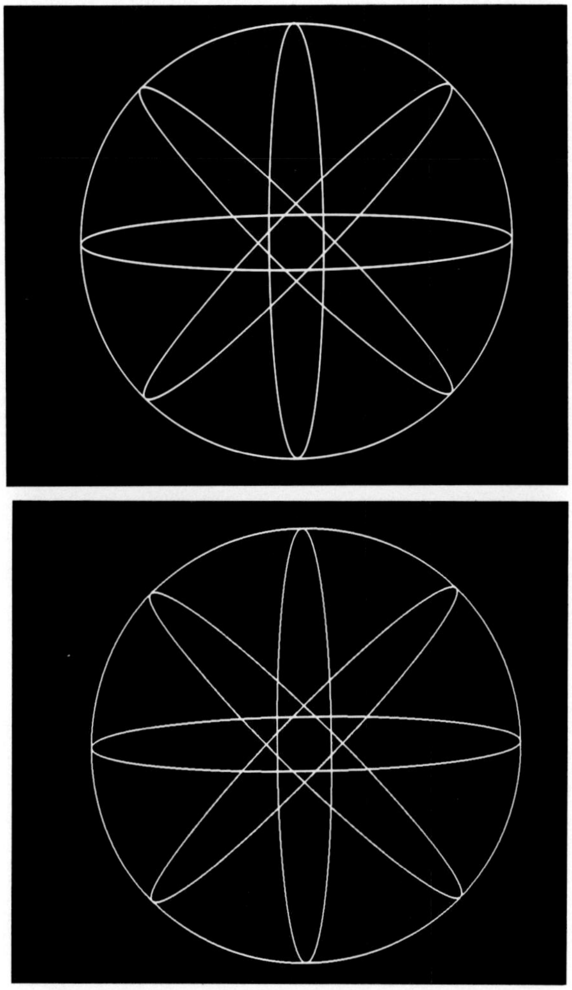

Figure 6. Comparison of antialiased and ordinary conics rendered with adaptive forward difference scheme.

Figure 7. Adaptive forward difference rendering of the Utah teapot using 80 patches.

Figure 8. Classical polygon rendering of the Utah teapot using 4060 triangles.

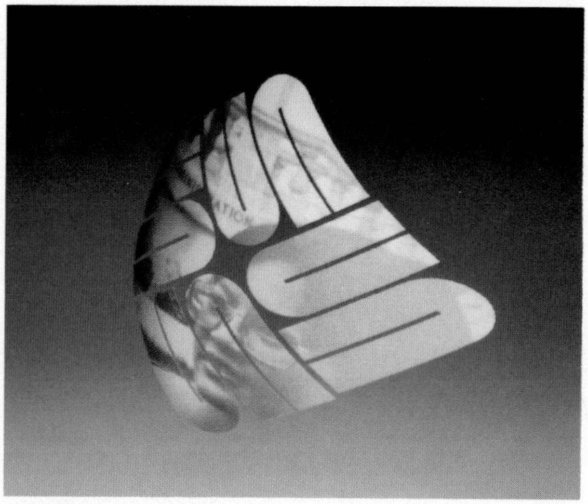

Figure 9. An image_mapped bicubic patch trimmed with a SUN logo.

Ray Tracing Complex Models Containing Surface Tessellations

John M. Snyder
Alan H. Barr
California Institute of Technology
Pasadena, CA 91125

Abstract

An approach to ray tracing complex models containing mathematically defined surfaces is presented. Parametric and implicit surfaces, and boolean combinations of these, are first tessellated into triangles. The resulting triangles from many such surfaces are organized in a hierachy of lists and 3D grids, allowing efficient calculation of ray/model intersections.

The technique has been used to ray trace models containing billions of triangles and surfaces never before ray traced. The organizing scheme developed is also independently useful for efficiently ray tracing any complex model, whether or not it contains surface tessellations.

KEYWORDS: Ray tracing, parametric surface, tessellation, triangle, list, 3D grid

1 Introduction

In the past, models suitable for ray tracing have contained too few and too simple primitives. Much work has been focused on solving these two problems independently.

To extend the set of "ray-traceable" surfaces beyond polygons and quadric surfaces, several schemes for intersecting rays with surfaces have been developed. Kajiya [Kajiya 82] has described an algorithm for ray tracing bicubic patches. Toth [Toth 85], Barr [Barr 86], and Joy and Bhetanabhotla [Joy 86] have studied algorithms for intersecting rays with general parameteric surfaces. These schemes are slow, require expensive evaluation of surface parameterizations, and are hard to robustly implement.

Alternatively, mathematically defined surfaces can be broken down into simple pieces. The resulting tessellation is an approximation to the real surface which can be made arbitrarily close to it by using tiny enough pieces. This approach has been avoided because ray tracers were unable to handle the vast numbers of primitives needed to approximate a surface.

Recently, organizing structures for large and complex collections of primitives have been proposed which make feasible ray tracing of models containing many fine tessellations. These structures fall into three categories — lists, octrees, and 3D grids. Each organizes a collection of objects into a single unit which may later be incorporated into a higher level structure. Each allows the ray tracing algorithm to determine which objects in the collection can potentially be intersected by a ray.

Lists were used in early ray tracers such as developed by Rubin and Whitted [Rubin 80]. A list is simply a grouping of objects. Hierarchies are built by grouping lists into higher level lists. Kay and Kajiya [Kay 86] investigated an algorithm to traverse the list hierarchy so that objects are considered in the order that they occur along the ray. This requires sorting of objects that can potentially be intersected by the ray.

Octrees and 3D grids partition space rather than objects and thus avoid object sorting. In these structures, each cell, a rectangular volume in space, contains all the objects that occur within it. The difference between the two structures is that octrees are hierarchical with variable sized cells, while 3D grids are nonhierarchical with cells of uniform size. Glassner [Glassner 84] and Kaplan [Kaplan 85] investigated octrees. Fujimoto, et al. [Fujimoto 86] developed 3D grids and compared their efficiency with octrees.

Fujimoto found the 3D grid structure superior to an octree for ray tracing models containing large numbers of primitives homogenously scattered through space. This finding can be explained in light of two 3D grid properties. First, because grid cells are of uniform size, tracing a ray from one grid cell to the next is an extremely fast, incremental calculation. Second, because grids are nonhierarchical, determining which cell contains the ray origin can be done in constant time, while the same operation is logarithmic in the number leaf cells in an octree. In fact, both lists and octrees require hierarchy traversal; lists through a hierarchy of bounding volumes around objects, and octrees through a hierarchy of octree cells. Set up time for a ray/grid intersection is large, however, making it impractical for collections of a few objects. A single grid is also impractical for organizing objects at widely varying lengths of scale.

The proposed algorithm uses a hybrid, hierarchical approach to organizing a complex model. In it, both lists and 3D grids are used to organize model elements, which are primitives, or themselves lists or 3D grids. Grids are used to organize large collections that are evenly distributed through space. Lists are used to organize small collections that are sparsely distributed through space. This scheme can adapt to complexity in a model at many scales; in fact, a hierarchy of 3D grids can be viewed as a generalization of an octree, in which arbitrary branching ratios are possible instead of a fixed branching ratio of eight.

Using this technique, we have ray traced a model containing 400 billion triangles, more primitives than have previously been rendered into a single image. We have generated complex images containing such shapes as teapots, grass blades, clover leaves, flower petals, and bumpy, twisted, and self-intersecting parametric surfaces. In short, this technique has established a new state of the art in the complexity of ray traced images.

2 Surface Tessellation

A surface *tessellation* is a connected mesh of pieces which approximates the surface. A *triangle* is the tessellation piece; a surface is thus approximated by a polyhedron with triangular faces. Triangles were chosen because their simplicity allowed fast con-

© 1987 ACM-0-89791-227-6/87/007/0119 $00.75

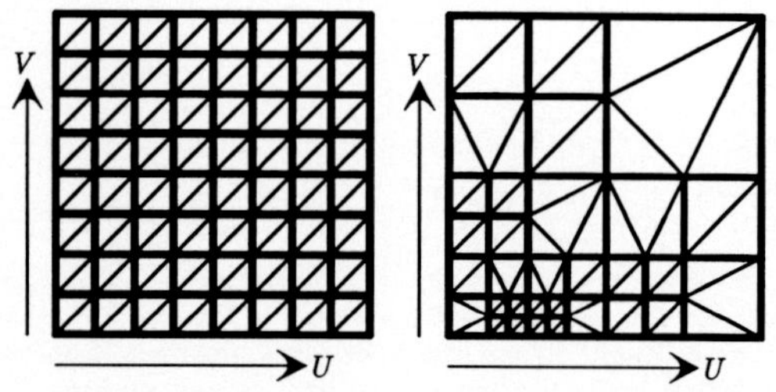

Figure 1: Parameter Space Tessellated Into Triangles

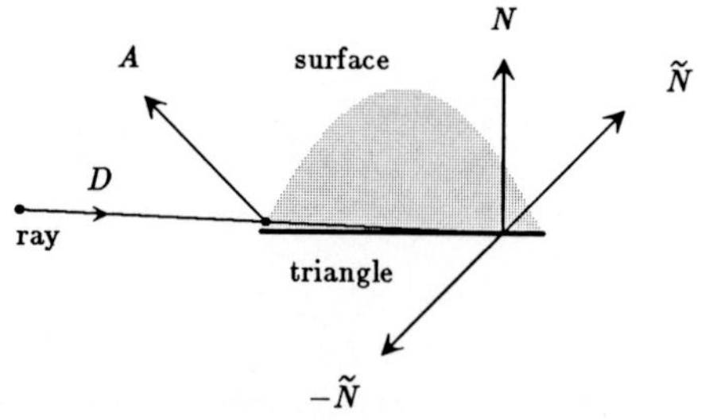

Figure 2: The Surface Sidedness Problem — The triangle normal vector N faces slightly toward the ray origin ($N \cdot D \leq 0$ implies outside intersection) but the interpolated normal vector $\tilde{N}$ faces away ($\tilde{N} \cdot D > 0$ implies inside intersection). The vector A is the normal to the surface at the intersection of the ray with the surface; it clearly indicates that the ray intersects the outside of the surface.

struction of surface tessellations and fast ray intersection with the mesh pieces (see Appendix).

Tessellation of surfaces is accomplished in a program separate from the ray tracer. Currently, this program tessellates several types of parametric surfaces $S(u,v)$: $R^2 \rightarrow R^3$ by uniformly sampling a rectangular region of parameter space using a specified number of divisions in u and v (see Figure 1a). Each set of four adjacent samples is then used to create two triangles. Surfaces can also be tessellated using adaptive sampling techniques (see Figure 1b) in which the fineness of the subdivision can vary over the parameter space. A technique for adaptive subdivision of parametric surfaces and boolean combinations of parametric surfaces is discussed in [Von Herzen 85]. In addition, a technique to tessellate implicit surfaces is currently being developed at Caltech [Kalra 86].

2.1 Tessellation Artifacts And Solutions

Experimentation has shown that surface tessellations can be ray traced without noticeable artifact. The organizational scheme can easily handle tessellations which are fine enough so that no silhouette or shadow polygonal segmentation is visible. Moreover, as the number of triangles in a tessellation is increased, the time to ray trace the tesselation grows slowly (see Section 6). In practice, while the algorithm had the capability to ray trace tessellations containing many more triangles in an allotted rendering time, some surfaces in very complex models remained inadequately tessellated because of memory limitations (typically about 16 megabytes). Visible artifacts were the result.

Artifacts take the form of polygonal shading facets, silhouettes, and shadows. Polygonal shading facets are largely controlled by using normal interpolation across triangles. Silhouette and shadow artifacts are most pronounced in regions where the surface has high curvature, and in regions where triangles in the tessellation have long edges. One solution is to tessellate the surface adaptively using variation in normal vector, and linear length of triangle edge as criteria for subdivision. In this way, parts of the surface requiring further sampling may be more finely tessellated without increasing the overall number of triangles.

Information concerning how the surface is positioned with respect to the camera, the lights, and other surfaces can also be used in a subdivision scheme to reduce artifacts. For example, given an eye position, surfaces can be subdivided more in regions where the normal to the surface is nearly perpendicular to the direction to the eye. Silhouette edges of objects will then appear less choppy. This approach has not been pursued because it depends on properties not inherent in the surface, creating tessellations which are only good in a particular scene. Also, determining the location of silhouettes and shadows is complicated by ray tracing effects such as reflections, refractions, diffuse shadows, and depth of field.

Artifacts can also be reduced by intelligent shading and ray casting techniques as well as by intelligent subdivision. The following sections describe two examples.

The Surface Sidedness Problem

When a ray intersects a triangle, the triangle's interpolated normal, $\tilde{N}$, is passed to the shader as the actual normal to the surface at the point of intersection. Let the ray be parametrized by $O + Dt$ where t is a scalar greater than 0 and O and D are vectors; O is the ray origin, and D, the ray direction. The vector $\tilde{N}$ is used to determine whether the inside or outside of the surface was hit according to the sided intersection test:

$$\tilde{N} \cdot D \leq 0 \implies \text{outside intersection}$$
$$\tilde{N} \cdot D > 0 \implies \text{inside intersection}$$

For an inside intersection, $\tilde{N}$ is flipped (scaled by -1), since the intersection algorithm always returns outward facing normals. The final $\tilde{N}$, flipped or unflipped, is used by the shader to compute diffuse (Lambert) shading, specular highlights, and directions for recursively generated reflection and refraction rays.

Let N be the normal to the plane embedding the triangle. It is the normal of the polyhedral tessellation of the surface at the point of intersection, whereas $\tilde{N}$ is an approximation to the actual (pre-tessellated) surface's normal. A problem arises if the result of the sided intersection test is different when applied to $\tilde{N}$ and N, as in Figure 2. Large shading discontinuities result when $\tilde{N}$ is erroneously flipped in this situation since it indicates an inside intersection. As Figure 2 shows, the unflipped $\tilde{N}$ is also a bad approximation to the actual surface normal.

Experimentation has shown that this problem can be made less severe by using the actual triangle normal N instead of $\tilde{N}$ whenever the sign of $\tilde{N} \cdot D$ is not equal to the sign of $N \cdot D$. For outside intersections (as in Figure 2), the normal must have some component toward the ray origin, rather than away from it. Thus N is closer to A than is either $\tilde{N}$ or $-\tilde{N}$. Although not a completely

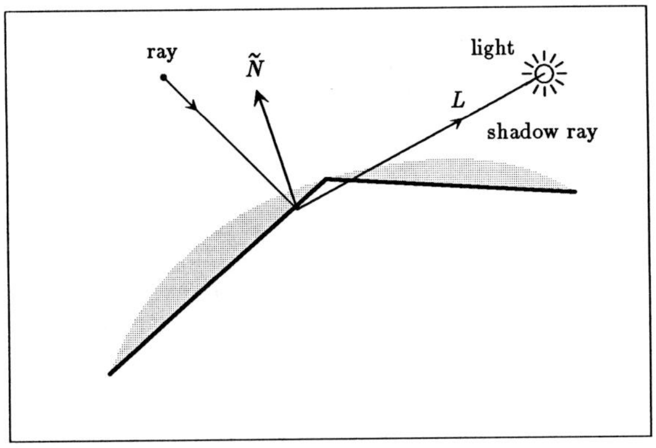

Figure 3: The Terminator Problem — Although $\tilde{N}$ indicates that a surface point is not self-shadowed, (i.e. $\tilde{N} \cdot L \leq 0$ where L is opposite to the shadow ray direction) the shadow ray is launched starting from inside the surface. The point is therefore found to be in shadow when the shadow ray intersects the surface on its way out. This problem manifests itself in a polygonal, segmented terminator, particularly evident with point light sources.

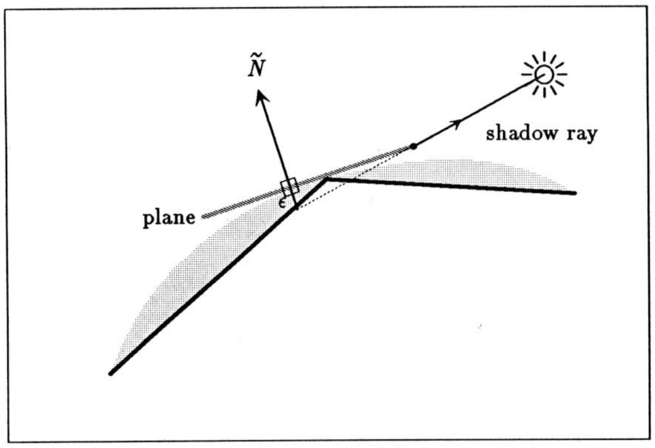

Figure 4: Solving The Terminator Problem Using Variable Shadow Tolerance — To allow the shadow ray to escape from inside the surface, we can shoot the shadow ray starting from its intersection with a plane ϵ from the point of intersection along the interpolated normal direction $\tilde{N}$.

satisfactory solution, this technique restored the brightness of a few unnaturally dark pixels along silhouettes of highly curved surfaces in experimental pictures. It is expected that adaptive surface tessellation which samples more highly in regions where the surface normals vary largely, coupled with this technique, will be an effective solution to surface sidedness artifacts. Such adaptive sampling will limit the maximum angular difference between N and A.

The Terminator Problem

A terminator is an area on a surface separating lit and self-shadowed areas. Let L be the direction of the light from a point on the surface. Whether or not a point on a surface is self-shadowed is determined according to the self-shadowing test:

$$\tilde{N} \cdot L \geq 0 \implies \text{potentially lit}$$
$$\tilde{N} \cdot L < 0 \implies \text{self-shadowing}$$

As in the previous case, artifacts occur in regions where the result of the self-shadowing test is different when applied to the actual triangle normal N and the interpolated normal $\tilde{N}$. In the case that N indicates that an intersection point is lit, and $\tilde{N}$ indicates that it is in shadow, we can use the solution discussed for the surface sidedness problem. Merely substituting the actual triangle normal N for the interpolated normal $\tilde{N}$ in subsequent shading calculations reduces terminator artifacts. In the case that N indicates that a surface point is in shadow and $\tilde{N}$ indicates that it is lit, as in Figure 3, a different solution is required. Here, the problem is that the shadow ray is launched from inside the surface so that the point is always in shadow, even though the actual surface point may be lit.

To solve this problem, the shadow ray is launched further from the point of intersection so that it can "escape" to the outside of the surface. Ray tracing algorithms incorporate a tolerance, called the shadow tolerance, which controls how far from the point of intersection to shoot the shadow ray. For most surfaces, simply making this number a parameter of the surface instead of a global constant eliminates terminator artifacts. When the shadow tolerance can not be made large enough over the whole surface to eliminate terminator artifacts without simultaneously creating other artifacts, a variable shadow tolerance can be used. Figure 4 shows one such scheme.

3 Organization Of The Model

Once the modeler has tessellated surfaces in the model into triangles, he must organize these triangles and other model components using lists and 3D grids. This organization takes place during the preprocessing phase. When preprocessing is complete, the model may be ray traced to generate an image. This section describes the structure of lists and 3D grids, and their use in organizing complex models. Section 4 describes how model components are inserted into lists and grids during preprocessing. Section 5 describes how the preprocessed model is ray traced.

A component of a model is called an *object*. The following is the C language definition of an object:

```
structure object {
    double bounding_box[3][2];
    structure transformation *trans;
    char *root_object;
    int object_type;
}
```

Each object can be transformed using an 3×3 transformation matrix and a 3×1 translation vector, pointed to by the **trans** field. Each object is also bounded by a simple box formed by three pairs of extents in the x, y, and z directions in the **bounding_box** field. The **root_object** field is a pointer to a structure containing parameters of a specific object, called the *root object*. Examples of root objects are polygons, spheres, cylinders, triangles, lists, and 3D grids. The **object_type** field indicates the type of the root object.

3.1 Structure Of Lists And 3D Grids

A *list* is a linked list of objects. Its C language definition is

```
structure list {
    structure object *list_object;
    structure list *next;
}
```

A *3D grid* is a three dimensional array of rectangular volumes, called *cells*, formed by regularly dividing a larger rectangular solid along the coordinate axes. Each cell contains a pointer to an object that is bounded by the cell extents. It is defined as:

```
structure grid {
    double grid_extent[3][2];
    int x_divisions, y_divisions, z_divisions;
    structure object *cells[];
}
```

Since many objects can occupy space within a cell extent, the object pointed to by a nonempty cell is always a list. This list has its own bounding box which bounds all the objects inside the grid cell. Its transformation pointer is always null. Empty cells are indicated by a null object pointer. Cells in the grid are stored in the `cells` field. The `grid_extent` field stores the extent of the volume that was divided into cells using `x_divisions` x divisions, `y_divisions` y divisions, and `z_divisions` z divisions.

3.2 Building the Model with Lists and Grids

The modeler specifies lists and 3D grids by opening a list or 3D grid and inserting a series of objects into it. Only one list or grid can be open at a time. When a grid is opened, the modeler specifies the number of x, y, and z divisions in the grid, and the x, y, and z extent of the grid. Opening a list requires no parameters. The specification of a list or grid also includes a unique name so that lists or grids built by the modeler can later be instantiated into other lists and grids. The entire model is hierarchically built in a bottom-up fashion using instantiation.

Triangles in a single surface tessellation are usually inserted into a single grid. This grid can then be instantiated many times in the model, and can be separately tranformed in each instance. This is accomplished by creating several objects whose `root_object` fields all point to a single copy of the grid, but whose `trans` field point to different transformation structures. In the same way, the modeler can also replicate lists by multiple instantiation.

Model building is currently a heuristic, modeller directed process. More work still remains to develop fully automatic algorithms that can organize complex models for efficient ray tracing. On the other hand, lists and 3D grids often naturally fit the model's organizational structure. For example, our model of a grassy plain (see image in Section 6) is a list containing a plain polygon and a grass field grid. The grass field was hierarchically constructed using two different grass blade surface tessellations. First, a grass patch was built by replicating these two blades many times with various rotations, scales, and translations and inserting them into a grid. Two of these patches were then replicated and inserted into a larger grid to form a field of grass. Fields were then replicated into a grass plain. In this way, without much modeler effort, we constructed a very complex model (4×10^{11} triangles) which could be ray traced quite quickly (12 hours on an IBM 4381).

4 Preprocessing Algorithm

Figure 5 describes the "generic" algorithm to insert a object into a list. The term "generic" is used because the algorithm works for any object that can be bounded in a simple xyz extent bounding box. Figure 5 refers to transforming and enlarging bounding boxes. A bounding box is transformed by transforming each vertex of the original bounding box, and bounding the result in x, y, and z. A bounding box is enlarged by another bounding box with simple maximum/minimum operations to produce a bounding box that

Let O be an object to be inserted into list L
Let B be O's bounding box
Let T be the current transformation
Transform B by T to give $\dot{B}$
Create an object $\hat{O}$ *whose*
  `root_object` *and* `object_type` *fields are equal to O's*
  `bounding_box` *field is* $\dot{B}$
  `trans` *field points to T*
Enlarge L's bounding box by $\dot{B}$
Add a pointer to $\hat{O}$ *to L's linked list of objects*

Figure 5: Generic Object Enlist Algorithm

Let O be an object to be inserted into grid G
Let B be O's bounding box
Let T be the current transformation
Transform B by T to give $\dot{B}$
For each cell in G within or intersecting $\dot{B}$ *Do*
  clip $\dot{B}$ *to this grid cell yielding a bounding box* $\ddot{B}$
  create an object $\hat{O}$ *whose*
    `root_object` *and* `object_type` *fields equal O's*
    `bounding_box` *field is* $\ddot{B}$
    `trans` *field points to T*
  add $\hat{O}$ *to the cell's object list, creating this*
   list if the cell was previously empty
Endfor

Figure 6: Generic Object Engrid Algorithm

bounds both. Figure 6 describes the generic algorithm for inserting an object into a grid.

The generic algorithms work for any primitive. Several optimizations can be made, however, to speed ray tracing of triangle and polygon primitives. First, instead of transforming objects by inverse transforming the ray (see Section 5), we can transform the primitives directly during preprocessing. This avoids many ray transformations and yields tighter bounding boxes around the primitives, allowing the ray tracing algorithm to cull more objects from ray intersection consideration.

Second, instead of clipping the primitive's bounding box to each grid cell, the primitive itself can be clipped as in Figure 7 [1]. This yields tight bounding boxes around the triangles and polygons inside of every grid cell, and appropriately ignores grid cells which intersect the bounding box but not the primitive inside. The bounding box of the primitive inside a grid cell becomes its bounding box after clipping to the grid cell's extents. On the other hand, the object inserted into the grid cell's list is still the original unclipped triangle or polygon. The unclipped primitive is inserted to conserve memory since only one copy of a triangle or polygon is stored instead of several clipped versions of the same thing. It is also more efficient to intersect a ray with a triangle than to intersect with the many-sided polygon that may result from clipping a triangle to a volume.

5 Ray/Model Intersection Algorithm

To intersect a ray with an object, the algorithm first determines if the ray intersects the object's bounding box (see Figure 8) [2]. If

[1] [Cyrus 78] discusses clipping polygons to convex volumes.

[2] The ray/bounding box intersection algorithm is adapted from that found in [Kay 86] to avoid intersections with planes behind the ray origin.

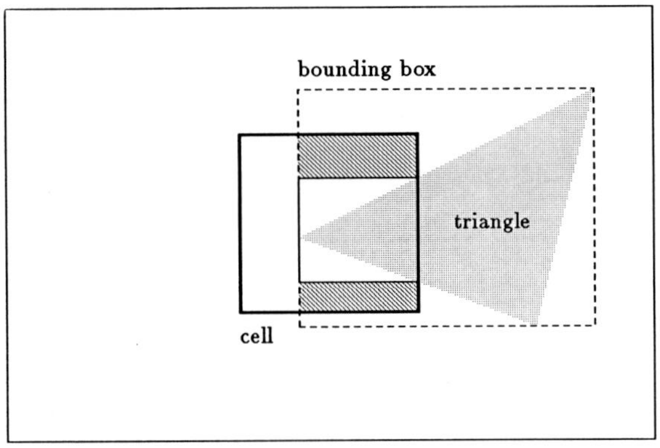

Figure 7: Clipping a Triangle to a Grid Cell — Clipping the triangle yields a bounding box that is smaller (by the diagonally shaded areas) than intersecting the triangle bounding box (dashed lines) with the cell extent.

it does, and the object's **trans** field is non-null, then it transforms the ray. Let A be a 3×3 matrix and B a 3×1 vector that transforms a point P to P' via $P' = AP + B$. Intersecting a ray $O + Dt$ with an object so transformed is equivalent to intersecting the untransformed object with a transformed ray $O' + D't$ where [3]

$$
\begin{aligned}
O' &= A^{-1}(O - B) \\
D' &= A^{-1}(D)
\end{aligned}
$$

The transformed ray and the root object pointed to by the object's `root_object` field are then passed to the intersection routine for the specific type of root object. If the root object is a primitive (e.g. a triangle) then this routine computes the ray/root object intersection directly. If the object is a list or 3D grid, then the routine traces the ray through the structure, recursively calling the ray/object intersection routine for individual objects it contains.

5.1 Tracing A Ray Through A List

Computing the intersection of a ray with a list can be accomplished by performing a ray/object intersection (defined in Section 5) on each object in the list. The intersection that occurs at the minimum t parameter of the ray is the desired frontmost intersection.

Alternatively, ray/bounding box intersections can be computed on each object first, so that objects whose bounding box is intersected by the ray can be sorted in increasing order of the ray's $t^{\min}$ intersection with the object's bounding box (see [Kay 86]). Then, when a ray/root object intersection is computed at some t, the algorithm can eliminate any root objects whose $t^{\min} > t$.

The implementation allows the modeler to specify whether sorting takes place in any list. The sort algorithm used is a simple linear insertion sort; [Kay 86] notes that a heap sort is faster for large lists.

5.2 Tracing A Ray Through A 3D Grid

The algorithm to trace a ray through a 3D grid is described in Figure 9. It visits each grid cell intersected by the ray in the order of intersection, and intersects the ray with the cell list in each grid cell visited. At the start of the while loop, t_x, t_y, and t_z are the

[3] The transformation structure should therefore store the matrix A^{-1} and the vector B.

Let the ray be $O + Dt$
Let t *be bounded by* $t^{\min} \le t \le t^{\max}$
Let the bounding box be $B^{\min}, B^{\max}$ *where*
  $B^{\min}$ *(*$B^{\max}$*) is a vector containing the minimum (maximum) xyz extents of the box*

For $i \leftarrow$ *x-index to z-index Do*
  If $D_i \ge 0$ *Then* $b^{\min} \leftarrow B_i^{\min}$, $b^{\max} \leftarrow B_i^{\max}$
  Else $b^{\min} \leftarrow B_i^{\max}$, $b^{\max} \leftarrow B_i^{\min}$
  If $b^{\max} - O_i < 0$ *Then Return no hit*
  $t \leftarrow (b^{\max} - O_i)/D_i$
  If $t \le t^{\max}$ *Then*
    If $t < t^{\min}$ *Then Return no hit*
    $t^{\max} \leftarrow t$
  Endif
  If $b^{\min} - O_i > 0$ *Then*
    $t \leftarrow (b^{\min} - O_i)/D_i$
    If $t \ge t^{\min}$ *Then*
      If $t > t^{\max}$ *Then Return no hit*
      $t^{\min} \leftarrow t$
    Endif
  Endif
Endfor
Return hit (intersection at $t = t^{\min}$ *and* $t = t^{\max}$*)*

Figure 8: Ray/Bounding Box Intersection Algorithm

Let the ray be parameterized by $O + Dt$
Let t *be bounded by* $t^{\min} \le t \le t^{\max}$
Let the grid volume origin be M
Let the cell extent be C *i.e. each grid cell has extent*
  C_x *in* x, C_y *in* y, *and* C_z *in* z

Compute t^0 *— the ray's minimum intersection with the whole grid volume*
Compute the position P *of this intersection*
Compute the grid cell g *where this intersection occurs*
For $\phi \leftarrow$ *x-index to z-index Do*
  Initialize t_ϕ *such that*
    $M_\phi + iC_\phi \le P_\phi < M_\phi + (i+1)C_\phi$ *and*
    $O_\phi + D_\phi t_\phi = M_\phi + iC_\phi$
  $\Delta_\phi \leftarrow C_\phi / D_\phi$
  $t_\phi \leftarrow t_\phi + \Delta_\phi$
Endfor

While $t^0 \le t^{\max}$ *and* g *is in grid Do*
  Let ψ *be the index such that* $t_\psi = \min(t_x, t_y, t_z)$
  $t^1 \leftarrow t_\psi$
  If g *is nonempty Then*
    Intersect ray with the list at cell g $(t^0 \le t \le t^1)$
    If intersects Then Return intersection
  Endif
  $t^0 \leftarrow t^1$
  $t_\psi \leftarrow t_\psi + \Delta_\psi$
  Update g *depending on* ψ *and the sign of* D_ψ
Endwhile

Return no intersection

Figure 9: Ray/3D Grid Intersection Algorithm

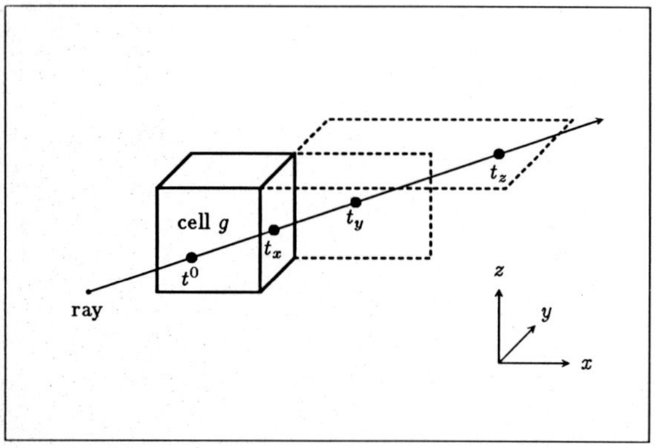

Figure 10: Tracing a Ray Through a Grid — The minimum t_ψ occurs when $\psi = x$, so the next grid cell intersected is adjacent in the increasing x direction. In this case, the algorithm will increment t_x by Δ_x after intersecting the ray with the list in grid cell g.

t values of the ray's maximum (second) intersection with the x, y, and z bounding extents of the current grid cell, g (see Figure 10). The next grid cell may be computed incrementally by finding the minimum of these (t_ψ). This gives the t value of the ray's second intersection with g. It is also the t value of the ray's minimum (first) intersection with the next grid cell intersected. The index ψ indicates which grid cell is intersected next — if D_ψ is positive, the next cell is adjacent in the increasing ψ direction; otherwise, it is adjacent in the decreasing ψ direction.

This grid traversal algorithm is different than the 3DDDA algorithm described in [Fujimoto 86]. Like 3DDDA, no multiply operations are used in the inner loop. Also, the algorithm can be performed using integer arithmetic by scaling the t variables by $1/(t^{\max} - t^{\min})$. Double precision arithmetic was actually used in the implementation, however, to eliminate inaccuracies in tracing the ray through the grid. Unlike 3DDDA, for each grid cell visited this algorithm computes t^0 and t^1 — the t extents of the ray through the grid cell. This is useful to check that root object intersections actually occur within the cell extent, and in further processing to cull objects in the grid cell list.

Checking Intersections in a 3D Grid Cell

Since a single object may occupy several grid cells, the ray's intersection with the object inside a grid cell should be checked to ensure it is actually within the grid cell. A ray/object intersection should occur in the cell where the ray actually intersects the object, not in the first grid cell visited which contains the primitive. The check for this situation is illustrated in Figure 11.

Culling Inside a 3D Grid Cell

The grid intersection algorithm must intersect the ray with the list in each grid cell the ray intersects. Two optimizations to the algorithm in Section 5.1 can be made for this list intersection.

The first concerns determining whether any object in the cell list is hit by the ray. A simple optimization speeds up detection of situations in which a ray intersects a nonempty grid cell, but misses the cell list bounding box, as in Figure 12. Many times, most of the extents of the cell list bounding box are identical to the cell extent. Since the grid traversal algorithm has already computed the ray's intersection with the cell extent, the algorithm need only process the cell list bounding planes that are different from the cell extent.

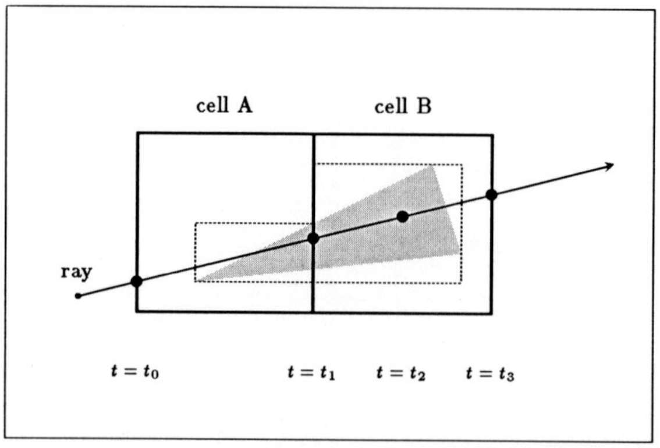

Figure 11: Intersecting a Ray with an Object in Multiple Grid Cells — A ray intersects a triangle in cell B at $t = t_2$. The ray also intersects the bounding box (dashed lines) of the triangle in cell A, but not the triangle itself. When it processes cell A, the algorithm checks that the ray intersection with the triangle is between t_0 and t_1. Since it is not ($t_2 > t_1$), it correctly returns the intersection of the ray with the triangle only after processing cell B, where $t_1 < t_2 < t_3$.

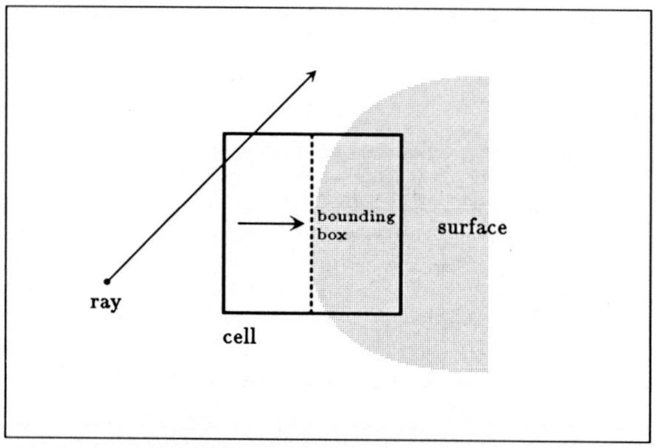

Figure 12: Bounding Box Inside a Grid Cell — The bounding box around the surface inside a grid cell differs from the cell extent in only one extent, identified with an arrow. We need only check one extent to see that the ray misses the bounding box inside this cell.

This is accomplished by storing six flags along with the cell list bounding box extents, which indicate whether or not the extent differs from the cell extent. These flags are trivially computed during preprocessing. The algorithm in Figure 8 is modified to disregard extents whose flag is false.

A second optimization concerns determining which objects in the list are intersected by the ray. A simple cull called the *ray box cull*, shown in Figure 13, determines if a ray misses an object's bounding box using only six comparison operations. The ray box cull is much faster than the bounding box intersection algorithm, but is less strict (note Object B, whose bounding box is not intersected by the ray, but whose bounding box does intersect the ray box). In practice, for very simple primitives like triangles, it has been effective enough to replace the bounding box test, since the bounding box test has complexity on the order of a ray/triangle intersection.

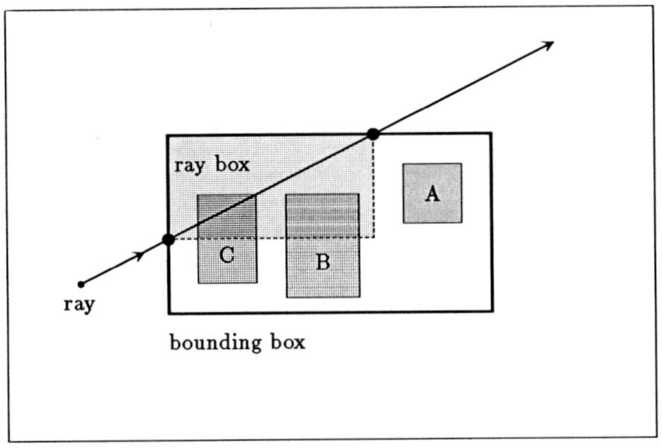

Figure 13: The Ray Box Cull — The t extents of the ray (t^{min} and t^{max}) through the cell list bounding box are used to construct a box, called the *ray box*, with corners at the ray's two intersections with the bounding box. If an object inside the cell extent is intersected by the ray, then its bounding box must overlap the ray box. By computing the ray box once for all the objects in the cell list, any object whose bounding box does not overlap the ray box can be culled, like Object A.

6 Results

Figures 14 and 15 show how time to render a tessellation of a single surface depends on the number of triangles in the tessellation. Times for both graphs are given in seconds to render a non-antialiased (one ray per pixel) 128 by 128 pixel resolution picture. Reported times are for an IBM 4381/Group 12 running Amdahl UTS. An example picture produced is shown in upper left corner of the graph. The dashed line is the time to render the non-tessellated surface using an analytic algorithm in the case of the sphere [4], and an iterative algorithm in the case of the superquadric (see [Barr 84] for an explanation of superquadrics). The solid lines represent graphs of time vs. number of triangles for grids of various cell sizes.

The graphs demonstrate that the time to render a tessellated surface grows quite slowly with increasing number of triangles. Further, in the case of superquadrics, the iterative approach is slower than tessellating and rendering. Only about 2000 triangles were required to produce an image of the superquadric which was indistinguishable from that produced by the iterative algorithm, while the rendering time for this tessellation was half that for the iterative algorithm. Tessellations containing up to 50,000 triangles were still faster than the iterative algorithm.

Yet, superquadrics are very simple parametric surfaces. Tessellation is even more advantageous for complex surfaces whose evaluation can cost hundreds of times more than a superquadric. In experiments, rendering time for tesselations depended on the number of triangles, surface area, and projected screen area of the tessellation. It was relatively independent of the mathematical definition and shape of the parametric surface. Numerical techniques, in contrast, depend on the complexity of the parameterization of the surface.

For example, the grass blade rendered in several included pictures is a parametric surface defined by an integral of a specified Jacobian function that governs how the surface normals behave.

[4]The sphere graph is included for comparison purposes only; tessellation is not necessary for quadric surfaces for which ray intersections may be computed analytically.

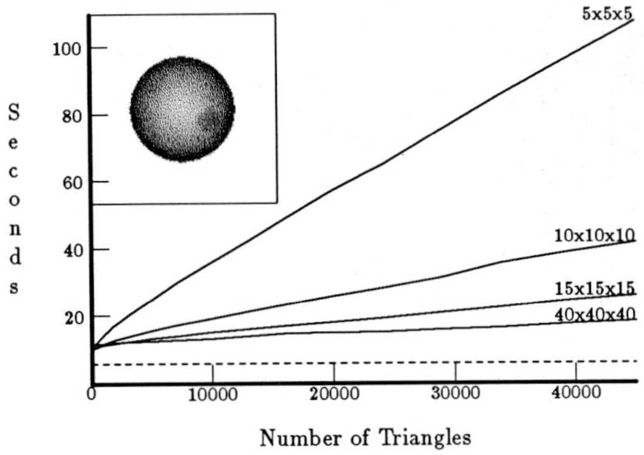

Figure 14: Time to Render Sphere Tessellation

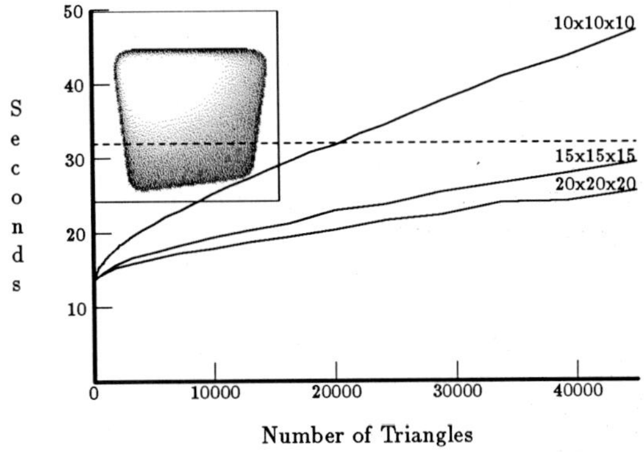

Figure 15: Time to Render Superquadric Tessellation

Evaluation of surface points requires numerical integration and is very expensive. After tessellating once, this surface was incorporated into many models at a rendering cost roughly equal to a tessellated sphere or superquadric of equal size, surface area, and number of triangles. Use of a numerical technique to ray trace the blades would be prohibitively slow, if it can be made to work at all.

The algorithm has been effective for fast rendering of models. For simple pictures (< 100,000 primitives), it consistently performed about twice as fast as the current implementation of the algorithm developed in [Kay 86], which claimed to out-perform competing algorithms such as octrees. It was also able to render complex models that have never been attempted using conventional ray tracers. Table 1 shows the rendering time in CPU hours and number of primitives for pictures included in this paper. All pictures were computed at 512 by 512 pixel resolution.

The times for ray tracing these images are comparable to times for conventional ray tracers to generate images containing a few hundred polygons and spheres. In this same rendering time, our ray tracer has generated pictures containing huge numbers of primitives, and surfaces that would require much greater rendering time using other published techniques.

7 Acknowledgements

Tim Kay and Jim Kajiya provided advice on ray tracing; Brian Von Herzen on tessellation of surfaces. Figures and monochrome

Title	Primitives	Rays/Pixel	Hours
graphics lab	100	16	12
teapot museum piece	10,000	16	8
reflective bristles	15,000	16	12
statue of liberty	100,000	16	14
brass ornament	100,000	16	9
flowers, grass, clovers	200,000	16	3.5
glass museum piece	400,000	16	8.5
grass and trees	$2x10^9$	16	16
field of grass	$4x10^{11}$	16	12

Table 1: Rendering Time For Pictures

raster images in this paper were incorporated using software written by Wen King Su and Brian Von Herzen.

8 References

[Barr 81] Barr, Alan H., "Superquadrics and Angle Preserving Transformations," *Computer Graphics and Applications*, 1(1).

[Barr 86] Barr, Alan H., "Ray Tracing Deformed Surfaces," Computer Graphics, 20(4), August 1986, pp. 287-296.

[Cyrus 78] Cyrus, M. and J. Beck, "Generalized two and three dimensional Clipping," Computers and Graphics, 3(1), 1978, pp. 23-28.

[Fujimoto 86] Fujimoto, Akira, Takayuki Tanaka, and Kansei Iwata, "ARTS: Accelerated Ray-Tracing System", IEEE Computer Graphics and Applications, 6(4), April 1986, 16-26.

[Glassner 84] Glassner, Andrew S., "Space Subdivision for Fast Ray Tracing," IEEE Computer Graphics and Applications, 4(10), October, 1984, pp. 15-22.

[Kalra 86] Kalra, Devendra, M.S. dissertation in preparation.

[Kaplan 85] Kaplan, Michael R., "The Uses of Spatial Coherence in Ray Tracing," ACM SIGGRAPH '85 Course Notes 11, July 22-26 1985.

[Kajiya 82] Kajiya, James T., "Ray Tracing Parametric Patches," Computer Graphics, 16(3), July 1983, pp. 245-254.

[Kay 86] Kay, Timothy L., James T. Kajiya, "Ray Tracing Complex Scenes," Computer Graphics, 20(4), August 1986, pp. 269-278.

[Joy 86] Joy, Kenneth I., Murthy N. Bhetanabhotla, "Ray Tracing Parametric Surface Patches Utilizing Numerical Techniques and Ray Coherence," Computer Graphics, 20(4), August 1986, pp. 279-286.

[Rubin 80] Rubin, Steve M. and T. Whitted., "A Three-Dimensional Representation for Fast Rendering of Complex Scenes," Computer Graphics 14(3), July 1980, pp. 110-116.

[Toth 85] Toth, Daniel L., "On Ray Tracing Parametric Surfaces," Computer Graphics 19(3), July 1985, pp. 171-179.

[Von Herzen 85] Von Herzen, Brian P.,"Sampling Deformed, Intersecting Surfaces with Quadtrees," Caltech CS Technical Report 5179:TR:85, pp. 1-40.

[Von Herzen 87] Von Herzen, Brian P.,"Accurate Sampling of Deformed, Intersecting Surfaces," to appear in Computer Graphics, 1987.

[Whitted 80] Whitted, Turner, "An Improved Illumination Model for Shaded Display," Communications of the ACM, 23(6), June 1980, pp. 343-349.

Appendix — Ray/Triangle Intersection

This appendix describes an efficient algorithm to compute ray/triangle intersections.

Let P_i for $i \in 0, 1, 2$ be the coordinates of the three vertices of the triangle. Let R_i be the corresponding normal vectors at these vertices which are to be used for normal interpolation across the triangle.

During the preprocessing stage, the above information is used to construct a triangle structure, the tessellation unit root object. We first compute and store the normal vector to the plane containing the triangle, N, by

$$N = (P_1 - P_0) \times (P_2 - P_0).$$

We also compute and store a scalar d such that any point, P, in the triangle's plane satisfies $P \cdot N + d = 0$. This scalar is computed by

$$d = -P_0 \cdot N.$$

Lastly, we compute and store an index i_0 such that

$$i_0 = \begin{cases} 0 & \text{if } |N_x| \text{ is maximum} \\ 1 & \text{if } |N_y| \text{ is maximum} \\ 2 & \text{if } |N_z| \text{ is maximum} \end{cases}$$

The triangle structure also stores the three vertices and normals, P_i and R_i. To conserve memory, the triangle structure should store pointers to these since, on average, each vertex in a tessellation is shared by six triangles.

To intersect a ray parametrized by $O + Dt$ with a triangle, first compute the t parameter of the ray's intersection with the triangle plane:

$$t = \frac{d - N \cdot O}{N \cdot D}. \tag{1}$$

Let i_1 and i_2 ($i_1, i_2 \in \{0, 1, 2\}$) be two unequal indices different from i_0. Using the t value obtained from Equation 1, compute the i_1 and i_2 components of the point of intersection, Q, by

$$Q_{i_1} = O_{i_1} + D_{i_1} t$$
$$Q_{i_2} = O_{i_2} + D_{i_2} t.$$

A point enclosure test can then be performed by computing scalars β_0, β_1, and β_2 according to [5]

$$\beta_i = \frac{[(P_{i+2} - P_{i+1}) \times (Q - P_{i+1})]_{i_0}}{[N]_{i_0}} \tag{2}$$

where addition in subscripts is modulo 3. Note that these β's are the barycentric coordinates of the point where the ray intersects the triangle plane. Only the i_0 component of the cross product is computed; the value of Q_{i_0} is therefore unnecessary. Q is inside the triangle if and only if $0 \le \beta_i \le 1$ for $i \in \{0, 1, 2\}$. Division by N_{i_0} can be eliminated by appropriate rearrangement of the test implied by Equation 2. The interpolated normal $\tilde{N}$ is given by

$$\tilde{N} = \beta_0 R_0 + \beta_1 R_1 + \beta_2 R_2.$$

[5] $[X]_i$ denotes the ith component of the vector X.

Figure 15: Graphics Lab — The carpet texture map in this image was created by ray tracing a simulated carpet containing roughly 125,000 triangles. Note the diffuse shadows from three extended light sources.

Figure 17: Statue of Liberty — The statue database was created using I-DEAS Geomod from SDRC, and contained about 12,000 triangles after processing. Each tree contains roughly 10,000 primitives.

Figure 16: Field of Grass — This image was rendered from a model description containing more than 400 billion primitives.

Figure 18: Flowers, Grass, and Clovers

Figure 19: Brass Ornament

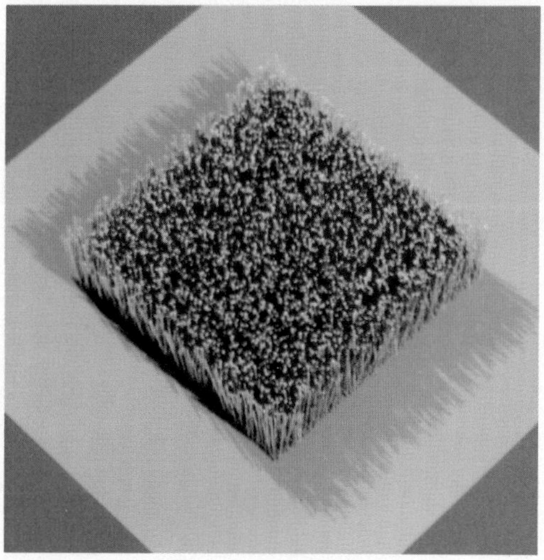

Figure 20: Reflective Bristles

Figure 21: Teapot Museum Piece

Figure 22: Glass Museum Piece

Figure 23: Trees and Grass

Boundary Evaluation of Non-Convex Primitives to Produce Parametric Trimmed Surfaces

Gary A. Crocker and William F. Reinke

Calma Company
Research and Development Center
9805 Scranton Road
San Diego, CA 92121-1765

1. ABSTRACT

To integrate a CSG-based solid modeler into an existing wireframe/surface modeling system, new boundary evaluation technology has been developed. This scheme uses exact representations for the simple quadric surfaces and both exact and approximate representations of higher-order curved surfaces. It supports parametric primitives (box, wedge, sphere, cylinder, cone, torus), procedural primitives (extrusion, revolution, tube) and a sculptured surface primitive. The output includes curves, parametric trimmed surfaces, and a data structure of adjacency information.

An existing boundary evaluator (PADL-2's) has been enhanced to allow a general non-convex faceted primitive with planar and quadric facets. This new hybrid evaluator combines two techniques for curve/primitive classification. PADL-2's existing halfspace-based classification is reserved for the simple convex primitives, and a new ray firing based classification is applied to the non-convex primitives. After evaluation, approximate intersection curves (from intersections involving higher order surfaces) are refined to a specified tolerance by exploiting an exact parametric representation of the surfaces of the primitives. The refined curves and the quadric surface intersection curves are used to create a parametric trimmed surface representation of the solid. This combination of techniques and representations offers advantages in accuracy, robustness and efficiency suitable to a production environment.

CR Categories and Subject Descriptors: I.3.5 [Computer Graphics]: Computational Geometry and Object Modeling-- Curve, surface, solid and object representations; Geometric algorithms, and systems; Modeling packages.

Key Words and Phrases: Computational geometry, Boolean set operations, solid modeling, boundary evaluation, constructive solid geometry, surface/surface intersection, parametric surfaces, curve/primitive classification.

2. INTRODUCTION

A Constructive Solid Geometry (CSG) representation is used by many solid modelers to define solids [17,18]. In this representation, complex solids are defined in terms of volumetric Boolean operations to be performed on simpler solid "primitives." A boundary representation (Brep) is a representation of a solid in terms of the bounding surfaces, curves and vertices, together with adjacency relationships. Boundary evaluation is the process which calculates a boundary representation of a solid from its CSG representation. Additional information on boundary evaluation can be found in [3,5,9,15,16,25].

Although the algorithms which perform boundary evaluation are very complex, at a high level of abstraction the overall approach is "generate-and-test"; that is generate a "sufficient set" of bounding geometry (surfaces and curves), then test (classify) each element of the sufficient set to see whether it lies on the boundary of the resulting solid. The set of surfaces belonging to the primitives is a sufficient set of surfaces, but the set of curves belonging to the primitives is not a sufficient set of curves; we need to add (some subset of) all possible surface/surface intersections between primitives. Thus, in its simplest form, a boundary evaluator needs to perform surface/surface intersection to generate curves and curve classification to determine which curves lie on the boundary of the resulting solid. This outlines an approach common to many boundary evaluators [15]. Differences between evaluators occur in areas such as geometric coverage (allowed input), methods of classification, algorithms for surface intersection, use of topological information, computational complexity reduction schemes, and so on.

A survey of published work on boundary evaluation algorithms shows two distinct classes of boundary evaluators: faceted and analytical [15,17,18]. Faceted evaluators approximate solids with planar facets [4,5,6,9,14,25]. Evaluation is then performed on the resulting polyhedron. These types of evaluators accept as input any primitive which can be expressed or approximated by planar facets. A limitation of this technique is that the intersection curves for nonplanar surfaces are all approximate. Analytical evaluators perform actual intersection between curved surfaces [2,3,8,15]. The curves which are created using this type of evaluator represent exact surface intersections. However, inrut to these evaluators is usually limited to primitives which can be represented as intersections of quadric and simple higher order halfspaces. Ways of extending the geometric coverage of the analytical evaluators are under investigation[13,19].

We have designed and implemented a hybrid boundary evaluator which produces intersection curves and accurate trimmed surfaces for simple quadric primitives and for certain procedural (revolved, extruded) and sculptured surface primitives. This has been accomplished using a two-stage boundary evaluator and a dual representation of the surfaces of the solid primitives. The first stage of the process is referred to as "Boolean evaluation" and the second stage as "parametric surface trimming." The Boolean evaluator consists of an existing analytical boundary evaluator (PADL-2) [15] which has been enhanced by adding a ray firing-based classification procedure to allow a general non-convex faceted primitive. The faceted primitive is a two-manifold representation [24] of a solid which allows both planar and quadric facets (cylindrical and conical). Quadric surfaces of faceted primitives are represented exactly, while other curved surfaces are approximated with planar or quadric facets. The output of the Boolean evaluator is a boundary file which contains analytical curves, approximate curves, topological information, and references to the original primitives.

Because the original analytical primitive definitions have been maintained outside the Boolean evaluator, a set of parametric surfaces can be created which exactly represent the surfaces of the primitives. These together with the output of the Boolean evaluator are used to create parametric trimmed surfaces (surfaces restricted to a closed bounded subset of the parameter space) [11]. A general iterative intersection technique uses the exact surfaces to refine the approximate curves (generated from intersections involving higher order surfaces) to a given tolerance. The refined curves and the analytical curves are used to create curves in the parameter space of the surfaces. Loops formed from these parametric curves define the parametric trimmed surface boundaries. The trimmed surfaces and existing adjacency information create a boundary representation which binds the trimmed surfaces together in an edge-based topology.

3. DESIGN OBJECTIVES

The main rationale for the development of a boundary evaluator was to integrate solid modeling into an existing wireframe/surface modeler (Prism/DDM). Given a constructive solid geometry definition of a solid, the boundary evaluator should produce curves for the various curve applications (dimensioning and tolerancing, graphic display, design documentation, etc.) and parametric trimmed surfaces suitable for the surface applications (NC tool path generation, hidden line/surface removal, mass properties, filleting, etc.). A boundary representation which explicitly represents the various face/edge/vertex adjacency relationships would also be useful for automatic NC tool path generation algorithms on multiple surfaces, and for other applications. The solid modeler would then be able to provide input to a large number of existing applications, and would thus be a viable piece of an end-to-end production system rather than simply a conceptual design tool for producing graphic images.

To accomplish this in a production system, the following goals were specified:

1) The curves produced should be analytical for at least the quadric surface (planar, cylindrical, conical, spherical) intersections.

2) The surfaces should be trimmed to user-specifiable tolerances that can practically be set tight enough for existing manual/automatic tool path generation algorithms.

3) The evaluator should allow as input parametric primitives (box, wedge, sphere, cylinder, cone, torus), procedural primitives (solid of extrusion, solid of revolution, tube) and sculptured surface primitives.

4) The boundary evaluator should be reliable enough to be used in a production environment.

5) The evaluator should be able to process models with as many as 5000 primitive faces.

6) The performance of the evaluator should be competitive with existing production evaluators.

4. PADL 2 OVERVIEW

PADL-2 is a well known solid modeling system developed with industrial and public resources by the Production Automation Project (PAP) at the University of Rochester, Rochester, New York. Calma Company was a participant in the PAP's Industrial Associates program. The decision to use the PADL-2 boundary evaluator as the basis of our Boolean evaluator gave us a reliable and robust set of boundary evaluation algorithms and geometric utilities [16].

The PADL-2 boundary evaluator accepts as input primitives which can be expressed as intersections of halfspaces. The quadric halfspaces supported by PADL-2 are planar, spherical, cylindrical and conical. There is also a toroidal halfspace, but it is not fully supported. PADL-2 fully supports box, wedge, cylinder, cone, and sphere primitives, and the latest version of PADL-2 contains a general halfspace primitive. With this, a user can define a primitive as the intersection of up to 100 of the halfspaces.

The PADL-2 evaluator is an edge-based analytical evaluator. It requires two major geometric operations: surface/surface intersection and curve/primitive classification. The surface intersection is analytical. The intersection curves are classified with respect to each primitive in a three-step process. First, a curve is intersected with the surface of the halfspace and divided into segments. Second, each segment is classified as inside/on/outside the halfspace by classifying a point on the segment with respect to the halfspace. Third, the results of the halfspace classification are combined to determine curve/primitive classification results. The classification of a segment with respect to a primitive is simplified by the constraint of convexity placed upon the input primitives [21].

The primitive classification results are propagated up the CSG tree using a set of Boolean combination rules [16] to determine the relationship of the curve to the resulting solid. If a curve lies on the boundary of the resulting solid, it is stored into the PADL-2 boundary file. When evaluation is finished, the boundary file contains a list of surfaces and the 3-D curves associated with each.

5. Boolean Evaluation of Non-Convex Primitives

We wanted to extend the geometric coverage of the PADL-2 boundary evaluator by removing the requirement of convexity. Many non-convex primitives could be expressed as Boolean combinations of convex primitives, but it may require a large number of convex primitives to represent or approximate a single non-convex primitive. Moreover, such an approach would not be practical for representing sculptured surface primitives. We considered keeping the existing algorithms and adding new geometric entities (halfspaces and curves) corresponding to the non-convex primitive types. That is, a halfspace definition would be created for surfaces of revolution, extrusion and the sculptured surface type, in much the same way that a toroidal halfspace is used in PADL-2 to represent a (non-convex) torus. It would then be necessary to add surface intersection capabilities for these surface types -- but that is not a simple task, because these intersections cannot be computed analytically. Using an iterative intersection algorithm for these new halfspace types would carry a stiff penalty in terms of performance and/or reliability. Our reluctance to introduce iterative techniques into the evaluator led to the decision to add a general non-convex faceted primitive and change the PADL-2 evaluation algorithms to accommodate it.

Convexity is needed only for the PADL-2 curve/primitive classification. More general classification techniques are available for non-convex solids, but there is a price to be paid in performance and in complexity of implementation [3]. The geometric coverage requirement overrode the considerations of complexity. Thus we have implemented a more general curve/primitive classification technique, based on ray firing, for the new non-convex primitives. The simpler technique has been retained for the convex primitives to which it is suited. All non-convex primitives are represented by a closed set of planar or quadric surfaces. The rest of the boundary evaluation algorithms (surface/surface intersection, curve/surface intersection, propagation of results up the CSG tree) remain largely unchanged.

5.1. New Non-Convex Primitive

The non-convex primitive is itself a boundary representation. The new primitive is defined by a closed set of facets (bounded surfaces). The facets are bound together by an edge-based topology. In our implementation, three facet types were allowed: convex planar, convex quadric, and non-convex planar. Note that we have broadened the term "facet" to remove the restriction of planarity.

The first type is a planar facet bounded by a convex three- or four- sided polygon. A set of these facets is used to approximate the free form surfaces and noncylindrical and nonplanar surfaces of the extrusion.

The second facet type is a convex quadric facet bounded by four curves. Our implementation limits these curves to linear and circular arcs, as the only two quadric facets required were the cylindrical facet and the conical facet. These facets, along with the planar facets, allow the exact representation of extrusion surfaces defined by linear and circular arcs; other curve types in the boundary of the extruded region result in surfaces which are approximated with convex planar facets. Linear arcs in a revolution create surfaces which are represented exactly by cylindrical and conical facets. Other curve types in the boundary of the revolved region result in surfaces which are approximated by cylindrical and conical facets. For example, a torus is approximated by a relatively small number of conical facets. To achieve roughly the same accuracy as 16 conical facets would require at least 256 planar facets.

The third facet type is a planar facet bounded by an unlimited number of linear or circular arcs, with no requirement of convexity. In fact, the curves may form nested loops, representing a facet with holes. This facet type is used to represent the end planes of an extrusion, planar surfaces in a revolution, and the end caps of the skinned solid.

With these three facet types it is possible to represent the quadric surfaces exactly and approximate the rest of the surfaces with either planar or quadric facets. Removing the requirement of convexity allows the representation of non-convex quadric primitives, without necessitating a Boolean combination of convex primitives. When non-quadric surfaces are approximated by a set of facets, these facets are treated as a single composite surface. No attempt is made to intersect two facets from the same surface. This is important in efficiently evaluating a primitive approximated by a large number of facets, such as the sculptured surface primitive.

5.2. Classification Method for Non-Convex Primitive

Ray firing can be used to determine if a point lies inside/outside/on the boundary of a non-convex faceted primitive. A ray is created starting at the point of interest and goes to effective infinity in some direction. This ray is intersected with all of the facets of the primitive, and the number of intersections are counted. If there is an odd number of intersections, the point lies inside the primitive. If the number is even or zero, the point lies outside the primitive. If the start point of the ray lies on a facet of the primitive, the point is on the primitive boundary.

A major problem with using ray firing in this application is processing speed. Typically, a large number of curves need to be classified for even moderately sized models. A single curve may intersect a primitive a number of times, creating several segments; each segment requiring a ray to be fired. Each ray then has to be intersected with each facet of the primitive.

A procedure which we refer to as *local transition detection* is used to reduce the number of ray/facet intersections and increase the efficiency of the ray firing algorithm [3]. Local transition detection determines an in/out/on classification using information available at a single intersection point. The classification is determined by comparing the curve tangents at the intersection point to the outward pointing normal of the facet at that point. If the tangent of the curve is in the same direction as the normal (dot product of tangent and normal greater then zero), then the curve segment is going out of the primitive. Special processing is required for cases where the curve just touches the surface. In our implementation, this problem was solved by stepping away from the intersection a small distance along the curve and recomputing the tangents on either side of the intersection. If a curve goes through an curve or a vertex rather than through the interior of the facet, the surface normals of facets adjacent to the curve or vertex are required for the transition detection. When a curve intersects a facet of a primitive, local transition detection can be used to determine which portions of it are inside/outside/on the primitive. Therefore, only curves which do not intersect the primitive require ray firing.

Two additional classification functions are used to apply ray firing to the bounded facets of the new primitive. A point-in-facet function determines if a point on the surface of a facet lies inside/outside/on the curves of the facet. An curve-in-facet function is also required to determine which portions of a curve, lying on the surface of a facet, lie inside/outside/on the curves of the facet. These functions are simple for the convex facets; a set of planes is constructed which bounds the facet on the surface, using the fact that all bounding curves are planar. Existing halfspace classification functions are then used to classify the point or curve with respect to the facet [21]. The nonconvex planar facet requires a special 2-D processor in which the facet is bounded by curves rather than halfspaces. This processor is based on 2-D ray firing with 2-D local transition detection [23].

The performance of this evaluation scheme is improved using several well known techniques (spatial sorting, bounding box tests, etc.) to decrease both the number of surface/surface intersections during curve generation and the number of facet/curve intersections during classification [7,20]. Without these techniques, this approach to boundary evaluation would be impractical for all but the simplest of models.

6. Parametric Surface Trimming

The Boolean evaluator produces curves and some adjacency information referencing the surfaces of the primitives. For our applications, this information does not constitute a trimmed surface representation. Our trimmed surface is a parametric surface restricted to a closed bounded region of its 2-D parameter space. The 2-D region is defined by closed oriented loops in parameter space. To obtain the parameter space loops we first obtain the model space loops. *Edge chasing* is the process of connecting the model space curves into loops, orienting the curves within the loops, and determining the relative loop containment. Up to this point the primitives have been represented by implicit surfaces and faceted approximations. The next step is to create the corresponding exact parametric surfaces using the original primitive definition. A representation of each model space curve in the parameter space of its incident surfaces is derived using projection along surface normals. At this stage the approximated model space curves, from intersections involving approximated surfaces, are refined by exploiting the exact surface representation. The parameter space loops defined by these curves along with the parametric surface definition constitute our trimmed surface representation. This approach has an advantage over repatching in that it does not alter the original surface definition [19]. The trimmed surfaces are joined together using the adjacency data carried over from the Boolean evaluator to create our boundary representation of a solid.

6.1. Edge chasing

At this point the boundary representation contains an unordered list of pointers to the curves bounding each surface. Seams are added to the list of curves bounding each closed surface, so that the model space loops formed from these curves will correspond to closed loops in the parameter spaces of the surfaces. Tolerance based comparisons of the endpoints of the curves associated with a surface are used to connect the curves into loops. The loops are then nested to differentiate between outer boundaries and holes of a surface, using a 2-D counterpart of the ray firing technique already discussed. Outer boundaries are oriented clockwise, inner boundaries counterclockwise, to maintain the convention that the part of the surface that is kept lies to the right of the boundary.

6.2. Parametric surface creation

Many surfaces of primitives in the original CSG model will not contribute to the evaluated representation. Other surfaces will appear in disjoint pieces, and multiple surfaces will have to be created, one for each piece. The information gained from edge chasing indicates how many copies of each surface need to be created. The parameters and positional information defining the parametric surface are extracted from the original CSG primitive definition. The normal direction of each surface is obtained from its dual in the Boolean evaluator; this allows us to expect that model space and parameter space loops will have the same orientation. The properly oriented surfaces are created and stored in the model database.

6.3. Projection

The role of surface projection is to find the parameter space representation of the curves that will bound each trimmed surface. For curves arising from intersections of simple surfaces, this could be done algebraically, but such an approach does not readily extend to all of the curves and surfaces which we support. An iterative algorithm based on Newton's method is used to project a sampling of points from each curve along surface normals [12]. A chord height test, using a user-specifiable tolerance, determines the density of the sampling. The resulting parameter space points are then used to create a curve which is an approximate parameter space representation of the original model space curve.

The most important requirement of the trimmed surface boundaries is that adjacent surfaces actually meet in model space; i.e., that intersection curves are accurately represented by parameter space curves. Gaps occur when the images of one or both of the parameter space curves representing an intersection differ from the actual intersection curve. For quadric surfaces, the Boolean evaluator obtains the actual analytical intersection curves, so any gaps in the trimmed surfaces will have been introduced by projection. The projection tolerance allows the user to specify an upper limit to the gap size relevant to the intended application.

6.4. Refinement of Approximated Curves

Intersections involving more advanced surfaces introduce a new difficulty. The trimmed surface boundary cannot be guaranteed to be any more accurate than the curve from Boolean evaluation, and in these cases the curve is only as accurate as the chord height allowed by the surface tessellation parameters. The resulting gaps may be unacceptable for many applications. One way to increase the accuracy of the original curve is to re-evaluate with a reduced surface tessellation tolerance, greatly increasing the number of facets, thus lowering the performance and even stretching the limits of capacity of the evaluator. The dual representation of surfaces allows the refinement of approximate curves without re-evaluation at a higher resolution.

The ideal result of boundary evaluation would include exact surface intersection curves and their exact representations in the parameter spaces of the surfaces. This method has achieved exact intersections for the simple quadrics, and accurate if not exact parameter space curves; however, by itself, the projection algorithm cannot give accurate parameter space intersection curves if the model space curve it begins with is inaccurate. To refine the approximated curves and simultaneously generate accurate parameter space representations of the refined curves, an iterative surface intersection algorithm is applied [12]. This provides point sets to define the two parameter space curves and the model space curve. By guiding the intersection using the approximate curve from the Boolean evaluator, the "hunting phase" is unnecessary and the "tracing phase" is simplified. The resulting model space and parameter space curves are still approximations, but the tolerance value of the intersection may be orders of magnitude finer than the surface tessellation tolerance that first captured the intersection. Figures 1 through 4 illustrate the success of this technique.

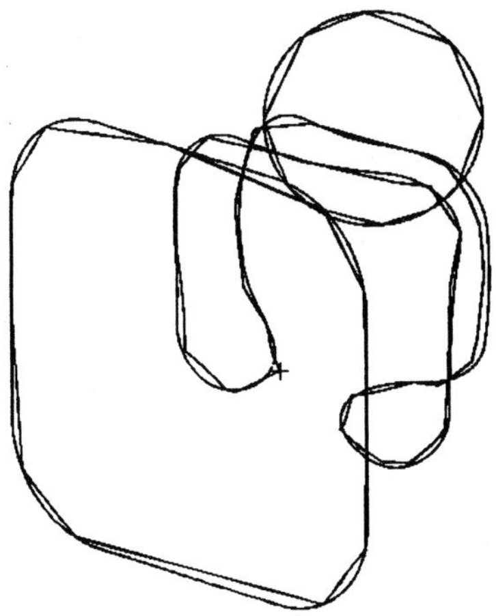

Figure 2. Intersection curves of primitive surfaces before and after curve refinement.

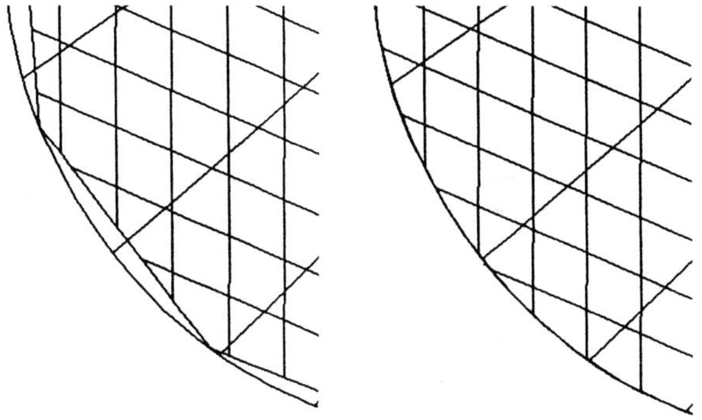

Figure 3. Example of gaps between trimmed surfaces in absence of curve refinement.

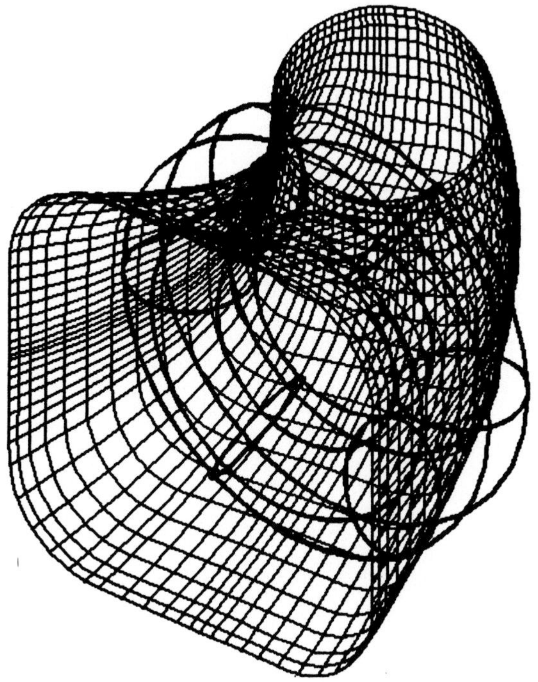

Figure 1. CSG wireframe display of sculptured primitive and torus.

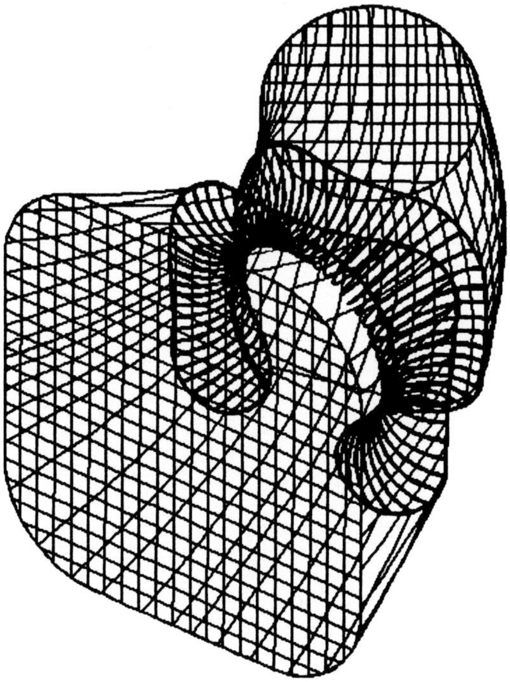

Figure 4. Boundary representation of torus subtracted from sculptured primitive.

Applying this algorithm to adjacent curves of an approximated surface may pull those curves away from their common endpoint (figure 5). To prevent this, the approximate position of the vertex should be refined first (using a three-surface intersection with the common endpoint of the incident approximated curves as a starting guess). Driven by constraints of time to a simpler approach, we found that we could clip or extend the refined parameter space curves to common endpoints without the vertex refinement preprocess. No effort has been made to implement a corresponding correction for the refined model space curves.

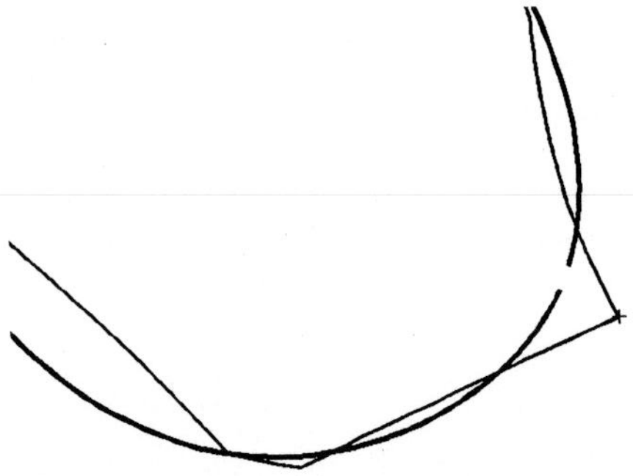

Figure 5. A detail from figure 2. The refined curves may tend to pull away from common verticies.

The curve refinement technique cannot correct topological errors caused by specifying tessellation values that are too coarse to capture the topology correctly. Also, the iterative technique may fail to attain its tolerances for completion within a maximum number of steps, particularly when adjacent surface normals are near-parallel along the intersection. Such failures can be detected, and the original coarse approximation used instead. Note that in the absence of such problems, the Boolean evaluator has only to approximate tessellated surfaces to an accuracy sufficient to correctly capture the topology of the solid boundary in order for accurate trimmed surfaces to be produced.

The parameter space curves are joined into loops according to the topology of their model space duals as derived from edge chasing. The loops can be tested for orientation, connectedness and disjointedness, each a test of the correctness of the final result. The parameter space loops are then stored with their original surfaces as parametric trimmed surfaces. The DDM/Prism system can use these surfaces in a variety of ways.

The adjacency information is also stored, to simplify automatic NC tool path generation across multiple surfaces. Work is in progress to expand the usefulness of this data.

7. Conclusion

We believe that our approach to boundary evaluation is unique in several ways. The "hybrid" nature of this evaluation scheme provides both the geometric coverage of a faceted evaluator and the intersection capabilities of an analytical approach. To the best of our knowledge, it is the first evaluator to combine halfspace based classification for simple convex primitives with ray firing for non-convex primitives, yielding both performance and geometric coverage suitable to a production environment. The dual surface representation and curve refinement make it possible to create an accurate parametric trimmed surface representation of a CSG model. The main ideas discussed here have been implemented in a modeling system which we believe represents a significant advancement toward the complete integration of solids modeling into a concept-to-manufacturing CAD/CAM/CAE system.

8. Future Research

It may be possible to extend these ideas and algorithms to allow incremental boundary evaluation for solids represented by quadric surfaces. For example, it should be possible to extend the idea of non-convex planar facets to curved surfaces. Analytical intersection and inversion of certain higher order surfaces (toroidal, extruded, revolved) is also of great interest. Techniques to improve performance and capacity warrant investigation in any commercial CAD/CAM system.

9. Results

Tests on a variety of models have demonstrated the suitability of this boundary evaluator in terms of reliability, capacity and performance, to a production environment. This evaluator has been in actual production use for a number of months in Calma Company's Prism/DDM CAD/CAM/CAE system. Figures 6 through 8 represent a cross section of the test results. The shaded images are generated directly from the CSG model using Calma Company's proprietary scanline based CSG rendering algorithm.

10. Acknowledgements

The boundary evaluator development team also included Kathleen Busker, Nga Dang, James Jou, Russell LaPuma, and Ted Valencia. Thanks also to Pierre Malraison, Thomas Check, Semyon Nisenzon and Pete Noel. Special thanks are due to Robert Smith for contributions to many of the ideas discussed here and for his encouragement and support.

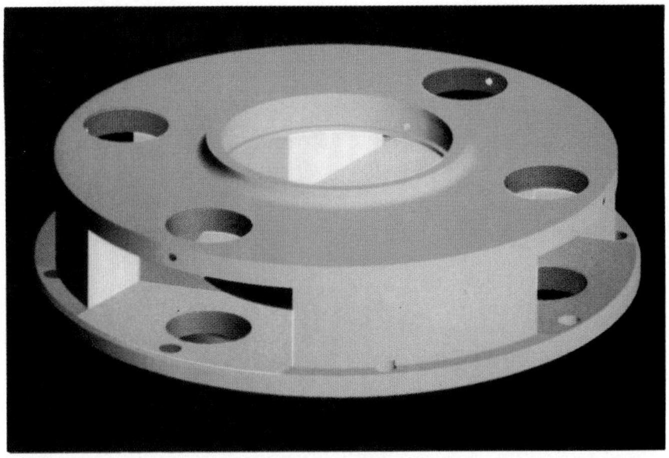

Figure 6a. Solid model with revolution primitive.

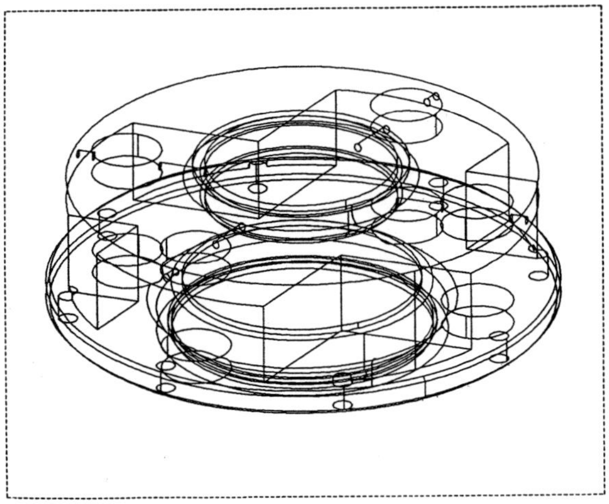

Figure 6b. Curves produced during evaluation.

Figure 7a. Model with sculptured and extruded primitives.

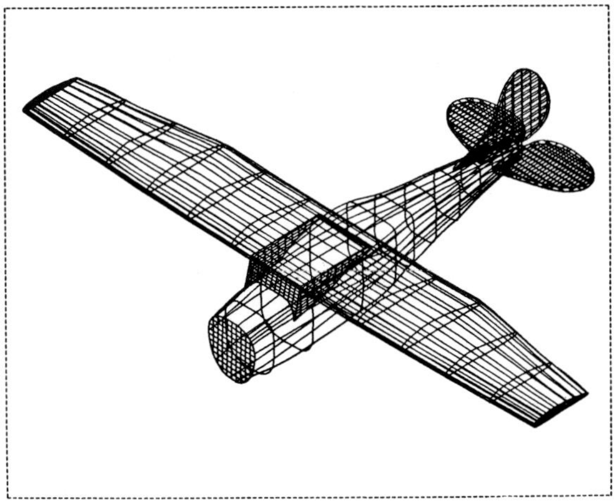

Figure 7b. Trimmed surfaces of Brep.

Figure 8a. Jet engine turbine disk.

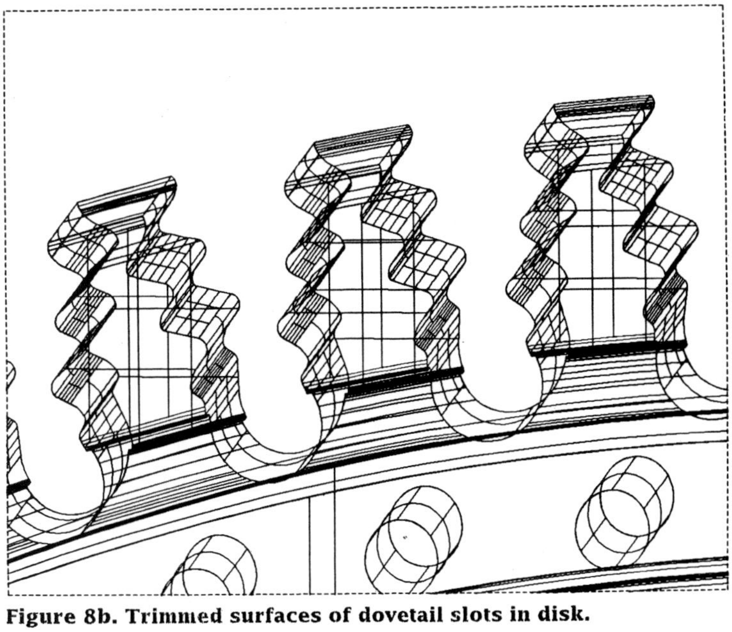

Figure 8b. Trimmed surfaces of dovetail slots in disk.

BIBLIOGRAPHY

[1] Baumgart B.G., "Geometric Modeling for Computer Vision," *rep. STAN-CS-74-463, Stanford Artificial Intelligence Lab.,* Stanford Univ., Stanford, CA 1974.

[2] Boyse, J.W., Gilchrist J.E., "GMSolid: Interactive Modeling for Design and Analysis of Solids," *IEEE Computer Graphics and Applications,* Vol. 2, No 2, pp. 27-40, Mar. 1982.

[3] Braid, I.C., "The Synthesis of Solids Bounded by Many Faces," *Communications of the ACM,* Vol. 18, No. 4, April 1975, pp. 209-216.

[4] Carlson, W.E., "An Algorithm and Data Structures for 3D Object Synthesis Using Surface Patch Intersections," *ACM Computer Graphics,* Vol. 16, No. 3, July 1982, pp. 255-263.

[5] Eastman C.M., Yessios C.J., "An Efficient Algorithm for Finding the Union, Intersection, and Differences of Spatial Domains," Tech. Rep 31, Institute of Physical Planning, Carnegie-Mellon Univ., Pittsburgh, PA. Sept. 1972.

[6] Franklin, W.R., "Efficient Polyhedron Intersection and Union," *Proc. Graphics Interface '82,* (Toronto, Canada, May 17-21, 1982), pp. 73-80.

[7] Glassner, A.S., "Space Subdivision for Fast Ray Tracing," *IEEE Computer Graphics and Applications,* Vol. 4, No. 10, October 1984, pp. 15-22.

[8] Hillyard R.C., "The Build Group of Solid Modelers," *IEEE Computer Graphics and Applications,* Vol. 2, No. 2, March 1982, pp. 43-52.

[9] Kalay Y.E., Eastman, C.M., "Shape Operations: An Algorithm for Spatial-Set Manipulations of Solid Objects," CAD Graphics Lab., Carnegie-Mellon Univ., Pittsburgh, PA, July 1980.

[10] Lee Y.T., Requicha, A.A.G., "Algorithms for Computing the Volume and Other Integral Properties of Solids. I. Known Methods and Open Issues," *Communications of the ACM,* Vol. 25, No. 9, September 1982, pp. 635-641.

[11] Miller, J.R., "Sculptured Surfaces in Solid Models: Issues and Alternative Approaches," *IEEE Computer Graphics and Applications,* Vol. 6, No. 12, December 1986, pp. 37-48.

[12] Mortenson, Michael E. *Geometric Modeling.* John Wiley & Sons, New York, 1985, ch. 6.

[13] Pfeifer, H., "Methods used for Intersecting Geometrical Entities in the GMP Module for Volume Geometry," *Computer-Aided Design,* Vol. 17, No. 7, September 1985, pp. 311-318.

[14] Putnam, L.K., Subrahmanyam, P.A., "Computation of the Union, Intersection and Difference of n-dimensional Objects via Boundary Classification," Department of Computer Science, University of Utah, Salt Lake City, UT, 1982.

[15] Requicha, A.A.G., Voelcker, H.B., "Boolean Operations in Solid Modeling: Boundary Evaluation and Merging Algorithms," *Proceedings of the IEEE,* Vol. 73, No. 1, January 1985, pp. 30-44

[16] Requicha, A.A.G., Voelcker, H.B., "Boolean Operations in Solid Modeling: Boundary Evaluation and Merging Algorithms," Tech. Memo. 26, Production Automation Project, Univ. of Rochester, Rochester, NY, Jan 1984.

[17] Requicha, A.A.G., Voelcker, H.B., "Solid Modeling: A Historical Summary and Contemporary Assessment," *IEEE Computer Graphics and Applications,* Vol. 2, No. 2, March 1982, pp. 9-24.

[18] Requicha, A.A.G., Voelcker, H.B., "Solid Modeling: Current Status and Research Directions," *IEEE Computer Graphics and Applications,* Vol. 3, No. 7, October 1983, pp. 25-37.

[19] Sarraga, R.F., Waters, W.C., "Free-Form Surfaces in GMSolid: Goals and Issues," *Solid Modeling by Computers.* Plenum Press, New York, 1984, pp. 187-210.

[20] Tilove, R.B., "Exploiting Spatial and Structural Locality in Geometric Modeling," Tech. Memo. 38, Production Automation Project, Univ. of Rochester, Rochester, NY, October 1981.

[21] Tilove, R.B., "Set Membership Classification: A Unified Approach to Geometric Intersection Problems," *IEEE Transactions on Computers,* Vol. C-29, No. 10, October 1980, pp. 874-883.

[22] Tilove, R.B., Requicha, A.A.G, "Closure of Boolean Operations on Geometric Entities," *Computer-Aided Des.,* Vol. 12, No. 5, September 1980, pp. 219-220.

[23] Weiler, K., "Polygon Comparison Using a Graph Representation," *ACM Computer Graphics,* Vol 14, No 3, July 1980, pp. 10-18.

[24] Weiler, K., "Edge-Based Data Structures for Solid Modeling in Curved-Surface Modeling Environments," *IEEE Computer Graphics and Applications,* Vol. 5, No. 1, January 1985, pp. 21-40.

[25] Yamaguchi, F., Tokieda, T., "A Unified Algorithm for Boolean Shape Operations," *IEEE Computer Graphics and Applications,* Vol. 4, No 6, pp. 24-37, June 1984.

Discrete Beta-Splines

Barry Joe

Department of Computing Science
University of Alberta
Edmonton, Alberta, Canada T6G 2H1

Abstract

Goodman (1985) and Joe (1986) have given explicit formulas for (cubic) Beta-splines on uniform knot sequences with varying β1 and β2 values at the knots, and nonuniform knot sequences with varying β2 values at the knots, respectively. The advantage of the latter formula is that it can also be used for knot sequences with multiple knots. Discrete Beta-splines arise when a Beta-spline curve is subdivided, i.e. the knot sequence is refined so that the curve is expressed in terms of a larger number of control vertices and Beta-splines. We prove that discrete Beta-splines satisfy the same properties as discrete B-splines, and present an algorithm for computing discrete Beta-splines and the new control vertices using the explicit formula of Joe (1986).

CR Categories and Subject Descriptors: I.3.5 [**Computer Graphics**]: Computational Geometry and Object Modeling - Curve, surface, solid, and object representations

Additional Key Words and Phrases: B-splines, subdivision, knot refinement, geometric continuity, computer-aided geometric design

1. Introduction

B-splines, discrete B-splines, and subdivision techniques are used in computer-aided geometric design and computer graphics for designing free-form curves and surfaces. B-spline curves can be described as weighted averages of control vertices, in which B-splines are taken as the weighting functions. The shape of the curve approximates the control polygon, which is formed by connecting consecutive control vertices by line segments. The subdivision problem for a B-spline curve is to express the curve in terms of a larger number of control vertices and B-spline weighting functions. The reasons for subdivision are (a) to allow a more local change to the B-spline curve (moving a new control vertex affects a smaller part of the curve than moving an original control vertex), (b) to split the B-spline curve into two separate pieces which are represented in a similar form, and (c) to use the new control polygon as a good approximation to the B-spline curve when the number of new control vertices is sufficiently large.

Discrete B-splines are used to express the new control vertices in terms of the original control vertices, and to express the original B-splines in terms of the new B-splines which are defined on a refined knot sequence. Cohen, Lyche, and Riesenfeld (1980) have presented the theory of discrete B-splines and the Oslo algorithm for computing the discrete B-splines and new control vertices using a recurrence relation. Lyche and Morken (1986) recently gave an improved version of the Oslo algorithm. An alternative way to compute the new control vertices, based on inserting one new knot at a time, was given by Boehm (1980) and Boehm and Prautzsch (1985).

Barsky (1981) introduced (cubic) Beta-splines as a generalization of cubic B-splines. They provide a means of constructing parametric spline curves in which the shape of a curve is controlled by bias parameter β1 and tension parameter β2. A cubic B-spline curve has second degree parametric continuity while a Beta-spline curve has second degree geometric continuity, i.e. continuity of the curve, the unit tangent vector, and the curvature vector. Barsky (1981) used a uniform knot sequence and constant β1 and β2 values at all knots or joints of the curve, and introduced the extension to varying β1 and β2 values at the joints to provide local control of bias and tension in the curve. This resulted in the paper of Barsky and Beatty (1983) in which quintic Hermite interpolation is used to give continuous β1 and β2 values throughout the curve. Recently, Bartels and Beatty (1984) and Goodman (1985) have extended Beta-splines to nonuniform knot sequences and varying β1 and β2 values at the knots without using interpolation.

Goodman (1985) has shown that these more general Beta-splines satisfy the local support, convex hull, and variation-diminishing properties, and gave an explicit formula for these Beta-splines on a uniform knot sequence. Goodman and Unsworth (1986) described the effects on the Beta-spline curve when β1 and β2 values at the knots are varied. Joe (1986) gave an alternative explicit formula for these Beta-splines on a nonuniform knot sequence with constant $\beta 1 = 1$ and varying β2 values at the knots. For distinct knot sequences, these two formulas are equivalent since it is possible to transform between the two knot sequences by appropriately changing the β1 and β2 values at the knots. The advantage of the latter formula is that it can also be used for knot sequences with multiple knots.

The books by Barsky (1986) and Bartels, Beatty, and Barsky (1987) provide background information on the above topics. The papers by Farin (1982), Farin (1985), and Boehm (1985) describe other ways to construct curvature continuous cubic spline curves. Boehm (1985) also gave a geometric approach for the insertion of a new knot.

Discrete Beta-splines are analogous to discrete B-splines, i.e. they arise in the subdivision of Beta-spline curves. Subdivision of a Beta-spline curve allows a more local change to the curve by modifying a new bias or tension parameter as well as moving a new control vertex. In Section 2, notation and definitions are given. In Section 3, we prove that discrete Beta-splines satisfy the same properties as discrete B-splines. In Section 4, we present an algorithm for computing discrete Beta-splines and the new control vertices using the explicit formula of Joe (1986). In Section 5, we give examples of refined control polygons obtained from this algorithm.

2. Notation and definitions

Let $t_0 \le t_1 \le \cdots \le t_{m+4}$ be a sequence of knots in which no knot has multiplicity greater than four. Let $\beta 1_i = 1$ and $\beta 2_i \ge 0$ be the bias and tension parameter at t_i, $1 \le i \le m+3$, and $h_i = t_i - t_{i-1}$, $1 \le i \le m+4$. There is no loss of generality in assuming $\beta 1_i = 1$ for all i, since any distinct knot sequence with varying $\beta 1$ and $\beta 2$ values at the knots can be linearly transformed to a different nonuniform distinct sequence with constant $\beta 1 = 1$ and different $\beta 2$ values. An effect similar to bias can be obtained by varying the spacing between knots.

Let $F_i(t)$ be the Beta-spline with nonzero support on the interval $[t_i, t_{i+4}]$, $0 \le i \le m$. The explicit formula of Joe (1986) for the $F_i(t)$ is as follows (any term with a zero denominator has a zero value). Let

$$\psi_i = \beta 2_i h_i h_{i+1} / [2(h_i + h_{i+1})], \quad 1 \le i \le m+3 \tag{2.1}$$

$$\phi_i = h_i + h_{i+1} + h_{i+2} + \psi_i (h_{i+1} + h_{i+2}) + \psi_{i+1}(h_i + h_{i+1}) + \psi_i \psi_{i+1} h_{i+1}, \; 1 \le i \le m+2.$$

$$F_i(t) = \begin{cases} s_{i,1}(t) = d_{i,1}u^3, & u = (t-t_i)/h_{i+1},\ t_i \le t < t_{i+1} \\ s_{i,2}(t) = a_{i,2} + b_{i,2}u + c_{i,2}u^2 + d_{i,2}u^3, & u = (t-t_{i+1})/h_{i+2},\ t_{i+1} \le t < t_{i+2} \\ s_{i,3}(t) = a_{i,3} + b_{i,3}u + c_{i,3}u^2 + d_{i,3}u^3, & u = (t_{i+3}-t)/h_{i+3},\ t_{i+2} \le t < t_{i+3} \\ s_{i,4}(t) = d_{i,4}u^3, & u = (t_{i+4}-t)/h_{i+4},\ t_{i+3} \le t < t_{i+4} \\ 0, & \text{otherwise} \end{cases} \tag{2.2}$$

where

$$\begin{aligned} d_{i,1} = a_{i,2} &= (1+\psi_{i+2}) h_{i+1}^2 / [\phi_{i+1}(h_{i+1} + h_{i+2})] \\ b_{i,2} &= 3(1+\psi_{i+2}) h_{i+1} h_{i+2} / [\phi_{i+1}(h_{i+1} + h_{i+2})] \\ c_{i,2} &= 3(1+\psi_{i+2}) h_{i+2} [h_{i+2}/(h_{i+1} + h_{i+2}) + \psi_{i+1}] / \phi_{i+1} \\ d_{i,2} &= -(1+\psi_{i+3}) h_{i+2}^2 / [\phi_{i+2}(h_{i+2} + h_{i+3})] - \\ &\quad h_{i+2}[(1+\psi_{i+2})(h_{i+2}/(h_{i+1}+h_{i+2}) + \psi_{i+1}) + \\ &\quad (1+\psi_{i+1})(h_{i+2}/(h_{i+2}+h_{i+3}) + \psi_{i+2})] / \phi_{i+1} \\ d_{i,4} = a_{i,3} &= (1+\psi_{i+2}) h_{i+4}^2 / [\phi_{i+2}(h_{i+3} + h_{i+4})] \\ b_{i,3} &= 3(1+\psi_{i+2}) h_{i+3} h_{i+4} / [\phi_{i+2}(h_{i+3} + h_{i+4})] \\ c_{i,3} &= 3(1+\psi_{i+2}) h_{i+3} [h_{i+3}/(h_{i+3} + h_{i+4}) + \psi_{i+3}] / \phi_{i+2} \\ d_{i,3} &= -(1+\psi_{i+1}) h_{i+3}^2 / [\phi_{i+1}(h_{i+2} + h_{i+3})] - \\ &\quad h_{i+3}[(1+\psi_{i+2})(h_{i+3}/(h_{i+3}+h_{i+4}) + \psi_{i+3}) + \\ &\quad (1+\psi_{i+3})(h_{i+3}/(h_{i+2}+h_{i+3}) + \psi_{i+2})] / \phi_{i+2}. \end{aligned} \tag{2.3}$$

The geometric continuity conditions satisfied by $F_i(t)$ are as follows. Let p be the multiplicity of knot t_j, $i \le j \le i+4$, in the sequence $t_i, t_{i+1}, \cdots, t_{i+4}$. If $p = 1$ then (a) $F_i(t_j^-) = F_i(t_j^+)$, (b) $F_i'(t_j^-) = F_i'(t_j^+)$, and (c) $F_i''(t_j^-) + \beta 2_j F_i'(t_j^-) = F_i''(t_j^+)$. If $p = 2$ then only conditions (a) and (b) are satisfied, and (c) is not satisfied. If $p = 3$ then only condition (a) is satisfied, and (b) is not satisfied. If $p = 4$ then condition (a) is not satisfied.

Goodman (1985) showed that the $F_i(t)$ are linearly independent and satisfy the convex hull property. The $F_i(t)$ also satisfy the *reflection symmetry property* : if the knots are negated to get $-t_{m+4} \le -t_{m+3} \le \cdots \le -t_0$ with tension parameter $\beta 2_i$ at $-t_i$, and $\bar{F}_i(t)$ is the Beta-spline with nonzero support on the interval $[-t_{i+4}, -t_i]$, then $\bar{F}_i(-t) = F_i(t)$.

A Beta-spline curve is defined by

$$Q(t) = \sum_{i=0}^{m} V_i F_i(t), \quad t_3 \le t < t_{m+1} \tag{2.4}$$

where the V_i are two- or three-dimensional control vertices. If the tension parameters $\beta 2_i$ are set to zero at all knots, then $Q(t)$ reduces to a cubic B-spline curve. $Q(t)$ does not depend on h_1, h_{m+4}, $\beta 2_1$, and $\beta 2_{m+3}$. In general, at a double (triple, quadruple, respectively) knot t_i, the curve $Q(t)$ has only first degree geometric continuity (only continuity, no continuity, respectively). In general, at all simple knots and non-knot values, $Q(t)$ has second degree geometric continuity, i.e. it has position, unit tangent vector, and curvature vector continuity. Exceptions to these geometric continuity conditions may occur for a few configurations of control vertices (Goodman and Unsworth (1986)). The shape of the curve can be controlled locally by changing a control vertex, a tension parameter, or a spacing between two knots.

For subdivision of the Beta-spline curve, the knot sequence is refined and new Beta-splines and control vertices are obtained. Let $u_0 \le u_1 \le \cdots \le u_{n+4}$, $n \ge m$, be a refined sequence of knots such that no knot has multiplicity greater than four, $u_0 = t_0$, $u_{n+4} = t_{m+4}$, and for all i, $t_i = u_j$ for some j. Let $\hat{h}_j = u_j - u_{j-1}$, $1 \le j \le n+4$, and let $\hat{\beta} 2_j$ be the tension parameter at u_j, $1 \le j \le n+3$. If u_j is one of the $n-m$ new knots, then $\hat{\beta} 2_j = 0$, otherwise $\hat{\beta} 2_j$ has the same tension value as the corresponding knot in the t_i sequence. If the multiplicity of a knot in the t_i sequence has been increased in the u_j sequence, then it does not matter how the tension parameters $\hat{\beta} 2_j$ are assigned to these multiple knots since the tension at a multiple knot t_i is effectively zero by (2.1) (because $\psi_i = 0$).

Let $G_j(t)$, $0 \le j \le n$, be the Beta-splines defined on the refined knot sequence. The coefficients, segment polynomials, and other variables associated with the $G_j(t)$ are similar to those for the $F_i(t)$, and will be denoted using variables with hats, e.g. $\hat{a}_{j,k}$, $\hat{b}_{j,k}$, $\hat{c}_{j,k}$, $\hat{d}_{j,k}$, $\hat{s}_{j,k}$, $\hat{\psi}_j$, $\hat{\phi}_j$. The Beta-spline curve $Q(t)$ can also be represented as

$$Q(t) = \sum_{j=0}^{n} W_j G_j(t), \quad t_3 \le t < t_{m+1} \tag{2.5}$$

where the W_j are the new (refined) control vertices. If new knots are added in the subinterval $[t_0, t_3]$ or $[t_{m+1}, t_{m+4}]$, then $G_j(t) = 0$ in the interval $[t_3, t_{m+1})$ for $j < L$ and $j > U$, where $L \ge 0$ is the number of new knots added in $[t_0, t_3]$ and $n - U \ge 0$ is the number of new knots added in $[t_{m+1}, t_{m+4}]$. So it may appear that it is useless to add knots in these two subintervals, but these knots must be added if it is desired to get a closer approximation to the curve at its two ends (see figures in Section 5). The new control polygon contains the vertices $W_L, \cdots, W_U$, since the W_j for $j < L$ and $j > U$ do not contribute to (2.5).

Since the space of functions spanned by the $F_i(t)$ is a subspace of that spanned by the $G_j(t)$ (Goodman (1985), Prautzsch (1984,1985)),

$$F_i(t) = \sum_{j=0}^{n} \alpha_i(j) G_j(t) \quad \text{for } i = 0, \cdots, m \tag{2.6}$$

for some constants $\alpha_i(j)$ called *discrete Beta-splines*. Substituting (2.6) into (2.4) results in

$$\sum_{i=0}^{m} V_i \sum_{j=0}^{n} \alpha_i(j) G_j(t) = \sum_{j=0}^{n} \left[\sum_{i=0}^{m} \alpha_i(j) V_i \right] G_j(t) . \qquad (2.7)$$

By comparing the coefficients of $G_j(t)$ in (2.5) and (2.7), and using the linear independence of the $G_j(t)$,

$$W_j = \sum_{i=0}^{m} \alpha_i(j) V_i \quad \text{for } j=0, \cdots, n . \qquad (2.8)$$

3. Properties of discrete Beta-splines

In this section, we prove that the discrete Beta-splines $\alpha_i(j)$ satisfy the same properties as discrete (cubic) B-splines. To simplify the proof, we add three arbitrary knots at the beginning and end of both knots sequences, so that the t_i sequence becomes $t_{-3} < t_{-2} < t_{-1} < t_0 \le \cdots \le t_{m+4} < t_{m+5} < t_{m+6} < t_{m+7}$, and $u_i = t_i$ for $i=-3, -2, -1$ and $u_{n+i} = t_{m+i}$ for $i=5, 6, 7$. The tension parameters at these six additional knots as well as t_0 and t_{m+4} can be arbitrarily set to zero. With these additional knots, (2.6) becomes

$$F_i(t) = \sum_{j=-3}^{n+3} \alpha_i(j) G_j(t) \quad \text{for } i=-3, \cdots, m+3 . \qquad (3.1)$$

The properties satisfied by the discrete Beta-splines are:

(1) $\sum_{i=-3}^{m+3} \alpha_i(j) = 1$ for $j=-3, \cdots, n+3$.

(2) For each index i, $\alpha_i(j)=0$ for all $j < \gamma(i)$ and for all $j > \delta(i)$, where $\gamma(i)$ and $\delta(i)$ are defined below. For each index j, there are at most four indices i such that $\alpha_i(j) \ne 0$.

(3) $\alpha_i(j) \ge 0$ for all i, j.

The proof of property (1) is the same as for discrete B-splines. From the convex hull property of Beta-splines,

$$\sum_{i=-3}^{m+3} F_i(t) = 1 , \quad t_0 \le t \le t_{m+4} \qquad (3.2)$$

$$\sum_{j=-3}^{n+3} G_j(t) = 1 , \quad t_0 \le t \le t_{m+4} . \qquad (3.3)$$

Substituting (3.1) into (3.2) results in

$$\sum_{i=-3}^{m+3} \sum_{j=-3}^{n+3} \alpha_i(j) G_j(t) = \sum_{j=-3}^{n+3} \left[\sum_{i=-3}^{m+3} \alpha_i(j) \right] G_j(t) = 1 , \qquad (3.4)$$

$$t_0 \le t \le t_{m+4} .$$

By comparing the coefficients of $G_j(t)$ in (3.3) and (3.4), and using the linear independence of the $G_j(t)$, property (1) is obtained.

Now we show when $\alpha_i(j)$ is zero, first for fixed index i and then for fixed index j. From (3.1) and the linear independence of the $G_j(t)$, $\alpha_i(j)=0$ if the nonzero part of $G_j(t)$ is partially outside interval $[t_i, t_{i+4}]$ (where $F_i(t)$ is nonzero), i.e. if $u_j < t_i$ or $u_{j+4} > t_{i+4}$. In addition, it is possible that $\alpha_i(j)=0$ if $u_j = t_i$ and u_j is a multiple knot or $u_{j+4} = t_{i+4}$ and u_{j+4} is a multiple knot. Let p and q be the integers such that $t_i = t_{i+p-1} < t_{i+p}$ and $t_{i+4-q} < t_{i+5-q} = t_{i+4}$ (note that $1 \le p, q \le 4$). Suppose $t_i = u_j < u_{j+4} \le t_{i+4}$ and $u_j = u_{j+p}$. Then $G_j(t)$ has a lower degree of geometric continuity at u_j than $F_i(t)$ has at t_i, hence $\alpha_i(j)=0$ (if $\alpha_i(j) \ne 0$ then $F_i(t)$ has a higher degree of geometric continuity at t_i than $\sum_{k=-3}^{n+3} \alpha_i(k) G_k(t)$, which contradicts (3.1)). Similarly, $\alpha_i(j)=0$ if $t_i \le u_j < u_{j+4} = t_{i+4}$ and $u_{j+4-q} = u_{j+4}$.

Therefore, for fixed index i, it is possible to determine which indices j satisfy $\alpha_i(j)=0$. Given that $t_i = t_{i+p-1} < t_{i+p}$, we define $\gamma(i)$ to be the index such that $u_{\gamma(i)} = t_i$ and $u_{\gamma(i)} = u_{\gamma(i)+p-1} < u_{\gamma(i)+p}$. Similarly, given that $t_{i-q} < t_{i-q+1} = t_i$, we define $\eta(i)$ to be the index such that $u_{\eta(i)} = t_i$ and $u_{\eta(i)-q} < u_{\eta(i)-q+1} = u_{\eta(i)}$. (Note that $\gamma(i) = \eta(i)$ if the multiplicity of knot t_i has not been increased in the refined knot sequence.) We also define $\delta(i) = \eta(i+4) - 4$. These indices satisfy $\gamma(i) \le \delta(i)$, $-3 = \gamma(-3) < \gamma(-2) < \cdots < \gamma(m+3)$, and $\delta(-3) < \delta(-2) < \cdots < \delta(m+3) = n+3$. From the previous paragraph, $\alpha_i(j)=0$ if $j < \gamma(i)$ or $j > \delta(i)$, i.e.

$$F_i(t) = \sum_{j=\gamma(i)}^{\delta(i)} \alpha_i(j) G_j(t) . \qquad (3.5)$$

We note that $\delta(i) - \gamma(i)$ is the number of new knots added in interval (t_i, t_{i+4}), and for all indices i between 0 and m inclusive, the total number of possibly nonzero $\alpha_i(j)$ is

$$\sum_{i=0}^{m} [\delta(i) - \gamma(i) + 1] \le m + 1 + 4(n-m) \qquad (3.6)$$

since $n-m$ is the number of new knots and each new knot u_j is in at most four intervals (t_k, t_{k+4}).

Now, for fixed index j, we determine the indices i for which $\alpha_i(j) \ne 0$ is possible. There is at least one such index i by property (1). Also, these indices must be consecutive since the interval of nonzero support of the $F_i(t)$ moves from left to right as i increases. Therefore $\alpha_i(j) \ne 0$ is possible for $i = \lambda(j), \cdots, \rho(j)$ where

$$\lambda(j) = \min \{ i \mid \gamma(i) \le j \le \delta(i) \}, \qquad (3.7)$$
$$\rho(j) = \max \{ i \mid \gamma(i) \le j \le \delta(i) \} .$$

These indices satisfy $-3 = \lambda(-3) \le \lambda(-2) \le \cdots \le \lambda(n+3)$ and $\rho(-3) \le \rho(-2) \le \cdots \le \rho(n+3) = m+3$. As discussed above, $\lambda(j)$ and $\rho(j)$ satisfy $t_{\rho(j)} \le u_j < u_{j+4} \le t_{\lambda(j)+4}$. Hence, $\rho(j) \le \lambda(j)+3$ and there are at most four indices i such that $\alpha_i(j) \ne 0$. This completes the proof of property (2).

Now we prove that the $\alpha_i(j)$ are nonnegative for all i and j. We consider the effect of adding the $n-m$ new knots one at a time into the refined knot sequence. The Beta-splines change as follows:

$$F_j = G_j^{(0)} \rightarrow G_j^{(1)} \rightarrow \cdots \rightarrow G_j^{(n-m)} = G_j$$

where $G_j^{(k)}(t)$, $-3 \le j \le m+k+3$, are the Beta-splines resulting from adding k new knots. For the same reason as (2.6), these Beta-splines satisfy

$$G_j^{(k)}(t) = \sum_{r=-3}^{m+k+4} \alpha_j^{(k)}(r) G_r^{(k+1)}(t), \; -3 \le j \le m+k+3, \qquad (3.8)$$

$$0 \le k \le n-m-1$$

for some constants $\alpha_j^{(k)}(r)$. If we can show that $\alpha_j^{(k)}(r) \ge 0$ for all j, k, r, i.e. adding one additional knot to a knot sequence results in nonnegative discrete Beta-splines, then the following induction argument shows that the $\alpha_i(j)$ are all nonnegative.

Suppose the inductive hypothesis is that

$$F_i(t) = \sum_{j=-3}^{m+k+3} \beta_i^{(k)}(j) G_j^{(k)}(t) , \; -3 \le i \le m+3, \qquad (3.9)$$

$$\text{where } \beta_i^{(k)}(j) \ge 0 \text{ for all } i, j.$$

Note that $\alpha_i(j) = \beta_i^{(n-m)}(j)$. The basis step, in which $k=0$, is true since $\beta_i^{(0)}(i) = 1$ and $\beta_i^{(0)}(j) = 0$ if $j \ne i$. Suppose (3.9) is true for $k < n-m$. Substituting (3.8) into (3.9) results in

$$F_i(t) = \sum_{r=-3}^{m+k+4} \beta_i^{(k+1)}(r) G_r^{(k+1)}(t),\ -3 \le i \le m+3$$

where

$$\beta_i^{(k+1)}(r) = \sum_{j=-3}^{m+k+3} \beta_i^{(k)}(j)\, \alpha_j^{(k)}(r).$$

If $\alpha_j^{(k)}(r) \ge 0$ for all j, r, then (3.9) is true for $k+1$.

Therefore the problem of proving property (3) has been reduced to the case in which the refined knot sequence contains one additional knot. Hence, for the remainder of this proof, we assume that $n = m+1$. There are two cases to consider:

(i) the new knot is not equal to t_i for any i,

(ii) the new knot increases the multiplicity of some knot t_i.

First suppose case (i) occurs. Suppose the new knot u_{k+1} is added in the nonvacuous interval (t_k, t_{k+1}) where $0 \le k \le m+3$, so that $u_i = t_i$ for $-3 \le i \le k$, $u_{i+1} = t_i$ for $k+1 \le i \le m+7$, and the $\hat{\beta}2_i$ are similarly defined with $\hat{\beta}2_{k+1} = 0$. For $i \le k-4$, $F_i(t) = G_i(t)$, so $\alpha_i(i) = 1$ and $\alpha_i(j) = 0$ for $j \ne i$. For $i \ge k+1$, $F_i(t) = G_{i+1}(t)$, so $\alpha_i(i+1) = 1$ and $\alpha_i(j) = 0$ for $j \ne i+1$. For $i = k-3, k-2, k-1$, and k, $\alpha_i(j) = 0$ for $j < i$ and $j > i+1$ by property (2), so

$$\begin{aligned}
&(a)\ F_{k-3}(t) = \alpha_{k-3}(k-3) G_{k-3}(t) + \alpha_{k-3}(k-2) G_{k-2}(t) \\
&(b)\ F_{k-2}(t) = \alpha_{k-2}(k-2) G_{k-2}(t) + \alpha_{k-2}(k-1) G_{k-1}(t) \\
&(c)\ F_{k-1}(t) = \alpha_{k-1}(k-1) G_{k-1}(t) + \alpha_{k-1}(k) G_k(t) \qquad (3.10) \\
&(d)\ F_k(t) = \alpha_k(k) G_k(t) + \alpha_k(k+1) G_{k+1}(t).
\end{aligned}$$

We will show that $\alpha_{k-3}(k-3)$, $\alpha_{k-3}(k-2)$, $\alpha_{k-2}(k-2)$, and $\alpha_{k-2}(k-1)$ are nonnegative, which implies that $\alpha_{k-1}(k-1)$, $\alpha_{k-1}(k)$, $\alpha_k(k)$, and $\alpha_k(k+1)$ are also nonnegative by the reflection symmetry property mentioned in Section 2. First, we consider the discrete Beta-splines in (3.10a). $\alpha_{k-3}(k-3) = 1$ since $\sum_{i=-3}^{m+3} \alpha_i(k-3) = 1$ and $\alpha_i(k-3) = 0$ for $i \ne k-3$. In interval $[u_{k+1}, u_{k+2}] = [u_{k+1}, t_{k+1}]$,

$$F_{k-3}(t) = s_{k-3,4}(t) = d_{k-3,4}[(t_{k+1}-t)/h_{k+1}]^3$$

$$G_{k-2}(t) = \hat{s}_{k-2,4}(t) = \hat{d}_{k-2,4}[(t_{k+1}-t)/\hat{h}_{k+2}]^3,\quad G_{k-3}(t) = 0.$$

Hence, by comparing coefficients of $(t_{k+1}-t)^3$ in (3.10a),

$$\alpha_{k-3}(k-2) = d_{k-3,4}\hat{h}_{k+2}^3 / (\hat{d}_{k-2,4} h_{k+1}^3) > 0 \qquad (3.11)$$

since all four variables are positive.

Now, we consider the discrete Beta-splines in (3.10b). If $t_{k-2} < t_{k-1}$, then in interval $[t_{k-2}, t_{k-1}]$,

$$F_{k-2}(t) = s_{k-2,1}(t) = d_{k-2,1}[(t-t_{k-2})/h_{k-1}]^3$$

$$G_{k-2}(t) = \hat{s}_{k-2,1}(t) = \hat{d}_{k-2,1}[(t-t_{k-2})/h_{k-1}]^3,\quad G_{k-1}(t) = 0.$$

Hence, by comparing coefficients of $(t-t_{k-2})^3$ in (3.10b),

$$\alpha_{k-2}(k-2) = d_{k-2,1} / \hat{d}_{k-2,1} > 0$$

since both variables are positive. If $t_{k-2} = t_{k-1}$, then $\alpha_{k-2}(k-2) = 1 - \alpha_{k-3}(k-2)$ where the value of $\alpha_{k-3}(k-2)$ is given in (3.11). The explicit formula given by (2.1) and (2.3), along with $h_{k-1} = 0$, $\hat{\beta}2_{k+1} = 0$ and $h_{k+1} = \hat{h}_{k+1} + \hat{h}_{k+2}$, imply that $\psi_{k-1} = \hat{\psi}_{k+1} = 0$ and

$$d_{k-3,4} / h_{k+1}^3 = 1 / [h_{k+1}(h_k + h_{k+1})(h_k + h_{k+1} + \psi_k h_k)] \qquad (3.12)$$

$$\hat{d}_{k-2,4} / \hat{h}_{k+2}^3 = (1 + \hat{\psi}_k) / [\hat{h}_{k+2} h_{k+1}(h_k + h_{k+1} + \hat{\psi}_k h_{k+1})].$$

From (3.11) and (3.12), $\alpha_{k-2}(k-2) > 0$ if and only if $\alpha_{k-3}(k-2) < 1$ if and only if

$$\begin{aligned}
&\hat{h}_{k+2}(h_k + h_{k+1}) + \hat{\psi}_k \hat{h}_{k+2} h_{k+1} \qquad (3.13)\\
&\quad < (h_k + h_{k+1})(h_k + h_{k+1} + \psi_k h_k) + \\
&\quad \hat{\psi}_k (h_k + h_{k+1})(h_k + h_{k+1} + \psi_k h_k).
\end{aligned}$$

$\hat{h}_{k+2} < h_{k+1}$ implies that (3.13) is true, hence $\alpha_{k-2}(k-2) > 0$.

If $t_{k+1} < t_{k+2}$, then in interval $[t_{k+1}, t_{k+2}] = [u_{k+2}, u_{k+3}]$,

$$F_{k-2}(t) = s_{k-2,4}(t) = d_{k-2,4}[(t_{k+2}-t)/h_{k+2}]^3$$

$$G_{k-1}(t) = \hat{s}_{k-1,4}(t) = \hat{d}_{k-1,4}[(t_{k+2}-t)/h_{k+2}]^3,\quad G_{k-2}(t) = 0.$$

Hence, by comparing coefficients of $(t_{k+2}-t)^3$ in (3.10b),

$$\alpha_{k-2}(k-1) = d_{k-2,4} / \hat{d}_{k-1,4} > 0$$

since both variables are positive. If $t_{k+1} = t_{k+2}$ (i.e. $h_{k+2} = 0$), then in interval $[u_{k+1}, t_{k+1}]$,

$$F_{k-2}(t) = s_{k-2,3}(t) = c_{k-2,3}[(t_{k+1}-t)/h_{k+1}]^2 + d_{k-2,3}[(t_{k+1}-t)/h_{k+1}]^3$$

$$G_{k-2}(t) = \hat{s}_{k-2,4}(t) = \hat{d}_{k-2,4}[(t_{k+1}-t)/\hat{h}_{k+2}]^3$$

$$G_{k-1}(t) = \hat{s}_{k-1,3}(t) = \hat{c}_{k-1,3}[(t_{k+1}-t)/\hat{h}_{k+2}]^2 + \hat{d}_{k-1,3}[(t_{k+1}-t)/\hat{h}_{k+2}]^3$$

since $a_{k-2,3} = b_{k-2,3} = \hat{a}_{k-1,3} = \hat{b}_{k-1,3} = 0$. By the linear independence of $(t_{k+1}-t)^2$ and $(t_{k+1}-t)^3$, and by comparing coefficients of $(t_{k+1}-t)^2$ in (3.10b),

$$\alpha_{k-2}(k-1) = c_{k-2,3}\hat{h}_{k+2}^2 / (\hat{c}_{k-1,3} h_{k+1}^2) > 0$$

since all four variables are positive.

Now suppose case (ii) occurs. Suppose the new knot u_{k+1} satisfies $u_k = u_{k+1} = t_k < t_{k+1}$ for index k in the range $0 \le k \le m+3$ (the case of $k > m+3$ can be taken care of by using the reflection symmetry property). For $i \le k-4$, $F_i(t) = G_i(t)$, so $\alpha_i(i) = 1$ and $\alpha_i(j) = 0$ for $j \ne i$. For $i \ge k$, $F_i(t) = G_{i+1}(t)$, so $\alpha_i(i+1) = 1$ and $\alpha_i(j) = 0$ for $j \ne i+1$. For $i = k-3, k-2$, and $k-1$, $\alpha_i(j) = 0$ for $j < i$ and $j > i+1$ by property (2), so

$$\begin{aligned}
&(a)\ F_{k-3}(t) = \alpha_{k-3}(k-3) G_{k-3}(t) + \alpha_{k-3}(k-2) G_{k-2}(t) \\
&(b)\ F_{k-2}(t) = \alpha_{k-2}(k-2) G_{k-2}(t) + \alpha_{k-2}(k-1) G_{k-1}(t) \\
&(c)\ F_{k-1}(t) = \alpha_{k-1}(k-1) G_{k-1}(t) + \alpha_{k-1}(k) G_k(t)
\end{aligned}$$

The proof that $\alpha_{k-3}(k-3)$, $\alpha_{k-3}(k-2)$, $\alpha_{k-2}(k-2)$, $\alpha_{k-2}(k-1)$, $\alpha_{k-1}(k-1)$, and $\alpha_{k-1}(k)$ are nonnegative is similar to that for case (i). For the same reason as for $\alpha_{k-3}(k-3)$ in case (i), $\alpha_{k-3}(k-3) = \alpha_{k-1}(k) = 1$. For the same reason as for $\alpha_{k-3}(k-2)$ in case (i), $\alpha_{k-3}(k-2) = d_{k-3,4} / \hat{d}_{k-2,4} > 0$ (note that $h_{k+1} = \hat{h}_{k+2}$).

If $t_{k-2} < t_{k-1}$, then for the same reason as for $\alpha_{k-2}(k-2)$ in case (i), $\alpha_{k-2}(k-2) > 0$. If $t_{k-2} = t_{k-1}$, then $\alpha_{k-2}(k-2) = 1 - \alpha_{k-3}(k-2)$ where the value of $\alpha_{k-3}(k-2)$ is given above. The explicit formula given by (2.1) and (2.3), along with $h_{k-1} = 0$ and $\hat{h}_{k+1} = 0$, imply that $\psi_{k-1} = \hat{\psi}_k = \hat{\psi}_{k+1} = 0$ and

$$d_{k-3,4} = h_{k+1}^2 / [(h_k + h_{k+1})(h_k + h_{k+1} + \psi_k h_k)]$$

$$\hat{d}_{k-2,4} = h_{k+1} / (h_k + h_{k+1}).$$

Clearly, $\alpha_{k-3}(k-2) = d_{k-3,4} / \hat{d}_{k-2,4} \le 1$, therefore $\alpha_{k-2}(k-2) \ge 0$.

For the same reason as for $\alpha_{k-2}(k-1)$ in case (i), $\alpha_{k-2}(k-1) > 0$ if $t_{k+1} < t_{k+2}$ or $t_{k+1} = t_{k+2}$. If $t_{k-1} < t_k$, then $\alpha_{k-1}(k-1) > 0$ for a reason similar to that for $\alpha_{k-2}(k-2)$ when $t_{k-2} < t_{k-1}$. If $t_{k-1} = t_k$, then $\alpha_{k-1}(k-1) = 0$ since $F_{k-1}(t) = G_k(t)$. This completes the proof of property (3).

Now we look more closely at the $\alpha_i(j)$ restricted to $0 \le i \le m$ and $0 \le j \le n$. The indices L and U, which were defined in Section 2, satisfy $L = \gamma(3) - 3$ and $U = \eta(m+1) - 1 = \delta(m-3) + 3$. Also, from (3.7), $\lambda(L) \ge 0$ since $u_{L+3} = t_3$ and $[u_{L+3}, u_{L+4}] \subseteq [t_3, t_4]$, and $\rho(U) \le m$ since $u_{U+1} = t_{m+1}$ and $[u_U, u_{U+1}] \subseteq [t_m, t_{m+1}]$. ($\lambda(L) > 0$ or $\rho(U) < m$ can occur only if $t_3 = t_4$ or $t_m = t_{m+1}$, respectively.) So property (1) becomes:

(1') $\sum_{i=0}^{m} \alpha_i(j) = 1$ for $j = L, \cdots, U$;

$\sum_{i=0}^{m} \alpha_i(j) \le 1$ for $j = 0, \cdots, L-1, U+1, \cdots, n$.

The indices $\gamma(i)$, $\delta(i)$ for $0 \le i \le m$, and $\lambda(j)$, $\rho(j)$ for $0 \le j \le n$, used in determining the nonzero $\alpha_i(j)$, can be computed in $O(n)$ time by the pseudocode below. For this computation, we restrict the index i in the definition of $\lambda(j)$ and $\rho(j)$ in (3.7) to the range $0 \le i \le m$. We note that $\gamma(0) \ge 0$ and $\delta(m) \le n$; $\gamma(0)$ and $n - \delta(m)$ are the increase in the multiplicity of knots t_0 and t_{m+4}, respectively, in the refined knot sequence. For $j < \gamma(0)$ and $j > \delta(m)$, $\alpha_i(j) = 0$ for $i = 0, \cdots, m$, so it is useless to increase the multiplicity of t_0 and t_{m+4}. For these indices j, the following pseudocode sets $\rho(j) - \lambda(j) = -1$.

```
i := m+3
for j := n+3 to 0 by -1 do
    if i ≥ 0 and t_i = u_j then
        if i ≤ m then γ(i) := j endif
        i := i-1
    endif
endfor

i := 1
for j := 1 to n+4 do
    if i ≤ m+4 and t_i = u_j then
        if i ≥ 4 then δ(i-4) := j-4 endif
        i := i+1
    endif
endfor

i := 0
for j := 0 to n do
    if i ≤ m and j > δ(i) then i := i+1 endif
    λ(j) := i
endfor

i := m
for j := n to 0 by -1 do
    if i ≥ 0 and j < γ(i) then i := i-1 endif
    ρ(j) := i
endfor
```

4. Computation of discrete Beta-splines

In this section, we give an algorithm for computing the discrete Beta-splines $\alpha_i(j)$ defined in Section 2. Our approach is to use (3.5) and the explicit formula given by (2.1), (2.2), and (2.3) to compute the discrete Beta-splines of fixed index i in the order $\alpha_i(\gamma(i)), \cdots, \alpha_i(\delta(i))$. This is different from the Oslo algorithm for computing discrete B-splines in which the nonzero $\alpha_{i,k}(j)$ of fixed index j are computed using a recurrence relation (k is the order of the B-splines).

If $\gamma(i) = \delta(i)$, then $\alpha_i(\gamma(i)) = 1$. Hence, suppose $\gamma(i) < \delta(i)$. There are four cases to consider for index j between $\gamma(i)$ and $\delta(i)$ inclusive:

(1) $u_j < u_{j+1}$

(2) $u_j = u_{j+1} < u_{j+2}$

(3) $u_j = u_{j+1} = u_{j+2} < u_{j+3}$

(4) $u_j = u_{j+1} = u_{j+2} = u_{j+3} < u_{j+4}$.

Case (1) : Let $k = 1, 2, 3,$ or 4 be the index such that $[u_j, u_{j+1}] \subseteq [t_{i+k-1}, t_{i+k}]$. Due to the local support of the $G_j(t)$, in interval $[u_j, u_{j+1}]$,

$$F_i(t) = \sum_{r=j-3}^{j} \alpha_i(r) G_r(t) = \sum_{r=j-3}^{j} \alpha_i(r) \hat{s}_{r,j+1-r}(t) \tag{4.1}$$

where $\alpha_i(r)$, $r < j$, is zero if $r < \gamma(i)$, or already computed otherwise. From the linear independence of t^3, t^2, t, and 1, the following equation for $\alpha_i(j)$ is obtained by comparing the coefficients of t^3 in (4.1):

$$\alpha_i(j) = [\sigma d_{i,k} \hat{h}_{j+1}^3 / h_{i+k}^3 + \hat{d}_{j-3,4} \alpha_i(j-3) + \hat{d}_{j-2,3} \alpha_i(j-2) - \hat{d}_{j-1,2} \alpha_i(j-1)] / \hat{d}_{j,1} \tag{4.2}$$

where $\sigma = 1$ if $k \le 2$ and $\sigma = -1$ if $k \ge 3$.

Case (2) : Let k be the index such that $[u_{j+1}, u_{j+2}] \subseteq [t_{i+k-1}, t_{i+k}]$. In interval $[u_{j+1}, u_{j+2}]$,

$$F_i(t) = \sum_{r=j-2}^{j+1} \alpha_i(r) G_r(t) = \sum_{r=j-2}^{j+1} \alpha_i(r) \hat{s}_{r,j+2-r}(t) \tag{4.3}$$

where $\alpha_i(r)$, $r < j$, is zero if $r < \gamma(i)$, or already computed otherwise. Since $\hat{h}_{j+1} = 0$,

$$\hat{s}_{j,2}(t) = \hat{c}_{j,2}[(t-u_{j+1})/\hat{h}_{j+2}]^2 + \hat{d}_{j,2}[(t-u_{j+1})/\hat{h}_{j+2}]^3$$
$$\hat{s}_{j+1,1}(t) = \hat{d}_{j+1,1}[(t-u_{j+1})/\hat{h}_{j+2}]^3.$$

From the linear independence of $(t-u_{j+1})^3$, $(t-u_{j+1})^2$, $t-u_{j+1}$, and 1, $\alpha_i(j)$ can be obtained by comparing the coefficients of $(t-u_{j+1})^2$ in (4.3). If $\hat{s}_{j-2,4}(t)$, $\hat{s}_{j-1,3}(t)$, and $s_{i,k}(t)$ are rewritten as linear combinations of $(t-u_{j+1})^3$, $(t-u_{j+1})^2$, $t-u_{j+1}$, and 1, then the coefficients of $(t-u_{j+1})^2$ are, respectively, $3\hat{d}_{j-2,4}/\hat{h}_{j+2}^2$, $(\hat{c}_{j-1,3} + 3\hat{d}_{j-1,3})/\hat{h}_{j+2}^2$, and c, where

$$c = \begin{cases} 3d_{i,k}\varepsilon / h_{i+k}^3, & \text{if } k = 1 \text{ or } 4 \\ c_{i,k}/h_{i+k}^2 + 3d_{i,k}\varepsilon / h_{i+k}^3, & \text{if } k = 2 \text{ or } 3, \end{cases}$$

$$\varepsilon = \begin{cases} u_{j+1} - t_{i+k-1}, & \text{if } k \le 2 \\ t_{i+k} - u_{j+1}, & \text{if } k \ge 3. \end{cases}$$

Therefore

$$\alpha_i(j) = [c\hat{h}_{j+2}^2 - 3\hat{d}_{j-2,4}\alpha_i(j-2) - (\hat{c}_{j-1,3} + 3\hat{d}_{j-1,3})\alpha_i(j-1)] / \hat{c}_{j,2}. \tag{4.4}$$

Case (3) : Let k be the index such that $[u_{j+2}, u_{j+3}] \subseteq [t_{i+k-1}, t_{i+k}]$. In interval $[u_{j+2}, u_{j+3}]$,

$$F_i(t) = \sum_{r=j-1}^{j+2} \alpha_i(r) G_r(t) = \sum_{r=j-1}^{j+2} \alpha_i(r) \hat{s}_{r,j+3-r}(t) \tag{4.5}$$

where $\alpha_i(r)$, $r < j$, is zero if $r < \gamma(i)$, or already computed otherwise. Since $\hat{h}_{j+2} = 0$,

$$\hat{s}_{j,3}(t) = \hat{a}_{j,3} + \hat{b}_{j,3}u + \hat{c}_{j,3}u^2 + \hat{d}_{j,3}u^3, \quad u = (u_{j+3} - t)/\hat{h}_{j+3}$$
$$\hat{s}_{j+1,2}(t) = \hat{c}_{j+1,2}[(t-u_{j+2})/\hat{h}_{j+3}]^2 + \hat{d}_{j+1,2}[(t-u_{j+2})/\hat{h}_{j+3}]^3$$
$$\hat{s}_{j+2,1}(t) = \hat{d}_{j+2,1}[(t-u_{j+2})/\hat{h}_{j+3}]^3.$$

From the linear independence of $(t-u_{j+2})^3$, $(t-u_{j+2})^2$, $t-u_{j+2}$, and 1, $\alpha_i(j)$ can be obtained by comparing the coefficients of $t-u_{j+2}$ in

(4.5). If $\hat{s}_{j-1,4}(t)$, $\hat{s}_{j,3}(t)$, and $s_{i,k}(t)$ are rewritten as linear combinations of $(t-u_{j+2})^3$, $(t-u_{j+2})^2$, $t-u_{j+2}$, and 1, then the coefficients of $t-u_{j+2}$ are, respectively, $-3\hat{d}_{j-1,4}/\hat{h}_{j+3}$, $-(\hat{b}_{j,3}+2\hat{c}_{j,3}+3\hat{d}_{j,3})/\hat{h}_{j+3}=3/\hat{h}_{j+3}$, and b, where

$$b=\begin{cases}3\sigma d_{i,k}\varepsilon^2/h_{i+k}^3, & \text{if } k=1 \text{ or } 4\\ \sigma(b_{i,k}+2c_{i,k}\varepsilon/h_{i+k}+ & \\ \quad 3d_{i,k}\varepsilon^2/h_{i+k}^2)/h_{i+k}, & \text{if } k=2 \text{ or } 3,\end{cases}$$

$$\sigma=1,\quad \varepsilon=u_{j+2}-t_{i+k-1},\quad \text{if } k\le 2$$

$$\sigma=-1,\quad \varepsilon=t_{i+k}-u_{j+2},\quad \text{if } k\ge 3.$$

Therefore

$$\alpha_i(j)=[b\hat{h}_{j+3}+3\hat{d}_{j-1,4}\alpha_i(j-1)]/3. \tag{4.6}$$

Case (4) : Let k be the index such that $[u_{j+3},u_{j+4}]\subseteq[t_{i+k-1},t_{i+k}]$. In interval $[u_{j+3},u_{j+4}]$,

$$F_i(t)=\sum_{r=j}^{j+3}\alpha_i(r)G_r(t)=\sum_{r=j}^{j+3}\alpha_i(r)\hat{s}_{r,j+4-r}(t). \tag{4.7}$$

Since $G_{j+1}(t)$, $G_{j+2}(t)$, and $G_{j+3}(t)$ are continuous at $t=u_{j+3}$ and $G_j(t)$ is not continuous at $t=u_{j+3}$, $G_{j+1}(u_{j+3})=G_{j+2}(u_{j+3})=G_{j+3}(u_{j+3})=0$ and $G_j(u_{j+3})=\hat{s}_{j,4}(u_{j+3})=1$. Therefore, from (4.7),

$$\alpha_i(j)=F_i(u_{j+3})=s_{i,k}(u_{j+3}). \tag{4.8}$$

In summary, the algorithm for computing the nonzero discrete Beta-splines is to first compute the coefficients of the $F_i(t)$ and $G_j(t)$ using the explicit formula (2.1) and (2.3), and then, for each index i, compute the $\alpha_i(j)$ in the order $j=\gamma(i),\cdots,\delta(i)$ using (4.2), (4.4), (4.6), and (4.8). If the nonzero $\alpha_i(j)$ are to be saved, then they can be stored in an n+1 by 4 array *alpha*[0..*n*,0..3] where $\alpha_i(j)$ is stored in *alpha*[$j,i-\lambda(j)$]. If the nonzero $\alpha_i(j)$ are to be computed only for determining the new control vertices W_j using (2.8), then, except for the four most recent values $\alpha_i(k)$, $k=j-3,\cdots,j$, they do not have to be saved, since $\alpha_i(j)V_i$ can be computed and accumulated immediately into W_j.

We now establish an upper bound on the number of floating point operations required to compute the discrete Beta-splines using our algorithm. From Joe (1986), the number of floating point operations required to compute the coefficients of $F_i(t)$, $0\le i\le m$, and $G_j(t)$, $0\le j\le n$, for distinct knot sequences (the worst case) is $26+34(m+n+2)$ multiplications/divisions and $12+19(m+n+2)$ additions/subtractions. The computation of each nonzero $\alpha_i(j)$ requires at most 11 multiplications/divisions and 5 additions/subtractions (these counts are 8 and 4, respectively, for distinct knot sequences). From (3.6), the number of nonzero $\alpha_i(j)$ is at most $4n-3m+1$. Therefore computation of all the nonzero $\alpha_i(j)$ requires an upper bound of $78n+m+105$ multiplications/divisions and $39n+4m+55$ additions/subtractions. In addition, the computation of the new control vertices W_j requires at most $(4n-3m+1)d$ multiplications and $(3n-3m)d$ additions where $d=2$ or 3 is the dimension of the control vertices.

Finally, we discuss the numerical stability of the algorithm. The computation of $\alpha_i(j)$, $j=\gamma(i),\cdots,\delta(i)$, is equivalent to solving a lower triangular banded system of linear equations using forward substitution. Hence the algorithm is stable in the sense that the forward substitution algorithm is stable (Stewart (1973)). However, if the tension parameters or knot spacings vary a lot, then the lower triangular matrix may be ill-conditioned and considerable roundoff errors can occur in the computed $\alpha_i(j)$. Therefore double precision should be used in these cases.

5. Examples

Examples of new control polygons, obtained from the algorithm of Section 4, are given in Figure 1. The same control polygon $V_0V_1\cdots V_9$ is used with different tension parameters and knot spacings. The control polygon is drawn in dashed lines, and the refined control polygons $W_LW_{L+1}\cdots W_U$ are drawn in solid lines.

Figures 1(a) to 1(d) are refined control polygons for a Beta-spline curve with knots $t_i=i$, $0\le i\le 13$, and tension parameters $\beta2_1=0$, $\beta2_2=10$, $\beta2_3=9$, $\beta2_4=8$, $\beta2_5=7$, $\beta2_6=6$, and $\beta2_i=0$ for $7\le i\le 12$. For Figure 1(a), knots $i+.5$, $3\le i\le 9$, are added to get the refined knot sequence. For Figure 1(b), knots $i+.25$, $i+.5$, and $i+.75$, $3\le i\le 9$, are added. For Figure 1(c), knots $i+.5$, $0\le i\le 12$, are added. For Figure 1(d), knots $i+.25$, $i+.5$, and $i+.75$, $0\le i\le 12$, are added. These figures illustrate that refined knots must be added in the intervals $[t_0,t_3]$ and $[t_{m+1},t_{m+4}]$ in order for the refined control polygon to be a good approximation to the Beta-spline curve at its two ends. If no knots are added in these two intervals, then $W_L=V_0$ and $W_U=V_m$.

Figures 1(e) and 1(f) are refined control polygons for a Beta-spline curve with quadruple knots at t_0 and t_{13} so that V_0 and V_9 are interpolated by the curve. The knots are $t_i=i-3$, $3\le i\le 10$, and the tension parameters are $\beta2_4=10$, $\beta2_5=8$, $\beta2_6=6$, $\beta2_7=4$, $\beta2_8=2$, and $\beta2_i=0$ otherwise. For Figure 1(e), knots $i+.5$, $0\le i\le 6$, are added to get the refined knot sequence. For Figure 1(f), knots $i+.2$, $i+.4$, $i+.6$, and $i+.8$, $0\le i\le 6$, are added.

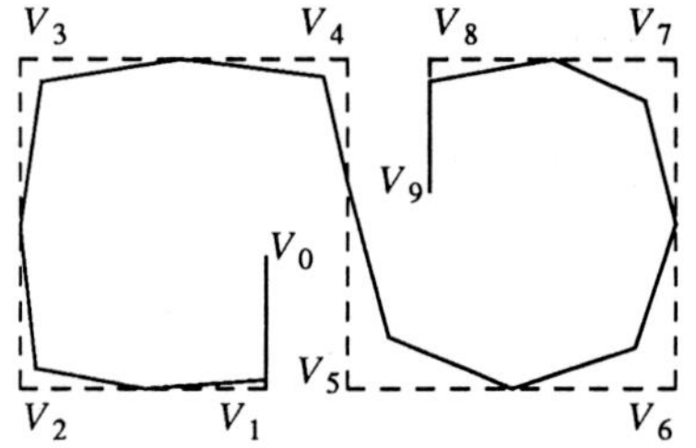

(a)

new knots $i+.5$, $3\le i\le 9$

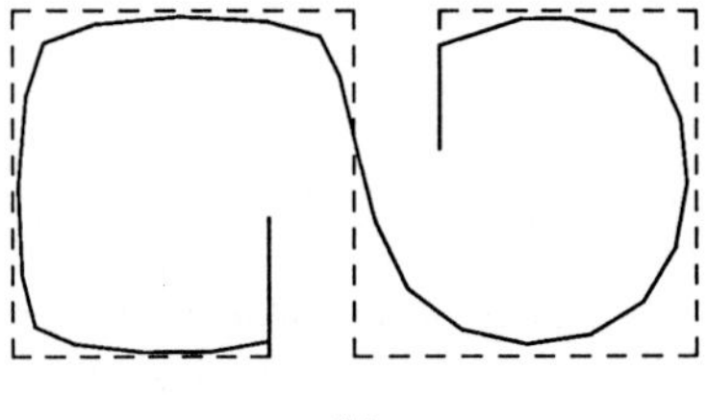

(b)

new knots $i+.25, i+.5, i+.75$, $3\le i\le 9$

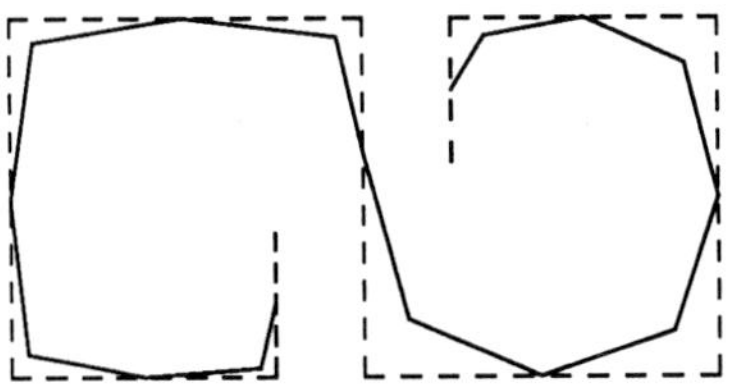

(c)

new knots $i+.5$, $0 \le i \le 12$

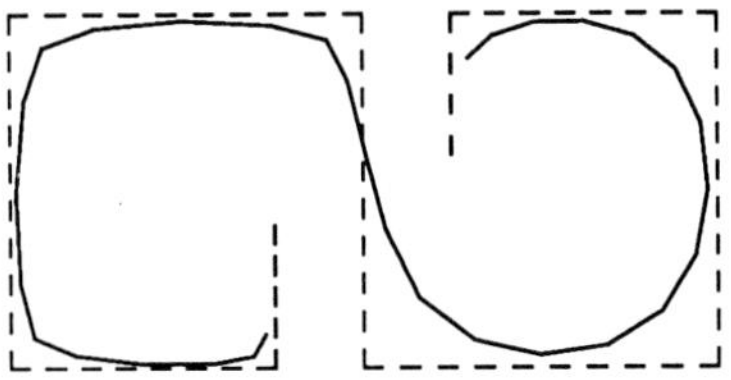

(d)

new knots $i+.25, i+.5, i+.75$, $0 \le i \le 12$

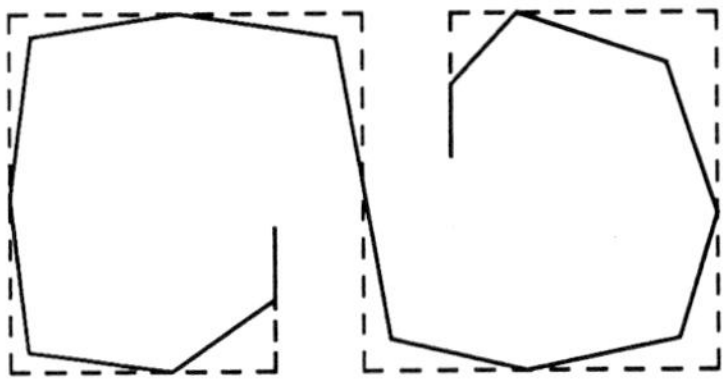

(e)

new knots $i+.5$, $0 \le i \le 6$

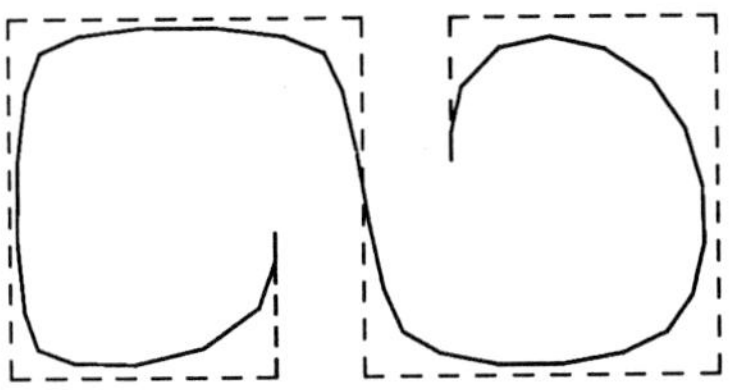

(f)

new knots $i+.2, i+.4, i+.6, i+.8$, $0 \le i \le 6$

Figure 1 Examples of refined control polygons

6. Concluding remarks

Discrete Beta-splines arise when a Beta-spline curve is subdivided, i.e. the knot sequence is refined so that the curve is expressed in terms of a larger number of control vertices and Beta-splines. We have proved that discrete Beta-splines satisfy the same properties as discrete B-splines, and presented an algorithm for computing discrete Beta-splines and the new control vertices using the explicit formula of Joe (1986). An alternative approach to computing discrete Beta-splines and the new control vertices, based on the proof of property (3) in which the new knots are inserted one at a time, is given by Joe (1987).

An open problem is whether discrete Beta-splines can be computed using a recurrence relation like the Oslo algorithm for discrete B-splines. Goodman and Unsworth (1985) have given a recurrence for Beta-splines in terms of quadratic B-splines, in which the coefficients of the recurrence are piecewise linear polynomials. Because of these piecewise linear polynomials, it is not possible to derive a recurrence for discrete Beta-splines in terms of discrete quadratic B-splines using the approach of Prautzsch (1984).

Acknowledgment

The author would like to thank R. H. Bartels for his comments on a preliminary draft of this paper, and the referees for their useful comments. This work was partially supported by grants from the Central Research Fund of the University of Alberta and the Natural Sciences and Engineering Research Council of Canada.

References

B. A. Barsky (1981), The Beta-spline: a local representation based on shape parameters and fundamental geometric measures, Ph.D. Dissertation, Dept. of Computer Science, Univ. of Utah.

B. A. Barsky and J. C. Beatty (1983), Local control of bias and tension in Beta-splines, *ACM Transactions on Graphics,* 2, pp. 109-134.

B. A. Barsky (1986), *Computer Graphics and Geometric Modelling Using Beta-splines,* Springer-Verlag, Tokyo.

R. H. Bartels and J. C. Beatty (1984), Beta-splines with a difference, Technical Report CS-83-40, Dept. of Computer Science, Univ. of Waterloo.

R. H. Bartels, J. C. Beatty, and B. A. Barsky (1987), *An Introduction to the Use of Splines in Computer Graphics,* to be published by Morgan Kaufman Publishers, Los Altos, California.

W. Boehm (1980), Inserting new knots into B-spline curves, *Computer-Aided Design,* 12, pp. 199-201.

W. Boehm and H. Prautzsch (1985), The insertion algorithm, *Computer-Aided Design,* 17, pp. 58-59.

W. Boehm (1985), Curvature continuous curves and surfaces, *Computer Aided Geometric Design,* 2, pp. 313-323.

E. Cohen, T. Lyche, and R. Riesenfeld (1980), Discrete B-splines and subdivision techniques in computer-aided geometric design and computer graphics, *Computer Graphics and Image Processing,* 14, pp. 87-111.

G. Farin (1982), Visually C^2 cubic splines, *Computer-Aided Design,* 14, pp. 137-139.

G. Farin (1985), Some remarks on V^2-splines, *Computer Aided Geometric Design,* 2, pp. 325-328.

T. N. T. Goodman (1985), Properties of Beta-splines, *J. Approximation Theory,* 44, pp. 132-153.

T. N. T. Goodman and K. Unsworth (1985), Generation of Beta-spline curves using a recurrence relation, in *Fundamental Algorithms for Computer Graphics,* Springer-Verlag, Berlin, pp. 325-357.

T. N. T. Goodman and K. Unsworth (1986), Manipulating shape and producing geometric continuity in Beta-spline curves, *IEEE Computer Graphics and Applications,* 6, No. 2, pp. 50-56.

B. Joe (1986), An explicit formula for nonuniform Beta-splines, Technical Report TR86-21, Dept. of Computing Science, Univ. of Alberta.

B. Joe (1987), Rational Beta-spline curves and surfaces and discrete Beta-splines, Technical Report TR87-04, Dept. of Computing Science, Univ. of Alberta.

T. Lyche and K. Morken (1986), Making the Oslo algorithm more efficient, *SIAM J. Numer. Anal.,* 23, pp. 663-675.

H. Prautzsch (1984), A short proof of the Oslo algorithm, *Computer Aided Geometric Design,* 1, pp. 95-96.

H. Prautzsch (1985), Letter to the editor, *Computer Aided Geometric Design,* 2, p. 329.

G. W. Stewart (1973), *Introduction to Matrix Computations,* Academic Press, New York.

Direct Least-Squares Fitting of Algebraic Surfaces

Vaughan Pratt
Sun Microsystems Inc.
and
Stanford University

Abstract. In the course of developing a system for fitting smooth curves to camera input we have developed several direct (i.e. noniterative) methods for fitting a shape (line, circle, conic, cubic, plane, sphere, quadric, etc.) to a set of points, namely exact fit, simple fit, spherical fit, and blend fit. These methods are all dimension-independent, being just as suitable for 3D surfaces as for the 2D curves they were originally developed for.

Exact fit generalizes to arbitrary shapes (in the sense of the term defined in this paper) the well-known determinant method for planar exact fit. Simple fit is a naive reduction of the general overconstrained case to the exact case. Spherical fit takes advantage of a special property of circles and spheres that permits robust fitting; no prior direct circle fitters have been as robust, and there have been no previous sphere fitters. Blend fit finds the best fit to a set of points of a useful generalization of Middleditch-Sears blending curves and surfaces, via a nonpolynomial generalization of planar fit.

These methods all require $(am + bn)n^2$ operations for fitting a surface of order n to m points, with $a = 2$ and $b = 1/3$ typically, except for spherical fit where b is larger due to the need to extract eigenvectors. All these methods save simple fit achieve a robustness previously attained by direct algorithms only for fitting planes. All admit incremental batched addition and deletion of points at cost an^2 per point and bn^3 per batch.

1. Introduction

Background. We began this project with the problem of recovering outline fonts from scanned-in camera images of large-scale drawings, as part of a larger project to automate the entry of such drawings. Such entry is usually done by hand, typically by entering points around the curve via a tablet and postediting the result to achieve smoothness and fidelity to the original. Such manual entry of curves is not only an expensive use of human resources but also less accurate than what can be achieved by working algorithmically with scanned-in camera images.

The techniques we developed for this application are of general interest to other domains where curve fitting is needed, as well as to situations involving surface fitting in three or more dimensions. This paper therefore emphasizes these general techniques at the expense of their motivating application, which we hope to report on elsewhere.

Our application is also the main application of similar work reported by Plass and Stone in this forum [21]. The two main differences of our work from theirs are our emphasis on algebraic as opposed to parametric curves (in the 2D case), and on one-step application of matrix-inversion-style least-squares methods, which we refer to as *direct* methods in distinction to slower iterative methods.

© 1987 ACM-0-89791-227-6/87/007/0145 $00.75

Problem Statement. We wish to fit an algebraic curve or surface of a given shape to m points in d-dimensional space $\mathbf{R}^d$. We cater for such shapes as circle, line-pair, cubic, cone, sphere, and quadric, all of which are definable in the form $f(x_1, \ldots, x_d) = 0$ where f is a polynomial in its arguments, but not, e.g., for space curves, which are defined as the intersection of two surfaces and require two such equations.

Goodness of fit is taken to be the length of the m-vector of distances of the m points from the surface. The fit is called exact, best, or good when this length is respectively zero, least possible, or close to least possible.

We take the length of an m-vector to mean its Euclidean length. Best fit then amounts to least-squared-distance fit.

We take the *geometric* distance of a point p from a surface S to be the distance from p to the nearest point of S, i.e. the minimum, over all points p' of S, of the Euclidean distance from p to p'. Unfortunately geometric distance is neither computationally nor algebraically convenient, particularly for higher-order surfaces. This leads to the use of distance metrics that approximate geometric distance. A distance metric is more or less *robust* when the best fit under it is a more or less good fit under geometric distance.

Performance. The main emphasis of this paper is on fast computation of good fits, to which end we confine ourselves to *direct* methods, by which we mean those least-squares methods that require roughly the work of a matrix inversion or an extraction of eigenvalues. Our typical cost to fit a surface of order n to m points is on the order of $(m+n)n^2$ operations, e.g. to fit circles to 20 points $m = 20$ and $n = 4$, so a few hundred operations. By contrast iterative methods may be much slower; Figure 2 of [21] suggests that an iterative method may require on the order of a hundred iterations to fit a parametric cubic to a set of $m = 20$ points, with each iteration itself requiring the application of a least squares algorithm.

Why algebraic surfaces? An algebraic presentation of a surface is an implicit presentation $f(x_1, \ldots, x_d) = 0$ for which f is a polynomial in its d arguments. The main rationale for our interest in algebraically presented surfaces is that they lend themselves to direct least-squares techniques at least as naturally as parametric surfaces. In addition, in some situations parameters constitute an inconvenient or unnatural artifact. Thirdly, although all algebraic surfaces are representable parametrically they are not all representable with a polynomial or even rational polynomial representation, whence algebraic methods have a greater domain of applicability. And fourthly, parametric curves and surfaces have received the lion's share of attention in the fitting literature, creating the misleading impression that algebraically presented curves and surfaces are less suitable for fitting purposes. Indeed our own experience has been that the situation is quite the opposite: we find the algebraic form more convenient and efficient for fitting.

Related work. There appears to be relatively little written about fitting algebraic curves. A fairly thorough search turned up only a few treatments of least-squares fitting of algebraic curves [1, 2, 3, 4, 9, 15, 16, 24, 25] and none whatsoever of least-squares fitting of nonplanar algebraic surfaces. By comparison least-squares fitting of parametric polynomial curves and surfaces is routinely treated in many papers and a number of textbooks [5, 7, 8, 13, 19]. In the case of least-squares fitting of surfaces there seems to be a universal impression that fitting is only feasible for parametrically presented surfaces.

Perhaps the single commonest failing of those papers that do treat algebraically presented curves is their casual adoption of computationally convenient distance metrics. These metrics generally measure the distance of a point (x_0, y_0) to a curve $q(x,y) = 0$ ($q(x,y)$ a polynomial in x and y) by first normalizing q according to some quadratic constraint on its coefficients and then taking the distance to be $q(x_0, y_0)$. We shall call this a *quadratic-norm* distance metric. Bookstein [3] faults several authors [1,2,4,9] for adopting quadratic-norm metrics that depend on choice of basis, and gives a similarity-invariant metric (relative to geometric distance) that is usable for both conic-fitting and circle-fitting, arguing that this is the only similarity-invariant exact-fit-preserving quadratic-norm metric.

Sampson [24] points out that even with these properties Bookstein's metric still departs sufficiently from geometric distance that when fitting highly elliptic conics to "very scattered" data the resulting fit can be perceptibly inferior. One might conclude that the application of Bookstein distance to circle-fitting would be less problematic since the ellipticity problem addressed by Sampson cannot arise. Actually it is the other way around: for circle fitting Bookstein's measure can fail far more convincingly than envisaged by Sampson, which we illustrate below with an example where curvature of the fitted circle increases when it should be decreasing.

Turner [25] and Sampson [24] apply the nonalgebraic distance metric $q/|\nabla q|$ to curve fitting. We show how to modify this metric to be algebraic – a quadratic normalization – for the case of circles (extending immediately to spheres), ironically the one case of ellipses to which Sampson did not evisage applying $q/|\nabla q|$.

Results. The techniques we have developed are as follows.

(i) Exact fit. We give a simple method for exact fitting of a surface of a given shape to the appropriate number of points, generalizing the well-known determinant method for fitting a hyperplane in d dimensions to d points.

(ii) Simple fit. We naively translate the problem of finding the best fitting surface for a surfeit of points into the exact-fit problem, via normal equations. The translation is very simple, has excellent performance, but lacks robustness. We give a variation on the method that substantially improves its robustness at negligible performance cost.

(iii) Spherical fit. We give a distance metric that leads to a robust direct algorithm for fitting spheres in d dimensions. For $d = 2$ this algorithm is the first direct least-squares circle fitter to achieve this level of robustness. For higher d this is still true, albeit vacuously since the problem of fitting spheres to points seems not to have previously been considered.

(iv) Blend fit. We first give a useful generalization of the Middleditch-Sears [14] approach to blending surfaces. Then, given a set of base surfaces to be blended, along with a set of points, we give a simple direct method for finding a blending surface of a given shape best fitting those points.

2. Samples, Surfaces, and Shapes

Given a *sample* consisting of an m-tuple of points in $\mathbf{R}^d$, we wish to find a *surface* of the form $Z(q) \subseteq \mathbf{R}^d$ consisting of the zeros of a function $q : \mathbf{R}^d \to \mathbf{R}$, that comes close to minimizing the sample-to-surface distance, which we define as the Euclidean norm (length) of the m-vector of the true (geometric) point-to-surface distances. The function q is to be drawn from a given set Q; for example if we are fitting circles then Q is the set Q_C of all polynomials of the form $A(x^2+y^2)+Dx+Ey+F$.

The techniques of this paper apply to sets of functions closed under linear combinations. For example it should be apparent that Q_C is so closed. Such a subset of the ring of all functions $q : \mathbf{R}^d \to \mathbf{R}$, is called an *ideal* of that ring; it also constitutes a vector space ($\mathbf{R}$ being a field). For example Q_C is a 4-dimensional vector space (of polynomials $q : \mathbf{R}^2 \to \mathbf{R}$) one of whose bases is $x^2+y^2, x, y, 1$. (The reader accustomed to thinking about the set of cubic polynomials as a four-dimensional vector space with $1, t, t^2, t^3$ as one basis and $(1-t)^3, 3t(1-t)^2, 3t^2(1-t), t^3$ as another should have no difficulty adapting to these concepts.) Our techniques are limited to the case where this space is of finite dimension n. We call a set of surfaces defined by an n-dimensional ideal a *shape* of order n, e.g. the set of all 2D circles constitutes a shape of order 4.

It is customary in geometry to work with just the ideals of the ring of all *polynomials* $q : \mathbf{R}^d \to \mathbf{R}$. However our methods extend immediately to the larger ring of all *functions* $f : \mathbf{R}^d \to \mathbf{R}$, which we take advantage of for blend fitting.

Every such Q contains the identically zero polynomial 0, defining the trivial surface consisting of the whole space. One additional requirement when fitting surfaces is that we do not allow this trivial fit. We nevertheless leave 0 in Q for algebraic convenience.

Examples. Many useful shapes are definable by finite-dimensional ideals. We list a few below along with suitable generators for their defining ideals, each set of generators constituting a basis for the ideal as a vector space.

horizontal line	$1, y$
diagonal line	$1, x+y$
line*	$1, x, y$
upright parabola	$1, x, y, x^2$
upright hyperbola	$1, x, y, xy$
diagonal hyperbola	$1, x, y, x^2-y^2$
circle at origin	$1, x^2+y^2$
circle	$1, x, y, x^2+y^2$
right hyperbola	$1, x, y, 2xy, x^2-y^2$
conic*	$1, x, y, x^2, xy, y^2$ or circle $\cup$ right hyperbola
cubic*	conic $\cup$ x^3, x^2y, xy^2, y^3
plane*	$1, x, y, z$
z-axis cylinder	$1, x^2+y^2$
z-axis cone	x^2+y^2, z^2
x=z-axis cone	$y^2, 2xz$
z-aligned cylinder	$1, x, y, x^2+y^2$
sphere	$1, x, y, z, x^2+y^2+z^2$
right hyperboloid	$1, x, y, z, x^2-y^2, y^2-z^2, 2xy, 2yz, 2zx$
quadric*	$1, x, y, z, x^2, y^2, z^2, xy, yz, zx$ or sphere $\cup$ right hyperboloid

Asterisks denote shapes invariant under linear transformations (and hence under change of basis), meaning that a linear transformation maps any object of that shape to an object of the same shape. Although the circle, right hyperbola (orthogonal asymptotes, useful for converting spherical fit to conic fit), sphere, and right hyperboloid (3D analog of the right hyperbola) shapes are not so invariant, they are invariant under similarities (angle-preserving linear transformations, i.e. rotations, scalings, and translations), while the properties of being a line of a given orientation (horizontal, diagonal, etc.), upright parabola, upright or diagonal hyperbola (asymptotes parallel to or at 45 degrees to the axes), or z-aligned cylinder are invariant under translations. The remaining properties are not even invariant under translations.

3. Algebraic Distance

A commonly used surrogate for geometric distance from a point p to a surface $Z(q)$ is the value of q at p. Since $Z(q) = Z(cq)$ for $c \neq 0$ q is first normalized in order to make this value meaningful, typically by scaling it so as to set to a constant (unity for definiteness) some quadratic function of its coefficients, which we call *quadratic normalization.* Since we seek to minimize the sum of the *squares* of the distances it changes nothing if we take the negation of a normal polynomial to also be normal. We shall refer to distance computed in this manner as *algebraic distance*; the essential characteristic of algebraic distance from p to $Z(q)$

is that it is computed by evaluating a fixed representative polynomial cq, *chosen independently of* p.

An important aspect of quadratic normalization for our purposes is that the best fit under such a distance metric can be computed directly via the computation of an $n \times n$ eigenvector in $O(n^3)$ operations [12]. Hence *any distance metric defined by a quadratic normalization leads automatically to a fitting method meeting our performance requirement.* The remaining concern is then with the quality of fit, which can vary substantially between normalizations.

Normalization can be visualized geometrically by thinking of the set $\{cq | c \text{ real}\}$ for any given q as the line containing the polynomials q and 0 in the vector space Q. This line is called the *principal ideal* generated by q, and pervades the algebraic geometry of surfaces. Normal polynomials then appear as complementary pairs of points (equidistant from the origin of Q) on principal ideals, and we may think of the set of all normal polynomials as forming a surface in the space Q, which we may call a *normalizing surface* in Q (not to be confused with surfaces comprising shapes, which exist in R^d).

If the normalizing surface is say a sphere then it will intersect all principal ideals (in two complementary points), but if it is say a cylinder then the principal ideal along its axis will contain no normal polynomial (equivalently, the normal polynomial can be regarded as being at the "end" of the ideal, i.e. at infinity). In this case a fitting algorithm will never fit such a principal ideal; furthermore, principal ideals very close to it will have very large normal polynomials and so will appear to be bad fits. We think of the unfittable polynomials as the *singularities* of the normalization, and their neighbors as being very hard to fit. In the actual fitting process the presence of singularities is felt as a sort of repulsive force pushing the fitted shape well away from the singularity.

A number of authors have proposed such normalizations for the conic shape. Paton [16] normalizes conics $Ax^2+Bxy+Cy^2+Dx+Ey+F=0$ subject to $A^2+B^2+C^2+D^2+E^2+F^2=1$, corresponding to taking the normalizing surface to be the unit sphere with center 0 (with respect to the basis $x^2, xy, y^2, x, y, 1$), having no singularities. Biggerstaff [2], Albano [1], and Cooper and Yalabik [4] take the plane $F = 1$ (equivalently, the two planes $F = \pm 1$), whose singularities correspond to those conics that pass through the origin. Gnanadesikan [9] takes the unit cylinder along the F-axis, that is, $A^2+B^2+C^2+D^2+E^2=1$, missing only the F-axis itself, defining the empty conic $Z(1)$, which is no great loss. Bookstein uses the ellipsoidal cylinder $A^2+B^2/2+C^2=2$, ruling out the subspace $A = B = C = 0$ of Q which can be seen to make straight lines singular and so unfittable.

Each of these metrics save Bookstein's varies (relative to geometric distance) under similarities (rotations, translations, and scaling) of the plane, as Bookstein points out. It is worth adding that the most popular normalization, $F = 1$, is a particularly poor one due to the singularity at the origin, which tends to push the fit away from the origin. (Hence to lie with statistics when fitting curves to data it suffices to choose as the origin for that data a point you want the curve to stay away from regardless of what the data says.) Gnanadesikan's normalization has the opposite problem, tending to push the fit towards the origin to keep D and E small.

For the circle shape, definable as the subshape $A = C, B = 0$ of the conic shape, Bookstein's normalization specializes to $A^2 + C^2 = 2$, i.e. $A = \pm 1$, still having lines as its singularities. One might then predict that Bookstein's normalization should prefer slightly more curved fits than the true best fit; in actuality it is easily encouraged to prefer absurdly curved fits, as we shall see in the section on spherical fits. To correct this we propose a new normalization for circles, namely $D^2+E^2-4AF=1$ ($D^2+E^2+F^2-4AG=1$ for spheres). Like Bookstein's normalization this is invariant relative to geometric distance under similarities but has only points (zero-radius circles) as singularities, which appear to cause less havoc than lines.

4. Nonalgebraic Distance

We mention here some of the principles behind metrics whose normalizations do depend on p, i.e. nonalgebraic distance metrics. Curiously enough, one of the insights from this section leads us to our above-mentioned algebraic distance metric for circles. Beyond this, an understanding of the principles will improve perspective on surface fitting techniques in general.

Sink or Swim. In visualizing the correspondence between geometric and algebraic distance we find the *sink or swim* picture helpful. In dimension $d = 2$, think of a point $p = (x, y)$ on the plane R^2 as a swimmer in the ocean and the 3D surface $z = q(x, y)$ as the land below him. $Z(q)$ is the shoreline, geometric distance $D(p, Z(q))$ is swimming distance to shore, unnormalized algebraic distance (the sign is unimportant) is sinking distance to bottom, and normalization is vertical rescaling. In this connection a useful additional concept is the gradient operator ∇: $\nabla q = (\partial q/\partial x, \partial q/\partial y)$ is a function which assigns to each point p on the ocean surface a vector $\nabla q(p)$ lying in the ocean surface whose direction is the uphill direction of the ocean bottom immediately below p and whose length $|\nabla q(p)|$ is the slope of the ocean bottom there.

When the surface $z = q(x, y)$ is planar, ∇q and hence $|\nabla q|$ are constant. We can therefore normalize q to $q/|\nabla q|$ to yield a surface with slope 1, for which algebraic distance coincides with geometric distance [18]. If $q(x, y) = Dx + Ey + F$ then $|\nabla q| = \sqrt{D^2 + E^2}$, so the appropriate normalization is $D^2 + E^2 = 1$, with only the trivial degeneracy $F = 0$. This leads to an eigenvector-based direct method for best geometric fitting of lines and planes in any R^d. (A slope-1 normalization is possible also for cones, pyramids, and much more complex surfaces; unfortunately none of these shapes appear to be definable in terms of an ideal of polynomials. They can in some cases be defined in terms of an ideal of algebraic functions, typically involving square roots of polynomials, but unlike the convenient setup with blending surfaces that we present below these ideals appear not to be of finite dimension, ruling out any direct application of our methods.)

Turner [25] and Sampson [24] have independently proposed using the above normalization $q/|\nabla q|$ for nonplanar shapes, for which $|\nabla q|$ is not constant. This normalization is a function of p and gives a nonalgebraic distance metric, albeit one that remains computationally more tractable than geometric distance. Nalwa and Pauchon [15] refine this metric to take into account second-order derivatives of q, which can be helpful with very scattered data.

These metrics offer the following benefits. First $q/|\nabla q|$ is insensitive to scaling of q. Secondly it is as invariant as geometric distance, being invariant under translations and rotations and varying in proportion to geometric distance under change of scale; hence the best fit is invariant under similarities (angle-preserving transformations or changes of basis). Thirdly it coincides with geometric distance for plane surfaces. Fourthly, for nonplanar surfaces, $q(p)/|\nabla q(p)|$ approximates geometric distance to the extent that q is approximately planar (i.e. approximates a linear combination of $1, x_1, \ldots, x_d$) on the (d-dimensional) ball with center p and radius $q(p)/|\nabla q(p)|$, which is almost invariably the case for only slightly scattered data.

The Turner-Sampson and Nalwa-Pauchon metrics are both nonalgebraic and seemingly unusable with direct methods. Rather, at least as envisaged by Sampson [24], one iteratively computes an algebraic fit q by a direct method, weighting the algebraic distance from each sample point p to $Z(q)$ by $1/|\nabla q^{(-1)}(p)|$ where $q^{(-1)}$ is the surface found at the previous iteration, using unit weights in the first iteration. This appears to us to be the most robust method for those situations where there is no appropriate quadratic normalization, e.g. highly elliptical conics, as we discuss in the section on spherical fits.

5. Exact Fit

We give a straightforward method for exactly fitting a surface of order n to $n-1$ points $p_1, \ldots, p_{n-1}$, which we want mainly for the more general problem of approximately fitting such a shape to at least that many points. The method is well-known for the case of planes, appears occasionally in textbooks for the case of circles, and in [22] and [20] (p.369) for conics. However we have been unable to locate any reference to the general method.

Let $A : Q \to \mathbf{R}^m$ map each polynomial $q \in Q$ to the m-vector of values of q at the m points, evidently a linear transformation. The exact fits are then the zeros of A. Given any basis $b_1, \ldots, b_n$ for Q, q is representable as the n-vector $\mathbf{q}$ of coefficients of b_i's A is representable as the $m \times n$ matrix A whose ij-th element is $b_j(p_i)$, and $A(q)$ is given by the product $A\mathbf{q}$. To fit a circle to five points we would have

$$A = \begin{pmatrix} 1 & x_1 & y_1 & x_1^2 + y_1^2 \\ 1 & x_2 & y_2 & x_2^2 + y_2^2 \\ 1 & x_3 & y_3 & x_3^2 + y_3^2 \\ 1 & x_4 & y_4 & x_4^2 + y_4^2 \\ 1 & x_5 & y_5 & x_5^2 + y_5^2 \end{pmatrix}$$

Then the matrix A amounts to a change of coordinates for (defining polynomials of) surfaces, namely from the given basis to a coordinate system in which the i-th coordinate gives the algebraic distance of the surface from p_i.

For the case $m = n - 1$ an exact fit is possible, and is easily found as follows. Let A^+ denote the square matrix obtained from A by adjoining an n-th row consisting of the basis polynomials themselves, making A^+ a matrix over polynomials, and form its determinant. In the circle example this determinant is

$$\begin{vmatrix} 1 & x_1 & y_1 & x_1^2 + y_1^2 \\ 1 & x_2 & y_2 & x_2^2 + y_2^2 \\ 1 & x_3 & y_3 & x_3^2 + y_3^2 \\ 1 & x & y & x^2 + y^2 \end{vmatrix}$$

This determinant, a polynomial q, can be seen to be a linear combination of the n (here $n = 4$) basis polynomials and so is in Q, whence we have a legal surface. Since the value of row n at p_i is row i it follows that the determinant vanishes at each p_i, so the surface passes through all $m = n - 1$ points.

We may compute q as the cofactors of the elements of the n-th row, giving its representation in terms of coefficients of the b_i's. For large n it is worthwhile to triangularize A first (i.e. make $A_{ij} = 0$ for $i > j$ via row operations) at cost $O(n^3)$ and then compute the cofactors at an additional cost of $O(n^2)$.
The one uninteresting case of this situation is when q is identically 0, which it is if and only if the rank of A is strictly less than $n-1$. In this case the points underdetermine the shape, a situation we do not treat here.

When $m \geq n$ but the rank of A is $n - 1$ we may select $n - 1$ linearly independent rows of A to form an $(n-1) \times m$ matrix whose rank is still $n - 1$. The above technique may then be applied to this matrix to yield a surface passing through these $n-1$ selected points. This surface will also pass through all points whose corresponding matrix rows are linear combinations of the $n-1$ selected rows, which is the case for the $m - (n-1)$ unselected rows, the rank of A being only $n - 1$. Again, if the rank of A is less than $n - 1$ the points still underdetermine the shape.

6. Simple Fit

The only remaining case now is $m \geq n$ and rank$(A) = n$. This is the overdetermined case (no exact fit), our primary interest. The goal is to find a good fit $Z(q)$ to the sample The following method is of interest partly for its simplicity, partly for its connection to Exact Fit, and partly for how it circumvents singularities.

We first state the method for the normalization which holds the last coefficient constant. This normalization has the obvious drawback that a fit having this coefficient zero constitutes a singularity, which we will attend to shortly.

The first step of the method is the basic step for the method of normal equations, the second step is novel in that the normal equations method is usually applied to systems with an independent variable, whereas here we are solving an implicit system in which none of the d variables can be identified as independent.

The Simple Fit algorithm can be obtained by combining the non-geometric ideas from equation (19.10) of [12] (taking their $\tilde{U}$ to be our U) with the above geometrically-oriented exact fit algorithm, as follows.

1. Given A as above, of size $m \times n$, compute the Cholesky decomposition $A'A = U'U$ [7,8,12,19]. That is, compute the unique $n \times n$ upper triangular U with nonnegative diagonal entries such that $U'U = A'A$.

2. Delete the last row of U to yield an $(n-1) \times n$ matrix and treat the result as though it were the $(n-1) \times n$ matrix A in the exact fit case. That is, append a row of polynomials and form the determinant.

The discussion of equation 19.10 in [12] shows that the resulting surface is the best algebraic fit subject to holding the n-th coefficient of q constant. (Hence the best algebraic fit under the normalization in which the n-th coefficient is 1 may be obtained by dividing q by its n-th coefficient.) The quality of fit (square root of sum of squares, amounting to standard deviation times $\sqrt{n}$) is given by U_{nn} (ρ in 19.10 [12]), the one nonzero element of the discarded last row.

Cholesky Without Square Roots. While the $U'U$ decomposition has the merit of conceptual simplicity it has the drawback of requiring the extraction of n square roots. Cholesky decomposition without square roots (Exercise 19.40 of [12]) modifies step 1 above by finding $n \times n$ matrices U and D satisfying $A'A = U'DU$ where D is diagonal and the leading diagonal of U consists of 1's. Step 2 is left unchanged.

A suitable procedure for this decomposition is as follows. An $n \times n$ matrix P is initialized to $A'A$. Only the upper triangles of P and U require storage since $A'A$ is symmetric and U is upper triangular.

```
for i := 1 to n do
  {U_ii := 1;
   for j := i+1 to n do
     {U_ij := P_ij/P_ii;
      for k := j to n do
        P_jk := P_jk - U_ij × P_ik}}
```

Note that the procedure modifies P. D is obtained as the diagonal of the final P. If $P_{ii} \leq 0$ (with negative P_{ii} being possible only on account of roundoff error) then U_{ij} is set to 0 for all $j \geq i$. The diagonal of U being 1 simplifies the computation of the cofactors in Step 2, which requires only $O(n^2)$ operations.

The quality of fit is now obtained as D_{nn} rather than U_{nn}, the latter now always being 1. D_{nn} is actually the square of the old U_{nn} and so is the sum of squares rather than its square root (amounting to variance times n). The rest of D may be discarded since q and hence each row of U need only be determined up to a constant factor. Besides avoidance of square roots this decomposition has the property that the last coefficient of q produced in Step 2 is 1; the resulting q is as for the $U'U$ decomposition after division by its n-th coefficient. (In this respect the method acts as though the n-th coordinate were the independent variable in a conventional least-squares regression.) Hence for conics the popular $F = 1$ normalization can be implemented with this method by putting 1 at the end of the basis, and for circles Bookstein's normalization $A = 1$ can be used by putting $x^2 + y^2$ at the end, when these normalizations are appropriate.

The principle novelty in the above is the application of well-understood least squares techniques, using normal equations and Cholesky decomposition, to fitting algebraic surfaces.

Basis Order Independence. Ideally a procedure for selecting a member of Q would be independent of the choice of basis for Q. This is possible using a somewhat more elaborate procedure than we shall consider here. With considerably less effort we are able to achieve independence of the order in which the elements of the basis are presented, via a procedure we shall now describe. A corollary of this property is that no one coefficient is singled out as having to be nonzero, eliminating this source of singularities from this application of Cholesky decomposition.

It would be particularly convenient if the algorithm were to hold constant (namely.1) the coefficient with maximum absolute value. Unfortunately this is not the case for the procedure we shall give – we have seen coefficients as large as $n - 1$ (n the size of the matrix). It is tempting to conjecture that this is the limit on size of coefficients. We do not understand at all the mechanism by which the algorithm selects which coefficient is to be held constant.

The idea is to perform row-and-column permutations of the (more or less) as-yet unprocessed P during the Cholesky decomposition. Just before the assignment of 1 to U_{ii}, the maximum P_{jj} for $j \geq i$ is found, and if $j \neq i$ a row-and-column permutation of P is performed in place, exchanging i with j; in effect the i-th and j-th basis elements are exchanged.

We omit the proof that the result is independent of basis order.

The method lends itself to partial permutations, in which some elements of the basis are not permuted. In fitting lines and planes for example the constant basis element (1) can be left undisturbed if it is put at the beginning of the basis, though we have not encountered a situation where it is actually beneficial to leave it alone.

Incremental addition and deletion of points. The matrix $A'A$ is $n \times n$, which is considerably smaller than A when $m >> n$. Yet despite the extent of the data reduction implied by this compaction it is very easy to update $A'A$ to reflect the addition *or* deletion of points. Each point, as a row of A, forms a $1 \times n$ matrix Z, with $Z'Z$ the same size as $A'A$. To add or delete point Z from A, add or subtract $Z'Z$ from $A'A$. In our implementation we compute $A'A$ exclusively by this method.

Weighting. To increase or decrease the contribution of a point, scale either Z or $Z'Z$ (as convenient) appropriately. Doubling $Z'Z$ has the same effect as having two occurrences of the point. One might decrease the weight of a point if it is relatively unreliable; conversely one might increase its weight to force the surface to pass closer to it.

Cost. If $A'A$ is maintained incrementally the cost to add or delete a point is n^2 multiplications (to form $Z'Z$) and n^2 additions (to add or subtract it). Hence adding or deleting m points in a batch (without then running Cholesky) costs mn^2 such operations. The constant factor in the cost of Choleski decomposition of $A'A$ makes it quite cheap in comparison with Gaussian elimination; the procedure requires only $n^3/6$ multiplications and additions. Because U is triangular computing the determinant of the modified U requires only n^2 multiplications and additions. Thus for circles, with $n = 4$, the cost is $16m + 26$ multiplications and additions. For conics, with $n = 6$, the cost rises to $36m + 36$. The additional cost of the row-and-column-permuting variant is $O(n^2)$ exchanges, which is dominated by the other costs.

Quality of Fit. We have not been able to analyze this method directly. Experience with its use however demonstrates the need for the basis-permuting variant, in the absence of which the singularities consisting of fits with zero n-th coefficient are very noticeable. Permuting the basis eliminates those singularities, but we have noticed in the case of planar fits a tendency to avoid exact 45-degree fits when the data is very badly scattered. It would be of considerable interest to know whether this situation could be understood in terms of the shape of a normalization surface associated with the algorithm.

Stability. In the method of normal equations, all steps save the computation of $A'A$ are numerically very stable; the replacement of A by $A'A$ has the destabilizing effect of squaring the condition number. When A is ill-conditioned, such as when sampling points from two nearly parallel coplanar lines to determine their common plane, normal equations aggravate the situation. This effect may be offset by either (i) doubling precision, (ii) using an alternative method based on Householder or Givens transformations of A [12], or (iii) designing the application to avoid geometric instabilities. Our preference has been a combination of (i) and (iii), (ii) having somewhat inferior performance to Cholesky decomposition, and considerably worse performance when points are to be added and deleted incrementally, which our application makes extensive use of.

7. Spherical Fit

In this section we give a quadratic-norm metric for circles and spheres which is substantially more robust than the only other such metric to have previously been proposed for circles, namely Bookstein's. As pointed out in the section on algebraic distance, the singularities for Bookstein's metric are lines. Such singularities tend to increase the curvature of the fit. The following illustration of this nonrobustness of Bookstein's metric should give some idea of the rate at which the fit deteriorates as the curve of best fit approaches a line.

Figure 1 shows, under each of the $A = 1$ and geometric distance metrics, the best fitting circle to the points $(-1,0)$, $(-.3,y)$, $(.3,.1)$, $(1,0)$ for $y = .1, .02, -.02, -.06$. The $A = 1$ circle is in each case the one with higher curvature, with equality only at $y = .1$.

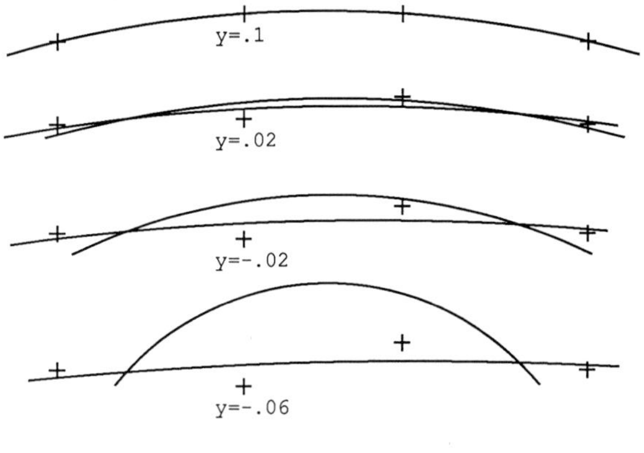

Figure 1. Best fitting circles under $A = 1$ and geometric metrics.

The $A = 1$ circle can be seen to become a very poor fit as the best geometric fit increases in radius.

We repair this problem as follows. The circle ideal consists of all polynomials $q(x,y) = A(x^2+y^2) + Dx + Ey + F$. For any such q the 3D surface $z = q(x,y)$ (z being the direction of sinking in the sink-or-swim model of Section 4) is a paraboloid of revolution. Our observation is that although $|\nabla q|$ is not constant, it *is* constant on $Z(q)$, by the circular symmetry of the paraboloid. This motivates normalizing q to make $|\nabla q| = 1$ on $Z(q)$.

Now the partial derivatives of q are $\partial q/\partial x = 2Ax + D$ and $\partial q/\partial y = 2Ay + E$. Hence $|\nabla q|^2 = 4A^2x^2 + 4DAx + D^2 + 4A^2y^2 + 4EAy + E^2 = 4A(Dx + Ey + A(x^2+y^2)) + D^2 + E^2 = 4A(q(x,y) - F) + D^2 + E^2$. The term $q(x,y)$ vanishes on $Z(q)$, where $|\nabla q|^2 = D^2 + E^2 - 4AF$. Hence we obtain the invariant $D^2 + E^2 - 4AF = 1$. (The normalization itself, meaning the quantity by which q must be divided to be normalized, is $\sqrt{D^2 + E^2 - 4AF}$. However we need not actually perform this operation; for finding the circle of best fit it suffices to hold the invariant constant.) The circles fitted with this metric to the data of Figure 1 are indistinguishable from the best geometric fits.

One way to visualize the effect of this invariant is to picture an inverted cone (apex at top) with vertical axis and 45-degree side. This cone may be translated arbitrarily (three degrees of freedom) to intersect the plane in an arbitrary circle. The normal paraboloid for that circle is the one which is tangent to the cone at the circle; our invariant finds exactly that paraboloid.

For spheres in R^3, $q(x,y,z) = A(x^2+y^2+z^2)+Dx+Ey+Fz+G = 0$, for which the corresponding form to be held constant is $D^2+E^2+F^2-4AG$, and similarly for higher dimensions.

Our normalization, like Bookstein's (taking his to be $\sqrt{A}$), is a *Euclidean invariant*, that is, its quotient with Euclidean distance is invariant, under similarities – translations, rotations, and scalings – of the plane. Bookstein argues that a normalization containing D, E, or F cannot be invariant even under translations because these quantities can individually grow without bound. The inapplicability of this argument to our normalization should be clear: although D and E can indeed grow without bound, their growth can nevertheless be cancelled by the growth of $4AF$.

Bookstein also argues that a normalization which is not positive-definite will fail to fit data lying exactly on certain curves. This seems to assume that when such a normalization passes through zero on its way to becoming negative it must represent an exact fit to something. The inapplicability of Bookstein's argument to our normalization follows from the fact that $D^2 + E^2 - 4AF$ is nonpositive only for circles of zero radius, which is not the exact or even best fit for any sample not having infinitely many exact fits.

The main adverse effect with our invariant arises from the radial curvature of the paraboloid, i.e. its departure from a cone. For scattered data $|\nabla q|$ will be larger for more outlying data, increasing linearly with distance from the axis of the paraboloid. This makes the fit more responsive to data lying further out, which tends to decrease the curvature of our fit. However this is a second order phenomenon, being tied to the radial curvature of the paraboloid, as opposed to the first order phenomenon illustrated by Figure 1, which depends on the value of $|\nabla q|$ itself rather than its radial variation.

The other drawback of our invariant is that it involves the extraction of eigenvectors. Bookstein's invariant $A = 1$ is simple enough to be used with our Simple Fit algorithm, taking the A coordinate to be the final basis element, which the nonpermuting version of our algorithm automatically sets to 1. The permuting version of our algorithm typically picks some other coefficient to be 1; in the case of the data of Figure 1 it picks E, the coefficient of y, which has the effect of yielding circles whose radius is larger than that of the best fitting circle by factors of 1, 1.03, 1.1, 1.5 respectively (top to bottom), rather than smaller. However in the absence of a good understanding of what Permuting Simple Fit is up to we remain uncertain as to its reliability for circle fitting.

The conclusion then is, for safety use the invariant $D^2 + E^2 - 4AF$, but if you are willing to take risks then use either Simple Fit with Bookstein's invariant, or Permuting Simple Fit which supplies its own incompletely understood invariant.

Application to Conics and Quadrics. Our method for circles does not generalize directly to ellipses and other conics, since these lack the circular symmetry on which our method depended. This problem is addressed by Sampson's iterative method [24], as we saw at the end of Section 4. In this method Sampson repeatedly fits a conic using Bookstein's invariant $A^2 + B^2/2 + C^2$, at each stage weighting each point p by $1/|\nabla q(p)|$ using the q fitted at the previous stage.

The difficulty we have observed with Bookstein's invariant for circles carries over to conics: conics of low curvature are avoided. Hence this problem can be inherited by Sampson's algorithm. We cure this by showing how to generalize our circle solution to conics.

Our solution is to use the basis $x^2 + y^2, 2xy, x^2 - y^2, x, y, 1$. The advantage of this basis over the customary conic basis $x^2, xy, y^2, x, y, 1$ is that it more cleanly separates out the circular (rotationally invariant) component of a conic, namely the $x^2 + y^2$ basis element. Taking the coefficients to be $A(x^2 + y^2) + 2Bxy + C(x^2 - y^2) + Dx + Ey + F$, we may continue to use our invariant $D^2 + E^2 - 4AF$, simply ignoring the coefficients B and C The effect is as though we had a circle whose diameter is in between the lengths of the major and minor axes, in the case of an ellipse; this is adequate to get a good initial fit of a conic. (Note that if B and C are normalized to $B^2 + C^2 = 1$ then they are respectively $\sin(2\theta)$ and $\cos(2\theta)$ where θ is the orientation of an axis of the conic to the X axis. This is where the 2 in $2xy$ is used.)

The generalization of this basis to higher dimensions is to take the sum of the squares (in four dimensions: $w^2 + x^2 + y^2 + z^2$) along with the differences of consecutive squares ($w^2 - x^2$, $x^2 - y^2$, $y^2 - z^2$) and the cross terms ($2wx$, $2wy$, $2wz$, $2xy$, $2xz$, $2yz$), along with all degree 0 and 1 terms ($w, x, y, z, 1$).

8. Blend Fit

Given a set $b_i = 0$, $i = 1, \ldots, k$, of *base* surfaces, a *blending surface* is a surface tangent to all of them. (In two dimensions substitute curve for surface.) The problem of finding blending surfaces has received considerable attention in the literature. Some particularly interesting recent approaches are those of Middleditch and Sears [14] and Hoffman and Hopcroft [10,11].

In this section we first describe a new method of constructing blending surfaces that generalizes both the Middleditch-Sears and Hoffman-Hopcroft methods. We then apply this construction to give a method of least-squares fitting of such surfaces; however the construction should prove to be of considerable utility in the theory and applications of blending surfaces independent of our fitting application.

The principle behind our construction can be understood in 2D by considering the lines $Z(x)$ and $Z(y)$, respectively the Y-axis and the X-axis. The zeros of any linear combination $\alpha x + \beta y$ will pass through the intersection of $Z(x)$ and $Z(y)$, but need not be tangent to either of these lines there. However the zeros of any linear combination $\alpha x^2 + \beta y$ with $\beta \neq 0$ will be tangent to $Z(y)$ (consider the curve $y = \alpha x^2$ for any α). The principle is that αx^2 initially grows more slowly with movement away from $Z(x)$ than does βy with movement away from $Z(y)$, provided $\beta \neq 0$. Hence in the neighborhood of the intersection the zeros of $\alpha x^2 + \beta y$ will tend to "stick" to $Z(y)$. The higher the power x^γ the less "sticky" is $Z(x^\gamma)$. This principle generalizes to two arbitrary polynomials in $x_1, \ldots, x_d$ in place of x and y; raising the first to a sufficiently high power will make it negligibly sticky compared to the second at the intersection of their respective zeros, whence the zeros of their linear combination will stick to the second.

For our blending surface construction the two polynomials are the product $\prod_i b_i$ of polynomials defining the base surfaces, and a polynomial t, defining the *truncating surface*, which intersects each base surface in the point(s) of tangency of the blending surface to that base surface. Then by the above principle there is an integer γ large enough that the zeros of any linear combination $\alpha t^\gamma + \beta \prod_i b_i$, $\beta \neq 0$, will be tangent to each b_i where $Z(b_i)$ intersects $Z(t)$.

The canonical example of this in the plane is given by the conic spline, which is a conic section inscribed in a triangle ABC, tangent to AB at A and to BC at C. If a, b, c are linear combinations of $x, y, 1$ such that their respective zeros are the lines BC, CA, and AB, then such conics are given by the zeros of the linear combinations of b^2 and ac. Here $Z(b)$ is the truncating surface, or rather line, and $Z(a), Z(c)$ are the two base lines.

A more interesting example, in 3D, is given by the problem of finding a blending surface (fillet) between equal-diameter cylinders $x^2 + z^2 = 1$ and $y^2 + z^2 = 1$ (unit radius cylinders along the Y and X axes respectively). We take $Z(t)$ to be the ellipsoid $\lambda x^2 + \mu y^2 + z^2 = 1$, where λ and μ are reals less than unity. This ellipsoid is tangent to both cylinders where they intersect the Z-axis, and otherwise intersects each cylinder in the curve where the blending surface will be tangent to that cylinder, with λ and μ providing some variety in the choice of curve. The blending surface is then the degree 4 surface $Z(\alpha(\lambda x^2 + \mu y^2 + z^2 - 1)^2 + \beta(x^2 + z^2 - 1)(y^2 + z^2 - 1))$, with α/β determining how "fat" the fillet is: larger is fatter (more metal if the fillet were a weld).

This generalizes the Middleditch-Sears method by allowing t to be arbitrary; Middleditch and Sears restrict t to be a linear combination of $b_1, \ldots, b_k, 1$ (the 1 being essential), which rules out the truncating surface we used to solve the above cylinder-blending problem. It also considerably simplifies the Hoffman-Hopcroft *potential method* [10], in particular eliminating the complexity in the case when the intersection curve is reducible (e.g. with the above equal-diameter-cylinders problem), as well as generalizing it by permitting more than two surfaces to be blended simultaneously.

Given this notion of a blending surface we turn to the problem of finding such a surface tangent to a given set of base surfaces that best fits a given set of data points. For example we may have two rods welded together, along with a large number of measurements of the fillet between them, and we want to reduce these samples to a good analytical model of the fillet. This includes discovery of the appropriate truncating surface $Z(t)$; in the rod-blending example we would assume that it was an ellipsoid, leaving only λ and μ to be found in order to determine t, corresponding to selecting a surface having the shape of order 3 generated by the basis $x^2, y^2, z^2 - 1$.

A weaker version of this problem assumes that the truncating surface is completely specified, as for example in [15]. This is not always a good assumption. While it is usually easy to determine the base surfaces – they are typically either given or are large enough as to be easily measured – the exact points of intersection of a sampled blending surface with the base surfaces are not so easily measured, since these points can move a long distance under a very small perturbation of the blending surface. Tangency is an inherently unstable condition in this respect.

We give a very simple method for choosing t of a given shape of order n so as to get the blending surface of best fit. Write the implicit equation of the blending surface as $(\alpha t)^\gamma = \prod_i b_i$. Rewrite it as $\alpha t = (\prod_i b_i)^{1/\gamma}$.

Treat this as the problem of fitting the shape whose ideal has the $n+1$ basis functions $t_1, \ldots, t_n, (\prod_i b_i)^{1/\gamma}$, where the t_i's are the basis for the truncating shape.

Previously all our ideals consisted of polynomials. We now have an ideal Q (of the ring of all functions $q : R^d \to R$) containing the nonpolynomial $(\prod_i b_i)^{1/\gamma}$. The beauty of least-squares fitting is that nothing in the theory depends on what functions appear in Q, just so long as Q forms a finite-dimensional vector space, here $n+1$. Of course we need to be able to compute the functions in order to construct the $m \times (n+1)$ matrix A, but $(\prod_i b_i)^{1/\gamma}$ is easily evaluated at each of the m sample points. We also need to be sure that the functions in the basis are independent; it is easily seen that this will be the case if there is only one nonpolynomial in the set and the polynomials form an independent set, which describes the case at hand.

In the case of conics we are given tangents $Z(a)$ and $Z(c)$, a and c being linear combinations of $x, y, 1$, and seek a linear combination b of $x, y, 1$ such that $Z(\alpha b^2 + \beta ac)$ best fits a given set of data points. In this case the above rather dry algebraic solution to this problem has a beautiful geometric visualization. If we take a, v, c to be the coordinates of a 3D space then the 3D surface $v^2 = 4ac$ turns out to be the cone illustrated in Figure 2 (which is taken from Figure 2 of [22], where we give a relatively novel analytic treatment of conic sections by treating them literally as plane sections of a cone).

For each data point p let $a(p)$ denote the value of a at p (the result of evaluating a given the x and y coordinates of p) and similarly for $c(p)$. Each such point then corresponds to a pair of points $(a(p), \pm v, c(p))$ on the cone, obtainable as $v = \pm\sqrt{4a(p)c(p)}$. Discard the $-v$ point. The resulting points, ranging over all the given data, should now approximate a plane in AVC space if as points in XY space they approximate a conic. Then the equation $b = 0$ of this plane yields the desired b. A conic of good fit is obtained by finding the plane of best fit. This is the geometric description of our method for the case of conics.

It will be noted that the method is more sensitive to noise in points in the neighborhood of either tangent. This is due to the cone being steeper (treating V as up) near the tangents. This increased sensitivity there corresponds to looking at the points more closely as they approach the tangent in order to tell exactly where the point of tangency is. This insight into the stability of the method is very easily deduced from this geometric picture of our fitting process.

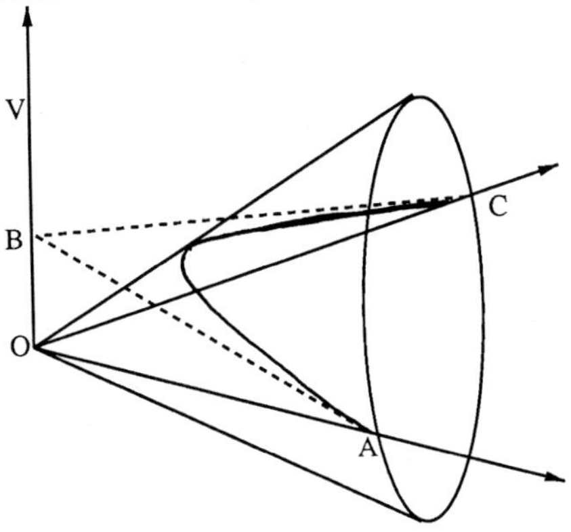

Figure 2. The AVC cone and ABC conic.

Additional Constraints. Sometimes the truncating surface t will be partially constrained, e.g. one or more points or curves of tangency may be given. When such a constraint can be represented as a linear dependence between the coefficients to be found, the dependence can be used to reduce the order of the shape of the truncating surface, thereby transforming the fitting problem to a simpler one. This is the situation that obtains when either or both of the points of tangency are known when fitting a conic given two of its tangents.

Typography Application. Our application for blend fit has been as part of a two-stage process for reconstructing font outlines from scanned-in images. The first stage finds tangents at lines, extrema, inflexion points, and other suitable articulation points. The second stage then fills in the remainder of the outline by finding the best fitting conic splines as blending curves to these tangents.

Acknowledgments

I am grateful to Gene Golub for some informative discussions.

Bibliography

[1] A. Albano, Representation of Digitized Contours in Terms of Conic Arcs and Straight-Line Segments, *Computer Graphics and Image Processing* **3**, 23-33, 1974.

[2] R.H. Biggerstaff, Three Variations in Dental Arch Form Estimated by a Quadratic Equation, *Journal of Dental Research* **51**, 1509, 1972.

[3] F.L. Bookstein, Fitting Conic Sections to Scattered Data, *Computer Graphics and Image Processing* **9**, 56-71, 1979.

[4] D.B. Cooper and N. Yalabik, On the Computational Cost of Approximating and Recognizing Noise-Perturbed Straight Lines and Quadratic Arcs in the Plane, *IEEE Transactions on Computers* **C-25**, 10, 1020-1032, October 1976.

[5] C. de Boor, **A Practical Guide to Splines**, Springer-Verlag, 1978.

[6] I.D. Faux and M.J. Pratt, **Computational Geometry for Design and Manufacture**, Ellis Horwood, 1978.

[7] Y. Gardan, **Numerical Methods for CAD**, MIT Press, 1986.

[8] A.A. Giordano and F.M. Hsu, **Least Squares Estimation with Applications to Digital Signal Processing**, Wiley, 1985.

[9] R. Gnanadesikan, **Methods for Statistical Data Analysis of Multivariate Observations**, Wiley, 1977.

[10] C. Hoffman and J. Hopcroft, Automatic Surface Generation in Computer Aided Design, *The Visual Computer*, **1**, 2, 92-100 (1985).

[11] C. Hoffman and J. Hopcroft, Quadratic Blending Surfaces, *Computer Aided Design*, **18**, 6, 301-306 (Jul-Aug. 1986).

[12] C.L. Lawson and R.J. Hanson, **Solving Least-Squares Problems**, Prentice-Hall, 1974.

[13] E.A. Lord and C.B. Wilson, **The Mathematical Description of Shape and Form**, Ellis Horwood, Chichester, 1984.

[14] A.E. Middleditch and K.H. Sears, Blend Surfaces for Set Theoretic Volume Modelling Systems, *Computer Graphics* **19**, 3 (Siggraph-85), 161-170, July 1985.

[15] V.S. Nalwa and E. Pauchon, Edgel-Aggregation and Edge-Description, *Eighth International Conference on Pattern Recognition,* 604-609, Paris, Oct. 1986,

[16] K. Paton, Conic Sections in Chromosome Analysis, *Pattern Recognition* **2**, 39-51, 1970.

[17] T. Pavlidis, Curve Fitting with Conic Splines, *ACM Transactions on Graphics* **2**, 1, 1-31, January 1983.

[18] K. Pearson, On lines and planes of closest fit to systems of points in space, *Philos. Mag. Ser. 6*, 2, 559, 1901.

[19] C. Pearson, **Numerical Methods in Engineering and Science**, Van Nostrand Reinhold, 1986.

[20] M.A. Penna and R.R. Patterson, **Projective Geometry and its Applications to Computer Graphics**, Prentice-Hall, New Jersey, 1986.

[21] M. Plass and M. Stone, Curve-Fitting with Piecewise Parametric Cubics, *Computer Graphics* **17**, 3 (Siggraph-83), 229-239, July 1983.

[22] V. Pratt, Techniques for Conic Splines, *Computer Graphics* **19**, 3 (Siggraph85), 151-159, July 1985.

[23] D. Proffitt, The Measurement of Circularity and Ellipticity on a Digital Grid, *Pattern Recognition* **15**, 5, 383-387, 1982.

[24] P.D. Sampson, Fitting Conic Sections to "Very Scattered" Data: An Iterative Refinement of the Bookstein Algorithm, *Computer Graphics and Image Processing* **18**, 97-108, 1982.

[25] K. Turner, Computer Perception of Curved Objects using a Television Camera, Ph.D. Thesis, Dept. of Machine Intelligence, University of Edinburgh, Nov. 1974.

Appendix

The following was generated using most of the techniques described in the paper. The first image is the result of filtering and thresholding an 18-point sans-serif m digitized using a Datacopy camera. The second is the result of fitting conic splines to the first. The fitted outline consists of 8 conic splines (2 per curve) and 11 lines. This example is intended only to demonstrate potential applications of the method and should not be regarded as any indication of the limits of general applicability of the fitting methods of this paper. In particular the curves are not particularly faithful to the original (the arrows point to two of the more objectionable portions), due to overemphasis of position fidelity at the expense of tangent fidelity. We plan to further apply the techniques of this paper to correct this.

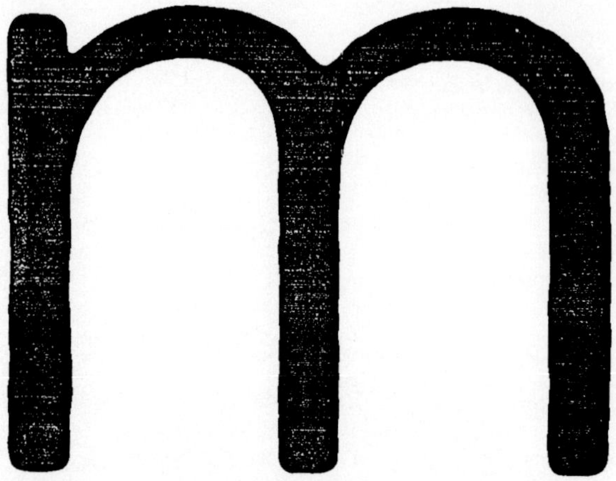

Set Operations on Polyhedra Using Binary Space Partitioning Trees

William C. Thibault
Georgia Institute of Technology
Atlanta, GA 30332
and
Bruce F. Naylor
AT&T Bell Laboratories
Murray Hill, NJ 07974

Abstract
We introduce a new representation for polyhedra by showing how Binary Space Partitioning Trees (BSP trees) can be used to represent regular sets. We then show how they may be used in evaluating set operations on polyhedra. The BSP tree is a binary tree representing a recursive partitioning of d-space by (sub-)hyperplanes, for any dimension d. Their previous application to computer graphics has been to organize an arbitrary set of polygons so that a fast solution to the visible surface problem could be obtained. We retain this property (in 3D) and show how BSP trees can also provide an exact representation of arbitrary polyhedra of any dimension. Conversion from a boundary representation (B-reps) of polyhedra to a BSP tree representation is described. This technique leads to a new method for evaluating arbitrary set theoretic (boolean) expressions on B-reps, represented as a CSG tree, producing a BSP tree as the result. Results from our language-driven implementation of this CSG evaluator are discussed. Finally, we show how to modify a BSP tree to represent the result of a set operation between the BSP tree and a B-rep. We describe the embodiment of this approach in an interactive 3D object design program that allows incremental modification of an object with a tool. Placement of the tool, selection of views, and performance of the set operation are all performed at interactive speeds for modestly complex objects.

CR Categories I.3.5 [Computer Graphics]: Computational Geometry and Object Modeling - object representation and geometric algorithms.

Keywords - polyhedra, set operations, geometric modeling, geometric search, point location.

1. Introduction

While the study of polyhedra has an ancient history, computer science has given it renewed attention in the various sub-disciplines of computational geometry, geometric modeling, computer graphics, robotics, and computer vision. Its attractiveness stems from the relative simplicity of linear computations when compared to non-linear, coupled with the fact that linear approximations of non-linear sets can often be quite satisfactory. An important example of this comparative simplicity is set operations: union, intersection, difference and exclusive-or (and their complements). The algebra of set operations defined on the collection of linear sets of any dimension $\leqslant$ some d is closed (assuming a countable number of operations). This is not true of non-linear sets; for example, the intersection of two quadrics (second degree) can be a fourth degree curve. When computational speed is important, such as in interactive object design, using polyhedral approximations of non-linear solids can provide a very effective alternative to non-linear computations. On the other hand, for operations which are not speed-critical, a second unapproximated non-linear representation can be used, if the greater accuracy is needed.

The most prominent method of representing polyhedra at this time would appear to be boundary representations (B-reps): in a d dimensional space, a d-polyhedron (also called a d-polytope) is represented by a set of $(d-1)$-polyhedra, called faces, which are in turn represented by $(d-2)$-polyhedra, and so on until d equals 0, at which point the d coordinates of a vertex are used. An alternative suitable for representing convex polyhedra is provided by the volumetric approach, where the intersection of a set of halfspaces determines a polyhedron.

In this paper, we develop a new approach first presented in [Nayl86] and describe in greater detail in [Thib87]. It is based on the dimension independent concept embodied in the Binary Space Partitioning Tree, abbreviated BSP tree, which, at its simplest, is a binary tree whose non-leaf nodes are labeled with hyperplanes and whose leaves correspond to cells of a convex polyhedral tessellation (partitioning) of d-space. The approach provides what is essentially a volumetric representation of general linear polyhedra. What we mean by general is that any genus (handles/holes) is permissible, any number of connected components (separate objects), and regions of connectivity with no interior, such as two parts connected only by a vertex. More generality is available in that the interior of the polyhedra need not be completely bounded, i.e. it may be (semi-)infinite.

Previous work has established the BSP tree as an effective representation of polyhedra for efficient visible surface determination, both in polygon tiling environments [Schu69] [Fuch80] [Nayl81] [Fuch83] and for ray-tracing [Nayl86] (Figure RAY-TRACING). In this paper, we concentrate on the problem of evaluating set operations, the set theoretic analog of boolean operations, defined on 3D polyhedra. This takes two forms. One begins with a set (theoretic) expression represented as a tree (i.e. a CSG tree) defined on a set of polyhedra represented by B-reps. The method produces the polyhedron defined by the CSG tree by constructing its (non-unique) BSP tree representation. The resulting tree can then be used for rendering by the techniques referred to above or as input to the second approach. The second approach takes a BSP tree as one operand and a B-rep as the other and produces a new BSP tree determined by the set operation via modification of the original tree. We have used this technique as the basis for an interactive program that supports modification of a work piece, represented by a BSP tree, through the adding, subtracting or intersecting of a tool, represented by a B-rep.

2. Representation of Polyhedra by BSP Trees

2.1 Generic BSP Trees[1]

A BSP tree represents a recursive, hierarchical partitioning, or subdivision, of d-dimensional space. It is most easily understood as a process which takes a subspace and partitions it by any hyperplane that intersects the interior of that subspace. This produces two new subspaces that can be further partitioned. Figure BSPT illustrates the relationship between the partitioning of space and the corresponding BSP tree. In (a), we see a recursive partitioning of the plane. Note how partitioning first by u produces two subspaces whose subsequent partitionings proceed independently of each other. The distinction between the two halfplanes formed by a line is indicated by the orientation of the normal vector to each line (indicated by arrows). Which of the two possible orientations is used is typically arbitrary. Now referring to (b), we see that in the corresponding BSP tree, each (sub-)line is associated with an internal node of the tree. The right subtree of each internal node represents the region of the plane lying to the side of the line pointed to by the normal. The left subtree represents the other side. The resulting partitioning produces a set of unpartitioned subspaces that correspond to leaves of the tree (labeled with digits).

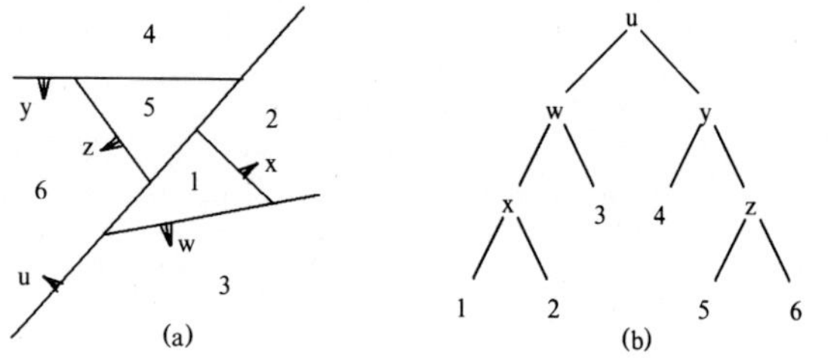

Figure BSPT. Geometry of a 2D partitioning (a) and its BSP tree (b).

More formally, for a hyperplane

$$H = \{(x_1, \dots, x_d) \mid a_1x_1 + \cdots + a_dx_d + a_{d+1} = 0\},$$

the *right* (or in B-rep parlance, the "front") halfspace of H is

$$H^+ = \{(x_1, \dots, x_d) \mid a_1x_1 + \cdots + a_dx_d + a_{d+1} > 0\},$$

and the *left* (or "back") halfspace of H is

$$H^- = \{(x_1, \dots, x_d) \mid a_1x_1 + \cdots + a_dx_d + a_{d+1} < 0\}).$$

The right side of H lies to the side of H in the direction of the hyperplane's normal, $(a_1,...,a_d)$.

Each node v represents a region of space $R(v)$ (to be defined below). Leaves correspond to un-partitioned polyhedral regions, which we call *cells*. Each internal node v of the tree is associated with a *partitioning hyperplane*, H_v, which intersects the interior of $R(v)$. The hyperplane partitions $R(v)$ into three sets: $R(v) \cap H_v^+$, $R(v) \cap H_v^-$, and $R(v) \cap H_v$. The d-dimensional region in H_v^+ is represented by the right child of v, *v.right*, and the region in H_v^- is represented by the left child, *v.left*. The intersection of H_v and $R(v)$ is called the *sub-hyperplane* of H_v, indicated by $SHp(v)$, and is of dimension $d-1$.

$R(v)$ is the intersection of open halfspaces on the path from the root to v. More precisely, for each edge (v_1,v_2) in the tree we associate a halfspace $HS(v_1,v_2)$ defined as follows: for any node v, let $HS(v,v.left)$ denote H_v^-, and $HS(v,v.right)$ denote H_v^+. Let $E(v)$ denote the set of edges on the path from the root to v. Then $R(v) = \bigcap_{e \in E(v)} HS(e)$. For the root node, whose $E(v)$ is empty, $R(v)$ is defined to represent all of d-space. Thus, $R(v)$ is convex, non-empty, may not be completely bounded, and is topologically open. It also follows that sub-hyperplanes have the same properties. An important relationship between sub-hyperplanes and regions is that the sub-hyperplanes associated with nodes on the path from the root to v contain the boundary of $R(v)$. Finally, a *trivial* BSP tree consists of only a single node (a cell).

2.2 Representation of Regular Sets

A regular set S has an interior, an exterior, and a boundary denoted by *int S*, *ext S*, and *bd S*, respectively. A set is *regular* if it is the closure of its interior [Requ78], i.e $S = cl(\, int\ S\,)$, where *cl* denotes closure. (The *closure* of a set consists of the set together with its boundary.) Given a BSP tree, we can use it to represent linear regular sets, and polyhedra in particular. We need to simply classify each cell as either *in* the set or *out* of the set. Each leaf then has at least one attribute, membership, with values $\in \{\, in,\ out\,\}$. For example, in Figure BSPT, consider the set defined when cells 1 and 5 are assigned the value *in* and the rest are assigned *out*. Since each cell is open (and therefore, has an interior) and is non-empty by construction, we can take the union of all in-cells and then form the closure of this union, to produce a regular set.

$$S = cl(\, \bigcup_i C_i), \ for\ all\ C_i = in$$

Note that points lying between two in-cells are included in S and are in *int S*. The boundary of the set consists of points between in-cells and out-cells, and all such points lie in sub-hyperplanes of the tree.

$$bd\ S = \bigcup_{i,j} cl(C_i) \cap cl(C_j), \ for\ all\ C_i = in,\ C_j = out$$

Methods of constructing such representations will be described in subsequent sections.

2.3 Point Classification

We can show the sufficiency of the above representation by solving a problem studied in computational geometry [Prep85]. The *point classification* problem can be stated: Given a set S and a point p, determine if p lies in *int S*, *ext S*, or *bd S*. We assume S is regular and we have a BSP tree representing S. Figure POINT-CLASSIFY gives an algorithm for solving this problem in d-space. The recursive process begins at the root of the tree and uses location of a point with respect to a hyperplane to control the search. To solve the problem, we must know whether the neighborhood of p is homogeneous, and therefore *in* or *out*, or non-homogeneous, and therefore *on*. If p lies in a cell, its neighborhood is known to be homogeneous. When p lies on some H_v, the search must be performed on both subtrees to determine all cells in whose closure p lies. If the value of all such cells are not the same, p is known to be *on*, otherwise it is known to be *in* or *out*, depending upon the value. (Note that the search could terminate whenever the first *on* value is encountered). While *bd S* has measure zero, it is given non-zero measure numerically by specifying an interval about zero which is mapped to "on the hyperplane", thus giving thickness to the hyperplanes. Machine precision determines a lower bound on this interval.

In [Kala82], this problem is solved for 3D in $O(n)$ for a B-rep with n faces. A result in [Nayl81] shows that this could be at most $O(n)$ for any BSP tree constructed from n faces (the tightest known upper-bound on tree size is $O(n^d)$). However, when a balanced BSP tree is of size $O(n)$ (which may or may not be possible for a given set of faces), this can be solved in $O(log\ n)$.

1. This section is an adaptation of work presented in [Nayl81].

```
procedure point_classify (p : point; v : BSPTreeNode)
                                        returns {in, out, on}
  if v is a leaf
    return the leaf's value (in or out)
  else
    let d = dot_product(p, H_v).
    if d < 0 then
      return point_classify (p, v.left)
    else if d > 0 then
      return point_classify (p, v.right)
    else (* p lies on the partitioning hyperplane *)
      l := point_classify (p, v.left)
      r := point_classify (p, v.right)
      if l = r then
        return r
      else
        return "on"
end point_classify ;
```

Figure POINT-CLASSIFY.

2.4 Augmented BSP Trees

A common means of augmenting the generic BSP tree is to include other sets within the BSP tree structure. In particular, leaves can each include a collection of sets (objects) contained completely within the corresponding cell, e.g. [Schu69], and similarly, internal nodes can include sets lying in the corresponding sub-hyperplane, e.g. [Fuch80]. Traditionally, the motivation for this has been the visible surface problem in 3D. Given an arbitrary viewing position, a traversal of the tree can induce a visibility priority ordering on the contents of the various subspaces (cells and sub-hyperplanes). Because of the usefulness of boundary representations for polygon tiling, polygons have been stored at the various nodes. We retain this visibility property by associating sets of polygons with internal nodes, where each set lies on the node's sub-hyperplane, and are in the boundary of the represented polyhedron. At each node v, these faces are separated into those whose normals have the *same* orientation as the normal of H_v and those whose orientation is *opposite*.

3. B-rep → BSP tree

We now examine converting a B-rep into an equivalent BSP tree. Essentially any of the many varieties of B-reps can be used, as long as they are sufficient and form a valid representation of a polyhedron. We use the term *face* to refer to the (d-1)-dimensional boundaries of a d-polyhedron, H_f to denote the hyperplane containing a face f, and we assume that face normals point to the exterior.

The approach is essentially one that first appeared in [Fuch80] with one significant extension : assignment of values to leaves. The algorithm begins with a set of faces forming one or more disjoint polyhedra. At each stage, the recursive process selects a hyperplane H and partitions the current set of faces F into three sets of faces, $F(H^+)$, $F(H^-)$, $F(H)$, corresponding respectively to the three subspaces H^+, H^-, H. The *partitioning of a face*, $f \in F$, is defined as the result of forming the following three sets, one or two of which will be empty:

$$f^+ = cl(H^+ \cap int\ f),\quad f^- = cl(H^- \cap int\ f),\quad f^0 = cl(int(H \cap int\ f)),$$

where int is with respect to H_f. Partitioning all faces of F produces $F(H^+)$, $F(H^-)$, $F(H)$, respectively. The set $F(H)$ is retained at a new BSP tree node v (separated into same and opposite lists). The process then proceeds recursively on the other two sets until the current list of faces is empty (Figure BUILD-BSPT).

Figure CONCAVE shows how the algorithm can create a BSP tree from a concave polygon. One note worthy consequence of this process is that each polyhedron is decomposed into a set of convex regions (in-

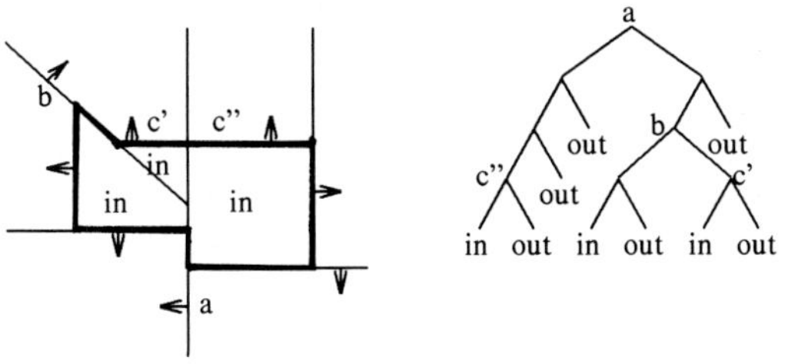

Figure CONCAVE. A concave set and its BSP tree.

```
procedure Build_BSPT ( F : set of faces ) returns BSPTreeNode

  Choose a hyperplane H that embeds a face of F;
  new_BSP := a new BSP tree node with H as its
             partitioning plane;
  <F_right, F_left, F_coincident, > := partition faces of F with H;
  Append each face of F_coincident to the appropriate face list
    of new_BSP;

  if (F_left is empty) then
    if (F_coincident has the same orientation as H) then
      (* faces point "outward" *)
      new_BSP.left := "in";
    else new_BSP.left := "out";
  else
    new_BSP.left := build_BSPT( F_left );

  if (F_right is empty) then
    if (F_coincident has the same orientation as H) then
      new_BSP.right := "out";
    else new_BSP.right := "in";
  else
    new_BSP.right := build_BSPT( F_right );

  return new_BSP;
end; (* Build_BSPT *)
```

Figure BUILD-BSPT. Algorithm to build a BSP tree from a boundary representation.

cells). Note that the only aspect of this algorithm dependent upon the particular B-rep variant is the splitting of a face by a hyperplane. While any order of selection will produce a BSP tree representing the same set, some orders produce more desirable trees. The issue of selecting partitioning hyperplanes can be somewhat complicated, and is discussed briefly in section 5.1.

It is necessary, however, that all points on the boundary of the polyhedra lie in sub-hyperplanes of the resulting BSP tree (section 2.2 above). This is accomplished most simply by always choosing a hyperplane that embeds some face among the current set of faces. Eventually, all points on the original faces will lie in sub-hyperplanes. The second requirement is the correct classification of cells. Assignment of values to leaves occurs when the partitioning of a set of faces finds no faces on one side of the partitioning hyperplane. That region is then known to be *homogeneous,* i.e. the region lies either entirely within the interior of one of the polyhedra or entirely in the exterior of all the polyhedra. We know this because for it to be non-homogeneous, there would be some part of a boundary to make it so, i.e. to mark the transition between inside and outside. Therefore, the region forms a cell and can be classified as *in* or *out*. In this algorithm, differentiating between the two cases is simple. When hyperplanes are chosen from the (hyper)plane equation of some face, we use the fact that normals point to the exterior to deduce the fact that a left leaf must be *in* (in the back-halfspace of the face) and a right leaf *out* (in the front-halfspace). Also, it is not difficult to show that when one subtree of v is a cell, any faces coincident with H_v will all have the same orientation.

Another quite similar approach involves an idea that we will need later: the concept of *inserting a face into a BSP tree.* Let us say that we had used the above algorithm to build a BSP tree out of only $n-1$ of the n faces. We could "add" the last face f to the tree in the following way. Let v be some node in the tree, initially equal to the root. Partition f by H_v. If it is coincident, add it to the appropriate face list of v. Otherwise, pass any part of f lying in H_v^- to *v.left*, and similarly any part in H_v^+ to *v.right*. Now repeat the process recursively on the subtrees. If and when a part of f reaches a leaf, create a new node. Now, if one begins with a trivial BSP tree, and inserts each face one-at-a-time, a BSP tree representing the polyhedra will be constructed.

Before leaving this discussion, we should point out that a much simpler case occurs when the input is a single convex polyhedron P of n faces. The above algorithm, when restricted to partitioning hyperplanes that embed a face, will always produce the same tree structure with n nodes independent of the order in which faces/hyperplanes are selected (Figure CONVEX). Each right child is a leaf with value *out* and the only left leaf has a value *in* representing *int P*. This structure is very similar to a list of the minimal set of (closed) halfspaces whose intersection equals P.

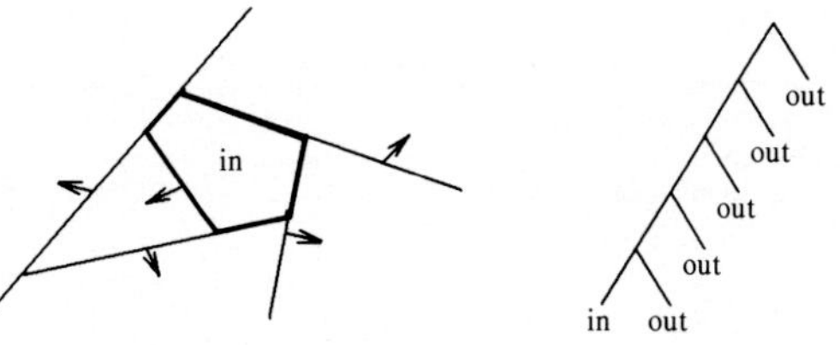

Figure CONVEX. A convex set and its BSP tree.

4. Evaluation of Set Operations Using BSP trees

Since we are concerned with regular sets, we are interested only in the regularized set operations [Requ78], which are denoted as such by an asterisk: $\cap^*$, $\cup^*$, $-^*$, and $\sim^*$. First, consider the unary complementation operator. Given a BSP tree representing a set S, a BSP tree representing its complement, $\sim^* S$, can be formed by simply complementing the cell values: all in-cells are changed to out-cells and all out-cells to in-cells. Any boundary polygons at internal nodes must have their orientations reversed as well. A boundary representation can be similarly complemented by reversing the orientation of every face.

To evaluate binary operators, we will use expression simplification in a geometric setting. Consider for example the expression $S_1 \cap^* S_2$. If we have determined that, for some region R, that $R \subseteq ext\ S_2$, then the expression in R may be simplified to $S_1 \cap^* \emptyset = \emptyset$, where $\emptyset$ denotes the empty set. If instead $R \subseteq int\ S_2$, the expression reduces to $S_1 \cap^* U_R = S_1$, where U_R is the universal set restricted to R. In either case, we can perform the simplification without any knowledge of the structure in R of S_1, which could be an arbitrarily complex sub-expression on arbitrarily complex objects. Analogous cases exist for the other operations (Figure SIMPLIFY). This has been called "pruning" in the context of CSG trees.

To utilize this technique we must partition the space into regions such that at least one operand is homogeneous in each region. That is, given the expression S_1 *op* S_2 defined on some space, one must find a partitioning of that space such that for each region R_i of the partitioning, $R_i \subseteq int\ S_j$ or $R_i \subseteq ext\ S_j$, j = 1 or 2. For an expression of n operands, this property may need to hold in each R_i for up to $n-1$ of the operands, depending on the expression. This technique appears in a number of places, e.g. [Wood82] [Tilo84], and seems fundamental to the problem. We use a BSP tree to partition space to achieve these conditions.

op	left operand	right operand	result
$\cup^*$	S	in	in
	S	out	S
	in	S	in
	out	S	S
$\cap^*$	S	in	S
	S	out	out
	in	S	S
	out	S	out
$-^*$	S	in	out
	S	out	S
	in	S	$\sim^*$ S
	out	S	out

Figure SIMPLIFY. Expression simplification rules. S **is an arbitrary regular set.**

4.1 BSP Tree <op> B-rep → BSP Tree

Given a BSP tree $\hat{T}$ representing a polyhedron T, and a B-rep $\hat{B}$ representing a polyhedron B, we wish to evaluate T *op* B or B *op* T, where *op* is a regularized set operation. In the case of the difference operator $S_1 -^* S_2$, we choose to complement the right operand and evaluate the equivalent $S_1 \cap^* \sim^* S_2$ [3]. Now, the approach is to perform the set operations on open sets only, since these are closed under standard (non-regularized) union and intersection. If the boundary of the result is needed, it is explicitly computed (see section 4.3 below). We will need to classify T and B with respect to each other. This is achieved by discovering parts of one that lie in the interior or exterior of the other. We refer parenthetically to Figure SET-OP, which illustrates $T -^* B$.

We begin by inserting collectively into $\hat{T}$ all of the faces of $\hat{B}$. As the faces filter down into $\hat{T}$ we can discover which if any of the subtrees of $\hat{T}$ lie entirely in *int B* or *ext B*. When at some node v, no part of $\hat{B}$ is found to lie on one side of H_v, say, the left side, then R(*v.left*) must be homogeneous with respect to B (e.g., x.right and z.right in the figure), as explained in section 3. A general method for determining whether the region is in *int B* or *ext B* is given below in Section 4.5. When this occurs, the subtree rooted at *v.left* is either left untouched, or is replaced by a leaf, depending upon the simplification rules (in our example, both x.right and z.right are not modified). If it is also the case that no face of B is coincident with H_v, then the sub-hyperplane of v has also been classified with respect to B. The faces of v are kept or deleted according to the same simplification rules (e.g, x's sub-hyperplane is in *ext B* and its face is kept). Deletion of v may also be possible (see section 4.4).

The insertion process results in $\hat{B}$ being distributed among some subset of the subspaces of $\hat{T}$, i.e. cells or sub-hyperplanes. The reaching of a leaf l by some subset of the boundary, $\hat{B}_l$, means that $\hat{B}_l$ has been classified with respect to T (e.g. the faces in y.right and z.left in (3)). The operation can then be evaluated since we have a region in which one operand, T, is homogeneous. The result is either T's value (e.g. y.right) or B's value (e.g. z.left) in the region represented by the leaf, depending upon the particular operation and the value of the leaf, as given in Figure SIMPLIFY. If the value is T's, then the faces of $\hat{B}_l$

3. It is possible to gain a little in efficiency by performing the complementation as part of the evaluation so that only the parts included in the result are actually complemented.

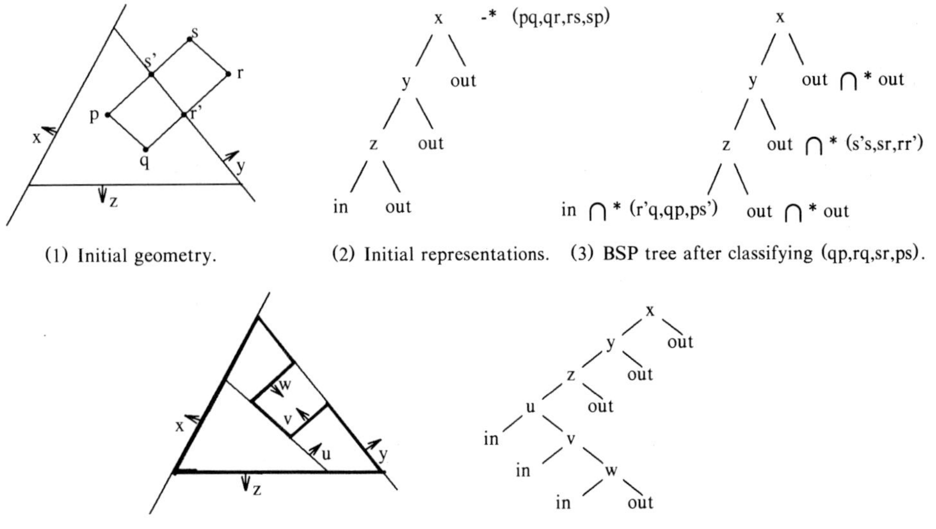

(1) Initial geometry. (2) Initial representations. (3) BSP tree after classifying (qp,rq,sr,ps).

(4) Resulting partitioning. (5) Final BSP tree.

Figure SET-OP. BSP tree −* B-rep → BSP tree.

are discarded (as in y.right); otherwise $\hat{T}$ is "extended" by replacing the leaf with a subtree built from the faces of $\hat{B}_l$ (as in z.left). This can be performed by the procedure Build-BSPT, given earlier. Thus, the cell is "refined" to reflect B's value in the region. The tree now represents the desired set. We refer to this algorithm as the *incremental* set-op evaluation algorithm because it can be used to create a polyhedron by a series of "incremental" modifications to an initial polyhedron. The algorithm is summarized in Figure INCREMENTAL SET-OP.

4.2 CSG on B-reps → BSP Tree

A Constructive Solid Geometry representation (CSG) of a set S is a binary tree in which the internal nodes represent (regularized) set operations and leaves are instanced primitives (such as blocks, cones, etc.) [Requ80]. One can classify some arbitrary set s with respect to S by first classifying s with respect to each primitive, and then combining the classifications according to the set theoretic expression represented by the CSG tree [Tilo80][Roth82]. An alternative is to convert the CSG representation to a more explicit form, such as a B-rep or BSP tree, and classify with respect to that representation. The algorithm we now present provides this latter approach.

We define a CSG evaluation problem π as a pair (τ, R), where τ is a CSG tree with polyhedral primitives represented as B-reps or as trivial BSP trees (representing $\varnothing$ or U), and where R is a convex region of d-space on which τ is defined. The algorithm returns a BSP tree which represents the same set in R as τ. Starting with the problem $\pi = (\tau, \mathrm{R})$, the algorithm chooses a hyperplane H to partition the problem into two sub-problems, $\pi_{left} = (\tau_{left}, R \cap H^-)$, and $\pi_{right} = (\tau_{right}, R \cap H^+)$. The root of the tree returned has H as its partitioning hyperplane, and its left and right subtrees are the results of the recursive evaluation of π_{left} and π_{right}, respectively. The recursion is terminated when the current CSG tree reduces to a trivial BSP tree (a cell).

The algorithm is quite similar to Build-BSPT of section 3, with one important difference: rather than having just a simple list of faces to partition, we have a CSG tree with faces at its leaves. Figure CSG-EVALUTATION describes the algorithm. As before, a hyperplane H is chosen at each stage that embeds a face using a heuristic (Section 5.1). Two copies of the CSG tree are generated and modified to represent the set in each of the two halfspaces of H. This entails for

```
if op = −* then
  B := Negate_B-rep( B )
  op := ∩*

procedure Incremental_Set_op
            ( op : set_operation ; v : BSPTreeNode ;
              B : set of Face ) returns BSPTreeNode
  if v is a leaf then
    case op of
      ∪* : case v.value of
        in  : return v
        out : return Build_BSPT( B )
      ∩* : case v.value of
        in  : return Build_BSPT( B )
        out : return v
  else
    <B_left, B_right, B_coincident> := partition B with H_v
    if B_left has no faces then
      status := Test_in/out(H_v, B_coincident, B_right)
      case op of
        ∪* : case status of
          in  : discard_BSPT( v.left )
                v.left := new "in" leaf
          out : do nothing
        ∩* : case status of
          in  : do nothing
          out : discard_BSPT( v.left )
                v.left := new "out" leaf
    else
      v.left := Incremental_Set_op( op, v.left, B_left )

    if B_right has no faces then
      (* similar to above *)
    else
      v.right := Incremental_Set_op(op, v.right, B_right)
    return v

end Incremental_Set_op ;
```

Figure INCREMENTAL SET-OP. Psuedo code for the incremental set evaluation algorithm.

each primitive replacing the faces of that primitive in the respective CSG trees with the subset of the faces that lies in each halfspace.

Faces coincident with H are retained at the new node. Detection of homogeneous regions allows CSG tree simplification using the rules in Figure SIMPLIFY. If the CSG tree is reduced to, in effect, a single value (in/out), the problem in that region has been solved and is represented by a cell of the BSP tree. The entire problem, then, is solved through the discovery/creation of regions which are homogeneous with respect to the defined set, where each region is represented by a different cell of the resulting BSP tree.

```
procedure Evaluate_CSG ( τ : CSGTree ) returns BSPTree

   choose a face f of a primitive of τ
   v := new BSPTreeNode; H_v := H_f
   <τ_left , τ_right> := Split_CSG ( τ, H_v )

   τ_left := Simplify_CSG ( τ_left )
   if τ_left represents ∅ then
      v.left := new "out" leaf
   else if τ_left represents U then
      v.left := new "in" leaf
   else
      v.left := Evaluate_CSG ( τ_left )

   (* similar code for τ_right *)

   return v
end;  (* Evaluate_CSG *)

procedure Split_CSG ( τ : CSGTree; H : plane_equation )
                                 returns <CSGTree, CSGTree>
   if τ is not a primitive then
      τ_left := copy ( τ.root )
      τ_right := copy ( τ.root )
      <τ_left.left, τ_right.left> := Split_CSG ( τ.left, H )
      <τ_left.right, τ_right.right> := Split_CSG ( τ.right, H )
   else
      <τ_left, τ_right, τ_coincident> := partition τ with H
      if τ_left = ∅ then
         τ_left = Test_in/out ( H, τ_coincident, τ_right )
      elseif τ_right = ∅ then
         τ_right = Test_in/out ( H, τ_coincident, τ_left )
      Add τ_coincident to v's face lists

   return <τ_left, τ_right>
end;  (* Split_CSG *)
```

Figure CSG-EVALUATION. Algorithm for converting from a CSG tree to a BSP tree.

4.3 Boundaries

The two algorithms described above produce, in effect, a generic BSP tree which is sufficient for point classification and ray-tracing. While certain faces were retained at internal nodes, these no longer correspond necessarily to the boundary of the set S represented by the tree $\hat{S}$. Since B-reps are useful for rendering via polygon tiling, and the BSP tree can induce a priority ordering on the faces, we may wish to generate the boundary faces of S. This requires that for each node v of $\hat{S}$, we find and store at v, $bd\ S \cap SHp(v)$ (where $SHp(v)$ is the sub-hyperplane of v). There are two alternatives. One is to discard the old faces entirely and generate the boundary faces directly from the generic BSP tree using a technique described in [Thib87]. The second, which we will describe here, constructs the new faces from the faces of the operands.

The boundary of the result of any set operation is known to be a subset of the boundaries of the operands. Now, since $bd\ S$ is known to lie entirely within the sub-hyperplanes of $\hat{S}$, only the parts of the original faces which lie in these sub-hyperplanes can possibly be in $bd\ S$. These two facts imply that the faces retained at $\hat{S}$'s nodes form a superset of $bd\ S$, i.e. their union contains $bd\ S$, and the discarded faces do not contain any subset of $bd\ S$. It also immediately follows that for a given node v, any part of $bd\ S$ lying in the $SHp(v)$ must be a contained in the region covered by the faces retained at v. However, parts of these faces may lie in either *int* S or *ext* S. To find the *on* parts of these faces, we can insert them into the subtrees of v, analogous to the technique used in point classification for points lying in sub-hyperplanes. This produces a set of new faces, a subset of which form $bd\ S \cap SHp(v)$, and this subset is retained at v (as opposed to extending the tree as in sections 3 and 4.1).

4.3.1 Classifying Faces. Consider for the moment the case where *v.right* is a cell with value *out*, as at node y in Figure SET-OP. Then the boundary contained in the $SHp(v)$ is precisely the points lying between this out-cell and those in-cells in *v.left* whose closure intersects H_v. Moreover, the orientation of the boundary faces must be that of H_v, since they are to point to the exterior, which by construction lies in *v.right*. Therefore, faces in the opposite-face list cannot be in $bd\ S$. Now, if we classify the same-faces by inserting them into *v.left*, the resulting faces which are classified as *in* with respect to *v.left*, i.e those which reach in-cells, must lie in $bd\ S$. Those in out-cells would be between two out-cells and thus known to lie in *ext* S. These can be discarded. As an example, in Figure SET-O, a face of the original tree at node y, when inserted into *y.left* would be split into three pieces, two of which are *in* and the third (middle piece) is *out*.

Now, to extend this for an arbitrary *v.right*, we first take the in-faces from the *v.left* insertion/classification above and insert/classify then with respect to *v.right*. The faces resulting from this insertion that are classified as *out* are then known to lie between an in-cell and an out-cell, and therefore in $bd\ S$. Now, the same process applied to the opposite-faces, but with the insertion sequence reversed (*v.right* then *v.left*), produces faces in $bd\ S$ whose orientation is opposite of H_v.

In the case of the incremental algorithm, we can exploit the fact that a single set operation is being evaluated, and use its semantics to avoid inserting faces into both subtrees. Consider union. We know that the neighborhood in the back-halfspace of a face of either operand is in the interior of the result. Therefore, we know *a priori* that same-faces inserted into *v.left* will all land in in-cells, and similarly for opposite-faces inserted into *v.right*. Thus, each face needs only to be classified with respect to one subtree: same-faces with respect to *v.right*, and opposite-faces with respect to *v.left*. The resulting faces that land in out-cells lie on the boundary, since the other side is known to be in-cells. For intersection, a similar analysis indicates that same-faces should be inserted into *v.left*, opposite-faces into *v.right*, and that resulting faces lying in in-cells should be kept.

While the above technique guarantees that the union of the remaining faces is exactly $bd\ S$, it does not guarantee that the set of faces at each node are disjoint. If the faces are given the same attributes, such as color, this redundancy will not affect renderings of the object, other than to possibly increase time and space requirements. However, this redundancy can be eliminated by merging the faces, i.e. by forming for each node independently the union of the same-faces and separately the union of the opposite-faces.

4.3.2 Face Merging. Merging of faces can be performed by the CSG evaluation algorithm in the dimension of the faces, optimizing for the fact that there is only one type of operator: union. Conceptually, we have a CSG tree representing $f_1 \cup f_2 \cup \cdots \cup f_n$, for n faces. The result is a BSP tree, in $(d-1)$-space, where the $(d-1)$ value of "in" corresponds to the d-value of "on", and similarly "out" corresponds to "not-on". Faces lying in a hyperplane H are orthogonally projected into a coordinate hyperplane by dropping the coordinate corresponding to the largest coordinate of H's normal. The tree building process proceeds as before, but in the lower dimension. The recursion terminates when regions are discovered that are either completely covered by some face or contain no faces.

Let us consider the case where $d = 3$. If convex polygons are the desired output, it is relatively straightforward to maintain a vertex-list representation of the regions of the 2D tree. All in-regions yield polygons whose vertices are projected back into H. Now, for concave polygons, we must find the $(d$-2) boundary of the in-regions. This means that finding the 2D boundary of a 3D set requires recursing in dimension and finding the 1D boundary of 2D set and subsequently the 0D boundaries of 1D sets. Thus, to perform the complete boundary evaluation requires that we apply our algorithm recursively in dimension. The recursion forms 1D BSP trees for each internal node of a 2D BSP tree. The in-cells of these trees lie on polygon edges. In this 1D-space, hyperplanes are forced to the form $[\ 1\ \ -x\ ]$. Vertices lie on these hyperplanes and have value x, and the left subtree of a node contains values $< x$ while the right subtree values are $>x$, i.e. they are binary search trees. To find the minimum boundary of these 1D in-regions, i.e. the pairs of vertices bounding each edge, we can traverse each 1D tree using the procedure in Figure GENERATE-EDGES. The vertices are projected back from 1D to 2D which are then projected back into H defined in 3D. This then produces a merged set of edges bounding the on-regions (with respect to the 3D polyhedron) lying in a given sub-hyperplane[4].

```
Global variables
  v1,v2 : scalar,   last_value : { in,out } := out
  edge_list : LIST OF ( v1,v2 )

Generate_Edges( root, [ 1  − −∞] )

procedure Generate_Edges( v : BSPTreeNode,
                          min : 1D-Hyperplane )
   if v = leaf then
      case ( last_value, v.value )
        ( out,in ) -> v1 := min.x
        ( in,out ) -> v2 := min.x
                      edge_list += NewEdge( v1, v2 )
      last_value := v.value
   else
      Generate_Edges( v.left, min )
      Generate_Edges( v.right, H_v )

end Generate_Edges
```

Figure GENERATE-EDGES

Another alternative for boundary generation from the CSG evaluator, described in [Thib87], uses a technique where each same-face is inserted into *v.left* and a copy, but with orientation reversed, is inserted into *v.right*. The complementary operation is performed for the opposite-faces. The resulting in-cell faces are retained and merged together as above, but with the following "glue" operator in place of union:

(same, same) -> same
(same, opposite) -> not-on
(opposite, same)-> not-on
(opposite, opposite) -> opposite

The 1D boundaries of same and opposite regions are constructed independently. This kind of operation has appeared elsewhere, e.g. [Putn86], to "regularize" the set.

4. Representing a set of arbitrary non-overlapping polygons by a set of edges is sufficient for many polygon processing algorithms.

4.4 BSP Tree Reduction

Once a BSP tree has been constructed as the result of the evaluation of set operations, it may be possible to *reduce* the tree by eliminating certain nodes without changing the represented set. We identify two cases in which this reduction is possible. The first case occurs when both subtrees of a node v are cells with identical values (Node z in Figure REDUCE). Since $R(v)$ is homogeneous, the subtree rooted at v can be replaced by a cell with the same value. Note that no boundary faces could lie in the sub-hyperplane of such a node. This case arises naturally from expression simplification during which a formerly non-homogeneous region is simplified to a homogeneous one, and is analogous to the "condensation" of quad/oct-trees. It can be performed as part of the tree construction.

We may also remove a node that has as one child a cell and, in addition, has no part of the boundary in its sub-hyperplane (node u in Figure REDUCE). This means that all cells in the other subtree bounded by this node's hyperplane have the same value as the cell. Since the sub-hyperplane does not contribute to the differentiation of space, the tree rooted at this node can be replaced by the node's non-trivial subtree (Node w). This reduction can be performed during the phase that generates the boundary faces. (With the incremental algorithm, this can be detected and effected during set-op evaluation.)

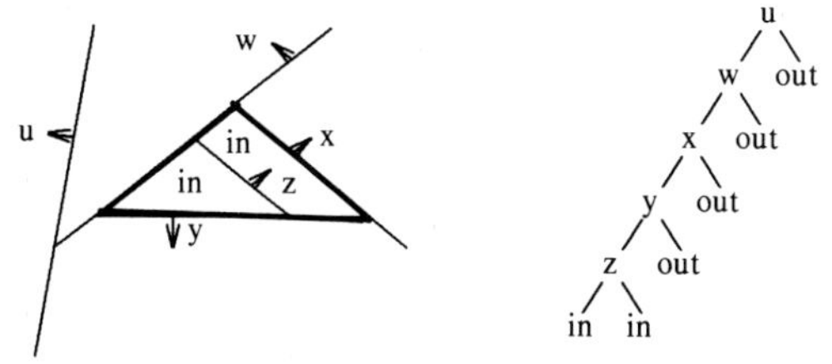

Figure REDUCE. Nodes u and z can be eliminated.

4.5 The In/Out Test

In all three of our algorithms that produce BSP tree representations of polyhedra, we discover regions that do not contain any faces of a polyhedron B represented by a B-rep $\hat{B}$. In these cases, we must determine whether that region lies in *int* B or *ext* B. In procedure Build_BSP, we saw that we could use the normal of a face, coincident with H, to answer this question. However, in the set operation algorithms, no such face may exist. We must then decide the status of this region based upon the subset of *bd* B lying on the non-homogeneous side of H. We solve this for dimensions 1, 2 and 3.

Let $\hat{B}_v = \hat{B} \cap R(v)$. (Note that since $R(v)$ is open, $\hat{B} \cap$ *bd* $R(v)$ is not included in $\hat{B}_v$). We assume, without loss of generality, that B_v lies entirely in H_v^+, and therefore in $R(v.right)$. We are then interested in determining the status of $R(v.left)$ with respect to B. In the case where $B \cap R(v)$ is convex, this is relatively simple. We can test some point lying in $SHp(v)$ for inclusion in the back half-spaces of all faces of $\hat{B}_v$. If the point is "behind" all of these faces, then $R(v.left) \subset$ *int* B, otherwise $R(v.left) \subset$ *ext* B. Such a point can be easily produced if each sub-hyperplane embeds some face: we use the centroid of three non-collinear vertices of this face.

We now address the problem for (sets of) arbitrary polyhedra. One alternative is the ray casting test [Laid86]. This method would intersect a ray emanating from a point on the sub-hyperplane with $\hat{B}_v$ to find the closest face, from whose orientation the classification can be obtained. If the closest intersection point lies on more than one face, the process is repeated with a randomly perturbed ray. We have, however, discovered a simpler method which uses the closest vertex b of $\hat{B}_v$ to H. This b can be found trivially during the partitioning of $\hat{B}_v$ by H_v. In the following, let p be a point in $SHp(v)$.

In 1D, the problem is solved exactly as in Build-BSPT, i.e from the orientation of the single face (a point). For 2D, the problem is illustrated in Figure 2D-IN/OUT. Vertex b is either in $bd\ R(v)$ or in $int\ R(v)$. If b lies in $bd\ R(v)$, then there is a single edge e in $\hat{B}_v$ incident with b. (A second edge could only lie in $bd\ R(v)$ or $ext\ R(v)$). If p lies in H_e^+, then $R(v.left)$ lies in $ext\ B$. Otherwise, $R(v.left)$ is in $int\ B$. Now, if b is in $int\ R(v)$, b is incident with two edges, e_1 and e_2. The region $R(v.left)$ is in $ext\ B$ if e_1 and e_2 lie in each other's back halfspace, i.e., if $e_1 \subset H_{e_2}^-$ and $e_2 \subset H_{e_1}^-$. This means that b is a point of "local convexity" of B. Otherwise $R(v.left)$ is in $int\ B$ (and b is a point of "local concavity").

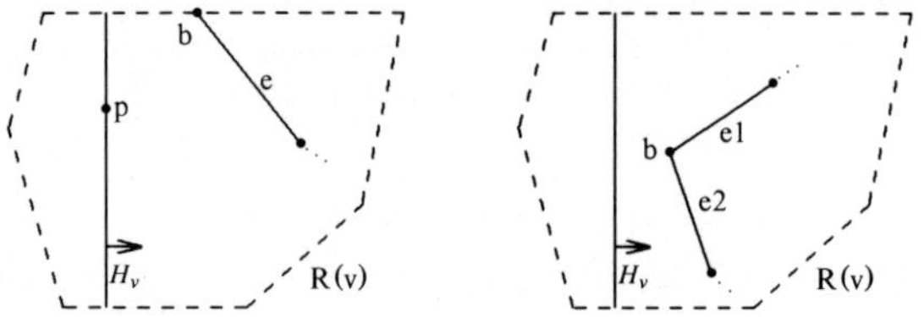

(a) closest vertex in $bdR(v)$. (b) closest vertex in $intR(v)$.

Figure 2D-IN/OUT.

In 3D, the situation is somewhat similar: either b lies in $bd\ R(v)$ and is not shared by any other face of $\hat{B}_v$, or b is shared by more than one face of $\hat{B}_v$ (and may lie in either $bd\ R(v)$ or $int\ R(v)$). The test for the first case is the same as above: p is tested against the hyperplane of the single face containing b. When b is shared by more than one face of $\hat{B}_v$, we select the edge which forms the smallest angle with the plane H_v (think of b lying on H_v). In the neighborhood of b, this is the closest edge of $\hat{B}_v$ to H_v (Figure 3D-IN/OUT). If f_1 and f_2 are the faces that share this edge, then $R(v.left)$ is in $ext\ B$ if, in a local region of b, f_1 and f_2 lie in each other's back halfspace; otherwise, $R(v.left)$ lies in $int\ B$. To determine this we first find a vertex of f_1 adjacent (connected by an edge) to b but not lying in f_2. The location with respect to the plane of f_2 of this vertex provides the same answer as in the 2D case above. If the faces are convex, any vertex of f_1 not lying in f_2 will do. If there is a tie for the closest vertex, we can choose the one that allows the simplest test.

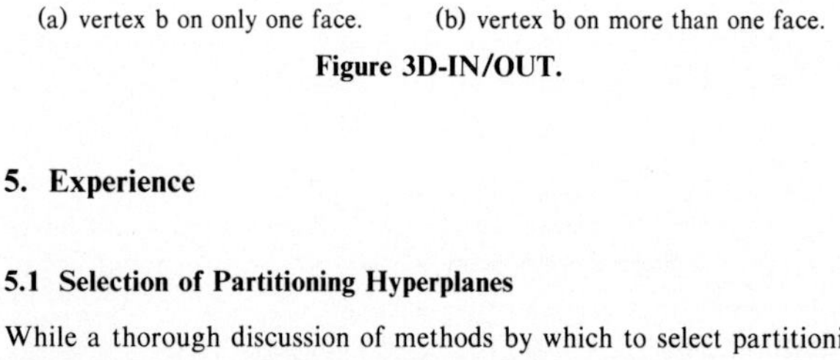

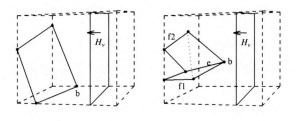

(a) vertex b on only one face. (b) vertex b on more than one face.

Figure 3D-IN/OUT.

5. Experience

5.1 Selection of Partitioning Hyperplanes

While a thorough discussion of methods by which to select partitioning hyperplanes is beyond the scope of this paper, we will at least describe the primary ones we have been using. The two principal properties of BSP trees that we are wanting to optimize are size and balance. Because finding the optimal is considered to be computationally hard, heuristics are employed. Most of our work has been with heuristics that select a hyperplane from among those that embed faces. For a set of faces, we define the *candidate set* to be those faces that are to be considered for generating partitioning hyperplanes. The *test set* consists of the faces against which each candidate hyperplane is tested, with possible outcomes being "in front of", "in back of", and "intersected by". The heuristic is a function of the number of outcomes of each type that occurred when a candidate was tested against the test set. The candidate chosen is that member of the candidate set that maximizes the heuristic. We investigated three heuristic functions:

$$Heur_1\ (front,back,split) = (-|back - front|) - w_{split} * split$$
$$Heur_2\ (front,back,split) = (front * back) - w_{split} * split$$
$$Heur_3\ (front,back,split) = front - w_{split} * split$$

The weight w_{split} allows "tuning" of the heuristics. The reason for applying a negative weight to intersected candidates is that splitting of faces tends to increase tree size and total computation time. The first two heuristics try to balance the number of faces on each side of the candidate. The third is motivated by CSG trees with convex primitives and attempts to maximize the number of faces in the exterior of some primitive. This can facilitate CSG tree simplification, since in one of the two subspaces, the value of the primitive will be *out*.

5.2 Implementation of the CSG evaluation algorithm

The CSG evaluation algorithm has been implemented in a dialect of Pascal running under Unix BSD 4.3. The CSG tree is described in a simple language of our design, translated using *lex* and *yacc*. Statistics obtained for various test objects are given in Figure STATS. Objects "stand" and "holed head" are depicted in Figure RAY-TRACING. In Figure CLUTCHPLATE, the edges (highlighted) reveal the spatial partitioning of that object. Tests were run on a VAX 8650. For each heuristic, $w_{split} = 8$, the candidate set consisted of 5 polygons chosen at random from each primitive in the current sub-problem, and the test set consisted of all polygons in the sub-problem. Early experience with various candidate set sizes shows that heuristics $Heur_1$ and $Heur_3$ are comparable. $Heur_2$ produces trees with a larger number of nodes, but with less CPU time than is required by the other heuristics for the same objects.

5.3 Implementation of the Incremental Algorithm

We have implemented the algorithm for incremental set operations in C on a Silicon Graphics IRIS workstation. The user modifies a "work piece", represented by a BSP tree, with a "tool", represented by a B-rep. The user can interactively control the view and the tool's position. Moving the tool results in a temporary union of the current work piece with the tool at its current position. Visibility is accomplished by transmitting the polygons in back to front order, using the visibility priority ordering produced from the BSP tree. The union we use for this is a "lazy" union because we do not re-evaluate boundary polygons in nodes of the resulting tree. We can do this because the visible surface of two objects that interpenetrate is the same as the visible surface of their union. Re-evaluation would only serve to eliminate invisible faces in the interior or overlapping faces on the boundary. Our impression is that the time required to draw the extra polygons is less than that needed to update the boundaries. In addition, subtrees lying inside the tool are saved and former cells that were refined by the tool's faces are noted. Thus to restore the original tree for use in the next frame requires reinstating the "removed" subtrees and cells, and removing any of the tool's faces lying in internal nodes of the tree. Finally, once the tool is positioned, the user chooses a set operation and the BSP tree is modified to reflect the result.

The initial work piece is obtained by either converting some B-rep to a BSP tree or using the result of the CSG evaluator. We have restricted the tools to be convex polyhedra so that we can take advantage of the

object	number of primitives	number of polygons	heuristic used	cpu (seconds)	tree size (nodes)	tree height	number of polygons
clutchplate	8	158	1	8.3	368	43	353
			2	7.2	408	27	362
			3	8.3	369	47	353
stand	31	623	1	41.9	713	31	1781
			2	41.1	814	31	1825
			3	152.9	896	93	1850
holed head	3	955	1	30.6	1536	104	1982
			2	24.5	1811	61	2167
			3	32.8	1532	90	2067

Figure STATS. Statistics for some test cases.

simpler algorithms for tree building and in/out testing. We have not found this to be an unnatural limitation for the user. Also, the IRIS workstation requires polygons to be convex. In forming the boundary during set operations, we take advantage of the convex decomposition generated by the BSP tree to provide us with convex polygons.

6. Concluding Comments

6.1 Comparison to Alternative Approaches

Space limitations prevent any but a limited discussion of the relationship of our work to others. The octree [Meag82] is similar in ways to the BSP tree. Both are tree structures that recursively subdivides space and assigns values to leaves, and both are dimension-independent. The most obvious difference is that octrees require the partitioning to be axis-aligned and the subdivision to be uniform. Of course, any partitioning of space by an octree can be modeled by a BSP tree[5]. The simplicity of octrees is attractive, and this can lead to certain advantages. But, for representation of polyhedra, the octree in general provides only an approximation, and it is typically a very verbose one. However, work described in [Carl85] [Ayal85] attempts to addresses these problems. While the verbosity is reduced, it still remains a problem. Set operations (in [Ayal85] and described for 2D only) require identifying and handling a number of cases, an aspect that tends to complicate implementations and makes extension to higher dimensions difficult. More importantly, axis-aligned partitioning schemes do not transform. To transform an octree it must be rebuilt. BSP trees do transform: simply apply the transformation to each hyperplane (the inverse of what would be applied to points). Also, we expect the generality of orientation to lead to smaller representations.

In B-rep algorithms, e.g. [Mant83] [Requ85] [Laid86] [Putn86], the geometric search structure, the set operations, and the visible surface determination are independent. In the BSP tree, they are all unified in a single structure (also true of octrees). While boundary representations transform, the search structures are typically axis-aligned. With one exception [Putn86], the algorithms for set operations are not dimension-independent and are somewhat complex with, once again, considerable case analysis. The principal "case analysis" per se for the BSP tree is the partitioning of a face by a hyperplane. On the other hand, B-reps are typically more concise (although not always).

6.2 Future Work

Other operations that we have examined include the calculation of metric properties such as volume, surface area, center of mass, etc. (see [Thib87]). We have also made a potentially important step by devising a closed set theoretic (boolean) algebra on BSP trees, thus dispensing with B-reps per se. In addition, the original ray-tracing techniques have been extended considerably, now exploiting non-linear hyperplanes. Utilization of non-linear hyperplanes is also possible with the fundamental techniques presented in this paper. However, the simplicity of linear computations would be lost in doing so. Nonetheless, we intend to explore this option. Heuristics are another area requiring greater study. All partitioning hyperplanes do not need to embed faces. One technique we have begun investigating is the use of a "median cut" algorithm similar to that used to build k-d trees [Bent79]. This can result in more well-balanced trees, especially for convex regions bounded by many faces.

5. To make the cost of determining the location of a point in a BSP tree more comparable to an octree, we use plane-equation-type = (x-axis, y-axis, z-axis, arbitrary) and optimize when not "arbitrary".

6.3 Conclusions

A new representation for something as fundamental as polyhedra introduces a new "algorithm space" to explore. Divide-and-conquer algorithms are often simple and efficient and we believe this is reflected in the BSP tree algorithms. Also, the dimension independent aspect allowed a solution to the boundary problem without introducing a different methodology. The unified framework provided for geometric searching, set operations, and visible surface rendering reduces the conceptual complexity as well as the complexity of implementations.

The representation can be viewed as something of a cross between octrees and boundary representations. It has the unifying quality of octrees, but is not as simple. It has the exactness, transformability and conciseness of boundary representations, although not generally as concise. In fact, one might view the greater verbosity as the cost of the unity, something which must be weighed against the other gains.

References

[Ayal85] D. Ayala, P. Brunet, R. Juan, and I. Navazo, "Object Representation by Means of Nonminimal Division Quad trees and Octrees," *ACM Transactions on Graphics Vol. 4(1)* pp. 41-59 (January 1985).

[Bent79] Jon Louis Bentley and Jerome H. Friedman, "Data Structures for Range Searching," *Computing Surveys Vol. 11(4)*, pp. 397-409 (December 1979).

[Carl85] Ingrid Carlbom, Indranil Chakravarty, and David Vanderschel, "A Hierarchical Data Structure for Representing the Spatial Decomposition of 3-D Objects," *IEEE Computer Graphics and Applications*, pp. 24-31 (April 1985).

[Fuch80] H. Fuchs, Z. Kedem, and B. Naylor, "On Visible Surface Generation by a Priori Tree Structures," *Computer Graphics Vol. 14(3)*, (June 1980).

[Fuch83] Henry Fuchs, Gregory D. Abram, and Eric D. Grant, "Near Real-Time Shaded Display of Rigid Objects," *Computer Graphics Vol. 17(3)* pp. 65-72 (July 1983).

[Kala82] Yehuda E. Kalay, "Determining the Spatial Containment of a Point in General Polyhedra," *Computer Graphics and Image Processing Vol. 19* pp. 303-334 (1982).

[Laid86] David H. Laidlaw, W. Benjamin Trumbore, and John F. Hughes, "Constructive Solid Geometry for Polyhedral Objects," *Computer Graphics Vol. 20(4)* pp. 161-170 (August 1986).

[Mant83] Martii Mantyla and Markku Tamminen, "Localized Set Operations for Solid Modeling," *Computer Graphics Vol. 17(3)* pp. 279-288 (July 1983).

[Meag82] D. Meagher, "Geometric Modeling using Octree Encoding," *Computer Graphics and Image Processing Vol. 19* (June 1982).

[Nayl81] Bruce F. Naylor, "A Priori Based Techniques for Determining Visibility Priority for 3-D Scenes," Ph.D. Thesis, University of Texas at Dallas (May 1981).

[Nayl86] Bruce F. Naylor and William C. Thibault, "Application of BSP Trees to Ray-Tracing and CSG Evaluation," Technical Report GIT-ICS 86/03, School of Information and Computer Science, Georgia Institute of Technology, Atlanta, Georgia 30332 (February 1986).

[Prep85] Franco P. Preparata and Michael Ian Shamos, *Computational Geometry: An Introduction,* Springer-Verlag, New York (1985).

[Putn86] L. K. Putnam and P. A. Subrahmanyam, "Boolean Operations on n-Dimensional Objects," IEEE Computer Graphics and Applications, pp. 43-51 (June 1986).

[Requ78] Aristides A. G. Requicha and Robert B. Tilove, "Mathematical Foundations of Constructive Solid Geometry: General Topology of Closed Regular Sets," TM-27a, Production Automation Project, University of Rochester, Rochester, New York 14627 (June 1978).

[Requ80] Aristides A. G. Requicha, "Representations for Rigid Solids: Theory, Methods, and Systems," *Computing Surveys Vol. 12(4)* pp. 437-464 (December 1980).

[Requ85] Aristides A. G. Requicha and Herbert B. Voelcker, "Boolean Operations in Solid Modeling: Boundary Evaluation and Merging Algorithms," Proceedings of the IEEE Vol. 73(1) pp. 30-44 (January 1985).

[Roth82] Scott D. Roth, "Ray Casting for Modeling Solids," *Computer Graphics and Image Processing Vol. 18* pp. 109-144 (1982).

[Schu69] R. A. Schumacker, R. Brand, M. Gilliland, and W. Sharp, "Study for Applying Computer-Generated Images to Visual Simulation," AFHRL-TR-69-14, U.S. Air Force Human Resources Laboratory (1969).

[Thib87] William C. Thibault, "Application of Binary Space Partitioning Trees to Geometric Modeling and Ray-Tracing", Ph.D. Dissertation, Georgia Institute of Technology, Atlanta, Georgia, (1987).

[Tilo80] Robert B. Tilove, "Set Membership Classification: A Unified Approach to Geometric Intersection Problems," *IEEE Transactions on Computers Vol. C-29(10)* pp. 874-883 (October 1980).

[Tilo84] Robert Tilove, "A Null-Object Algorithm for Constructive Solid Geometry," *Communications of the ACM Vol. 27(7)* (July 1984).

[Wood82] J. R. Woodwark and K. M. Quinlan, "Reducing the effect of complexity on volume model evaluation," *Computer Aided Design Vol. 14(2)* (1982).

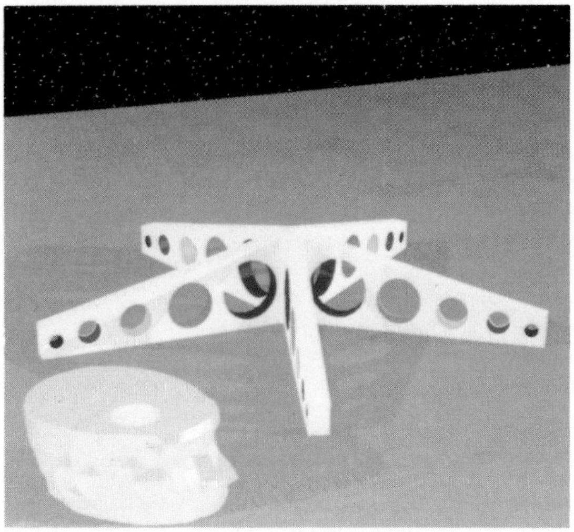

Figure RAY-TRACING. Two objects defined with BSP trees and rendered by ray-tracing.

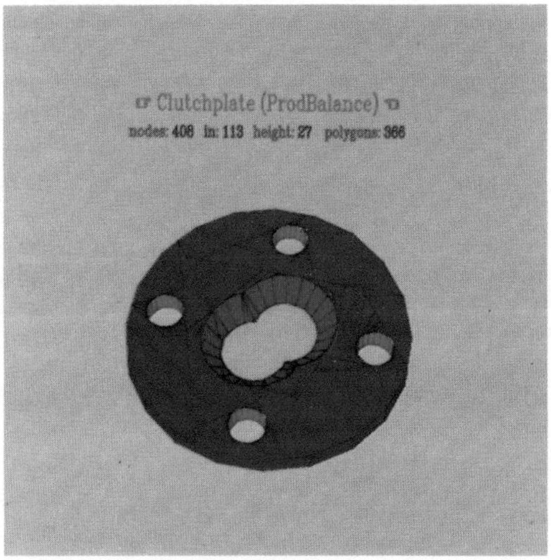

Figure CLUTCHPLATE. Edges reveal the partitioning.

MARCHING CUBES: A HIGH RESOLUTION 3D SURFACE CONSTRUCTION ALGORITHM

William E. Lorensen
Harvey E. Cline

General Electric Company
Corporate Research and Development
Schenectady, New York 12301

Abstract

We present a new algorithm, called *marching cubes*, that creates triangle models of constant density surfaces from 3D medical data. Using a divide-and-conquer approach to generate inter-slice connectivity, we create a case table that defines triangle topology. The algorithm processes the 3D medical data in scan-line order and calculates triangle vertices using linear interpolation. We find the gradient of the original data, normalize it, and use it as a basis for shading the models. The detail in images produced from the generated surface models is the result of maintaining the inter-slice connectivity, surface data, and gradient information present in the original 3D data. Results from computed tomography (CT), magnetic resonance (MR), and single-photon emission computed tomography (SPECT) illustrate the quality and functionality of *marching cubes.* We also discuss improvements that decrease processing time and add solid modeling capabilities.

CR Categories: 3.3, 3.5

Additional Keywords: computer graphics, medical imaging, surface reconstruction

1. INTRODUCTION.

Three-dimensional surfaces of the anatomy offer a valuable medical tool. Images of these surfaces, constructed from multiple 2D slices of computed tomography (CT), magnetic resonance (MR), and single-photon emission computed tomography (SPECT), help physicians to understand the complex anatomy present in the slices. Interpretation of 2D medical images requires special training, and although radiologists have these skills, they must often communicate their interpretations to the referring physicians, who sometimes have difficulty visualizing the 3D anatomy.

Researchers have reported the application of 3D medical images in a variety of areas. The visualization of complex acetabular fractures [6], craniofacial abnormalities [17,18], and intracranial structure [13] illustrate 3D's potential for the study of complex bone structures. Applications in radiation therapy [27,11] and surgical planning [4,5,31] show interactive 3D techniques combined with 3D surface images. Cardiac applications include artery visualization [2,16] and nongraphic modeling applications to calculate surface area and volume [21].

Existing 3D algorithms lack detail and sometimes introduce artifacts. We present a new, high-resolution 3D surface construction algorithm that produces models with unprecedented detail. This new algorithm, called *marching cubes,* creates a polygonal representation of constant density surfaces from a 3D array of data. The resulting model can be displayed with conventional graphics-rendering algorithms implemented in software or hardware.

After describing the information flow for 3D medical applications, we describe related work and discuss the drawbacks of that work. Then we describe the algorithm as well as efficiency and functional enhancements, followed by case studies using three different medical imaging techniques to illustrate the new algorithm's capabilities.

2. INFORMATION FLOW FOR 3D MEDICAL ALGORITHMS.

Medical applications of 3D consist of four steps (Figure 1). Although one can combine the last three steps into one algorithm, we logically decompose the process as follows:

1. *Data acquisition.*
   This first step, performed by the medical imaging hardware, samples some property in a patient and produces multiple 2D slices of information. The data sampled depends on the data acquisition technique.

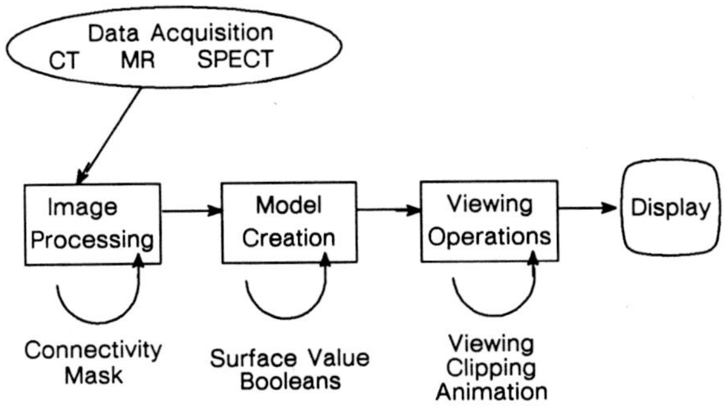

Figure 1. 3D Medical Information Flow.

X-ray computed tomography (CT) measures the spatially varying X-ray attenuation coefficient [3]. CT images show internal structure. For 3D applications, CT is frequently used to look at bone structure, although we have had success visualizing soft tissue.

Magnetic resonance (MR) measures three physical properties [20]. One property is the distribution of "mobile" hydrogen nuclei and shows overall structure within the slices. The other two properties measure relaxation times of the nuclei. MR, a recent technique, shows excellent contrast between a variety of soft tissues. However, the variety of surfaces presents a challenge to 3D surface construction and requires techniques for selective surface extraction and display.

A third acquisition technique, single-photon emission computed tomography (SPECT) measures the emission of gamma rays [24]. The source of these rays is a radioisotope distributed within the body. In addition to structure, SPECT can show the presence of blood in structures with a much lower dose than that required by CT.

2. *Image processing.*
Some algorithms use image processing techniques to find structures within the 3D data [1,32,30,29] or to filter the original data. MR data, in particular, needs image processing to select appropriate structure.

3. *Surface construction.*
Surface construction, the topic of this paper, involves the creation of a surface model from the 3D data. The model usually consists of 3D volume elements (voxels) or polygons. Users select the desired surface by specifying a density value. This step can also include the creation of cut or capped surfaces.

4. *Display.*
Having created the surface, the final step displays that surface using display techniques that include ray casting, depth shading, and color shading.

3. RELATED WORK.

There are several approaches to the 3D surface generation problem. An early technique [23] starts with contours of the surface to be constructed and connects contours on consecutive slices with triangles. Unfortunately, if more than one contour of surface exists on a slice, ambiguities arise when determining which contours to connect [14]. Interactive intervention by the user can overcome some of these ambiguities [8]; however, in a clinical environment, user interaction should be kept to a minimum.

Another approach, developed by G. Herman and colleagues [19] creates surfaces from cuberilles. A cuberille is "dissection of space into equal cubes (called voxels) by three orthogonal sets of parallel planes [7]." Although there are many ways to display a cuberille model, the most realistic images result when the gradient, calculated from cuberilles in a neighborhood, is used to find the shade of a point on the model [15]. Meagher [25] uses an octree representation to compress the storage of the 3D data, allowing rapid manipulation and display of voxels.

Farrell [12] uses ray casting to find the 3D surface, but rather than shade the image with a gray scale, uses hue lightness to display the surface. In another ray casting method, Hohne [22], after locating the surface along a ray, calculates the gradient along the surface and uses this gradient, scaled by an "appropriate" value, to generate gray scales for the image.

A different approach, used at the Mayo Clinic [26], displays the density volume rather than the surface. This method produces, in effect, a conventional shadow graph that can be viewed from arbitrary angles. Motion enhances the three-dimensional effect obtained using the volume model.

Each of these techniques for surface construction and display suffer shortcomings because they throw away useful information in the original data. The connected contour algorithms throw away the inter-slice connectivity that exists in the original data. The cuberille approach, using thresholding to represent the surface as blocks in 3D space, attempts to recover shading information from the blocks. The ray casting methods either use depth shading alone, or try to approximate shading with an unnormalized gradient. Since they display all values and not just those visible from a given point of view, volume models rely on motion to produce a three-dimensional sensation.

Our approach uses information from the original 3D data to derive inter-slice connectivity, surface location, and surface gradient. The resulting triangle model can be displayed on conventional graphics display systems using standard rendering algorithms.

4. MARCHING CUBES ALGORITHM.

There are two primary steps in our approach to the surface construction problem. First, we locate the surface corresponding to a user-specified value and create triangles. Then, to ensure a quality image of the surface, we calculate the normals to the surface at each vertex of each triangle.

Marching cubes uses a divide-and-conquer approach to locate the surface in a logical *cube* created from eight pixels; four each from two adjacent slices (Figure 2).

The algorithm determines how the surface intersects this cube, then moves (or *marchs*) to the next cube. To find the surface intersection in a cube, we assign a one to a cube's vertex if the data value at that vertex exceeds (or equals) the value of the surface we are constructing. These vertices are inside (or on) the surface. Cube vertices with values below the surface receive a zero and are outside the surface. The surface intersects those cube edges where one vertex is outside the surface (one) and the other is inside the surface (zero). With this assumption, we determine the topology of the surface within a cube, finding the location of the intersection later.

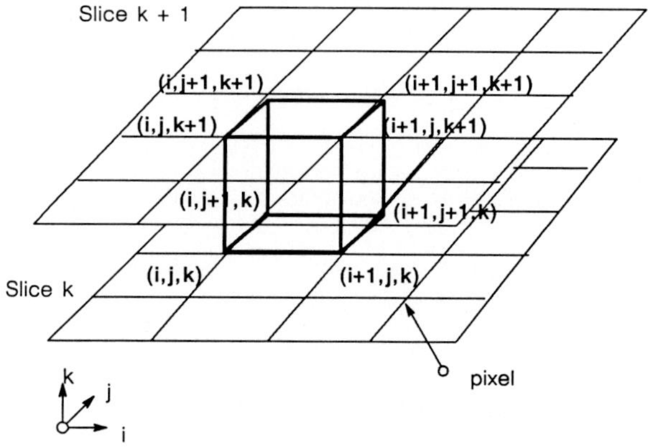

Figure 2. Marching Cube.

Since there are eight vertices in each cube and two states, inside and outside, there are only $2^8 = 256$ ways a surface can intersect the cube. By enumerating these 256 cases, we create a table to look up surface-edge intersections, given the labeling of a cubes vertices. The table contains the edges intersected for each case.

Triangulating the 256 cases is possible but tedious and error-prone. Two different symmetries of the cube reduce the problem from 256 cases to 14 patterns. First, the topology of the triangulated surface is unchanged if the relationship of the surface values to the cubes is reversed. Complementary cases, where vertices greater than the surface value are interchanged with those less than the value, are equivalent. Thus, only cases with zero to four vertices greater than the surface value need be considered, reducing the number of cases to 128. Using the second symmetry property, rotational symmetry, we reduced the problem to 14 patterns by inspection. Figure 3 shows the triangulation for the 14 patterns.

The simplest pattern, 0, occurs if all vertex values are above (or below) the selected value and produces no triangles. The next pattern, 1, occurs if the surface separates on vertex from the other seven, resulting in one triangle defined by the three edge intersections. Other patterns produce multiple triangles. Permutation of these 14 basic patterns using complementary and rotational symmetry produces the 256 cases.

We create an index for each case, based on the state of the vertex. Using the vertex numbering in Figure 4, the eight bit index contains one bit for each vertex.

This index serves as a pointer into an edge table that gives all edge intersections for a given cube configuration.

Using the index to tell which edge the surface intersects, we can interpolate the surface intersection along the edge. We use linear interpolation, but have experimented with higher degree interpolations. Since the algorithm produces at least one and as many as four triangles per cube, the higher degree surfaces show little improvement over linear interpolation.

The final step in *marching cubes* calculates a unit normal for each triangle vertex. The rendering algorithms use this normal to produce Gouraud-shaded images. A surface of constant density has a zero gradient component along the surface tangential direction; consequently, the direction of the gradient vector, $\vec{g}$, is normal to the surface. We can use this fact to determine surface normal vector, $\vec{n}$, if the magnitude of the gradient, $|\vec{g}|$, is nonzero. Fortunately, at the surface of interest between two tissue types of different densities, the gradient vector is nonzero. The gradient vector, $\vec{g}$, is the derivative of the density function

$$\vec{g}(x,y,z) = \nabla \vec{f}(x,y,z). \tag{1}$$

To estimate the gradient vector at the surface of interest, we first estimate the gradient vectors at the cube vertices and linearly interpolate the gradient at the point of intersection. The gradient at cube vertex (i, j, k), is estimated using central differences along the three coordinate axes by:

$$G_x(i,j,k) = \frac{D(i+1,j,k) - D(i-1,j,k)}{\Delta x} \tag{2}$$

$$G_y(i,j,k) = \frac{D(i,j+1,k) - D(i,j-1,k)}{\Delta y} \tag{3}$$

$$G_z(i,j,k) = \frac{D(i,j,k+1) - D(i,j,k-1)}{\Delta z} \tag{4}$$

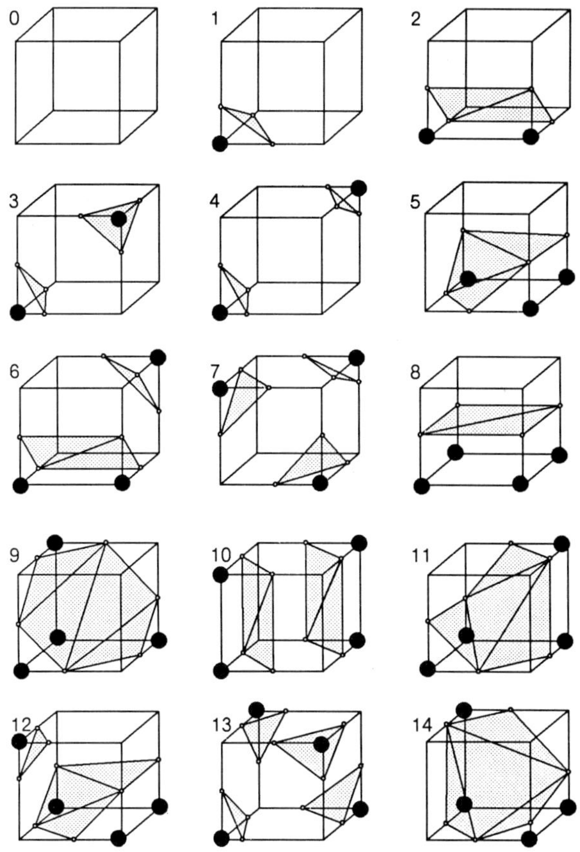

Figure 3. Triangulated Cubes.

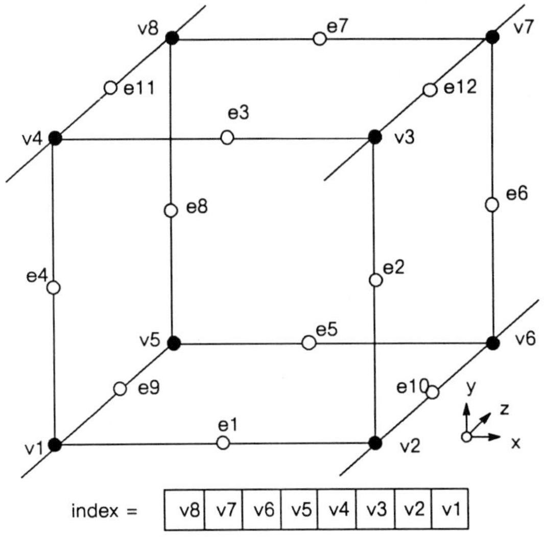

Figure 4. Cube Numbering.

where $D(i,j,k)$ is the density at pixel (i,j) in slice k and $\Delta x, \Delta y, \Delta z$ are the lengths of the cube edges. Dividing the gradient by its length produces the unit normal at the vertex required for rendering. We linearly interpolate this normal to the point of intersection. Note that to calculate the gradient at all vertices of the cube, we keep four slices in memory at once.

In summary, *marching cubes* creates a surface from a three-dimensional set of data as follows:

1. Read four slices into memory.
2. Scan two slices and create a cube from four neighbors on one slice and four neighbors on the next slice.
3. Calculate an index for the cube by comparing the eight density values at the cube vertices with the surface constant.
4. Using the index, look up the list of edges from a precalculated table.
5. Using the densities at each edge vertex, find the surface-edge intersection via linear interpolation.
6. Calculate a unit normal at each cube vertex using central differences. Interpolate the normal to each triangle vertex.
7. Output the triangle vertices and vertex normals.

5. ENHANCEMENTS TO THE BASIC ALGORITHM.

We have made several improvements to the original *marching cubes* that make the algorithm run faster and that add solid modeling capabilities.

5.1 Efficiency Enhancements.

The efficiency enhancements allow the algorithm to take advantage of pixel-to-pixel, line-to-line, and slice-to-slice coherence. For cubes interior to the original data limits (those not including slice 0, line 0, or pixel 0), only three new edges need to be interpolated for each cube. We can obtain the other nine edges from previous slices, lines, or pixels. In Figure 5, the shaded circles represent values available from prior calculations; only edges 6, 7, and 12 have to be calculated for the new cube.

Special cases are present along the boundaries of the data, but, by enumerating these cases, we can limit vertex calculations to once per vertex. In practice, we only save the previous pixel and line intersections because the memory required to save the previous slice's intersections is large. Using the coherence speeds up the algorithm by a factor of three.

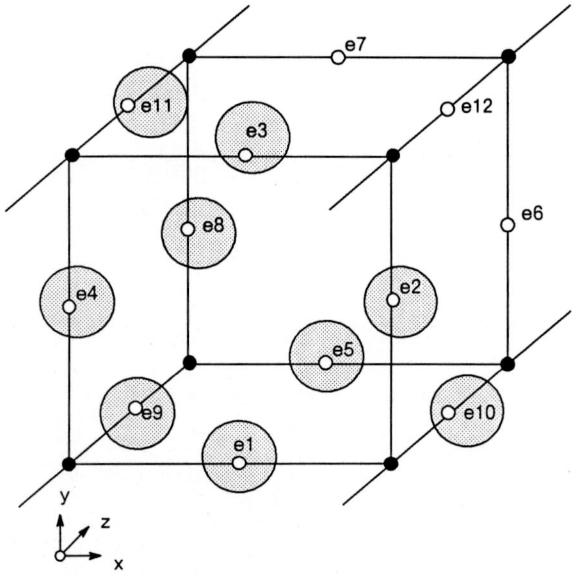

Figure 5. Coherence.

Reducing the slice resolution, by averaging four pixels into one, decreases the number of triangles, improves the surface construction efficiency and smooths the image. Although there is some loss of detail in the averaged slices, the averaging makes the number of triangles more manageable for high-resolution slices.

5.2 Functional Enhancements.

We have added a solid modeling capability to the algorithm. Boolean operations permit cutting and capping of solid models, as well as the extraction of multiple surfaces. In a medical application, cutting is analogous to performing surgery and capping (and texture mapping) is analogous to the medical imaging technique of reformatting.

We use the cube index described earlier to do Boolean operations on the surfaces. Here, just consider three values of the index:

index = *0* for cubes outside the surface.
index = *255* for cubes inside the surface.
0 < *index* < *255* for cubes on the surface.

Solid modeling uses these notions of *inside*, *outside*, and *on* to create a surface. Analytic functions also provide the same information; so, for example the equation of a plane, $ax + by + cz - d$, tells where a given point lies with respect to the plane. Let $\sim$**S**, δ**S**, and **S** represent sets of points that are outside, on, and inside a surface, respectively. Referring to Figure 6, we build a truth table, shown in Figure 7, for the Boolean intersection operation.

Nine entries in the truth table describe what to do when two surfaces have a given index. With **x**'s representing no operation, the entry for (**S**, $\sim$**P**) shows that the cube in question is inside one surface but outside the other, resulting in no triangles. The (δ**S**, **P**) entry produces triangles from the *S* surface, while the (**S**, δ**P**) entry produces triangles from the *P* surface. The (δ**S**, δ**P**) entry, created when a cube is on both surfaces, requires special processing. We clip

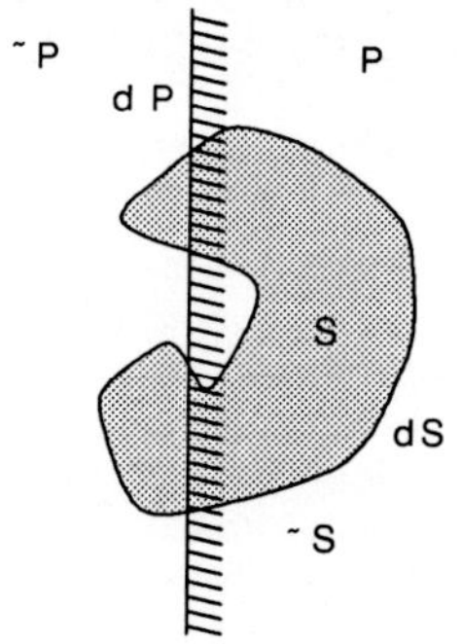

Figure 6. Point/Surface Relations.

	P	~P	d P
S	x	x	P
~S	x	x	x
d S	S	x	*

Figure 7. Truth Table.

each triangle from one surface against each triangle from the other, using the Sutherland-Hodgman clipping algorithm [28].

This technique applies to any surfaces that have inside/outside functions. We have used it with planes and with connectivity masks generated by separate image processing algorithms [9]. Application of a "logical or" truth table provides the capability for multiple surface extraction.

We implement texture mapping by finding the triangles on a plane's surface and attenuating the normal's length using the original slice data.

6. IMPLEMENTATION.

Marching cubes, written in C, runs on Sun Workstations[1] under Unix[2], VAX's under VMS[3], and an IBM 3081 under IX/370[4]. We display the models using an in-house z-buffer program or a General Electric Graphicon 700[5]. For our models, the Graphicon displays at a rate of 10,000 triangles per second. In addition to surfaces of constant density, the software allows any number of planes that can be transparent, capped with triangles, or textured with interpolated density data. Medical practitioners refer to this texture mapping as reformatting. Execution times depend on the number of surfaces and resolution of the original data. Model creation times on a VAX 11/780 vary from 100 seconds for 64 by 64 by 48 SPECT data to 30 minutes for 260 by 260 by 93 CT studies. Times for the same studies on the IBM 3081 are twelve times faster. The number of triangles in a surface model is proportional to the area of the surface. This number can get large (over 500,000 in some cases), so we reduce it using cut planes and surface connectivity. Also, sometimes we reduce the resolution of the original data by filtering, producing a somewhat smoother surface with some loss of resolution.

7. RESULTS.

We have applied *marching cubes* to data obtained from CT, MR, and SPECT, as well as data generated from analytic functions. We present three case studies that illustrate the quality of the constructed surfaces and some modeling options. Each image was rendered at 512 by 512 resolution without antialiasing.

7.1 Computed Tomography.

The first case is a CT study of the head of a twelve year old male with a hole in the skull near the left side of the nose. The 93 axial slices are 1.5 mm thick, with pixel dimensions of 0.8 mm. This study by D.C. Hemmy, MD, of the Medical College of Wisconsin, illustrates the detail present in surfaces constructed by *marching cubes.* Figures 8 and 9 show the bone and soft tissue surfaces respectively. The tube in the patient's mouth is present to administer anesthetic during the scanning process. The soft tissue image shows fine detail that includes the patient's pierced ear and the impression of adhesive tape on the face. Although these details are not clinically significant, they do show the resolution present in the constructed surface. Figure 10 is a tilted view of the soft tissue surface that shows nasal and ear passages. In Figure 11, a sagittal cut, texture mapped with the original

1 Sun Workstation is a trademark of Sun Microsystems.

2 Unix is a trademark of Bell Laboratories.

3 VAX and VMS are trademarks of Digital Equipment Corporation

4 IX/370 is a trademark of IBM.

5 Graphicon is a trademark of General Electric Company.

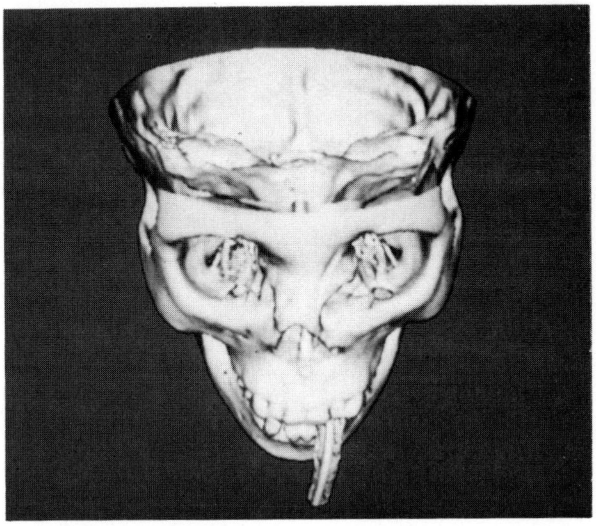

Figure 8. Bone Surface.

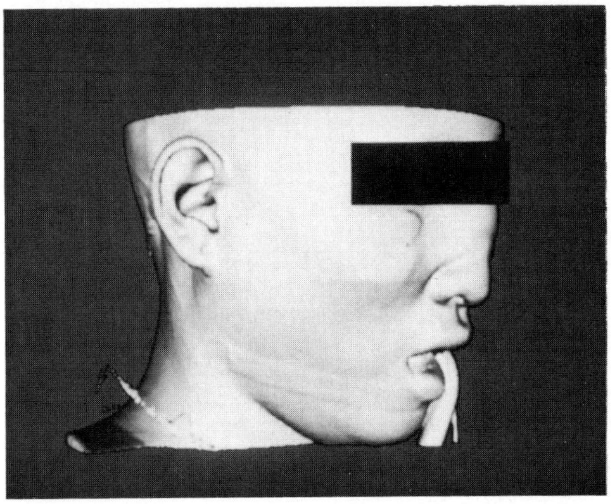

Figure 9. Soft Tissue Surface.

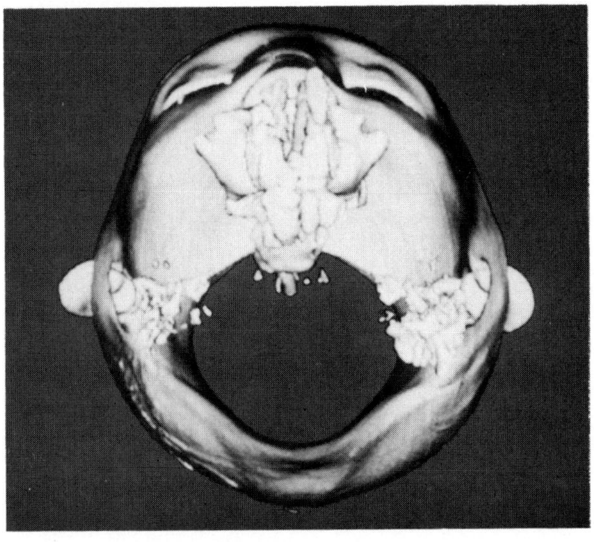

Figure 10. Soft Tissue, Top View.

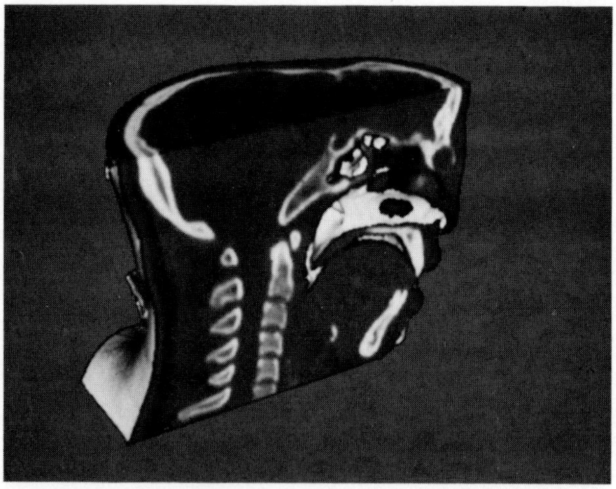

Figure 11. Sagittal Cut with Texture Mapping.

CT data, shows the slice data in relation to the constructed surface. The bone surface contains 550,000 triangles while the soft tissue surface has 375,000.

7.2 Magnetic Resonance.

The MR case of an adult male volunteer consists of 128 1.9 mm coronal slices. A 3D FT, flow compensated, fast sequence acquired the 128 slices in only 9 minutes. This pulse sequence, contrasting the unsaturated spins of the fresh blood flowing into the excited region of saturated spins, was produced by G. Glover of GE Medical Systems Group. Because of the complex anatomy present in the MR slices, we show, in Figure 12, the texture mapped cut surfaces intersected with the surface of the skin. Although the original slices are coronal, we show sagittal cuts to illustrate the algorithm's ability to interpolate texture on a cut plane. The largest surface model in the sequence contains 330,000 triangles, including triangles on the cut surface.

7.3 Single-Photon Emission Computed Tomography.

The SPECT study consisting of 29 coronal slices of the heart shows the algorithm's performance on low resolution data. D. Nowak from GE Medical Systems provided the 64 by 64 pixel data. Figure 13, showing the surface of the blood pool in the diastolic heart, contains 5,000 triangles. The descending aorta is the large vessel in the left of the picture.

8. CONCLUSIONS.

Marching cubes, a new algorithm for 3D surface construction, complements 2D CT, MR, and SPECT data by giving physicians 3D views of the anatomy. The algorithm uses a case table of edge intersections to describe how a surface cuts through each *cube* in a 3D data set. Additional realism is achieved by the calculation, from the original data, of the normalized gradient. The resulting polygonal structure can be displayed on conventional graphics display systems. Although these models often contain large numbers of triangles, surface cutting and connectivity can reduce this number. As CAD hardware increases in speed and capacity, we expect that *marching cubes* will receive increased use in practical, clinical environments.

Recently we developed another high-resolution surface construction algorithm called *dividing cubes* that generates points rather than triangles [10]. As the resolution of the 3D medical data increases, the number of triangles approaches the number of pixels in the displayed image. The density of surface points is chosen to cover the raster display. Both algorithms produce the same quality images, since the shading governs the perceived quality of the image.

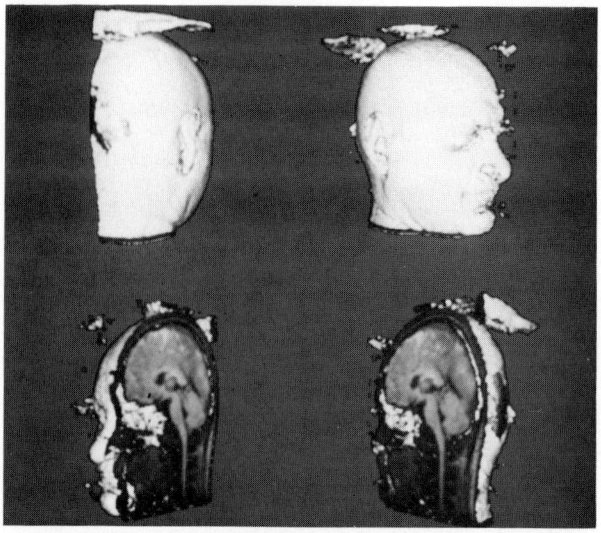

Figure 12. Rotated Sequence of Cut MR Brain.

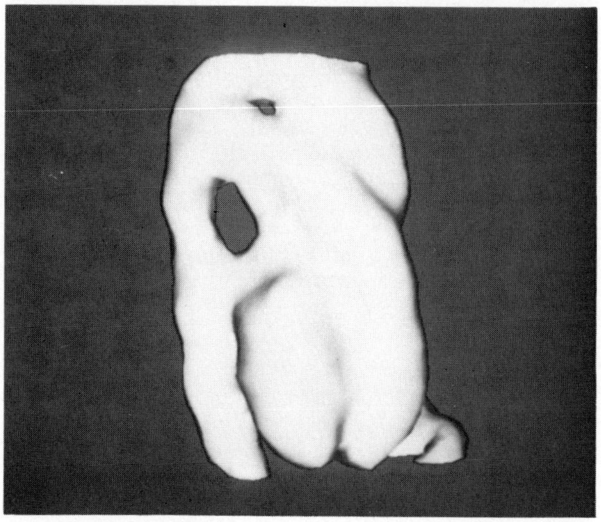

Figure 13. Blood Pool in the Diastolic Heart.

9. ACKNOWLEDGMENT.

We thank C. Crawford from General Electric's Medical Systems for stimulating our work in this area. Throughout the project, he has provided us with data and encouragement to improve the algorithm. R. Redington from our laboratory's Medical Diagnostics Branch provided a stable research environment and insight into the practical applications of 3D in medicine. W. Leue assisted us in converting between the different medical data formats and provided interfaces to our MR equipment.

10. REFERENCES

[1] Artzy, E., Frieder, G., and Herman, G. T. The Theory, Design, Implementation and Evaluation of a Three-Dimensional Surface Detection Algorithm. *Computer Graphics and Image Processing 15*, 1 (January 1981), 1-24.

[2] Barillot, C., Gibaud, B., Scarabin, J., and Coatrieux, J. 3D Reconstruction of Cerebral Blood Vessels. *IEEE Computer Graphics and Applications 5*, 12 (December 1985), 13-19.

[3] Bates, R. H., Garden, K. L., and Peters, T. M. Overview of Computerized Tomography with Emphasis on Future Developments. *Proc. of the IEEE* 71, 3 (March 1983), 356-372.

[4] Bloch, P. and Udupa, J. K. Application of Computerized Tomography to Radiation Therapy and Surgical Planning. *Proc. of the IEEE 71*, 3 (March 1983), 351-355.

[5] Brewster, L. J., Trivedi, S. S., Tut, H. K., and Udupa, J. K. Interactive Surgical Planning. *IEEE Computer Graphics and Applications 4*, 3 (March 1984), 31-40.

[6] Burk, D. L., Mears, D. C., Kennedy, W. H., Cooperstein, L. A., and Herbert, D. L. Three-Dimensional Computed Tomography of Acetabula Fractures. *Radiology 155*, 1 (1985), 183-186.

[7] Chen, L., Herman, G. T., Reynolds, R. A., and Udupa, J. K. Surface Shading in the Cuberille Environment. *IEEE Computer Graphics and Applications 5*, 12 (December 1985), 33-43.

[8] Christiansen, H. N. and Sederberg, T. W. Conversion of Complex Contour Line Definitions into Polygonal Element Meshes. *Computer Graphics 12*, 3 (August 1978), 187-192.

[9] Cline, H. E., Dumoulin, C. L., Lorensen, W. E., Hart, H. R., and Ludke, S. 3D Reconstruction of the Brain from Magnetic Resonance Images. *Magnetic Resonance Imaging* (1987, to appear).

[10] Cline, H. E., Lorensen, W. E., Ludke, S., Crawford, C. R., and Teeter, B. C. High-Resolution Three-Dimensional Reconstruction of Tomograms. *Medical Physics* (1987, to appear).

[11] Cook, L. T., Dwyer, S. J., Batnitzky, S., and Lee, K. R. A Three-Dimensional Display System for Diagnostic Imaging Applications. *IEEE Computer Graphics and Applications 3*, 5 (August 1983), 13-19.

[12] Farrell, E. J. Color Display and Interactive Interpretation of Three-Dimensional Data. *IBM J. Res. Develop 27*, 4 (July 1983), 356-366.

[13] Farrell, E. J., Zappulla, R., and Yang, W. C. Color 3D Imaging of Normal and Pathologic Intracranial Structures. *IEEE Computer Graphics and Applications 4*, 9 (September 1984), 5-17.

[14] Fuchs, H., Kedem, Z. M., and Uselton, S. P. Optimal Surface Reconstruction from Planar Contours. *Comm. of the ACM 20*, 10 (October 1977), 693-702.

[15] Gordon, D. and Reynolds, R. A. Image Space Shading of 3-Dimensional Objects. *Computer Graphics and Image Processing 29*, 3 (March 1985), 361-376.

[16] Hale, J. D., Valk, P. E., and Watts, J. C. MR Imaging of Blood Vessels Using Three-Dimensional Reconstruction: Methodology. *Radiology 157*, 3 (December 1985), 727-733.

[17] Hemmy, D. C., David, D. J., and Herman, G. T. Three-Dimensional Reconstruction of Craniofacial Deformity Using Computed Tomography. *Neurosurgery 13*, 5 (November 1983), 534-541.

[18] Hemmy, D. C. and Tessier, P. L. CT of Dry Skulls with Craniofacial Deformities: Accuracy of Three-Dimensional Reconstruction. *Radiology 157*, 1 (October 1985), 113-116.

[19] Herman, G. T. and Udupa, J. K. Display of 3D Digital Images: Computational Foundations and Medical Applications. *IEEE Computer Graphics and Applications 3*, 5 (August 1983), 39-46.

[20] Hinshaw, W. S. and Lent, A. H. An Introduction to NMR Imaging: From the Bloch Equation to the Imaging Equation. *Proc. of the IEEE 71*, 3 (March 1983), 338-350.

[21] Hoffman, E. A. and Ritman, E. L. Shape and Dimensions of Cardiac Chambers: Importance of CT Section Thickness and Orientation. *Radiology* 155, 3 (June 1985), 739-744.

[22] Hohne, K. H. and Bernstein, R. Shading 3D-Images from CT Using Gray-Level Gradients. *IEEE Trans. on Medical Imaging MI-5*, 1 (March 1986), 45-47.

[23] Keppel, E. Approximating Complex Surfaces by Triangulation of Contour Lines. *IBM J. Res. Develop 19*, 1 (January 1975), 2-11.

[24] Knoll, G. F. Single-Photon Emission Computed Tomography. *Proc. of the IEEE 71*, 3 (March 1983), 320-329.

[25] Meagher, D. J. Geometric Modeling Using Octree Encoding. *Computer Graphics and Image Processing 19*, 2 (June 1982), 129-147.

[26] Robb, R. A., Hoffman, E. A., Sinak, L. J., Harris, L. D., and Ritman, E. L. High-Speed Three-Dimensional X-Ray Computed Tomography: The Dynamic Spatial Reconstructor. *Proc. of the IEEE 71*, 3 (March 1983), 308-319.

[27] Sunguroff, A. and Greenberg, D. Computer Generated Images for Medical Application. *Computer Graphics 12*, 3 (August 1978), 196-202.

[28] Sutherland, I. E. and Hodgman, G. W. Reentrant Polygon Clipping. *Comm. of the ACM 17*, 1 (January 1974), 32-42.

[29] Trivedi, S. S., Herman, G. T., and Udupa, J. K. Segmentation Into Three Classes Using Gradients. *IEEE Trans. on Medical Imaging MI-5*, 2 (June 1986), 116-119.

[30] Udupa, J. K. Interactive Segmentation and Boundary Surface Formation for 3-D Digital Images. *Computer Graphics and Image Processing 18*, 3 (March 1982), 213-235.

[31] Vannier, M. W., Marsh, J. L., and Warren, J. O. Three Dimensional CT Reconstruction Images for Craniofacial Surgical Planning and Evaluation. *Radiology 150*, 1 (January 1984), 179-184.

[32] Zucker, S. W. and Hummel, R. A. A Three-Dimensional Edge Operator. *IEEE Trans. on Pattern Analysis and Machine Intelligence PAMI-3*, 3 (May 1981), 324-331.

Efficient Algorithms for 3D Scan-Conversion of Parametric Curves, Surfaces, and Volumes

Arie Kaufman

Department of Computer Science
State University of New York at Stony Brook
Stony Brook, NY 11794-4400

Abstract

Three-dimensional (3D) scan-conversion algorithms, . that scan-convert 3D parametric objects into their discrete voxel-map representation within a Cubic Frame Buffer (CFB), are presented. The parametric objects that are studied include Bezier form of cubic parametric curves, bicubic parametric surface patches, and tricubic parametric volumes. The converted objects in discrete 3D space maintain pre-defined application-dependent connectivity and fidelity requirements.

The algorithms introduced here employ third-order forward difference techniques. Efficient versions of the algorithms based on first-order decision mechanisms, which employ only integer arithmetic, are also discussed. All algorithms are incremental and use only simple operations inside the inner algorithm loops. They perform scan-conversion with computational complexity which is linear in the number of voxels written to the CFB. All the algorithms have been implemented as part of the *CUBE Architecture*, which is a voxel-based system for 3D graphics.

CR Categories and Subject Descriptors: I.3.3 [**Computer Graphics**]: Picture/Image Generation; I.3.5 [**Computer Graphics**]: Computational Geometry and Object Modeling; I.3.7 [**Computer Graphics**]: Three-Dimensional Graphics and Realism.

General Terms: Algorithms, Computer Graphics.

Additional Key Words and Phrases: Bezier curves, Bezier surfaces, Bezier volumes, cubic frame buffer, three-dimensional scan conversion, voxel.

This work was supported by the National Science Foundation under grant DCR-86-03603.

1. Introduction

Three primary representation domains are common for graphical data: the *continuous geometric model*, the *discrete pixel image*, and the *discrete voxel image*. The former two representations have received considerable attention in the literature, and there is an abundance of 2D scan-conversion algorithms which are fundamental to raster systems. Such an algorithm converts a 2D continuous geometric representation into a set of pixels in the pixel-image plane. Recent papers [16, 18] have introduced and developed the notion of a *three-dimensional (3D) scan-conversion algorithm*, which converts a 3D analytic representation into a set of voxels in the discrete voxel domain. We focus here on 3D scan-conversion algorithms for the following 3D parametric objects:

- Cubic parametric curves
- Bicubic parametric surface patches
- Tricubic parametric volumes

There are four voxel-image space architectures, CUBE [13-15], GODPA [11], PARCUM [12], and $3DP^4$ [21], and many other voxel-based software systems that have been reported in the literature. The theme of these systems is that the 3D inherently continuous scene is discretized, sampled, and stored in a large 3D cubic frame buffer of unit cells called volume elements or *voxels*. A CFB with 512^3 resolution and 8-bit-deep voxels, for example, is a large memory buffer of size 128M bytes. As computer memories are getting significantly cheaper and more compact, such huge memories and consequently voxel-based hardware systems are becoming more and more practical.

All the four voxel-based architectures utilize high performance multi-processing architecture to generate shaded projections of the 3D scene within the cubic buffer. They all assume that a database of voxel-based objects exists for loading into the CFB. Unlike the other systems that operate solely in the discrete voxel-image space, CUBE further provides object space capabilities and ways to intermix the two ([17]). The object-space capabilities are enabled using a spectrum of 3D scan-conversion algorithms [16, 18], those that pertain to parametric curves, surfaces and volumes are discussed in this paper. All these algorithms have been implemented as part of the 3D geometry processor of the CUBE architecture. They enable CUBE to cater to a wide variety of applications which accept a geometric representation of the 3D scene as well as sampled experimental data.

Although the voxel representation is more effective for empirical imagery, it also has a significant utility in synthetic 3D graphics or in applications merging empirical and synthetic images. For example, a synthetic injection needle or a scalpel can be superimposed on an ultrasound image, or a model of the skull can be overlaid, possibly with semi-transparent colors, upon a computed tomography scan of the skull. As a consequence of the proliferation of voxel-based systems, there is a growing need for mechanisms to input geometric models into such systems. The uniqueness of the CUBE architecture is in providing such a mechanism for a geometric model to be discretized and optionally overlaid upon and/or compared with the experimental data.

Terms used in the rest of the paper and the requirements from a 3D scan-converter are outlined in Section 2. The basic avenues to access the CFB are sketched in Section 3, followed by the 3D scan-conversion algorithms for curves (in Sections 4, 5 and 6), for surfaces (in Sections 7, 8 and 9), and for volumes (in Sections 10 and 11). The algorithms are described in pseudo-C where the C keywords are in **bold** face. Variables are shown in *italics* font. Comments are enclosed between a pair of double quotes and printed in "*italics*". Definitions are C language type definitions. Subscripts, superscripts and array notations are used interchangeably.

2. Terminology and Requirements

Most of the terms used in this paper for 3D discrete topology are generalizations of those used in 2D discrete topology (see e.g., [19, 22, 24, 25]). Let us mark the continuous 3D space by R^3, and the discrete 3D voxel-image space, which is a 3D array of grid points, by Z^3. We shall term a *voxel* or the *region contained by a 3D discrete point* (x, y, z), as the continuous region (u, v, w) such that $x-0.5<u\leq x+0.5$, $y-0.5<v\leq y+0.5$ and $z-0.5<w\leq z+0.5$. This assumes that the voxel "occupies" a unit cube centered at the grid point (x,y,z), and the array of voxels tessellates Z^3. Although there is a slight difference between a grid point and a voxel, they will be used interchangeably.

Each voxel $(x,y,z)\in Z^3$ has three kinds of *neighbors*:

(1) It has six *direct neighbors (face neighbors)*: $(x+1,y,z)$, $(x-1,y,z)$, $(x,y+1,z)$, $(x,y-1,z)$, $(x,y,z+1)$, and $(x,y,z-1)$.

(2) It has twelve *indirect neighbors (edge neighbors)*: $(x+1,y+1,z)$, $(x-1,y+1,z)$, $(x+1,y-1,z)$, $(x-1,y-1,z)$, $(x+1,y,z+1)$, $(x-1,y,z+1)$, $(x+1,y,z-1)$, $(x-1,y,z-1)$, $(x,y+1,z+1)$, $(x,y-1,z+1)$, $(x,y+1,z-1)$, and $(x,y-1,z-1)$.

(3) It has eight *remote neighbors (corner neighbors)*: $(x+1,y+1,z+1)$, $(x+1,y+1,z-1)$, $(x+1,y-1,z+1)$, $(x+1,y-1,z-1)$, $(x-1,y+1,z+1)$, $(x-1,y+1,z-1)$, $(x-1,y-1,z+1)$, and $(x-1,y-1,z-1)$.

We further define in Z^3 the six direct neighbors as *6-neighbors*. Both the six direct and twelve indirect neighbors are defined as *18-neighbors*. All three kinds of neighbors are defined as *26-neighbors*. A *6-connected path* is a sequence of voxels such that consecutive pairs are 6-neighbors. An *18-connected path* is a sequence of 18-neighbor voxels, while a *26-connected path* is a sequence of 26-neighbor voxels.

Three metrics on Z^3, which correspond to the three connectivity kinds, are defined. The *6-distance* between two voxels (x_1,y_1,z_1) and (x_2,y_2,z_2) is:

$$d_6 = |x_2-x_1| + |y_2-y_1| + |z_2-z_1| \quad (1)$$

which is the length of the shortest 6-connected path between them. The *26-distance* between two voxels is:

$$d_{26} = \max(\ |x_2-x_1|,\ |y_2-y_1|,\ |z_2-z_1|\ ) \quad (2)$$

which is the length of the shortest 26-connected path between them. The *18-distance* between two voxels is:

$$d_{18} = \max\left(d_{26}, \left\lceil \frac{d_6}{2} \right\rceil\right) \quad (3)$$

which is the length of the shortest 18-connected path between them.

A 3D scan-converter is required to obey some fidelity, connectivity, and efficiency requirements. These requirements are met by the algorithms presented in this paper. The basic fidelity requirements in scan-converting an object from R^3 to Z^3 are:

1) The discrete points, for which the region contained by them is entirely inside the continuous object, are in the converted discrete object.

2) The discrete points, for which the region contained by them is entirely outside the continuous object, are not in the converted discrete object.

Obviously, some discrete points will not belong to either of the above cases, and more guidelines are necessary. Those are:

3) If the object is a curve (1D object), the converted object will meet certain connectivity requirements. The converted endpoints will be in the converted object.

4) If the object is a surface (2D object), it will meet certain "lack of tunnels" connectivity requirements. The converted curved "edges" will be in the converted object.

5) If the object is a volume (3D object), its "inside" will be converted according to requirement 1. Other points will be treated by majority decision - the discrete point is in the object if more than half its region is in the continuous object.

For curves we shall require 6-connectivity, 18-connectivity or 26-connectivity, depending on implementation needs. For surfaces we shall require lack of 6-connected tunnels. 18-connectivity or 26-connected tunnels can also be disallowed depending on implementation requirements. For solid volumes 6-connectivity will be required in order to avoid any internal cavities.

As we show later the computational complexity of the algorithms is equal to the number of discrete points converted multiplied by a constant. The goals are, thus, to attempt to decrease the constant, and to use simple operations within inner algorithm loops. Furthermore, we will strive to use integer arithmetic whenever possible, and fixed-point arithmetic only when impossible otherwise.

3. Cubic Frame Buffer Access

We assume here that the CFB access system of the CUBE architecture accepts the point/voxel location in three (X, Y and Z) registers, and its color in a fourth register, *COLOR*. The algorithms access the CFB using the following auxiliary functions. Each of the first 3 functions executes in one machine instruction and should therefore be fast:

1) *NEW_POS (axis, value);*
This function assigns *value* to the *axis* register (*X, Y*, or *Z*).

2) *UPDATE_POS (axis, increment);*
Increments (decrements) the *axis* register in one machine instruction, where *increment* is the coordinate step.

3) *PUT_VOXEL ();*
Writes the voxel, whose address is in the X, Y, and Z registers with color as in the *COLOR* register, into the CFB.

4) *WRITE_VOXEL (x, y, z, c);*
Updates the *X, Y, Z* and *COLOR* registers with the specified parameters, and then calls *PUT_VOXEL* to "put" the voxel into the CFB.

4. Parametric Polynomial Curves

A parametric polynomial 3D curve is defined as polynomials of some parameter t, one for each x, y, and z. Varying the parameter, e.g., from 0 to 1, defines all the points along the curve segment. Many systems, including ours, use polynomials of the third degree, since this is the lowest degree parametric polynomial that can describe a well-formed 3D curve with four boundary constraints. Matrix notation of the cubic polynomial of the curve f is:

$$f(t) = T\ M\ G \qquad 0 \le t \le 1 \tag{4}$$

$$T = [t^3\ \ t^2\ \ t\ \ 1] \qquad G = \begin{bmatrix} G_1 \\ G_2 \\ G_3 \\ G_4 \end{bmatrix} \tag{5}$$

the 4×4 matrix M is the geometric basis matrix, G is the geometric vector (G_i are the geometric *control points*), and $M\ G$ is the coefficients of the cubic polynomial.

Common cubic representations are *Hermite* form [7, 10], *B-Spline* form [8, 23], and *Bezier* form [1-3]. In the latter, G_1 and G_4 are the curve endpoints, while $3(G_2-G_1)$ and $3(G_4-G_3)$ are the end tangents. The matrix M for the Bezier representation is:

$$M_b = \begin{bmatrix} -1 & 3 & -3 & 1 \\ 3 & -6 & 3 & 0 \\ -3 & 3 & 0 & 0 \\ 1 & 0 & 0 & 0 \end{bmatrix} \tag{6}$$

In Bezier form the curve resides wholly within the convex hull of its control points G_i. In this paper, curves are assumed to be in Bezier form which is widely used in graphics and geometric design. There is no loss of generality in this assumption, since all cubic curves have their Bezier representation.

Direct evaluation of the 3D curve points from the polynomial of Equation 4 is computationally intensive, even when Horner's rule is employed. An alternative method for scan-conversion is repeated bisection of the curve until the segments reside within a single discrete point (e.g., [6, 20]). Another mechanism, which is the one explored in this paper, is using the curve's third order finite forward difference matrix for a step size ϵ along the parameter t [6, 9]. The initial difference vector Δf_0 is obtained by:

$$\Delta f_0 = \begin{bmatrix} \Delta^0 f_0 \\ \Delta^1 f_0 \\ \Delta^2 f_0 \\ \Delta^3 f_0 \end{bmatrix} = E_\epsilon\ M\ G = \begin{bmatrix} 0 & 0 & 0 & 1 \\ \epsilon^3 & \epsilon^2 & \epsilon & 0 \\ 6\epsilon^3 & 2\epsilon^2 & 0 & 0 \\ 6\epsilon^3 & 0 & 0 & 0 \end{bmatrix} M\ G \tag{7}$$

Now, it is used to repeatedly obtain the differences of the next step using the following third order DDA (Digital Differential Analyzer) calculations:

$$\begin{aligned} \Delta^0 f_{i+1} &= \Delta^0 f_i + \Delta^1 f_i \\ \Delta^1 f_{i+1} &= \Delta^1 f_i + \Delta^2 f_i \qquad 0 \le i < \frac{1}{\epsilon} \\ \Delta^2 f_{i+1} &= \Delta^2 f_i + \Delta^3 f_i \\ \Delta^3 f_{i+1} &= \Delta^3 f_i \end{aligned} \tag{8}$$

and $\Delta^0 f_{i+1}$ is the next step polynomial value. These calculations require only three additions per step per ordinate, while the alternative method of utilizing the Horner's rule requires three additions and three multiplications per step per ordinate.

5. 3D Scan-Conversion of Curves

The formal data type **curve** is:

```
typedef struct curve {
        int g [3][4];           "x, y, z for 4 control points"
        color c;                "color of curve"
} curve;
```

where the 3×4 control matrix g is the four Bezier geometric control points. The coordinates are assumed to be integers or fixed-point which can be scaled up to some finite resolution integer domain. The algorithm *CURVE*, presented in Figure 1, scan-converts a 3D third degree parametric curve in the parameter t according to the forward difference equations (Eq. 8). The only problem remaining is to calculate a step size ϵ along the parameter t so as to guarantee at least 26-connectivity, that is, guaranteeing that the first difference along any dimension is not greater than 1 in magnitude. In first approximation, this is the same as:

$$\max_{0 \le t \le 1} \left(\left|\frac{dx}{dt}\right|, \left|\frac{dy}{dt}\right|, \left|\frac{dz}{dt}\right| \right) \le 1 \tag{9}$$

To find the maximum, the extrema of the second degree derivatives of the parametric equations in the range $0 \le t \le 1$ are found by differentiation. The maximum for each component is thus:

$$n_x = \max \left(\left|\frac{dx(0)}{dt}\right|, \left|\frac{dx(1)}{dt}\right|, \left|\frac{dx(\alpha)}{dt}\right| \right) \tag{10}$$

$$n_y = \max \left(\left|\frac{dy(0)}{dt}\right|, \left|\frac{dy(1)}{dt}\right|, \left|\frac{dy(\beta)}{dt}\right| \right) \tag{11}$$

$$n_z = \max \left(\left|\frac{dz(0)}{dt}\right|, \left|\frac{dz(1)}{dt}\right|, \left|\frac{dz(\gamma)}{dt}\right| \right) \tag{12}$$

where α, β, and γ are the t values for which the linear second derivatives of the curve equation are respectively 0, provided that $0 \le \alpha, \beta, \gamma \le 1$. The maximum magnitude of these extrema, $n = \max(n_x, n_y, n_z)$, is the inverse of the required algorithm step ϵ. A small term is first added to n, e.g., rounding up, to compensate for the approximation. The one time

```
Find maximum absolute value of dx/dt, dy/dt, dz/dt for
0 ≤ t ≤ 1 (Eqs. 10-12), set n to maximum of these maxima;
ε = 1/CEILING (n);

Calculate initial difference vectors Δx, Δy, Δz by multiplying
matrix E_ε by matrix M_b and control points g (Eq. 7);

WRITE_VOXEL (ROUND(Δ⁰x), ROUND(Δ⁰y), ROUND(Δ⁰z), c);

for (t = 0; t ≤ 1; t += ε) {          "follow the curve"

      Δ⁰x += Δ¹x;                      "apply Eq. 8 for x"
      Δ¹x += Δ²x;
      Δ²x += Δ³x;

      Δ⁰y += Δ¹y;                      "apply Eq. 8 for y"
      Δ¹y += Δ²y;
      Δ²y += Δ³y;

      Δ⁰z += Δ¹z;                      "apply Eq. 8 for z"
      Δ¹z += Δ²z;
      Δ²z += Δ³z;

      WRITE_VOXEL(ROUND(Δ⁰x),ROUND(Δ⁰y),ROUND(Δ⁰z),c);
}
```

Figure 1: *CURVE* - Algorithm for 3D Scan-Converting Curves

floating-point computation of the step ϵ requires 9 multiplications, 9 additions, 4 divisions, 8 comparisons, and one rounding.

Algorithm time complexity is linear in the maximum magnitude n, which should come near the number of painted voxels. This is so for all curves which are not too oscillative, wavy or self-intersecting. It is reasonable to assume that the curves, or series of sub-curves, dealt with here, which are third degree Bezier polynomials, belong to this class.

Each step of the algorithm loop, i.e., each voxel written into the CFB, takes 10 floating-point additions, one floating-point test, 3 roundings of floating-point numbers to integer coordinates, and one *WRITE_VOXEL*. These heavy floating-point computations are a result of the fact that the forward differences, being the first, second, and third order slopes, are floating-point numbers or fractional binary numbers (powers of the step ϵ). These difficulties with *CURVE* computations can be overcome by converting the variables to integers. A more efficient curve algorithm, *FAST_CURVE*, which uses only integer arithmetic, is discussed in the next section.

6. Efficient 3D Scan-Conversion of Curves

The forward differences are acting as first, second, and third order DDA's, where the vector $\Delta^1 f_i$ is the first order x, y, z slopes of the curve, which is used incrementally to update the voxel position $\Delta^0 f_{i+1}$ at step $i+1$ (Equation 8). The rounded coordinates of $\Delta^0 f_{i+1}$ are then used as the three integer coordinates of the $(i+1)$-st voxel written into the CFB.

Instead, a decision process can determine at each step of the algorithm which of the 26 neighbors of the current voxel lies closer to the curve being approximated. The process selects the next voxel by considering one dimension at a time, and the decision on any dimension, i.e., no change, increment, or decrement the coordinate, is independent of the other two dimensions. The variables $\Delta^0 x, \Delta^0 y, \Delta^0 z$ are used now as the *decision variables* of the algorithm, representing the residual change in the respective coordinate.

The decision process for x, for example, is as follows. Assuming that x is the current coordinate, then if $\Delta^0 x \geq 0.5$, i.e., the curve is passing closer to $x+1$ than to x, the register X is incremented (using *UPDATE_POS* function) and $\Delta^0 x$ is decremented by 1. Similarly if $\Delta^0 x \leq -0.5$, then X is decremented and $\Delta^0 x$ is incremented. Otherwise, X and $\Delta^0 x$ are unchanged. The residual value of $\Delta^0 x$ is passed to the next step, where it is first being updated by the first order slopes. Similar decision processes hold for y and z. These decision processes enable the algorithm to avoid the rounding of the three coordinates.

Furthermore, since the same decision processes hold also after scaling up the algorithm variables by a positive value, they can be transformed to all-integer processes (cf. [5]). In order to convert the forward differences to integers and to avoid the use of the fractional step ϵ at all, the E_ϵ matrix of Equation 7 is redefined by scaling it up by the positive integer scalar $2n^3$:

$$E_n = 2n^3 E_\epsilon = \begin{bmatrix} 0 & 0 & 0 & 2n^3 \\ 2 & 2n & 2n^2 & 0 \\ 12 & 4n & 0 & 0 \\ 12 & 0 & 0 & 0 \end{bmatrix} \tag{13}$$

As a result the initial difference vector is redefined as:

$$\Delta f_0 = \begin{bmatrix} \Delta^0 f_0 \\ \Delta^1 f_0 \\ \Delta^2 f_0 \\ \Delta^3 f_0 \end{bmatrix} = E_n \; M \; G \tag{14}$$

Since both E_n and $M\,G$ are integer matrices the initial difference vector and consequently the forward differences (computed by Equation 8) are all integers. The variables of the algorithm are also scaled up by $2n^3$, and thus the use of the step ϵ and the floating-point variables within the loop of the algorithm are completely avoided. In particular, the parameter t is now an integer, stepping by one from 0 to n. Note that the constants n^3 and $2n^3$ should be computed only once at initialization.

The algorithm *FAST_CURVE*, displayed in Figure 2, is the algorithm *CURVE* modified to include the all-integer decision processes. The time complexity of this efficient version of the algorithm is also linear with the number of voxels written into the CFB. However, writting a single voxel requires now between 9 to 12 additions, 4 to 7 tests, an increment, all in integer, and 0 to 3 *UPDATE_POS* calls and one *PUT_VOXEL*. Note also that 0 to 3 calls to *UPDATE_POS* and one *PUT_VOXEL* are faster than a single *WRITE_VOXEL* (see Section 3). This cost per voxel is much more attractive than the original all floating-point loop (cf. Section 5).

```
Find maximum absolute value of dx/dt, dy/dt, dz/dt for
0 ≤ t ≤ 1 (Eqs. 10-12), set n to maximum of these maxima;
Calculate initial difference vectors Δx, Δy, Δz by Eq. 14;
Set Δ⁰x, Δ⁰y, Δ⁰z to 0;
NEW_POS (g[0][0], g[1][0], g[2][0]);            "start point"
for (t = 0; t ≤ n; t++) {                        "follow the curve"
    if (Δ⁰x > n³) {                              "decision for x"
        UPDATE_POS (X,1);                        "increment x"
        Δ⁰x -= 2n³; }
    else if (Δ⁰x < -n³) {
        UPDATE_POS (X,-1);                       "decrement x"
        Δ⁰x += 2n³; }
    Δ⁰x += Δ¹x;
    Δ¹x += Δ²x;
    Δ²x += Δ³x;

    if (Δ⁰y > n³) {                              "decision for y"
        UPDATE_POS (Y,1);                        "increment y"
        Δ⁰y -= 2n³; }
    else if (Δ⁰y < -n³) {
        UPDATE_POS (Y,-1);                       "decrement y"
        Δ⁰y += 2n³; }
    Δ⁰y += Δ¹y;
    Δ¹y += Δ²y;
    Δ²y += Δ³y;

    if (Δ⁰z > n³) {                              "decision for z"
        UPDATE_POS (Z,1);                        "increment z"
        Δ⁰z -= 2n³; }
    else if (Δ⁰z < -n³) {
        UPDATE_POS (Z,-1);                       "decrement z"
        Δ⁰z += 2n³; }
    Δ⁰z += Δ¹z;
    Δ¹z += Δ²z;
    Δ²z += Δ³z;

    PUT_VOXEL ();                                "in CFB"
}
```

Figure 2: *FAST_CURVE* - An Efficient Algorithm for 3D Scan-Converting Curves

Both algorithms *CURVE* and *FAST_CURVE* handle the three coordinates independently, and therefore one, two and/or three coordinates may be simultaneously changed at any step. Consequently, the resulting curve is a 26-connected path in Z^3 of length $n_{26} = \max(n_x, n_y, n_z)$ voxels. In order to obtain a 6-connected path, that is, one coordinate at the most changes at any step, the algorithm may increment (decrement) only the coordinate with the largest magnitude decision variable. For example, if $|\Delta^0 x|$ is the largest, then x is the only candidate for a change, which is contingent to $|\Delta^0 x| > n^3$. The length in voxels of this curve is $n_6 = n_x + n_y + n_z$.

Similarly, in order to obtain an 18-connected path, i.e., two coordinates at the most change at any step, the algorithm does not change the coordinate with the smallest magnitude of the decision variable. The other two coordinates, however, may or may not be incremented (decremented), depending on whether their respective decision variable magnitude is greater than n^3. The length in voxels of this curve is $n_{18} = \max(n_{26}, \lceil n_6/2 \rceil)$.

7. Parametric Polynomial Surfaces

Bicubic parametric polynomial surfaces are cubic polynomials of two parameters t and u. As both parameters vary across the (0, 1) range, all the points on the surface patch are defined. The two-parameter representation is:

$$f(t,u) = T\ M\ G\ M^{\dagger}\ U^{\dagger} \qquad 0 \le t, u \le 1 \tag{15}$$

$$U = [u^3\ \ u^2\ \ u\ \ 1] \tag{16}$$

T and M are the same as for curves. Again, we use the Bezier form where G is the 4×4 control point matrix, and G_{11}, G_{14}, G_{41}, G_{44} are the surface patch "corners". The properties of the Bezier curves also hold for the Bezier surfaces. Therefore, the forward difference method can be used for surfaces too. The initial 4×4 forward difference matrix Δf_{00} is obtained by multiplying the difference operator by the algebraic matrix $M\ G\ M^{\dagger}$ [9]:

$$\Delta f_{00} = E_{\epsilon}\, M\ G\ M^{\dagger}\, E_{\delta}^{\dagger} \tag{17}$$

where ϵ and δ are the step size in the t and the u parameters, respectively. A bicubic surface in t and u can be drawn as a sequence of cubic curves, where u is a constant and t varies from 0 to 1 using a curve forward difference process. The inter-curve iteration is very similar to that of the intra-curve, but it is performed on all rows of Δf_{00}. This is further explained in the next section in the context of the 3D scan-conversion algorithm for surfaces.

8. 3D Scan-Conversion of Surfaces

The formal data type **surface** represents a bicubic surface patch:

```
typedef struct surface {
        int g[3][4][4];          "x, y, z for 16 control points"
        color c;                 "surface color"
} surface;
```

The 3×4×4 control matrix g is the 16 Bezier geometric control points of the bicubic Bezier patch. When scan-converting such a surface we guarantee lack of 6-connected tunnels. This is achieved if the first difference (in first approximation - the partial derivative) of the surface in each of the parameters is bounded by 1 in magnitude. Thus, we must find the extrema of the derivatives over the surface patch, n for t and m for u, and set the step size in each parameter to their inverse. These extrema are difficult to compute, so we shall use the maxima of the derivatives of the components, and require that they be less than $1/\sqrt{3}$ to guarantee the above requirement. Unfortunately, even finding these extrema is not trivial and requires solving high-degree equations which is very time consuming, and therefore not acceptable.

Instead, we will show that the derivatives of a Bezier surface are also Bezier surfaces, and the convex hull property guarantees bounding derivatives. Finding the bound on $\partial f / \partial t$ is as follows. The D_t-differentiating operator and the derivative of the surface with respect to the parameter t are:

† means transposed

$$D_t = \begin{bmatrix} 0 & 0 & 0 & 0 \\ 3 & 0 & 0 & 0 \\ 0 & 2 & 0 & 0 \\ 0 & 0 & 1 & 0 \end{bmatrix} \quad (18)$$

$$\frac{\partial f\,(t\,,u\,)}{\partial t} = T\ D_t\ M_b\ G\ M_b^{\dagger}\ U^{\dagger} \quad (19)$$

$$= T\ M_b\ (M_b^{-1}\ D_t\ M_b\ G\ )\ M_b^{\dagger}\ U^{\dagger}$$

The term in parentheses in Equation 19 is the control point matrix $G_f^{'}$ for the $\partial f\ /\partial t$ surface in Bezier representation, thus its D_{t_b}-differentiating operator in Bezier representation is:

$$D_{t_b} = M_b^{-1}\ D_t\ M_b = \begin{bmatrix} -3 & 3 & 0 & 0 \\ -1 & -1 & 2 & 0 \\ 0 & -2 & 1 & 1 \\ 0 & 0 & -3 & 3 \end{bmatrix} \quad (20)$$

Now we find the bound on the derivative as the maximum of the offset between all the control points of the $\partial f\ /\partial t$ surface. After finding all the offsets, set:

$$n_x^{'} = \max(G_x^{'}\ )\text{-}\min(G_x^{'}\ )$$

$$n_y^{'} = \max(G_y^{'}\ )\text{-}\min(G_y^{'}\ )$$

$$n_z^{'} = \max(G_z^{'}\ )\text{-}\min(G_z^{'}\ ) \quad (21)$$

$$\epsilon = \frac{1}{n} = \frac{1}{\sqrt{3}} \min\left(\frac{1}{n_x^{'}}, \frac{1}{n_y^{'}}, \frac{1}{n_z^{'}} \right)$$

Similarly, calculate δ and m using the D_u matrices. Note that symmetry provides $D_u = D_t^{\dagger}$.

The algorithm to scan-convert a 3D bicubic parametric surface employs the forward differences iteration to evaluate the surface as a sequence of cubic curves $f\ (t\,,0)$, $f\ (t\,,\delta)$, $f\ (t\,,2\delta)$, $\cdots$, each of which is computed using a 1D curve forward difference iteration similar to the one described for curves. The computation of the initial endpoint of each of the curves is done by a similar 2D iteration.

The algorithm first calculates the difference matrix $\Delta f_{\ 00}$ (using Equation 17) for each of its components, i.e., the 4×4 matrices Δx_{tu}, Δy_{tu}, and Δz_{tu}. The zero column of Δx_{tu} contains the initial values $\Delta^0 x_t$, $\Delta^1 x_t$, $\Delta^2 x_t$, $\Delta^3 x_t$ used as the x forward differences of the curve $f\ (t\,,u_0)$ for the current u_0 (u_0 is constant, t varies). Similarly the zero column of Δy_{tu} and Δz_{tu} are utilized for the y and z components. After scan-converting the curve $f\ (t\,,u_0)$ the difference matrices Δx_{tu}, Δy_{tu}, and Δz_{tu} are updated as 2D forward differences. Namely, column 1 of these matrices is added to their column 0, column 2 is added to column 1, and column 3 is added to column 2. Now column 0 contains the initial difference vectors for the next curve $f\ (t\,,u_0{+}1)$.

The algorithm complexity is $\mathbf{O}(n\ m\,)$ which is linear in the number of painted voxels. Each voxel drawn in the inner loop of such an algorithm requires the calculation of 10 non-integer additions, a voxel write (including 3 *ROUND* operations), and an inner loop completion test. This is in addition to 37 non-integer additions, copying 12 elements, and a loop completion test for each u. Initialization involves the non-integer computation of the coefficients, ϵ, δ, and the initial difference matrices.

9. Efficient 3D Scan-Conversion of Surfaces

Like for the curve algorithm, the heavy non-integer computations can be replaced by a more efficient all-integer algorithm, *FAST_SURFACE*, presented in Figure 3. The idea is very similar to that used by the *FAST_CURVE* algorithm, namely, scaling the program variables up by a large constant so that all the algorithm variables, including the forward differences, are integers, and using decision processes to set the coordinates of the next voxel. More specifically, the matrix E_δ is redefined as E_m:

$$E_m = m^3\ E_\delta = \begin{bmatrix} 0 & 0 & 0 & m^3 \\ 1 & m & m^2 & 0 \\ 6 & 2m & 0 & 0 \\ 6 & 0 & 0 & 0 \end{bmatrix} \quad (22)$$

while the matrix E_ϵ is redefined as E_n (Equation 13). As a result the initial difference matrix $\Delta f_{\ 00}$, defined originally in Equation 17, is redefined as:

$$\Delta f_{\ 00} = E_n\ P\ E_m^{\ \dagger} = 2n^3 m^3 E_\epsilon\ P\ E_\delta^{\ \dagger} \quad (23)$$

The coordinates of the next voxel along the curve $f\ (t\,,u_0)$ are selected based on three decision processes, one for each dimension. In the x decision process, for example, the absolute magnitude of the decision variable $\Delta^0 x_t$ is tested against the threshold $n^3 m^3$ to determine whether to increment, decrement or leave unchanged the X register holding the x ordinate. These inner loop decision processes are identical to those employed by the *FAST_CURVE* algorithm.

The curve scan-conversion process is repeated for all the $m+1$ curves, $u=0,1,...,m$. In order to get the initial difference values for the next curve, the algorithm updates the difference matrices as a 2D forward difference and then steps along the curve $f\ (0,u\,)$ (see Figure 3). The scan-conversion of this curve also involves three decision processes. The decision process for x, for example, tests the decision variable $\Delta^{00} x_{tu}$, and the variable x_u is accordingly incremented, decremented, or remains unchanged. The point $(x_u\,, y_u\,, z_u\,)$ is the starting point of the next curve to be scan-converted by the inner loop. Note, that unlike the variables Δx_{tu}, Δy_{tu}, Δz_{tu} which are scaled up by the scalar $2n^3 m^3$, the coordinates $(x_u\,, y_u\,, z_u\,)$, starting at the first endpoint, represents all along actual voxel coordinates.

The time complexity of the efficient version of the algorithm is also linear in the number of voxels written into the CFB. However, writting one voxel in the inner loop requires the same number of integer operations as for *FAST_CURVE*, namely, 9-12 additions, 4-7 tests, an increment, 0-3 *UPDATE_POS* calls, and one *PUT_VOXEL*. The outer loop requires the following integer operations for each u: 36-39 additions, 1-4 increments, 4-7 tests, 15 copies, and one *NEW_POS* call. This is much more attractive than the original surface scan-conversion algorithm (cf. Section 8).

10. Parametric Polynomial Volumes

Parametric polynomial curves and surfaces have their trivariate version, i.e, a volume element. Varying the three parameters t, u, v from 0 to 1 defines all the points of the volume element. The extension to volumes is similar to the way curves have been extended into surfaces. Namely, if one parameter, say v, is assigned a constant value, and the other

```
Find n and m as described by Eq. 21;
Find initial difference matrices Δx_tu , Δy_tu , Δz_tu using Eq. 17;
Set Δ^00 x_tu , Δ^00 y_tu , Δ^00 z_tu to 0;
x_u = g[0][0][0];
y_u = g[1][0][0];
z_u = g[2][0][0];

for (u = 0; u ≤ m; u++) {
      NEW_POS(x_u ,y_u ,z_u );                    "start point"
      Copy column 0 of Δx_tu to Δx_t ;            Set Δ^0 x_t to 0;
      Copy column 0 of Δy_tu to Δy_t ;            Set Δ^0 x_t to 0;
      Copy column 0 of Δz_tu to Δz_t ;            Set Δ^0 x_t to 0;
      for (t = 0; t ≤ n; t++) {                   "follow f(*,u)"
            if (Δ^0 x_t > n^3 m^3) {
                  UPDATE_POS (X,1);
                  Δ^0 x_t -= 2n^3 m^3;
            }
            else if (Δ^0 x_t < -n^3 m^3) {
                  UPDATE_POS (X,-1);
                  Δ^0 x_t += 2n^3 m^3;
            }
            Δ^0 x_t += Δ^1 x_t ;
            Δ^1 x_t += Δ^2 x_t ;
            Δ^2 x_t += Δ^3 x_t ;
            Same decisions for Δy_t and Δz_t ;
            PUT_VOXEL ();
      }
      Update Δx_tu : col 0 += col 1;
                     col 1 += col 2;
                     col 2 += col 3;
      Same update for Δy_tu and Δz_tu ;

      if (Δ^00 x_tu > n^3 m^3) {                  "decision for f(0,*)"
            x_u ++;
            Δ^00 x_tu -= 2n^3 m^3;
      }
      else if (Δ^00 x_tu < -n^3 m^3) {
            x_u --;
            Δ^00 x_tu += 2n^3 m^3;
      }
      Same decisions for Δy_tu and Δz_tu ;
}
```

Figure 3: *FAST_SURFACE* - An Efficient Algorithm for 3D Scan-Converting Surfaces

two parameters, t and u, are varied in the range 0 to 1, a bivariate surface is defined. As v varies from 0 to 1 a sequence of bivariate surfaces sweeps the entire volume element.

Since the geometric matrix for volume representations is a tensor of 3-component vectors, the following summation notation is used:

$$f(t,u,v) = \sum_{i=0}^{3} \sum_{j=0}^{3} \sum_{k=0}^{3} h_i(t)\, h_j(u)\, h_k(v)\, g_{ijk} \qquad (24)$$

where $h_i(t)$, $h_j(u)$, and $h_k(v)$ are the geometric basis functions, and g_{ijk} are the components of the geometric tensor. The properties of the Bezier curves and surfaces hold also for the Bezier type volumes. More specifically, the forward difference method can be generalized to volumes.

11. 3D Scan-Conversion of Volumes

The trivariate Bezier volume is formally represented by the data type **volume**:

```
typedef struct volume {
      int g[3][4][4][4];          "x, y, z for 64 control points"
      color c;                    "volume color"
} volume;
```

The $3{\times}4{\times}4{\times}4$ control matrix g is the 64 Bezier geometric control points of a tricubic Bezier volume element in the parameters t, u, and v, each varies from 0 to 1. A volume element is scan-converted as a sequence of bicubic surfaces, where v is constant and t and u vary. Consequently, the scan-conversion algorithm for tricubic volumes is an extension of the associated algorithm for bicubic surfaces.

Furthermore, the all-integer version of the surface algorithm, *FAST_SURFACE*, can be generalized to volumes. An efficient volume algorithm, *FAST_VOLUME*, employing only integer arithmetic is displayed in Figure 4. The complexity of the algorithm is $\mathbf{O}(n\ m\ l)$, which is linear in the number of painted voxels. The numbers n, m and l are the inverse of the step sizes in t, u and v, respectively, and their computation is similar to that for surfaces and 6-connected curves. In order to avoid internal cavities in the solid volume, the algorithm generates a 6-connected volume, i.e., at each step of the algorithm only one coordinate may be changed. This coordinate is the one with the largest magnitude decision variable.

12. Concluding Remarks

We have described 3D scan-conversion algorithms for Bezier parametric cubic curves, bicubic surfaces, and tricubic volumes, from their geometric R^3 representation to the Z^3 voxel-image space. The conversion was achieved while obeying the fidelity, connectivity and efficiency requirements. For the curve algorithms 6-, 18- and 26-connected versions have been discussed. The surface algorithm guarantees lack of 6-connected tunnels in the converted surface, while the volume element generated by the volume algorithm has no internal cavities. All the algorithms are incremental and use only simple operations within their inner loops. Furthermore, efficient integer-only algorithms for 3D scan-conversion of curves, surfaces and volumes have been developed.

All the algorithms do scan-conversion with computational and temporal complexities which are linear in the number of voxels in the object. An object given for scan-conversion is assumed to be completely within the CFB bounds. However, if it extends slightly outside the CFB, scissoring can be applied, which can be easily incorporated within all the algorithms with no added time complexity.

All the 3D scan-conversion algorithms were implemented as part of the 3D geometry processor of the CUBE architecture. The geometry processor has been simulated in software, written in C under UNIX running on VAX computers and SUN workstations. Special purpose hardware (third order DDAs) has also been designed to improve conversion speed. Figure 5, generated in less than 30 seconds on a color SUN 3/160C, shows a straw dipped in a semi-transparent goblet filled with semi-transparent wine. The goblet was scan-converted by the geometry processor into a 128^3 CFB using the efficient surface algorithm. The image was then projected and rendered (with semi-transparency and shading) by the viewing processor of

```
Find n, m, l;  Find initial matrices Δx_tuv , Δy_tuv , Δz_tuv ;
Set Δ^000 x_tuv , Δ^000 y_tuv , Δ^000 z_tuv  to 0;
x_v = g[0][0][0][0];  y_v = g[1][0][0][0];  z_v = g[2][0][0][0];
for (v = 0;  v ≤ l;  v++) {
        Δx_tu  = 0 t-u layer of Δx_tuv ;
        Δy_tu  = 0 t-u layer of Δy_tuv ;
        Δz_tu  = 0 t-u layer of Δz_tuv ;
        Set Δ^00 x_tu , Δ^00 y_tu , Δ^00 z_tu  to 0;
        x_u = x_v ;   y_u = y_v ;   z_u = z_v ;
        for (u = 0;  u ≤ m;  u++) {                    "surface f(*,*,v)"
                NEW_POS(x_u , y_u , z_u );
                Δx_t  = 0 col of Δx_tu ;
                Δy_t  = 0 col of Δy_tu ;
                Δz_t  = 0 col of Δz_tu ;
                Set Δ^0 x_t , Δ^0 y_t , Δ^0 z_t  to 0;
                for (t = 0;  t ≤ n;  t++) {  "curve f(*,u,v)"
                        if ( | Δ^0 x_t | is the largest) {
                                if (Δ^0 x_t > n^3 m^3 l^3) {
                                        UPDATE_POS (X,1);
                                        Δ^0 x_t -= 2n^3 m^3 l^3;  }
                                else if (Δ^0 x_t < -n^3 m^3 l^3) {
                                        UPDATE_POS (X,-1);
                                        Δ^0 x_t += 2n^3 m^3 l^3;  }
                                Δ^0 x_t  += Δ^1 x_t ;
                                Δ^1 x_t  += Δ^2 x_t ;
                                Δ^2 x_t  += Δ^3 x_t ;
                        }                                  "step only in x"
                        else if ( | Δ^0 y_t | is the largest)
                                Same decisions for Δy_t ;
                        else    Same decisions Δz_t ;
                        PUT_VOXEL ();
                }
                Update Δx_tu ,Δy_tu ,Δz_tu :        col 0 += col 1;
                                                   col 1 += col 2;
                                                   col 2 += col 3;
                if ( | Δ^00 x_tu | is the largest) {
                        if (Δ^00 x_tu > n^3 m^3 l^3) {  x_u ++;
                                Δ^00 x_tu  -= 2n^3 m^3 l^3;  }
                        else if (Δ^00 x_tu < -n^3 m^3 l^3) {  x_u --;
                                Δ^00 x_tu  += 2n^3 m^3 l^3;  }
                }                                          "step only in x"
                else if ( | Δ^00 y_tu | is the largest)
                        Same decisions for Δy_tu ;
                else    Same decisions for Δz_tu ;
        }
        Update Δx_tuv ,Δy_tuv ,Δz_tuv :  layer 0 += layer 1;
                                        layer 1 += layer 2;
                                        layer 2 += layer 3;
        if ( | Δ^000 x_tuv | is the largest) {
                if (Δ^000 x_tuv > n^3 m^3 l^3) {  x_v ++;
                        Δ^000 x_tuv  -= 2n^3 m^3 l^3;  }
                else if (Δ^000 x_tuv < -n^3 m^3 l^3) {  x_v --;
                        Δ^000 x_tuv  += 2n^3 m^3 l^3;  }
        }                                                  "step only in x"
        else if ( | Δ^000 y_tuv | is the largest)
                Same decisions for Δy_tuv ;
        else    Same decisions for Δz_tuv ;
}
```

Figure 4: *FAST_VOLUME* - An Efficient Algorithm for 3D Scan-Converting Volumes

the CUBE architecture.

The algorithms developed here are by no means limited to cubic Bezier objects and apply equally well to other forms, and can also be extended to higher degree objects. Furthermore, the 3D scan-conversion algorithms for curves, surfaces and volumes, and more specifically the efficient all-integer decision mechanisms can also be exploited in conventional pixel-based algorithms (cf. [4]) which generate directly (after eliminating hidden surfaces) a set of pixels representing a projection of the desired parametric object.

Acknowledgment

This work was supported by the National Science Foundation under grant DCR-86-03603. The author would like to thank Eyal Shimony of the Center of Computer Graphics, Ben-Gurion University, for his work on an early version of some of the algorithms.

Figure 5: A Goblet Scan-Converted into a 128^3 CFB Using the Surface Algorithm and Projected/Rendered with Semi-Transparencies and Shading

13. References

1. Bezier, P., "UNISURF System: Principles, Program, Language", in *Computer Languages for Numerical Control*, J. Hatvany, (ed.), North-Holland, Amsterdam-London, 1972, 417-426.
2. Bezier, P., *Numerical Control - Mathematics and Applications*, A. R. Forrest (Trans.), Wiley, London, 1972.
3. Bezier, P., "Mathematical and Practical Possibilities of UNISURF", in *Computer Aided Geometric Design*, R. E. Barnhill and R. F. Riesenfeld, (eds.), Academic, New York, 1974, 127-152.
4. Blinn, J. F., Carpenter, L., Lane, J. and Whitted, T., "Scan Line Methods for Displaying Parametrically Defined Surfaces", *Communications of the ACM*, **23**, 1 (January 1980), 23-34.
5. Bresenham, J. E., "Algorithm for Computer Control of a Digital Plotter", *IBM Systems Journal*, **4**, 1 (1965), 25-30.
6. Clark, J. H., "Parametric Curves, Surfaces, and Volumes in Computer Graphics and Computer-Aided Geometric Design", Technical Report 221, Computer Systems Laboratory, Stanford University, Stanford, CA, November 1981.
7. Coons, S. A., "Surfaces for Computer-Aided Design of Space Forms", MIT Project MAC Tech. Rep.-41, June 1967.
8. deBoor, C., "On Uniform Approximation with Splines", *Journal of Approximation Theory*, **1**, (1968), 249-274.
9. Foley, J. D. and van Dam, A., *Fundamentals of Interactive Computer Graphics*, Addison-Wesley, Reading, MA, 1982.
10. Forrest, A. R., "On Coons and Other Methods for the Representation of Curved Surfaces", *Computer Graphics and Image Processing*, **1**, 4 (December 1972), 341-354.
11. Goldwasser, S. M., "A Generalized Object Display Processor Architecture", *IEEE Computer Graphics and Applications*, **4**, 10 (October 1984), 43-55.
12. Jackel, D., "The Graphics PARCUM System: A 3D Memory Based Computer Architecture for Processing and Display of Solid Models", *Computer Graphics Forum*, 1985, 21-32.
13. Kaufman, A. and Bakalash, R., "CUBE - An Architecture Based on a 3-D Voxel Map", in *Theoretical Foundations of Computer Graphics and CAD*, R. A. Earnshaw, (ed.), Springer-Verlag, 1987.
14. Kaufman, A. and Bakalash, R., "A 3-D Cellular Frame Buffer", *Proc. EUROGRAPHICS'85*, Nice, France, September 1985, 215-220.
15. Kaufman, A. and Bakalash, R., "Memory and Processing Architecture for 3-D Voxel-Based Imagery", Technical Report 87/06, Department of Computer Science, SUNY at Stony Brook, February 1987.
16. Kaufman, A., "An Algorithm for 3D Scan-Conversion of Polygons", *Proc. EUROGRAPHICS'87*, Amsterdam, Netherlands, August 1987.
17. Kaufman, A., "Voxel-Based Architectures for Three-Dimensional Graphics", *Proc. IFIP'86*, Dublin, Ireland, September 1986, 361-366.
18. Kaufman, A. and Shimony, E., "3D Scan-Conversion Algorithms for Voxel-Based Graphics", *Proc. ACM Workshop on Interactive 3D Graphics*, Chapel Hill, NC, October 1986.
19. Kim, C. E., "Three-Dimensional Digital Planes", *IEEE Transactions on Pattern Analysis and Machine Intelligence*, **PAMI-6**, 5 (September 1984), 639-645.
20. Lane, J. M. and Riesenfeld, R. F., "A Theoretical Development for the Computer Generation and Display of Piecewise Polynomial Surfaces", *IEEE Transactions on Pattern Analysis and Machine Intelligence*, **PAMI-2**, 1 (January 1980), 35-46.
21. Ohashi, T., Uchiki, T. and Tokoro, M., "A Three-Dimensional Shaded Display Method for Voxel-Based Representation", *Proc. EUROGRAPHICS'85*, Nice, France, September 1985, 221-232.
22. Pavlidis, T., *Algorithms for Graphics and Image Processing*, Computer Science Press, Rockville, MD, 1982.
23. Riesenfeld, R. F., "Applications of B-spline Approximation to Geometric Problems of Computer Aided Design", University of Utah UTEC-CSc-73-126, March 1973.
24. Rosenfeld, A., "Three-Dimensional Digital Topology", Computer Science Center, Univ. of Maryland, Tech. Rep.-936, 1980.
25. Srihari, S. N., "Representation of Three-Dimensional Digital Images", *Computing Surveys*, **4**, 13 (December 1981), 399-424.

Real-Time Manipulation of Texture-Mapped Surfaces

Masaaki Oka, Kyoya Tsutsui, Akio Ohba
Yoshitaka Kurauchi, Takashi Tago

Information Systems Research Center
Sony Corporation
Asahi-cho, Atsugi-shi 243
Japan

ABSTRACT

A system for real-time texture mapping was constructed. Here, "real-time" means that the system reacts to changes in parameter values which define the shape of surfaces and the viewing point that are given by its operator 30 times per second. This real-time processing enables interactive manipulation of texture-mapped free-form surfaces and various application software has been developed taking advantage of this ability. The system owes its performance to a new algorithm for texture mapping which is based on a newly proposed approximation scheme of mapping functions. In this scheme, a mapping function from the texture plane into the output screen is approximated by a linear function on each of the small regions which form the texture plane altogether. The algorithm is very simple and applicable to any smooth surface. It is especially efficient when implemented by a special-purpose hardware.

1. Introduction

Texture mapping is one of the most popular techniques in computer graphics and several algorithms have been proposed for it. Catmull [2] first introduced texture mapping and developed a subdivision algorithm. Blinn and Newell [1] proposed an algorithm which calculates the inverse image of each pixel on the output screen and assigns the average intensity of the inverse image to the pixel. Catmull and Smith [3] proposed a 2-pass algorithm which works in scanline order and can be implemented by video-rate hardware if the inverse mapping function for the 2nd pass is available. Unfortunately, in order to obtain the inverse mapping function, it is necessary to solve various equations and this difficulty restricts the kinds of surfaces available in these algorithms.

The goal of our research is to provide a means for easy manipulation of texture-mapped surfaces and to make texture mapping useful in such applications as free-form surface design and facial animation production. This requires a fast texture-mapping algorithm applicable to surfaces of arbitrary shapes. In this paper, we introduce a new algorithm which suits such purposes. It is very simple and efficient and is applicable to a wide variety of surfaces. The algorithm approximates a mapping function by a linear function on each of small regions which form the texture plane altogether (locally linear approximation). Its only constraint is that the mapping function be smooth enough. (The meaning of "smooth" is discussed later.) A practical method for anti-aliasing which works well with this algorithm is also proposed.

A real-time texture-mapping system was constructed using the above-mentioned algorithm. The system runs in real time in the sense that it not only transforms 30 images per second but also reacts to changes in transformation parameter values which are given by its operator at the same rate. The system is flexible in the sense that it can deal with free-form surfaces. Due to its real-time processing, the system allows its users to manipulate the shape of texture-mapped surfaces in an interactive manner and various application software has been developed taking advantage of this ability.

In the following section, the texture-mapping algorithm based on a locally linear approximation of mapping functions and the method for anti-aliasing are presented. In Section 3, how they have been integrated into a flexible system is explained. In Section 4, two applications of this system are introduced. In Section 5, some possible improvements are discussed.

2. Locally Linear Approximation

Texture mapping transforms a texture plane, $\{(u,v)\}$, onto a 3D surface, $\{(x',y',z')\}$, and then projects it into the output screen, $\{(x,y)\}$. Let f be the transformation from $\{(u,v)\}$ to $\{(x',y',z')\}$ and p the projection from $\{(x',y',z')\}$ to $\{(x,y)\}$. Then, $g(u,v)=p(f(u,v))$ is a mapping function from the texture plane into the output screen (see Fig.2.1).

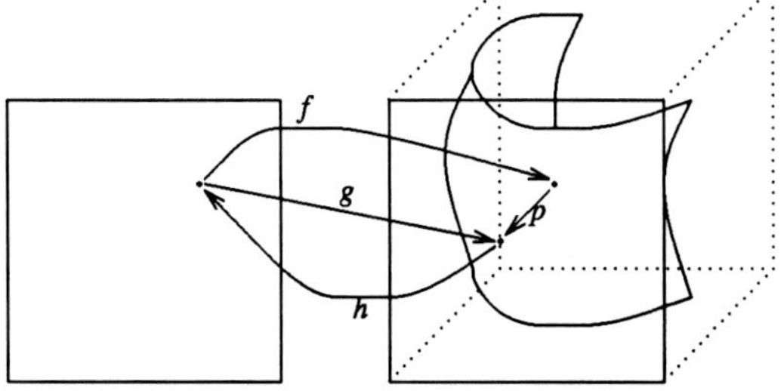

Fig.2.1
Functions in Texture Mapping

Note that the inverse of g, namely h, is not defined for all (x,y) on the output screen. Moreover, even for (x,y) such that $(x,y)=g(u,v)$ for some (u,v), $h(x,y)$ is not uniquely defined. Given (x,y), it is hidden-surface removal that assigns (u,v)-value such that $f(u,v)$ has the maximum z-value (the closest to the viewing point) among the candidates. Once h has been explicitly given, texture mapping is almost trivial, but it is difficult to compute h in general. So here, instead of calculating h, we approximate g using a locally linear function, namely $\hat{g}$, and calculate the inverse of $\hat{g}$, namely $\hat{h}$. Suppose g is in C^3.

$$\begin{bmatrix} x \\ y \end{bmatrix} = g(u,v) = \begin{bmatrix} \overset{1}{g}(u,v) \\ \overset{2}{g}(u,v) \end{bmatrix}. \qquad (2.1)$$

We first divide the (u,v)-plane into a 2D array of small square regions with edges of length d. We refer to each of these regions as a "block" in this paper. Let B be one of such blocks and (u_0,v_0) its center. Taking Taylor's expansion of g about (u_0,v_0), we have

$$\overset{1}{g}(u_0+d,v_0) = \overset{1}{g}(u_0,v_0) + d\cdot\overset{1}{g}_u(u_0,v_0) + d^2\cdot\overset{1}{g}_{uu}(u_0,v_0) + O(d^3) \qquad (2.2)$$

$$\overset{1}{g}(u_0-d,v_0) = \overset{1}{g}(u_0,v_0) - d\cdot\overset{1}{g}_u(u_0,v_0) + d^2\cdot\overset{1}{g}_{uu}(u_0,v_0) + O(d^3). \qquad (2.3)$$

We define

$$a_{11} \equiv \frac{\overset{1}{g}(u_0+d,v_0)-\overset{1}{g}(u_0-d,v_0)}{2d} = \overset{1}{g}_u(u_0,v_0)+O(d^2). \qquad (2.4)$$

Similarly,

$$a_{12} \equiv \frac{\overset{1}{g}(u_0,v_0+d)-\overset{1}{g}(u_0,v_0-d)}{2d} = \overset{1}{g}_v(u_0,v_0)+O(d^2) \qquad (2.5)$$

$$a_{21} \equiv \frac{\overset{2}{g}(u_0+d,v_0)-\overset{2}{g}(u_0-d,v_0)}{2d} = \overset{2}{g}_u(u_0,v_0)+O(d^2) \qquad (2.6)$$

$$a_{22} \equiv \frac{\overset{2}{g}(u_0,v_0+d)-\overset{2}{g}(u_0,v_0-d)}{2d} = \overset{2}{g}_v(u_0,v_0)+O(d^2). \qquad (2.7)$$

Then $\hat{g}$, a linear approximation of g on B, is given as follows:

$$\hat{g}(u,v) = \begin{bmatrix} \overset{1}{\hat{g}}(u,v) \\ \overset{2}{\hat{g}}(u,v) \end{bmatrix} = \begin{bmatrix} \overset{1}{g}(u_0,v_0) \\ \overset{2}{g}(u_0,v_0) \end{bmatrix} + \begin{bmatrix} a_{11} & a_{12} \\ a_{21} & a_{22} \end{bmatrix} \begin{bmatrix} h_1 \\ h_2 \end{bmatrix}, \qquad (2.8)$$

where

$$h_1=u-u_0 \quad , \quad h_2=v-v_0.$$

By this linear transformation, a block is transformed onto a parallelogram (see Fig.2.2). Note that the approximation was applied directly to g, a mapping into the output screen, but not to f, a mapping onto the surface.

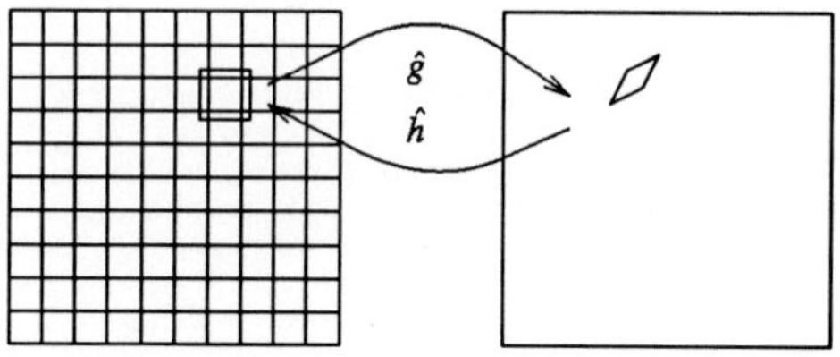

texture plane — output screen

Fig.2.2
Locally Linear Approximation

Now, let's estimate the error caused by this approximation scheme. Since g can be expressed by

$$g(u,v) = \begin{bmatrix} \overset{1}{g}(u_0,v_0) \\ \overset{2}{g}(u_0,v_0) \end{bmatrix} + \begin{bmatrix} \overset{1}{g}_u(u_0,v_0) & \overset{1}{g}_v(u_0,v_0) \\ \overset{2}{g}_u(u_0,v_0) & \overset{2}{g}_v(u_0,v_0) \end{bmatrix} \begin{bmatrix} h_1 \\ h_2 \end{bmatrix} + \frac{1}{2} \begin{bmatrix} (h_1\frac{\partial}{\partial u}+h_2\frac{\partial}{\partial v})^2 \overset{1}{g}(u_0+\theta_1\cdot h_1, v_0+\theta_1\cdot h_2) \\ (h_1\frac{\partial}{\partial u}+h_2\frac{\partial}{\partial v})^2 \overset{2}{g}(u_0+\theta_2\cdot h_1, v_0+\theta_2\cdot h_2) \end{bmatrix} \qquad (2.9)$$

for some $0\le\theta_1,\theta_2\le 1$, taking (2.3) through (2.6) and $|h_1|,|h_2|\le d$ into consideration, we have

$$\hat{g}(u,v)-g(u,v) = \frac{1}{2} \begin{bmatrix} (h_1\frac{\partial}{\partial u}+h_2\frac{\partial}{\partial v})^2 \overset{1}{g}(u_0+\theta_1\cdot h_1, v_0+\theta_1\cdot h_2) \\ (h_1\frac{\partial}{\partial u}+h_2\frac{\partial}{\partial v})^2 \overset{2}{g}(u_0+\theta_2\cdot h_1, v_0+\theta_2\cdot h_2) \end{bmatrix} + \begin{bmatrix} O(d^3) \\ O(d^3) \end{bmatrix} = \begin{bmatrix} O(d^2) \\ O(d^2) \end{bmatrix}. \qquad (2.10)$$

That is, if we measure the approximation error in terms of length, it is proportional to the square of the length of the edge of a block. This rapid convergence of the error is well illustrated in Fig.2.3, where the finely divided quadrilaterals look almost like parallelograms.

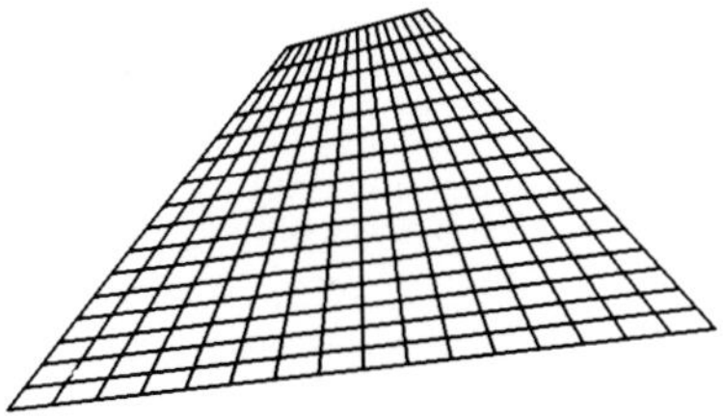

Fig.2.3
Effect of Fine Division

Given a mapping function, although we can reduce the approximation error by increasing the fineness of division, there will always remain some error. This may cause a crack between two adjacent parallelograms, resulting in a serious degradation of the image quality. Fortunately, these cracks can be avoided by setting some common area between two adjacent blocks (see Fig.2.4).

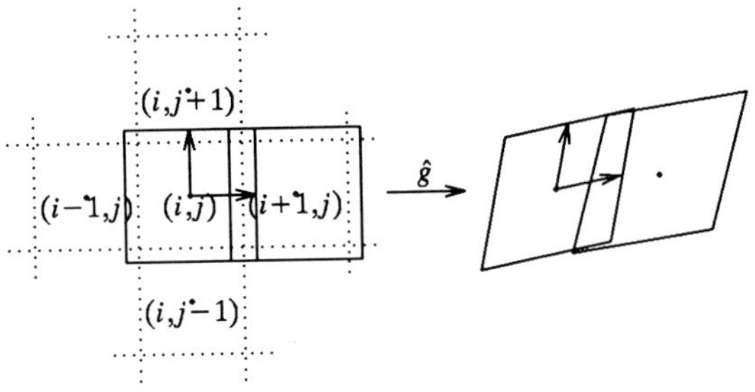

Fig.2.4
Transformation of Blocks with Common Area

Some pixels on the output screen will be accessed more than once, but if the blocks are sufficiently small, the approximation becomes sufficiently accurate and we do not care which access resulted in the final image. As is shown in (2.10), the approximation error is dominated by the second partial derivatives of g. Unfortunately, the values of these derivatives depend on many factors, such as the curvature of the surface and the location of the viewing point, so it is impossible to determine the appropriate block size in terms of surface parameters. It has been shown by experiment that division of a 512×512-pixel texture plane into 8×8-pixel blocks with 0.5-pixel-wide common areas works in most practical applications. As a general aid to understanding, in this paper we refer to mapping functions with reasonably small second partial derivatives as "smooth" mapping functions and surfaces which lead to smooth mapping functions as "smooth surfaces".

The employment of the locally linear approximation described above makes the algorithm for texture mapping very simple. First of all, the inverse of a linear function $\hat{g}$, namely $\hat{h}$, is also a linear function and is obtained by simply calculating the inverse matrix of A, namely $B(b_{ij})$, as follows:

$$D = a_{11} \cdot a_{22} - a_{12} \cdot a_{21} \qquad r = \frac{1}{D}$$
$$b_{11} = r \cdot a_{22} \qquad b_{12} = -r \cdot a_{12} \tag{2.11}$$
$$b_{21} = -r \cdot a_{21} \qquad b_{22} = r \cdot a_{11}.$$

This requires only 1 division, 6 multiplications, 1 subtraction and 1 change of sign. Moreover, since h is also a linear function, its own calculations are quite simple. Let $p_0 = (x_0, y_0)$ be the center of an output pixel within the parallelogram and q_0 the image of p_0 by h. Let p_{mn} be the output pixel which lies m-pixels to the right of and n-pixels above p_0, and q_{mn} the image of p_{mn} by $\hat{h}$. Then,

$$q_{mn} = q_0 + \begin{bmatrix} m \cdot b_{11} + n \cdot b_{12} \\ m \cdot b_{21} + n \cdot b_{22} \end{bmatrix}. \tag{2.12}$$

(2.12) can be used to calculate $\hat{h}$ in an incremental manner. To calculate $\hat{h}(p_{2m2n})$, for example, we repeat (2.12) twice. Alternatively, (2.12) can be used to calculate $\hat{h}$ for various m and n directly. A combination of these two methods leads to the efficient algorithm shown in Fig.2.5.

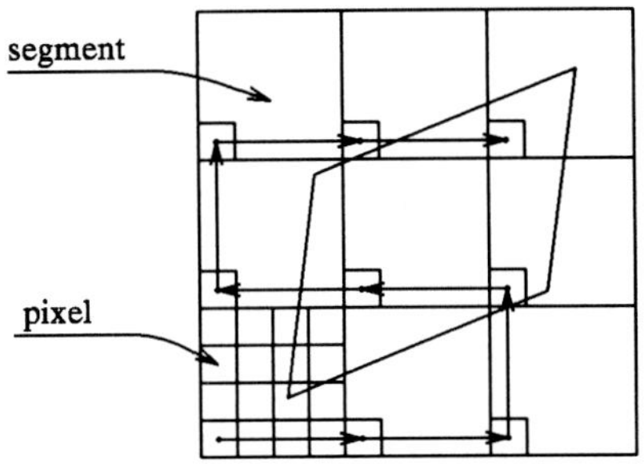

Fig.2.5
Calculation of Inverse Linear Transformation

The output screen is divided into rectangular segments. $\hat{h}$ is calculated by the former method for one pixel in each of the segments which intersect the parallelogram. To the rest of the pixels in each segment, the latter method is applied. Notice that the calculations within a segment can be processed in parallel. Also notice that the second term of the right hand side of (2.12) is a constant for fixed values of m and n. By synthesizing all the transformed blocks based on their z-coordinate, transformation of the whole texture image is completed.

As is well known, assigning to a given pixel on the output screen the intensity value of the texture point which corresponds to the center of the pixel causes serious aliasing problems. A popular method which produces results which are visually acceptable is to assign to the pixel the average intensity value over the texture area that corresponds to the output pixel square (see, for example, [5]). Another method, which was employed by Williams [6] and Crow [4] , is to assign to the pixel the average value of the texture in the minimal rectangle (or square) which covers the area that corresponds to the output pixel. Although this may cause an over-blurred image due to the extraneous areas considered for the average, it simplifies the calculation greatly. Since an output pixel corresponds to a parallelogram defined by the two vectors, (b_{11}, b_{21}) and (b_{12}, b_{22}) in our algorithm, the minimal rectangle is bounded by edges of length $|b_{11}| + |b_{12}|$ and $|b_{21}| + |b_{22}|$ (see Fig.2.6). Assuming that the center of the parallelogram coincides with the center of a pixel, pre-filtering of the texture image, whose coefficient values vary from one block to another, is possible. Pixels lying near boundary or silhouette edges of the transformed image may partially cover the background and the texture pattern in a remote location. Anti-aliasing along these edges is computationally much more expensive and is not considered in this paper.

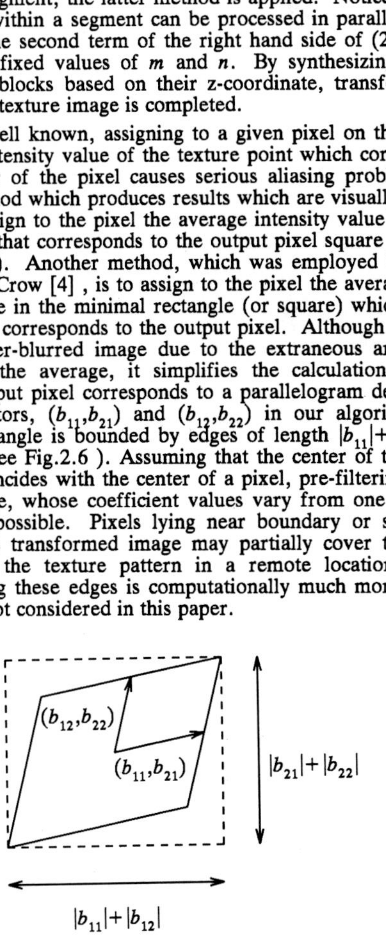

Fig.2.6
Texture Area Corresponding to One Output Pixel

3. Real-Time Texture-Mapping System

The methods described in the previous section were integrated to construct a texture-mapping system. In order to allow easy manipulation of free-form surfaces, the system was designed so that:

[1] Transformation into any smooth surface is possible.

[2] Transformation of texture image is done in real time.

[3] Response to changes in transformation data is made in real time.

Although our algorithm runs fast, it is impossible for any current single processor to satisfy these requirements. Fortunately, processing of texture mapping can be done as shown in Fig.3.1:

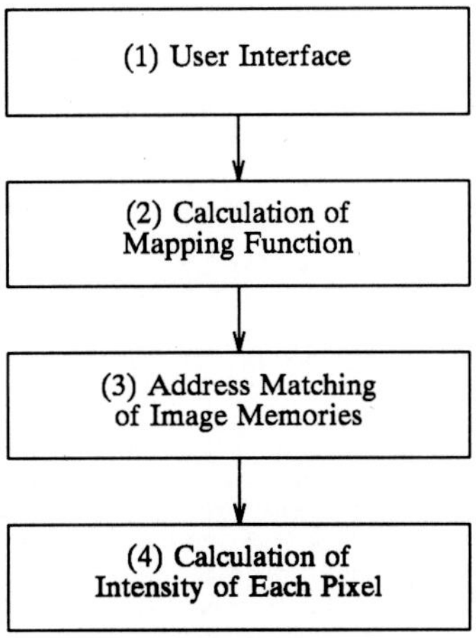

Fig.3.1
Processing of Texture Mapping

A notable characteristics of this process is that calculations done at an early step are unaffected by subsequent calculations. Making use of this characteristics, we constructed a hierarchical system which consists of software-driven processors and special hardware and implements pipeline processing.

There are several ways to define the shape of a surface, for example by equations and by interpolation of two given surfaces. In any case, the system has to cope with changes in the shape of surfaces. Among the processing steps in Fig.3.1, (1) and (2) require this flexibility and hence, should be controlled by software. For (2), our algorithm calculates the transformation of the central point of each block. Although the number of blocks is much smaller than that of pixels, it is still several thousands, so the processing for (2) has to be much faster than that for (1), which only has to be done once for a frame. In the constructed system, (1) is implemented by a versatile micro-processor and (2) is implemented by parallel micro-coded processors. On the other hand, the processings for (3) and (4) are only linear transformations which are substantially the same for any curved surface. These calculations are simple but as they must be done for each pixel, the system implements them by hardware.

Figure 3.2 shows the actual composition of the system. It has two major data channels, one for transformation data, the other for image data. Host Computer (HC) conducts user interface. It accepts transformation data from input devices and transfers programs and data to Micro-Coded Processors (MP) every frame according to the kind of curved surface. MP first calculates the 3D location of the central point of each block, applies 3D affine transformations to it and projects it onto the screen. Then it generates locally linear approximation data based on (2.4) through (2.7) and (2.11) in the previous section. It also controls hidden-surface removal by sorting the blocks according to the z-coordinate of their central points. This sorting is done by a bucket-sort and a linear list of these blocks is constructed. The data calculated by MP are stored in Block Data Memory (BDM) and transferred to Address Controller (AC) by double-buffering. AC calculates the inverse linear transformation using the algorithm described in the previous section and gives the read address to Input Image Memory (IIM) and write address to Output Image Memory (OIM). AC processes the blocks in the order of the linear list, from the furthest to the nearest. Thus the hidden-surface removal is automatically carried out. Pixel Processor (PP) interpolates the texture data of the nearest 4 pixels in IIM and writes it to OIM. Texture image is filtered for anti-aliasing before it is stored in IIM. Double buffering is also applied to IIM and OIM and one frame of transformed image is output every 33msec.

4. Applications

Various application software which makes use of the real-time processing of this system has been developed. In this section, two of them are introduced.

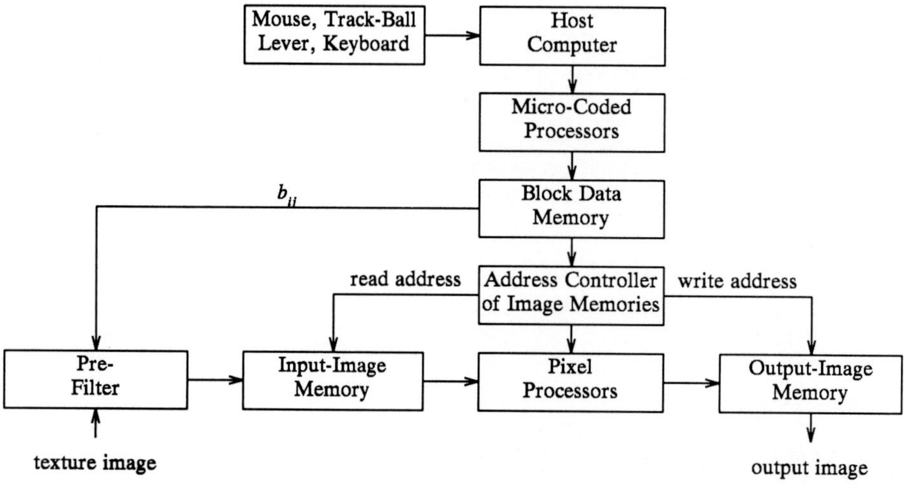

Fig.3.2
System Composition

4.1. Free-Form Surface Design

This application is to design and manipulate free form surfaces such as human faces in an interactive way by locally deforming a displayed curved surface by trial and error and step by step.

A non-deformed plane is taken as the initial shape of the surface and deformations are repeatedly added to it. Let p be a point on the texture plane. At the i-th deformation, p is transformed to a point in a 3D space, namely P_i. P_i is calculated as

$$P_i = P_{i-1} + V_i \cdot F(p, c_i, a_i), \quad (4.1)$$

where V_i is a deformation 3D vector at the i-th step and F is a scalar valued function which regulates the deformation area. F is controlled by two kinds of parameters, c_i and a_i. c_i is the central point of the deformation and a_i is a 2D vector which gives its extent. To restrict the deformation within the neighborhood of c_i, F should have an essentially finite support. For example, the following Gaussian Distribution Function, whose value is nearly 0 outside a certain limit, can be used as F:

$$F(p, c_i, a_i) = \exp(-((\frac{p_{iu} - c_{iu}}{a_{iu}})^2 + (\frac{p_{iv} - c_{iv}}{a_{iv}})^2)) \quad (4.2)$$

Each point on the surface is moved by the action of $V_i \cdot F(p, c_i, a_i)$, and the surface is locally deformed near c_i. Deformations are repeatedly added to the surface until a satisfactory shape is obtained.

Figure 4.1 shows the surface obtained by adding a deformation to the initial plane. The "+" cursor indicates the central point of deformation and the oval shows its extent. Figure 4.2 is a schematic block diagram of the apparatus of this free-form surface design system. The trackball is used to control the viewing point and the lever and the mouse are used to control the above V_i, c_i and a_i. Figure 4.3 is a flowchart of this free-form surface design. In the Loop-1, a deformation which corresponds to (4.1) is implemented. Thanks to the real-time processing, the user can control the deformation interactively and check it from various viewing points quite easily. In the Loop-2, deformations are repeatedly added and the surface data are renewed. At the same time, deformation parameters such as V_i, c_i and a_i are added to a data list. Since the shape of a surface is independent from the order of the deformations and each deformation is reversible, it is easy to edit this list to modify the shape of the surface. Figure 4.4 is a relief generated from a picture of a face using the above-mentioned method. Fifty deformations were added to generate this surface. Figure 4.5 shows other examples which were generated from the same picture as Fig.4.4, where S_0 was created first and then some modifications were added to it to generate S_1 through S_9.

4.2. Multiple 3D Inbetweening and Real-Time Animation

3D inbetweening, a popular technique in 3D computer animation, interpolates two surfaces to define new surfaces. It is not necessary to restrict the number of surfaces to be interpolated to two if some means of controlling the interpolation is provided. Increasing the number of the surfaces gives more potential variety to the shape of the interpolated surface. So, we extend 3D inbetweening to a multiple 3D inbetweening and apply it to a real-time animation.

In a multiple 3D inbetweening, a weighted sum of several surfaces is calculated as

$$T = \sum_{i=0}^{n} I_i \cdot S_i, \quad (4.3)$$

where S_i's are the given surfaces, I_i's the coefficients and T the interpolated surface. The sum of the coefficient values, I_i's, is 1, but each of them is not necessarily restricted to between 0 and 1. Coefficient values which do not lie between 0 and 1 extrapolate the given surfaces instead of interpolating them.

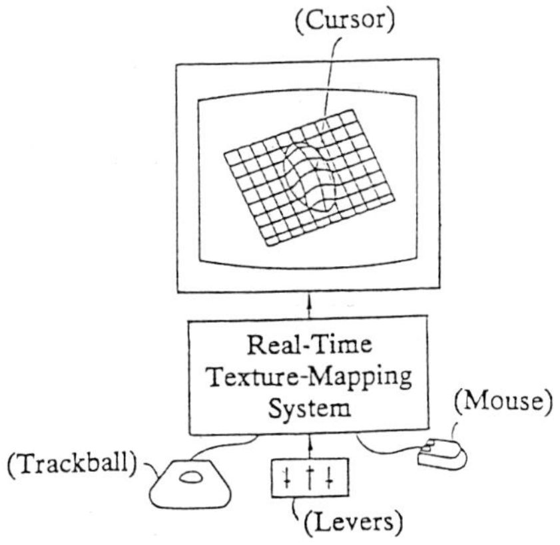

Fig.4.2
Apparatus for Free Form Surface Design

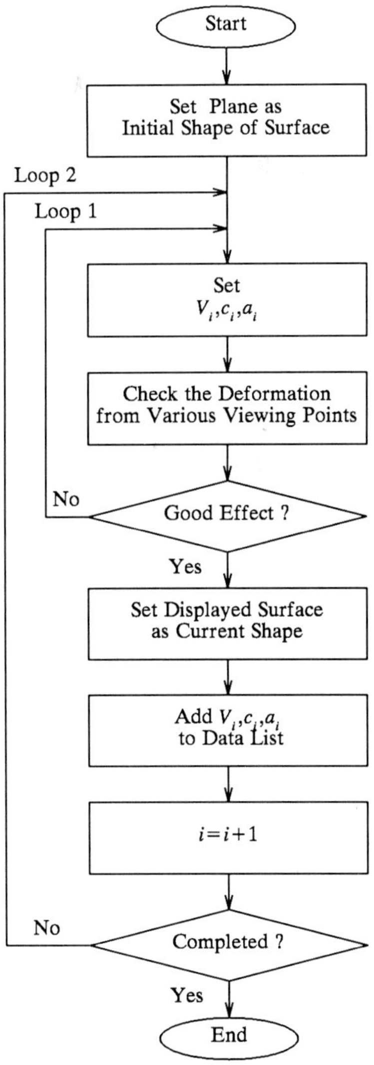

Fig.4.3
Flowchart of Free Form Surface Design

It is easy to generate smooth movement of a free-form surface using a multiple 3D inbetweening. A key-frame animation is produced with this system in the following manner. First, the animator selects several surfaces and stores them in the internal memories of MPs. Then, key frames are designated and the coefficients of the multiple 3D inbetweening are given at each of the key frames in an interactive way. Finally, the system interpolates the parameters along the time axis and an animated texture mapping is realized.

Animation of facial expressions proved to be an interesting application of this method and will be quite useful when combined with speech recognition and synthesis. It is possible to synthesize a variety of facial expressions with fewer surfaces if they have been chosen in an efficient way. For this purpose, deformations of different parts of a face should be put into separate surfaces. Reduction of the number of surfaces helps the control of animation as well as saving storage space. The facial expressions in Fig.4.6 were synthesized from the surfaces in Fig.4.5 using the coefficient values shown in the table. Notice that T_0 in Fig.4.6 was generated by extrapolating the original facial relief, S_0, and the one with a closed mouth, S_5.

5. Some Possible Improvements

Although in the interest of simplicity we did not integrate them into our first system, improvements on hidden-surface removal and shading are possible at a rather small expense. As stated in Section 3, hidden-surface removal was realized by sorting the blocks according to the z-coordinate of their central points and processing them from the furthest to the nearest. So, if two blocks intersect with each other or two non-adjacent blocks are positioned too close, this hidden-surface removal does not work correctly. This is avoided by calculating the z-coordinate of each pixel and implementing a z-buffer algorithm. Locally linear approximation in z-direction will be useful for calculating the z-coordinate of each pixel. Gouraud and Phong-type shadings are also possible by linearly approximating the intensity or the normal direction in each block.

6. Conclusions

A real-time texture mapping system was constructed. The system works in real time in the sense that it reacts to changes in parameter values of the surfaces and the viewing point which are interactively given by its operator 30 times per second. The system makes use of a newly proposed algorithm based on a locally linear approximation of mapping functions. The algorithm is simple, runs fast and can be applied to any smooth surface. A practical anti-aliasing method was also proposed and integrated into the system. Real-time texture mapping proved to be very useful for human-machine interface and several applications were introduced.

Acknowledgements

The authors would like to express their appreciation to Mr. Y. Kodera, Mr. H. Yoshida and Mr. M. Morizono of Sony Corporation, for giving them the opportunity to study this subject and the permission to publish this paper. They also wish to thank Mr. H. Kanemaki, Mr. N. Asamizuya and many other colleagues in Sony Corporation who have contributed to the work described in this paper.

References

1. Blinn, James F., Newell, Martin E. Texture and Reflection in Computer Generated Images. Communications of the ACM, 19,10 (October 1976), 542-547.

2. Catmull, Edwin. Computer Display of Curved Surfaces. Proceedings of IEEE Conference on Computer Graphics, Pattern Recognition, and Data Structures (Los Angeles, California, May 1975), 11-17.

3. Catmull, Edwin., Smith, Alvy R. 3-D Transformation of Images in Scanline Order. Proceedings of SIGGRAPH'80. In Computer Graphics 14,3 (July 1980), 279-285.

4. Crow, Franklin C. Summed-Area Tables for Texture Mapping. Proceedings of SIGGRAPH'84 (Minneapolis, Minnesota, July 23-27). In Computer Graphics 18,3 (July 1984), 207-212

5. Glassner, Andrew. Adaptive Precision in Texture Mapping. Proceedings of SIGGRAPH'86 (Dallas, Texas, August 18-22, 1986). In Computer Graphics 20,4 (August 1986), 297-306.

6. Williams, Lance. Pyramidal Parametrics. Proceedings of SIGGRAPH'83 (Detroit, Michigan, July 25-29, 1983). In Computer Graphics 17,3 (July 1983), 1-11.

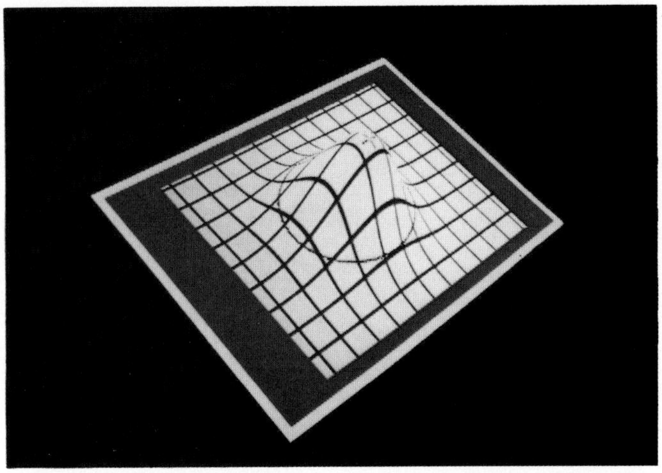

Fig.4.1
Surface with One Deformation

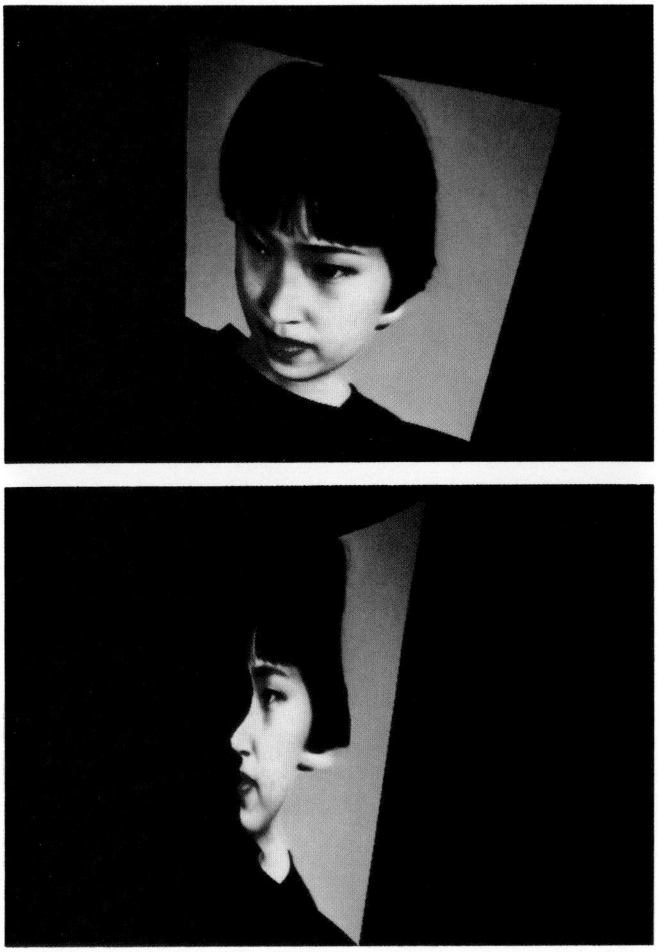

Fig.4.4
Facial Relief

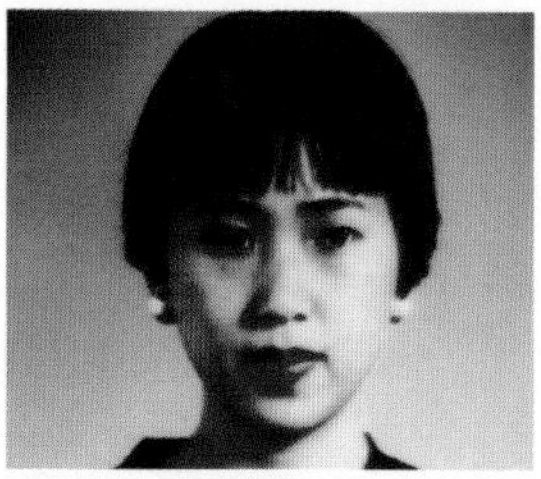

S_1: (Eyes)

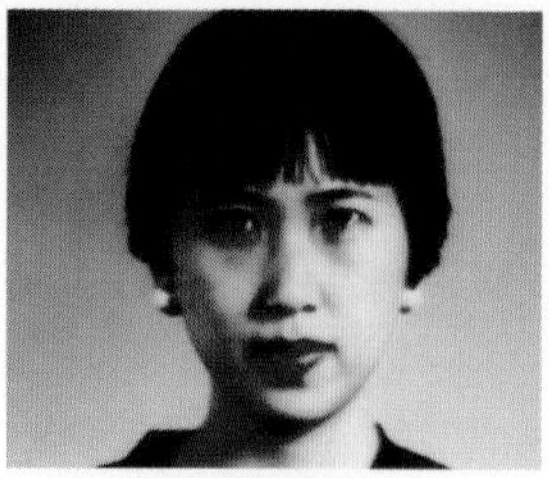

S_2: (Eyes)

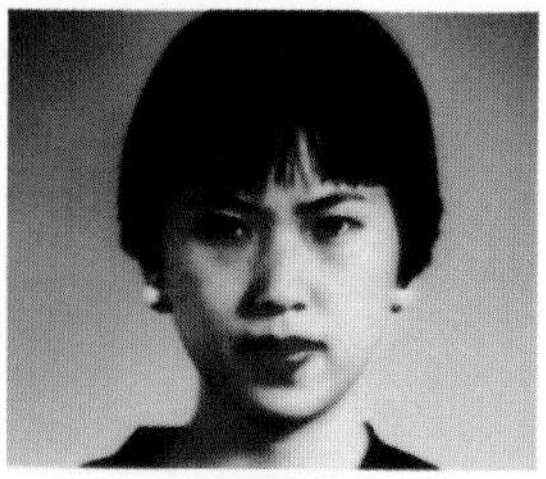

S_3: (Eyebrows)

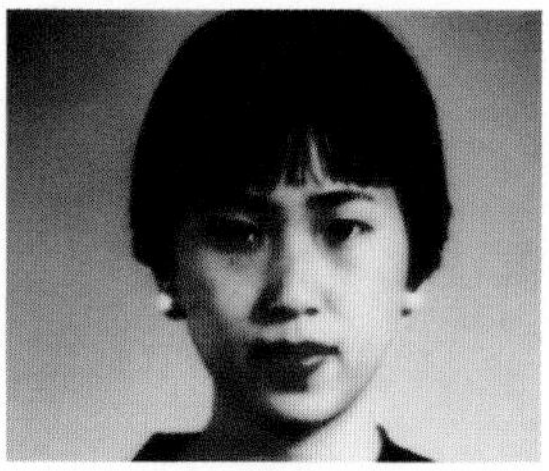

S_0:
Original Facial Relief

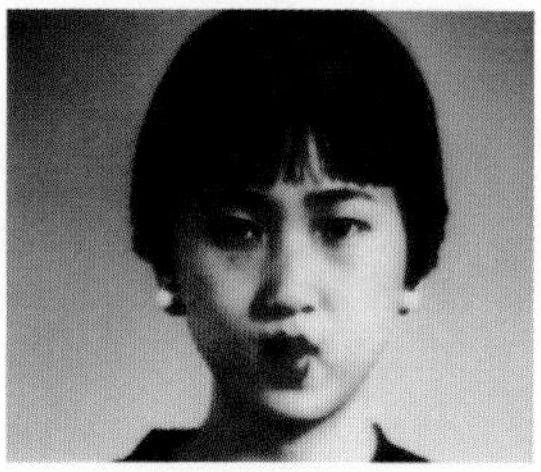

S_4: (Lips)

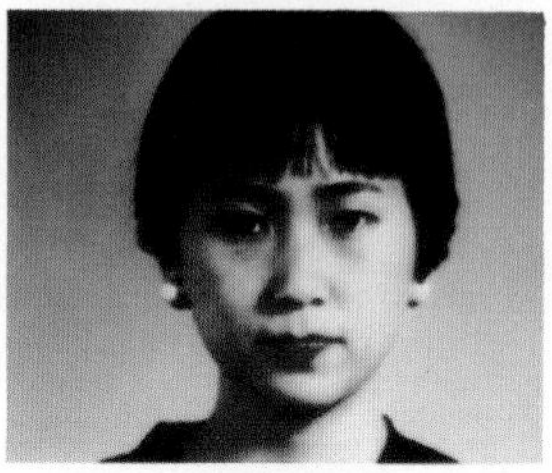

S_5: (Lips & Jaw)

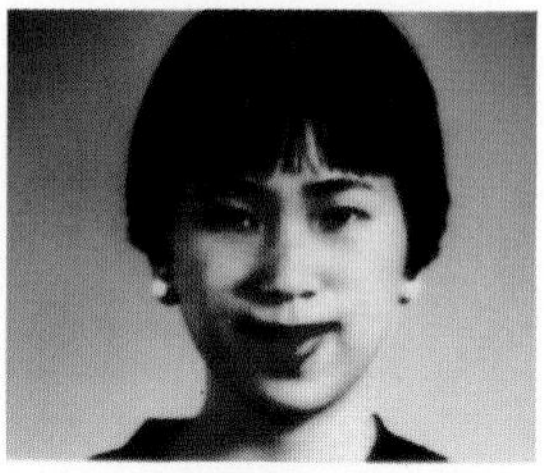

S_6: (Lips & Cheeks)

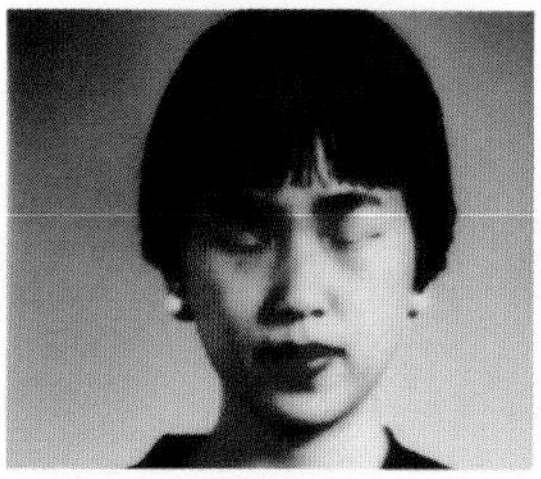

S_7: (Eyelids)

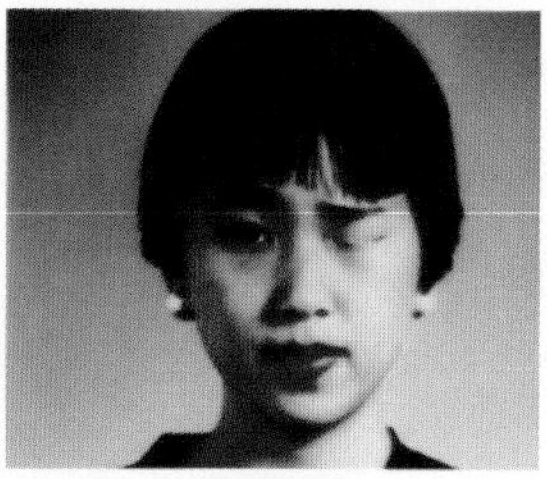

S_8: (Eyelid)

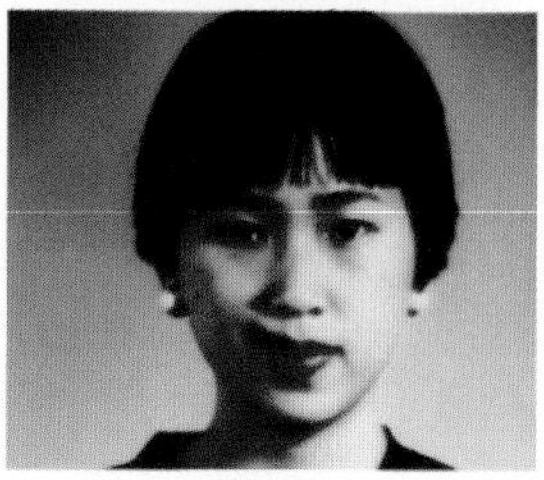

S_9: (Lips & Cheek)

Fig.4.5
Various Facial Relieves

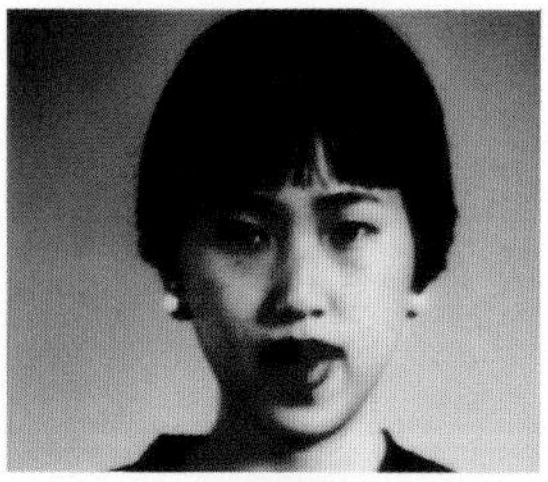

T_0

$$T=\sum_{i=0}^{9} I_i \cdot S_i$$

$$\sum_{i=0}^{9} I_i = 1.0$$

	I_0	I_1	I_2	I_3	I_4	I_5	I_6	I_7	I_8	I_9
T_0	2.30	0.00	0.00	0.00	0.00	-1.30	0.00	0.00	0.00	0.00
T_1	-0.28	0.26	-0.32	1.30	-0.14	0.26	-0.34	0.26	0.00	0.00
T_2	0.61	-0.55	0.72	-0.68	-0.28	0.52	0.66	0.00	0.00	0.00
T_3	1.74	-0.52	-0.46	-0.68	0.78	0.56	-0.46	0.04	0.00	0.00
T_4	-1.13	0.36	0.00	0.68	-0.08	0.00	0.36	0.77	-0.68	0.72

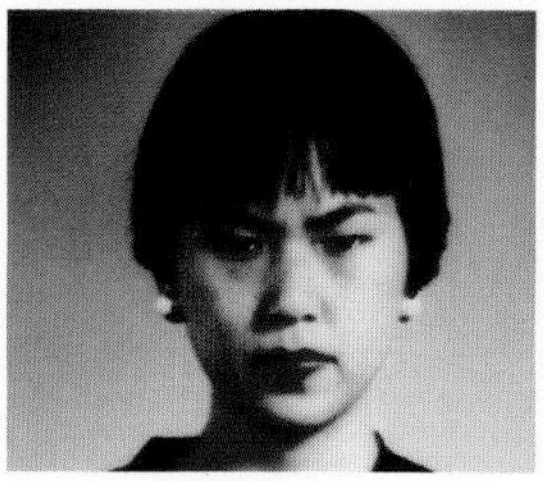

T_1

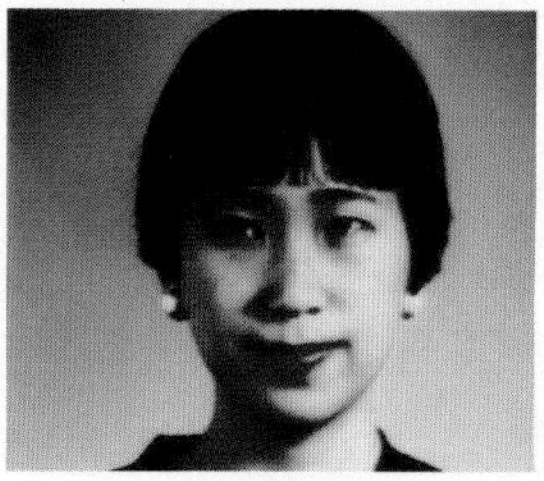

T_2

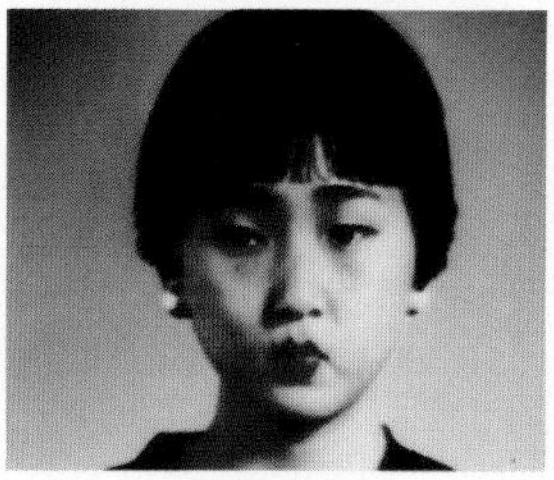

T_3

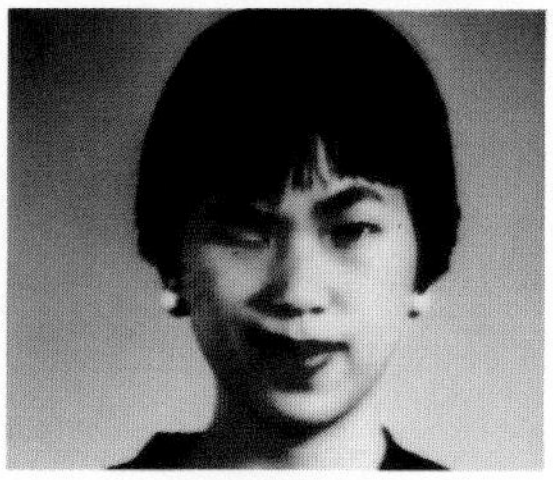

T_4

Fig.4.6
Facial Expressions by Multiple 3D Inbetweening

Shading Bicubic Patches

Michael Shantz and Sheue-Ling Lien

Sun Microsystems, Inc.
2500 Garcia Avenue
Mountain View, CA 94043

Abstract

We present several techniques for implementing Phong shading in hardware for bicubic patches. Patches are shaded, not by subdividing into polygons, but by drawing many curves close together leaving no pixel gaps. Each curve is drawn using an adaptive forward difference algorithm which generates the coordinates as well as the shading parameters as cubic functions incrementally evaluated along the curve. The forward difference step size is adaptively adjusted so that it generates approximately one pixel along the curve per forward difference step. The hardware implements Phong shading directly with a surprisingly simple configuration built from general purpose compute units and look-up tables. Two new methods are presented for deriving bicubic approximations to the shading parameters over a bicubic patch. One method uses two Coons patches to approximate the unnormalized $N{\cdot}L$, and $N{\cdot}H$, and a third Coons patch for $N{\cdot}N$, where N is the surface normal, L is the light direction, and H is the direction of maximum highlight. In this case the hardware performs the normalization per pixel. The second method uses two Coons patches to approximate the normalized dot products $N{\cdot}L$, and $N{\cdot}H$. The method is suitable for both hardware and software implementations.

CR Categories and Subject Descriptors: I.3.3 [**Computer Graphics**]: Picture/Image Generation - Display algorithms; I.3.7 [**Computer Graphics**]: Three-dimensional Graphics and Realism - Color, shading, shadowing, and texture.

Additional Key Words and Phrases: image synthesis, shading, adaptive forward differencing, graphics VLSI, parametric surfaces.

Introduction

Phong[7] shading is a well known technique for generating smoothly shaded images of surfaces approximated by patches or polygons. This shading technique is attractive because it gives a fairly realistic rendering with a modest computational cost. Most 3D MCAD applications give highest priority to interactive performance and are satisfied with the realism afforded by Phong shading. Indeed, linear interpolation of color over the individual polygons is often acceptable for interactive design.

Polygonal approximations for curved surfaces are used for performance reasons, since most high speed graphics hardware is built for fast rendering of polygons. A typical bicubic patch may require 25 or more polygons to give a usably accurate approximation. Many design applications would be facilitated if smooth, high speed, curved surface rendering were available. Existing scanline algorithms for rendering curved surfaces[5] are too complex for hardware implementation.

In this paper we describe a method for smoothly shading bicubic patches which is suitable for hardware implementation. Hardware adaptive forward difference units are used to evaluate bicubic functions which approximate the shading parameters over a patch. Patches are rendered by drawing many cubic curves spaced closely together. Each curve is shaded with the cubic approximations to the shading parameters. The result is high speed rendering of bicubic patches. The hardware referred to in this paper has not been built. All images were generated by software simulations of the algorithms. †

Background

We use the following Phong approximation to compute the color at a point on a surface illuminated by a single light source at infinity.

$$color = (A + D\,(N{\cdot}L))\,objectcolor$$
$$+ S\,(N{\cdot}H)^m\,lightcolor$$

Where A, D and S are the ambient light intensity, the diffuse coefficient, and the specular coefficient, respectively, m is

† Sun Microsystems, Inc. is pursuing patent protection in the United States and abroad on the technology described in this paper.

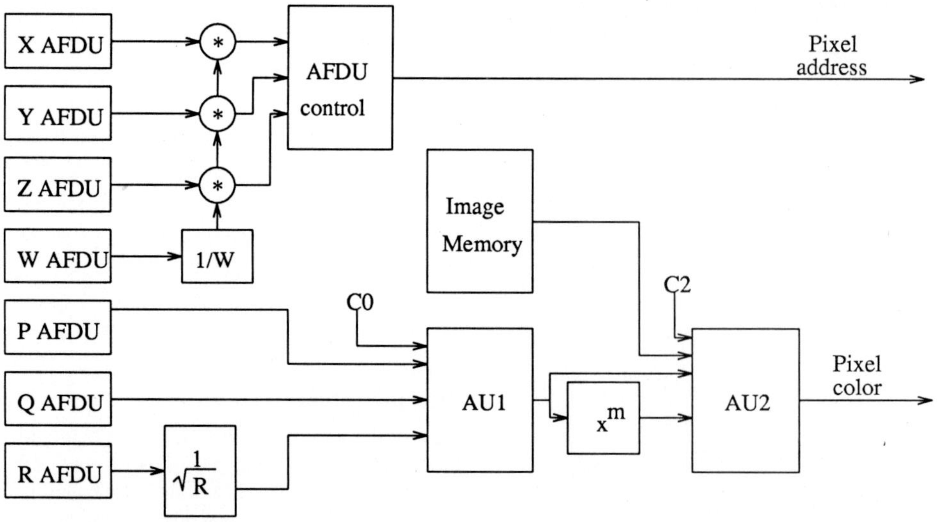

Figure 1. Simplified block diagram of the shading hardware. The AFDUs (Adaptive Forward Difference Units) are cubic function generators and the AUs (Arithmetic Unit) perform $\alpha A + (1-\alpha)B$, $\alpha A + B$, or $A*B$.

the specular power, L is a unit vector toward the light source, and H is a unit vector in the direction of maximum highlight (ie. the vector in the direction halfway between the viewer and the light source). The surface normal unit vector N varies across the surface.

Duff[4] derived a difference equation for efficiently interpolating $N \cdot L$ or $N \cdot H$ between two points A and B on a polygon with normalization at each intermediate point. This expression requires 3 additions, a divide, and a square root per pixel.

$$N \cdot L = \frac{\alpha(N_b \cdot L) + (1-\alpha)(N_a \cdot L)}{\sqrt{1-2\alpha(1-\alpha)(1-N_a \cdot N_b)}}$$

Bishop and Weimer[1] further reduced the computation per pixel by approximating Duff's expression with a quadratic. The difference equation for this quadratic requires only 2 additions per pixel but the setup per polygon to obtain the quadratic expression is significant. They quoted the overhead as equivalent to computing Duff's expression directly for 10 pixels, including the square root. If the pixel loop additions were performed in fast hardware, the setup overhead would likely be the performance bottleneck. The quadratic approximation produces visible artifacts if the angle between N_a and N_b is greater than 60 degrees. The robustness of this method would be improved if cubic interpolation were used for $N \cdot N$ and the normalization was done per pixel in hardware.

Bishop and Weimer correctly point out that Phong's proposal for hardware implementation is somewhat complicated since he suggests a circuit for actually computing the square root. However, current hardware technology provides some very simple ways to compute Duff's expression directly and at the same time reduce the polygon overhead. Our approach for high performance bicubic patches computes cubic approximations and normalization directly in hardware.

The new method we propose has the following advantages.

1) Fast rendering of bicubic patches using adaptive forward differencing
2) Simple hardware implementation with pixel rates at frame buffer memory speeds. The circuit uses general purpose units which may be implemented in VLSI and used for other geometry and shading tasks.
3) Allows for up to cubic approximation of $N \cdot L$ and $N \cdot N$.

The Shading Hardware

Patches are shaded by drawing many curves spaced closely together so that no pixel gaps remain between the adjacent curves. Each curve is a univariate cubic obtained by setting one of the bicubic parameters to a constant. The hardware uses adaptive forward difference units to compute the cubic equations for x,y,z,w and for the shading parameters such as $N \cdot L$ along the curve. Polygons are shaded by drawing horizontal line segments with the shading parameters along the segment computed by adaptive forward difference units. The details of the adaptive forward differencing technique are presented in another paper.[6] This paper will concentrate on the shading computations along the cubic curves across a bicubic patch.

Figure 1 shows the cubic adaptive forward difference units which together with the arithmetic units compute the Phong shading along a scanline or along a cubic curve. Polygon shading doesn't require cubics but they are used as basic building blocks for many graphics hardware tasks, and are used to shade bicubic patches.

The arithmetic unit consists of three subunits, one for red, green, and blue. Each computes one of the following expressions on the A, B, and α components of their input. The output may be clamped to a maximum value.

$$out = \alpha A + (1-\alpha)B$$

$$out = \alpha A + B$$

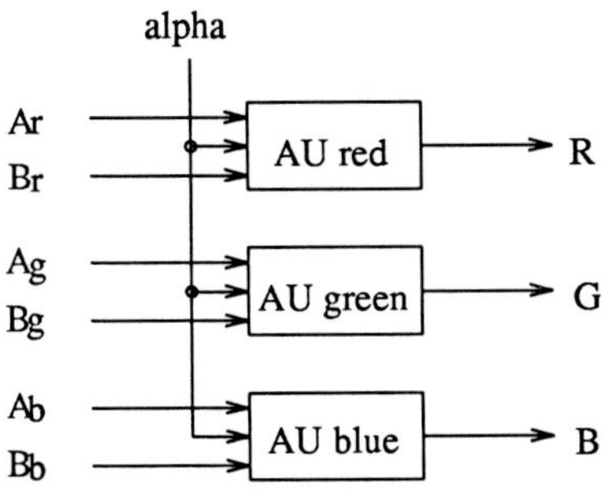

Figure 2. Detailed block diagram of an arithmetic unit.

$$out = A*B$$

Here, A and B are RGB colors or other shading parameters, and α is a shading parameter or coefficient used for blending A and B. The inputs A, B, and α may be selected from various sources depending on the function being performed. These functions include shading, depth cueing, image mapping, and antialiasing.

The AFD units are third order digital differential analyzers which implement an adaptive forward difference solution to a parametric cubic function of v. The parameter v varies from 0 to 1 along the curve. The dv step size for v is adaptively adjusted so that the curve steps along in approximately one pixel steps. The same dv is used for the AFDUs involved in the shading calculations so that the shading is mapped correctly along the curve. We use the forward difference basis functions:

$$B_3 = \frac{v(v-1)(v-2)}{6}$$

$$B_2 = \frac{v(v-1)}{2}$$

$$B_1 = v$$

$$B_0 = 1$$

A parametric cubic function f(v) is represented in this basis as

$$f = aB_3(v) + bB_2(v) + cB_1(v) + dB_0(v)$$

A cubic curve is defined by four cubic functions x(v), y(v), z(v), and w(v), each implemented by a separate AFD unit.

$$x(v) = a_x B_3 + b_x B_2 + c_x B_1 + d_x B_0$$

$$y(v) = a_y B_3 + b_y B_2 + c_y B_1 + d_y B_0$$

$$z(v) = a_z B_3 + b_z B_2 + c_z B_1 + d_z B_0$$

$$w(v) = a_w B_3 + b_w B_2 + c_w B_1 + d_w B_0$$

The coefficients a, b, c, and d are loaded into the 4 coefficient registers of each AFD unit. At each clock event the parameter v increases by dv and the four AFD units generate the coordinates of one pixel. The P, Q, and R AFDUs are used as function generators in Phong shading. The R AFDU computes $N \cdot N$ along a scanline or a curve. The Q and P AFDUs compute cubic approximations (linear for polygon scanlines) for the dot products between light and normal $N \cdot L$, and between highlight and normal $N \cdot H$.

The AU1 A input is $<N \cdot L, N \cdot H, 0>$. A look-up table is used to obtain the reciprocal square root of $N \cdot N$. AU1 multiplies $N \cdot L$ and $N \cdot H$ by $\frac{1}{\sqrt{N \cdot N}}$ and adds the ambient light constant, C0, to the $N \cdot L$ term. The output from AU1 is

$$\begin{bmatrix} AU1(R) \\ AU1(G) \\ AU1(B) \end{bmatrix} = \begin{bmatrix} diff \\ spec \\ 0 \end{bmatrix} = \begin{bmatrix} ambient \\ 0 \\ 0 \end{bmatrix} + \frac{1}{\sqrt{N \cdot N}} \begin{bmatrix} N \cdot L \\ N \cdot H \\ 0 \end{bmatrix}$$

The specular coefficient from AU1(G) is raised to a power by the x^m look-up table. This look-up table generates 24bit specular color values from one of 4 look-up tables, one table for white light, and three others for other light source colors. This allows a limited selection of light source colors. The AU2 operation $\alpha A + B$ multiplies the diffuse coefficient α times the object color A, and adds this to the specular coefficient B times the light color. The object color can either be the constant color C2, or a mapped sample from image memory. The resulting pixel color is

$$pixel\_color = \left[ambient + \frac{N \cdot L}{\sqrt{N \cdot N}} \right] object\_color + \left[\frac{N \cdot H}{\sqrt{N \cdot N}} \right]^m light\_color$$

The design allows high speed diffuse and specular shading and image mapping on curved surfaces, at frame buffer memory speeds.

Shading Bicubic Patches

We develop two methods for fast shading of ordinary bicubic patches. The first is to approximate the un-normalized $N \cdot L$, the un-normalized $N \cdot H$, and $N \cdot N$ over a bicubic patch using three bicubic functions $F(u,v)$. The second method is to approximate the normalized functions $N \cdot L$ and $N \cdot H$ over a bicubic patch using two bicubic functions. The shading hardware described above then generates the Phong shading values of each pixel along the curve $F(u{=}u_i, v)$. A δu is adaptively calculated so that adjacent curves have no unshaded pixel gaps between them [6]. Coons patches are used because they give tangent continuity across patch boundaries.

1. Un-normalized Coons Patch

The components of the normal vector to a bicubic patch are fifth order polynomials in u and v. Catmull[2] gives a method for approximating these biquintic functions with bicubic functions, using Coons[3] matrix C

$$C = \begin{bmatrix} 2 & -2 & 1 & 1 \\ -3 & 3 & -2 & -1 \\ 0 & 0 & 1 & 0 \\ 1 & 0 & 0 & 0 \end{bmatrix}$$

For a bicubic patch defined as

$$x(u,v) = U\ X\ V^T$$

$$y(u,v) = U\ Y\ V^T$$

$$z(u,v) = U\ Z\ V^T$$

the normal vector is

$$N = <\frac{\partial x}{\partial u}, \frac{\partial y}{\partial u}, \frac{\partial z}{\partial u}> \times <\frac{\partial x}{\partial v}, \frac{\partial y}{\partial v}, \frac{\partial z}{\partial v}>$$

$$= <n_x, n_y, n_z>$$

where

$$n_x(u,v) = y_u z_v - y_v z_u$$

$$n_y(u,v) = z_u x_v - z_v x_u$$

$$n_z(u,v) = x_u y_v - x_v y_u$$

Each component of the normal vector $<n_x, n_y, n_z>$ can be approximated by a Coon's patch $n_x(u,v) \approx UCP_xC^TV^T$, where matrix

$$P_x = \begin{bmatrix} n_x(0,0) & n_x(0,1) & \frac{\partial n_x}{\partial v}(0,0) & \frac{\partial n_x}{\partial v}(0,1) \\ n_x(1,0) & n_x(1,1) & \frac{\partial n_x}{\partial v}(1,0) & \frac{\partial n_x}{\partial v}(1,1) \\ \frac{\partial n_x}{\partial u}(0,0) & \frac{\partial n_x}{\partial u}(0,1) & \frac{\partial^2 n_x}{\partial u \partial v}(0,0) & \frac{\partial^2 n_x}{\partial u \partial v}(0,1) \\ \frac{\partial n_x}{\partial u}(1,0) & \frac{\partial n_x}{\partial u}(1,1) & \frac{\partial^2 n_x}{\partial u \partial v}(1,0) & \frac{\partial^2 n_x}{\partial u \partial v}(1,1) \end{bmatrix}$$

and similarly for n_y and n_z. (The derivation of the derivatives of the vector functions is in Appendix A.) These functions approximate *unnormalized* normal vector functions, therefore, at each pixel the shading function is calculated with an inner product, a "one over square root" look up, and a multiply:

$$N \cdot L = \frac{n_xL_x + n_yL_y + n_zL_z}{\sqrt{n_x^2 + n_y^2 + n_z^2}}$$

where $L=<L_x, L_y, L_z>$ is the light source direction. Figure 4 shows the Utah teapot rendered with a software simulation of this shading method and using the adaptive forward difference technique [6].

2. $N \cdot N$ Coons Patch

Our first approach is to apply Catmull's technique to the unnormalized normal function $N \cdot L$ as in Catmull's thesis, and to use another Coons patch to approximate $N \cdot N$. The Coons patches are converted to the forward difference basis [6] for hardware evaluation. Three AFD units are used to calculate these cubic functions $N \cdot L$, $N \cdot H$, and $N \cdot N$. This approach eliminates the calculation of $N \cdot N$ per pixel, but still needs the "one over square root" look up and a multiply.

The un-normalized $N \cdot L$ is interpolated by a matrix

$$\overline{M} = P_xL_x + P_yL_y + P_zL_z$$

and the bicubic patch is $N \cdot L(u,v) = UC\overline{M}C^TV^T$.

The inner product $N \cdot N = n_x^2 + n_y^2 + n_z^2$. We approximate this function by a bicubic function $f(u,v)$

$$N \cdot N \approx f(u,v) = UCFC^TV^T$$

where C is the Coons matrix and F is the Coons data matrix.

We derive F below. The lighting function $N \cdot L$ is given by

$$N \cdot L = \frac{N \cdot L(u,v)}{\sqrt{N \cdot N}} = \left[\frac{1}{\sqrt{f}}\right](N \cdot L(u,v))$$

It remains to obtain the elements of the matrix F for the $N \cdot N$ Coons patch. We need

$$F = \begin{bmatrix} f(0,0) & f(0,1) & \frac{\partial f}{\partial v}(0,0) & \frac{\partial f}{\partial v}(0,1) \\ f(1,0) & f(1,1) & \frac{\partial f}{\partial v}(1,0) & \frac{\partial f}{\partial v}(1,1) \\ \frac{\partial f}{\partial u}(0,0) & \frac{\partial f}{\partial u}(0,1) & \frac{\partial^2 f}{\partial u \partial v}(0,0) & \frac{\partial^2 f}{\partial u \partial v}(0,1) \\ \frac{\partial f}{\partial u}(1,0) & \frac{\partial f}{\partial u}(1,1) & \frac{\partial^2 f}{\partial u \partial v}(1,0) & \frac{\partial^2 f}{\partial u \partial v}(1,1) \end{bmatrix}$$

These elements are given by

$$\frac{\partial f}{\partial u} = 2\left[n_x\frac{\partial n_x}{\partial u} + n_y\frac{\partial n_y}{\partial u} + n_z\frac{\partial n_z}{\partial u}\right]$$

$$\frac{\partial f}{\partial v} = 2\left[n_x\frac{\partial n_x}{\partial v} + n_y\frac{\partial n_y}{\partial v} + n_z\frac{\partial n_z}{\partial v}\right]$$

$$\frac{\partial^2 f}{\partial u \partial v} = 2\left[\frac{\partial n_x}{\partial u}\frac{\partial n_x}{\partial v} + \frac{\partial n_y}{\partial u}\frac{\partial n_y}{\partial v} + \frac{\partial n_z}{\partial u}\frac{\partial n_z}{\partial v}\right] + 2\left[n_x\frac{\partial^2 n_x}{\partial u \partial v} + n_y\frac{\partial^2 n_y}{\partial u \partial v} + n_z\frac{\partial^2 n_z}{\partial u \partial v}\right]$$

and for example

$$f(0,0) = n_x^2(0,0) + n_y^2(0,0) + n_z^2(0,0)$$

We now have a bicubic function for the un-normalized $N \cdot L$ and for $N \cdot N$. Figure 5 shows the teapot rendered using this $N \cdot N$ approximation with the reciprocal square root lookup table and normalization performed at each pixel. This approximation for $N \cdot H$ starts to exhibit some visual artifacts in the specular regions on less smooth patches. The Coons patch can overshoot in the center of the patch to produce $N \cdot H$ values greater than 1. When these values are raised to a high power, some specular "blooming" occurs, as can be seen under the knob on the teapot lid.

3. Normalized Coons Patch

An alternative method is to apply Catmull's technique to the normalized functions. The normal vector for a patch is given by the cross product of the patch tangent vectors

$$N = <n_x, n_y, n_z>$$

Normalizing the normal vector functions gives

$$\hat{n}_x(u,v) = \frac{n_x}{G}$$

$$\hat{n}_y(u,v) = \frac{n_y}{G}$$

$$\hat{n}_z(u,v) = \frac{n_z}{G}$$

where G is the length of the normal vector

$$G(u,v) = \sqrt{n_x^2 + n_y^2 + n_z^2}$$

We then use a Coons patch to approximate the normalized normal vector function by

$$\hat{n}_x(u,v) \approx UC\hat{P}_x C^T V^T$$

$$\hat{n}_y(u,v) \approx UC\hat{P}_y C^T V^T$$

$$\hat{n}_z(u,v) \approx UC\hat{P}_z C^T V^T$$

where $\hat{P} = \langle \hat{P}_x, \hat{P}_y, \hat{P}_z \rangle$ is the Coons patch data matrix. The x component $\hat{P}_x$ is

$$\hat{P}_x = \begin{bmatrix} \hat{n}_x(0,0) & \hat{n}_x(0,1) & \frac{\partial \hat{n}_x}{\partial v}(0,0) & \frac{\partial \hat{n}_x}{\partial v}(0,1) \\ \hat{n}_x(1,0) & \hat{n}_x(1,1) & \frac{\partial \hat{n}_x}{\partial v}(1,0) & \frac{\partial \hat{n}_x}{\partial v}(1,1) \\ \frac{\partial \hat{n}_x}{\partial u}(0,0) & \frac{\partial \hat{n}_x}{\partial u}(0,1) & \frac{\partial^2 \hat{n}_x}{\partial u \partial v}(0,0) & \frac{\partial^2 \hat{n}_x}{\partial u \partial v}(0,1) \\ \frac{\partial \hat{n}_x}{\partial u}(1,0) & \frac{\partial \hat{n}_x}{\partial u}(1,1) & \frac{\partial^2 \hat{n}_x}{\partial u \partial v}(1,0) & \frac{\partial^2 \hat{n}_x}{\partial u \partial v}(1,1) \end{bmatrix}$$

At first glance this matrix is somewhat terrifying, however, the calculations involve many common subexpressions so that the computational cost is reasonable. Appendix A shows how to calculate the elements of the $\hat{P}_x$, $\hat{P}_y$, and $\hat{P}_z$ matrices. We now have a Coons patch which approximates the normalized normal vectors over the patch. Clearly, if the light source is transformed into world coordinates and the Coons patch is derived in world coordinates, the resulting bicubic function for $N \cdot L$ can be used for ordinary bicubic patches which undergo perspective transformations. It remains only to transform the Coons patch into the forward difference basis so that the parameters of the cubic $N \cdot L$ curves at $u=u_i$ can be loaded directly into the hardware. Figure 6 shows the teapot rendered as bicubic patches using adaptive forward differencing and shaded with the above approximations to the normalized $N \cdot L$ and $N \cdot H$. With this approximation method, only two Coons patches are required and no normalization per pixel is required.

4. Surface Rendering

Shading and image mapping onto rational bicubic or rational biquadratic patches is performed by drawing many cubic or rational cubic curves very close to each other. Each curve is a cubic in v formed by setting $u=u_i$. We therefore need to find the maximum δu between curves such that no gaps exist between the pixels of the curve $g(u_i,v)$ and the curve $g(u_i+\delta u,v)$.

To obtain this δu we use the adaptive forward difference hardware. The first partial derivative of a rational bicubic at $u = u_i$ is a 6th order rational equation. We cannot solve this directly, however, we can use the AFD units to find the maximum δu for which no gaps will exist between the curves. We first draw a series of test curves at constant v and monitor the adjustments that are made to δu along these curves. The AFDUs automatically adjust δu along the curve so as to generate one pixel steps. We need to find the smallest δu used by the hardware anywhere along these test curves. A register is maintained in the hardware which accumulates the maximum net up-down adjustments made by the AFDUs. The estimated minimum value for δu over the entire patch is obtained by looking at the number of adjusts done on these test curves by the hardware. The patch is then rendered by drawing the curves corresponding to $u = n\delta u$, for $0 \le n \le \frac{1}{\delta u}$.

For each curve we load the hardware with six sets of cubic coefficients, four for the geometry, one for the normalized $N \cdot L$, and one for the normalized $N \cdot H$. The AFDUs for x,y control the δv for all the AFDUs. The color values over a single curve of the patch are thus generated in lock step with the geometry.

Conclusions

We have described a method for shading bicubic patches suitable for hardware implementation. We presented two new methods for approximating the shading parameters over a bicubic patch. These methods both produce higher quality images than polygonal renderings. The advantages of rendering bicubic patches directly, instead of breaking them down into polygons for rendering, can be seen by comparing figures 3 and 4. The 4000 polygon teapot of figure 3 is still noticeably faceted whereas the 80 patch teapot shown in figure 4 is quite smooth. No antialiasing has been performed and the hidden surface elimination is via Z-buffer.

Further work is necessary to better understand how to approximate $N \cdot H$ with no overshoot (never greater than 1). The specular areas tend to "bloom" if the approximation exceeds 1.0 in the interior of the Coons patch. Figure 7 shows a sequence of increasingly subdivided patches using the normalized Coons method. The four examples represent 1, 4, 16, and 64 patches, respectively, used on the visible side of the teapot spout. With finer subdivision of the patches, the shading approximations improve as the patches become smoother. We use Coons patches because of their tangent continuity properties, but other approximations such as Bezier patches should be investigated.

Shading approximations for curved surfaces that are rational cubics or rational quadratics in world coordinates is an area that also needs further investigation. We are currently applying the techniques in this paper to the rational quadratic case.

Acknowledgements

Sue Carrie and David Elrod contributed to the architecture of the shading section by improving its Phong shading capabilities. Jerry Evans, Nola Donato, Bob Rocchetti, and Jim Van Loo gave many helpful suggestions on various aspects of this project.

Appendix A

A bicubic patch is defined by

$$x(u,v) = UXV$$

$$y(u,v) = UYV$$

$$z(u,v) = UZV$$

where $U = [u^3\ u^2\ u\ 1]$, $V = [v^3\ v^2\ v\ 1]^T$, $U' = [3u^2\ 2u\ 1\ 0]$, $V' = [3v^2\ 2v\ 1\ 0]^T$, $U'' = [6u\ 2\ 0\ 0]$, and $V'' = [6v\ 2\ 0\ 0]^T$. The normal vector to this patch is given by the following cross product.

$$N = <\frac{\partial x}{\partial u}, \frac{\partial y}{\partial u}, \frac{\partial z}{\partial u}> \times <\frac{\partial x}{\partial v}, \frac{\partial y}{\partial v}, \frac{\partial z}{\partial v}>$$

$$= <n_x, n_y, n_z>$$

where

$$n_x = U'YVUZV' - UYV'U'ZV$$

$$n_y = U'ZVUXV' - UZV'U'XV$$

$$n_z = U'XVUYV' - UXV'U'YV$$

The derivatives of the normal vector function are given by

$$\frac{\partial n_x}{\partial u} = U''YVUZV' + U'YVU'ZV' - U'YV'U'ZV - UYV'U''ZV$$

$$\frac{\partial n_x}{\partial v} = U'YV'UZV' + U'YVUZV'' - UYV''U'ZV - UYV'U'ZV'$$

$$\frac{\partial^2 n_x}{\partial u \partial v} = U''YV'UZV' + U''YVUZV'' + U'YV'U'ZV' + U'YVU'ZV'' - U'YV''U'ZV - U'YV'U'ZV' - UYV''U''ZV - UYV'U''ZV'$$

The normalized normal vector function or unit normal function is

$$\hat{n}_x(u,v) = \frac{n_x}{\sqrt{n^2_x + n^2_y + n^2_z}}$$

$$\hat{n}_y(u,v) = \frac{n_y}{\sqrt{n^2_x + n^2_y + n^2_z}}$$

$$\hat{n}_z(u,v) = \frac{n_z}{\sqrt{n^2_x + n^2_y + n^2_z}}$$

To interpolate the unit normal vector function by a bicubic function, we need

$$\hat{P}_x = \begin{bmatrix} \hat{n}_x(0,0) & \hat{n}_x(0,1) & \frac{\partial \hat{n}_x}{\partial v}(0,0) & \frac{\partial \hat{n}_x}{\partial v}(0,1) \\ \hat{n}_x(1,0) & \hat{n}_x(1,1) & \frac{\partial \hat{n}_x}{\partial v}(1,0) & \frac{\partial \hat{n}_x}{\partial v}(1,1) \\ \frac{\partial \hat{n}_x}{\partial u}(0,0) & \frac{\partial \hat{n}_x}{\partial u}(0,1) & \frac{\partial^2 \hat{n}_x}{\partial u \partial v}(0,0) & \frac{\partial^2 \hat{n}_x}{\partial u \partial v}(0,1) \\ \frac{\partial \hat{n}_x}{\partial u}(1,0) & \frac{\partial \hat{n}_x}{\partial u}(1,1) & \frac{\partial^2 \hat{n}_x}{\partial u \partial v}(1,0) & \frac{\partial^2 \hat{n}_x}{\partial u \partial v}(1,1) \end{bmatrix}$$

Let

$$G(u,v) = (n^2_x + n^2_y + n^2_z)^{-1/2}$$

so that, for example

$$\hat{n}_x(0,0) = n_x(0,0)G(0,0)$$

The derivatives in the u and v directions, and the cross derivatives are given by.

$$\frac{\partial \hat{n}_x(u,v)}{\partial u} = \frac{\partial n_x}{\partial u}G + \frac{\partial G}{\partial u}n_x$$

$$\frac{\partial \hat{n}_x(u,v)}{\partial v} = \frac{\partial n_x}{\partial v}G + \frac{\partial G}{\partial v}n_x$$

$$\frac{\partial^2 \hat{n}_x}{\partial u \partial v} = \frac{\partial^2 n_x}{\partial u \partial v}G + \frac{\partial n_x}{\partial u}\frac{\partial G}{\partial v} + \frac{\partial^2 G}{\partial u \partial v}n_x + \frac{\partial G}{\partial u}\frac{\partial n_x}{\partial v}$$

The only terms remaining to compute are those involving G

$$\frac{\partial G}{\partial u} = -(n^2_x + n^2_y + n^2_z)^{-3/2}\left(n_x\frac{\partial n_x}{\partial u} + n_y\frac{\partial n_y}{\partial u} + n_z\frac{\partial n_y}{\partial u}\right)$$

$$= -G^3\left(n_x\frac{\partial n_x}{\partial u} + n_y\frac{\partial n_y}{\partial u} + n_z\frac{\partial n_y}{\partial u}\right)$$

$$\frac{\partial G}{\partial v} = -(n^2_x + n^2_y + n^2_z)^{-3/2}\left(n_x\frac{\partial n_x}{\partial v} + n_y\frac{\partial n_y}{\partial v} + n_z\frac{\partial n_y}{\partial v}\right)$$

and

$$\frac{\partial^2 G}{\partial u \partial v} = \frac{\partial}{\partial v}\left[\frac{\partial G}{\partial u}\right]$$

$$= \frac{3}{G}\left[\frac{\partial G}{\partial v}\right]\left[\frac{\partial G}{\partial u}\right]$$

$$- G^3\left[\frac{\partial n_x}{\partial v}\frac{\partial n_x}{\partial u} + \frac{\partial n_y}{\partial v}\frac{\partial n_y}{\partial u} + \frac{\partial n_z}{\partial v}\frac{\partial n_z}{\partial u}\right]$$

$$- G^3\left[n_x\frac{\partial^2 n_x}{\partial u \partial v} + n_y\frac{\partial^2 n_y}{\partial u \partial v} + n_z\frac{\partial^2 n_z}{\partial u \partial v}\right]$$

References

1. Gary Bishop and David M. Weimer, "Fast Phong Shading," *Computer Graphics*, vol. 20, no. 4, pp. 103 - 106, August 1986.
2. Edwin Catmull, *A Subdivision Algorithm for Computer Display of Curved Surfaces,* Computer Science, University of Utah, UTEC-CSc-74-133, December 1974.
3. Steven A. Coons, *Surfaces for Computer-Aided Design of Space Forms,* Project MAC, Massachusetts Institute of Technology, MAC-TR-41, June 1967.
4. Tom Duff, "Smoothly Shaded Renderings of Polyhedral Objects on Raster Displays," *Computer Graphics*, vol. 13, no. 2, August 1979.
5. Jeffrey Lane, Loren Carpenter, Turner Whitted, and James Blinn, "Scan Line Methods for Displaying Parametrically Defined Surfaces," *CACM*, vol. 23, no. 1, January 1980.
6. Sheue-Ling Lien, Michael Shantz, and Vaughan Pratt, "Adaptive Forward Differencing for Rendering Curves and Surfaces," *Computer Graphics*, vol. 21, no. 4, July 1987.
7. Bui Tuong Phong, *Illumination for Computer-Generated Images,* UTEC-CSc-73-129, July 1973.

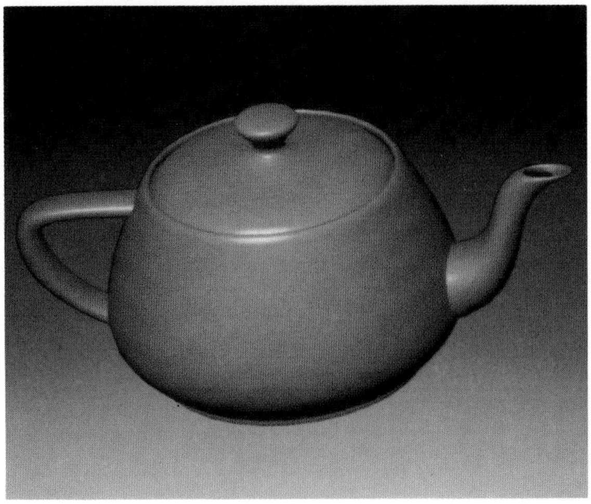

Figure 3. Classical polygon rendering of the Utah teapot using 4060 Phong shaded triangles.

Figure 4. Un-normalized Coons Patch: 80 Bicubic patches rendered using Coons patches to approximate the normal vector components n_x, n_y, n_z. The normalized $N \cdot L$ and $N \cdot H$ are computed from these components at each pixel.

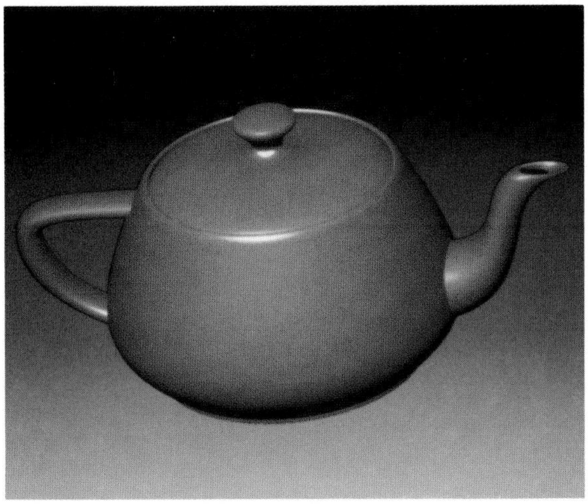

Figure 5. $N \cdot N$ Coons Patch: Bicubic patches rendered using three Coons patches to approximate the un-normalized $N \cdot L$, un-normalized $N \cdot H$ and $N \cdot N$. The normalization is performed per pixel using the square root of the $N \cdot N$ approximation.

Figure 6. Normalized Coons Patch: Bicubic patches rendered using two Coons patches to approximate the normalized $N \cdot L$ and normalized $N \cdot H$. No additional normalization is performed per pixel.

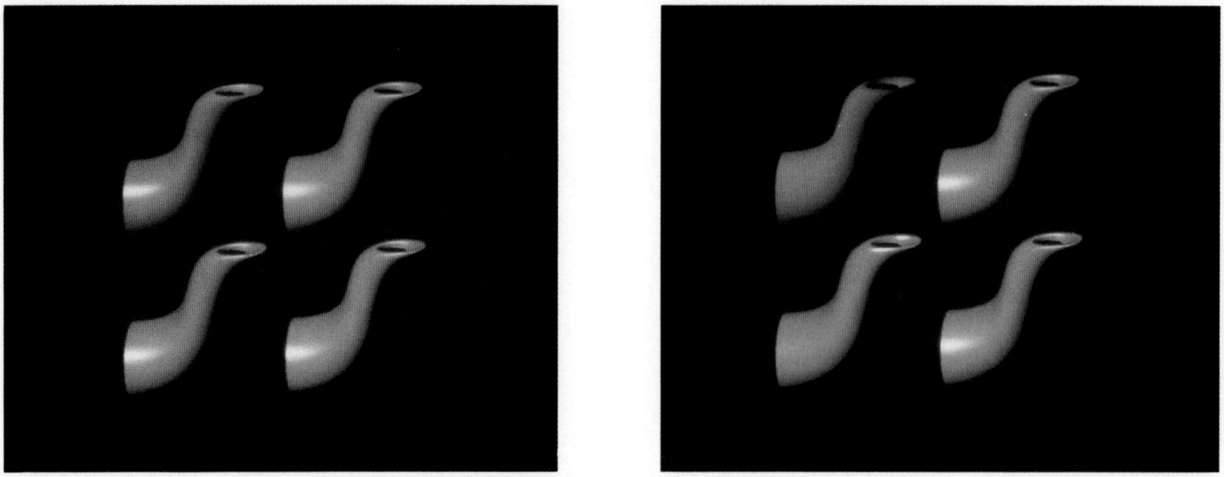

Figure 7. Patch rendering showing the improvement in the shading approximations with succesive subdivision. Here 1, 4, 16, and 64 patches are used on the visible side of the teapot spout (not including the backside or the very small patches forming the tip of the spout). The left group of four are done using the un-normalized Coons Patch method. Those on the right are done using the Normalized Coons Patch method.

A Parallel Processor Architecture for Graphics Arithmetic Operations

John G. Torborg

Raster Technologies, Inc.
Two Robbins Road
Westford, Mass. 01886

ABSTRACT

Interactive 3D graphics applications require significant arithmetic processing to handle complex models, particularly if realistic rendering techniques are used. Current semiconductor technology cannot provide the necessary performance without some form of multiprocessing.

This paper describes a graphics processor architecture which can be configured with an arbitrary number of identical processors operating in parallel. Each of the parallel processors can be programmed identically as if it were a single processor system, substantially simplifying software development and allowing complex rendering functions to take advantage of the multiple processors. The architecture described is able to achieve extremely high performance while allowing the price/performance of the system to be optimized for a given application.

Techniques are described for handling graphics command distribution, sequencing of commands which must be processed in order, parallel processing of graphics primitive picking, and handling inquiry (readback) commands.

CR Categories and Subject Descriptors: B.2.1 [Arithmetic and Logic Structures]: Design Styles - Parallel; C.1.2 [Processor Architectures]: Multiprocessors - Parallel processors; I.3.5 [Computer Graphics]: Computational Geometry and Object Modeling - Geometric algorithms, languages, and systems.

Additional Key Words and Phrases: parallel processing, arithmetic processing, graphics command processing.

INTRODUCTION

Multiprocessor architectures have been used for several years to meet the demanding computational requirements of interactive 3D graphics. Simple graphics operations such as 3D wireframe manipulation can easily be divided into a sequence of pipelined operations. If independent processors are used to handle these operations, very high performance can be attained [Clark 1982]. However, more complex operations such as surface tesselation and lighting calculations can not easily be handled by a highly pipelined architecture because of the difficulty in reconfiguring the pipeline to execute a wide variety of different graphics operations efficiently.

Although parallel processing architectures have been explored by many researchers for performing drawing operations [Fuchs 1981, Niimi 1984, Fuchs 1986], relatively little work has been done to take advantage of parallel processing for front end geometric and arithmetic operations. A graphics processor architecture is presented which employs an arbitrary number of identical graphics arithmetic processors. This architecture is currently being implemented in a high performance graphics system which can be configured with one to eight processors.

The graphics system has been designed to run an extended version of the ANSI proposed Programmer's Hierarchical Interactive Graphics Standard called PHIGS+. PHIGS+ has been jointly developed by several industrial and university contributors to provide a standard for high performance 3D graphics systems. Extensions to the ANSI proposed PHIGS are provided for shading and hidden surface removal, lighting models, arbitrary clipping planes, 3D curves and surfaces, depth cueing, segment extents, and several other extensions. Many of these capabilities have been available on a smattering of high performance graphics systems although no attempt has been made to standardize them. [van Dam, et. al. 1987].

While some of the specifics of the graphics processor implementation are unique to PHIGS+, most of the concepts can be easily applied to other graphics command sets.

A parallel processing architecture for graphics must provide two basic attributes to be effective. First, graphics commands must be adequately distributed between the processors for efficient processor utilization. And second, the multiple processors must produce the same apparent results as a single processor performing the same operations. In other words, as additional processors are added, the user should notice no differences in the operation of the system other than an almost linear improvement in graphics performance.

ORDER INDEPENDENCE OF GRAPHICS COMMANDS

An order-independent series of graphics commands is defined as a list of graphics primitives (polylines, polygons, etc.) in which the order in which the primitives are drawn has no effect on the display. For example, consider a series of vectors which define an arbitrary wireframe object. As long as all of these vectors are drawn into the frame buffer with the same pixel value (color), the order in which they are actually drawn has no effect on the resultant image.

Analysis of a shaded surface representation of the same object indicates that if depth buffering is used to perform hidden surface removal, the resultant image will be determined by the depth priority of each pixel on each patch and is again independent of the order in which the primitives (patches in this case) are drawn.

The order-independent nature of the most frequently encountered graphics primitives allows a parallel processing architecture to be used very efficiently. There are, however, some graphics primitives and other operators which may be encountered in a display list which are not order-independent. The parallel processing architecture should also handle these operations with minimal degradation to the overall system performance.

Sequential Commands

A sequential graphics command is defined to be one which must be processed (written into the frame buffer if it is a drawing primitive) after all preceding graphics commands, and must be processed before any succeeding graphics commands. An example of a sequential command is one which changes the pixel value with which succeeding drawing primitives will be written.

A simple approach to handling sequential commands would be to wait until all graphics processors are idle, process the command by a single processor, then continue the distribution of order-independent commands to the parallel processors. This approach dramatically reduces system performance if the command stream contains a significant percentage of sequential commands dispersed throughout.

The inefficiencies which result from this situation can be greatly minimized by providing a mechanism which can reorder the sequential commands as they are drawn into the frame buffer. There will still be a degree of inefficiency due to the forced delay of the processors which are processing other commands (to wait for the sequential command to be transferred), but this will be shown to be minimal.

GRAPHICS SYSTEM ARCHITECTURE AND DATA FLOW

The overall architecture of the graphics display system is split into three main sections as shown in Figure 1. The display list manager contains a dual-ported memory system and memory management processor. Graphics commands are stored in this memory system as a hierarchical structure of linked blocks. The memory management processor reads graphics commands from a particular structure (as specified by the applications processor) and sends each command to a graphics arithmetic processor as shown in Figure 2.

The graphics arithmetic processors handle all of the complex computational functions such as transformations, clipping, tesselation, lighting models, picking, and general command processing. After processing, the graphics arithmetic processors transfer low-level drawing primitives (points, vectors, triangles, etc.) to the image memory units (as shown in Figure 2). The uniqueness of this architecture is in determining the order in which these low-level drawing primitives are transferred.

The image memory units contain a frame buffer and video output section, as well as a VLSI drawing processor which directly handles vectors, triangles, rectangles, and bitblts. By offloading the low-level drawing operations to the image memory units, the processing time for each graphics command (by the graphics arithmetic processors) is independent of the number of pixels that are modified, thereby increasing the uniformity of command processing time and improving the efficiency of parallel processing of order dependent commands.

The VLSI drawing processor has been designed to allow very fast update of image memory. A master controller IC and four scan line processor ICs make up the drawing processor. The master control parses the low-level drawing command stream and performs setup calculations for the various operations. Each scan-line processors each control one quarter of the scan-lines using a four-way interleaved organization. The image memory is five-way interleaved to each scan-line processor allowing the entire system to access twenty pixels every memory cycle. This allows a peak drawing performance of over 60 million pixels per second including full intensity interpolation and depth buffering.

The master controller IC directly controls vector and triangle operations and performs the necessary setup calculations. The setup calculations, as well as the pixel drawing performance, can limit the primitive drawing rate. The vector setup time is 1 microsecond allowing 1 million short vectors/second to be rendered. The triangle setup time is 3 microseconds allowing 330,000 small triangles/second to be rendered (including interpolated shading and depth buffering). Substantial floating point arithmetic power is necessary to fully utilize the drawing performance of this processor.

COMMAND DISTRIBUTION

The display list manager interfaces with the graphics arithmetic processors over a unidirectional 32-bit synchronous bus (called the CMD Bus). Data will be transferred to the arithmetic processors whenever data is available and the appropriate arithmetic processor is ready. Graphics commands are distributed to arithmetic processors in one of four ways as determined by information in the first word of each command.

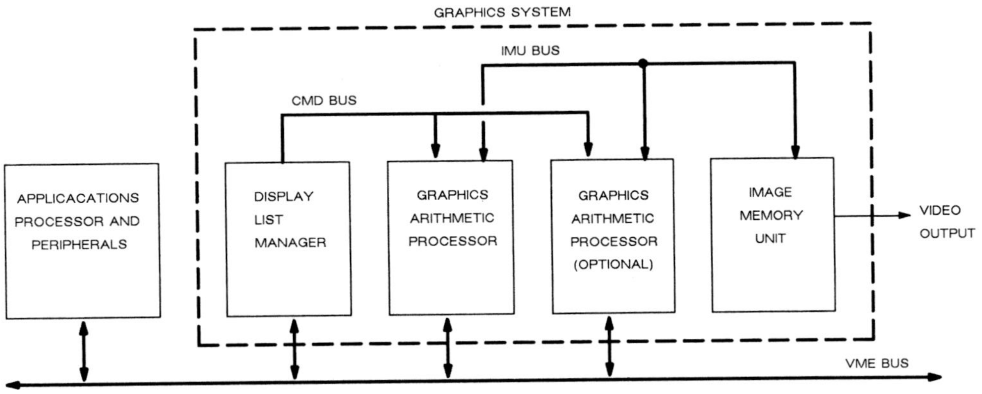

FIGURE 1 GRAPHICS SYSTEM ARCHITECTURE

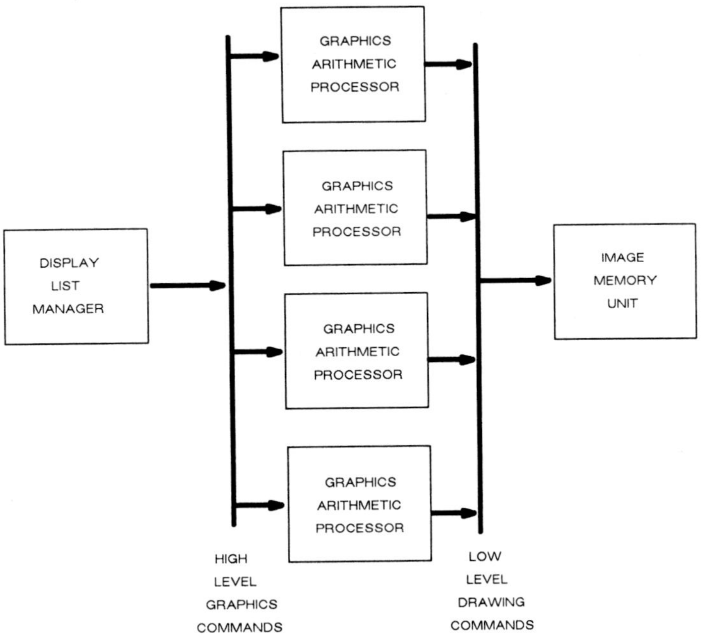

FIGURE 2 GRAPHICS COMMAND PROCESSING DATA FLOW

1) The command is not sent to any arithmetic processor. This command type is used to insert labels and other non-graphics information into the display list.

2) The command is sent to all arithmetic processors. This is used for commands that affect state on the arithmetic processors, such as the transformation matrix, the clipping planes, or the light sources.

3) The command is sent to the arithmetic processor which is most ready to accept the command. This is determined by a command arbitration mechanism described later. This command type is used for all graphics drawing primitives and all other graphics commands which only affect the image memory units.

4) The command is sent to a specific arithmetic processor. In this case, the first word in the command specifies a particular processor number. This mode is currently not used but could allow specialized processors to be incorporated into the architecture for certain command types in the future.

Command Format

The first word of each command is called the command header and is used to indicate how the command should be distributed between the parallel processors. An eight bit field in the header indicates the command type. The remainder of the header bits provide command dependent information to the arithmetic processors.

The command type field in the header is defined as follows:

Distribution Mode	Order Dependence	Hidden Command	Pick Mode
3 bits	3 bits	1 bit	1 bit

The distribution mode field is used by the display list manager and graphics arithmetic processors to determine how the command should be distributed. The order dependence field is used by the arithmetic processor in determining whether the command must be processed sequentially. The hidden command bit and pick mode bits are used for graphics primitive picking and are described later.

Order Dependence Classification

Parallel command processing falls into two categories - order-independent and sequential. The order dependence field in the command header is used to determine how the command will be processed by the arithmetic processors. All commands fall into one of six classifications as described below.

1) Non-shaded Drawing Primitive Command. This classification includes all drawing primitives which use preset value registers (registers on the image memory unit which have been loaded by a previous command) to determine the pixel value in which the primitive will be drawn. Examples of these commands are vectors (other than depth-queued vectors), circles, arcs, and polygons. This command type is order-independent and therefore can always be processed in parallel and transferred to the image memory unit in any order.

2) Shaded Drawing Primitive Command. All drawing primitives where the value of the pixel data is computed using light source calculations or where the value is included in the command (other than image transfers) fall into this category. Examples of these commands are shaded patches, 3D surfaces, and depth-queued lines. This type of command is order-independent if depth buffering is used to determine depth priority. If depth buffering is not enabled, this command is sequential and must be transferred to the image memory unit in the same order as the command appeared in the original command stream.

3) Sequential Image Memory Unit Command. All commands of this type must be transferred from the arithmetic processor(s) to the image memory unit in the same order in which it occurred in the original command stream. Examples of these commands are set value register, set area pattern, and set vector pattern.

4) Inquire Image Memory Unit Commands. All inquire commands are sequential commands to insure that the application will receive the inquire responses in order and to insure that the data is current. This command category is used for inquire commands which read data from the image memory units. Inquiries to the image memory unit will occur in the same order as the command appeared in the original command stream. Likewise, data transfers back to the application processor must occur in order. Examples of these commands are inquire value register, inquire pixel data, and inquire look-up table entry.

5) Inquire Arithmetic Processor State. This classification is used for inquire commands which respond with state contained on the arithmetic processors. As described above, all inquire commands are sequential commands requiring response data to be transferred to the application processor in order. Examples of this command category are inquire transformation matrix, inquire clipping plane, and inquire light source.

6) Order-Independent Image Memory Unit Command. This command type is used to specify a command which accesses the image memory unit and is order independent. This command type is not currently used.

Command Arbitration

Command arbitration is used to determine which arithmetic processor should receive the command if it can be processed in parallel. This arbitration mechanism attempts to fairly distribute commands between processors and gives priority to processors which are most ready to accept the command.

Each processor has a command input FIFO which is used to buffer commands from the display list manager. This FIFO is 512 long-words deep so that it can contain several commands simultaneously. The processor will request commands on two priority levels based on the amount of data in its input FIFO. If the FIFO is empty, it will request a command using the high priority request. If the FIFO is not empty but is less than half full, the lower priority request will be used.

No request will be made if the input FIFO is more than half full. This insures that the processor will not request a command if it cannot buffer the entire command in the remaining space in the FIFO (at least for the vast majority of commands). This prevents one processor from tying up the bus when another processor may be idle.

A fair arbitration mechanism is used to insure that all processors requesting a command on a given arbitration level will be serviced before any other processor can request. If all commands took the same amount of processing time, this would result in a round-robin command distribution. However, since command processing time is usually not evenly distributed, distribution priority is given to the processors executing the commands which take the least amount of time to process.

GRAPHICS ARITHMETIC PROCESSOR ARCHITECTURE

A simplified block diagram of the graphics arithmetic processor is shown in Figure 3. This diagram shows the basic blocks that are necessary for graphics drawing operations. The programmable element of the graphics arithmetic processor is designated the processor core. This is implemented using a horizontally microcoded 32 bit processor running at 12.5 Mhz providing a peak performance of 12.5 MIPs and 25 MFLOPs (using independent multiply and ALU pipelines).

Graphics Command Input Controller

The graphics command input controller includes the CMD Bus interface and the command input FIFO. This controller determines which commands and which command headers need to be clocked into the input FIFO, based on the result of the command arbitration and the information in the command header. All commands (including headers) to be executed by the processor core are clocked into the FIFO. In addition, command headers are clocked into the FIFO for commands which are sequential or potentially sequential (for example, shaded drawing primitives are sequential if depth buffering is disabled, but are otherwise order-independent). During pick mode (described later), all command headers are clocked into the FIFO.

In addition to the data, two control bits are clocked into the FIFO. These two bits indicate whether the data is a header and whether the header is part of a command to be executed by this particular arithmetic processor. The processor core only executes commands which are so indicated.

Graphics Command Tag FIFO

As each command header is fetched from the command input FIFO, an entry is loaded into another small tag FIFO (64 x 2). This FIFO is used to keep track of the ordering of all sequential commands being processed by all arithmetic processors and all commands being processed by this processor. The two bit entry in the tag FIFO indicates whether the command is being processed by this arithmetic processor and whether the command is a sequential command. The appropriate mode bits are checked to determine if a potentially sequential command is actually sequential before loading the tag FIFO. (A potentially sequential command which is determined to be order-independent and is not being processed by this arithmetic processor will not cause an entry to be loaded into the tag FIFO).

This tag FIFO is the key to providing optimum performance for parallel commands and insuring sequential processing of order dependent commands. The output of this FIFO is used to control the order in which image memory unit commands are transferred over the image memory unit bus (IMU Bus).

Drawing Command Output Controller

This controller is used to transfer data from the processor core to the image memory units over a 32-bit multimaster synchronous data bus (IMU Bus). Included in this logic is a 512 x 36 output FIFO and the mechanism used to maintain proper ordering of sequential commands.

The processor core writes image memory unit commands into the output FIFO as required. The first 32-bit word of each command is a command header which indicates the destination of the command as well as certain command specific information. In addition to the data word, the FIFO contains several control bits which indicate the first word (header) and last word of each image memory unit command. If the entry is the last word, control bits indicate whether the command is the last of a sequence of indivisible commands, and whether it is the last of a group of commands spawned by a single high-level graphics input command.

The control information allows multiple image memory unit commands to be associated with a single high-level graphics input command. These commands may be divisible in which case the output controller will release the IMU Bus between commands (assuming that the graphics input command was not sequential), or may be indivisible in which case all the image memory commands will be sent as a group before releasing the bus.

The output of the tag FIFO is used to control arbitration for the IMU Bus. If the two control bits indicate that the command is not sequential, then the output controller will request the IMU Bus as soon as a complete command block is available. In this case, the order in which commands are transferred to the image memory unit will depend on the processor load and command distribution of all processors. The tag FIFO output will be clocked after each command group associated with a single graphics input command is transferred over the IMU Bus.

If the tag FIFO indicates a sequential command, the output controller will wait until all other arithmetic processor output controllers have reached the same point in the original command stream. Since every processor places an entry into its tag FIFO for every

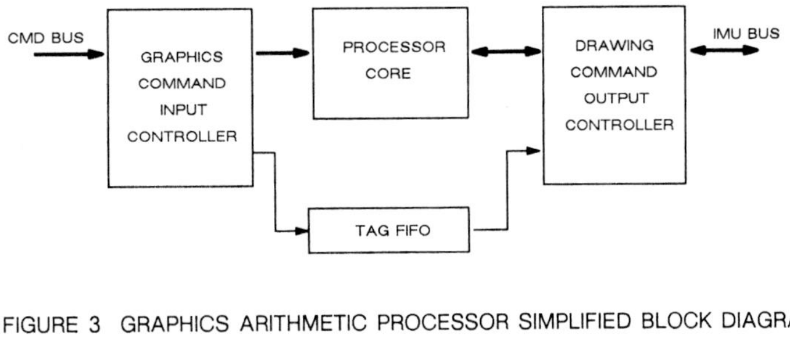

FIGURE 3 GRAPHICS ARITHMETIC PROCESSOR SIMPLIFIED BLOCK DIAGRAM

sequential command (even if the command is not executed on that processor), all processors' tag FIFOs will indicate a sequential command but only one will indicate that the command was processed by that processor. The processor which has processed the sequential command will then request the bus and send the group of commands associated with the graphics input command. Once this command transfer has completed, the tag FIFO output on all arithmetic processors will be clocked.

Since the processor core can still continue to transfer commands into the output FIFO, processor performance is usually not affected when the IMU interface is held up to maintain sequentiality.

GRAPHICS COMMAND PREFETCHER

The command headers of all potentially sequential commands are transferred to all arithmetic processors. If a significant number of potentially sequential commands (such as 3D patches) are being processed in a large configuration (several processors), each processor will receive many more command headers than commands. A command prefetcher is added to eliminate the overhead associated with these extra command headers. This prefetcher will fetch data out of the FIFO before it is required by the processor core. If the data is a header which is not to be processed by the processor core, it is handled directly by the prefetcher. The tag FIFO is also controlled by the prefetcher, allowing the processor core to completely ignore the parallel processing aspects of the architecture.

SEQUENCING OF RESPONSE DATA

Response data is sent to the application processor over the VME bus. This allows inquiry commands to be processed without interrupting the command pipeline from the display list manager. All response data is written back to the application processor in the same order as the high-level graphics commands occurred in the command stream.

As with the IMU Bus, some mechanism must be provided to insure that response data transfers are performed sequentially. The mechanism provided for the VME Bus is the same as the IMU Bus with two exceptions. First, the response commands are always sequential so no distinction is made between sequential and order-independent commands. Second, some commands do not always have response data to send (such as drawing primitives in pick mode) so a mechanism must be provided to allow processing to continue without requesting the VME Bus.

The VME Bus interface incorporates a small (64 x 1) tag FIFO to keep track of sequential inquiry commands. This FIFO is clocked whenever a command header is fetched from the command input FIFO which potentially has response data to transfer back to the application processor. The FIFO input bit is set if the command will be processed by the processor core and is cleared if the command will be processed by a different arithmetic processor.

The output of the tag FIFO is used to control arbitration for the VME Bus. If the FIFO is not empty, a VME response transfer is pending from some processor. A mechanism is provided to suspend VME arbitration until all processor VME bus controllers have reached the same point in the command stream (indicated by a tag FIFO not-empty condition). If the processor executing the command has response data to send to the application processor, it can then request the VME Bus and transfer the data. After the processor has transferred all its response data, or if no data is to be sent, all processor VME bus controllers will clock their tag FIFO outputs.

Two enhancements are added to this basic mechanism to improve parallel processing performance. The VME Bus controller will assume that the processor core did not require the VME Bus if another command is fetched from the input FIFO. This eliminates the need for the processor to inform the bus controller. Further, the VME Bus controller incorporates a counter which keeps track of the number of potential response commands which did not require VME Bus access. This counter allows the processor core to continue processing potential response commands without waiting for the VME Bus sequential transfer mechanism to catch up. Only when the processor actually needs to transfer data over the VME Bus will it wait for the other arithmetic processors (which are performing response transfers from commands earlier in the command stream). These enhancements are particularly important when the system is operating in pick mode (described below) because all primitive drawing commands are potentially response commands although only a small percentage of commands actually transfer data over the VME Bus.

GRAPHICS PRIMITIVE PICKING

Primitive picking performance is as important as display performance in an interactive system. The arithmetic processors operate in a special mode for primitive picking operations. This pick mode is controlled by the display list manager and causes drawing primitives to be handled differently. As the display list is traversed, all geometry is transformed and clipped normally, and is also clipped to the pick aperture. The pick aperture is a small 2D window (or 3D cube) which surrounds the pick point (normally the pointing device position). Primitives which intersect the pick aperture cause a pick hit. When this occurs, the arithmetic processor will inform the application processor with information identifying the picked primitive.

All drawing primitives are potentially response commands when the system is in pick mode. This requires that all command headers for pickable commands be loaded into the input FIFO of all arithmetic processors. (Note that all command headers must be clocked in to support the primitive counting mechanism described below). Only those primitives which are picked will actually generate a response to the application processor.

Some commands, such as segment ID, are only needed by the arithmetic processors when in pick mode. The command header contains a bit, called the Pick Mode bit, which is set for commands required only during pick mode. These commands are not transferred to the arithmetic processors unless the system is in pick mode, thus reducing processor overhead when the system is not in pick mode.

PRIMITIVE COUNTING MECHANISM

When a pick hit is detected by the arithmetic processor, information is returned to the application processor identifying the location in the structure of the primitive. The PHIGS graphics standard includes a primitive count as part of this information. The primitive count specifies the number of the primitive within the structure.

A 24-bit counter is provided on each arithmetic processor. This counter is incremented for each command header as it is fetched from the command input FIFO except for those headers with the hidden bit set. The hidden bit allows non-PHIGS commands (such as display list labels) to be inserted in the command stream transparently to the primitive count and the application program. Since all headers are clocked into the input FIFO of all arithmetic processors when the system is in pick mode, each arithmetic processor can maintain a count of the PHIGS primitive which is being processed.

The primitive count is pushed onto a stack and the counter is reset when a segment reference is encountered. The primitive count is restored when the segment ends.

A latch is loaded with the primitive count when a header is fetched from the input FIFO which is to be executed by the processor core. This allows the command prefetcher to continue prefetching headers from the input FIFO while the processor core is testing the primitive against the pick aperture. If the processor core determines that the primitive is a valid pick hit, it can then write the primitive count and appropriate tree (structure) information to the application processor.

PERFORMANCE

At the time that this paper was written, the system was in debug and was unavailable for system benchmarking. The image memory unit and VLSI drawing processor has been fabricated and the performance of this part of the system has been validated. Detailed simulation software has been developed to allow accurate system analysis. A wireframe and shaded patch representation of an automobile (shown in Figure 4 and 5) have been run through this simulator to show the performance of the parallel processing architecture. The expected performance is shown below.

Wire Frame Database of Chrysler Laser
courtesy of Chrysler Corporation

Number of Vectors: 99,236

Average Vector Length: 4.8 pixels

Number of Processors	Time to Process Image	Processor Efficiency
1	690 ms	100%
2	345 ms	100%
3	230 ms	100%
4	176 ms	98%
5	143 ms	96%
6	124 ms	93%
7	109 ms	90%
8	104 ms	84%

Shaded Patch Database of Chrysler Laser
courtesy of Chrysler Corporation

Number of Triangles: 64,696

Average Triangle Size: 19 pixels

Number of Processors	Time to Process Image	Processor Efficiency
1	5.7 sec	100%
2	2.9 sec	100%
3	1.9 sec	100%
4	1.4 sec	100%
5	1.1 ms	100%
6	950 ms	100%
7	820 ms	100%
8	720 ms	100%

Perspective transformations were applied to both the wireframe and surface models. Approximately half of the triangles were culled because the normal vectors were facing away from the viewer. Diffuse, ambient, and specular terms were calculated at each vertex of the remaining triangles to determine the colors to be interpolated.

The efficiency of this architecture when processing a large number of the same command is extremely high (until other system constraints are reached). This makes the system well suited for interactive manipulation of complex models. Processor efficiency degrades as the processing time for each command becomes less uniform and as the percentage of sequential commands increases. Our simulations have shown that this becomes a factor only when the total drawing command output rate (from all graphics arithmetic processors) starts to exceed 50% of the drawing processor bandwidth. Below this level, the output FIFOs of the graphics arithmetic processors are never filled so the processor core never has to wait. On the current implementation, the maximum vector drawing performance of 104 ms (for the given example) is reached with just over seven processors. The maximum shaded patch rendering performance of 150 ms is not reached with the maximum complement of processors.

SUMMARY

A parallel processing architecture has been presented which allows an arbitrary number of identical processors to be applied to graphics arithmetic calculations. This system provides the necessary floating point computational power to handle sophisticated tesselation and lighting models, while still operating very efficiently and cost effectively for simple operations such as transformations and clipping.

The processors are each programmed identically and each processor is programmed as if it were a uniprocessor system, thus substantially simplifying software development. The number of processors can be optimized for the computational requirements of the problem, allowing a cost effective system to be implemented for a wide range of applications. Also, since all processors are identical, systems in the field can be upgraded to higher performance by simply plugging in additional processor boards.

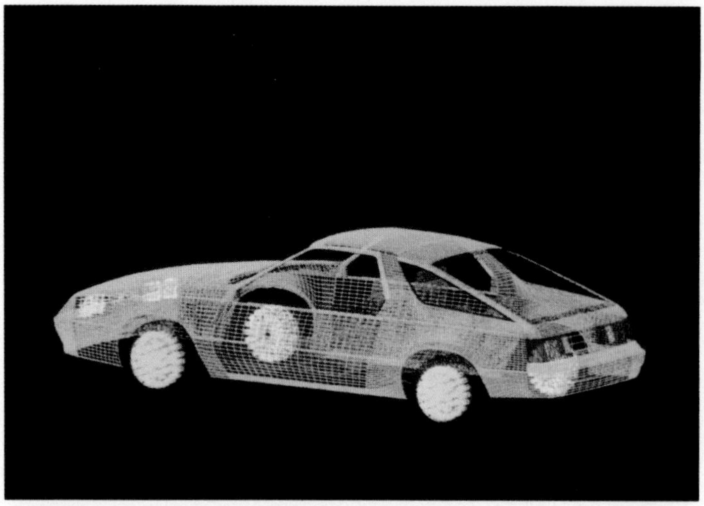

FIGURE 4 WIRE FRAME IMAGE (Database Courtesy Chrysler Corporation)

FIGURE 5 SHADED IMAGE (Database Courtesy Chrysler Corporation)

ACKNOWLEDGMENTS

Thanks to the entire graphics system design team for their participation in the implementation of this architecture. Special thanks to Fred Oliver and Mary Ellen Natusch for their help in the details and implementation of the parallel processors, Chan Verbeck for the development of the simulator used to estimate the performance of the graphics system, and Dave Youatt for generating the images, and Greg Bartlett for generating the figures.

REFERENCES

Clark, J.H., "The Geometry Engine, a VLSI Geometry System for Graphics", Computer Graphics (ACM) 16,3 (1982), 127.

Fuchs, H. and Poulton, J., "Pixel-Planes: A VLSI-Oriented Design for a Raster Graphics Engine," VLSI Design, No. 3 (1981), 20.

Fuchs, H., Goldfeather, J., Hultquist,, J. "Fast Constructive Solid Geometry Display in the Pixel-Powers Graphics System," Computer Graphics (ACM) 20,4 (1986), 107.

Niimi, H., Imai, Y., Murakami, M., Tomita, S., and Hagiwara, H., "A Parallel Processor System for Three-Dimensional Color Graphics," Computer Graphics (ACM) 18,3 (1984), 67.

Torborg, John G., "Computer Graphics System Having Arbitrary Number of Parallel Arithmetic Processors," US Patent Application, (1987).

van Dam. A., et. al., "PHIGS+ Functional Description Rev. 2," Jointly developed PHIGS+ specification. (1987) Contact Andries van Dam - Committee Chairman, Stellar Computer Inc., 100 Wells Ave., Newton, MA, 02159. (1987).

Elastically Deformable Models

Demetri Terzopoulos[†]
John Platt[‡]
Alan Barr[‡]
Kurt Fleischer[†]

[†]Schlumberger Palo Alto Research, 3340 Hillview Avenue, Palo Alto, CA 94304
[‡]California Institute of Technology, Pasadena, CA 91125

Abstract: The theory of elasticity describes deformable materials such as rubber, cloth, paper, and flexible metals. We employ elasticity theory to construct differential equations that model the behavior of non-rigid curves, surfaces, and solids as a function of time. Elastically deformable models are active: they respond in a natural way to applied forces, constraints, ambient media, and impenetrable obstacles. The models are fundamentally dynamic and realistic animation is created by numerically solving their underlying differential equations. Thus, the description of shape and the description of motion are unified.

Keywords: Modeling, Deformation, Elasticity, Dynamics, Animation, Simulation
CR categories: G.1.8—Partial Differential Equations; I.3.5—Computational Geometry and Object Modeling (Curve, Surface, Solid, and Object Representations); I.3.7—Three-Dimensional Graphics and Realism

1. Introduction

Methods to formulate and represent instantaneous shapes of objects are central to computer graphics modeling. These methods have been particularly successful for modeling rigid objects whose shapes do not change over time. This paper develops an approach to modeling which incorporates the physically-based dynamics of flexible materials into the purely geometric models which have been used traditionally. We propose models based on elasticity theory which conveniently represent the shape and motion of deformable materials, especially when these materials interact with other physically-based computer graphics objects.

1.1. Physical Models versus Kinematic Models

Most traditional methods for computer graphics modeling are kinematic; that is, the shapes are compositions of geometrically or algebraically defined primitives. Kinematic models are passive because they do not interact with each other or with external forces. The models are either stationary or are subjected to motion according to prescribed trajectories. Expertise is required to create natural and pleasing dynamics with passive models.

As an alternative, we advocate the use of active models in computer graphics. Active models are based on principles of mathematical physics [5]. They react to applied forces (such as gravity), to constraints (such as linkages), to ambient media (such as viscous fluids), or to impenetrable obstacles (such as supporting surfaces) as one would expect real, physical objects to react.

This paper develops models of deformable curves, surfaces, and solids which are based on simplifications of elasticity theory. By simulating physical properties such as tension and rigidity, we can model static shapes exhibited by a wide range of deformable objects, including string, rubber, cloth, paper, and flexible metals. Furthermore, by including physical properties such as mass and damping, we can simulate the dynamics of these objects. The simulation involves numerically solving the partial differential equations that govern the evolving shape of the deformable object and its motion through space.

The dynamic behavior inherent to our deformable models significantly simplifies the animation of complex objects. Consider the graphical representation of a coiled telephone cord. The traditional approach has been to represent the instantaneous shape of the cord as a mesh assembly of bicubic spline patches or polygons. Making the cord move plausibly is a nontrivial task. In contrast, our deformable models can provide a physical representation of the cord which exhibits natural dynamics as it is subjected to external forces and constraints.

1.2. Outline

The remainder of the paper develops as follows: Section 2 discusses the connections of our work to other physical models in computer graphics. Section 3 gives differential equations of motion describing the dynamic behavior of deformable models under the influence of external forces. Section 4 contains an analysis of deformation and defines deformation energies for curve, surface, and solid models. Section 5 lists various external forces that can be applied to deformable models to produce animation. Section 6 describes our implementation of deformable models. Section 7 presents simulations illustrating the application of deformable models. Section 8 discusses our work in progress.

2. Related Graphics Models

Interestingly, the classical spline representations of shape have characterizations based in elasticity theory [7]. However, in adopting splines as a representation of curve and surface shape, the graphics literature has deemphasized the physical basis of splines. The cubic interpolating spline, for instance, is an abstraction of the shape exhibited by a thin elastic beam (the elastica used in boat construction) whose minimal bending energy configuration may be characterized by a fourth-order differential equation. The elasticity theory perspective leads to generalized spline representations of curves, surfaces, and solids. Our work in this paper can be viewed as an extension, including physically-based dynamics, of the mixed-order generalized splines employed in computer vision by Terzopoulos [24].

Special purpose physical models have begun to capture the attention of the computer graphics community. Fluid mechanics was used by Peachey [20] and Fournier and Reeves [11] to model water waves, as well as Kajiya and von Herzen [17] and Yaeger *et al.* [28] for cloud simulation. Also, the physics of imaging has been applied to rendering [16, 15]. Weil [26] used catenaries to approximate cloth, while Feynman [10] used a more sophisticated thin plate flexure model for the same purpose.

Terzopoulos [23] employed deformable models based on variational principles to reconstruct surfaces from scattered visual constraints. To create deformable models, Barr [3] subjected solid primitives to prescribed deformations using Jacobian matrices. Sederberg and Parry [21] imposed similar deformations to solids modeled as free-form surfaces. We extend these approaches by adding equations governing the evolution of deformations.

Our models are compatible with and complementary to the constraint-based modeling approach for rigid primitives proposed by Barzel and Barr [4], as well as with the dynamics-based approaches of Wilhelms and Barsky [27] and Armstrong and Green [1] to animating articulated rigid bodies. Finally, since computer vision is the inverse problem of computer graphics, the models presented in this paper are of value for reconstructing mathematical representations of non-rigid objects from their images [25].

3. Dynamics of Deformable Models

We begin the mathematical development by giving the equations of motion governing the dynamics of our deformable models under the influence of applied forces. The equations of motion are obtained from Newtonian mechanics and balance the externally applied forces with the forces due to the deformable model.

Let $\mathbf{a}$ be the intrinsic or material coordinates of a point in a body Ω. For a solid body, $\mathbf{a}$ has three components: $[a_1, a_2, a_3]$. Similarly, for a surface $\mathbf{a} = [a_1, a_2]$, and a curve $\mathbf{a} = [a_1]$. The Euclidean 3-space positions of points in the body are given by a time-varying vector valued function of the material coordinates $\mathbf{r}(\mathbf{a}, t) = [r_1(\mathbf{a}, t), r_2(\mathbf{a}, t), r_3(\mathbf{a}, t)]$. The body in its natural rest state (see Figure 1) is specified by $\mathbf{r}^0(\mathbf{a}) = [r_1^0(\mathbf{a}), r_2^0(\mathbf{a}), r_3^0(\mathbf{a})]$.

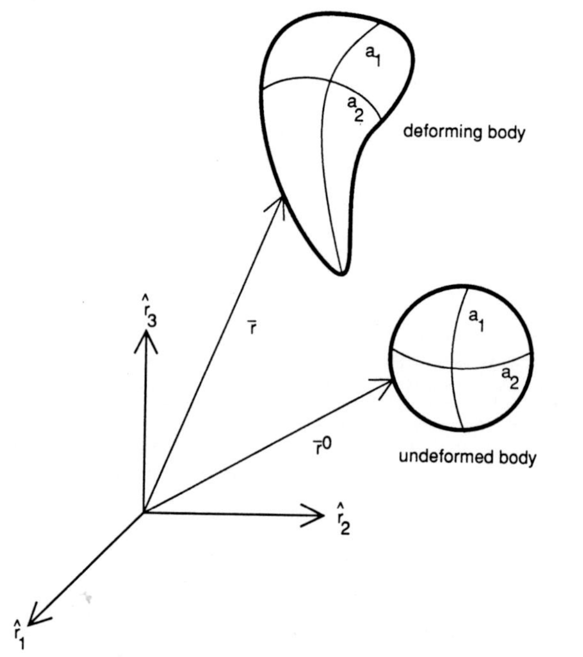

Figure 1. Coordinate systems.

The equations governing a deformable model's motion can be written in Lagrange's form [14] as follows:

$$\frac{\partial}{\partial t}\left(\mu \frac{\partial \mathbf{r}}{\partial t}\right) + \gamma \frac{\partial \mathbf{r}}{\partial t} + \frac{\delta \mathcal{E}(\mathbf{r})}{\delta \mathbf{r}} = \mathbf{f}(\mathbf{r}, t), \tag{1}$$

where $\mathbf{r}(\mathbf{a}, t)$ is the position of the particle $\mathbf{a}$ at time t, $\mu(\mathbf{a})$ is the mass density of the body at $\mathbf{a}$, $\gamma(\mathbf{a})$ is the damping density, and $\mathbf{f}(\mathbf{r}, t)$ represents the net externally applied forces. $\mathcal{E}(r)$ is a *functional* which measures the net instantaneous potential energy of the elastic deformation of the body.

The external forces are balanced against the force terms on the left hand side of (1) due to the deformable model. The first term is the inertial force due to the model's distributed mass. The second term is the damping force due to dissipation. The third term is the elastic force due to the deformation of the model away from its natural shape.

The elastic force is conveniently expressed as $\delta\mathcal{E}(\mathbf{r})/\delta\mathbf{r}$, a *variational derivative* of the potential energy of deformation $\mathcal{E}(\mathbf{r})$ (as approximated in equation 14). More information on variational derivatives can be found in textbooks on the calculus of variations [5, 13].

4. Energies of Deformation

This section develops potential energies of deformation $\mathcal{E}(\mathbf{r})$ associated with the elastically deformable models. These energies are employed to define the internal elastic forces of the models (see Section 6).

4.1. Analysis of Deformation

Elasticity theory involves the analysis of deformation [18, 12]. We will define measures of deformation using concepts from the differential geometry of curves, surfaces, and solids [8]. One requirement of our present approach is that the measures should be insensitive to rigid body motion since it imparts no deformation.

The shape of a body is determined by the Euclidean distances between nearby points. As the body deforms, these distances change. Let $\mathbf{a}$ and $\mathbf{a} + d\mathbf{a}$ be the material coordinates of two nearby points in the body. The distance between these points in the deformed body in Euclidean 3-space is given by

$$dl = \sum_{i,j} G_{ij} da_i da_j, \qquad (2)$$

where the symmetric matrix

$$G_{ij}(\mathbf{r}(\mathbf{a})) = \frac{\partial \mathbf{r}}{\partial a_i} \cdot \frac{\partial \mathbf{r}}{\partial a_j} \qquad (3)$$

is known as the metric tensor or first fundamental form [9] (the dot indicates the scalar product of two vectors).

Two 3-dimensional solids have the same shape (differ only by a rigid body motion) if their 3×3 metric tensors are identical functions of $\mathbf{a} = [a_1, a_2, a_3]$. However, this no longer need be true when the body becomes infinitesimally thin in one or more of its dimensions.

Thus, the lengths between nearby points do not determine the shape of a surface, since curvature can be altered without affecting lengths. The fundamental theorem of surfaces [8] states that two surfaces have the same shape if their metric tensors $\mathbf{G}$ as well as their curvature tensors $\mathbf{B}$ are identical functions of $\mathbf{a} = [a_1, a_2]$. The 2×2 matrices $\mathbf{G}$ and $\mathbf{B}$ are the first and second fundamental forms of the surface [9]. The components of the curvature tensor are

$$B_{ij}(\mathbf{r}(\mathbf{a})) = \mathbf{n} \cdot \frac{\partial^2 \mathbf{r}}{\partial a_i \partial a_j}, \qquad (4)$$

where $\mathbf{n} = [n_1, n_2, n_3]$ is the unit surface normal.

For the case of space curves, the metric and curvature tensors are scalars called the arc length $s(\mathbf{r}(a))$ and the curvature $\kappa(\mathbf{r}(a))$. Again, arc length and curvature do not entirely determine the shape of a space curve; the curve can twist. Thus, the fundamental theorem of curves [8] states that two curves have the same shape if their arc length, curvature, and torsion $\tau(\mathbf{r})$ are identical functions of $\mathbf{a} = a$ [9].

4.2. Energies for Curves, Surfaces, and Solids

Using the above differential quantities, we now define potential energies of deformation for elastic curves, surfaces, and solids. These energies restore deformed bodies to their natural shapes, while being neutral with respect to rigid body motion (see Figure 2). Thus, the potential energy should be zero when the model is in its natural state, and the energy should grow larger as the model gets increasingly deformed away from its natural state.

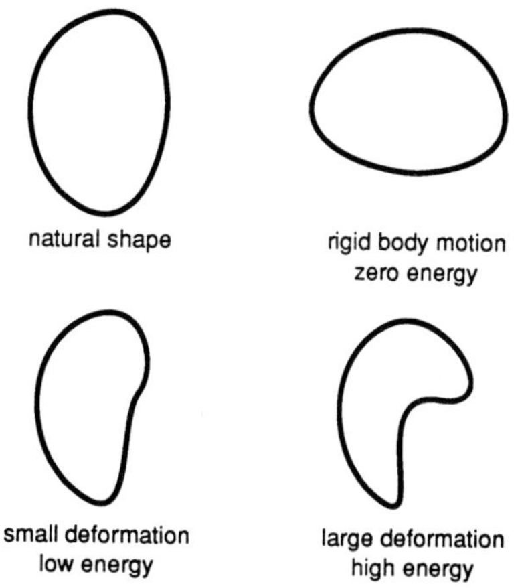

Figure 2. Energy of deformation.

A reasonable strain energy for elastic bodies is a norm of the difference between the fundamental forms of the deformed body and the fundamental forms of the natural, undeformed body. This norm measures the amount of deformation away from the natural state.

In the rest of the paper, the fundamental forms associated with the natural shapes of deformable bodies will be denoted by the superscript 0. For example,

$$\mathbf{G}^0_{ij} = \frac{\partial \mathbf{r}^0}{\partial a_i} \cdot \frac{\partial \mathbf{r}^0}{\partial a_j}. \qquad (5)$$

Thus, for a curve, we use the strain energy

$$\mathcal{E}(\mathbf{r}) = \int_\Omega \alpha(s - s^0)^2 + \beta(\kappa - \kappa^0)^2 + \gamma(\tau - \tau^0)^2 da \qquad (6)$$

where α, β, and γ are the amount of resistance of the curve to stretching, bending, and twisting, respectively. An analogous strain energy for a deformable surface in space is

$$\mathcal{E}(\mathbf{r}) = \int_\Omega ||\mathbf{G} - \mathbf{G}^0||^2_\alpha + ||\mathbf{B} - \mathbf{B}^0||^2_\beta \, da_1 da_2, \qquad (7)$$

where $||\cdot||_\alpha$ and $||\cdot||_\beta$ are weighted matrix norms. Similarly, a strain energy for a deformable solid is

$$\mathcal{E}(\mathbf{r}) = \int_\Omega ||\mathbf{G} - \mathbf{G}^0||^2_\alpha \, da_1 da_2 da_3. \qquad (8)$$

The deformation energies (6), (7), and (8) are zero for rigid motions, and they include the fewest partial derivatives necessary to restore the natural shapes of non-rigid curves, surfaces, and solids, respectively. However, higher-order derivatives can be included to further constrain the smoothness of the admissible deformations of these bodies [24].

5. Applied Forces

Applying external forces to elastic models yields realistic dynamics. This section lists representative examples of external forces, including the effects of gravity, fluids, and collisions with impenetrable objects. The net external force $\mathbf{f}(\mathbf{r}, t)$ in (1) is the sum of the individual external forces. Various types of external forces, each a vector function of $\mathbf{r}$, are presented below.

A gravitational force acting on the deformable body is given by

$$\mathbf{f}_{\text{gravity}} = \mu(\mathbf{a})\mathbf{g}, \tag{9}$$

where $\mu(\mathbf{a})$ is the mass density and $\mathbf{g}$ is the gravitational field.

A force that connects a material point $\mathbf{a}_0$ to a point in world coordinates $\mathbf{r}_0 = [x_0, y_0, z_0]$ by an ideal Hookean spring is

$$\mathbf{f}_{\text{spring}} = k(\mathbf{r}_0 - \mathbf{r}(\mathbf{a}_0)), \tag{10}$$

where k is the spring constant.

The force on the surface of a body due to a viscous fluid is

$$\mathbf{f}_{\text{viscous}} = c(\mathbf{n} \cdot \mathbf{v})\mathbf{n}, \tag{11}$$

where c is the strength of the fluid force, $\mathbf{n}(\mathbf{a})$ is the unit normal on the surface, and

$$\mathbf{v}(\mathbf{a}, t) = \mathbf{u} - \frac{\partial \mathbf{r}(\mathbf{a}, t)}{\partial t} \tag{12}$$

is the velocity of the surface relative to some constant stream velocity $\mathbf{u}$. The force is a flow field projected onto the normal of the surface, is linear in the velocity, and models a viscous medium [2].

We simulate collision dynamics between elastic models and immobile impenetrable objects by creating a potential energy $c\exp(-f(\mathbf{r})/\epsilon)$ around each object, where f is the object's inside/outside function. The constants c and ϵ determine the shape of the potential and are chosen such that the energy becomes prohibitive if the model attempts to penetrate the object. The resulting force of collision is

$$\mathbf{f}_{\text{collision}} = -\left(\frac{\nabla f(\mathbf{r})}{\epsilon} \exp\left(-\frac{f(\mathbf{r})}{\epsilon}\right) \cdot \mathbf{n}\right) \mathbf{n}, \tag{13}$$

where $\mathbf{n}(\mathbf{a})$ is the unit normal vector of the deformable body's surface. This force ignores frictional effects at contact points, but it is a straightforward matter to define friction forces which impede sliding motions along the object's surface.

Elastic bodies should not self-intersect as they deform. Self-intersection can be avoided by surrounding the surface of the object with a self-repulsive collision force. The repulsive force requires an implicit description of the surface of the object, which is only available locally in our models. Thus, each object decomposes into many small patches and the repulsive force computation can become expensive. However, greater efficiency may be obtained by placing the patches into hierarchical bounding boxes.

6. Implementation of Deformable Models

To create animation with deformable models, the differential equations of motion are simulated numerically. We concentrate on the case of surfaces in order to illustrate the implementation of deformable models. Curves (solids) represent a straightforward restriction (extension) of the discrete two-parameter equations developed in this section. Discrete equations of motion are sought that are tractable and stable. We first propose a simplification of the elastic forces $\delta\mathcal{E}(\mathbf{r})/\delta\mathbf{r}$. The partial differential equation (1) is then discretized in space. Finally, the resulting system of coupled ordinary differential equations is integrated through time using standard techniques.

6.1. A Simplified Elastic Force

We will use a weighted matrix norm in (7) to obtain the following simplified deformation energy for a surface:

$$\mathcal{E}(\mathbf{r}) = \int_\Omega \sum_{i,j=1}^{2} \left(\eta_{ij}(G_{ij} - G^0_{ij})^2 + \xi_{ij}(B_{ij} - B^0_{ij})^2\right) da_1 da_2, \tag{14}$$

where $\eta_{ij}(\mathbf{a})$ and $\xi_{ij}(\mathbf{a})$ are weighting functions.

The first variational derivative $\delta\mathcal{E}(\mathbf{r})/\delta\mathbf{r}$ of (14) can be approximated by the vector expression:

$$\mathbf{e}(\mathbf{r}) = \sum_{i,j=1}^{2} -\frac{\partial}{\partial a_i}\left(\alpha_{ij}\frac{\partial \mathbf{r}}{\partial a_j}\right) + \frac{\partial^2}{\partial a_i \partial a_j}\left(\beta_{ij}\frac{\partial^2 \mathbf{r}}{\partial a_i \partial a_j}\right), \tag{15}$$

where $\alpha_{ij}(\mathbf{a}, \mathbf{r})$ and $\beta_{ij}(\mathbf{a}, \mathbf{r})$ are constitutive functions describing the elastic properties of the material.

Now,

$$\alpha_{ij}(\mathbf{a}, \mathbf{r}) = \eta_{ij}(\mathbf{a})\left(G_{ij} - G^0_{ij}\right). \tag{16}$$

When α_{ij} is positive the surface wants to shrink in extent, and when α_{ij} is negative, it wants to grow. Thus, the α_{ij} are controlling surface tensions which minimize the deviation of the surface's actual metric from its natural metric G^0_{ij}. As $\eta_{ij}(\mathbf{a}_0)$ is increased, the material's resistance to such deformation increases at material point $\mathbf{a}_0$. η_{11} and η_{22} determine the resistance to length deformation along the coordinate directions, while $\eta_{12} = \eta_{21}$ determine the resistance to shear deformation.

Unfortunately, the calculus of variations applied to the second term in (14) yields unwieldy expressions. One alternative which follows by analogy to (16) is to use

$$\beta_{ij}(\mathbf{a}, \mathbf{r}) = \xi_{ij}(\mathbf{a})\left(B_{ij} - B^0_{ij}\right). \tag{17}$$

When β_{ij} is positive, the surface wants to be flatter, and when β_{ij} is negative, the surface wants to be more curved. Thus, β_{ij} are controlling surface rigidities which act to minimize the deviation of the surface's actual curvature from it's natural curvature B^0_{ij}. As $\xi_{ij}(\mathbf{a}_0)$ is increased, the material becomes more resistant to such deformation at material point $\mathbf{a}_0$. ξ_{11} and ξ_{22} determine the resistance to bending deformation along the coordinate directions, while $\xi_{12} = \xi_{21}$ determines the resistance to twist deformation.

To simulate a stretchy rubber sheet, for example, we make η_{ij} relatively small and set $\xi_{ij} = 0$. To simulate relatively stretch resistant cloth, we increase the value of η_{ij}. To simulate paper, we make η_{ij} relatively large and we introduce a modest value for ξ_{ij}. Springy metal is simulated by increasing the value of ξ_{ij}. The ability to set η and ξ independently at each material point $\mathbf{a}$ allows the introduction of local singularities such as fractures and creases [24].

Note that for the special case where $\alpha_{12} = \alpha_{21} = 0$ and where α_{11}, α_{22}, and the β_{ij} are linearized so as to be independent of $\mathbf{r}$, we obtain the "thin plate surface under tension" [24]. The thin plate surface under tension further reduces to the traditional "spline under tension" in the case of curves.

6.2. Discretization

Expression (15) for the elastic force is continuous in the material coordinates of the deformable surface. For simulating the dynamics of the model, (15) can be discretized by applying finite element or finite difference approximation methods [19]. Discretization transforms the partial differential equation of motion (1) into a system of linked ordinary differential equations. We illustrate the discretization step using standard finite difference approximations.

The discrete representation of the unit square domain $0 \le a_1, a_2 \le 1$ on which the surface is defined is a regular $M \times N$ discrete mesh of nodes with horizontal and vertical inter-node spacings h_1 and h_2. The nodes are indexed by integers $[m,n]$ where $1 \le m \le M$ and $1 \le n \le N$. We approximate an arbitrary continuous vector function $\mathbf{u}(a_1, a_2)$ by the grid function $\mathbf{u}[m,n] = \mathbf{u}(mh_1, nh_2)$ of nodal variables.

The elastic force requires approximations to the first and second derivatives of the nodal variables. Given a grid function $\mathbf{u}[m,n]$, we first define the forward first difference operators

$$\begin{aligned} D_1^+(\mathbf{u})[m,n] &= (\mathbf{u}[m+1,n] - \mathbf{u}[m,n])/h_1 \\ D_2^+(\mathbf{u})[m,n] &= (\mathbf{u}[m,n+1] - \mathbf{u}[m,n])/h_2 \end{aligned} \tag{18}$$

and the backward first difference operators

$$\begin{aligned} D_1^-(\mathbf{u})[m,n] &= (\mathbf{u}[m,n] - \mathbf{u}[m-1,n])/h_1 \\ D_2^-(\mathbf{u})[m,n] &= (\mathbf{u}[m,n] - \mathbf{u}[m,n-1])/h_2. \end{aligned} \tag{19}$$

Using (18) and (19), we can define the forward and backward cross difference operators

$$\begin{aligned} D_{12}^+(\mathbf{u})[m,n] &= D_{21}^+(\mathbf{u})[m,n] = D_1^+(D_2^+(\mathbf{u}))[m,n], \\ D_{12}^-(\mathbf{u})[m,n] &= D_{21}^-(\mathbf{u})[m,n] = D_1^-(D_2^-(\mathbf{u}))[m,n], \end{aligned} \tag{20}$$

and the central second difference operators

$$\begin{aligned} D_{11}(\mathbf{u})[m,n] &= D_1^-(D_1^+(\mathbf{u}))[m,n], \\ D_{22}(\mathbf{u})[m,n] &= D_2^-(D_2^+(\mathbf{u}))[m,n]. \end{aligned} \tag{21}$$

Using the above difference operators, we can discretize the constitutive functions (16) and (17) as follows:

$$\begin{aligned} \alpha_{ij}[m,n] &= \eta_{ij}[m,n](D_i^+(\mathbf{r})[m,n] \cdot D_j^+(\mathbf{r})[m,n] - G_{ij}^0[m,n]), \\ \beta_{ij}[m,n] &= \xi_{ij}[m,n](\mathbf{n}[m,n] \cdot D_{ij}^{(+)}(\mathbf{r})[m,n] - B_{ij}^0[m,n]), \end{aligned} \tag{22}$$

where $\mathbf{n}[m,n]$ is the surface normal grid function and the $(+)$ superscript indicates that the forward cross difference operator is used when $i \ne j$.

The elastic force (15) can then be approximated by

$$\mathbf{e}[m,n] = \sum_{i,j=1}^{2} -D_i^-(\mathbf{p})[m,n] + D_{ij}^{(-)}(\mathbf{q})[m,n], \tag{23}$$

where

$$\mathbf{p} = \alpha_{ij}[m,n]D_j^+(\mathbf{r})[m,n] \text{ and } \mathbf{q} = \beta_{ij}[m,n]D_{ij}^{(+)}(\mathbf{r})[m,n]. \tag{24}$$

Jump discontinuities will generally occur in the surface: for example, at its external boundaries. However, a free (natural) boundary condition can be simulated by setting to zero the value of any difference operator D_i^+ or $D_{ij}^{(+)}$ in (24) involving $\mathbf{r}[m,n]$ on opposite sides of a boundary.

If the nodal variables comprising the grid functions $\mathbf{r}[m,n]$ and $\mathbf{e}[m,n]$ are collected into the MN dimensional vectors $\underline{\mathbf{r}}$ and $\underline{\mathbf{e}}$, (23) may be written in the vector form

$$\underline{\mathbf{e}} = \mathbf{K}(\underline{\mathbf{r}})\underline{\mathbf{r}} \tag{25}$$

where $\mathbf{K}(\underline{\mathbf{r}})$ is an $MN \times MN$ matrix known as the *stiffness matrix*. Due to the local nature of the finite difference discretization, $\mathbf{K}$ has the desirable computational properties of sparseness and bandedness.

Consider, for simplicity, the case of time invariant mass density $\mu(\mathbf{a},t) = \mu[a_1,a_2]$ and damping density $\gamma(\mathbf{a},t) = \gamma[a_1,a_2]$ in (1). The resulting discrete densities are $\mu[m,n]$ and $\gamma[m,n]$. Let $\mathbf{M}$ be the *mass matrix*, a diagonal $MN \times MN$ matrix with the $\mu[m,n]$ variables as diagonal components, and let $\mathbf{C}$ be the *damping matrix* constructed similarly from $\gamma[m,n]$. The discrete form of the equations of motion (1) can be expressed in grid vector form using (25) by the following coupled system of second-order ordinary differential equations:

$$\mathbf{M}\frac{\partial^2 \underline{\mathbf{r}}}{\partial t^2} + \mathbf{C}\frac{\partial \underline{\mathbf{r}}}{\partial t} + \mathbf{K}(\underline{\mathbf{r}})\underline{\mathbf{r}} = \underline{\mathbf{f}}, \tag{26}$$

where $\underline{\mathbf{f}}$ is the grid vector representing the discrete net external force.

6.3. Numerical Integration Through Time

To simulate the dynamics of an elastic model, the system of ordinary differential equations (26) is integrated through time. We integrate these equations using a numerical step-by-step procedure, which converts the system of nonlinear ordinary differential equations into a sequence of linear algebraic systems.

A time interval from $t = 0$ to $t = T$ is subdivided into equal time steps Δt, and the integration procedure computes a sequence of approximate solutions at times Δt, $2\Delta t, \ldots, t, t+\Delta t, \ldots, T$. Evaluating $\underline{\mathbf{e}}$ at $t+\Delta t$ and $\underline{\mathbf{f}}$ at t, and substituting the (second-order accurate) discrete time approximations

$$\begin{aligned} \frac{\partial^2 \underline{\mathbf{r}}}{\partial t^2} &= (\underline{\mathbf{r}}_{t+\Delta t} - 2\underline{\mathbf{r}}_t + \underline{\mathbf{r}}_{t-\Delta t})/\Delta t^2 \\ \frac{\partial \underline{\mathbf{r}}}{\partial t} &= (\underline{\mathbf{r}}_{t+\Delta t} - \underline{\mathbf{r}}_{t-\Delta t})/2\Delta t \end{aligned} \tag{27}$$

into (26), we obtain the semi-implicit integration procedure

$$\mathbf{A}_t \underline{\mathbf{r}}_{t+\Delta t} = \underline{\mathbf{g}}_t, \tag{28}$$

where the matrix

$$\mathbf{A}_t = \mathbf{K}(\underline{\mathbf{r}}_t) + \left(\frac{1}{\Delta t^2}\mathbf{M} + \frac{1}{2\Delta t}\mathbf{C} \right) \tag{29}$$

and the effective force vector

$$\underline{\mathbf{g}}_t = \underline{\mathbf{f}}_t + \left(\frac{1}{\Delta t^2}\mathbf{M} + \frac{1}{2\Delta t}\mathbf{C} \right) \underline{\mathbf{r}}_t + \left(\frac{1}{\Delta t}\mathbf{M} - \frac{1}{2\Delta t}\mathbf{C} \right) \underline{\mathbf{v}}_t, \tag{30}$$

with

$$\underline{\mathbf{v}}_t = (\underline{\mathbf{r}}_t - \underline{\mathbf{r}}_{t-1})/\Delta t. \tag{31}$$

This implicit procedure therefore evolves the dynamic solution from given initial conditions $\underline{\mathbf{r}}_0$ and $\underline{\mathbf{v}}_0$ by solving a time sequence of static equilibrium problems for the instantaneous configurations $\underline{\mathbf{r}}_{t+\Delta t}$. Thus, the original nonlinear partial differential equation (1) has been reduced to a sequence of sparse linear algebraic systems (28), each of size proportional to MN, the number of nodes comprising the discrete deformable model.

We have used both direct methods, such as Choleski decomposition, and relaxation methods, such as the Gauss-Seidel method, to solve the sparse linear systems (28) (see [6]). Note that in the special case of linear elasticity, where α_{ij} and β_{ij} are constants independent of $\mathbf{r}$, then $\mathbf{A}_t = \mathbf{A}$ is time-invariant, so a matrix decomposition solver need only perform a single initial decomposition of $\mathbf{A}$, which significantly reduces the total amount of computation required. A detailed description of our linear equation solvers is beyond the scope of this paper.

7. Simulation Examples

The following simulations have been selected to convey the broad scope of elastically deformable models.

Figure 3 shows two different static behaviors of an elastic surface. The surface is lifted by a spring attached to the rightmost corner and constrained at the remaining corners. Figure 3a simulates a thin plate, whose rest state is flat ($\eta_{ij} = 0$, β_{ij} = positive constant). Figure 3b simulates a membrane resistant to stretch away from the prescribed metric $\mathbf{G}^0$ (a prescribed-metric membrane) whose curvature is not regulated ($\eta_{ij} > 0$, $\xi_{ij} = 0$).

Figure 4 illustrates a ball resting on a supporting elastic solid. The solid has a prescribed metric tensor. The internal elastic force interacts with the collision force to deform the solid.

Figure 5 shows a shrink wrap effect. Figure 5a shows a model of a rigid jack. In Figure 5b, a spherical membrane is stretched to surround the jack. The membrane shrinks and the jack exerts an attractive force on the membrane until a balance is achieved with the collision force. The remaining figures are extracted from a motion sequence which simulates the shrinking membrane.

Figure 6 illustrates a simulation of a flag waving in the wind. The flag material is modeled as a fixed metric membrane. The wind is constant and its effect on the flag is modeled by the viscous force (11). The flag is fixed to

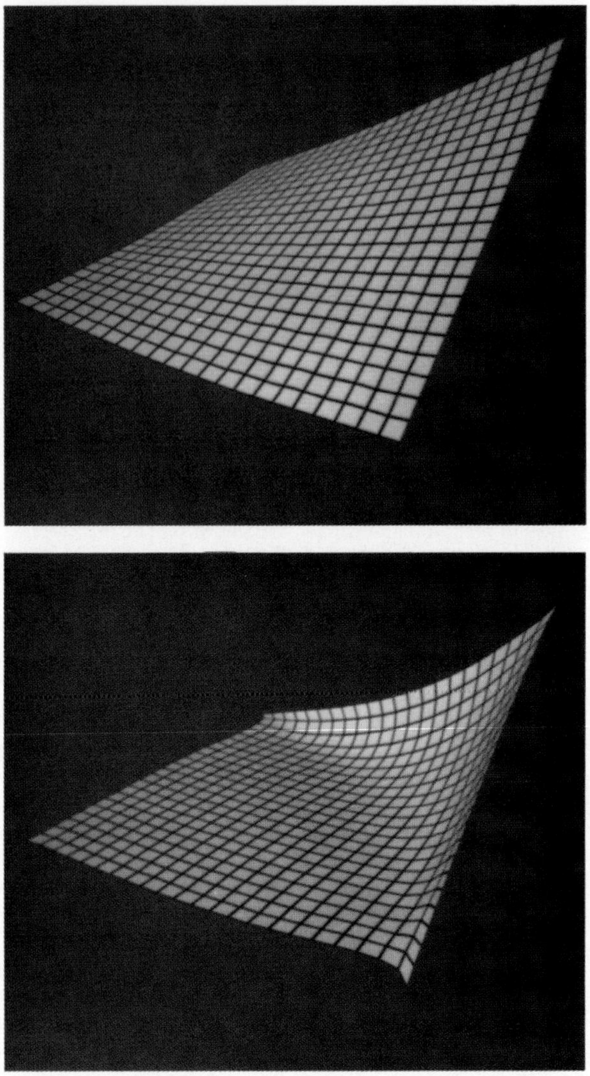

Figure 3. Lifting elastic surfaces.

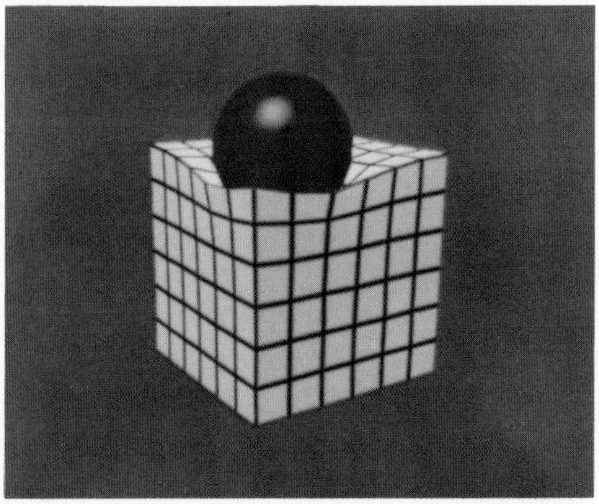

Figure 4. Ball on a deformable solid.

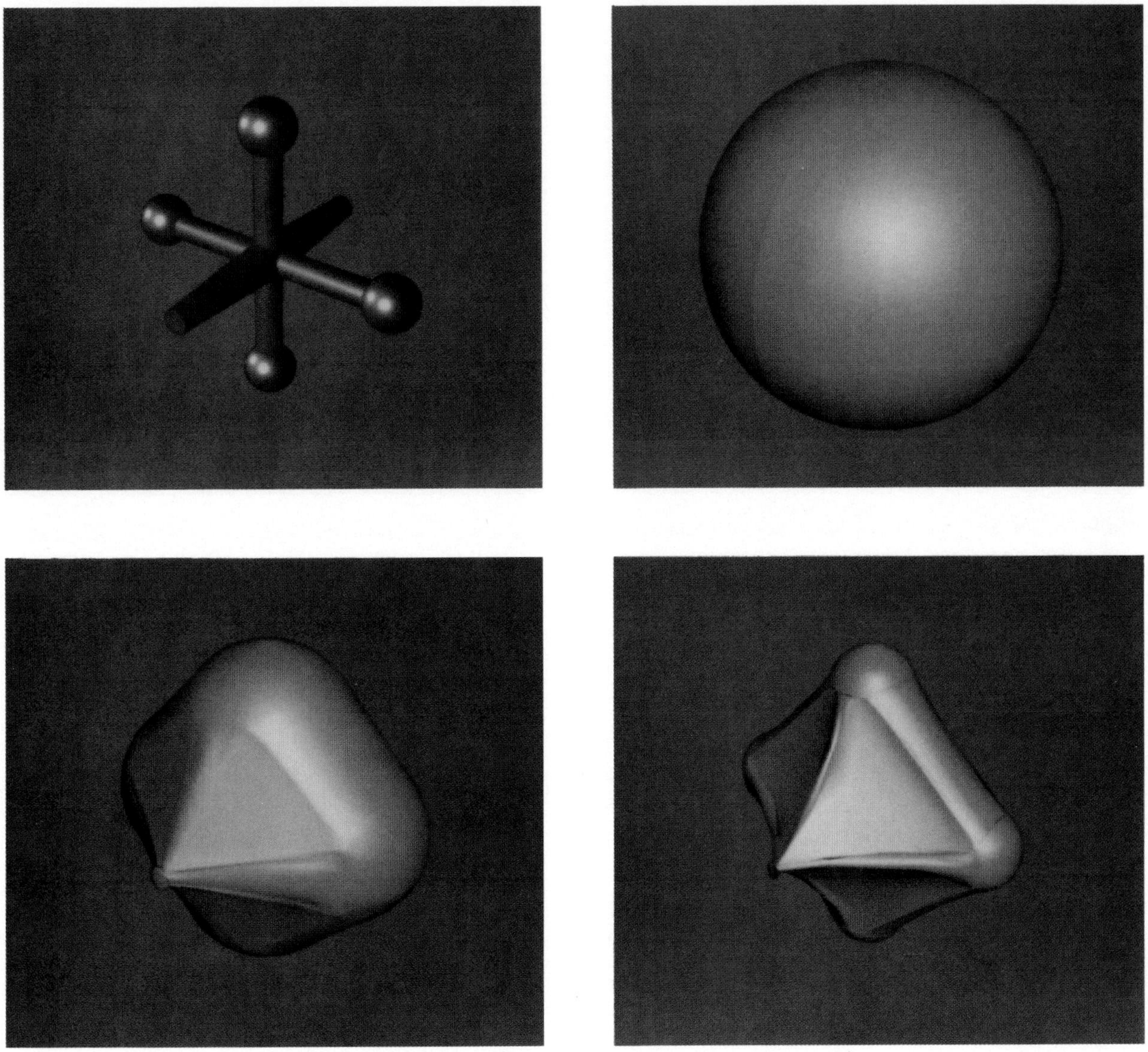

Figure 5. Membrane shrinking around a jack.

a rigid flagpole along one of its edges by imposing a fixed-position (Dirichlet) boundary condition [19].

Figure 7 illustrates a simulation of a carpet falling onto two rigid bodies in a gravitational field. The carpet material is modeled as a prescribed-metric membrane with a small amount of plate rigidity ($\eta_{ij} > 0$, $\beta_{ij} > 0$). The carpet slides off the bodies due to the interaction between gravity and the repulsive collision force. The frictional component is due to the damping term in (1).

8. Work in Progress

We are currently experimenting with alternative formulations of deformable models. The elastic forces developed in this paper are nonlinear expressions involving 3-space position functions $\mathbf{r}$. In principle, we can use such expressions to simulate nonlinear elastic phenomena such as the bending of shells [22]. Unfortunately, the discrete nonlinear approximations, especially the β_{ij} terms in (17), tend to be poorly conditioned numerically. One way to improve conditioning is to linearize the second term of (15) by making β_{ij} a function of $\mathbf{a}$, not of $\mathbf{r}$, resulting in the less general "thin plate" expression.

As an alternative, we have implemented linear elastic forces expressed in terms of the displacement $\mathbf{d} = \mathbf{r} - \mathbf{r}^0$ away from a reference 3-space configuration $\mathbf{r}^0$. The reference configuration $\mathbf{r}^0$ must, however, be allowed to undergo explicit rigid body motion, which amounts to solving the dynamical equations for rigid bodies [14]. The displacement formulation has allowed us to easily implement interesting visco-elasticity effects.

Another focus of our current work is on the topic of discretization and numerical solution of the deformable

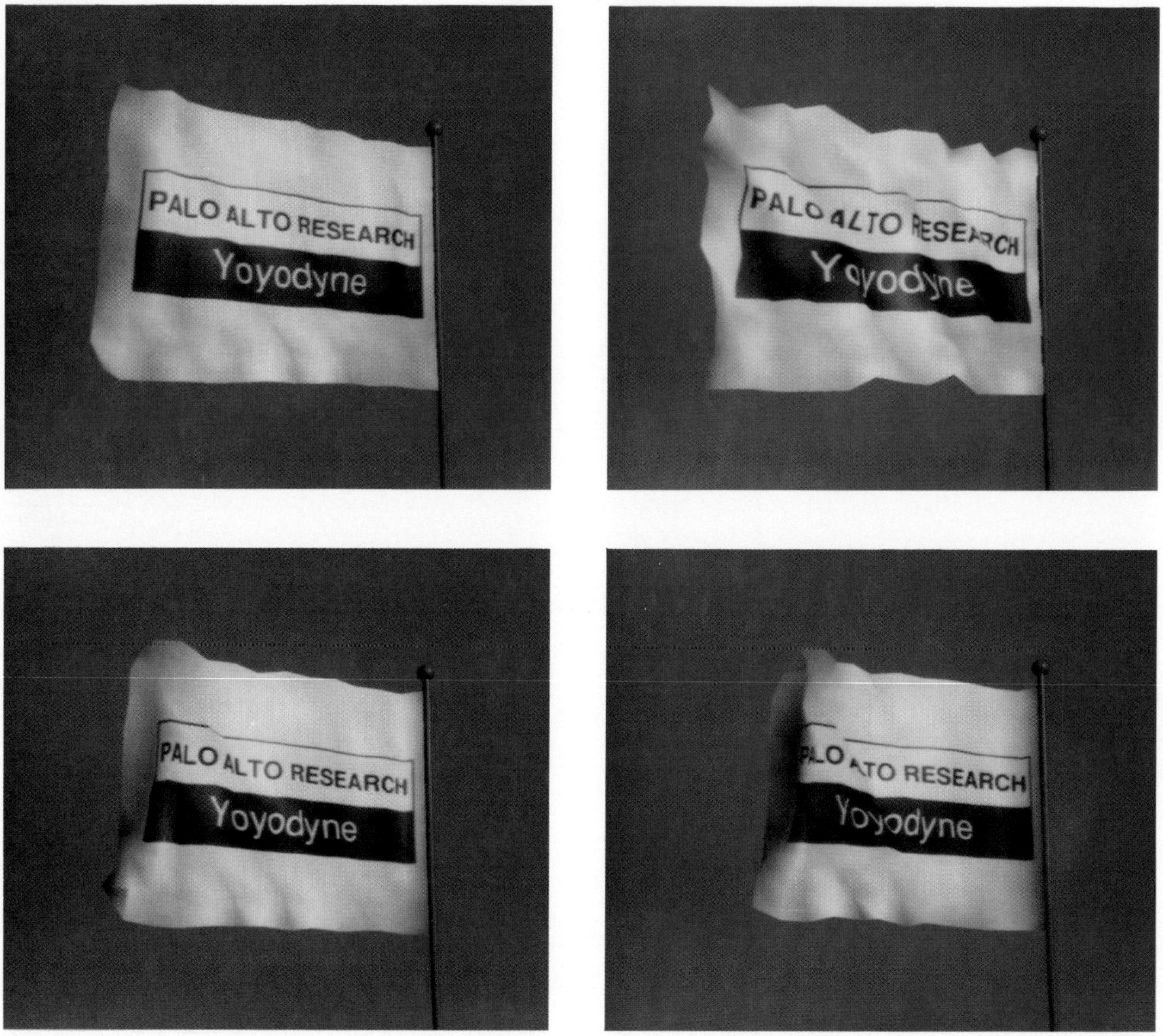

Figure 6. Flag waving in a wind.

model equations. In the present paper we have employed finite difference discretization techniques. We are presently implementing more sophisticated discretizations using the finite element method [29]. We have also experimented with higher-order time integration procedures such as a fourth-order Runge-Kutta method [6]. Our results indicate that adaptive time-step control can be beneficial in increasing stability, especially during collisions with impenetrable objects. We are also developing a multigrid relaxation solver that promises to accelerate the solution of the very large discrete equations arising from detailed approximations [23].

9. Conclusion

This paper has proposed a class of elastically deformable models for use in computer graphics. Our goal has been to create models for non-rigid curves, surfaces, and solids that inherit the essential features of elastic materials, while still maintaining computational tractability. Because our models are physically-based, they are active: they respond to external forces and interact with other objects in a natural way. Our models yield realistic dynamics in addition to realistic statics; they unify the description of shape and motion. We therefore believe that physically-based modeling will prove to be an increasingly powerful technique for computer graphics animation.

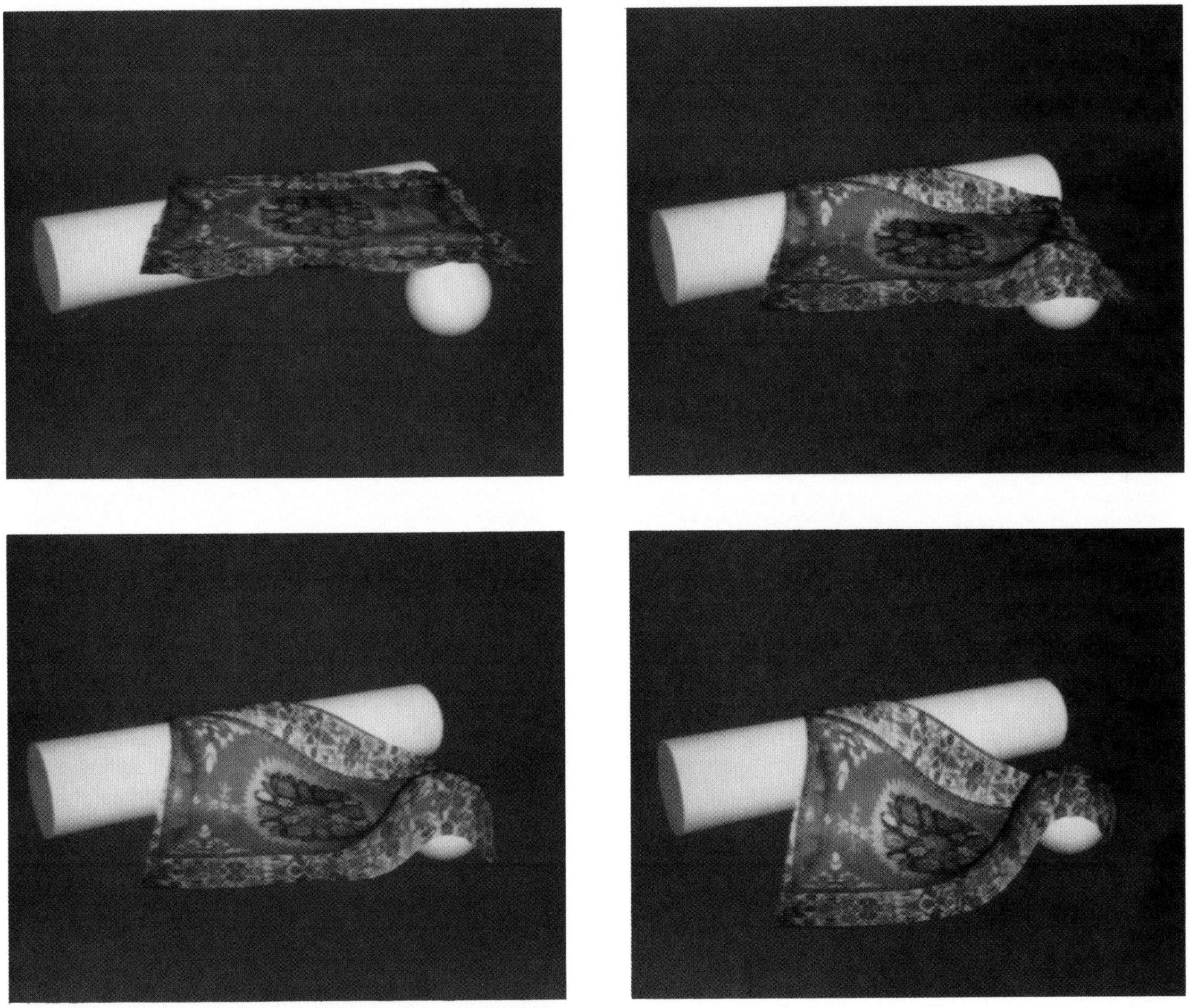

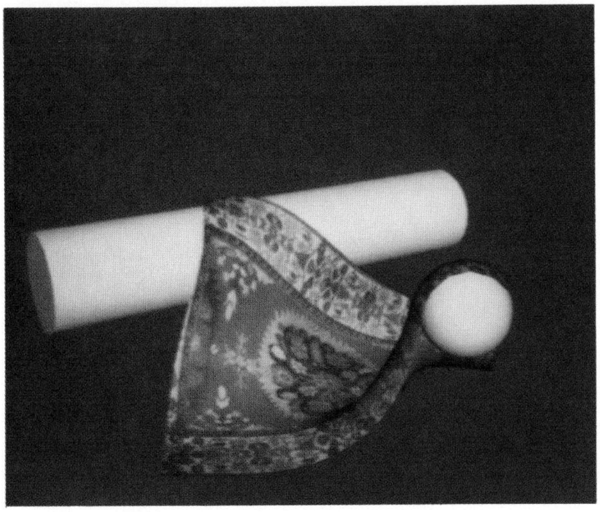

Figure 7. Persian carpet falling over immobile obstacles.

Acknowledgements

The figures in this paper were rendered by Kurt Fleischer using his modeling testbed system implemented on a LISP Machine. We wish to thank Andy Witkin for valuable discussions and goop. This research was funded, in part, by Schlumberger Palo Alto Research, Hewlett-Packard, Symbolics Inc., and by an AT&T Bell Labs Fellowship (JCP).

References

1. **Armstrong, W.W., and Green, M.**, "The dynamics of articulated rigid bodies for purposes of animation," *Proc. Graphics Interface '85*, Montreal, Canada, 1985, 407–415.
2. **Barr, A.H.**, Geometric Modeling and Fluid Dynamic Analysis of Swimming Spermatozoa, PhD thesis, Department of Mathematical Sciences, Rensselaer Polytechnic Institute, Troy, NY, 1983.
3. **Barr, A.H.**, "Global and local deformations of solid primitives," *Computer Graphics*, **18**, 3, 1984, (Proc. SIGGRAPH) 21-29.
4. **Barzel, R.**, Dynamic Constraints, MSc thesis, Department of Computer Science, California Institute of Technology, Pasadena, CA, 1987.
5. **Courant, R., and Hilbert, D.**, *Methods of Mathematical Physics*, Vol. I, Interscience, London, 1953.
6. **Dahlquist, G., and Bjorck, A.**, *Numerical Methods*, Prentice–Hall, Englewood Cliffs, NJ, 1974.
7. **de Boor, C.**, *A Practical Guide to Splines*, Springer–Verlag, New York, NY, 1978.
8. **do Carmo, M.P.**, *Differential Geometry of Curves and Surfaces*, Prentice–Hall, Englewood Cliffs, NJ, 1974.
9. **Faux, J.D., and Pratt, M.J.**, *Computational Geometry for Design and Manufacture*, Halstead Press, Horwood, NY, 1981.
10. **Feynman, C.R.**, Modeling the Appearance of Cloth, MSc thesis, Department of Electrical Engineering and Computer Science, MIT, Cambridge, MA, 1986.
11. **Fournier, A., and Reeves, W.T.**, "A simple model for ocean waves," *Computer Graphics*, **20**, 4, 1986, (Proc. SIGGRAPH), 75–84.
12. **Fung, Y.C.**, *Foundations of Solid Mechanics*, Prentice–Hall, Englewood Cliffs, NJ, 1965.
13. **Gelfand, I.M., and Fomin, S.V.**, *Calculus of Variations*, Prentice–Hall, Englewood Cliffs, NJ, 1963.
14. **Goldstein, H.**, *Classical Mechanics*, Addison-Wesley, Reading, MA, 1950.
15. **Immel, D.S., Cohen, M.F., and Greenberg, D.P.**, "A radiosity method for non-diffuse environments," *Computer Graphics*, **20**, 4, 1986, (Proc. SIGGRAPH), 133–142.
16. **Kajiya, J.T.**, "The rendering equation," *Computer Graphics*, **20**, 4, 1986, (Proc. SIGGRAPH), 143–150.
17. **Kajiya, J.T., and von Herzen, B.**, "Ray tracing volume densities," *Computer Graphics*, **18**, 3, 1984, (Proc. SIGGRAPH), 165–174.
18. **Landau, L.D., and Lifshitz, E.M.**, *Theory of Elasticity*, Pergamon Press, London, UK, 1959.
19. **Lapidus, L., and Pinder, G.F.**, *Numerical Solution of Partial Differential Equations in Science and Engineering*, Wiley, New York, NY, 1982.
20. **Peachey, D.R.**, "Modeling waves and surf," *Computer Graphics*, **20**, 4, 1986, (Proc. SIGGRAPH), 65–74.
21. **Sederberg, T.W., and Parry, S.R.**, "Free-form deformation of solid geometric models," *Computer Graphics*, **20**, 4, 1986, (Proc. SIGGRAPH), 151–160.
22. **Stoker, J.J.**, *Nonlinear Elasticity*, New York, NY, 1968.
23. **Terzopoulos, D.**, "Multilevel computational processes for visual surface reconstruction," *Computer Vision, Graphics, and Image Processing*, **24**, 1983, 52–96.
24. **Terzopoulos, D.**, "Regularization of inverse visual problems involving discontinuities," *IEEE Trans. Pattern Analysis and Machine Intelligence*, **PAMI-8**, 1986, 413–424.
25. **Terzopoulos, D.**, "On matching deformable models to images: Direct and iterative solutions," *Topical Meeting on Machine Vision, Technical Digest Series, Vol. 12., Optical Society of America*, Washington, DC, 1987, 160–167.
26. **Weil, J.**, "The synthesis of cloth objects," *Computer Graphics*, **20**, 4, 1986, (Proc. SIGGRAPH), 49–54.
27. **Wilhelms, J., and Barsky, B.A.**, "Using dynamic analysis to animate articulated bodies such as humans and robots," *Proc. Graphics Interface '85*, Montreal, Canada, 1985, 97–104.
28. **Yaeger, L., Upson, C., and Myers, R.**, "Combining physical and visual simulation — creation of the planet Jupiter for the film "2010"," *Computer Graphics*, **20**, 4, 1986, (Proc. SIGGRAPH), 85-94.
29. **Zienkiewicz, O.C.**, *The Finite Element Method; Third edition*, McGraw–Hill, London, 1977.

CONTROLLING DYNAMIC SIMULATION WITH KINEMATIC CONSTRAINTS, BEHAVIOR FUNCTIONS AND INVERSE DYNAMICS

Paul M. Isaacs and Michael F. Cohen
Program of Computer Graphics, Cornell University
Ithaca, New York, 14853

ABSTRACT

Theoretical and numerical aspects of the implementation of a DYNAmic MOtion system, dubbed DYNAMO, for the dynamic simulation of linked figures is presented. The system introduces three means for achieving control of the resulting motion which have not been present in previous dynamic simulation systems for computer animation. (1) "Kinematic constraints" permit traditional keyframe animation systems to be embedded within a dynamic analysis. Joint limit constraints are also handled correctly through kinematic constraints. (2) "Behavior functions" relate the momentary state of the dynamic system to desired forces and accelerations within the figure. (3) "Inverse dynamics" provides a means of determining the forces required to perform a specified motion.

The combination of kinematic and dynamic specifications allows the animator to think about each part of the animation in the way that is most suitable for the task. Successful experimental results are presented which demonstrate the ability to provide control without disrupting the dynamic integrity of the resulting motion.

1.0 INTRODUCTION

The specification of motion for computer graphic sequences has traditionally been controlled explicitly by an animator. Motion occurs in the physical world, however, due to forces acting on objects which have shape and mass. The explicit control of traditional animation methods might be compared to utilizing a paint program for image creation, as opposed to simulating light propagation in an environment. To achieve the degree of realism found in other areas of computer graphics, the motion of objects must be simulated by the physical principles of dynamics governing the motion.

There are good reasons that this has not yet occurred. The mathematical principles governing the motion of objects are both complex and computationally time consuming. Perhaps even more difficult is establishing some intuitive link between the parameters of a dynamic simulation and the resulting motion. For example, it is clear that to pick up an object we must move our hand from its current position to the object. It is much more difficult to describe the same motion through dynamics, i.e., as a series of forces and torques on joints of a skeletal structure. It is at this level, however, that the simulation must have its roots.

The term "simulation", itself, rather than "animation", denotes a shift in control from the animator to the underlying physics of the environment. One would like a system for specifying motion which combines the realism of dynamic simulation without removing control from the animator.

A DYNAmic MOtion system, dubbed DYNAMO, has been implemented to perform dynamic simulation on linked figures. In addition to performing dynamic simulation, the system contains three means for achieving control which have not been present in previous dynamic simulation systems for computer animation.
(1) The imposition of "kinematic constraints" permits traditional animation systems to be embedded within a dynamic analysis. Motion of portions of the figure can be explicitly specified while allowing the remaining sections of the body to react to the dynamic forces created by this motion. Joint limits are also handled in a coherent means through kinematic constraints.
(2) The ability to define "behavior functions" allows the figure to react to its surroundings. Behavior functions relate the momentary state of the dynamic system to desired forces and accelerations within the figure.
(3) A process of "inverse dynamics" provides a means of determining the forces required to perform a specified motion. Thus, a previously specified action can be transformed into equivalent forces for development of behavior functions or evaluation of stresses within the linkage.
The above mechanisms provide control without disrupting the dynamic integrity of the resulting motion.

After a short look at previous work in the field,

theoretical and numerical aspects of the DYNAMO system are described. Simulations which have been run to date have provided some exciting results. These are briefly described following the system's description. After a concluding discussion, a derivation of the equations of motion is provided in the appendix.

2.0 FROM ANIMATION TO SIMULATION

Computer animation methodologies can be characterized as belonging to one of three categories: Keyframe Animation, Procedural Animation, and Dynamic Simulation.

2.1 Keyframe Animation

Keyframe animation is derived directly from traditional animation techniques in which the animator specifies what is to appear in each frame and thus explicitly specifies the "kinematics" or motion of the system. The computer adds efficiency by interpolating "in-between" frames from user supplied "keyframes" [10],[12]. Although this type of system gives almost complete control to the animator, it lacks the tools for creating dynamically correct sequences.

2.2 Procedural Animation

Procedural methods rely on the computer's ability to determine the kinematics based on implicit instructions rather than explicit positions. One class of procedural methods is "inverse kinematics," where the motion of end links in a chain is specified by the animator, but the motion of interior links is determined algorithmicly [2],[5],[6],[8]. In Girard's work, some dynamic principals are invoked to enable the figure to interact with the ground plane in realistic ways. Although procedural methods have produced some of the best animation to date, they often lack dynamic integrity.

2.3 Dynamic Simulation

General systems for dynamic simulation of linked figures have been described in recent literature relating to robotics and biomechanics as well as computer graphics. Wilhelms and Barsky [13] describe a system for dynamic simulation similar to the one presented here, but without the incorporation of kinematic constraints and the associated control mechanisms. Armstrong and Green [1] have also taken steps towards describing figure animation based on an alternative dynamic formulation. Williams and Seireg [14] have developed a system for simulating dynamic systems in order to study optimizing strategies for actuator forces. Development of robot machines through simulation relies heavily on similar principles. Experiments reported by Raibert [11] of hopping and running machines reinforce the need for dynamic simulation methods.

While based on a dynamic formulation, the methods presented in this paper provide a means to incorporate the three types of animation techniques within a single coherent system. Among the numerous texts on dynamics of jointed figures, Wittenberg [15] has been found to be of the most use for developing the DYNAMO system and many of the mathematical formulations in this paper are derived from it.

3.0 THE DYNAMO SYSTEM

3.1 Overview

The dynamic simulation for this work was done using the DYNAMO system written in the C programming language at the Cornell University Program of Computer Graphics. The flow of control of the system is illustrated in figure 1.

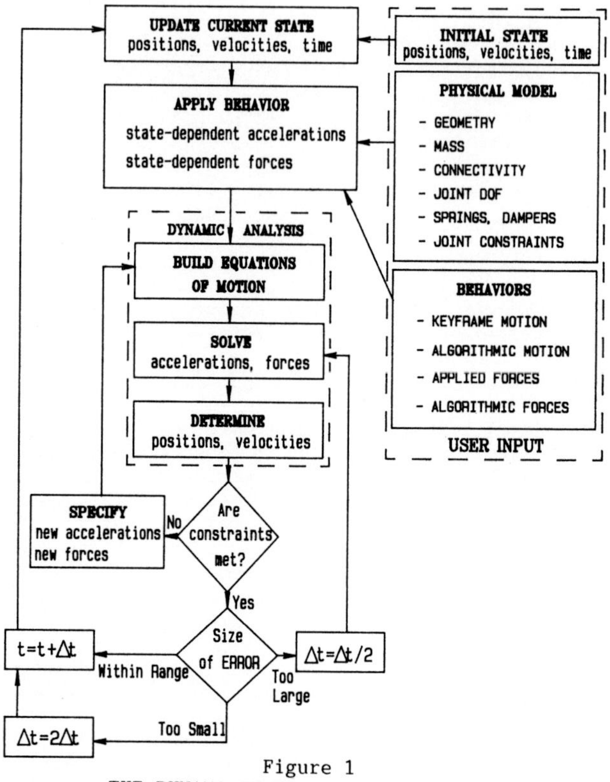

Figure 1
THE DYNAMO SYSTEM: FLOW OF CONTROL

DYNAMO requires as input the physical and behavioral characteristics of a linked figure placed in an initial state. The physical model includes descriptions of all links and joints, as well as their connectivity. The initial state of the system contains the starting position and velocity of the links and an initial time. Behavior functions relate the current state of the system to external forces or to specified motion.

The dynamic simulation is treated as an explicit time series analysis. A simultaneous solution is performed at each time increment for the accelerations of each degree of freedom of the system. These accelerations are integrated with the current state to determine a new set of positions and velocities. The solution is checked to see if any constraints have been exceeded and to see if the accuracy is within a tolerable range. If these tests are passed, the new state becomes the current state and the process is repeated for the following time increment. Time increments corresponding to frame times are recorded for display and playback.

3.2 Links, Joints and Forces

Each link has size, shape and mass and, thus, a center of gravity (COG) and a moment of inertia. The linkage for each figure forms a tree structure. Each link possesses one joint at which it is attached to its parent link and may possess one or more joints at which child links are attached. Links move relative to each other via one to six translational or rotational degrees of freedom, (DOF), associated with each joint. (figures 2,3)

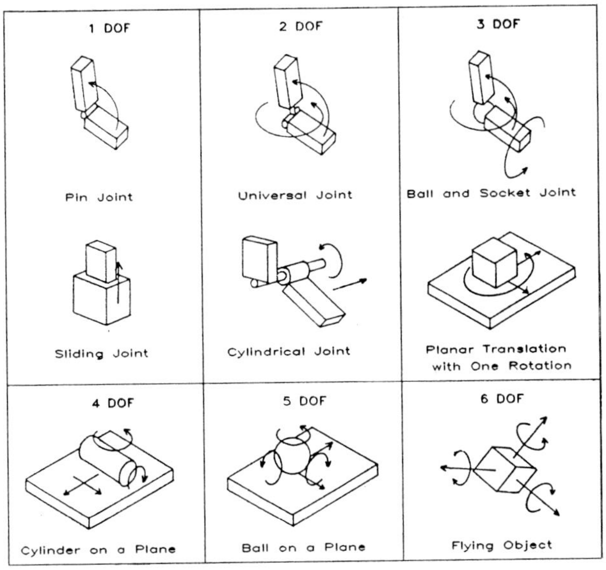

Figure 2: Types Of Joints

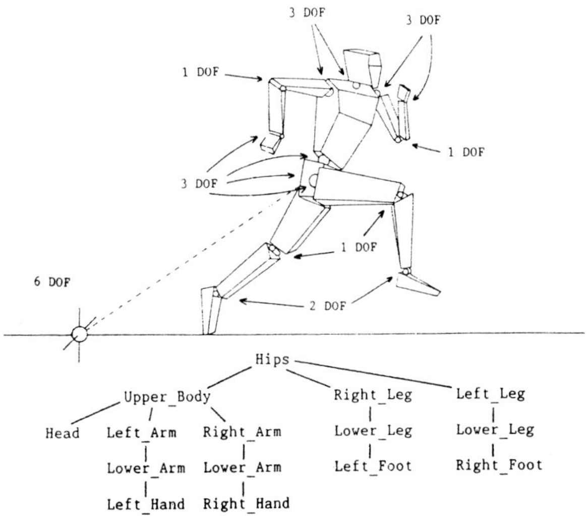

Figure 3
The Human Figure As A Linkage

Each joint may have associated springs and/or dampers which act to exert internal forces or torques within that joint. Joints may also have associated limits which act to keep the DOFs from moving beyond some point, e.g., the lower arm can bend only within a defined arc about the elbow. (figure 4)

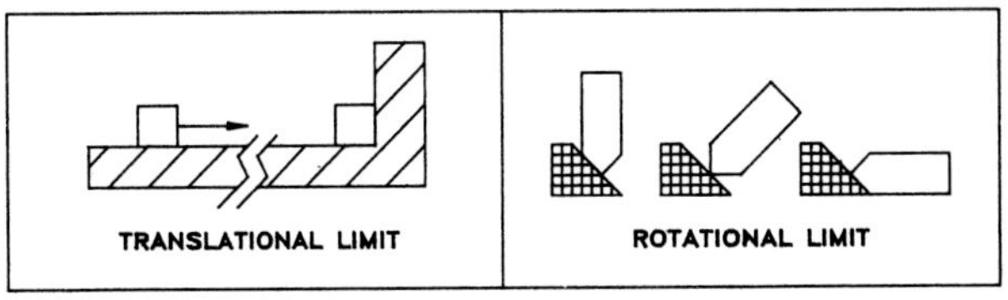

Figure 4: Joint Limits

In addition, the linkage responds to externally applied forces . External forces can be specified as applied torques, point vector forces, or force fields. Most animate figures are actually driven by tensile forces caused by contraction of a muscle attached to the skeletal frame. Muscles can be modeled as physical entities attached to the links (figure 5). Muscle contractions apply equal but opposite tensile forces between adjacent attachment points. All forces are resolved into force/torque pairs acting at the link center of gravity.

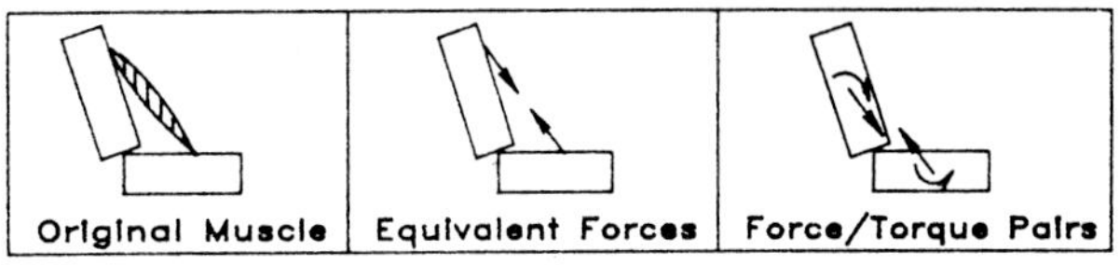

Figure 5: Representation Of A Muscle

The links, joints, forces, and position and velocity of the DOFs form a complete description of the state of the dynamic system at any given time.

3.3 Dynamic Simulation

The dynamic simulation for each time increment can be broken down into four phases. These are: 1) execution of the behaviors, 2) calculation of joint forces 3) formation of the equations of motion, and 4) matrix solution and evaluation of results.

3.31 Execution of Behavior Functions

Behavior functions determine, at each moment, forces acting on a linkage and/or specific motion which is to occur. The forces or specified motion can be determined through any algorithm of the user's choosing, based on any currently available information about the state of the system (e.g. time, geometry, etc.) Examples of useful input and associated output for behaviors are illustrated in figure 6.

A behavior function's output can specify a single force or a force field such as gravity. Gravity's simple behavior function always exerts a downward force equal to the mass times the acceleration of gravity with its point of action at the center of gravity of each link. Contributions from all external forces are summed for each link into an aggregate force and torque vector expressed in the global or "inertial" spatial frame.

Motion may also be output from a behavior function using time or other input parameters. The specified motion can be defined by keyframed paths which depend only on time, or by procedural means which may depend on other criteria.

The user-designed behavior algorithms can make decisions in virtually any way, ranging from "begin

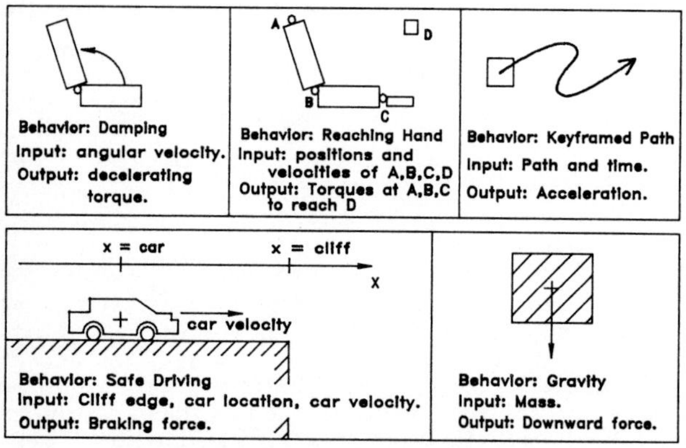

Figure 6: Some Sample Behaviors

the keyframed motion of the car when the starting gun sounds" to "apply torques to all motors that will lift the right leg." In addition, these algorithms may be nested; thus one behavior function may invoke others, allowing for higher level behaviors such as walking.

The mixture of specified forces and specified motion expressed through the behavior functions provides the combination of kinematic control and dynamic integrity.

3.32 Calculation of Joint Forces

Given the current positions of the degrees of freedom, internal spring and damper forces are calculated through the equations:

F(spring) = spring_k * offset_from_center_position (Eq. 1)

F(damper) = damper_k * velocity_of_DOF (Eq. 2)

where spring_k and damper_k are the spring and damper constants for that DOF. These equations are used for both translational and rotational DOFs. The resulting forces are summed into internal force and torque vectors for each joint.

3.33 Building the Equations of Motion.

At this stage all the physical parameters have been determined. Thus, each creature may be regarded as a passive linkage moving in response to applied loads. The links and joints of a creature have a given position and velocity, and they are subjected to internal and external forces. The primary unknowns are the momentary accelerations of the DOF's (q").

A linear equation can be derived for each DOF relating the current state of the creature and the accelerations it undergoes to the forces which are acting on it. (Equations relating to DOFs with accelerations pre-specified by the behavior functions are eliminated. See section 3.4) The simplest view of this relationship is Newton's 2nd law, that force equals mass times acceleration. The series of equations can be written:

$$[A] \lfloor q'' \rfloor = \lfloor B \rfloor \quad \text{(Eq. 3)}$$

where: $[A]$ is a generalized mass matrix.
$\lfloor q'' \rfloor$ is a vector of the accelerations of each of the DOF's.
$\lfloor B \rfloor$ is a vector of force terms.

The $[A]$ matrix coefficients dependent only on the geometry and mass of the system. This includes the current configuration of all joints and links as well as the mass and moments of inertia of the links. The $\lfloor B \rfloor$ vector includes terms for all applied forces as they relate to each DOF.

A brief derivation for the equations of motion appears in the appendix. More details can be found in Wittenberg [15].

3.34 The Equation Solution

The set of simultaneous equations must be formed and solved for each time increment. A simple Gaussian elimination scheme works well.

More efficient recursive schemes have been devised to replace the simultaneous equation solution outlined here. The recursive solutions have been shown efficient for the determination of motion from specified forces [4] or for finding actuator forces required to execute specified motion [9]. Unfortunately, they do not allow the combination of partial force and partial motion specification within the same linkage. This combination permits the control that is central to the DYNAMO system.

The solution provides the accelerations of the DOFs for the current time increment. From these accelerations and the current position and velocity of each DOF, new positions and velocities are calculated for the following time step. If constraints are exceeded during the time increment, their constraining accelerations are determined and explicitly specified, the constrained DOF's are removed from the system, and the time increment is repeated.

The size of the time increment is crucial to the accuracy and stability of the simulation since the geometric terms are assumed to remain constant throughout a time increment. If the geometry is changing rapidly, this assumption can quickly lead to inaccurate solutions. To overcome this problem without overburdening the machine by enforcing very small time increments, an adaptive time step sequence has been implemented (figure 1).

A variation on a predictor corrector method [7],[3] allows the time step to vary based on momentary conditions of the stability of the equations. A starting sequence is achieved by more expensive Runge-Kutta methods for the initial three time increments to provide a history for following time steps. After the initial time increments, predictions for the positions and velocities of the DOFs are made for the following time step based on recent past history through a polynomial extrapolation. The equations of motion are then formed from these "predicted" results and solved to find new accelerations for the same time step. The new accelerations are interpolated with past accelerations and integrated to find "corrected" results for the positions and velocities.

If the predicted positions agree sufficiently with the corrected results, then the time step is held constant. If they do not coincide, then the results are thrown out and the time increment is halved and repeated. If the agreement is very good, the result is kept and the increment is doubled for subsequent time steps. In this way the size of the time increment adapts to changing conditions throughout the simulation. At no time is the time increment allowed to exceed a frame time, i.e., 1/24th of a second. Results from time increments representing frames are recorded for later playback.

3.4 Kinematic Constraints and Inverse Dynamics

If solving an equation for accelerations when the forces are given is called Forward Dynamics, then solving for forces when the accelerations are given can be called Inverse Dynamics. Since it is often difficult to think of motion in terms of the given forces, a system capable of performing both forward and inverse dynamics is desirable.

Equation 1, simply stated, is a relationship between geometry, acceleration, and forces. If all the values of matrix [A] are known, then there are really two ways to view the situation. Specify the force vector, B, and solve for the resultant accelerations:

$$q'' = [A]^{-1}\ B \qquad \text{(Eq. 4: Forward Dynamics)}$$

or in the simpler case: specify the acceleration vector, (i.e., the kinematic constraints), solving for the forces that would cause such an acceleration:

$$B = [A]q'' \qquad \text{(Eq. 5: Inverse Dynamics)}$$

In mechanical engineering terms, one can specify a set of Force Boundary Conditions (the first case), or a set of Displacement Boundary Conditions (the second case). In addition, the whole problem does not have to be specified in only one way. Each degree of freedom can be given either a Force Boundary Condition or a Displacement Boundary Condition (a kinematic constraint), but not both.

3.41 Kinematic Constraints

A kinematic constraint consists of an explicit specification for the acceleration of some DOF during the current time increment, thus removing an unknown degree of freedom from the system. Kinematic constraints may arise in three ways: they may be prespecified by an animator as part of a prescribed sequence; they may come into effect only when some inequality is satisfied, such as when the maximum rotation of an elbow joint constraint is exceeded; or they may be invoked by a behavior based on current criteria in the system, (e.g., a ball stays in the hand after being caught until thrown).

Within the context of the mathematical formulation, a kinematic constraint consists of removing a row and column from the system of equations. As an example, in a system with four DOF's, if the first and third are prescribed through kinematic constraints:

$$\begin{bmatrix} A_{11} & A_{12} & A_{13} & A_{14} \\ A_{21} & A_{22} & A_{23} & A_{24} \\ A_{31} & A_{32} & A_{33} & A_{34} \\ A_{41} & A_{42} & A_{43} & A_{44} \end{bmatrix} \begin{bmatrix} q''_1 \\ X \\ q''_3 \\ X \end{bmatrix} = \begin{bmatrix} X \\ B_2 \\ X \\ B_4 \end{bmatrix} \qquad \text{(Eq. 6:) (X's are unknown)}$$

The unknown DOF's, q''_2 and q''_4 can be solved for using the following general method:

A-- For each i where q''_i is given, move all terms involving q''_i to the right side by subtracting from the load vector the product of q''_i and the ith column of the [A] matrix.

$$\begin{bmatrix} 0 & A_{12} & 0 & A_{14} \\ 0 & A_{22} & 0 & A_{24} \\ 0 & A_{32} & 0 & A_{34} \\ 0 & A_{42} & 0 & A_{44} \end{bmatrix} \begin{bmatrix} q''_1 \\ X \\ q''_3 \\ X \end{bmatrix} = \begin{bmatrix} X \\ B_2 \\ X \\ B_4 \end{bmatrix} - \begin{bmatrix} A_{11} \\ A_{21} \\ A_{31} \\ A_{41} \end{bmatrix} q''_1 - \begin{bmatrix} A_{13} \\ A_{23} \\ A_{33} \\ A_{43} \end{bmatrix} q''_3$$

B-- Remove the rows and columns for each equation, i, for which an acceleration, q''_i is prescribed.

$$\begin{bmatrix} A_{22} & A_{24} \\ A_{42} & A_{44} \end{bmatrix} \begin{bmatrix} X \\ X \end{bmatrix} = \begin{bmatrix} B_2 \\ B_4 \end{bmatrix} - \begin{bmatrix} A_{21} * q''_1 \\ A_{41} * q_1 \end{bmatrix} - \begin{bmatrix} A_{23} * q''_3 \\ A_{43} * q_3 \end{bmatrix} = \begin{bmatrix} B_2\text{new} \\ B_4\text{new} \end{bmatrix}$$

C-- Solve the reduced system for the unknown accelerations, q''_2 and q''_4.

$$\begin{bmatrix} q''_2 \\ q_4 \end{bmatrix} = \begin{bmatrix} A_{22} & A_{24} \\ A_{42} & A_{44} \end{bmatrix}^{-1} \begin{bmatrix} B_2\text{new} \\ B_4\text{new} \end{bmatrix}$$

It is important to note that the new accelerations found by this method are, in a sense, a response to the given ones. This is because in step A, for each DOF with a prescribed force, a reactant force to the given accelerations is added to the original load. Hence, the solved motion is reactant to the prescribed motion.

The specification of some portion of a figure's motion leaves the remaining DOF's free to respond to the constrained motion under the control of the dynamic simulation. The ability to prespecify some motion within a dynamically based model provides the animator with the power of dynamic simulation while maintaining the control found in traditional animation methods. Thus, keyframe techniques can be embedded within a dynamic simulation system. If all parts of the body are constrained then there are no unknowns and the system reverts completely to a traditional animation system.

3.42 Inverse Dynamics

Continuing with the above example, once the unknown DOF accelerations have been found, the unknown forces can be found from the newly computed accelerations through inverse dynamics.

A-- Substitute the new-found accelerations (q''_2 and q''_4) into the original equation (Eq. 6).

B-- For each DOF, i, with q''_i originally given, multiply row i of [A] by the acceleration vector to find $B_i$new, the unknown force.

A specific desired motion can thus be converted to the equivalent set of forces. The reader may recall that in the original formulation of equation 12, values were found for B_i of all degrees of freedom. These original B_i contained all known internally and externally applied, centripital, coriolis, and coupling forces. We can use this knowledge to our advantage, if we say that:

$$B_i new - B_i = F_{actuator} \qquad \text{(Eq. 7)}$$

for the DOFs with prescribed motion. $F_{actuator}$ is then the additional force that a motor or muscle would have to exert on that degree of freedom to bring about the prescribed q_i''. This permits the determination of robot actuator forces needed to perform a specified task or the forces within the joints of a biomechanical system such as strain in a knee joint due to a given movement.

The ability to mix forward and inverse Dynamics has two direct implications for animation purposes. First, a keyframing animation system may be directly embedded within a Dynamic system. The key visual elements of a sequence can be programmed by keyframing them while allowing the other elements to react to them. Secondly, knowledge of the actuator forces can greatly increase the ability to develop behavior functions.

4.0 RESULTS

A series of short simulations has been performed to test the abilities of the DYNAMO system. The selected models were chosen in order to isolate various features which are of particular interest to the research effort being reported. Five experiments were conducted: a series of hanging chains, a tree blown by wind, a whip, a person on a swing, and an arm catching and throwing a ball.

The computation for the following simulations was run on a DEC VAX 8700. The display was performed on an Evans and Sutherland Picture System 2. The computation time is inversely dependent on the time step needed to maintain accuracy within the solution and exponentially dependent on the number of DOFs.

	# of DOFs	CPU_Minutes/Simulation_Seconds
CHAIN	6	0.35
TREE	39	14.00
WHIP	9	0.77
SWINGER	4	0.21
CATCHER	6	1.43
KICKER	39	30.00

4.1 A Series of Hanging Chains

A series of hanging chains ranging from a simple suspended weight to a branching tree of chains were constructed (figure 7). A simple behavior function exerted a force field due to gravity. Each chain was given an initial configuration and allowed to swing unconstrained. The resulting motion was complex, as primary and secondary waves passed through the chains, illustrating the dynamic coupled force interactions between links. The effects of damping within the DOFs produces expected settling of the motion over time.

4.2 A Tree Being Blown by a Time Varying Wind

A tree was constructed as a branching set of links and joints (figure 8). Each joint had three rotational DOFs and associated springs and dampers. The tree was given a density, thus, the mass of each link was a function of its volume. The spring and damper constants associated with each joint were described as a function of the cross-sectional area of the branch. A behavior for the wind exerted a time varying horizontal force on each branch as a function of the branch size.

The simulation resulted in a very complex swaying motion portraying the various natural frequencies of each of the branches of the tree. The tree and branches swayed in response to the wind, to coupled reactions between parent and child branches and to their individual resonances. Thus, a very simple set of instructions based on natural parameters to both construct and act on the tree resulted in a complex motion sequence.

4.3 A Whip Driven by a Kinematically Controlled Arm

A linear formation of links connected by one rotational degree of freedom formed an arm holding a whip (figure 9). The first two links represented the upper and lower arm, while the remaining links represented the whip. As in the tree example above, the diminishing size, mass and spring/dampers of each link and joint of the whip were parametrically determined from natural criteria.

The motion of the two arm rotations were prespecified as kinematic constraints through standard keyframing techniques.

The remaining links, the whip, were unconstrained and therefore reacted to the motion of the hand by whipping out and snapping. This example illustrates the combination of constrained and unconstrained motion and the complexity achieved by a relatively simple set of inputs.

4.4 A Swing

A swing illustrates a familiar dynamics problem; how does one get a swing to go by kicking out and contracting one's legs and body? The problem was simulated using a simplified model of a body on a swing. (figure 10) A person on a swing gains height by rapidly rotating the body and lower legs about the seat at appropriate times, thus adding rotational energy to the system . A functional description of the rotation of the upper body and lower legs, in terms of the natural period of the swing, specified the kinematic constraints on the fly.

After starting from an initial height, because of the body's pumping action, the swing did in fact gain height after each swing. This example illustrates how a simple behavior can be created without exact knowledge of the underlying physics to achieve a resulting motion with dynamic integrity.

4.5 An Arm Catching and Throwing a Ball

This example consisted of a ball and a three link arm: upper arm, lower arm, and hand (figure 11). The three arm joints had one rotational degree of freedom and the shoulder and elbow had associated springs and dampers.

Each joint possessed different types of constraints. The elbow was constrained not to bend

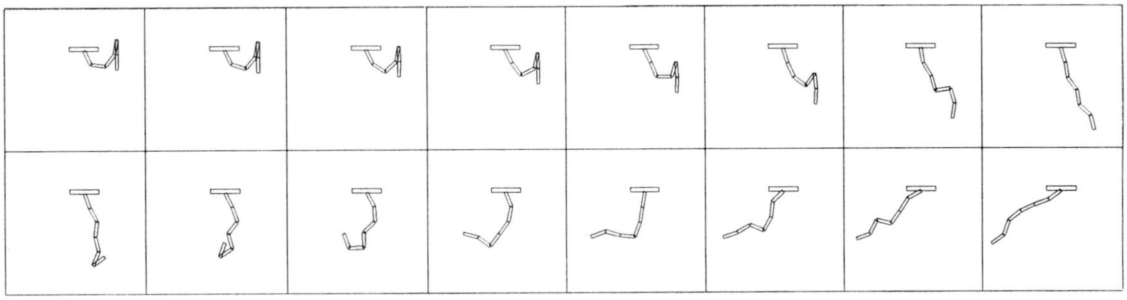

Figure 7: A Hanging Chain

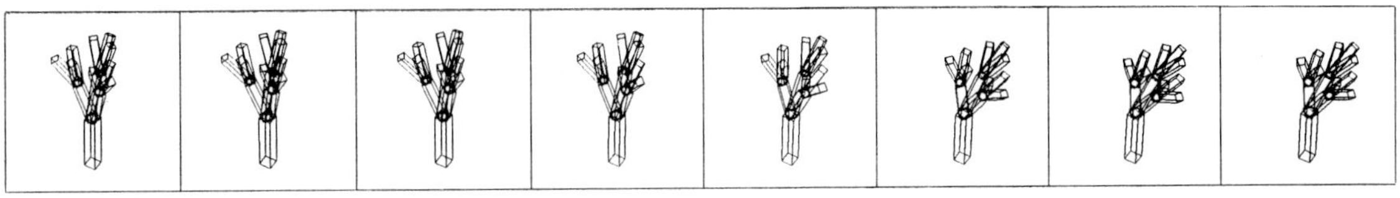

Figure 8: A Tree Swaying In The Wind

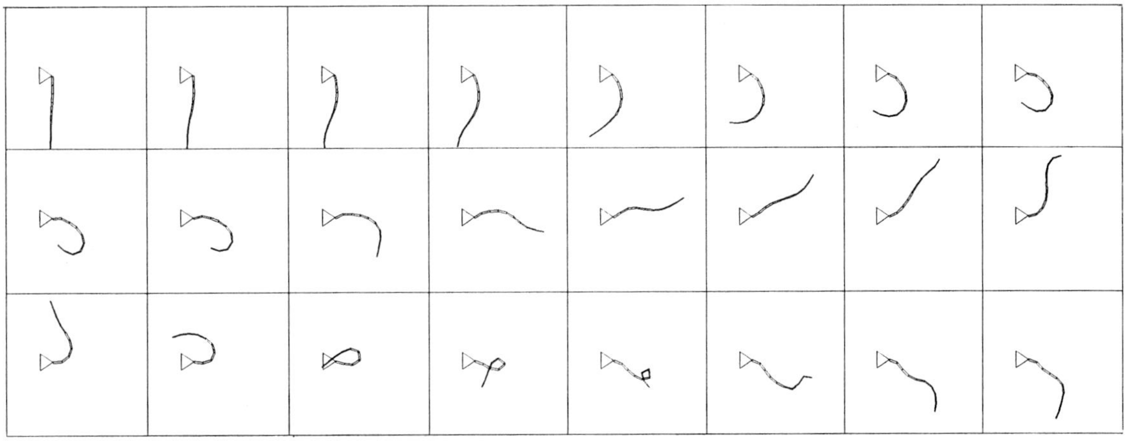

Figure 9: A Whip Driven By A Kinematically Controlled Arm

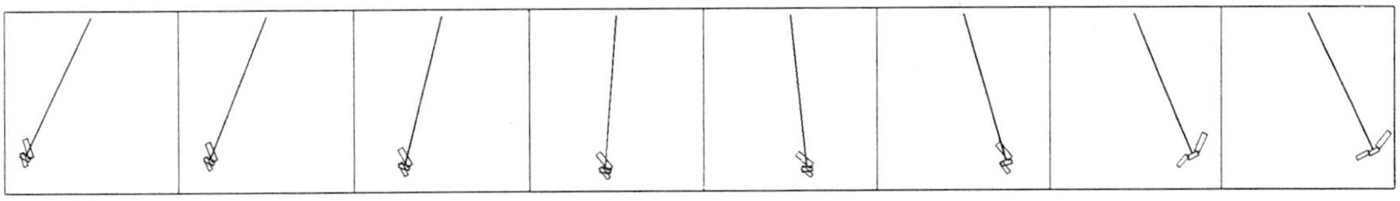

Figure 10: A Swing

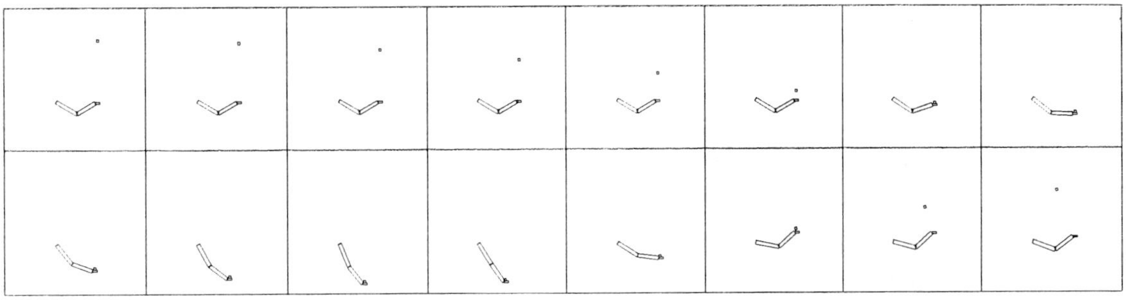

Figure 11: An Arm Catching And Throwing A Ball

backwards. The hand was always constrained to remain horizontal, thus the wrist had a positional constraint based on the unknown position of the shoulder and elbow.

A ball completed the system. The ball was free to move in the plane of the arm and was constrained to move with the hand while in contact with it.

An actuator force (programmed to mimic a strong spring) was added to the shoulder from the time that arm became fully cocked until the ball was released. This additional force threw the ball back into the air. This same actuator exerted a damping force after the release of the ball to bring the arm smoothly back to rest in its original position. The results produced a very natural action arising from the variety of constraint types and a simple set of behaviors.

The values of the wrist actuator torques were found by employing Inverse Dynamics. The required accelerations of the wrist to maintain the horizontality of the hand were determined during the dynamic simulation. After solving for all other accelerations, the actual torque on the wrist was calculated. Subtracting all other known torques on the wrist, the necessary actuator torque was found. Figure 12 shows a graph of the wrist actuator torques with time, as well as the shoulder spring and motor torques, which were given by forward dynamics.

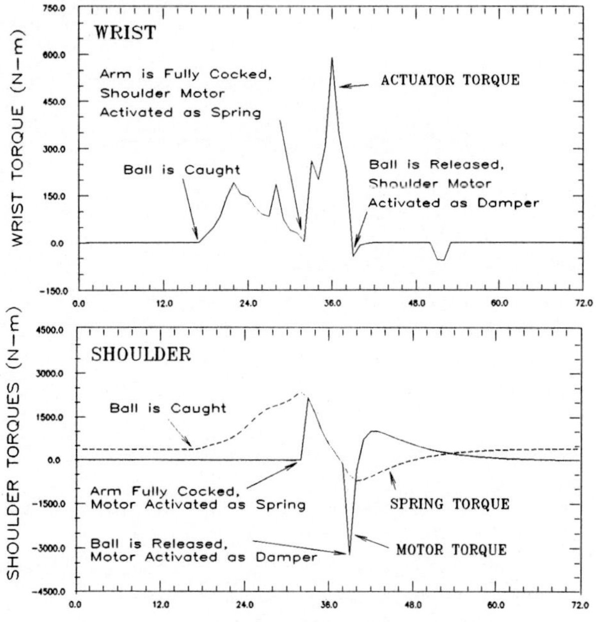

Figure 12: Torques In The Catcher Arm

4.6 A Man Kicking on Two Types of Floors

This last example illustrates how inverse dynamics can be used to create behaviors which produce different sequences under different conditions. A man executing a kick was first animated with a keyframing system (figure 13a). Through inverse dynamics, DYNAMO found the actuator forces and torques needed to produce the same motion.

Two subsequent runs of DYNAMO were then executed. In the first, these actuator force and torque values were used to drive the figure. As expected, the resulting motion was nearly identical to the original keyframed sequence. In the second (figure 13b), the horizontal forces between the foot and floor were removed, producing the conditions of a frictionless surface. The figure exerted the same pattern of forces on itself, but in a different environment. Since the horizontal support was gone and the figure was not perfectly balanced, the leg

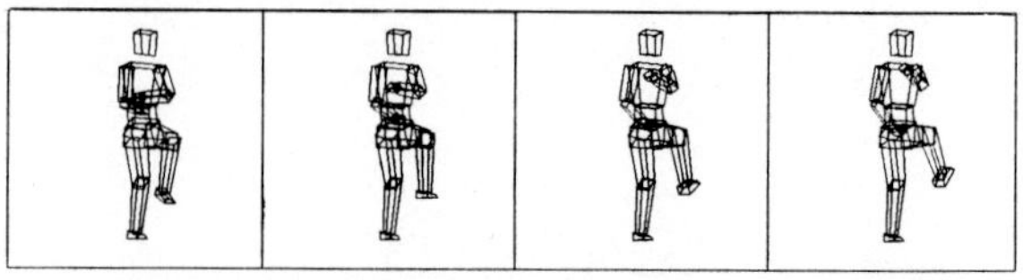

Figure 13a: A Man Executing A Kick

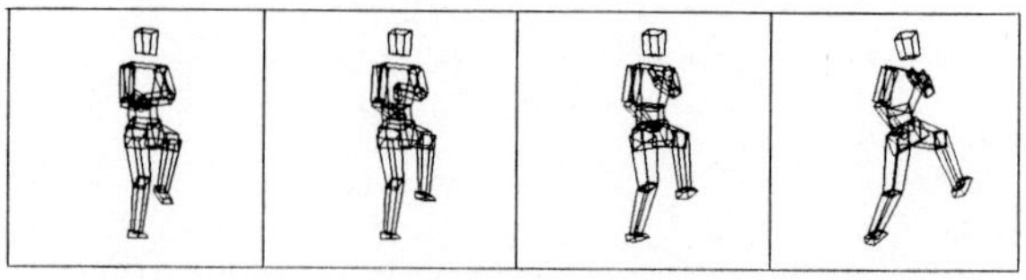

Figure 13b: The Same Kick On A Frictionless Floor

slid out from under the hip as the figure executed the motion.

5.0 CONCLUSION

A system for performing dynamic simulation of linked figures has been presented. The definition of the figures includes behavioral as well as physical characteristics. The behaviors cause the figures to react to their momentary state through the imposition of external or internal forces or through explicit specification of motion. The formulation of the equations of motion permits the imposition of kinematic and limiting constraints on the unknown degrees of freedom associated with each joint. An inverse dynamics procedure evaluates the equivalent force(s) which would be required to create the same motion as that specified by kinematic constraints. The dynamic simulation is run as an explicit time series analysis with predictor corrector methods maintaining accuracy and efficiency in the solution. A series of experimental runs of the DYNAMO system illustrating the methods outlined in the paper have produced some exciting results and are reported in the previous section.

The catcher-arm example illustrates one of the prime advantages of mixing kinematic and dynamic specifications through the behavior functions. It allows the user to think of each part of the animation in the way that is most suitable for the job: The motion of the hand is controlled visually -- it is simply kept level. The ball and lower arm are passive links, each with simple constraints on their motions. Lastly, the torque in the shoulder is controlled through forward dynamics, by specifying the torque in the motor based on information about the state of the system.

The behaviors, kinematic constraints, and inverse dynamics which were introduced in this paper provide control mechanisms to achieve a desired motion while maintaining dynamic integrity throughout the simulation.

There remains a large body of related research to be done. The system was written in C, which requires that behaviors be compiled and linked with the simulation code. Higher level interpreted languages would be a natural choice to enhance the process of developing behavior functions.

Additional desirable features which have not been

implemented to date include: the implementation of closed kinematic chains, behaviors that learn, collision detection between links, a more flexible user interface for defining linkages and behaviors, and the ability for figures to interact in parallel through message passing, i.e. messages passed from behavior to behavior. The use of a muscle based model may aid modeling techniques by relating muscle tension and contraction to shape and size.

The methods outlined in the paper should provide a base for further research for both the animator creating a particular motion sequence and the scientist simulating physical phenomena.

6.0 APPENDIX - DERIVING THE EQUATIONS OF MOTION

The equations of motion are derived from D'Alembert's principle of virtual work [15], which states that if a system is in dynamic equilibrium and the bodies are allowed to move a small amount (called a virtual displacement) then the sum of the work of applied forces, the work of applied torques, and the work of internal forces will be equal and opposite to the work of changes in momentum. This is equivalent to saying that all work done in the system is accounted for. For a system of n links, D'alembert's equation is:

$$\sum_{i=0}^{n} [dr_i(F_i - m_i r_i'') + d\theta_i(M_i - L_i') + dW_i] = 0 \qquad \text{(Eq. A1)}$$

Work of applied forces minus work of changes in linear momentum.	Work of applied torques minus work of changes in angular momentum.	Work of internal forces.	None left over.

where:

- dr_i = virtual linear displacement of link number i (3d coordinate)
- F_i = the total applied force through the COG of link i (coord)
- m_i = the mass of link i (scalar)
- r_i, r_i', r_i'' = the linear position, velocity and acceleration of link i (coord)
- $d\theta_i$ = virtual angular displacement of link number i (coord)
- M_i = total applied torque on link i (coord)
- L'_i = the change in angular momentum of link number i (coord),
  where: $L_i' = J_i \cdot \theta_i'' + \theta_i' \times J_i \cdot \theta_i'$
  J_i = moment of inertia tensor of link i (3x3 matrix)
  θ_i, θ_i', θ_i'' = the angular position velocity and acceleration of link i (coord)
- dW_i = virtual work done by internal forces on link i (coord) (i.e., the work done by springs and dampers in joint i)

D'Alembert's equation is written in terms of variables for position (r) and orientation (θ). If we treat this sum as a system of n independent linear equations, then each equation will have six unknowns: the linear acceleration in the x, y and z directions (r_x'', r_y'', r_z'') and the angular acceleration about the three axes (θ_x'', θ_y'', θ_z''). All other variables are calculated as known quantities from the current state of the system, except for the virtual displacements, which are later eliminated from the equations. This gives a total of (6 * n) unknowns.

If, instead, D'Alembert's principle is expressed in terms of the system's degrees of freedom, the total number of unknowns is reduced to total number of degrees of freedom, n_{DOF}, which is typically much less than (6 * n), because most links have parent joints with fewer than six degrees of freedom. If the number of unknowns is not reduced in this way, then ($6 - n_{DOF}$) additional constraint equations would have to be written, one for each disallowed direction of motion. Thus, by formulating the equations in terms of the DOFs, the number of unknowns are reduced and the simulation runs more efficiently. In addition, the resulting motion is expressed in terms of the joint DOFs as they were constructed.

To express the motion of the system in terms of the DOFs, four generalized coordinate vectors are used. Each vector has one entry for each DOF:

- q — a vector of positions (either r or θ)
- q' — a vector of velocities
- q" — a vector of accelerations (unknowns)
- and dq, — a vector of virtual displacements

Matrix equations describing each of the vector quantities dθ, dr, θ", r", and dW in terms of generalized coordinates and other known quantities are derived:

$$d\theta = -T^T p^T dq \qquad \text{(Eq. A2)}$$

$$dr = [p \times T(C + Z)T - kT]^T dq \qquad \text{(Eq. A3)}$$

$$\theta'' = -T^T (p^T q'' + f) + \theta_0'' \qquad \text{(Eq. A4)}$$

$$r'' = [p \times T(C + Z)T - kT]^T q'' + U \qquad \text{(Eq. A5)}$$

$$dW = -dq^T (k \cdot X + p \cdot Y) \qquad \text{(Eq. A6)}$$

and the following new (known) terms are introduced:

- T = matrix expressing connectivity of the system
- p = matrix of the unit axes of rotation of all rotational DOFs of the system. (zero for translational DOFs)
- C = matrix of distances from the joints to the COGs of the links which they connect
- Z = matrix of current displacement vectors along translational axes of freedom. (zero for rotational DOFs)
- k = matrix of partial derivatives of relative translation vectors with respect to each translational DOF.
- f = matrix of values relating angular velocity of one rotational DOF to a resulting angular acceleration of another DOF.
- θ_0'' = vector of coordinates each equal to angular acceleration of inertial frame of reference.
- U = array of values, one per link, which relate its linear acceleration to known quantities in the system.
- X = vector of internal applied forces, one per DOF.
- Y = vector of internal applied torques, one per DOF.

[details can be found in Wittenberg, pages 147-163]

All of these new terms above are calculated based on the pre-defined model of the system, the known values for q and q′, and the current internally applied forces and torques.

The derivation continues by substituting equations A2 through A6 into equation A1 to yield:

$$\begin{aligned} dq^T\{ & [p \times T(C + Z)T - kT] \\ & \cdot\{F - m[p \times T(C + Z)T - kT]^T q'' - mU\} \\ & - pT\cdot\{M - J\cdot[-T^T (p^T q'' + f) + \Theta_0'] - \theta' \times J\cdot\theta'\} \\ & - k\cdot X - p\cdot Y \\ \} & = 0 \end{aligned} \qquad \text{(Eq. A7)}$$

Isolating the terms involving q", we have:

$$dq^T (-A q'' + B) = 0 \qquad \text{(Eq. A8)}$$

where

$$\begin{aligned} A = & [p \times T(C + Z)T - kT] \cdot m[P \times T(C + Z)T - kT]^T \\ & + (pT)\cdot J\cdot(pT)^T \end{aligned} \qquad \text{(Eq. A9)}$$

$$\begin{aligned} B = & [p \times T(C + Z)T - kT] \cdot (F - mU) \\ & - pT \cdot [M + J \cdot (T^T f - \Theta_0') - \theta' \times J\cdot\theta'] \\ & - k\cdot X - p\cdot Y \end{aligned} \qquad \text{(Eq. A10)}$$

Since the motion of all generalized coordinates is independent, the dq term from equation A8 can be removed, yielding the original equation 3:

$$[A] \lfloor q'' \rfloor = \lfloor B \rfloor$$

Although the final form of the equations for A and B appear complicated, it should be stressed that all of the quantities are based on a relatively small set of very natural parameters (mass, size, type of joint, etc.). The only unknowns are q", and the only required user inputs are F and M, the applied forces and torques.

A note on the coordinate systems used: When forming the A matrix and B vector, it does not matter which coordinate system is used to represent vectors in 3-space, so long as they are consistent. In DYNAMO, the final equation is calculated in the inertial (world) reference frame. In many cases, as with axes of a joint and moment of inertia tensors, it is convenient to store the variables in local coordinates and convert them into inertial coordinates as they enter the equations.

7.0 ACKNOWLEDGEMENTS

This paper would not have been possible without the input and support of our colleagues at the Cornell Program of Computer Graphics. Special thanks go to Donald Greenberg, for providing unlimited freedom and constant enthusiasm, to Stewart Feldman, for helping with the diagrams, to Dave Salmon and Jerome Hajjar, for their depth of knowledge and generosity with their time, and to Susan Morgenstein, for her inspiration. This research was conducted under grant No. DCR-8203979 from the National Science Foundation and was supported by generous equipment grants from the Digital Equipment Corporation and Hewlett-Packard.

8.0 REFERENCES

[1] Armstrong, William W., and Green, Mark W., "The Dynamics of Articulated Rigid Bodies for Purposes of Animation," The Visual Computer, Vol. 1, 4, Springer Verlag, December 1985, pp.231-240

[2] Badler, Norman I., et al., "Multi-Dimensional Input Techniques and Articulated Figure Positionaing By Multiple Constraints," 1986 Workshop on Interactive 3D Graphics, Chapel Hill, North Carolina, October 1986.

[3] Conte, Samuel D., and de Boor, Carl, Elementary Numerical Analysis, An Algorithmic Approach, (Third Edition), McGraw-Hill Book Company, New York, N.Y., 1980, pp.379-389.

[4] Featherstone, R., "The Calculation of Robot Dynamics Using Articulated-Body Inertias," The International Journal of Robotics Research, Vol. 2, No. 1, Spring 1983, pp.13-30.

[5] Girard, Michael, and Maciejewski, A. A., "Computational Modelling for the Computer Animation of Legged Figures," ACM COMPUTER GRAPHICS (Siggraph Proc. '85), July 1985, pp.263-270.

[6] Girard, Michael, "Interactive Design of 3-D Computer-Animated Legged Animal Motion," 1986 Workshop on Interactive 3D Graphics, Chapel Hill, North Carolina, October 1986.

[7] Hornbeck, Robert W., Numerical Methods, Quantum Publishers, New York, NY, 1974, pp.199-202.

[8] Korein, James U., and Badler, Norman I., "Techniques for Generating the Goal-Directed Motion of Articulated Structures," IEEE Computer Graphics Applications, November 1982, pp.71-81.

[9] Luh, J., Walker M., Paul R., "On-line Computational Scheme for Mechanical Manipulators," in Robot Motion, Planning and Control, edited by Brady et. al., M.I.T. Press, pp.89-106.

[10] O'Donnell, T.J., and Olson, Arthur J. "GRAMPS - A Graphics Language Interpreter for Real-Time, Interactive, Three-Dimensional Picture Editing and Animation," ACM COMPUTER GRAPHICS (Siggraph Proc. '81), August 1981, pp. 133-142.

[11] Raibert, Marc H., et. al., "Experiments in Balance with a 3D One-Legged Hopping Machine," The International Journal of Robotics Research, Vol. 3, No. 2, Summer 1984, pp.75-92.

[12] Stern, Garland, "Bbop - A Program for 3-Dimensional Animation," Nicograph '83 Proceedings, December 1983, pp.403-404.

[13] Wilhelms, Jane, and Barsky, Brian. "Using Dynamic Analysis to Animate Articulated Bodies Such as Humans and Robots," Proceedings, Graphics Interface '85, May 1985, pp.97-104.

[14] Williams, R.J., and Seireg, A., "Interactive Modeling and Analysis of Open or Closed Loop Dynamic Systems with Redundant Actuators," Journal of Mechanical Design (Transactions of the ASME), Vol. 101, July 1979, pp.407-416

[15] Wittenberg, Jens, Dynamics of Systems of Rigid Bodies, B.G. Teubner, Stuttgart, Germany, 1977.

Energy Constraints On Parameterized Models

Andrew Witkin†
Kurt Fleischer†
Alan Barr‡
†Schlumberger Palo Alto Research, 3340 Hillview Avenue, Palo Alto, CA 94304
‡California Institute of Technology, Pasadena, CA 91125

Abstract

A simple but general approach to imposing and solving geometric constraints on parameterized models is introduced, applicable to animation as well as model construction. Constraints are expressed as energy functions, and the energy gradient followed through the model's parameter space. Intuitively, energy constraints behave like forces that pull and parametrically deform the parts of the model into place. A wide variety of geometric constraints are amenable to this formulation, and may be used to influence arbitrary model parameters. A catalogue of basic constraints is presented, and results are shown.

Keywords — Constraints, Modeling, Animation

I. Introduction

A widely-used approach to modeling is to combine geometric primitives—such as cylinders, blocks, and bicubic patches—with a variety of operators—such as translations, rotations, booleans, and deformations—to form a model hierarchy. The task of constructing a model within this framework has two parts: building the hierarchy, and setting the internal parameters of the primitives and operators. Experience tells us that the second task is usually by far the more difficult and time-consuming, particularly when complex operators such as deformations are used. As the complexity of the model increases, the number of parameters becomes large, and they tend to interact in ways that make the model difficult to control.

The user knows at the outset what the objects being modeled are supposed to look like—how the pieces are supposed to fit together and move. The difficulty lies in finding settings of the parameters that achieve the desired effect. The utility of hierarchic modeling systems would be greatly enhanced if this tedious process could be performed automatically, permitting the user to state in terms of constraints the properties the model is supposed to have, without the need to manually adjust parameters to give it those properties.

In this paper we present a simple but general approach to expressing and solving constraints on parameterized model hierarchies. We formulate constraints as *"energy"* functions on the model's parameter space, non-negative functions with zeroes at points satisfying the constraints. We then sum the constraints' energy functions to create a single scalar function of the parameters, and move through parameter space to minimize the energy.

We refer to the constraint functions as energy functions not because they always model the energy of actual physical systems, but because they play a role similar to that of physical energy functions during the constraint solving process. For example, an energy constraint attaching points on the surfaces of two objects acts much like a spring that pulls the objects together. However, in addition to translating and rotating, the objects are free to vary their internal parameters, so, for example, a cylinder may vary its length or radius to meet the constraint. Although no familiar physical material deforms in this stylized way in response to applied forces, it is easy enough to imagine an unphysical material that does. Since we are using the energy analogy as a mechanism for building models, rather than for simulating physical phenomena, this kind of non-physical behavior poses no problem.

Our approach provides:

- *Self-assembling* models, whose parts move and deform parametrically from an initial configuration to one that satisfies the specified constraints.
- *Animated* models that, once assembled, may move in response to time-varying constraints while continuing to satisfy static ones.
- Generality and modularity: we can formulate a wide range of constraints as energy functions, and use them to influence arbitrary model parameters. To implement a new constraint we need not know the details of other constraints, nor of the primitives and operators to which they will be applied. Similarly, new parameterized primitives and operators may be implemented without modifying existing constraints.
- Additivity: Energy functions compose by addition. The solution to a system of constraints is the so-

lution to a single equation, the sum of the energy terms. This property is particularly valuable in dealing with overdetermined systems. While conventional algebraic methods return no solution to an overdetermined system, the energy minimum is a "compromise" that is sometimes acceptable, nearly always informative, and often easily repaired.

- Interactive control: since we satisfy constraints by moving through a curve in parameter space, the initial constraint solving process can itself be animated, permitting the user to assist the solver in escaping local energy minima, resolving ambiguities, etc.

A significant body of work in constraint-based and dynamics modeling for computer graphics is concerned with the the specialized problem of animating articulated bodies, particularly human and animal forms. These include Armstrong and Green, [1], Girard and Maciejewski, [6], and Wilhelms and Barksy [13]. Nelson's *Juno* editor employs non-linear geometric constraints in the context of a 2-D image editor. Dynamic models of elastic bodies for computer graphics are treated by Terzopoulos *et al.* in [12]. Closest to ours in approach are Barzel and Barr's dynamic constraints [3], although their current work focuses on constraining the motion of rigid bodies.

II. Energy constraints

A model hierarchy is a tree that defines the model's geometry through a collection of mathematical functions, three of which will concern us here. These are a *parametric position* function, $\mathbf{P}(u, v)$ that returns a 3-space point for each (u, v) pair, a *surface normal* function, $\mathbf{N}(u, v)$, that returns a surface normal vector, and an *implicit* or inside-outside function, $I(\mathbf{X})$, that returns a scalar given a 3-space point, such that $I = 0$ for points on the object's surface, $I < 0$ for points inside the object, and $I > 0$ for points outside the object. One such collection of functions is defined for each leaf in the tree, and represents the combined effects of the primitive at the leaf and of all the operators on the path from that leaf to the root. Definitions of these functions are given in Appendix A.

In general, each primitive or operator possesses some real-valued parameters, for instance the radius of a sphere, a translation vector, or the bend angle of a parameterized deformation. The position, normal and implicit functions each depend on these parameters: when they change, objects' surfaces move. We refer to the union of all these parameters as $\mathbf{\Psi}$. Once the hierarchic structure is fixed, the state of the model is completely determined by the value of $\mathbf{\Psi}$. The notion of parameter spaces, and of motion along curves through parameter space, is familiar in computer graphics in the context of keyframe interpolation (see, e.g. [11].)

We will express geometric constraints in terms of the functions $\mathbf{P}$, $\mathbf{N}$, and I. For instance, if we wish to attach two surface points $\mathbf{P}_1(u_1, v_1)$ and $\mathbf{P}_2(u_2, v_2)$, at least one condition we must satisfy is $\mathbf{P}_1 = \mathbf{P}_2$. A solution is a value of $\mathbf{\Psi}$ such that all the imposed conditions are met.

Rather than solving the constraint equations algebraically, we formulate constraints as energy functions, and move through parameter space according to the energy gradient. In general, to formulate an energy constraint, we must construct a non-negative smooth function $E(\mathbf{\Psi})$ such that $E(\mathbf{\Psi}) = 0$ at all and only values of $\mathbf{\Psi}$ for which the constraint is satisfied. The solutions to a set of n constraints are values of $\mathbf{\Psi}$ such that

$$E(\mathbf{\Psi}) = \sum_i^n E_i(\mathbf{\Psi}) = 0,$$

so to combine constraints, the corresponding energy terms are simply summed. We are free to express E in terms of position, normal, or implicit functions, or any other quantities that may be extracted from the model tree.

Intuitively, energy constraints may be viewed as "forces" that pull the parts of the model into the desired configuration and hold them there, although they are not necessarily intended to be physically realistic forces. For instance, a simple attachment constraint might be implemented as a spring connecting the points, in which case we have

$$E_{spring} = \kappa \left| P_1(u_1, v_1) - P_2(u_2, v_2) \right|^2,$$

where κ is a spring constant, and the "force" vector in parameter space is ∇E_{spring}.

From an initial condition $\mathbf{\Psi}_0$, the energy E is minimized by numerically solving the differential equation

$$d\mathbf{F}(t)/dt = \nabla E, \mathbf{F}(0) = \mathbf{\Psi}_0,$$

for a fixed point of the parameter-space curve $\mathbf{F}(t)$, i.e. a point at which $\nabla E = 0$. The solution is a local minimum, although it is not guaranteed to be a zero. This is a steepest descent method for solving $\nabla E = 0$.

A variety of standard numerical methods may be used to solve the energy equation. The simplest of these, Euler's method, has

$$F(t_{i+1}) = F(t) + h \nabla E,$$

with h the step size. More sophisticated methods, such as Gear's method [5] should be used to obtain accurate, reliable results. Any solution method requires evaluation of ∇E. To do so, the summed energy must be differentiated with respect to each model parameter, which may be done numerically by varying each parameter in turn, re-evaluating E, and taking differences. The structure of the tree may be used to avoid the needless expense of differentiating energy terms with respect to parameters on which they do not depend.

A limitation of the method is that it may be trapped at spurious (i.e. non-zero) local minima of E. Our solution to this problem is user interaction. Such minima are usually easy to interpret geometrically, e.g. a single part has become stuck or been turned backwards. Presented with a bad answer, the user can often correct the situation by manually repositioning a part. In fact, with fast enough rendering to view the evolving solution dynamically, the user can literally push or pull on parts of the model with a pointing device, introducing a time-varying energy term, E_{user}, into the equation, to bump it out of local minima. This style of user interaction has been used to good effect in interactive image interpretation [7]. A different form of user control is obtained by selectively freezing and unfreezing model parameters, to decompose a large problem into a sequence of smaller ones.

III. A catalogue of useful constraints

A wide range of geometric constraints may be cast in the form of energy functions. Here we list a few basic constraints, most of which are used in the examples to follow. Many are subject to alternative formulations. Each energy function is multiplied by a weighting factor; these factors are not shown below.

- **Attachment to a fixed point in space:** The energy term

$$E = |\mathbf{P}^a(u_a, v_a) - \mathbf{Q}|^2$$

attaches a specific point on the surface of object a, defined by parameter point (u_a, v_a), to a specific point in space, $\mathbf{Q}$.

- **Surface-to-surface attachment:** Place specified points on two surfaces in contact. To acheive contact, the points must coincide. In addition, their tangent planes at those points must coincide, and the surfaces should not (locally) interpenetrate. These conditions can be encoded by

$$\begin{aligned} E &= \left|\mathbf{P}^a(u_a, v_a) - \mathbf{P}^b(u_b, v_b)\right|^2 + \\ &\quad \mathbf{N}^a(u_a, v_a) \cdot \mathbf{N}^b(u_b, v_b) + 1, \end{aligned}$$

where P^a and P^b are the positions at the two attachment points, and N^a and N^b are the unit surface normals at those points. This function is zero when the points coincide and the dot product of the normals is -1.

- **Floating attachment:** Attach a specified point on an object to *some* point on a second object, allowing the point of contact to slide freely on the second object. Our implementation of this constraint is similar to that for simple surface-to-surface attachment, but uses the second object's implicit function instead of its parametric position function:

$$\begin{aligned} E &= I^b(\mathbf{P}^a(u_a, v_a))^2 + \\ &\quad \mathbf{N}^a(u_a, v_a) \cdot \frac{\nabla I^b}{|\nabla I^b|} + 1, \end{aligned}$$

noting that $\nabla I^b / |\nabla I|$ is a unit normal to surface b where $I^b = 0$. A useful variation is double floating attachment, in which both points float on their respective surfaces.

- **Slider constraint:** Constrain a specified point on an object to a line in space:

$$E = PLD(\mathbf{P}^a(u_a, v_a), \mathbf{P}_1, \mathbf{P}_2)^2,$$

where PLD is the point-to-line distance function, and $\mathbf{P}_1$ and $\mathbf{P}_2$ are points on the line. Useful variations constrain the point to a line *segment*, or constrain two line segments to be colinear and to overlap (like segments of a telescope.)

- **Collision using the implicit function:** For objects possessing inside-outside functions, interference or collision constraints may be imposed without calculating surface intersections. The implicit function is zero everywhere on the object's surface, and, by our convention, negative inside and positive outside the object. To impose an anti-interference constraint, we transform the implicit function into a thin repulsive "force field" surrounding the object. At a single point, $P^a(u_a, v_a)$ on object a, a suitable energy function is

$$E = e^{-\kappa I^b(P^a(u_a, v_a))},$$

where κ is a positive scale factor. This makes the energy high inside object b, tending to zero far from object b. Thus a point inside the object is repelled, the repulsion approaching zero off the object's surface. To implement a general interference constraint, this function must be integrated over u and v. An efficient implementation must make use of intelligent sampling, hierarchic bounding boxes, etc., which are beyond the scope of this paper.

- **Direct constraints on parameters:** It is sometimes useful to impose constraints directly on model parameters, for instance to establish default values, or to constrain relations among parameters. If α is some model parameter, then a defaulting constraint may be written as $E = (\alpha - \alpha_0)^2$, where α_0 is the default value. If α and β are two model parameters, then a linear relational constraint may be written as $E = (\alpha - k_1\beta - k_2)^2$, which says that the linear relation $\alpha = k_1\beta + k_2$ should hold between α and β. For instance, if we want one rod to be twice as long as another, we have $E = (l_1 - 2l_2)^2$, where l_1 and l_2 are the lengths of the rods.

IV. Examples

This section presents three examples of the use of energy constraints to build and animate models. The first, a relatively simple one, is described in detail as a concrete illustration of the method. The second and third are described more briefly.

Pipefitting: A simple example illustrating self-assembly and adjustment of a variety of model parameters is shown in figure 1. A cylindrical pipe, subjected to a translation, a rotation, and a parameterized bend is to be fitted to other pipes at either end. All other parts of the model have already been assembled, and their parameters frozen.

The model hierarchy for the adjustable tube is described schematically by $Trans(Rot(Bend(Tube)))$:

- A tube is a primitive, whose axis is coincides with the x-axis in model space, and whose dimensions are controlled by three parameters —length, radius, and thickness.
- A bend (after [2]) is a parameterized deformation that maps the x-axis into a circular arc in the x, z plane. Its effect on shape is controlled by three parameters—start, stop, and amount. Start and stop determine the "tightness" of the bend, and amount is the angle between the ends of the curved axis.
- A quaternion rotation is specified by a 4-vector. Although any rotation may be specified by three Euler angles, we use quaternions to avoid gimbal lock.
- A translation is specified by a 3-vector of x, y, and z displacements.

The union of these parameters, $\mathbf{\Psi}$, is a 13-dimensional vector. Motion along a curve through $\mathbf{\Psi}$-space corresponds to some combination of bending, translating, rotating, and changing the tube's dimensions. Despite the simplicity of the example, this means that we have to come up with 13 independent numbers to pin down the model in the desired configuration. Doing this manually, or writing a special purpose program to do it, would have been unpleasant.

For our purposes, two pipes are attached if their axes join smoothly and they have the same radius and thickness. An "attach-pipes" (AP) energy constraint may be built by combining a surface-to-surface attachment constraint, as defined in the previous section, with relational constraints that make the radii and thicknesses agree. Let $\mathbf{P}_1$ and $\mathbf{P}_2$ be the endpoints of the two pipes' axes, i.e. the points to be joined, and let $\mathbf{N}_1$ and $\mathbf{N}_2$ be two unit vectors extending outward from the axis endpoints in a direction tangent to the axes. Then we want $P_1 = P_2$ and $N_1 \cdot N_2 = 0$. Additionally, we want $r_1 = r_2$ and $t_1 = t_2$ for the radii and thicknesses. In energy form, this gives us

$$E_{AP} = |\mathbf{P}_1 - \mathbf{P}_2|^2 + \mathbf{N}_1 \cdot \mathbf{N}_2 + 1 + (r_1 - r_2)^2 + (t_1 - t_2)^2.$$

To attach both ends of the moving pipe, we have as the total energy the sum of two terms of this form.

Prior to bending, rotation, and translation, the endpoints of the moving tube's axis are situated at the points $\mathbf{P}_1 = (length/2, 0, 0)$, and $\mathbf{P}_2 = (-length/2, 0, 0)$, with unit normals $\mathbf{N}_1 = (1, 0, 0)$ and $\mathbf{N}_2 = (-1, 0, 0)$ pointing outward from the ends. The two fixed pipes to which the moving one is to be attached each have a similarly defined endpoint and normal, which are constants. The transformed endpoints are $Trans(Rot(Bend(\mathbf{P}_1)))$ and $Trans(Rot(Bend(\mathbf{P}_2)))$, respectively, so their positions in model space depend on all the model parameters except radius and thickness. Using the fact that surface normals transform under deformations by multiplication with the inverse transpose of the deformation's jacobian ([2]), the transformed normals are $Rot(\mathbf{J}_{Bend}^{-1T}\mathbf{N}_1)$ and $Rot(\mathbf{J}_{Bend}^{-1T}\mathbf{N}_2)$, where J_{Bend}^{-1T} is the inverse transpose of the bend operator's jacobian, evaluated at P_1 and P_2 respectively (see [2] for the formula.)

To solve the constraints, we solve the equation $\frac{d}{dt}\mathbf{\Psi}(t) = \nabla E$ from a starting point $\mathbf{\Psi}(t_0)$, until we reach a point at which $\nabla E \leq \epsilon$, where ϵ is a small tolerance value. At any point $\mathbf{\Psi}$ in parameter space, we can evaluate $\mathbf{P}_1$, $\mathbf{P}_2$, $\mathbf{N}_1$, and $\mathbf{N}_2$, and hence the energy function defined in terms of them. To compute ∇E numerically, we first evaluate E at the current $\mathbf{\Psi}$, then add a small Δ to each parameter (i.e. each component of $\mathbf{\Psi}$) in turn, re-evaluate E and subtract the central value of E, obtaining the corresponding component of ∇E. Using Euler's method the new value of $\mathbf{\Psi}$ is given by $\mathbf{\Psi}_{t+1} = \mathbf{\Psi}_t + h\nabla E$, where h is a step size.

Figure 1 shows the model at the initial condition, at several steps toward the solution, and at the solution. Finally, we show a new solution obtained when one of the fixed pipes is moved.

Oldham linkage: An oldham linkage is used to transfer rotation between shafts that are offset in a plane perpendicular to their axes, by means of a system of tongues and grooves. Figure 2 shows several frames from the self-assembly sequence for an oldham linkage, and several frames from an animation sequence. The specification of this mechanism involved a variety of constraints, including sliders, surface-to-surface contact, and position and orientation constraints. This example illustrates the use of energy constraints both for assembly and for animation of the assembled model.

Cam and rocker arm: This example (figure 3) shows an already-assembled cam and rocker arm at several points in its cycle. This is a working model: the pressure of the spring on the valve head pushes the follower against the cam via the fulcrum. The follower "feels" the cam using an implicit-function interference constraint, so that if the cam were reshaped, the motion of the arm would change accordingly.

V. Conclusion

Energy constraints were shown to provide an effective means of building and controlling parameterized models. A principle advantage of the energy method is its generality: it does not depend on the details of the constraints used or the models to which they are applied. It is tolerant of over- and under-determined systems, and amenable to user interaction. Among its disadvantages, it can be numerically intensive—particularly when the equations become stiff—and it can be trapped in local minima. The second difficulty is largely overcome by effective user interaction.

Appendix A

In this appendix we define the position, normal and implicit functions in terms of the structure of the model tree. Our definition describes the SPAR modeling testbed [4], but is typical of hierarchic modelers in most relevant respects. Each leaf in the tree represents a primitive. The root is a camera, and the intermediate nodes represent operators. We denote the leaves by L^i, and the n nodes on the ascending path from leaf L^i to the camera as $O^{i,j}$, where $O^{i,1}$ is L^i, $O^{i,2}$ is the first operator above L^i, and O^i, n is the camera. (When we refer to the objects comprising the tree without regard to the paths they lie on, we index them as O_i.) For the purpose of sampling and rendering, each such path defines a distinct object, characterized by a coordinated bundle of mathematical functions. These include:

- A parametric position function, $\mathbf{P}^i(u,v)$, $\Re^2 \rightarrow \Re^3$, defined recursively by

$$\begin{aligned} \mathbf{P}^i(u,v) &= \mathbf{P}^{i,n}(u,v), \\ \mathbf{P}^{i,j}(u,v) &= \mathbf{T}^{i,j}(\mathbf{P}^{i,j-1}(u,v)), j \neq 1, \\ \mathbf{P}^{i,1}(u,v) &= \mathbf{P}^{L^i}(u,v), \end{aligned}$$

  where $\mathbf{T}^{i,j}$, $\Re^3 \rightarrow \Re^3$ is associated with operator $O^{i,j}$, defining the transformation it performs, and $\mathbf{P}^{L^i}$ is the primitive position function associated with L^i. By convention, the domain of $\mathbf{P}$ is the unit square $0 \leq u \leq 1$, $0 \leq v \leq 1$. In words, the primitive L^i generates 3-space positions on the object's surface as a function of u and v, and each operator transforms those positions.

- A parametric normal function, $\mathbf{N}^i(u,v)$, similar to the position function but generating surface normals. This is defined by

$$\begin{aligned} \mathbf{N}^i(u,v) &= \mathbf{N}^{i,n}(u,v), \\ \mathbf{N}^{i,j}(u,v) &= \mathbf{N}^{i,j-1}(u,v)\mathbf{J}^{-1\mathrm{T}}(\mathbf{T}^{i,j}), j \neq 1, \\ \mathbf{N}^{i,1}(u,v) &= \frac{\partial \mathbf{P}^{L^i}(u,v)}{\partial u} \times \frac{\partial \mathbf{P}^{L^i}(u,v)}{\partial v}, \end{aligned}$$

  where $\mathbf{J}^{-1\mathrm{T}}$ is the inverse transpose of the Jacobian matrix [2].

- An implicit (inside-outside) function, $I^i(\mathbf{X})$, $\Re^3 \rightarrow \Re^1$, such that the solution to $I^i(\mathbf{X}) = 0$ is the same surface defined by $\mathbf{P}^i$. The implicit function is defined recursively by

$$\begin{aligned} I^i(\mathbf{X}) &= I^{i,n}(\mathbf{X}), \\ I^{i,j}(\mathbf{X}) &= I^{i,j-1}((T^{i,j})^{-1}(\mathbf{X}), j \neq 1, \\ I^{i,1}(\mathbf{X}) &= I^{L^i}(\mathbf{X}), \end{aligned}$$

  where $\mathbf{T}^{-1}$ is the inverse of $\mathbf{T}$, and I^{L^i} is the primitive implicit function associated with L^i.

References

[1] William W. Armstrong and Mark W. Green, *The dynamics of articulated rigid bodies for purposes of animation,* in *Visual Computer,* Springer-Verlag, 1985, pp. 231-240.

[2] Alan H. Barr, *Global and Local Deformations of Solid Primitives,* Proc. SIGGRAPH, 1984, pp. 21–29,.

[3] Ronen Barzel and Alan H. Barr, *Dynamic Constraints,* to appear.

[4] Kurt Fleischer and Andrew Witkin, *The SPAR modeling testbed,* to appear.

[5] William C. Gear, *Numerical Initial Value Problems in Ordinary Differential Equations,* Prentice-Hall, Englewood Cliffs, NJ, 1971

[6] Michael Girard and Anthony a Maciejewski, *Computataional Modeling for the Computer Animation of Legged Figures,* Proc. SIGGRAPH, 1985, pp. 263–270

[7] Michael Kass, Andrew Witkin, and Demetri Terzopoulos, *Snakes: Active Contour Models,* Proc. International Conference on Computer Vision, 1987.

[8] V. C. Lin, D. C. Gossard, and R. A. Light, *Variational Geometry in Computer-Aided Design,* Proc. SIGGRAPH, 1981, pp. 171–178

[9] Greg Nelson, *Juno, a constraint-based graphics system* Computer Graphics, Vol. 19 No. 3, July 1985, pp. 235-243.

[10] Thomas W. Sederberg and Scott R. Parry, *Free-Form Deformation of Solid Geometric Models,* Proc. SIGGRAPH, 1986, pp. 151–160.

[11] Scott N. Steketee and Norman I. Badler, *Parametric Keyframe Interpolation Incorporating Kinetic Adjustment and Phrasing Control,* Proc. SIGGRAPH, 1985, pp. 255–262.

[12] Demetri Terzopoulos, John Platt, Alan Barr, and Kurt Fleischer, *Elastically Deformable Models,* Proc. SIGGRAPH, 1987.

[13] Jane Wilhelms and Brian Barsky, *Using Dynamic Analysis To Animate Articulated Bodies Such As Humans and Robots,* Graphics Interface, 1985.

Acknowledgements

All images were rendered by Kurt Fleischer using his modeling testbed system (M-BLORB) on a Symbolics LISP Machine. Michael Kass helped design some of the constraints, and provided helpful comments on early verions of this paper. We thank Demetri Terzopoulos, John Platt, and Michael Kass for valuable discussions and goop.

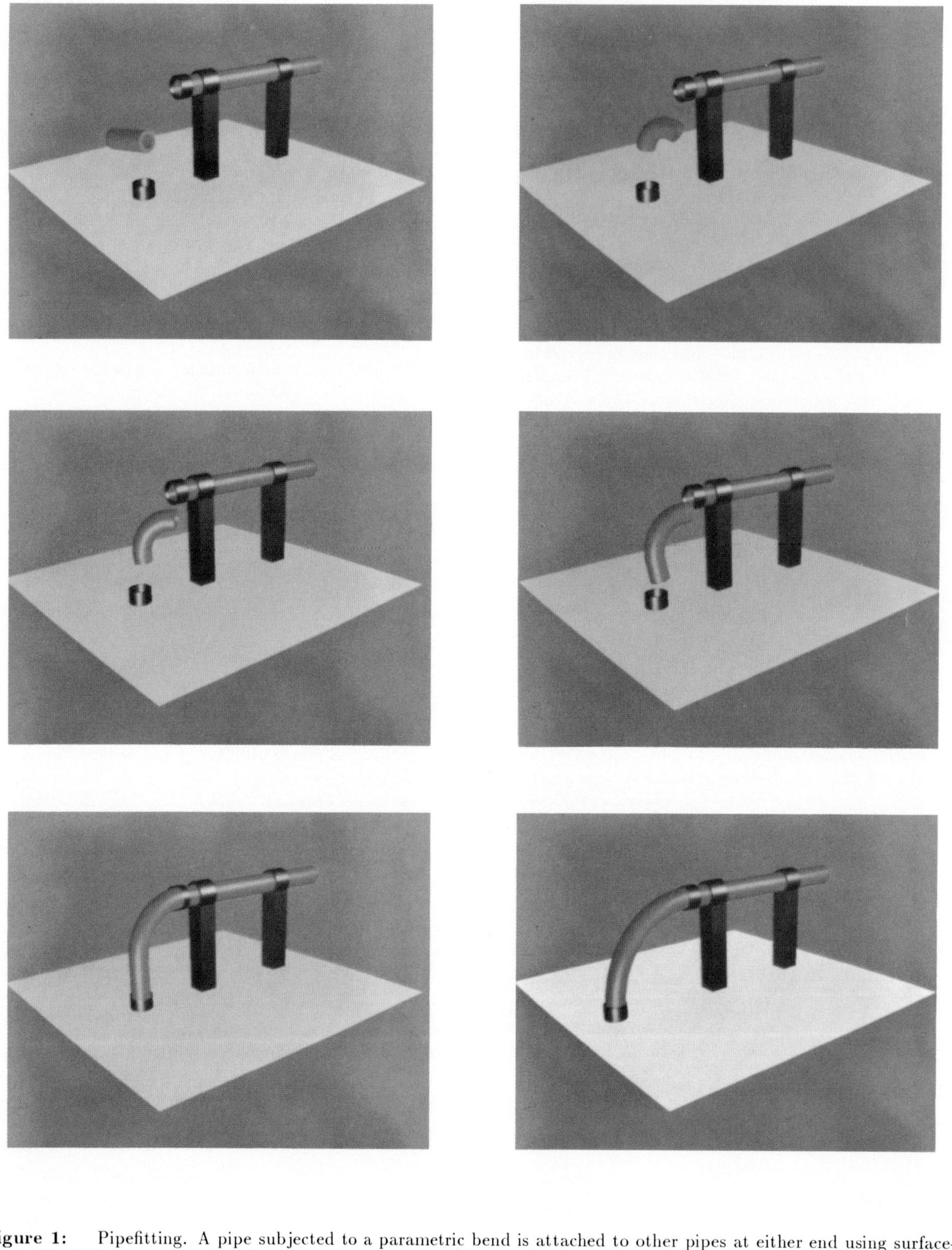

Figure 1: Pipefitting. A pipe subjected to a parametric bend is attached to other pipes at either end using surface-to-surface attachments. Starting with the upper left we see the initial configuration, three steps in the assembly process, and the final solution. At the lower right is shown a new solution obtained by moving one of the fixed pipes.

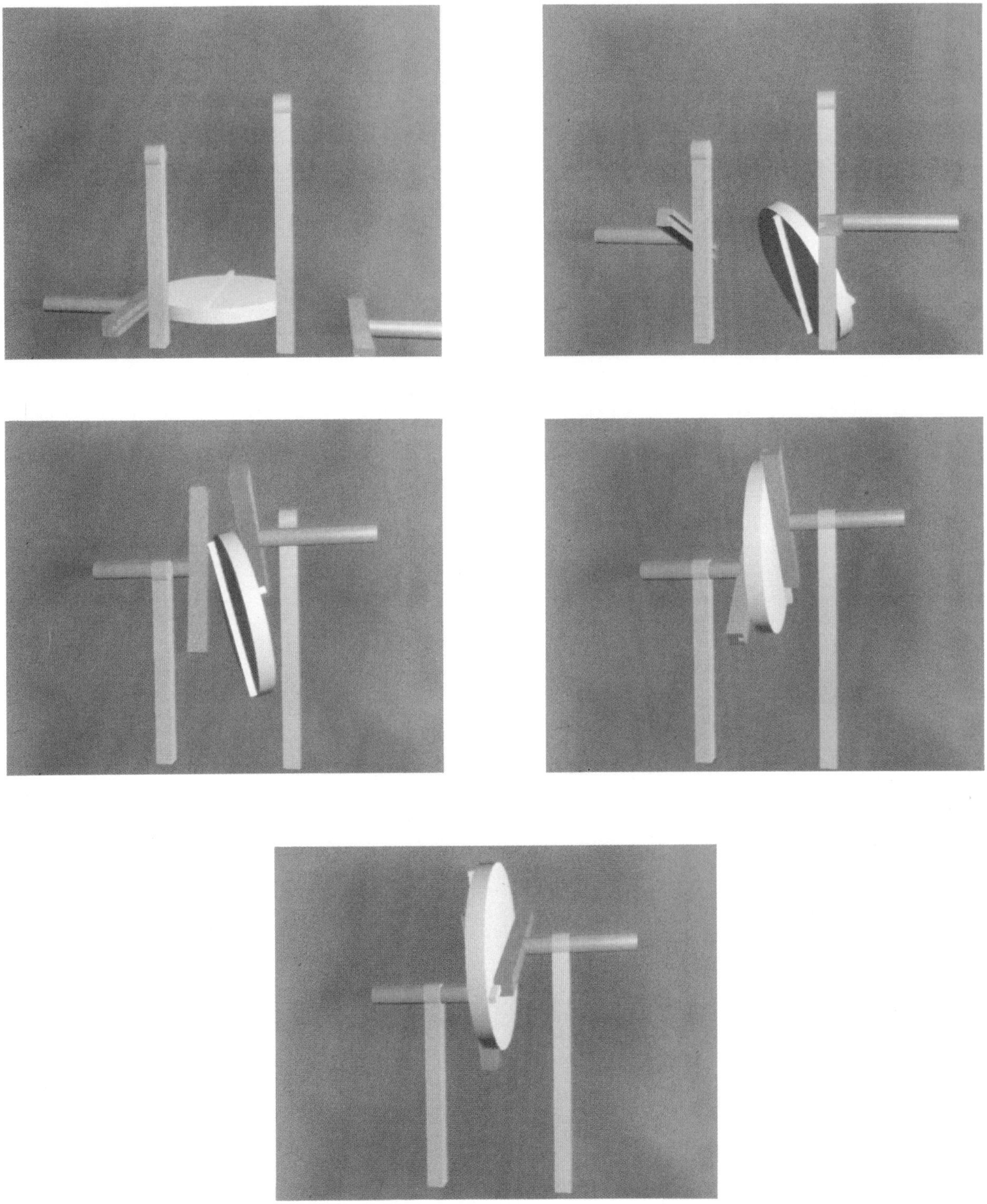

Figure 2: An Oldham's linkage being assembled and moved using a variety of energy constraints including sliders. The system of tongues and grooves serves to transfer rotation through the floating disc while allowing translations of either shaft in the plane of the disc.

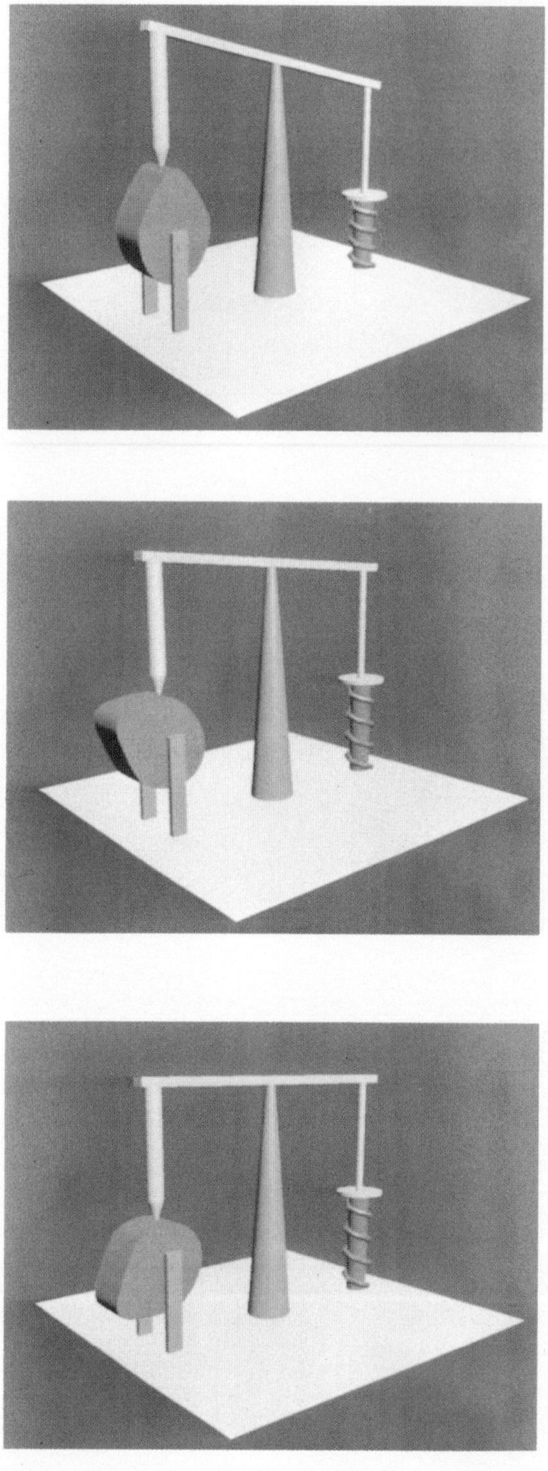

Figure 3: A working model of a cam and rocker arm, specified using energy constraints, shown at several points in its cycle. The spring creates a torque around the fulcrum, pushing the follower against the cam. The follower "feels" the cam using an implicit-function interference constraint.

Rectangular Convolution for Fast Filtering of Characters

Avi Naiman
Alain Fournier

Computer Systems Research Institute
Department of Computer Science
University of Toronto
Toronto, Ontario M5S 1A4
{avi|alain}@csri.toronto.edu

Abstract

While the race towards higher-resolution bitmap displays is still on, many grayscale displays have appeared on the scene. To fully utilize their capabilities, grayscale fonts are needed, and these can be produced by filtering bi-level masters. Most of the efficient filtering techniques cannot directly be applied. For example, prefiltering is impractical, due to the number of character masters and the requirement of sub-pixel positioning. Furthermore, we would like to impose as few restrictions as possible on the characteristics of the filter, in order to facilitate exploration into the quality of various filters.

We describe a fast filtering technique especially adapted to this task. The characters are decomposed into rectangles, and a summed-area representation of the filter is efficiently convolved with each individual rectangle to construct the grayscale character. For a given filter, the number of operations is *O(linear size of the grayscale character)*, which is optimal.

We give an analysis of the efficiency of this technique, and examples of its implementation applied to various families of fonts and point sizes. The performance of the implementation is such that filtering characters for grayscale displays is feasible in realtime on personal workstations.

CR Categories: I.3.3 [**Computer Graphics**]: Picture/Image Generation — *display algorithms*; I.4.3 [**Image Processing**]: Enhancement — *filtering, smoothing*.

General Terms: digital typography, algorithms.

Additional Keywords and Phrases: grayscale fonts, summed-area filters, rectangular decomposition.

Introduction

Until recently, most text on raster displays used characters represented as binary matrices, the ones and zeros corresponding to the black and white dots to be displayed. Typically, only one set of characters was provided, simple and tuned to the characteristics of the display.

While bi-level matrix representations of characters work quite well when high-resolution characters and display devices are available, at low resolutions — such as on terminals and low-end laser printers — the one-bit characters do not resemble their analog predecessors accurately enough [Bige83]. With the availability of grayscale devices, we can increase our *effective* resolution by using gray pixels in the representation of a character, as well as black and white ones (figure 1).

Figure 1. Sampled and filtered versions of several characters from Latin 725 Medium.

The success of grayscale fonts is based on the principle that, as objects become too small to resolve spatially, size and intensity become interchangeable [Corn70]. One of the principle functions carried out by the human visual system is to find edges in the scene being viewed [Blac46]. When objects are too small to resolve spatially — such as a pixel from a sufficient viewing distance — the gray intensity of that object may be 'misinterpreted' as spatial components of light and dark; i.e., an 'edge' will be inferred where there really is an area of uniform illumination. It is this perceptual effect which is exploited in the use of grayscale.

Note that the grayscale pixel provides no information about the orientation of the inferred edge; that information is deduced by the visual system based on the intensities of the surrounding pixels. For example, assuming for the moment that only the immediately adjacent pixels will influence the perception of the grayscale pixel, if the pixels to the left are black, the pixels to the right are white, and those above and below are the same gray as the center pixel, a vertical edge will be perceived in the center column, whose sub-pixel position depends on the intensity of the gray pixels. On the other hand, if the pixels above are white, the pixels below are black, and the pixels to the left and right are gray, a horizontal edge will be perceived in the center row, whose sub-pixel position again depends on the intensity of the gray pixels.

Notice, therefore, that the same value of (for example) 25% gray in the center pixel will at one time be interpreted as resolution in the horizontal direction and at another time in the vertical direction (or even some other orientation, depending on the surrounding pixels). In other words, once orientation information of the perceived edge is resolved with respect to the surrounding pixels, the grayscale is utilized as resolution information. Therefore, to a first approximation, the added number of grayscale *levels* (not the added number of bits) is advantageously exploited regardless of the orientation of the edge; it merely serves to *position* the edge more precisely.

For many applications (such as text entry), it will be sufficient to provide a single version of a grayscale font for each size and style which is needed on a particular display device. However, since grayscale can be used to achieve sub-pixel positioning of edges, one could generate many grayscale versions of the same font at a particular size and for a specific device, each differing only slightly from the next in terms of the sub-pixel position of the character's edges. By using the particular grayscale version which best approximates the sub-pixel position of the edge, one could reduce the spacing error that would otherwise result from positioning characters on whole pixel boundaries.

Prior Work

Although grayscale text has gotten some limited commercial exposure lately (e.g., IBM's Yoda terminal [Shol82] and Bitstream Inc.'s grayscale fonts), two factors have combined to restrict its usage mainly to specialized environments such as paint programs and slide preparation packages, where the grayscale value is used as a weight for interpolating between the text color and a variegated background.

First, the techniques previously discussed in the literature are computationally expensive, and second, there has been little quality control over the resultant fonts. Since the generation of gray pixels depends on the characteristics of the display device (pixel size, shape (point spread function), and overlap; intensity gamma; spatial inhomogeneities), a model of each device must be incorporated into the font generation system [Kaji81]. Otherwise, good-looking fonts produced for one monitor may not perform well on another.

One can envision a font-production tool which allows parametrization of a display device's characteristics, and produces device-dependent grayscale fonts from a master font library. For the benefit of researchers exploring models of display devices and the appropriateness of particular grayscaling algorithms, it is important to increase the efficiency of robust, filter- and display-independent techniques for generating grayscale fonts.

Once appropriate filters and models have been developed, we will be faced not only with producing numerous fonts at numerous sizes, but also for various devices, and perhaps with more than one filter. In order for this task to be feasible, fonts must be producible at rates far greater than have heretofore been reported. We will demonstrate how, by meeting a few reasonable assumptions, we can drastically reduce the computational expense of generating grayscale fonts, in particular for experimentation purposes, but more generally for font production.

Filtering

The common method for generating a grayscale character is *filtering*, whereby a high-resolution raster-encoded master character is convolved with a filter. The filters can be defined in various ways, very often analytically [Prat78]. For the rest of the paper, we will assume that values of the filter are needed only at the locations of the master and therefore, without loss of generality (though perhaps some loss of precision), we can represent a filter with a digitized array of values at the resolution of the master. In the process described below, we will assume that all two-dimensional arrays are square and we will adopt the following notation (this development is along the lines of [Warn80] — see figure 2):

- we have an $m \times m$ binary-valued pixel array, M, representing a high-resolution master character
- we want a $g \times g$ multi-valued pixel array, G, representing a low-resolution grayscale (filtered) character
- for a given filter type and filter overlap, o, we compute an $f \times f$ multi-valued weighted pixel array, F, representing a filter kernel, where $f = o \times m/g$, and $\sum_{y=1}^{f} \sum_{x=1}^{f} F_{xy}$ is normalized to 1.0
- M is overlaid with S, an $s \times s$ sampling grid where $s = g$, with a spacing interval of $i = m/g$ (the ratio between the master and grayscale sizes) between samples; note that there are $i \times i$ different *phases* at which S can be overlaid onto M
  - — if $p \times p$ different phases (i.e., grayscale character versions) are needed, then $s = pg$ with $i = m/pg$ spacing intervals
  - — if *all* of the possible phases are needed, then $s = m$ and $i = 1$
- F is centered at each of the sampling points S_{xy} and convolved with M, producing up to $p \times p$ different $g \times g$ grayscale characters

In our work, then, we assume an appropriate filter (or filters) is available for convolution with the character master, which sufficiently models the display device so that we can regard it as a linear device in both intensity [Catm79] and space. This allows us to concentrate our efforts on generating accurately-spaced grayscale characters in a minimum amount of time, independent of the other important issues affecting the success of grayscale fonts, namely the appropriateness of particular filters [Warn80], reconstruction of the character's signal (master) with the displayed samples (grayscale) [Kaji81], modeling of the characteristics of display devices [Shur80], the number of grayscale bits necessary [Lele80, Bruc86], and possible fatigue of the visual system [Goul84].

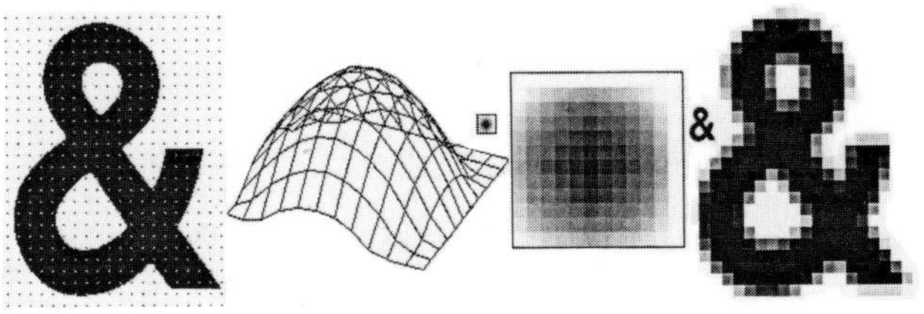

Figure 2. From left to right: character master ($m \times m$) overlaid with sampling grid ($s \times s$); continuous filter; digitized filter ($f \times f$); digitized filter enlarged; filtered character ($g \times g$); filtered character enlarged.

Character Size	Filter		Grayscale Percentage	
	Overlap	Size	Swiss 721	Latin 725
16	1.0	16	16	18
32	1.0	8	8	9
64	1.0	4	3	3
16	1.25	20	21	22
32	1.25	10	10	11
64	1.25	5	5	6
16	1.5	24	25	26
32	1.5	12	12	14
64	1.5	6	5	6

Table 1. Grayscale Percentage of two fonts (Swiss 721 Bold and Latin 725 Medium) at various character and filter sizes (in pixels).

The Problem

The straightforward solution to generating the grayscale pixels is *direct convolution*, where F is centered at each of the sampling points S_{xy} and all the elements of M under F are multiplied by the values of F and summed. Note that since, in our case, M is binary, only the summing operation is necessary. The cost of this method is $O(s^2 \times f^2)$ [Warn80, Schm83, Negr80, Shol82, Koba80, Crow78, Seit79].

Not all of this work is necessary. Specifically, the same amount of computation is performed regardless of the 'gray' outcome of a grayscale pixel (which could be black or white): F is centered over the sample point S_{xy} and is convolved with M. However, if all of the $f \times f$ pixels of M within $\pm f/2$ of S_{xy} are on (off), the grayscale pixel will be black (white). In other words, the direct convolution operation will have generated a black (white) pixel at the expensive cost of generating a gray one. Furthermore, much of the summing operation in direct convolution is repeated over and over for the same regions of F, especially when more than one phase is needed.

While the actual gray percentage of a character — the number of gray pixels divided by the total number of pixels — is a function of font, character, size, resolution, filter size, filter shape, and sampling phase, except for very low resolutions, most of the pixels will be either white or black (table 1). Clearly, it is disadvantageous to be performing the relatively expensive direct convolution operation for each of these black or white pixels, rather than the much cheaper operation of, for example, straight sampling.

Positioning Accuracy

If we want to position a vertical edge and can only position the edge on pixel boundaries, then we may be off by as much as one half of a pixel in positioning accuracy. If we want to position the edge 25% of the way into the pixel, we can prefilter it so that the left pixel column has values interpolated 25% of the way between the background (white) and foreground (black) colors. However, if this is now our only representation of the edge, we can still be off by as much as a half a pixel. It is only if we can *dynamically* filter the edge to the needed sub-pixel position (or, prefilter for all of the possible sub-pixel positions) that we can reduce the positioning error. If filtering of the edge can be done for any of p equally-spaced sub-pixel positions, then our positioning error is reduced to $1/2p$.

In our context, if we have a ½ pixel error in the positioning of a character, one character pair may appear too *closely* set by ½ a pixel, while the next pair seems too *loosely* set by ½ a pixel. Where the size of a pixel is large relative to the size of the character, this can lead to disastrous spacing problems. Even for state-of-the-art monitors with a resolution of approximately two pixels per typographer's point (in each of x and y), when setting 10-point text (about .35 cm), a ½ pixel of error is about 10% of the average inter-character spacing (one quarter of the point size) while the variation between the spacing of pairs of characters can be as much as 20%. By using 8 different phases in generating the grayscale characters, this error can be reduced to 1.25% and 2.5%. For more common monitors (about 1 pixel per typographer's point), the errors are 20% and 40%, and 8 phases can reduce this to 2.5% and 5% (figure 3).

In some contexts, the use of a single phase for each grayscale character may be sufficient. However, because the accurate spacing of characters is such an important part of generating high-quality text, the need for utilizing the best of the possible phases is crucial. Furthermore, not only are different phases needed in the horizontal dimension for accurate positioning of proportionally-spaced text, but in the vertical direction as well, in order not to be restricted to leading (i.e., line spacing) of an integral number of pixels and for the proper positioning of superscripts, subscripts, equations, and tabular information.

For many applications, grayscale characters may be needed for several fonts at numerous sizes and for each of (say) 8×8 phases. Because exactly which characters will be called for may not be known ahead of time, if precomputing the fonts is deemed necessary, all of the possible renditions must be generated. However, this may be impractical due to limited storage space. For example, if Roman, Bold, Italic, and Bold-Italic versions of a 128-character serif and sans-serif font are needed (not including special characters and mathematical symbols) for a 72 pixels-per-inch, 8 bits-per-pixel screen, at 8-, 10-, 12-, 14-, and 18-points, it will take approximately 51.75 Mb to store the 64 phases (without any encoding). Throw in a more generous selection of fonts (two families is very limited for all but the most mundane tasks) and sizes (6-, 9-, 11-, 24-, and 36-point), as well as a few monitors of different resolutions and filters of varying suitability, and the numbers become astronomical.

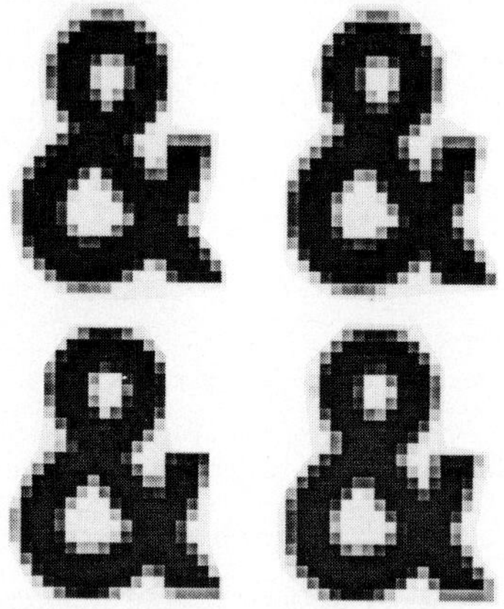

Figure 3. Four phases of the filtered ampersand character. Note the different gray levels along the sides of the characters, which will influence the perception of where the edges lie at sub-pixel resolution.

Naiman discusses an average-phase representation of a grayscale character — and a heuristic by which to modify it — to generate alternative phases without reconvolving the character [Naim85]. However, the technique is only valid in the horizontal dimension, and, at small character sizes, the error term in the approximation becomes too large to generate reasonable-looking fonts.

Therefore, except for very common tasks such as text editing with fixed-pitch screen fonts of a single style, precomputing the grayscale characters may be impractical. What we need, then, is the capability to dynamically generate the requested characters at the appropriate size, resolution, and phase, coupled with font-caching software to reduce the need to recompute already-generated characters [Fuch82].

Rectangular Convolution

Let us re-examine where the work is being done during direct convolution. For a particular sampling-grid position $S_{x_g y_g}$,† the filter F is centered over the sampling point and is convolved with the master; namely, for each master pixel $M_{x_f y_f}$ within the filter boundary, the weighted value in $F_{x_f y_f}$ is added to the output grayscale pixel $G_{x_g y_g}$. Since the master pixels which fall within the filter support (size) can form an arbitrary pattern, each pixel must be examined to determine contribution from the filter. This is why the computational expense for the direct convolution operation is $O(f^2)$ per sample.

Alternatively, if, instead of unrelated master pixels, we have a data structure for the master character which describes it in terms of regions of specific shapes, then the convolution operation for $S_{x_g y_g}$ amounts to intersecting the filter array with the r regions of the master character which fall within the filter support to produce $O(r)$ subregions, and extracting the contribution of each of those subregions to the corresponding grayscale pixel $G_{x_g y_g}$. Then the computational expense is $O(r \times (\textit{cost of intersection} + \textit{cost of extracting contribution}))$.

† The second-level subscript refers to the native matrix of the x and y indices.

What we are looking for, then, is a shape which meets the following criteria:

- it is easy to generate from a bitmap;
- it is compact in storage;
- it is easy to intersect with the filter; and
- it is simple to extract the filter contribution from the intersection.

Rectangles are a particularly appealing shape to use, since, for characters, they fulfill each of these criteria.

Certainly, encoding a bitmap into 1×1-pixel rectangles is trivial (we will discuss below the issues regarding optimal decomposition into rectangles). Although, in general, rectangular encoding may increase the size of the representation (in the limit, there could be f^2 1×1-pixel rectangles), since characters are very well-connected objects — often with rectilinearly oriented components — an encoding into rectangles is likely to be very compact.

Because the filter is stored in a rectangular array, the cost of intersecting a rectangle with the filter amounts to four comparisons to determine the rectilinear lines of intersection, and generates at most one subrectangle. Furthermore, if we use a summed-area array representation of the filter — analogous to the summed-area texture arrays discussed in [Crow84, Ferr84] — the cost of extracting the filter contribution of an intersecting subrectangle becomes constant. In such a representation, the entries of a summed-array are computed as the sum of all the entries of the original array (say) to the left of and below the entry. Extracting the sum of an arbitrary rectangular area of the summed-array costs four summed-array accesses and three additions (two subtractions and one addition — figure 4).

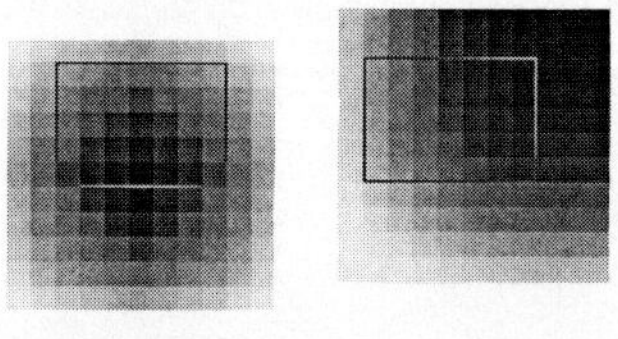

Figure 4. Digitized filter and summed-area representation. To evaluate the sum of the entries within the box on the left, it is sufficient to sum the four values at the corners of the box on the right.

Although the cost of generating the *summed-filter* is $O(f^2)$, it need be computed only once for each filter array that is needed (filter type and size combinations), and can be stored in a file for retrieval when needed. Therefore, for r rectangles which fall within the filter support, the computational expense of *rectangular convolution* is $O(r)$, or, more exactly, $r \times (\textit{4 comparisons} + \textit{4 array accesses} + \textit{3 additions})$, per sample.

Another issue to consider is the cost of determining which of the master rectangles fall within the filter support, when the filter is centered over a sampling point $S_{x_g y_g}$. However, there is no cost involved whatsoever if, instead of looping on the sampling points and convolving the filter at each sample point to determine a grayscale pixel, we loop on the rectangles and add their 'gray' contribution to each grayscale pixel affected by the rectangle. In this manner, a particular grayscale character pixel $G_{x_g y_g}$ may be computed in several stages, and when all of the master character rectangles which affect it have been processed, it will have the correct gray value.

The basic process for an arbitrary rectangle, then, is as follows (see figure 5):

for each rectangle in the master character
 determine area in master affected by rectangle
 for each sampling point in affected area
  center summed-filter over sample point
  intersect summed-filter with rectangle
  extract subrectangle sum from summed-filter
  add sum to sampling point's grayscale pixel

For the general case of convolving the summed-filter with each sampling point relative to an arbitrary rectangle, 4 intersections between the filter (centered at the sampling point) and the rectangle must be computed: one each for the *left*, *right*, *bottom*, and *top* of the intersecting subrectangle. Using the boundaries of the subrectangle as indices into the summed-filter, 4 accesses and 3 additions suffice to extract the sum of the filter within the intersecting subrectangle. For definiteness, the sum is $F_{tr}-F_{br}-F_{tl}+F_{bl}$.

However, when the rectangle spans the full width and height of the filter array, grayscale pixels corresponding to sampling points which are inside the rectangle's boundaries and at least $f/2$ pixels from the boundary, will turn out black when the filter is centered over the sampling point and convolved with the intersecting subrectangle. This is because *left* and *bottom* will be zero, while *right* and *top* will be f; i.e., the intersecting subrectangle is really the whole filter and we need only add the sum of the whole filter (which is 1.0). In fact, the area in the master affected by the rectangle has 8 more regions of interest — above, below, to either side, and in the corners (figure 6) — each of which allows for some initialization of constant values for all sampling points within the region (table 2).

If there is one sampling point in each of the 9 regions, then instead of requiring 36 index computations, 36 summed-filter table accesses, and 27 additions, 12 index computations, 12 summed-filter table accesses, and 7 additions suffice. In particular, note that any sampling points in the central region (corresponding to totally turned on — i.e., black — grayscale pixels) require no computation at all.

Although the numbers of intersection calculations in each of the four corner regions (2) and four non-corner, non-central regions (1) are uniform, note that the order of summation used in producing the summed-filter introduces a bias (in the direction of summation) regarding the extraction of the sum. One consequence of this can be seen in the top-right region (row TR), where only one table access is needed (and no additions), while the bottom-left region (row BL) requires 3 table accesses and 3 additions.

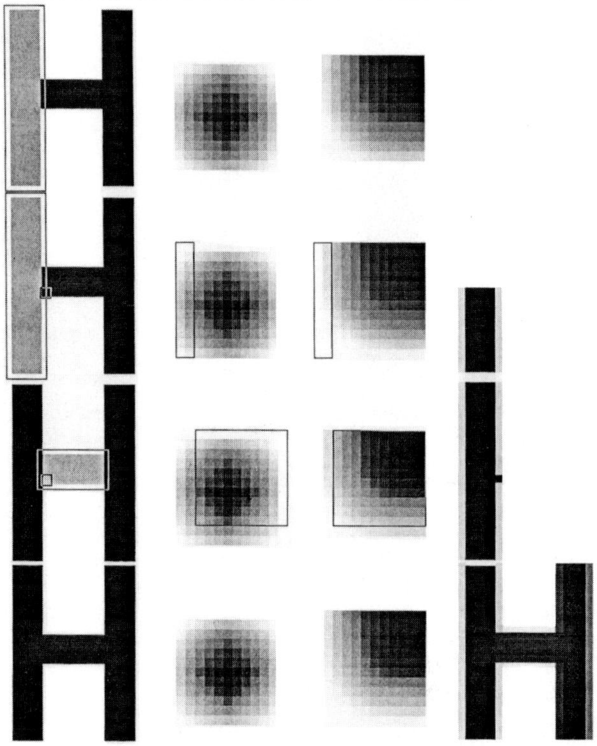

Figure 5. From left to right: master character; filter; summed-filter; (partially) filtered character. From top to bottom: the first rectangle and the affected area in master; rectangular convolution at a particular sampling point; rectangular convolution at the same sampling point for the next rectangle; completed convolution process.

We can exploit this bias to our benefit, by precomputing 4 different summed-filters from the original filter, each one using a different order of summation. This allows for extracting the summed-filter contribution in *any* of the regions of interest in only one table access (except, of course, for the central region, which does not require any table accesses) and no additions, simply by using the appropriately-biased summed-filter. Now, if there is one sampling point in each of the 9 regions, other than the 12 intersection comparisons, only 8 summed-filter table accesses and *zero* additions are needed.†

If the rectangle only spans the width *or* height of the filter, there are only 6 different regions of interest; if it does not span either the width or height of the filter, the different regions of interest are reduced to 4. However, the optimizations just discussed still apply, until, finally, if the rectangle does not cross any grayscale pixel boundaries, we are back to the general case which requires 4 intersection computations, 4 summed-filter table accesses, and 3 additions per sampling point.

† Of course, one addition per sampling point is always needed to add to the current intermediate value of the grayscale pixel.

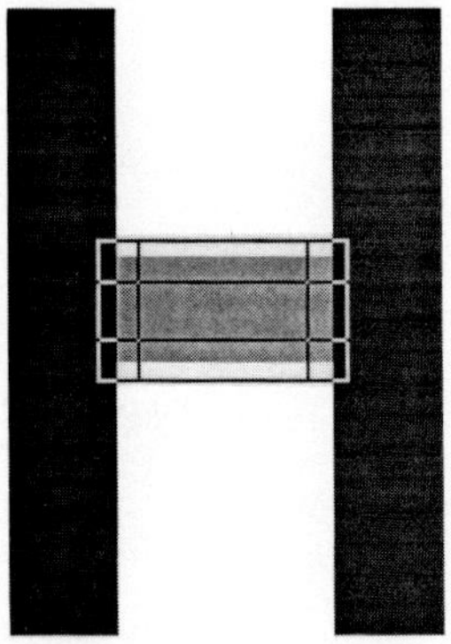

Figure 6. The nine areas of interest in a rectangle which spans the width and height of the filter.

Region	Size of Region	Intersection				Filter Access			
		l	r	b	t	tr	-br	-tl	+bl
Generic	$(w+f)(h+f)$	√	√	√	√	√	√	√	√
BL	f^2	√	f	√	f	1.0	√	√	√
BM	$f(w-f)$	0	f	√	f	1.0	√		
BR	f^2	0	√	√	f	√	√		
ML	$f(h-f)$	√	f	0	f	1.0		√	
MM	$(w-f)(h-f)$	0	f	0	f	1.0			
MR	$f(h-f)$	0	√	0	f	√			
TL	f^2	√	f	0	√	√		√	
TM	$f(w-f)$	0	f	0	√	√			
TR	f^2	0	√	0	√	√			

Table 2. Intersection calculations and summed-filter accesses (as well as additions) needed for a single sampling point for the generic rectangle (*width×height*) and 9 regions of interest (BottomLeft, BottomMiddle, etc.), when the rectangle is larger than the filter and only one summed-filter is used (with each entry representing the sum of the lower-left rectangle). A √ indicates that the computation specified in that column must be performed; 0, f, and 1.0 are constants within the loops; an empty entry means no work need be done. See text for further optimization when four summed-filters are computed.

Not only has the asymptotic cost of computing gray pixels been greatly reduced, but — given a 'good' rectangular decomposition of the master character — the cost of generating the black pixels of the grayscale character has become trivial, and the generation of white pixels comes for free. This meets our original goal of reducing the amount of work for non-gray pixels.

Cost of Rectangular Convolution

The only limitations to the filter used are that it has to be of finite width of support, and be space-invariant within a single rectangle. Note that it is possible without increased cost to switch filters between rectangles. This allows the implementation of a limited case of space-variant filters. The screen space can be divided into a grid where each cell has its own filter, and the rectangles of the decomposition of the characters are split at the boundaries of the grid cells as they are processed. Within each cell, the appropriate filter is selected by lookup using the cell indices.

As mentioned above, the filters have been digitized at the resolution of the font masters, and the summed versions of the filters are computed. Both computations require $O(f^2)$ operations, but this only has to be done once per filter in the initialization steps. Once generated, the cost of the algorithm is totally independent of the cost of the filter computation. Therefore, there is no penalty in using high-quality filters.

We already saw that for direct convolution the number of operations to filter an $m \times m$ master with an $f \times f$ kernel to produce a $g \times g$ grayscale character is $O(g^2 \times f^2)$, assuming constant cost for access into the master. The convolution can also be computed using the discrete Fast Fourier Transform, whose cost is $O(g^2 + m^2 \times \log m)$. However, this is an improvement only for large kernels and large numbers of samples.

Most of the efficient filtering techniques known in Computer Graphics — in particular to filter textures — are aimed at quite different circumstances. Usually there are only a few images which must be repeatedly filtered — often with space-variant filter kernels — and they are all available in advance. In such a case, prefiltering the images is a good strategy, as in MIP-maps [Will83] and summed-area tables [Crow84]. In both techniques, the cost after prefiltering is $O(g^2)$. However, the storage is $O(m^2)$ per image, and both the type of allowable filters and the positioning of the kernel are limited.

Note the connection between the approach taken here and Crow's summed-area tables: here the image is constrained to being a box signal (i.e., the bi-level rectangles) and is convolved with an arbitrary summed-area filter (which is, in general, smaller than the rectangles), while in [Crow84] an arbitrary image is convolved with a box filter (and the textures are, in general, larger than the pixels). Although Heckbert generalized the summed-area table technique to a class of filters that can be represented by repeated convolutions of box filters [Heck86], again, the context is quite different. In particular, the large number of character masters and the requirement of sub-pixel positioning makes the use of prefiltered masters quite impractical.

In asymptotic terms, the cost of performing rectangular convolution to produce a grayscale character is $\sum_{i=1}^{g^2} r_i \times$ *cost per subrectangle*, where r_i is the number of subrectangles which fall under the filter centered over g_i. In the worst case, $r_i = f^2$, and the cost for a grayscale character is $O(g^2 \times f^2)$. However, this would only occur when the decomposition results in rectangles which cover only one master pixel for each of the g^2 filter positions.

In general, the number of rectangles in a decomposition is directly related to the number of *reflex* vertices in the outline, which, for characters, is usually very small. Therefore, a more useful bound is obtained by looking at the cost per master rectangle, rather than per grayscale pixel. From this point of view, the influence of the size of the kernel is only felt because a larger kernel increases, for each rectangle, the size of the regions where more operations are needed.

In particular, for a $w \times h$ rectangle and an $f \times f$ filter, $4f^2+2f(w+h)$ intersections and $2f(\mathrm{MAX}(w,f)+\mathrm{MAX}(h,f))$ table accesses and additions are needed to process *all* sampling points that fall under the support of the rectangle (including adding the gray contribution to the intermediate grayscale pixels). As the number of operations for each rectangle is $O(f^2+f(w+h))$, when the filter is large relative to the rectangle, the cost is proportional to the *area* of the filter; however, when the filter is small relative to the rectangle, the cost becomes proportional to the *perimeter* of the rectangle. Since, for alphabetic characters, decomposition will generate $O(m)$ rectangles† — and a good portion of these will be large relative to the filter size — the cost of rectangular convolution is proportional only to the linear size of the characters.

Restrictions

Note that there are a few conditions which must be satisfied in order to exploit rectangular convolution:

- *The filter F has to be computed at the resolution of the master character M.* This is not a severe restriction however, since the filter is only computed once, before any convolution takes place, and can be easily computed from an analytical representation at the resolution of the master character (which in itself may have been generated at a specified resolution from an outline description).
- *The grayscale character G must be randomly accessible.* Since a grayscale pixel may be contributed to from several rectangles, we must be able to store partial gray sums for each pixel, and randomly access them to add the contribution when processing a rectangle. Given today's main memory capabilities, this poses no limitation at all. Even for a 128×128 grayscale character, only 16 Kb of memory are needed. Note that this technique is *not* $O(m^2)$ space (unlike previous techniques); therefore, very-high-resolution masters (e.g., 1024×1024) can be used even on relatively small computers.
- *The master character must be bi-level (i.e., black and white).* As the summed-table extraction method cannot weight the individual entries, each pixel in the master must be either on or off. However, other than in specialized texture fonts, characters are by nature bi-modal.

Rectangular Decomposition

The algorithm described in this paper is dependent on the representation of the filter as a rectangular summed-table, and on the decomposition of the character into rectangles. While it is obvious that every bitmap character can be decomposed into either possibly overlapping (*covering*) or non-overlapping (*partitioning*) rectangles, we should worry about algorithms to do so, metrics to characterize the goodness of the decomposition for our purpose, and optimality according to these metrics.

The most straightforward and immediately available decomposition is into scan segments, and they are indeed rectangles, all of height one. These are commonly stored in run-length encoded form. From these, the number of rectangles can be reduced by taking into account a *replication count*, that is, the count of how many times the same scan segment is repeated on successive scan lines without change. This is the representation, fully described in [Naim85], which was used in most of the examples presented in this paper.

† This is intrinsic in rectangular decomposition having an upper bound of run-length encoding, which is $O(m)$.

The goal of any decomposition should be to minimize the added edge length. To prove this, consider a rectangle of dimensions $w \times h$. With a filter of size $f \times f$, the number of totally black pixels in the central region of interest is $(w-f)\times(h-f)$ or 0 if $w \le f$ or $h \le f$. The number of gray pixels to be processed is the total number of pixels to be processed $(w+f)\times(h+f)$ minus the number of black pixels, that is, $2\times f\times(w+h)$.

Considering now a decomposition into r rectangles, possibly overlapping, the total number of gray pixels is:

$$f\sum_{i=1}^{r} 2\times(w_i+h_i)$$

where $2\times(w_i+h_i)$ is the perimeter of rectangle i, and the sum in the above expression is the sum of the perimeters of all the rectangles. This sum is made up of three terms: the initial perimeter p of the master character, which is independent of the decomposition, the sum of the lengths of the internal overlapping edges l_o, and the sum of the lengths of the internal abutting edges, l_a (figure 7), which counts double since these parts of edges are processed twice in the algorithm (once each for the two abutting rectangles). So the total number of gray pixels is:

$$f\sum_{i=1}^{r} 2\times(w_i+h_i) = f\,(p+l_o+2l_a)$$

Since f and p are constant, one has to minimize l_o+2l_a □

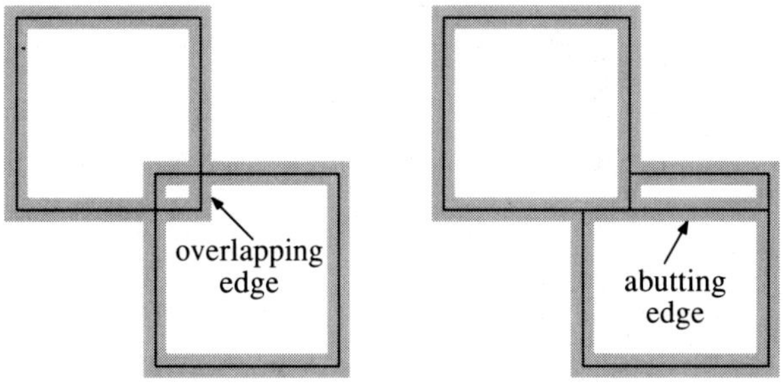

Figure 7. Example where the minimal decomposition with overlapping rectangles (left) generates fewer gray pixels than a minimal decomposition with disjoint rectangles (right).

Overlapping rectangles cannot be eliminated on the basis of non-optimality as far as added edge length is concerned. Figure 7 shows an example where the decomposition into two overlapping squares leads to fewer intermediate gray pixels than any partition into three rectangles. Overlapping rectangles, however, will not be considered, because they cannot be processed independently of each other. Doing so would cause the pixels within the overlap to be given an incorrect weight by being found under the filter too many times (i.e., the number of times the pixel is covered by a rectangle). Therefore, we will consider only non-overlapping rectangles.

Unfortunately, like many similar optimization algorithms, the general problem of decomposing a rectilinear polygon into rectangles such that the total perimeter is minimal is NP-hard [Ling82]. If a polygon is without holes, the problem is solvable in polynomial time ($O(n^4)$ for n corners [Ling82]), but, of course, many characters do have holes. Lingas presents various heuristics for finding a rectangular decomposition within some constant factor of the minimum edge length when there are holes [Ling83]. They are all theoretically interesting, but, for the relatively small number of holes involved in our application, the best approach seems to be to eliminate the holes by adding approximately minimum-length edges from the holes to the boundaries. This can be done in $O(n^2)$ time and gives a solution within a factor of 2 of the minimum length for this step [Kou81]. Once the holes have been eliminated, the aforementioned algorithm for rectilinear polygons with no holes can be run.† It should be stressed that all of this has only to be done once per master, and the cost of this preprocessing is therefore not an issue, as long as it is polynomial.

Implementation

In order to explore the quality of various filters in generating grayscale characters, we have implemented a subset of the rectangular convolution technique on a Motorola 68020 class machine (HP 9000-320). As our goal is to explore the problems inherent to this process, we did not want to take any short cuts which a production environment might use for wholesale font production. In particular, we did not use the optimizations discussed above concerning the reduced intersection calculations for the various regions of interest of a rectangle.

We used 32-bit fixed-point integer representations of the filter entries, where the sum of all the filter entries is normalized to 1.0, and the grayscale pixels are computed in the range of [0..256). Each addition, then, is a 32-bit add operation,

As mentioned above, the rectangular decomposition we used is the repeating-RLE described in [Naim85] (at a master size of 256×256), which does not generate optimal rectangles for the rectangular convolution process, but does a fairly good job on the Swiss 721 Bold seen in many of the figures.

Therefore, the timings listed in tables 3, 4, 5, and 6 should be considered for the relative improvement of rectangular convolution over direct convolution rather than as absolute benchmarks for generating grayscale fonts. We foresee another order of magnitude speedup for production software over the 2 orders of magnitude we have already achieved. Conservatively, this would result in a production rate on the order of 100-1000 characters per second for the filter/character size combinations listed in the tables.

† An alternative way to deal with holes would be to decompose them into *negative contribution* rectangles, that is, their gray value is subtracted from — rather than added to — the intermediate results. Although this will produce equivalent results, it must allow for intermediate values which could either overflow the maximum (1.0) or underflow the minimum (0.0), which may be impractical.

The timings reported are the average of 52 convolution operations (once for each of the upper and lower case characters), do not include rectangular decomposition or display time, and were obtained with the UNIX™ profiling utility *prof* at a 20 millisecond resolution.

Grayscale Size	Filter		Convolution Time	
	Overlap	Size	Rectangular	Direct
16	1.0	16	46	930
32	1.0	8	69	1010
64	1.0	4	139	1340
16	1.25	20	49	1310
32	1.25	10	78	1520
64	1.25	5	153	1860
16	1.5	24	55	2040
32	1.5	12	87	2120
64	1.5	6	168	2510

Table 3. Swiss 721 Bold, single phase timings (in milliseconds).

GS Size	Filter		Total Time		Per-Phase Time	
	Overlap	Size	Rect.	Direct	Rect.	Direct
16	1.0	16	4605	232690	18	909
32	1.0	8	2559	64210	40	1003
64	1.0	4	1673	21240	105	1328
16	1.25	20	5594	323840	22	1265
32	1.25	10	3060	96170	48	1503
64	1.25	5	1887	29260	118	1829
16	1.5	24	7147	526650	28	2057
32	1.5	12	3497	138220	55	2160
64	1.5	6	2073	41700	130	2606

Table 4. Swiss 721 Bold, all phases timings (in milliseconds).

Grayscale Size	Filter		Convolution Time	
	Overlap	Size	Rectangular	Direct
16	1.0	16	58	910
32	1.0	8	79	1000
64	1.0	4	139	1330
16	1.25	20	62	1270
32	1.25	10	87	1530
64	1.25	5	152	1870
16	1.5	24	69	2070
32	1.5	12	102	2160
64	1.5	6	169	2450

Table 5. Latin 725 Medium, single phase timings (in milliseconds).

Conclusions

The timings reported have demonstrated that the rectangular convolution technique is effective, leading to a considerable speedup in the computation of grayscale fonts, without compromising the characteristics of the kernels that can be used. This technique can be employed for realtime display of grayscale characters on systems with the comput-

™ UNIX is a registered trademark of AT&T Bell Laboratories.

GS Size	Filter		Total Time		Per-Phase Time	
	Overlap	Size	Rect.	Direct	Rect.	Direct
16	1.0	16	4844	235440	19	920
32	1.0	8	2477	64380	39	1006
64	1.0	4	1562	21340	98	1334
16	1.25	20	5820	320610	23	1252
32	1.25	10	2955	94900	46	1483
64	1.25	5	1753	29150	110	1822
16	1.5	24	7723	502240	30	1962
32	1.5	12	3616	133060	57	2079
64	1.5	6	1983	38940	124	2434

Table 6. Latin 725 Medium, all phases timings (in milliseconds).

ing power of a personal workstation. Several improvements described in this paper, but not included in the implementation used to generate the timings — such as optimal rectangular decomposition and the use of four summed-area filters — would further reduce the cost of filtering.

Note that filtering inherently takes care of mismatched aspect ratios, whether they arise from the master character, grayscale character, or display device pixel. Furthermore, as in previous methods, the grayscale pixel value can be used as a weight for interpolating between colored text and a variegated background.

Another aspect of the algorithm is that the rectangles in the decomposition do not have to be stored in any particular data structure and can be processed independently of each other and in any order. This suggests a straightforward implementation on multiprocessor systems, whether general-purpose or specialized for this particular task.

The ability to generate grayscale fonts very quickly changes the parameters of the 'font caching equation'. As mentioned earlier, precomputing all of the phases of all the characters needed is quite out of the question. With the technique described here, many applications will be able to justify the cost of dynamically computing grayscale characters, and not have to rely on a small selection of poor-quality fonts.

Extensions and Applications

One additional improvement in speed can easily be achieved by determining, for a given filter support, the pixels that will always be black, and separating them from the rest of the character, so that they are not included in the processing of the rectangles. Since these pixels are already processed very efficiently, this would result in only a modest improvement.

In many applications there is a demand for rotated text. Bitmaps can of course be rotated, and there are clever algorithms to do so [Guib82]. Our technique is not well adapted to this, however, since the rectangular decomposition would have to be recomputed for every new rotated master. The best way to apply our technique to generate rotated text is to rotate the sampling grid and apply it to the unrotated master. This rotation has to be done only for one point; the other grid points can be computed by incremental techniques. While the rectangular decomposition of the master is still valid, the filter and its summed-area representation would have to be rotated as well, but this has to be done only once per rotation angle. In fact, for radially-symmetric filters this does not even have to be done. The main loss in efficiency is in the computation of the intersection between the filter and the rectangles. For each rectangle, one has to find the sample point closest to one of its corners and then move along the grid points using some form of incremental technique. Each move would, in general, be in both the X and Y directions, and therefore also a little more costly than in the original case.

Lastly, one can also put to good use the flexibility of the choice of the filter. It has been advocated to use different filters for different parts of a character (for example, to emphasize the serifs, or treat leading and trailing edges differently). To this end, we can mark the rectangles of the decomposition based on the parts of the character to which they belong (e.g., vertical stem, diagonal hairline) and use a filter appropriate to that type of shape when displayed on a particular device.

These techniques were developed precisely to facilitate such investigations.

Acknowledgements

This work has been partially funded by the Natural Sciences and Engineering Research Council of Canada. The authors are grateful to Bitstream Inc. for providing high-quality fonts for this research project, and to the Hewlett Packard Co. (John Wilkes in particular) for the use of their facilities in producing the timings and preparing this manuscript. The second author also thanks the Imaging group at Xerox PARC for providing a very congenial environment while this paper was written. Lastly, the party of the first part would like to thank the party of the second part for encouraging him to become a party of the first part in the first place.

References

Bige83 Bigelow, C. and D. Day, "Digital Typography," *Scientific American*, Volume 249, Number 2, August 1983, pp. 106-119.

Blac46 Blackwell, H. R., "Contrast Thresholds of the Human Eye," *Journal of the Optical Society of America*, Volume 36, 1946, pp. 642-643.

Bruc86 Bruckstein, A. M., "On Optimal Image Digitization," Electrical Engineering Publication Number 577, Faculty of Electrical Engineering, Technion Israel Institute of Technology, Haifa, Israel, February 1986.

Corn70 Cornsweet, T. N., *Visual Perception*, Academic Press, New York, 1970.

Catm79 Catmull, E., "A Tutorial on Compensation Tables," *Computer Graphics*, Volume 13, Number 2, August 1979, pp. 1-7. SIGGRAPH 1979 Proceedings.

Crow78 Crow, F. C., "The Use of Grayscale for Improved Raster Display of Vectors and Characters," *Computer Graphics*, Volume 12, Number 3, August 1978, pp. 1-6. SIGGRAPH 1978 Proceedings.

Crow84 Crow, F. C., "Summed-Area Tables for Texture Mapping," *Computer Graphics*, Volume 18, Number 3, July 1984, pp. 207-212. SIGGRAPH 1984 Proceedings.

Ferr84 Ferrari, L. A. and J. Sklansky, "A Fast Recursive Algorithm for Binary-Valued Two-Dimensional Filters," *Computer Vision, Graphics, and Image Processing*, Volume 26, 1984, pp. 292-302.

Fuch82 Fuchs, D. R. and D. E. Knuth, "Optimal Font Caching," STAN-CS-82-901, Department of Computer Science, Stanford University, Stanford, California, March 1982.

Goul84 Gould, J. D. and N. Grischkowsky, "Doing the Same Work with Hard Copy and with Cathode-Ray Tube (CRT) Computer Terminals," *Human Factors*, Volume 26, Number 3, June 1984, pp. 323-337.

Guib82 Guibas, L. J. and J. Stolfi, "A Language for Bitmap Manipulation", *ACM Transaction on Graphics*, Volume 1, Number 3, July 1982, pp. 191-214.

Heck86 Heckbert, P. S., "Filtering by Repeated Integration," *Computer Graphics*, Volume 20, Number 4, August 1986, pp. 315-321. SIGGRAPH 1986 Proceedings.

Kaji81 Kajiya, J. and M. Ullner, "Filtering High Quality Text for Display on Raster Scan Devices," *Computer Graphics*, Volume 15, Number 3 August 1981, pp. 7-15. SIGGRAPH 1981 Proceedings.

Koba80 Kobayashi, S. C., "Optimization Algorithms for Grayscale Fonts," B. Sc. Thesis, Department of Electrical Engineering and Computer Science, Massachusetts Institute of Technology, Cambridge, Massachusetts, June 1980.

Kou81 Kou, L., G. Markowski and L. Berman, "A Fast Algorithm for Steiner Trees," *Acta Informatica*, Volume 15, 1981.

Lele80 Leler, W. J., "Human Vision, Anti-Aliasing, and the Cheap 4000 Line Display," *Computer Graphics*, Volume 14, Number 3, July 1980, pp. 308-313. SIGGRAPH 1980 Proceedings.

Ling82 Lingas, A., R. Pinter, R. Rivest, and A. Shamir, "Minimum Edge Length Decompositions of Rectilinear Figures," *Proceedings of the 12th Annual Allerton Conference on Communication, Control, and Computing*, Illinois, 1982.

Ling83 Lingas, A., "Heuristics for Minimum Edge Length Rectangular Partitions of Rectilinear Figures," in *Theoretical Computer Science*, Edited by A. B. Cremers and H. P. Kriegel, Springer-Verlag, Berlin, January 1983, pp. 199-219.

Naim85 Naiman, A. C., "High-Quality Text for Raster Displays," M. Sc. Thesis, Department of Computer Science, University of Toronto, Toronto, Ontario, 1985.

Negr80 Negroponte, N., "Soft Fonts," *Proceedings, Society for Information Display*, 1980.

Prat78 Pratt, W. K., *Digital Image Processing*, John Wiley and Sons, New York, 1978.

Schm83 Schmandt, C., "Fuzzy Fonts," *Proceedings of the National Computer Graphics Association*, 1983.

Seit79 Seitz, C., *et al.*, "Digital Video Display System with a Plurality of Gray-Scale Levels," United States Patent Number 4,158,200.

Shol82 Sholtz, P. N., "Making High-Quality Colored Images on Raster Displays," Computer Science Research Report RC9632 (#42528), IBM T. J. Watson Research Center, Yorktown Heights, NY 10598, October 1982.

Shur80 Shurtleff, D. A., *How to Make Displays Legible*, Human Interface Design, La Mirada, California, 1980.

Warn80 Warnock, J. E., "The display of Characters Using Gray Level Sample Arrays," *Computer Graphics*, Volume 14, Number 3, July 1980, pp. 302-307. SIGGRAPH 1980 Proceedings.

Will83 Williams, L., "Pyramidal Parametrics," *Computer Graphics*, Volume 17, Number 3, July 1983, pp. 1-11. SIGGRAPH 1983 Proceedings.

CHARACTER GENERATION UNDER GRID CONSTRAINTS

Roger D. HERSCH
Swiss Federal Institute of Technology, Lausanne

Abstract

An original and fast filling algorithm based on vertical scan line sweep and contour tracking of a presorted shape description allows filling of character shapes with real subpixel resolution. Identical parts of a character lying at a different phase in respect to the grid will have a dissimilar discrete look. Grid constraints are applied in order to force given parts of a character (stems, serifs) to attain identical phasing. So that several contraints may be applied, degrees of freedom are provided in the form of stretchable null-segments inserted at particular locations in the character outline description. Grid constraints are also applied to avoid discrete arcs with an isolated pixel or a long horizontal or vertical run. The type of constraints applied to parts of a character consists only of horizontal or vertical subpixel translations. The resulting character description therefore remains nearly identical to the original description. The processing time used to apply grid constraints is negligible, compared with the time needed for character scan-conversion and filling. Hence, this method is very well adapted for direct character generation on non-impact printers. It is also suitable for character rasterization in typographic computer-aided design systems.

Keywords

raster graphics, digital typography, outline fonts, analytical character generation, constraints application, shape filling, real scan-conversion

1. Introduction

For many years, digital character generation has been dedicated to high-resolution photocomposing devices [1]. In the seventies, fidelity of character generation was less important than minimization of computer power and memory requirements. The new laser printer technology developed in the eighties led to a first generation of raster image processors using bitmap characters. A second generation of imaging devices capable of representing and printing pages independently of the target's printer output resolution arose as a result of proprietary research [2]. For today's manufacturers of laser printer and plotting devices, the ability to interpret resolution-independent page description languages is becoming a crucial issue. The main problem of device-independent raster imaging is character generation from a resolution-independent character description.

Traditional typography has evolved into digital typography. Font designers use CAD systems for assistance and to generate output fonts compatible with the needs of today's photocomposers and laser printers. A major step, which may be very work-intensive, concerns the rasterization of character fonts. Commonly used systems [3] generate raster characters which generally entail interactive modification of their discrete representation by skilled typographers. The techniques described in this paper can be used in order to automatically generate raster characters of improved quality.

The main problem of typographic character generation on a discrete grid is the preservation of important geometrical properties by the scan-conversion process. For example, parts of a character which have an identical outline description like stems or serifs must remain identical after scan-conversion. Replication of identical parts should lead to identical configurations of darkened pixels. Simple scan-conversion of shapes outlines does not respect exactly implicit properties such as stem width or serif outlook (figure 1). In order to improve character rendering, selected segments of shapes are considered to be locally elastic. Important geometrical properties are described by constraints and applied to the character shape outline. The resultant character description allows the subsequent scan-conversion process to respect the given constraints.

A second key point concerns the generation of attractively curved character parts. As it has already been pointed out [4], strange rasterization effects may appear depending on the relative position of a curved character part in respect to the grid. In order to obtain acceptable discrete characters, it is imperative to allow only attractively discrete curves to be generated. This can be done by applying constraints specifying the domain through which the curvilinear outline must pass.

Shape of original character:
printed at 150 dots/inch
(physical height: 174 pixels)

scan-converted character
without constraint application
physical height: 23 pixels

scan-converted character
with constraint application
(physical height: 23 pixels)

Fig. 1 Identical stems before and after scan-conversion

Furthermore, the graphic filling algorithm used for analytical character generation should be able to fill degenerate shapes (figure 2). Filling speed becomes an essential factor for characters directly generated on a target printer.

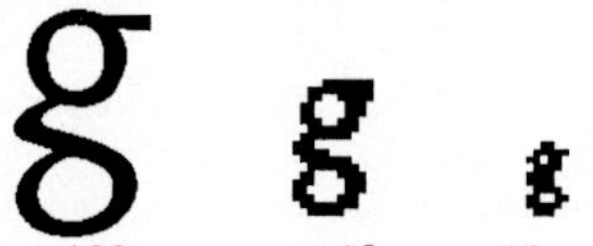

physical height (pixels) :	120	18	10
enlargment:	*2*	*8*	*8*

height:	8	5	3
enlargment:	*16*	*16*	*16*

Fig. 2 Example of degenerating character shape: vanishing white interior shape part

The filling algorithm developed for character generation [5] is based on vertical scan-line sweep and contour tracking of a presorted shape description. By working on presorted shapes, character generation time can be greatly reduced. Presorted shapes can only be filled if their topology remains unmodified by the scan-conversion process. Rounding operations may modify the shape´s topology. To avoid this, the traditional incremental straight line and circular arc scan-conversion algorithms are extended to work with real segment departure and arrival points, as well as with real parameters like slope or radius [6].

2. Elements of real scan-conversion

Traditional scan-conversion algorithms [7], [8] for straight line and circular arc segments are defined for integer coordinates of departure and arrival points. Traditional scan-conversion and shape filling implies preliminary rounding of shape vertices.

Real number scan-conversion is introduced to avoid rounding operations and to provide higher precision for the selection of discrete pixels. Furthermore, real scan-conversion allows the generation of many slightly different discrete shapes based on the same contour description, by applying to it horizontal or vertical subpixel displacements.

Real fixed-point scan-conversion of straight line segments is a simple extension of integer scan-conversion. Let us consider a line segment with real extremities lying on its support line. Real scan-conversion applied to the considered segment should generate exactly the same discrete pixels as those which would have been generated by scan conversion of the support line (figure 3).

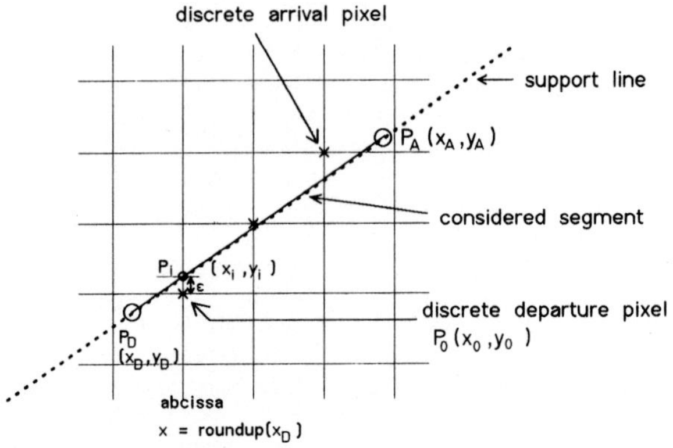

Fig. 3 Support line, real segment and associated pixels

After scan conversion, a real straight line segment $\overline{P_D(x_D,y_D)P_A(x_A,y_A)}$ lying in the first octant will have one pixel on each integer abcissa intersecting it. The discrete departure pixel $P_0(x_0,y_0)$ is the closest grid pixel to the intersection point $P_i(x_i,y_i)$ of the real segment with the integer abcissa on the right of departure point P_D.

Coordinates of intersection point $P_i(x_i, y_i)$:

$$x_i = \text{roundup}\ (x_D)$$

$$y_i = y_D + \frac{y_A - y_D}{x_A - x_D}\ (x_i - x_D)$$

Discrete departure pixel $P_0(x_0,y_0)$:

$$x_0 = x_i$$

$$y_0 = \text{round}\ (y_i)$$

where x_D, y_D, x_A, y_A, y_i : real numbers in fixed point representation
x_0, y_0, x_i : integer numbers

In order to run the extended Bresenham algorithm, the initial error $\varepsilon_0 = y_i - y_0$ is used for the computation of error e_1 which helps to select next grid pixel P_1. The following recurrence formula is used to get pixel P_{K+1} from pixel P_K and error coefficient ε_K.

$$e_{K+1} = \varepsilon_K + \frac{y_A - y_D}{x_A - x_D}$$

$$x_{K+1} = x_K + 1$$

$$y_{K+1} = y_K + \text{round}\ (e_{K+1})$$

$$\varepsilon_{K+1} = e_{K+1} - \text{round}(e_{K+1})$$

This recurrent formulation is equivalent to Bresenham's algorithm but real error and slope coefficents are expressed in fixed point digital representation (for example 16 bit signed integer part and 16 bit fractional part). The last discrete pixel is the one lying on the integer abcissa on the left of real line arrival point P_A.

In a similar way, real scan-conversion of circular arcs can be introduced for scan-converting arcs having real center, departure and arrival points. Consider a circular arc lying in the first octant (figure 4). Discrete departure pixel P_0 is one of the candidate pixels $T_0(x'_{t0}, y'_{t0})$, $T_1(x'_{t1}, y'_{t1})$ or $T_2(x'_{t2}, y'_{t2})$.

Compute, in fixed-point coordinates relative to the center of the arc, the quadratic error criterion

$$C_i = x_i^2 + y_i^2 - r^2$$

for each of the candidate pixels T_0, T_1, T_2. Select as the first discrete pixel P_0 the candidate pixel T_i for which $|C_i|$ is minimal.

In absolute coordinates:

$P_D : (x_D, y_D)$ real departure point

$P_A : (x_A, y_A)$ real arrival point

in absolute coordinates:	in coordinates relative to the center of the arc:
T_0 : x'_{t0} = roundup(x_D)	$x_{t0} = x'_{t0} - x_q$
y'_{t0} = roundup(y_D)	$y_{t0} = y'_{t0} - y_q$
T_1 : x'_{t1} = trunc(x_D)	$x_{t1} = x'_{t1} - x_q$
y'_{t1} = roundup(y_D)	$y_{t1} = y'_{t1} - y_q$
T_2 : x'_{t2} = trunc(x_D) − 1	$x_{t2} = x'_{t2} - x_q$
y'_{t2} = roundup(y_D)	$y_{t2} = y'_{t2} - y_q$

× discrete pixel center having integer coordinates

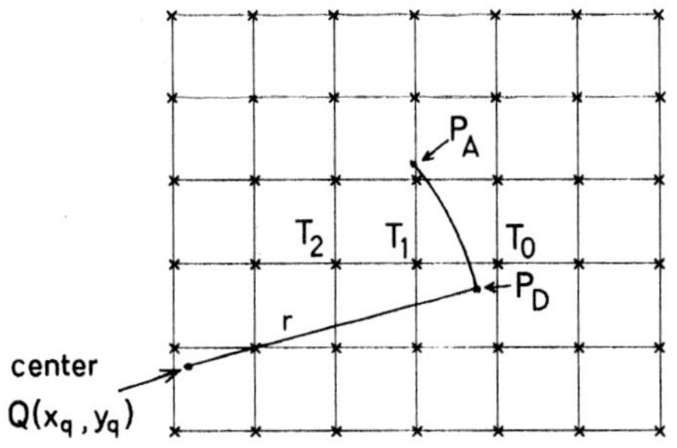

Fig. 4 Candidate pixels T_0, T_1, T_2 for discrete departure pixel P_0

Bresenham demonstrated that minimization of quadratic error criterion $|C_K| = |x_K^2 + y_K^2 - r^2|$ and minimization of radial error criterion $|D_K| = |\sqrt{x_K^2 + y_K^2} - r|$ agree for integer circle center and integer arc departure points. In the general case of real center and departure points, they may disagree [9], but the additional error introduced by quadratic error criterion minimization remains smaller than two, respective one percent of a grid unit, for radii $\geqslant 6$, respective $\geqslant 13$ pixels [6].

The next arc pixels are computed incrementally in the traditional way [10]. The discrete arrival pixel is the last pixel of the arc inferior to real arrival point P_A.

3. Filling of scaled shapes and characters

In an early comparision of filling algorithms [11], the category of edge tracking algorithms was shown as being one of the fastest.

Within this category, an original filling algorithm called *Descriptive Contour Fill* was developed for the generation of typographic characters. It allows filling of shapes scaled down by any factor [5].

Descriptive contour fill is based on the fact that a straight line has an even number of intersections with a closed shape. The parity of the intersection count (figure 5) indicates whether an intersected segment lies inside or outside the shape. By scanning the shape description vertically with horizontal scan lines and applying scan conversion, we obtain the coordinates of each discrete pair of pixels indicating the extremities of the horizontal segments to be filled.

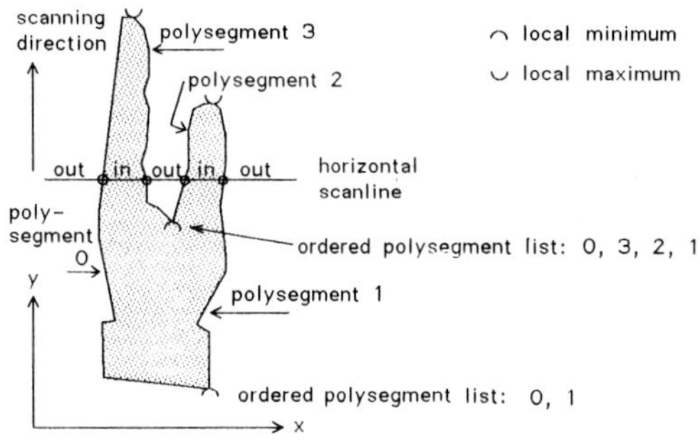

Fig. 5 Shape filling by vertical contour description sweep

Local minima and maxima play a major role :

1) Their intersection with a horizontal scan line is a *double intersection*.

2) By defining the description of the contour between a local minimum and a local maximum as one polysegment, we can associate with each local minimum an ordered set of polysegments which are intersected by the real horizontal tangent through the local minimum.

The filling process requires the segmentation of the contour description along local minima (birth points) and local maxima (death points). For each local minimum, intersected polysegments must be sorted along increasing x-coordinates. We assume that the shape has no self-intersections, thus ensuring that the intersection order of polysegments and horizontal scan lines does not change between two birth points.

During filling, the ordered contour description is swept on each horizontal scan line. If the new scan line does not intersect a local minimum (birth point), scan-conversion of previously intersected polysegments proceeds; pairs of intersected contour pixels are obtained and corresponding horizontal line segments are filled. If a local minimum lies between the previous and the actual new scan line, scan conversion and filling proceed on the ordered set of polysegments related to the new birth point.

Outlines of characters are generally described by cubic splines. Scan-conversion can proceed directly from the cubic spline equation, for example by forward differentiation [12]. If characters are described by conics [13], their outline can be scan-converted by fast incremental Bresenham-like algorithms [14]. For fast incremental scan-conversion, the original cubic spline description can be approximated by straight line, conic or circular arc segments.

In order to attain fastest possible scan-conversion and to be able to handle degeneration cases easily, we segment the original character description given in natural and closed splines [15] into circular arc segments. A sufficiently flat spline segment given by two interpolation points and their respective tangents can be approximated by two circular arcs having first derivative continuity at their meeting point [16]. A character shape approximated by circular arcs can be scaled down without loss of quality. When enlarged, the quality of its contour approximation will decrease. Therefore, spline to circular arc conversion should be accomplished on the full-scaled character outline description. In order to ease character filling, we ensure that local minima and maxima lie on circular arc vertices and that each arc is located within one octant.

The approximated contour described by a list of subsequent circular arcs and straight line segments must be sorted and converted to a description suitable for direct shape filling. Such a description (figure 6), which includes information about the order of occurrence of intersections between scan lines and contour parts, contains the following elements :

1) An ordered list of birth points
2) An ordered list of death points
3) An ordered list of polysegments associated with each birth point. This list contains the order in which polysegments are intersected by a horizontal scan line just above the corresponding birth point.
4) A description of each polysegment containing all circular arc and straight line segments from a local minimum (birth point) to a local maximum (death point).

Such a presorted character description can be referenced whenever a new raster character with horizontal or vertical orientation is generated. For characters rotated by any angle, circular arc extraction and presorting is applied again on the original spline outline description.

The character filling algorithm, working on a presorted description, can be described in the following way for non-degenerated shapes:

```
Initialize current scan line to the closest integer ordinate
inferior to the first birthpoint

FOR first birthpoint TO last birthpoint DO
   fetch list of ordered polysegments belonging to current
   birthpoint
   WHILE current scan line inferior to the next birthpoint DO
      with real scan-conversion, intersect each polysegment of
      the ordered polysegment list with the current scan line
      and fill the horizontal run between each pair of
      scan-converted pixels
      Increment the current scan line ordinate
   END (*while*)
END (*for*)
```

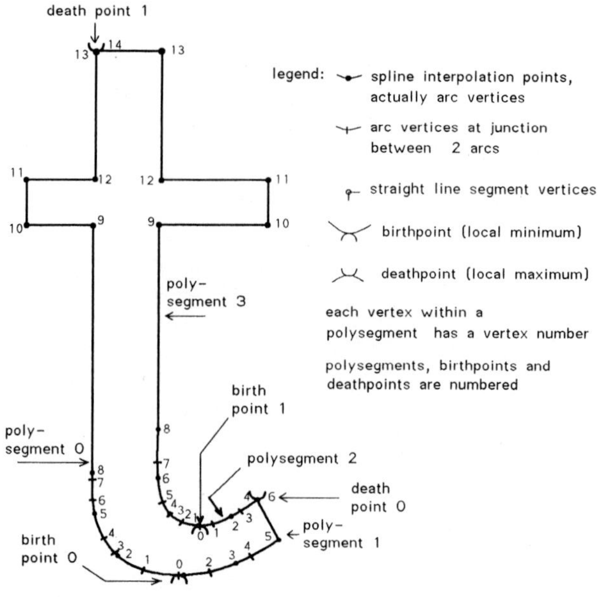

Description of character t:

birthpoint list: birthpoint 0 (polysegment 0, vertex 0)
birthpoint 1 (polysegment 2, vertex 0)

deathpoint list: deathpoint 0 (polysegment 2, vertex 4)
deathpoint 1 (polysegment 0, vertex 13)

ordered lists of polysegments:
ordered list at birthpoint 0: polysegment 0, polysegment 1
ordered list at birthpoint 1: polysegment 0, polysegment 3, polysegment 2, polysegment 1

polysegment description:

polysegment 0: departure vertex (p0x0,p0y0), arc vertex (p0x1,p0y1), .. , arc vertex (p0x8,p0y8), segment vertex (p0x9,p0y9), .. , segment vertex (p0x13,p0y13)

polysegment 1: departure vertex (p1x0,p1y0), arc vertex (p1x1,p1y1), .., arc vertex (p1x5,p1y5), segment vertex (p1x6,p1y6)

polysegment 2: departure vertex (p2x0,p2y0), arc vertex (p2x1,p2y1), .., arc vertex (p2x4,p2y4)

polysegment 3: departure vertex (p3x0,p3y0), arc vertex (p3x1,p3y1), .. ,arc vertex (p3x8,p3y8), segment vertex (p3x9,p3y9), .. segment vertex (p3x14,p3y14)

Fig. 6 Example of a presorted character description suitable for subsequent filling

This filling algorithm is restricted to shapes without self-intersections. Characters with self-intersections are segmented into one or more distinct shapes which are filled separately. For handling degeneration effects the reader should refer to a previous paper describing filling of degenerate shapes [5].

Characters generated by simple descriptive contour fill may lose some geometrical properties. For example, the first two stems of character **m** (figure 1), which have an identical description, appear in their rasterized unconstrained form as two different elements. Scan-converted originally identical stems appear differently because they are drawn at a different phase relative to the grid. Applying constraints to the character description can cause identical parts to be drawn at the same subpixel displacement relative to the grid.

4. Grid constraints applied to the character

The filling algorithm based on real scan-conversion allows the production of many slightly different discrete shapes at various subpixel displacements based on one original contour description (figure 7).

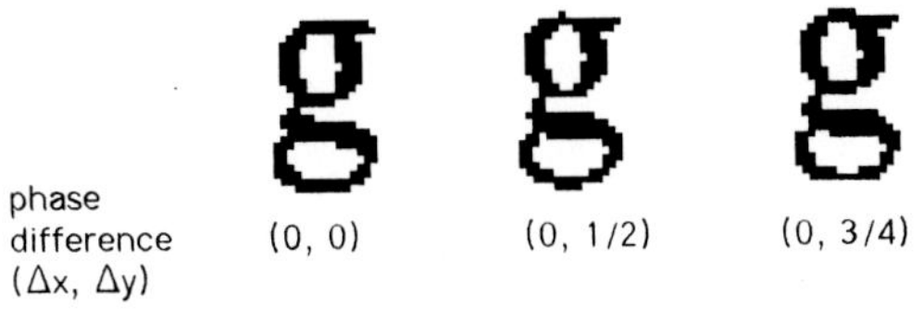

Fig. 7 Typographic character generated at different vertical subpixel displacements

The freedom to apply to a character horizontal or vertical displacements relative to the grid can be used to keep some geometrical relationships (⩾, =, ⩽) between discrete character parts. A simple analysis of phasing artifacts on a vertical bar shows that phasing may generate the same discrete bar for two real bars having, at worst, a width difference of 1 pixel on each side. By centering the real bar outline relative to the grid, the same discrete bar is generated for two real bars having a maximal width difference of half a pixel on each side (figure 8).

The centering operation ensures that a maximum number of discrete pixel centers come to lie within the real shape border. Therefore geometrical relations (⩾, =, ⩽) between real centered bars can be kept on the generated discrete bars (figure 9).

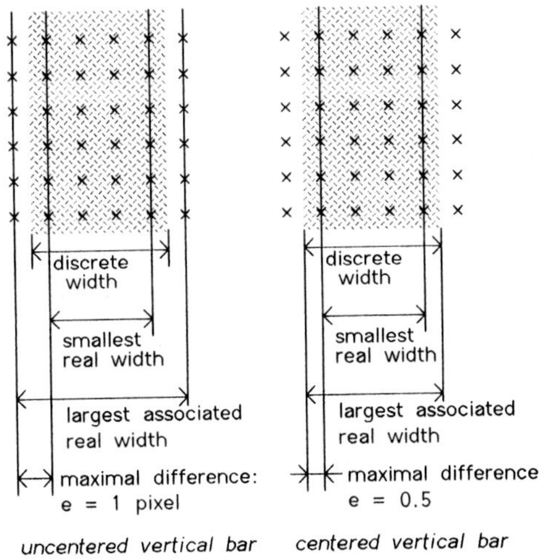

Fig. 8 Real and discrete vertical bars

Consider character **L** with vertical stroke width slightly larger than horizontal stroke width. By specifying that horizontal and vertical strokes of the scaled character must be drawn centered relative to the grid, we ensure that the discrete width of the vertical stroke remains larger or becomes equal to the discrete width of the horizontal stroke (figure 10).

For more complex characters, like character **E**, freedom of horizontal and vertical character displacement is not enough. More freedom may be given to a character

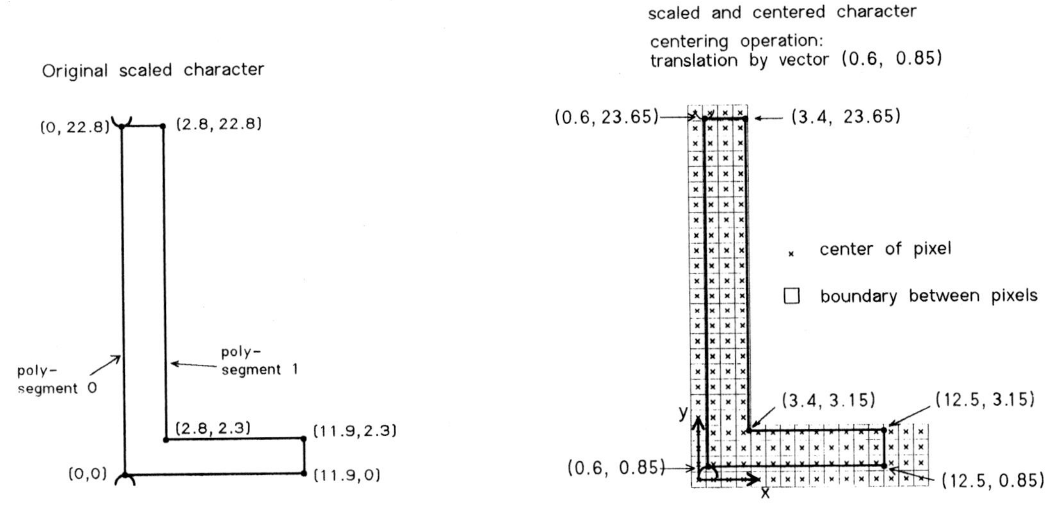

original coordinates after scaling:

polysegment 0: departure point (0,0)
segment arrival point (0, 22.8)

polysegment 1: departure point (0,0)
segment arrival point (11.9, 0)
segment arrival point (11.9, 2.3)
segment arrival point (2.8, 2.3)
segment arrival point (2.8, 22.8)
segment arrival point (0.0, 22.8)

original coordinates after scaling and centering:

polysegment 0: departure point (0.6, 0.85)
segment arrival point (0.6, 23.65)

polysegment 1: departure point (0.6, 0.85)
segment arrival point (12.5, 0.85)
segment arrival point (12.5, 3.15)
segment arrival point (3.4, 3.15)
segment arrival point (3.4, 23.65)
segment arrival point (0.6, 23.65)

Fig. 10 Centering the horizontal and vertical bars of character L description by considering some particular straight line segments to be elastic (figure 11). As an example, we consider some segments of the original character description of letter **E** to be stretchable in the vertical direction. Thus, it becomes easy to center every horizontal bar in respect to the pixel grid.

Elasticity is applied only at specific locations in order to leave the general shape description unchanged. Therefore, the segment which becomes elastic must be chosen carefully. In order to simplify the application of constraints, only straight line segments may acquire a stretchable end. Such segments are not always available, so that generally an additional stretchable segment called *null-segment* is inserted in the character description. By adding a horizontal or vertical displacement to parts of a character, this additional segment may acquire a positive fractional length.

A *constraint description* specifies the actions that must be taken in order to modify the coordinates of the character outline. Such a description contains a *constraint qualifier* specifying how to compute the horizontal or vertical displacement parameter. The *constraint application part* contains commands which specify on which parts of a character the current subpixel displacement must be applied (figure 12).

Before filling a character, the presorted character description is modified by a constraint interpretation routine. This routine computes horizontal or vertical displacements

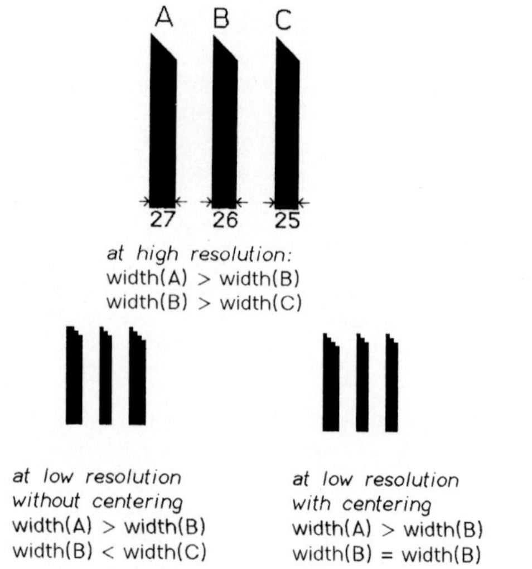

Fig. 9 Continuous and discrete relationships between shape parts

using the constraint qualifier information. These subpixel displacements are applied to the parts of the character specified by the constraint application description. The constraint interpreter can be compared to a linker: just before filling, it adjusts the coordinate values of the character description parameters.

Original scaled character description

character with modified description having vertical and horizontal bars centered on the grid

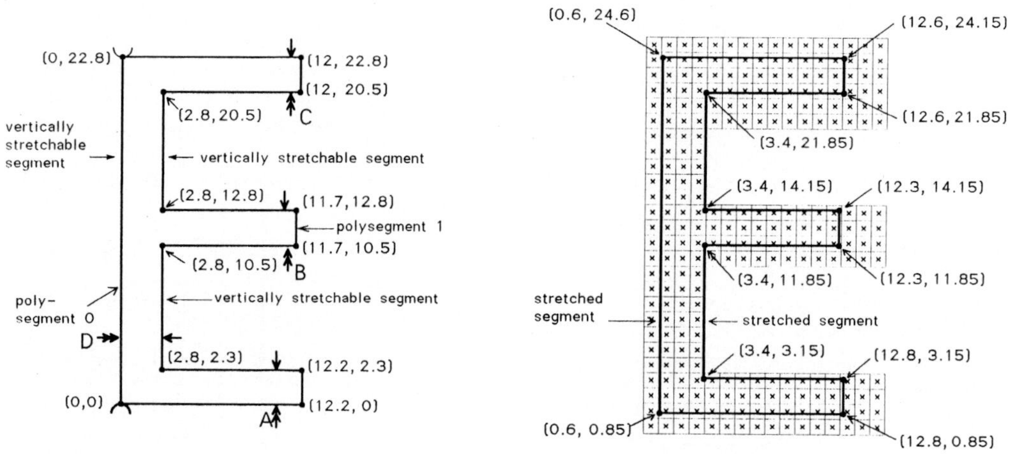

Outline coordinates before constraint application

Outline coordinates after constraint application

Constraints:

A. *constraint qualifier:*
centering lower horizontal segment in vertical direction

resulting constraint application:
vertical translation of whole character by 0.85

B. *constraint qualifier:*
centering middle horizontal segment in vertical direction

resulting constraint application:
translation of middle and upper character part by 0.5

C. *constraint qualifier:*
centering upper horizontal segment in vertical direction

resulting constraint application:
vertical translation of upper character part by 0.0

D. *constraint qualifier:*
centering of vertical bar to the right

resulting constraint application:
horizontal translation of whole character by 0.6

Fig. 11 Example of simple character outline with stretchable segments before and after centering vertical and horizontal bars

5. Generation of discrete curvilinear contour pieces by application of grid constraints

The problem of generating attractive curvilinear discrete contour pieces can be solved by specification of adequate grid constraints. Let us look at the same arc portion, at different subpixel displacements (figure 13) :

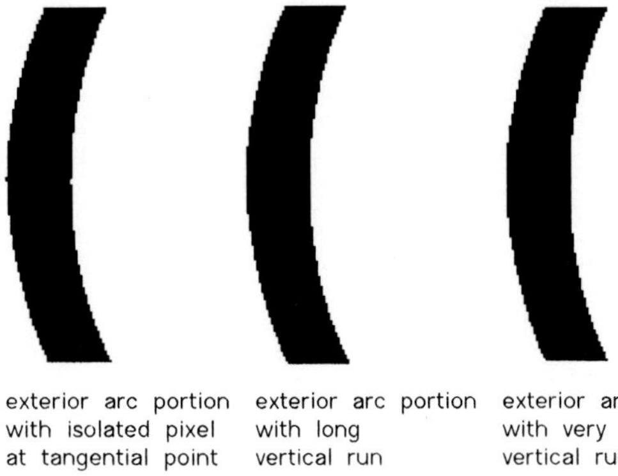

Fig. 13 Discrete curved shape at different subpixel displacements

Discrete curvilinear shapes look ugly when they contain, at their vertical or horizontal tangential points, an isolated pixel or a long run. Real scan-conversion generates an isolated pixel or a long run if the horizontal or vertical tangential point of a curve segment lies approximately halfway between two pixels (figure 14).

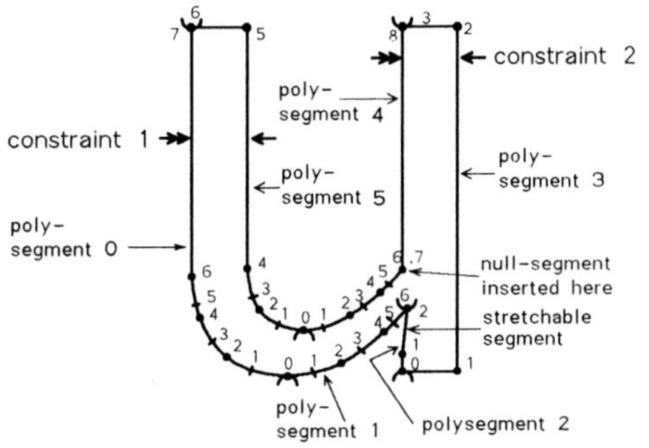

constraint descriptions

1. *constraint qualifier:*
   center horizontally between
   polysegment 0, vertex 6 and
   polysegment 5, vertex 4
   constraint application:
   horizontal displacement applied
   to the whole character
2. *constaint qualifier:*
   center horizontally between
   polysegment 4, vertex 6 and
   polysegment 3, vertex 2
   constraint application:
   apply horizontal displacement to:
   polysegment 3: whole polysegment
   polysegment 4: vertex 7, vertex 8
   polysegment 2: vertex 0, vertex 1

Fig. 12 Example of constraint descriptions with qualifier and application parts

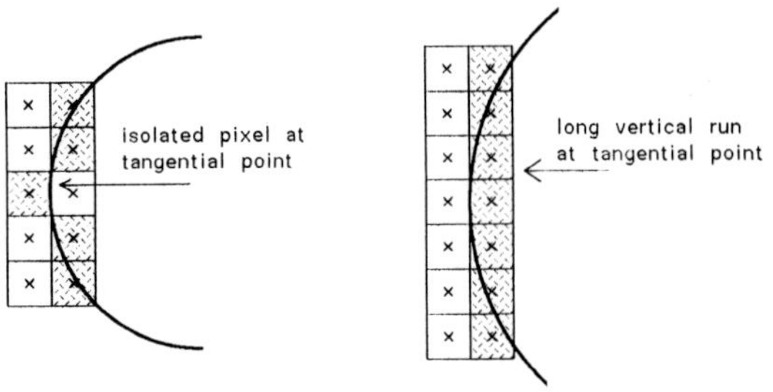

Fig. 14 Ugly discrete arcs produced by scan-converted real arc passing halfway between pixel centers

By allowing tangential points of arcs to pass only within a certain distance range from pixel centers, neither isolated pixels nor long vertical runs will be generated (figure 15).

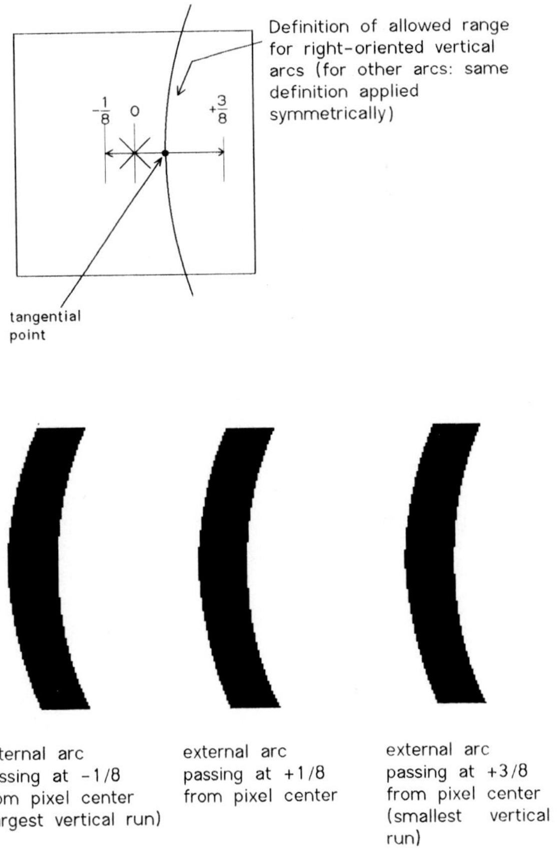

Fig. 15 Allowed placement of tangential points and corresponding results

These curve generation constraints can be added to the other character generation constraints. They may require stretchable segments at strategic places. In most cases however, it is enough to apply a horizontal or vertical displacement to the whole character in order to obtain attractive curvilinear contour parts. For character **u** (figure 16), a vertical displacement is calculated so that the inner and outer tangential points lie within the allowed range.

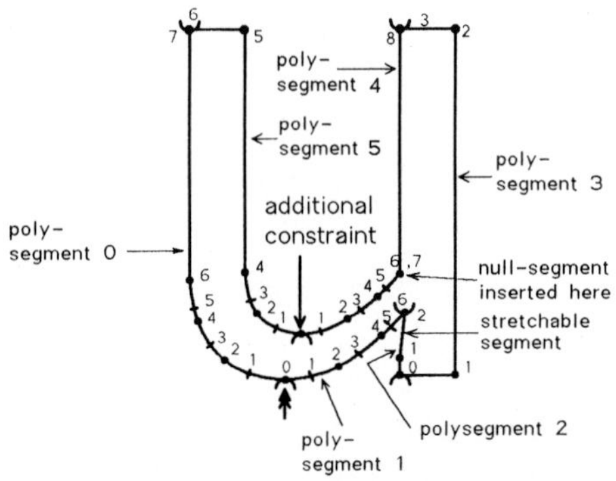

additional constraint to obtain attractive discrete arcs:

constraint qualifier:
horizontal positive arc - horizontal positive arc
between polysegment 0, vertex 0 and
polysegment 5, vertex 0
constraint application:
vertical displacement applied
to the whole character

Fig. 16 Application of a vertical constraint to get a nicely curvilinear character shape

The visual impact of exterior arcs is more important than the impact of interior arcs. Experience has shown that arc constraints should be applied to exterior arcs. Interior arcs can be left without constraints. An isolated "background pixel" on an interior arc does not disturb the overall visual impression too much.

6. Definition and application of grid constraints

Constraints should be defined in such a way that constraint application will not modify important topological attributes of the original shape. The ordered birthpoint and deathpoint lists as well as the ordered polysegment lists should remain valid for the shape undergoing constraint application. Cases of constraint applications arise in which subpixel translations of shape parts completely modify the original shape topology (figure 17). They may occur when selected stretchable segments are smaller than one pixel.

A simple solution to this problem consists in defining conditional constraints, which are applied only if a vertical or horizontal distance between two shape support points is bigger than a specified value.

By applying grid constraints to a character shape, we ensure that identical character parts (serifs, stems) remain identical on the discrete shape. We also ensure that relationships ($\leqslant$, =, $\geqslant$) between real shape parts are maintained on the generated discrete parts. Grid constraint application essentially implies local modifications at specific shape locations. Stretchable segments become longer or shorter by a fractional value. Null-segments acquire a positive length. Are these local shape modifications noticeable on the generated discrete shapes? Null-segments are generally inserted at corner points between distinct shape parts. The local discrete shape modification produced by null-segments acquiring a fractional length is hardly noticeable. Fractional modification of a stretchable segment length may result in a local difference of one or two pixels.

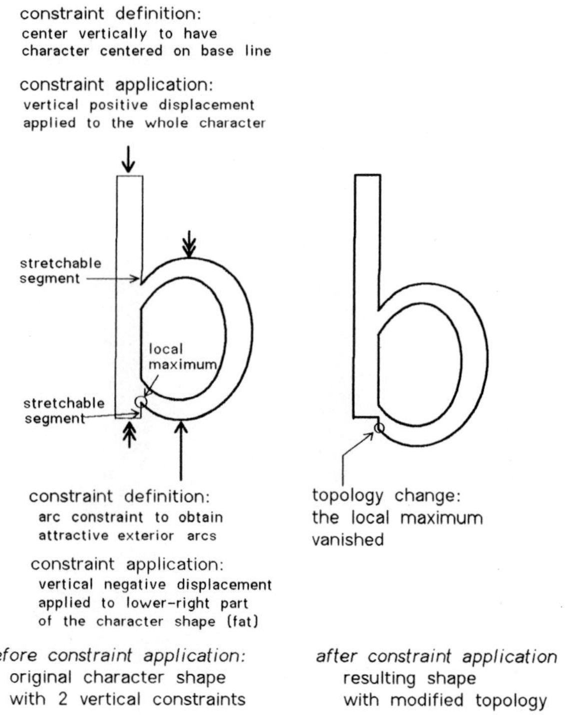

Fig. 17 Topological modifications by constraint application

The concept of constraints presented in this paper provides the framework within which further research is needed for defining optimal constraints, both from a topological and from an esthetical point of view. At present, constraints are added individually to each shape description. They should be extracted and formalized by partly automatic, partly interactive means.

7. Conclusion

An attempt to solve the problem presented by generation of typographic characters for middle resolution raster devices becomes possible with a fast shape-filling algorithm working on real shape coordinates and capable of filling degenerated shapes.

The fundamental problem of producing attractive and regular characters on middle resolution devices (200..600 dots/inch) is essentially a phasing problem. By providing a means to apply subpixel dephasing to critical parts of a character, identical parts of a character like stems or serifs may remain identical throughout scan-conversion. The proposed solution consists in appending to the character description a constraint description part. Each constraint descriptor contains a qualifier specifying how to compute horizontal or vertical subpixel displacements. The constraint application part belonging to a constraint descriptor specifies to which parts of the character the computed subpixel displacement should be applied. Between the part of a character where a constraint is applied and the part where it is not applied, stretchable null-segments are inserted. They will acquire a positive fractional length after constraint application. Similar constraints can be defined and applied in order to obtain attractively discrete curvilinear contour pieces at character generation time.

These constraint application techniques distinguish themselves from previous attempts to adapt character shapes to the grid [3] by the fact that the character description is modified only at very specific places. The inserted stretchable null-segments define separations between character parts. Character parts are translated by the constraint application process. Their outline description therefore remains nearly identical to the original one.

The presented techniques allow the drawing of sharp character edges. This approach contrasts with other character generation algorithms which generate half-tone rasters on character edges in order to compensate for phasing errors. Sharp edges produce the desirable crisp typographic effect on middle resolution printing devices.

Due to their simplicity, grid constraints can be applied satisfactorily to characters generated directly on non-impact printers. Compared to the time needed for character generation and filling, constraint application time is negligible.

The character designer should be aware that similar looking pieces of a character must have a strictly identical outline description. Furthermore, the computer aided character design system should allow the typographer to specify in a transparent way which are the constraints and where they must be applied. Constraint descriptions should be considered as an integral part of character outline descriptions. They provide the means to generate typographical characters of acceptable quality on middle resolution output devices.

8. Acknowledgments

This research was partly accomplished during a four months leave at Vrije Universiteit Brussel. I wish to thank Prof. T. d'Hondt (VUB) and E. Kohen (ETH) for the stimulating discussions. Also many thanks to Prof. Nicoud and to my colleagues at Laboratoire de Microinformatique for having developed powerful programming and document production environments.

9. References:

[1] Coueignoux, P.,"Character Generation by Computer," *Computer Graphics and Image Processing,* Vol 16, pp 240-269, 1981

[2] Adobe Systems Inc, *Postscript Language Reference Manual*, Addison-Wesley, 1985

[3] Karow, P., "Elektronische Modifikation grafischer und verbalgrafischer Zeichen," *Deutscher Drucker,* Nr. 25, pp.4-8, August 1979

[4] Knuth, D., *Tex and Metafont,* American Mathematical Society, Digital Press, 1979

[5] Hersch, R.D., "Descriptive Contour Fill of Partly Degenerated Shapes," *IEEE Computer Graphics and Applications,* Vol 6, No 7, July 1986.

[6] Hersch, R.D., "Real Scan-Conversion of Shape Contours," *Proceedings Computer Graphics International 87,* Karuizawa, Japan, Ed. T.L. Kunii, Springer Verlag, 1987

[7] Bresenham, J.E.,"Algorithm for computer control of a digital plotter," *IBM Systems Journal,* Vol 4, No 1, 1965, pp 25-30

[8] Bresenham, J.E., "A Linear Algorithm for Incremental Digital Display of Circular Arcs," *Communications of the ACM,* Vol 20, No 2, Febrary 1977

[9] McIlroy, M.D., "Best Approximate Circles on Integer Grids," *ACM Transactions on Graphics*, Vol. 2, No 4, pp 237-263, Oct 83.

[10] Foley, J.D., Van Dam, A., *Fundamentals of Interactive Computer Graphics*, Addison-Wesley, 1982

[11] Ackland, B.D., Weste, N.H., "The Edge Flag Algorithm - A Fill Method for Raster Scan Displays," *IEEE Trans. on Computers,* Vol 30, No 1, January 1981, pp. 41-48

[12] Newman, W.M., Sproull, R.F., *Principles of Interactive Computer Graphics,* McGraw-Hill, 1979

[13] Pratt, V., "Techniques for Conic Splines," Proceedings of SIGGRAPH'85, (San Francisco, July 22-26,1985). In *ACM Computer Graphics*, Vol 19, No 3, (July 1985), pp 151-159

[14] Pitteway, M., "Algorithm for Drawing Ellipses or Hyperbolae with digital plotters," Computer Journal, Vol 10, No 3, pp 282-289, Nov. 1967

[15] Rogers, D.F., *Mathematical Elements for Computer Graphics*, McGraw-Hill, New-York, 1976

[16] Hourdequin, M., Coueignoux, P., "Specifying arbitrary planar smooth curves for fast drawing", Proceedings Eurographics Conference, Bologna 1979, pp 193-211

Appendix

Typographic characters generated under grid constraints at several sizes:

original character at 150 dots/inch physical height: 243 pixels

reduced character physical height: 32 pixels

physical height: 27 pixels

physical height: 23 pixels

physical height: 19 pixels

physical height: 14 pixels

physical height: 10 pixels

physical height: 5 pixels

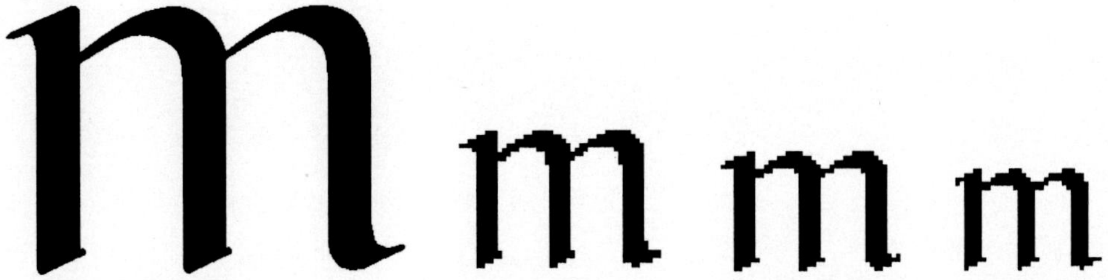

scan-converted character at 150 dots/inch physical height: 243 pixels

physical height: 31 pixels

physical height: 27 pixels

physical height: 23 pixels

physical height: 18 pixels

physical height: 14 pixels

physical height: 10 pixels

physical height: 5 pixels

scan-converted character at 150 dots/inch physical height: 243 pixels

physical height: 32 pixels

physical height: 27 pixels

physical height: 23 pixels

physical height: 19 pixels

physical height: 14 pixels

physical height: 10 pixels

physical height: 5 pixels

AN EFFICIENT NEW ALGORITHM FOR 2-D LINE CLIPPING: ITS DEVELOPMENT AND ANALYSIS

Tina M. Nicholl*, D. T. Lee+ and Robin A. Nicholl*

*Department of Computer Science, The University of Western Ontario, London, CANADA N6A 5B7

and

+Department of Electrical Engineering and Computer Science, Northwestern University, Evanston, Illinois 60201, U.S.A.

ABSTRACT

This paper describes a new algorithm for clipping a line in two dimensions against a rectangular window. This algorithm avoids computation of intersection points which are not endpoints of the output line segment. The performance of this algorithm is shown to be consistently better than existing algorithms, including the Cohen-Sutherland and Liang-Barsky algorithms. This performance comparison is machine-independent, based on an analysis of the number of arithmetic operations and comparisons required by the different algorithms. We first present the algorithm using procedures which perform geometric transformations to exploit symmetry properties and then show how program transformation techniques may be used to eliminate the extra statements involved in performing geometric transformations.

Categories and Subject Descriptors: D.2.2 [Software Engineering]: Tools and Techniques; F.2.2 [Analysis of Algorithms and Problem Complexity]: Nonnumerical Algorithms and Problems – geometrical problems and computations; I.3.3 [Computer Graphics] Picture/Image Generation – display algorithms; I.3.5 [Computer Graphics] Computational Geometry and Object Modeling – geometric algorithms, languages and systems; hierarchy and geometric transformations

General Terms: Algorithms, design, measurement, performance

Additional Key Words and Phrases: Clipping, line clipping, program transformation

I. INTRODUCTION

In the most general sense, clipping is the evaluation of the intersection between two geometrical entities. These geometrical entities may be points, line segments, rectangles, polygons, polyhedrons, curves, surfaces and so on, or assemblies of these. In this paper we will restrict ourselves to computing the intersection between a line segment and a rectilinear rectangle (which we call a window) in two dimensions.

Assume that we have a line segment with endpoints (x1,y1) and (x2,y2), and a window represented by four real numbers xleft, ytop, xright and ybottom. The window is defined as the set of all points (x,y) such that xleft ≤ x ≤ xright and ybottom ≤ y ≤ ytop. The intersection (if not empty) is a continuous portion of the line segment, and so can be represented by two endpoints. Thus we must determine if the intersection is empty, and if not, compute the coordinates of its endpoints.

II. BACKGROUND

The Cohen-Sutherland (CS) algorithm [1] appears, until recently, to be the only line-clipping algorithm known to the graphics community. (Sproull and Sutherland's midpoint subdivision algorithm [2] is designed for machines with no hardware support for multiplication and division.) The CS algorithm uses an encoding scheme to indicate the positions of the endpoints of line segments.

The Cyrus-Beck (CB) algorithm [3], though published in 1978, is not very well known to most of the graphics community. This algorithm is based on a parametric representation of the line segments. The theoretical model of this algorithm is very general. However, it is rather inefficient. To clip a line segment which is neither vertical nor horizontal and lies entirely within the window it will perform 12 additions, 16 subtractions, 20 multiplications and 4 divisions. The CS algorithm performs *no* arithmetic operations for the same line segment.

The Liang-Barsky (LB) algorithm [4], published in 1984, may be the first attempt to improve on the performance of the CS algorithm. The algorithm is a lot more efficient than the CB algorithm, even though the two use the same theoretical model. Experimental analysis was used to show that this algorithm is faster than the CS algorithm. However the approach of running the algorithms many times, with random line segments and windows, is inadequate. The results of the experiments are dependent on characteristics of the machine used, for example, whether or not a floating point accelerator is used.

A very recent technical report by Sobkow, Pospisil and Yang [5] describes an algorithm (the SPY algorithm) which also uses an encoding scheme for line segments. They also used experimental analysis to show that their algorithm is faster than both of the CS and the LB algorithms. In the experiment they showed that the LB algorithm is slower than the CS algorithm when the windows used are large. This inconsistency demonstrates further the weakness of experimental analysis.

Experimental analysis suffers from other problems too. The probabilistic model used to generate random input data may not be realistic. Even when it is realistic, the experiment provides little insight into *why* one algorithm is faster than another.

A common weakness of all the previous algorithms is the need to evaluate intersection points which are not part of the result. For example, given the line and window shown in Figure 1 both the CS and SPY algorithms will compute the intersection point I_L before rejecting the entire line segment (i.e. concluding that the intersection is empty), whereas the LB algorithm will compute parametric values of all the intersection points I_L, I_R, I_B and I_T before rejecting the line segment.

There are many trivial cases in two-dimensional line clipping, and they should be handled with as little computation as possible. For example, when both endpoints lie within the boundaries of the window the LB algorithm computes parametric values of the intersection points with all four window boundaries before deciding that the line needs no clipping. In fact, the LB algorithm always computes these four parametric values when the intersection is non-empty. This explains why the LB algorithm is slower than the CS algorithm when the window is large and there are more line segments with non-empty intersection with the window.

Both the CS and SPY algorithms use an encoding system. This approach divides the problem into a manageable number of cases and thus probably leads to a shorter program. However an encoding system can be the cause of inefficiency. To encode the location of a line segment some comparisons must be performed. Further comparisons on the encoding are then needed before the appropriate calculation of an intersection is done. If we can manage all possible cases without going through an encoding scheme then the appropriate calculations can be done immediately after the initial comparisons.

III. MACHINE-INDEPENDENT EVALUATION OF EFFICIENCY

To evaluate the efficiency of a clipping algorithm, we count up the number of times particular operations are executed in all possible cases. This is possible because clipping is a particularly simple and symmetrical problem. The operations to be counted should be generally recognised as most time-consuming and should also be indispensible in a clipping algorithm. What these operations should be depends on the level of abstraction we think about the algorithm and the assumptions we make of the computing environment.

The operations we have chosen are comparisons and the four arithmetic operations: addition, subtraction, multiplication and division. However, a clipping algorithm which relies heavily on operations other than these will be compared rather unjustly favourably in our evaluation. For example, the CS algorithm relies heavily on set operations on codes which are absent in the LB algorithm. This is indeed the most difficult hurdle in designing a machine-independent evaluation, namely, all operations are different and we are not comparing like with like.

To be able to progress from an evaluation scheme to the design of an efficient clipping algorithm, we also need to make some assumptions on the relative speeds (or costs) of these operations to be counted. The assumptions should be true in most computing environments. We have assumed that the operations comparison, addition, subtraction, multiplication and division are decreasing in speed in that order. This is true in most computing environments without a floating point accelerator. With a floating point accelerator, addition and subtraction are about the same speed with the latter slightly slower, multiplication and division are about the same speed with the latter slightly slower, and addition and subtraction are slower than multiplication and division. So, the most general assumption that applies to both kinds of environments is that subtraction is slower than addition and division is slower than multiplication. Even though we designed our algorithm with the initial assumption in mind, our algorithm is shown to be faster than the LB algorithm in all cases with the most general assumption, and faster than the CS algorithm in all cases averaged over symmetry with the most general assumption if the difference in speed between division and multiplication is greater than the difference between subtraction and addition.

IV. DEFINITIONS

The lines x = xleft, x = xright, y = ybottom and y = ytop are called the left, right, bottom and top boundaries of the window respectively. A point, a line segment or a portion of a line segment which lies entirely inside the window is *visible*. A point, a line segment or a portion of a line segment which lies entirely outside the window is *invisible*. A line segment which lies partly inside the window and partly outside is *partially visible*. If a line segment is invisible then no part of the line segment appears in the output, and the line segment is said to be *rejected* by the clipping algorithm. The boundaries of the window divide the 2-dimensional Cartesian plane into 9 *regions*. We call regions which are bounded by only 2 boundaries the *corner regions*, and the regions which are bounded by 3 boundaries, the *edge regions*. (See Figure 2)

V. A HIERARCHICAL ANALYSIS OF THE PROBLEM

Given a line segment with endpoints P1=(x1,y1) and P2=(x2,y2), P1 is located in the window, an edge region or a corner region. In each of these cases, P2 may be at any point on the 2-dimensional Cartesian plane. We can divide all possible positions of P2 (i.e. the whole plane) into regions each of which corresponds to intersection points at the same boundaries (or none) to be output. Figures 3 to 5 show the subdivisions. In those figures, if P2 lies in a region filled with character L, R, B or T, the line P1P2 will intersect the left, right, bottom or top boundary respectively. Combinations of two characters indicate the need for two intersection points. Unfilled regions require calculation of no intersection points. These three figures are sufficient to represent all cases, because all other cases are the same as one of them up to a rotation of a multiple of 90° about the origin or a reflection about the line x = −y, or a combination of the two.

This analysis leads naturally to an algorithm. Given the input P1 and P2, characterize the location of P1 among the 9 regions. According to that, characterize the location of P2 among the appropriate subdivisions. Then, calculate the intersection points according to the characterization. In this way, only the intersection points required for output are calculated.

VI. DESIGN OF THE ALGORITHM

1. Characterization of the endpoints

Characterization of P1 is straightforward. Characterization of P2 could involve a lot of arithmetic operations, because not all boundaries of the subdivision are vertical or horizontal. Observe that all oblique parts of the subdivision boundaries are formed by a line joining P1 to a corner of the window. For example, consider the line joining P1 to the left-top corner in Figure 4. P2 is above this line if and only if

$$(ytop-y1) * (x2-x1) < (xleft-x1) * (y2-y1).$$

Note that the arithmetic operations involved in making this comparison must be performed if intersection points at the top and left boundaries are to be calculated, so the effort involved in this comparison can be useful.

2. Geometric Transformations

Since P1 may be in any one of the 9 regions, each of which corresponds to a different subdivision, a different procedure can be written to handle each case. However, this can be very error-prone because the programmer will be writing similar but not identical code many times. A more satisfactory way is to exploit the symmetry of the problem as much as possible so that all cases symmetrical to each other are transformed geometrically to the same case and are handled by only one piece of code. This approach raises the fear that geometric transformations may involve a lot of arithmetic operations. However, a closer examination of the required geometric transformations revealed that the only operations involved are unary minus and assignment. A complete list of the required geometric transformations and their Pascal implementations are as follows:

Rotation of 90° clockwise about the origin:
```
procedure rotate90c (var x,y : real);
  var t: real; begin t := x; x := y ; y := -t end;
```

Rotation of 180° clockwise about the origin:
```
procedure rotate180c (var x,y : real);
begin x := -x; y := -y end;
```

Rotation of 270° clockwise about the origin:
```
procedure rotate270c (var x,y : real);
  var t: real; begin t := x; x := -y; y := t end;
```

Reflection about the line x = −y :
```
procedure reflectxminusy (var x,y : real);
  var t: real; begin t := x; x := -y; y := -t end;
```

Reflection about the x-axis:
```
procedure reflectxaxis (var x,y: real);
begin y := -y end;
```

By employing these simple transformations, the number of different cases becomes manageable and we can optimize each of them with confidence. However, we are not limiting ourselves from bringing the algorithm to its most efficient form – a form that is free from these geometrical transformations and procedure calls. As will be explained in a later section, a mechanical software transformation can be applied to the code to bring it to such a form.

VII. DETAILS OF THE ALGORITHM

P1 can be beyond the left boundary, beyond the right boundary or between the two boundaries. The first two cases are symmetrical up to a rotation of 180° about the origin, and can be handled together. A Pascal implementation of the main procedure is:

```
procedure clip
  (xleft, ytop, xright, ybottom,
   x1,y1,x2,y2: real);
  var display : boolean;
begin
  if x1 < xleft then
    leftcolumn (xleft, ytop, xright, ybottom,
          x1, y1, x2, y2, display)
  else if x1 > xright then begin
    rotate180c (x1, y1); rotate180c (x2, y2);
    leftcolumn (-xright, -ybottom, -xleft, -ytop,
          x1, y1, x2, y2, display);
    rotate180c (x1, y1); rotate180c (x2, y2);
  end else
    centrecolumn (xleft, ytop, xright, ybottom,
           x1, y1, x2, y2, display);

  if display then
    {display the visible part of the line segment,
     which is now between the current values of
     (x1,y1) and (x2,y2)}
end { clip } ;
```

Now we need consider only the cases where P1 is beyond the left boundary or between the left and right boundaries.

1. P1 is beyond the left boundary

Now, it is pointless to further characterize P1, if P2 is also beyond the left boundary. So, we should check that before proceeding on. P1 can be beyond the top boundary, beyond the bottom boundary or between the two boundaries. Again, the first two cases are symmetrical up to a certain transformation, and can be handled together. The transformation should not only map the left-bottom corner region to the left-top corner region, but should also preserve the fact that P2 is not beyond the left boundary. A reflection about the x-axis satisfies the criteria. A Pascal implementation of the procedure is:

```
procedure leftcolumn
  (xleft, ytop, xright, ybottom: real;
   var x1,y1,x2,y2: real; var display: boolean);
begin
  if x2 < xleft then display := false
  else if y1 > ytop then
    topleftcorner (xleft, ytop, xright, ybottom,
           x1, y1, x2, y2, display)
  else if y1 < ybottom then begin
    reflectxaxis (x1, y1); reflectxaxis (x2, y2);
    topleftcorner (xleft, -ybottom, xright, -ytop,
           x1, y1, x2, y2, display);
    reflectxaxis (x1, y1); reflectxaxis (x2, y2)
  end else leftedge (xleft, ytop, xright, ybottom,
           x1, y1, x2, y2, display)
end { leftcolumn } ;
```

1.1. P1 is in the left-top corner region and P2 is not beyond the left boundary

Now, it is pointless to proceed if P2 is beyond the top boundary. We check that first, and then start to characterize P2 among the subdivisions in Figure 5. To reduce the number of different cases by half (approximately), we compare P2 against the line joining P1 and the left-top corner. The case in which P2 is on one side of this line is symmetrical to the case in which it is on the other side. So, we only need to handle one of the two cases. Notice that up to this point, we still do not know whether the subdivisions are as in Figure 5 or its reflection about the line x = -y. If the line segment P1P2 is partially visible then this comparison is unavoidable. A Pascal implementation of the procedure is:

```
procedure topleftcorner
  (xleft, ytop, xright, ybottom: real;
   var x1,y1,x2,y2: real; var display: boolean);
  var relx2, rely2, topproduct, leftproduct: real;
begin
  if y2 > ytop then display := false
  else begin
    relx2 := x2 - x1; rely2 := y2 - y1;
    topproduct := (ytop - y1) * relx2 ;
    leftproduct := (xleft - x1) * rely2;
    if topproduct > leftproduct then
      leftbottomregion
        (xleft, ytop, xright, ybottom,
         x1, y1, x2, y2, display,
         relx2, rely2, leftproduct)
    else begin
      reflectxminusy (x1, y1);
      reflectxminusy (x2, y2);
      leftbottomregion
        (-ytop, -xleft, -ybottom, -xright,
         x1, y1, x2, y2, display,
         -rely2, -relx2, topproduct);
      reflectxminusy (x1, y1);
      reflectxminusy (x2, y2)
    end
  end
end { topleftcorner } ;
```

1.1.1. P1 is in the left-top corner, P2 is not beyond the left boundary, and P2 is to the right of the vector from P1 to the left-top corner

If P2 is above the bottom boundary, then no more oblique boundaries need to be compared. The intersection point(s) that should be calculated are as shown in Figure 5. If P2 is below the bottom boundary, then there are 3 possibilities. The boundary formed by the line joining P1 to the left-bottom corner has to be compared no matter which side of the right boundary P2 happens to be on. So, we do this comparison first. Now, if P2 is to the left of the right boundary, we have no more oblique boundaries to be compared. Otherwise, one more comparison with an oblique boundary will decide which subdivision P2 is in. A Pascal implementation is as follows:

```
procedure leftbottomregion
  (xleft, ytop, xright, ybottom: real;
   var x1,y1,x2,y2: real; var display: boolean;
   relx2, rely2, leftproduct : real);
  var bottomproduct, rightproduct : real;
begin
  if y2 >= ybottom then begin
    if x2 > xright then begin
      y2 := y1 + (xright - x1) * rely2/relx2;
      x2 := xright
    end;
    y1 := y1 + leftproduct/relx2; x1 := xleft;
    display := true
  end else begin
    bottomproduct := (ybottom - y1) * relx2;
    if bottomproduct > leftproduct then
      display := false
    else begin
      if x2 > xright then begin
        rightproduct := (xright - x1) * rely2;
        if bottomproduct > rightproduct then begin
          x2 := x1 + bottomproduct/rely2;
          y2 := ybottom;
        end else begin
          y2 := y1 + rightproduct/relx2;
          x2 := xright;
        end;
      end else begin
        x2 := x1 + bottomproduct/rely2;
        y2 ;= ybottom;
      end;
      y1 := y1 + leftproduct/relx2; x1 := xleft;
      display := true
    end
  end
end { leftbottomregion } ;
```

1.2. P1 is in the left edge region

If P2 is beyond the left boundary, then the line segment should be rejected. Otherwise, P2 can be above the top boundary, below the bottom boundary, or between the two boundaries. The first two cases are symmetrical to each other and should be handled together. The last case is quite obvious from Figure 4. A Pascal implementation is as follows:

```
procedure leftedge
  (xleft, ytop, xright, ybottom : real;
   var x1,y1,x2,y2: real; var display: boolean);
  var relx2, rely2: real;
begin
  if x2 < xleft then display := false
  else if y2 < ybottom then
    p2bottom (xleft, ytop, xright, ybottom,
           x1, y1, x2, y2, display)
  else if y2 > ytop then begin
    reflectxaxis (x1, y1); reflectxaxis (x2, y2);
    p2bottom (xleft, -ybottom, xright, -ytop,
           x1, y1, x2, y2, display);
    reflectxaxis (x1, y1); reflectxaxis (x2, y2)
  end else begin
    relx2 := x2 - x1; rely2 := y2 - y1;
    if x2 > xright then begin
      y2 := y1 + rely2 * (xright - x1)/relx2;
      x2 := xright
    end;
    y1 := y1 + rely2 * (xleft - x1)/relx2 ;
    x1 := xleft;
    display := true
  end
end { leftedge } ;
```

1.2.1. P1 is in the left edge region, P2 is not beyond the left boundary and P2 is beyond the bottom boundary

Comparing with the boundary joining P1 to the left-bottom corner cannot be avoided by comparing with any vertical or horizontal boundaries first. We, therefore, perform the comparison first before comparing with the right boundary which may save us from further comparisons. A Pascal implementation is as follows:

```
procedure p2bottom
  (xleft, ytop, xright, ybottom :real;
   var x1,y1,x2,y2: real; var display: boolean);
  var leftproduct, bottomproduct, rightproduct,
     relx2, rely2: real;
begin
  relx2 := x2 - x1; rely2 := y2 - y1;
  leftproduct := (xleft - x1) * rely2;
  bottomproduct := (ybottom - y1) * relx2;
  if bottomproduct > leftproduct then
    display := false
  else begin
    if x2 <= xright then begin
      x2 := x1 + bottomproduct/rely2;
      y2 := ybottom;
    end else begin
      rightproduct := (xright - x1) * rely2;
      if bottomproduct > rightproduct then begin
```

```
      x2 := x1 + bottomproduct/rely2;
      y2 := ybottom;
    end else begin
      y2 := y1 + rightproduct/relx2;
      x2 := xright;
    end;
  end;
  y1 := y1 + leftproduct/relx2; x1 := xleft;
  display := true
 end
end { p2bottom } ;
```

2. P1 is between the left and right boundaries

If P1 is above the top boundary or below the bottom boundary, the case is symmetrical to that if P1 is in the left edge region, and we will use the same procedure. A Pascal implementation is as follows:

```
procedure centrecolumn
  (xleft, ytop, xright, ybottom: real;
   var x1,y1,x2,y2: real; var display: boolean);
begin
  if y1 > ytop then begin
    rotate270c (x1, y1); rotate270c (x2, y2);
    leftedge (-ytop, xright, -ybottom, xleft,
          x1, y1, x2, y2, display);
    rotate90c (x1, y1); rotate90c (x2, y2)
  end else if y1 < ybottom then begin
    rotate90c (x1, y1); rotate90c (x2, y2);
    leftedge (ybottom, -xleft, ytop, -xright,
          x1, y1, x2, y2, display);
    rotate270c (x1, y1); rotate270c (x2, y2)
  end else
    inside (xleft, ytop, xright, ybottom,
          x1, y1, x2, y2, display)
end { centrecolumn } ;
```

2.1. P1 is in the window

If P2 is in an edge region then the intersection point to be calculated is obvious from Figure 3. If P2 is in a corner region then comparison with one oblique boundary is necessary before the appropriate intersection points are calculated. Again, symmetry is used to reduce the number of different cases. A Pascal implementation is as follows:

```
procedure inside
  (xleft, ytop, xright, ybottom: real;
   var x1,y1,x2,y2: real; var display: boolean);
  procedure p2left
    (xleft, ytop, xright, ybottom: real;
     var x1,y1,x2,y2: real);
    procedure p2lefttop
      (xleft, ytop, xright, ybottom: real;
       var x1,y1,x2,y2: real);
    var relx2, rely2,
       leftproduct, topproduct: real;
    begin relx2 := x2 - x1; rely2 := y2 - y1;
      leftproduct := rely2 * (xleft - x1);
      topproduct := relx2 * (ytop - y1);
      if topproduct > leftproduct then begin
        x2 := x1 + topproduct / rely2; y2 := ytop
      end else begin
        y2 := y1 + leftproduct / relx2; x2 := xleft
      end
    end { p2lefttop } ;
  begin
    if y2 > ytop then
      p2lefttop (xleft, ytop, xright, ybottom,
            x1, y1, x2, y2)
    else if y2 < ybottom then begin
      rotate90c (x1, y1); rotate90c (x2,y2);
      p2lefttop (ybottom, -xleft, ytop, -xright,
            x1, y1, x2, y2);
      rotate270c (x1, y1); rotate270c (x2,y2)
    end else begin
      y2 := y1 + (y2-y1) * (xleft-x1)/(x2-x1);
      x2 := xleft
    end
  end { p2left } ;
begin
  display := true;
  if x2 < xleft then
    p2left (xleft, ytop, xright, ybottom,
         x1, y1, x2, y2)
  else if x2 > xright then begin
    rotate180c (x1, y1); rotate180c (x2, y2);
    p2left (-xright, -ybottom, -xleft, -ytop,
         x1, y1, x2, y2);
    rotate180c (x1, y1); rotate180c (x2, y2)
  end else if y2 > ytop then begin
    x2 := x1 + (x2 -x1) * (ytop - y1)/(y2 - y1);
    y2 := ytop
  end else if y2 < ybottom then begin
    x2 := x1 + (x2-x1) * (ybottom-y1)/(y2-y1);
    y2 := ybottom
  end
  {else P2 is inside,
  just display, no need to clip}
end { inside } ;
```

Now, we have handled all possible cases.

VIII. ANALYSIS OF THE ALGORITHM

To analyse the efficiency of the algorithm, we insert extra variables in our Pascal implementation to count up the number of comparisons, additions, subtractions, multiplications and divisions in all the different cases. For the sake of comparison, we do the same to the CS algorithm and the LB algorithm. To normalize the effect of the different order in which the window boundaries are considered in the algorithms, we average the result over symmetry. For the cases in which P1 is in the window or in an edge region, we average over the 4 rotations of a multiple of 90°. For the case in which P1 is in a corner region, we average over the 4 rotations of a multiple of 90° and their reflections about the line x = -y. The results are displayed in Figures 6 to 8. From the analysis, we can draw the following conclusions (and these conclusions are machine independent) :

1. Our algorithm has the fewest number of divisions, equal to the number of intersection points for output.

2. Our algorithm has fewest comparisons, in most cases about 1/3 of the CS algorithm and about 1/2 of the LB algorithm.

3. If we assume only that (i) subtraction is slower than addition, (ii) division is slower than multiplication and (iii) the difference in speed between subtraction and addition is smaller than that between division and multiplication, then our algorithm is the most efficient.

4. The LB algorithm requires the largest number of multiplications + divisions in all cases, and the largest number of arithmetic operations in most cases.

5. The CS algorithm requires the largest number of comparisons in most cases. (To allow for possible *short-circuit evaluation* we treat the while condition as 2 comparisons instead of 3.)

6. The LB algorithm is the slowest in most trivial reject cases.

7. When the window is large, the dominating case is when P2 is in the window in Figure 6. In this case, the CS algorithm does very few set operations, and so the LB algorithm is the slowest.

8. When the window is small, the dominating cases are the four corner regions of Figure 8. If P1 and P2 are in corner regions at opposite ends of a diagonal of the window, then the CS algorithm may require twice as many comparisons as the LB algorithm. In this case the CS algorithm performs many set operations, so it may be slower than the LB algorithm. A floating point accelerator makes this more likely, because the CS algorithm has more additions and subtractions than the LB algorithm in this case.

The LB algorithm clips vertical and horizontal line segments faster than oblique line segments, hence a detailed analysis of the LB algorithm has been performed. This detailed analysis does not alter the conclusions.

IX. TRANSFORMATION OF THE ALGORITHM

The algorithm presented above uses explicit geometric transformations (rotations and reflections) to exploit the symmetries present in the problem. Thus sections of the algorithm have the form:

1) transform the positions of the line and the window ;
2) clip the line to that window ;
3) transform the clipped line to its original position ;

illustrated by the following statements from the main procedure "clip":

```
rotate180c (x1, y1) ; rotate180c (x2, y2) ;
leftcolumn (-xright, -ybottom, -xleft, -ytop,
        x1, y1, x2, y2, display) ;
rotate180c (x1, y1) ; rotate180c (x2, y2) ;
```

In addition to the arithmetic operations and comparisons of procedure leftcolumn, we have additional assignments and negations in precedure rotate180c, as well as the negations (and passing) of parameters to procedure leftcolumn. We will now explain how correctness-preserving program transformations are used to eliminate these extra operations. In this way we can construct a highly efficient algorithm from a form in which it is less efficient, but easier to follow.

1. Basic transformations

Let x and y be lists of variable names, with no names in common. Let E be a list of expressions, of the same length as x. Let F(x) be a list of expressions, of the same length as x and possibly involving some of the names in x. Then:

(a) (x,y := E,y) = (x := E)
For example,
(x1,y1,x2,y2 := -x1,-y1,x2,y2) = (x1,y1 := -x1,-y1)

(b) (x := E ; x := F(x)) = (x := F(E))
For example,
(x1,y1 := -x1,-y1; x1,y1 := x1,-y1)
= (x1,y1 := -x1,-(-y1)) = (x1,y1 := -x1,y1)

(c) (x := E ; if p(x) then S1 else S2) =
(if p(E) then begin x := E ; S1 end
else begin x := E ; S2 end)
For example,
(x2,y2 := -x2,-y2; if x2 < xl then S1 else S2)
= (if -x2 < xl then begin x2,y2 := -x2,-y2; S1 end
else begin x2,y2 := -x2,-y2; S2 end)

(d) (x := x) = ()   – the empty statement

(e) (if b then S1 else S2 ; x := E) =
(if b then begin S1 ; x := E end
else begin S2 ; x := E end)
For example,

```
(if tp > lp then S1 else S2 ; x1,y1 := -y1,x1)
= (if tp > lp then begin S1 ; x1,y1 := -y1,x1 end
  else begin S2 ; x1,y1 := -y1,x1 end)
```

These transformations (identified by Hoare *et al.* in [6]) may be used to eliminate many assignments by modifying statements following the assignments, as seen particularly in transformations (b) and (c). We illustrate this process by transforming the text of the procedure p2left.

2. Example: Transformation of p2left

p2left has the form:

```
if y2 > ytop then p2lefttop ...
else if y2 < ybottom then
  (rotate90c ... ; p2lefttop ... ; rotate270c ...)
else (y2 := ... ; x2 := ...)
```

The section of text to be transformed is

```
rotate90c ... ; p2lefttop ... ; rotate270c ...
```

which may be written as

```
x1,y1,x2,y2 := y1,-x1,y2,-x2 ;
p2lefttop ... ;
x1,y1,x2,y2 := -y1,x1,-y2,x2 ;
```

which is, expanding the parameter substitution involved in the call to p2lefttop,

```
x1,y1,x2,y2 := y1,-x1,y2,-x2 ;
xleft,ytop,xright,ybottom :=
          ybottom,-xleft,ytop,-xright ;
... body of procedure p2lefttop ... ;
x1,y1,x2,y2 := -y1,x1,-y2,x2 ;
```

Using transformation rules (a) and (b) and simplifying arithmetic expressions, the first four assignments of p2lefttop, which read

```
relx2 := x2 - x1 ; rely2 := y2 - y1 ;
leftproduct := rely2 * (xleft - x1) ;
topproduct := relx2 * (ytop - y1) ;
```

will become simply

```
relx2 := y2 - y1 ; rely2 := x1 - x2 ;
leftproduct := rely2 * (ybottom - y1) ;
topproduct := relx2 * (x1 - xleft) ;
```

Similarly transformation rules (c) and (e) allow us to rewrite the if statement of p2lefttop as

```
if topproduct > leftproduct then begin
  x1,y1,x2,y2 := y1,-x1,y2,-x2 ;
  xleft,ytop,xright,ybottom :=
          ybottom,-xleft,ytop,-xright ;
  x2 := x1 + topproduct / rely2 ; y2 := ytop ;
  x1,y1,x2,y2 := -y1,x1,-y2,x2
end else begin
  x1,y1,x2,y2 := y1,-x1,y2,-x2 ;
  xleft,ytop,xright,ybottom :=
          ybottom,-xleft,ytop,-xright ;
  y2 := y1 + leftproduct / relx2 ; x2 := xleft ;
  x1,y1,x2,y2 := -y1,x1,-y2,x2
end
```

which can be further transformed by rules (a) and (b) and then simplified to

```
if topproduct > leftproduct then begin
  x2 := xleft ; y2 := y1 + topproduct / rely2
end else begin
  x2 := x1 - leftproduct / relx2 ; y2 := ybottom
end ;
```

Thus after transformation, including removal of procedure calls, the text of p2left appears as:

```
procedure p2left
  (xleft, ytop, xright, ybottom: real ;
   var x1, y1, x2, y2: real) ;
  var relx2, rely2, leftproduct, topproduct: real ;
begin
  if y2 > ytop then begin
    ... text of p2lefttop ...
  end else if y2 < ybottom then begin
    relx2 := y2 - y1 ; rely2 := x1 - x2 ;
    leftproduct := rely2 * (ybottom - y1) ;
    topproduct := relx2 * (x1 - xleft) ;
    if topproduct > leftproduct then begin
      x2 := xleft ; y2 := y1 + topproduct / rely2
    end else begin
      x2 := x1 - leftproduct / relx2 ;
      y2 := ybottom
    end
  end else begin
    y2 := y1 + (y2-y1) * (xleft-x1) / (x2-x1) ;
    x2 := xleft
  end
end { p2left } ;
```

3. Observations on the transformations

Performing the above transformations reduces the number of assignments and negations executed in clipping a line. However the size of the program text increases considerably, so that it is not practical to provide the complete text here. Furthermore, since considerable effort is required to apply the transformations throughout the program, the transformations should be applied by a program (and not manually). Program transformation systems do exist (for example [7]), but we have not used such software to support development of this algorithm.

X. CONCLUSIONS AND FUTURE WORK

We have developed a new 2-dimensional line clipping algorithm. Using a machine-independent analysis, we have shown that this algorithm is faster than both the Cohen-Sutherland algorithm and the Liang-Barsky algorithm. Using program transformation techniques we showed how geometric transformations on the line to be clipped could be performed by modified program text without the overhead of actually executing statements to perform the transformation. Currently, we are investigating the possibility of extending it to polygons and to the 3-dimensional case.

Acknowledgements The authors would like to acknowledge the useful discussions with colleagues and students at the University of Western Ontario, especially Tim Walsh. We are very grateful for the reviewers' suggestions, which we have incorporated, within the space allowed. Financial upport for this research was provided by the National Science and Engineering Research Council (NSERC) of Canada.

REFERENCES

[1] Newman, W. M. and R. F. Sproull. Principles of Interactive Computer Graphics, 2nd ed., McGraw-Hill, New York, 1979.

[2] Sproull, R. F. and I. E. Sutherland. A Clipping Divider, FJCC 1968, Thompson Books, Washington, D.C., pp. 765-775.

[3] Cyrus, M. and J. Beck. Generalised Two- and Three-Dimensional Clipping, Computers and Graphics, Vol. 3, No. 1, 1978, pp. 23-28.

[4] Liang, Y.-D. and B. A. Barsky. A New Concept and Method for Line Clipping, ACM Transactions on Graphics, Vol. 3, No. 1, 1984, pp. 1-22.

[5] Sobkow, M. S., Pospisil, P. and Y.-H. Yang. A Fast Two-Dimensional Line Clipping Algorithm, University of Saskatchewan Technical Report, 86-2.

[6] Hoare, C. A. R. et al. Laws of Programming: a tutorial paper, Oxford University Programming Research Group PRG-45, 1985.

[7] Arsac, J. J. Syntactic Source to Source Transforms and Program Manipulation, Communications of the ACM, Vol. 22, No. 1, 1979, pp. 43-54.

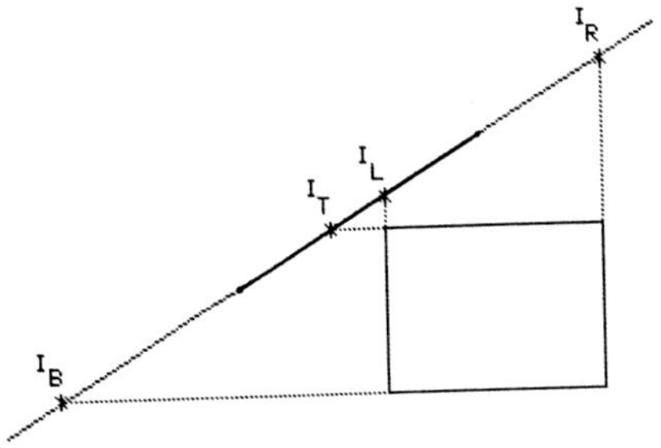

Fig. 1 Intersection points computed by previous algorithms

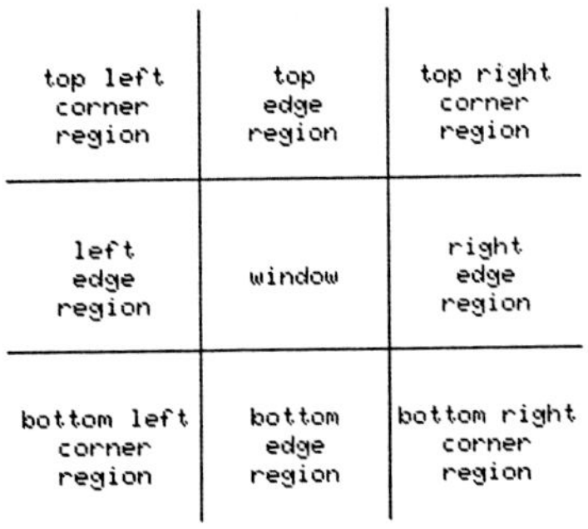

Fig. 2 Subdivision of the plane into regions

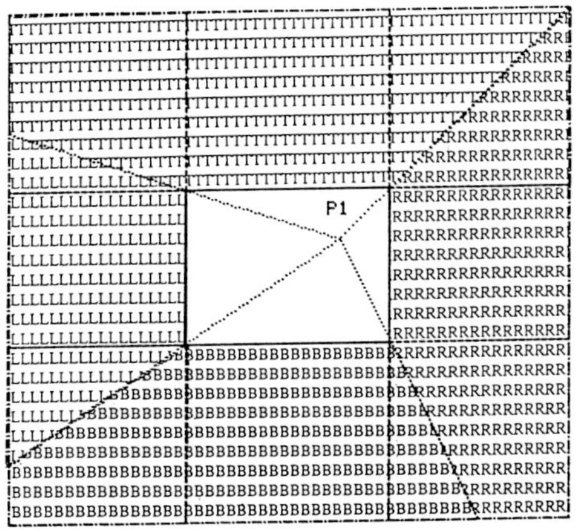

Fig. 3 Subdivision of the plane when P1 is in the window

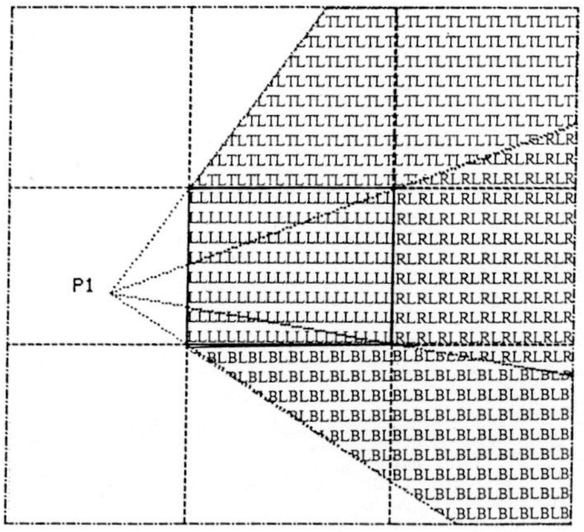

Fig. 4 Subdivision of the plane when P1 is in an edge region

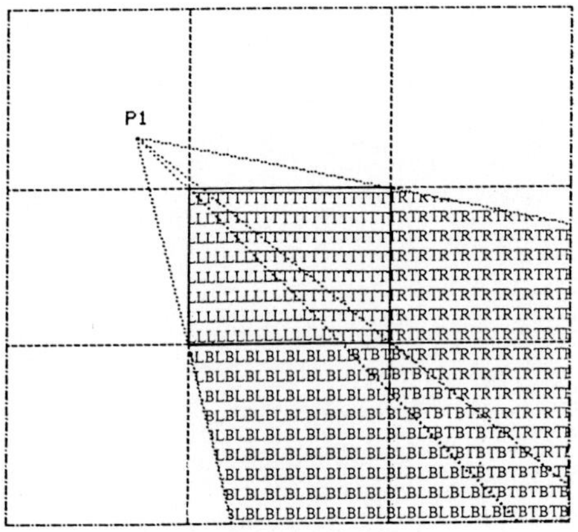

Fig. 5 Subdivision of the plane when P1 is in a corner region

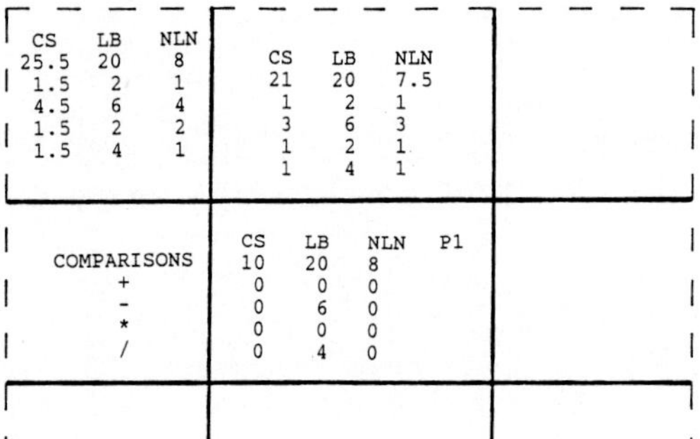

FIG.6 Analysis of the three algorithms when P1 is in the window

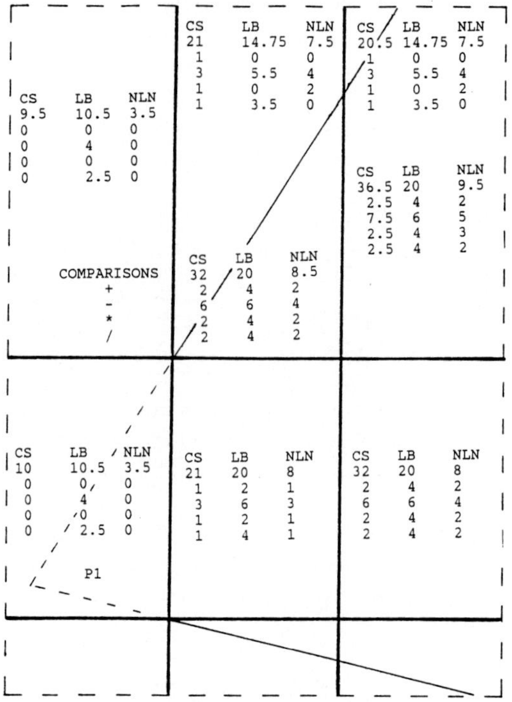

FIG.7 Analysis of the three algorithms when P1 is in an edge region

"Further subdivision is needed. Average shown is for the largest unbounded subregion."

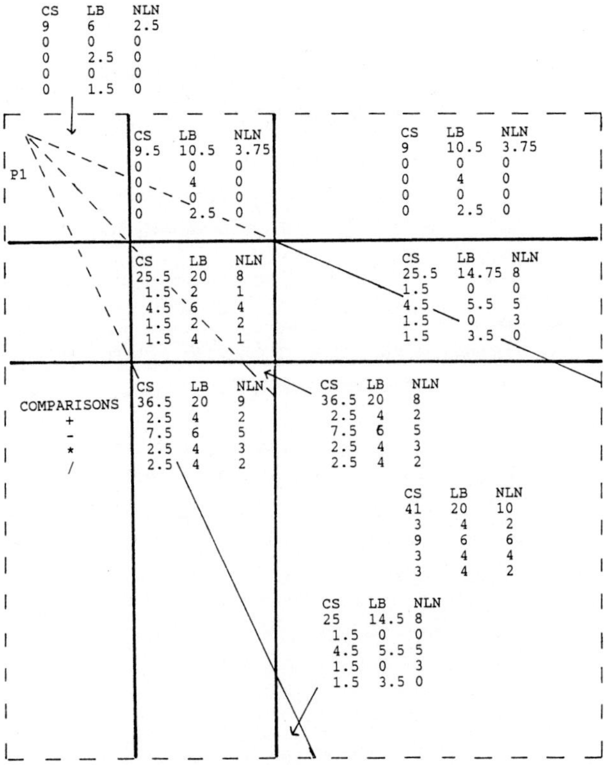

FIG.8 Analysis of the three algorithms when P1 is in a corner region

PLANAR 2-PASS TEXTURE MAPPING AND WARPING

Alvy Ray Smith
Pixar

ABSTRACT

The 2-pass transformation replaces a 2-D (2-dimensional) transformation with a sequence of orthogonal, simpler 1-D transformations. It may be used for the closely related processes of texture mapping and warping in computer graphics and image processing. First, texture maps onto planar quadric and superquadric surfaces and, second, planar bicubic and biquadratic warps of images are shown to be 2-pass transformable. A distinction between serial and parallel warps is introduced to solve a confusion in terms between computer graphics and image processing. It is shown that an n-th order serial polynomial warp is equivalent to an (n^2+n)-th order parallel polynomial warp. It is also shown that the serial equivalent to a parallel polynomial warp is generally not a polynomial warp, being more complicated than a polynomial. The unusual problem of bottlenecking and the usual one of antialiasing are discussed in the 2-pass context.

KEY WORDS AND PHRASES

2-pass, texture mapping, warping, serial warp, parallel warp, quadrics, superquadrics, bicubic warp, biquadratic warp, bottleneck, antialiasing

CR CATEGORY

8.2

INTRODUCTION

The term *warping* is often used in image processing to mean a 2-D resampling of an image. For example, when a photo of the Earth's surface is transmitted from a satellite to ground, it is typically warped to correct the surface patch for surface curvature, an oblique viewing angle, or lens aberrations. In general, warping is a continuous mapping of a 2-D planar region into another 2-D planar region. In image processing, it is the digital approximation of such a mapping which is of interest.

The term *texture mapping* is used in computer graphics to also mean 2-D resampling of an image, particularly when the target is the 2-D projection of a 3-D surface, viewed through a viewing transformation with perspective. It is the digital approximation of a presumably continuous mapping that is of interest in computer graphics also.

A useful distinction may be made between the use of warping in image processing and texture mapping in computer graphics. Image processing uses the mapping to correct or rectify images - to map a nonrectangular patch onto a rectangular one - while computer graphics proceeds the other direction to map a rectangular patch onto a nonrectangular one.

Another distinction - a confusion really - between the two historically separate disciplines is not helpful. The terms *biquadratic* and *bicubic* are used differently by the two groups. The terms *serial map (warp)* and *parallel map (warp)* are introduced to clarify this situation.

Examples from each of computer graphics and image processing are examined here and shown to be effectively simplified using the 2-pass technique [3]. First, the 2-pass texture mapping of a texture onto a planar superquadric surface is derived. For example, a rectangular framebuffer picture may be mapped onto a disk by the technique. Then the 2-pass warping of an image onto a planar bicubic or biquadratic patch is derived. The case where the edge of an image remains a rectangle but the interior points are warped - which is called a *frozen-edge warp* - is particulary suitable for image processing. Then the mathematical relationship between serial and parallel warps is derived using some of these results as examples.

Finally, two generic problems with the 2-pass technique are emphasized. The mathematical problem of *bottlenecking* is reexamined, and since it is the digital approximation of the 2-pass technique which is of primary interest, the important subject of antialiasing is investigated.

The work here builds on the original paper [3] and contains results derived in a series of internal technical memos [7-10].

2-PASS NOTATION AND REVIEW

If u_s and v_s are the coordinates of a source picture and u_t and v_t those of a target, then a general *parallel 2-D coordinate mapping* - or *parallel map* for short - may be defined by any two functions x and y such that

$$(u_t, v_t) = (\, x(u_s, v_s),\, y(u_s, v_s)\,)\,.$$

In this paper, u and v are understood to be parameterizations of the horizontal and vertical coordinates of a picture. Parameters u and v with no subscript are assumed to be u_s and v_s.

A *picture* of course is a mapping of each point of uv parameter space to a set of colors - e.g., the grays. The term *image* will be used here to mean picture - as in "image computing" or "image processing" - as well as for its usual mathematical meaning, with the context distinguishing which use is intended. The term *image computing* will be used to mean all of traditional computer graphics plus all of traditional image processing. This paper is an image computing paper because parallel maps include the texture maps of computer graphics and the warps of image processing. Thus parallel maps will also be called *parallel warps*.

The objects on which digital image computing focuses are digitized pictures - *sampled* versions of continuous images, where each sample is of course a pixel. Although we will talk of mappings of the set of continuous pictures to itself, it is really the sampled source and target pictures which are of ultimate interest.

Sampling and filtering theory is now a well-understood discipline for correctly representing continuous pictures by arrays of pixels, but it is computationally expensive. The *2-pass technique* is interesting because it suggests a cheaper solution for parallel maps on sampled pictures although it is a technique described in terms of continuous functions and pictures.

Perhaps the most general presentation of the 2-pass technique appears in [3], but approximately simultaneous work was occurring in industry [2] and in image processing [5]. All of these in turn refer to earlier works on the special case of image rotation in the plane.

The basic idea is to replace a parallel map with a sequence, or composition, of parallel maps, where each mapping in the sequence is computationally more interesting (e.g., cheaper) than the original map. The 2-pass technique replaces a given parallel map with a sequence of two parallel maps, where the first applied is called the *first pass,* or *horizontal pass,* and takes the form

$$(u_i, v_i) = (f_{v_s}(u_s), v_s)$$

where u_i and v_i are the coordinates of the *intermediate* image. The *second pass,* or *vertical pass* takes the form

$$(u_t, v_t) = (u_i, g_{u_i}(v_i))\,.$$

The decomposition of a parallel map into a sequence of mappings results in an overall mapping from source to target called a *serial 2-D coordinate mapping* or a *serial map (serial warp)* for short. (It has been shown that three mappings in the sequence is of interest in the case of rotation in the plane [6].)

It is sometimes important to reverse the order of the decomposition, with the vertical pass first, the horizontal pass second. The functional expressions are generally different for the two orderings. When a distinction between the two orderings is required, "horizontal pass first" or the "vertical pass first" will be used. The horizontal pass first is assumed unless otherwise stated. See Figure 1.

Each of the two mappings, the first and second passes, is considered simpler than the given parallel map because f_{v_s} applies across a line of constant v_s and g_{u_i} down a line of constant u_i. In the digital approximation, lines of constant v_s are the horizontal scanlines and those of constant u_i are vertical scanlines. Resampling along a scanline is a 1-D problem. Thus, in a sense, the 2-pass technique is the replacement of a 2-D resampling problem with a sequence of two 1-D resamplings. A more careful analysis shows that a true 1-D resampling is sometimes inadequate, but a simplified 2-D resampling may suffice. This will be explored further below.

The 2-Pass Technique

The problem of replacing a given parallel map with a serial equivalent was solved in [3]. It is restated and solved again here to show the use of the current notation. Given parallel map

$$(x(u_s, v_s),\, y(u_s, v_s)) = (u_t, v_t)\,,$$

it is desired to decompose it into two sequential mappings

$$(x'(u_s, v_s),\, v_s) = (u_i, v_i)$$

$$(u_i,\, y'(u_i, v_i)) = (u_t, v_t)\,.$$

The problem is to express x' and y', the two sequential *scanline functions,* as functions of the given mappings x and y and the source coordinates u_s and v_s for x' or the intermediate coordinates u_i and v_i for y'. The horizontal-pass scanline function is obvious:

$$x'(u_s, v_s) \equiv f_{v_s}(u_s) = x(u_s, v_s)\,.$$

We shall call this the *first step* of the 2-pass technique. For the vertical-pass scanline function, note that $u_i = x(u_s, v_s)$ and $v_s = v_i$. Let h_{u_i} be the solution of $u_i = x(u_s, v_s)$ for u_s. This solution is the *second step.* So h_{u_i} is a function of $v_s = v_i$ and

$$y'(u_i, v_i) \equiv g_{u_i}(v_i) = y(h_{u_i}(v_i), v_i)$$

for the *third step.* Vertical-pass-first scanline functions are derived in an analogous manner.

A difficulty with the 2-pass technique is obtaining a closed form for the second-pass scanline function. Sometimes this is not possible and numerical techniques must be used. In other cases, such as when there are multiple solutions h_{u_i}, numerical techniques are preferred. The bicubic and biquadratic warping techniques in this paper are of this variety [8, 9].

Another difficulty is the so-called *bottleneck problem.* There are cases [3] where the two scanline functions exist in closed form but are useless. If the source picture is mapped to a point or to a line segment by the first pass, then it hardly matters that a mapping exists which takes this intermediate image to the desired target picture. Although the shape would be correct, the color information would have been lost in the vanishing area bottleneck of the intermediate image. Although experience has shown that a bottleneck can always be avoided - e.g., by reversing the order of horizontal and vertical passes - this has not yet been proved to be the case.

A final difficulty appears only in the digital approximation of the 2-pass technique. This is the antialiasing problem alluded to earlier. If only 1-D sampling and filtering is used along scanlines, then serious aliasing can occur. In many interesting cases studied in [2, 3, 5], this is not a problem, but in others - such as in this paper (and in [7]) - it is. Again, experience has shown that aliasing artifacts can always be avoided - e.g., by reversing the order of horizontal and vertical passes - but this has not yet been proved to be the case.

SUPERQUADRIC TEXTURE MAPPING

Following Al Barr [1], given a "horizontal" plane curve **h** and a "vertical" modulating plane curve **m**

$$\mathbf{h}(v) = [h_1(v) \;\; h_2(v)], \quad v_0 \le v \le v_1,$$

$$\mathbf{m}(u) = [m_1(u) \;\; m_2(u)], \quad u_0 \le u \le u_1,$$

a *spherical product surface* is defined to be

$$\mathbf{S}(u,v) = [m_1(u)h_1(v) \;\; m_1(u)h_2(v) \;\; m_2(u)]$$

where $u_0 \le u \le u_1$, $v_0 \le v \le v_1$. We have reversed the orientation of **h** and **m** from [1], so **h** is actually vertical here - i.e., it is a function of the vertical parameter v - and **m** is horizontal. A *projected* spherical product surface has $m_2(u) = 0$ - i.e., is the orthographic projection of a spherical product surface into the xy-plane.

Barr [1] has shown how the (super)quadrics - (super)ellipsoids, (super)hyperboloids of one and two sheets, and (super)toroids - can be represented as rescaled spherical product surfaces. A (super)toroid may be thought of as an extended (super)ellipsoid; it has the same form except the modulating function is offset by a constant α and u varies over 2π radians. Table 1 gives the details of the defining functions for the superquadric family. An n-hyperboloid is an hyperboloid with n sheets. In all cases, the superquadrics give the quadrics if the two *squareness parameters* ε and ε' are set to 1.

It will be shown below (see also [7]) that the projected (super)quadrics, under "standard computer graphics transformations", are 2-pass transformable. A parallel map is *2-pass transformable* if it can be converted into an equivalent serial map by the 2-pass technique described above.

The standard computer graphics transformations are the following: In computer graphics, objects are flown through 3-space and projected into 2-space with a perspective projection using a 4x4 matrix multiplication followed with division by the homogeneous coordinate. These classic transformations shall be called *CG transforms*. The 4x4 matrix will be represented here by

$$\mathbf{T} = \begin{bmatrix} \mathbf{a} & \mathbf{e} & \mathbf{i} & \mathbf{m} \\ \mathbf{b} & \mathbf{f} & \mathbf{j} & \mathbf{n} \\ \mathbf{c} & \mathbf{g} & \mathbf{k} & \mathbf{o} \\ \mathbf{d} & \mathbf{h} & \mathbf{l} & \mathbf{p} \end{bmatrix}.$$

The transformation of a point $[X(u,v) \; Y(u,v) \; Z(u,v) \; 1]$ by a CG transform is accomplished by

$$[X' \; Y' \; Z' \; W'] = [X \; Y \; Z \; 1]\mathbf{T}.$$

The homogeneous divide by W' after this transform gives

$$x(u,v) = \frac{X'}{W'} = \frac{\mathbf{a}X + \mathbf{b}Y + \mathbf{c}Z + \mathbf{d}}{\mathbf{m}X + \mathbf{n}Y + \mathbf{o}Z + \mathbf{p}}$$

$$y(u,v) = \frac{Y'}{W'} = \frac{\mathbf{e}X + \mathbf{f}Y + \mathbf{g}Z + \mathbf{h}}{\mathbf{m}X + \mathbf{n}Y + \mathbf{o}Z + \mathbf{p}}.$$

For example, if $X(u,v) = u$, $Y(u,v) = v$, and $Z(u,v) = 0$ and we apply the 2-pass technique, the simple rectangle under CG transform result of [2, 3] is obtained.

The 2-D Superquadric 2-Pass Functions

The 2-D superquadrics are just the projected 3-D superquadrics - i.e., with $m_2(u) = 0$. The horizontal and vertical scanline functions for the 2-D superquadrics under CG transforms are derived to show a typical application of the 2-pass technique.

The general class of 2-D superquadrics under 3-D CG transforms is given by

$$[\, m_1(u)h_1(v) \;\; m_1(u)h_2(v) \;\; 0 \;\; 1 \,] \begin{bmatrix} \mathbf{a} & \mathbf{e} & \mathbf{i} & \mathbf{m} \\ \mathbf{b} & \mathbf{f} & \mathbf{j} & \mathbf{n} \\ \mathbf{c} & \mathbf{g} & \mathbf{k} & \mathbf{o} \\ \mathbf{d} & \mathbf{h} & \mathbf{l} & \mathbf{p} \end{bmatrix}.$$

Scaling factors for the two axes of the projected superquadric have been subsumed into the diagonal elements of the CG transform matrix. Thus

$$x(u,v) = \frac{\mathbf{a}m_1(u)h_1(v) + \mathbf{b}m_1(u)h_2(v) + \mathbf{d}}{\mathbf{m}m_1(u)h_1(v) + \mathbf{n}m_1(u)h_2(v) + \mathbf{p}}$$

$$y(u,v) = \frac{\mathbf{e}m_1(u)h_1(v) + \mathbf{f}m_1(u)h_2(v) + \mathbf{h}}{\mathbf{m}m_1(u)h_1(v) + \mathbf{n}m_1(u)h_2(v) + \mathbf{p}}.$$

Application of the first step of the 2-pass technique immediately yields, as the horizontal scanline function for scanline v_s:

$$f_{v_s}(u) = \frac{\mathbf{A}(v_s)m_1(u) + \mathbf{d}}{\mathbf{M}(v_s)m_1(u) + \mathbf{p}}$$

where

$$\mathbf{A}(v) = \mathbf{a}h_1(v) + \mathbf{b}h_2(v)$$

$$\mathbf{M}(v) = \mathbf{m}h_1(v) + \mathbf{n}h_2(v)\,.$$

The second step is to solve

$$u_i = \frac{\mathbf{A}(v)m_1(u) + \mathbf{d}}{\mathbf{M}(v)m_1(u) + \mathbf{p}}$$

for $u = h_{u_i}(v)$ for vertical scanline u_i. Expanding and rearranging gives

$$m_1(u) = \frac{\mathbf{d} - \mathbf{p}u_i}{\mathbf{M}(v)u_i - \mathbf{A}(v)}.$$

As will be seen immediately, it is unnecessary to complete the solution of this equation for u.

The third step yields the vertical scanline function by substituting the expression just obtained for $m_1(u)$ into the expression above for $y(u,v)$:

$$g_{u_i}(v) = \frac{(\mathbf{d} - \mathbf{p}u_i)(\mathbf{e}h_1(v) + \mathbf{f}h_2(v)) + \mathbf{h}(\mathbf{M}(v)u_i - \mathbf{A}(v))}{(\mathbf{d} - \mathbf{p}u_i)(\mathbf{m}h_1(v) + \mathbf{n}h_2(v)) + \mathbf{p}(\mathbf{M}(v)u_i - \mathbf{A}(v))}.$$

Since $v_i = v_s$, we will drop the subscript from v_i also. The scanline function may be rearranged to give

$$g_{u_i}(v) = \frac{\mathbf{E}(u_i)h_1(v) + \mathbf{F}(u_i)h_2(v)}{\mathbf{G}h_1(v) + \mathbf{H}h_2(v)}.$$

$\mathbf{E}(u)$, $\mathbf{F}(u)$, $\mathbf{G}$, and $\mathbf{H}$ are defined in Table 3, which, with

Table 2, summarizes the application of the formulas just derived to the superquadric family. All quantities are as defined above if not otherwise specified.

The vertical-pass-first scanline functions may be derived similarly by exchanging x and y and also u and v in the expression for the parallel mapping and then applying the 2-pass technique. To get an analytic solution, $\varepsilon' = 1$ must be assumed. This will be called a *semi-superquadric* case.

Suppose it is desired to map the contents of a framebuffer onto a disk with **T** the identity transformation. The parameterization used thus far is awkward for this case since it generates a polar view. A more natural mapping is that used for Figure 2. It corresponds to an ellipsoid expressed as the spherical product surface

$$\mathbf{S}(u,v) = [\ m_2(u)h_1(v)\ \ h_2(v)\ \ m_1(u)h_1(v)\ ]$$

with $m_1(u)$, $m_2(u)$, $h_1(v)$, $h_2(v)$ as before but with $-\pi \le u \le \pi$, $-\frac{\pi}{2} \le v \le \frac{\pi}{2}$. This is nothing more than a permutation of the 3-D coordinates used before and a swapping of the parameter space axes. For the example of mapping a framebuffer to a disk, the horizontal-pass-first formulas hold for the superquadric case in the alternative parameterization, just as before, and the vertical-pass-first functions are similarly good only up to the semi-superquadrics. Figure 2 also illustrates exercise of the two squareness parameters.

BICUBIC AND BIQUADRATIC WARPING

A bicubic patch may be described parametrically by two parameters u and v, each varying over the interval [0.,1.], and the two equations below:

$$x(u,v) = [\ u^3\ u^2\ u\ 1\ ] \begin{bmatrix} a_0 & a_1 & a_2 & a_3 \\ a_4 & a_5 & a_6 & a_7 \\ a_8 & a_9 & a_{10} & a_{11} \\ a_{12} & a_{13} & a_{14} & a_{15} \end{bmatrix} \begin{bmatrix} v^3 \\ v^2 \\ v \\ 1 \end{bmatrix} \equiv \mathbf{uAv}^T$$

$$y(u,v) = [\ u^3\ u^2\ u\ 1\ ] \begin{bmatrix} b_0 & b_1 & b_2 & b_3 \\ b_4 & b_5 & b_6 & b_7 \\ b_8 & b_9 & b_{10} & b_{11} \\ b_{12} & b_{13} & b_{14} & b_{15} \end{bmatrix} \begin{bmatrix} v^3 \\ v^2 \\ v \\ 1 \end{bmatrix} \equiv \mathbf{uBv}^T$$

The addition of a third equation of similar form, $z(u,v) = \mathbf{uCv}^T$, defines a full 3-D bicubic patch, and a fourth, $w(u,v) = \mathbf{uDv}^T$, may be added for the homogeneous coordinate convenient for perspective transformations. However, attention shall be restricted here to the planar case. Moreover, it will be computationally advantageous to consider only those planar patches which are *nonfolded,* or single valued. That is, no point (x,y) is the image of more than one point (u,v).

The equations for x and y expand into

$$x(u,v) = a_0u^3v^3+a_1u^3v^2+a_2u^3v+a_3u^3+a_4u^2v^3+a_5u^2v^2+a_6u^2v+a_7u^2+$$
$$a_8uv^3+a_9uv^2+a_{10}uv+a_{11}u+a_{12}v^3+a_{13}v^2+a_{14}v+a_{15}$$
$$y(u,v) = b_0u^3v^3+b_1u^3v^2+b_2u^3v+b_3u^3+b_4u^2v^3+b_5u^2v^2+b_6u^2v+b_7u^2+$$
$$b_8uv^3+b_9uv^2+b_{10}uv+b_{11}u+b_{12}v^3+b_{13}v^2+b_{14}v+b_{15}$$

which may be cast into expressions of the known coordinates x_i and y_i by solving for the boundary conditions. For example, $v = 0$ corresponds to one edge of the bicubic patch and $v = 1$ to the opposite edge, and similarly for $u = 0$ and $u = 1$. Define matrix **X** to be the following array of sixteen specific x coordinates (see Figure 3):

$$\mathbf{X} = \begin{bmatrix} x(0,0) & x(u_0,0) & x(u_1,0) & x(1,0) \\ x(0,v_0) & x(u_0,v_0) & x(u_1,v_0) & x(1,v_0) \\ x(0,v_1) & x(u_0,v_1) & x(u_1,v_1) & x(1,v_1) \\ x(0,1) & x(u_0,1) & x(u_1,1) & x(1,1) \end{bmatrix} \equiv \begin{bmatrix} x_0 & x_1 & x_2 & x_3 \\ x_4 & x_5 & x_6 & x_7 \\ x_8 & x_9 & x_{10} & x_{11} \\ x_{12} & x_{13} & x_{14} & x_{15} \end{bmatrix}$$

Then it can be shown that the x_i are related to the a_i by a compact matrix equation:

$$\mathbf{X} = \mathbf{VA}^T\mathbf{U}^T$$

where

$$\mathbf{U} = \begin{bmatrix} 0 & 0 & 0 & 1 \\ u_0^3 & u_0^2 & u_0 & 1 \\ u_1^3 & u_1^2 & u_1 & 1 \\ 1 & 1 & 1 & 1 \end{bmatrix}$$

and **V** is defined similarly in terms of v_0 and v_1.

This equation can be solved for the a_i in terms of the x_i :

$$\mathbf{A} = \mathbf{U}^{-1}\mathbf{X}^T\mathbf{V}^{-T}$$

where $\mathbf{V}^{-T}$ represents the inverse of the transpose of **V**. Similarly, the b_i in terms of the y_i are given by

$$\mathbf{B} = \mathbf{U}^{-1}\mathbf{Y}^T\mathbf{V}^{-T}$$

where **Y** is defined similarly to **X**, but for specific y coordinates. It can be shown that $\mathbf{U}^{-1}$ may be represented as follows, where for notational convenience, we let $\overline{u}_0 = 1-u_0$, $\overline{u}_1 = 1-u_1$, $\underline{u}_0 = 1+u_0$, $\underline{u}_1 = 1+u_1$, $u_{10} = u_1-u_0$, $u_{01} = u_0+u_1$, $\underline{u}_{01} = u_0+u_1+1$, and $\overline{u}_{01} = u_0u_1+u_0+u_1$, and similarly for v_0 and v_1 :

$$\mathbf{U}^{-1} = \begin{bmatrix} -1 & 1 & -1 & 1 \\ \underline{u}_{01} & -\underline{u}_1 & \underline{u}_0 & -u_{01} \\ -\overline{u}_{01} & u_1 & -u_0 & u_0u_1 \\ u_0u_1 & 0 & 0 & 0 \end{bmatrix} \begin{bmatrix} \frac{1}{u_0u_1} & 0 & 0 & 0 \\ 0 & \frac{1}{u_0\overline{u}_0u_{10}} & 0 & 0 \\ 0 & 0 & \frac{1}{u_1\overline{u}_1u_{10}} & 0 \\ 0 & 0 & 0 & \frac{1}{\overline{u}_0\overline{u}_1} \end{bmatrix}$$

and similarly for $\mathbf{V}^{-1}$ in terms of the v_i.

A special case is the *cubic patch,* a bicubic patch with terms which have exponents summing to three or less. This is equivalent to matrices **A** and **B** being all zeros above the bend-sinister diagonal. Several other special cases of interest are discussed below.

A Special Case: The Bicubic Frozen Edge

A simple special case (Figure 4) requires that the boundary of the bicubic patch be a rectangle. If the uv parameter space is thought of as a rectangular source picture and its image under $x(u,v)$ and $y(u,v)$ as a bicubic patch target picture, then the special case requires that the rectangle around the rectangular patch map to itself - hence the Frozen Edge. Only the four internal control points (x_5,y_5), (x_6,y_6), (x_9,y_9), and (x_{10},y_{10}) move from source to target. Thus

$$\mathbf{X}_s = \begin{bmatrix} 0 & u_0 & u_1 & 1 \\ 0 & x_5 & x_6 & 1 \\ 0 & x_9 & x_{10} & 1 \\ 0 & u_0 & u_1 & 1 \end{bmatrix}$$

$$\mathbf{Y}_s = \begin{bmatrix} 0 & 0 & 0 & 0 \\ v_0 & y_5 & y_6 & v_0 \\ v_1 & y_9 & y_{10} & v_1 \\ 1 & 1 & 1 & 1 \end{bmatrix}$$

And these collapse the expressions for **A** to

$$\mathbf{A}_s = \begin{bmatrix} a_0 & -(a_0+a_2) & a_2 & 0 \\ -(a_0+a_8) & a_0+a_2+a_8+a_{10} & -(a_2+a_{10}) & 0 \\ a_8 & -(a_8+a_{10}) & a_{10} & 1 \\ 0 & 0 & 0 & 0 \end{bmatrix} = \mathbf{U}^{-1}\mathbf{X}_s^T\mathbf{V}^{-T}$$

and similarly for **B**, both of which become particularly simple for the special case of the cubic frozen edge.

A Special Case: The Biquadratic Patch

By a derivation analogous to that for the bicubic patch above and using the notation of Figure 5,

$$\mathbf{A}_2 = \mathbf{U}_2^{-1}\mathbf{X}_2^T\mathbf{V}_2^{-T}$$

where the subscript 2 denotes the biquadratic case (3×3 matrices) and

$$\mathbf{U}_2^{-1} = \begin{bmatrix} 1 & -1 & 1 \\ -\underline{u}_1 & 1 & -u_1 \\ u_1 & 0 & 0 \end{bmatrix} \begin{bmatrix} \frac{1}{u_1} & 0 & 0 \\ 0 & \frac{1}{u_1\bar{u}_1} & 0 \\ 0 & 0 & \frac{1}{\bar{u}_1} \end{bmatrix}$$

and similarly for $\mathbf{V}_2^{-1}$ and also $\mathbf{B}_2$.

Common examples of biquadratic warps are the pincushion and barrel distortions of video - see Figure 7. So biquadratic warps may be used to correct for these distortions.

Analogous to the cubic patch, a *quadratic patch* (or *quadric patch)* is defined to have only those terms with exponents summing to two or less, so all elements above the bend-sinister diagonals of the corresponding 3×3 $\mathbf{A}_2$ and $\mathbf{B}_2$ matrices are zeros.

A Special Case: The Biquadratic Frozen Edge

There is a Frozen Edge special case of the general biquadratic patch analogous to that for the bicubic patch discussed above. See Figure 6. Using the techniques above, it can be readily shown that

$$\mathbf{A}_{2s} = \begin{bmatrix} a_0 & -a_0 & 0 \\ -a_0 & a_0 & 1 \\ 0 & 0 & 0 \end{bmatrix} = \mathbf{U}_2^{-1}\mathbf{X}_{2s}^T\mathbf{V}_2^{-T}$$

$$\mathbf{B}_{2s} = \begin{bmatrix} b_0 & -b_0 & 0 \\ -b_0 & b_0 & 0 \\ 0 & 1 & 0 \end{bmatrix} = \mathbf{U}_2^{-1}\mathbf{Y}_{2s}^T\mathbf{V}_2^{-T}$$

where

$$a_0 = \frac{x_4 - u_1}{u_1\bar{u}_1v_1\bar{v}_1}$$

$$b_0 = \frac{y_4 - v_1}{u_1\bar{u}_1v_1\bar{v}_1}$$

and point (x_4, y_4) is the only control point that moves.

The quadratic frozen edge is a particularly simple special case of the biquadratic frozen edge. The bilinear patch was fully treated in [3].

The Horizontal Function $f_{v_s}(u)$

For subsequent convenience, let the rows of **A** be denoted by $\mathbf{a}_0$, $\mathbf{a}_1$, $\mathbf{a}_2$, and $\mathbf{a}_3$. Also let

$$\mathbf{f}(v) = \mathbf{A}\mathbf{v}^T = [\ f_0(v)\ f_1(v)\ f_2(v)\ f_3(v)\ ]^T =$$
$$[\ \mathbf{a}_0\mathbf{v}^T\ \ \mathbf{a}_1\mathbf{v}^T\ \ \mathbf{a}_2\mathbf{v}^T\ \ \mathbf{a}_3\mathbf{v}^T\ ]^T$$

Direct application of the 2-pass technique first step yields

$$f_{v_s}(u) = \mathbf{u}\mathbf{A}\mathbf{v_s}^T = \mathbf{u}\mathbf{f}(v_s)$$

for horizontal scanline v_s and

$$\mathbf{v_s}^T = [\ v_s^3\ v_s^2\ v_s\ 1\ ]\ .$$

The biquadratic case may also be represented in an analogous fashion.

The Auxiliary Function $h_{u_i}(v)$

The 2-pass technique second step requires that

$$x(u,v) - u_i = 0$$

be solved for $u = h(v)$. (The subscript u_i is dropped from h and g for convenience in this and the following section.) In words, the set of u's is desired which map into u_i under the horizontal scanline functions. Since $x(u,v) = \mathbf{u}\mathbf{f}(v)$ is cubic in u, the equation may be written as a general cubic equation, the *auxiliary cubic* equation,

$$\alpha u^3 + \beta u^2 + \gamma u + \delta = 0$$

where the coefficients are the following functions of v :

$$\alpha = f_0(v) = \mathbf{a}_0\mathbf{v}^T$$
$$\beta = f_1(v) = \mathbf{a}_1\mathbf{v}^T$$
$$\gamma = f_2(v) = \mathbf{a}_2\mathbf{v}^T$$
$$\delta = f_3(v) - u_i = \mathbf{a}_3\mathbf{v}^T - u_i\ .$$

In general, the auxiliary cubic has three (non-polynomial) solutions, $h_0(v)$, $h_1(v)$, and $h_2(v)$, which may be obtained using classic cubic equation solution techniques. It is difficult to determine which of the three are the valid solutions, and two of them may be complex. The solution method suggested below capitalizes on the restriction to planar nonfolded patches to avoid these difficulties.

A Special Case: The Planar Nonfolded Bicubic Patch

Nonfolded patches can have only one valid solution; only one u on each horizontal scanline can map to the current vertical scanline u_i. This set of u's is a smooth function of v, $u = h(v)$. Hence, if we find a solution $u = h(0)$ for the first horizontal scanline, it can be assumed to be in the vicinity of the solution for the next adjacent scanline and hence be used as a first approximation in a Newton iteration to the solution for the second scanline. Then this solution can be used as a starting value for an iteration to a solution for the next scanline, and so forth, exploiting the coherence.

So the problem of solving for h reduces to that of finding good starting values for the Newton iteration. A crude value would be u_i itself. A more refined value comes from the fact that the horizontal scanline functions have already been derived in the first pass. For a given v, the scanline function $f_v(u)$ can be computed for a small number, say n, of values of u equally spaced along [0, 1] to find two images which bracket u_i. Either of the corresponding values of u could be used as a starting value for the iteration or a linear interpolation between them. A set of starting values could be generated for all vertical scanlines by such a procedure applied along just one horizontal scanline between passes. Figure 1 illustrates the use of Newton iteration to solve a planar nonfolded bicubic patch with the 2-pass technique.

The Vertical Function $g_{u_i}(v)$

Direct application of the 2-pass technique third step yields three functions g_i, depending on which of the three auxiliary functions h_i, is used. Assuming only the planar nonfolded case, this reduces to one function $g(v)$. Thus, for vertical scanline u_i,

$$g(v) = \mathbf{u_h B v}^T$$

where

$$\mathbf{u_h} = [\ h^3(v)\ \ h^2(v)\ \ h(v)\ \ 1\ ]\ .$$

In general, this vector changes from (vertical) scanline to scanline u_i. The biquadratic case is analogously handled.

A nonfolded patch would have $g(v)$ one-to-one on the domain [0, 1] *for those points which are images of [0, 1] under some horizontal scanline function.* The fourth, or alpha, channel of a framebuffer could be used to determine if a point fit this condition; its alpha channel would be empty if it were the image of a point outside [0, 1]. So nonfolded means that all scanline functions, horizontal and vertical, are one-to-one mappings on the domain [0, 1], subject to this condition. This can be shown to be equivalent to the definition of nonfolded given in the Bicubic and Biquadratic Warping section. Ordinary B-spline or Bezier patch techniques may be used to ensure a patch is nonfolded.

SERIAL VS PARALLEL WARPS

Summarizing, polynomial warps may defined by

$$x(u_s,v_s) = \mathbf{u}_s \mathbf{A} \mathbf{v}_s^T$$

$$y(u_s,v_s) = \mathbf{u}_s \mathbf{B} \mathbf{v}_s^T$$

where **A** and **B** are matrices of polynomial coefficients and $\mathbf{u}_s$ and $\mathbf{v}_s$ are vectors of powers of u_s and v_s. A third-order parallel polynomial warp would have **A** and **B** be 4×4 matrices of constants and

$$\mathbf{u}_s = [\ u_s^3\ u_s^2\ u_s\ \ 1\ ]$$

$$\mathbf{v}_s = [\ v_s^3\ v_s^2\ v_s\ \ 1\ ]$$

Since x and y are third-order polynomials in two variables, the resulting warp is called a *bicubic* warp. The *biquadratic* warp is defined similarly but for **A** and **B** both 3×3 matrices and

$$\mathbf{u}_s = [\ u_s^2\ u_s\ \ 1\ ]$$

$$\mathbf{v}_s = [\ v_s^2\ v_s\ \ 1\ ]$$

A second- or third-order serial polynomial warp would have

$$f_{v_s}(u_s) = x(u_s,v_s) = \mathbf{u}_s \mathbf{A} \mathbf{v}_s^T$$

$$g_{u_i}(v_i) = y(u_i,v_i) = \mathbf{u}_i \mathbf{B} \mathbf{v}_i^T$$

which is quite similar in form to the parallel polynomial warp described above. The parallel equivalent of this serial polynomial warp is derived below where it is seen to be a higher-order polynomial mapping and hence quite different in form from the parallel polynomial warp.

The Parallel Equivalent of a Serial Warp

Given a general serial warp

$$(x(u_s,v_s),v_s) = (u_i,v_i)$$

$$(u_i,y(u_i,v_i)) = (u_t,v_t)$$

the problem is to find $x'(u_s,v_s) = u_t$ and $y'(u_s,v_s) = v_t$ in terms of u_s, v_s, x, and y.

The solution is straightforward using the notation:

$$u_t = u_i = x(u_s,v_s)$$

is already the desired solution for x'. That is,

$$x'(u_s,v_s) = x(u_s,v_s)\ .$$

Since $v_i = v_s$ and $u_i = x(u_s,v_s)$,

$$y'(u_s,v_s) = y(u_i,v_i) = y(x(u_s,v_s),v_s)\ .$$

Example

The parallel equivalent of a serial biquadratic polynomial warp is given immediately by

$$x'(u_s,v_s) = \mathbf{u}_s \mathbf{A} \mathbf{v}_s^T$$

$$y'(u_s,v_s) = [\ (\mathbf{u}_s \mathbf{A} \mathbf{v}_s^T)^2\ \ \mathbf{u}_s \mathbf{A} \mathbf{v}_s^T\ \ 1\ ]\mathbf{B} \mathbf{v}_s^T\ .$$

Thus the parallel equivalent of a second-order serial polynomial warp is fourth order in u_s and sixth order in v_s. Similarly, a third-order serial polynomial warp is equivalent to a parallel polynomial warp which is ninth order in u_s and twelfth order in v_s. In general, the parallel equivalent of an n-th order serial polynomial warp is n^2-th order in u_s and (n^2+n)-th order in v_s.

In particular, for the biquadratic Frozen Edge case discussed above and implemented serially by Thomas Porter as part of the Pixar Image Computer demonstration at the National Computer Graphics Association (NCGA) convention in Dallas, April, 1985,

$$x(u_s,v_s) = a_0 u_s(1-u_s)v_s(1-v_s)+u_s \equiv a_0 u_s \overline{u}_s v_s \overline{v}_s + u_s$$

$$y(u_i,v_i) = b_0 u_i(1-u_i)v_i(1-v_i)+v_i \equiv b_0 u_i \overline{u}_i v_i \overline{v}_i + u_i$$

The parallel equivalent of this is easily shown to be

$$x'(u_s,v_s) = a_0 u_s \overline{u}_s v_s \overline{v}_s + u_s$$

$$y'(u_s,v_s) = a_0 b_0 u_s \overline{u}_s v_s^2 \overline{v}_s^2 (1 - u_s \overline{u}_s v_s \overline{v}_s) + v_s$$

which is a sixth-order parallel polynomial warp. Clearly, it is important to know if a "biquadratic" warp is serial or parallel.

Similarly the "bicubic" warp of the scarab beetle in [5] is a serial third-order warp equivalent to a twelfth-order parallel polynomial warp. The mappings in [5] are in reverse order to those given here with $u_s = \mathbf{u}_i \mathbf{A} \mathbf{v}_i^T$ and $v_i = \mathbf{u}_t \mathbf{B} \mathbf{v}_t^T$, but the argument still holds, in the reverse direction. The problem of converting between the order presented here and the reverse order is another whole problem not considered further here.

The Serial Equivalent of a Parallel Warp

The problem here is to find a serial decomposition of a parallel mapping. But, of course, this is exactly the 2-pass problem. In particular, it is shown above that parallel polynomial warps are equivalent to serial warps with

$$x'(u_s,v_s) = \mathbf{u}_s \mathbf{A} \mathbf{v}_s^T$$

and

$$y'(u_i,v_i) = [\, h^3 \;\; h^2 \;\; h \;\; 1 \,] \mathbf{B} \mathbf{v}_i^T$$

for the bicubic case and similarly for the biquadratic case, where h is the solution of $\mathbf{u}_s \mathbf{A} \mathbf{v}_s^T - u_i = 0$ for u_s. There are three solutions h for the bicubic case and two for the biquadratic case. The solutions are not polynomials, which proves that, in general, the serial equivalent of a parallel polynomial warp is not a serial polynomial warp.

SHADING, DEPTH, MATTING, AND NORMALS

Normals and z information at each point may be carried along through the 2-pass technique just as are colors (where alpha, or opacity, is assumed to be a fourth component of each color). Then shading information is computed from the normal information and color information, and depth from the z information, as traditionally done. The alpha channel is correctly transformed by the 2-pass technique. Therefore it serves as a matte channel so that a 2-pass transformed object may be correctly composited with other images.

BOTTLENECK PROBLEM

The area of the intermediate picture can be much less than that of either the source or the target pictures. This is called [3] the bottleneck problem. In fact, the intermediate area can be zero. This happens, for example, for a rotate about the picture plane normal by 90 degrees.

In general there are several paths from source to target using the 2-pass technique. First, there is the horizontal pass followed by the vertical pass - the method usually assumed in this paper. Second, there is the vertical pass followed by the horizontal pass. Then there are variations on these two which incorporate a "preprocessing" step for which there is subsequent compensation. For example, in the case of rotation by almost 90 degrees - say 87 degrees - the bottleneck can be avoided by doing a simple transpose of rows and columns to effect a 90-degree rotation then a normal 2-pass transformation to get the remaining -3 degrees.

The method which has been used successfully for CG transforms of a simple rectangle is to compute the intermediate areas which would obtain via a set of four paths and select the path with the largest intermediate area. The four paths are (1) horizontal pass first, (2) vertical pass first, (3) transpose rows and columns then horizontal pass first, and (4) transpose then vertical pass first. The intermediate areas can be readily computed - the formulas are given in [3]. As mentioned in The 2-Pass Technique section, this has always worked but has not been proved to do so.

The bottlenecking solution for the projected superquadrics used here is simply that above. The justification is that a CG transform of a projected superquadric is the same as a mapping onto a projected superquadric in canonical position followed by a CG transform of the resulting 2-D image. The first step is non-degenerate - see Figure 2. Since this image falls within a rectangle, the second step is exactly that solved with the technique above.

The bottlenecking problem for the bicubic and biquadratic warps is ignored here because warping is generally not used for large geometric distortions - such as scalings and rotations - but rather for relocation of points within the vicinity of the original positions - i.e., for scale factors of about 1. and rotations of about 0.

ANTIALIASING

Most of this paper may be read independently of a digital realization of the technique presented. In this section we address those artifacts which arise strictly because digital approximations of the scanline functions are implemented. The 2-pass technique is attractive because it promises to cheapen the antialiasing computations required by the equivalent serial mapping. How true is it that the 2-pass technique replaces a full 2-D antialiasing problem with a sequence of two simpler 1-D antialiasing problems - in the case of 2-D quadrics under CG transform?

Suppose the 2-D antialiasing method we would have chosen in a full 2-D antialiasing application would integrate all the pixels in neighborhood $N(p)$ of source pixel p to obtain the target pixel p'. Presumably $N(p)$ would be the pixel support of some antialiasing filter. Then a necessary condition that a serial map perform the same filtering would be that all these same pixels be used in the computation of p'. This implies that all pixels in $N(p)$ map into the same vertical scanline during the first pass, so that the vertical pass can then map all of them - their intermediate images actually - into p'.

This condition is rarely met, so it is surprising how often the use of two serial 1-D filtering steps actually works. Intuitively, it works whenever the horizontal pass does not skew neighboring horizontal scanlines in $N(p)$ very far with respect to one another. Another way to say this is that the 1-D filtering trick works whenever there is not a high frequency change, in the vertical direction, of the object being transformed. "High frequency" in this case means near or greater than the spatial frequency of the horizontal scanlines. Figure 8 illustrates the point, and also the fact that changing the order sometimes corrects the problem. As pointed out earlier, there is no proof that this is always the case.

It should be no surprise that 1-D filtering in the discrete 2-pass should occasionally result in aliasing artifacts - one whole dimension cannot be thrown away without seeing some effect. The *continuous* 2-pass technique, of course, isn't plagued by this problem.

A higher-order antialiasing technique to use when the 1-D filtering trick fails is easily described. Consider a horizontal scanline of pixels, modeled as a row of abutting squares. The input domain image of an output pixel which intersects this scanline is an area bounded above and below by parallel line segments and left and right by curves (straight lines for several interesting transformations). The average intensity over this area is a more accurate average than the strictly 1-D average over say the midline of this area. Notice that this "scanline area" technique takes the 1-D passes back into 2-D computations. It is essentially a box filtering technique. Higher order filters would give better results as usual.

All 1-D sampling and filtering used for the figures in this paper is derived from the standard theories as described, for example, in [11, 12].

ACKNOWLEDGEMENTS

Colleagues Ed Catmull, Charlie Gunn, Pat Hanrahan, and Tom Porter have all provided important ideas for this 2-pass work. Ed and I worked on the original idea together. Charlie championed Newton iteration. Tom implemented the serial biquadratic frozen-edge and Pat the full planar serial biquadratic on the Pixar Image Computer. Tom's implementation - and subsequent arguments about what a biquadratic warp really is - inspired the resolution, presented herein, of the long-standing confusion between serial and parallel maps.

REFERENCES

[1] Barr, Alan H. *Superquadrics and Angle-Preserving Transformations,* **IEEE Computer Graphics and Applications,** January, 1981, pp. 11-23.

[2] Bennett, Philip P., and Steven A. Gabriel, *System for Spatially Transforming Images,* **United States Patent 4,472,732,** September 18, 1984. (Assigned to Ampex Corporation. This is one of the patents for the very successful ADO (Ampex Digital Optics) product. See also U. S. Patents 4,463,372 and 4,468,688.)

[3] Catmull, Edwin, and Alvy Ray Smith. *3-D Transformations of Images in Scanline Order,* **Computer Graphics,** Vol. 14, No. 3, pp. 279-285, July, 1980. (SIGGRAPH 80 Conference Proceedings).

[4] Fant, Karl M. *A Nonaliasing, Real-Time Spatial Transform Technique,* **IEEE Computer Graphics and Applications,** January, 1986, pp. 71-80. (See also the *Letters to the Editor* section of **IEEE Computer Graphics and Applications,** March, 1986, pp. 66-67, and July, 1986, pp. 3 and 8.)

[5] Fraser, Donald, Robert A. Schowengerdt, and Ian Briggs. *Rectification of Multichannel Images in Mass Storage Using Image Transposition,* **Computer Vision, Graphics, and Image Processing,** Volume 29, Number 1, January, 1985, pp. 23-36. (See also *Corrigendum,* Volume 31, Number 3, September, 1985, p. 395.)

[6] Paeth, Alan. *A Fast Algorithm for General Raster Rotation,* **Graphics Interface '86 Proceedings,** May, 1986, pp. 77-81.

[7] Smith, Alvy Ray. *Projected Superquadrics are 2-Pass Transformable,* **Technical Memo 54,** Computer Graphics Department, Computer Division, Lucasfilm Ltd., August, 1982 (now Technical Memo 54, Pixar).

[8] Smith, Alvy Ray. *A 2-Pass Solution to the Planar Biquadratic Patch,* **Technical Memo 128,** Computer Graphics Department, Computer Division, Lucasfilm Ltd., May, 1985 (now Technical Memo 128, Pixar).

[9] Smith, Alvy Ray. *A 2-Pass Solution to the Planar Bicubic Patch,* **Technical Memo 132,** Computer Graphics Department, Computer Division, Lucasfilm Ltd., June, 1985 (now Technical Memo 132, Pixar).

[10] Smith, Alvy Ray. *Serial vs Parallel Warps,* **Technical Memo 134,** Computer Graphics Department, Computer Division, Lucasfilm Ltd., June, 1985 (now Technical Memo 134, Pixar).

[11] Smith, Alvy Ray. *Digital Filtering Tutorial for Computer Graphics* **Technical Memo 27,** Computer Graphics Department, Computer Division, Lucasfilm Ltd., March, 1983 (now Technical Memo 27, Pixar). Also in Tutorial Notes for Siggraph 1983 and Siggraph 1984.

[12] Smith, Alvy Ray. *Digital Filtering Tutorial, Part II* **Technical Memo 44,** Computer Graphics Department, Computer Division, Lucasfilm Ltd., May, 1983 (now Technical Memo 44, Pixar). Also in Tutorial Notes for Siggraph 1983 and Siggraph 1984.

(Figures 1, 2, 7, and 8 are on next page.)

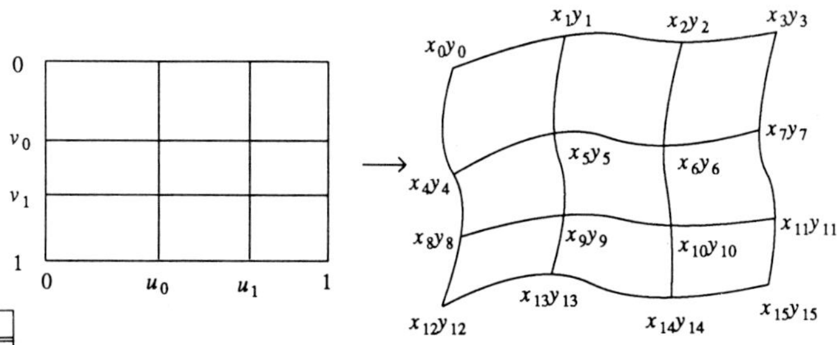

Figure 3. Bicubic patch transformation.

Table 1. Superquadric Defining Functions

Type	$m_1(u)$	$m_2(u)$	u domain	$h_1(v)$	$h_2(v)$	v domain
Ellipsoid	$\cos^{\varepsilon} u$	$\sin^{\varepsilon} u$	$-\frac{\pi}{2} \le u \le \frac{\pi}{2}$	$\cos^{\varepsilon'} v$	$\sin^{\varepsilon'} v$	$-\pi \le v < \pi$
1-Hyperboloid	$\sec^{\varepsilon} u$	$\tan^{\varepsilon} u$	$-\frac{\pi}{2} < u < \frac{\pi}{2}$	$\cos^{\varepsilon'} v$	$\sin^{\varepsilon'} v$	$-\pi \le v < \pi$
2-Hyperboloid	$\sec^{\varepsilon} u$	$\tan^{\varepsilon} u$	$-\frac{\pi}{2} < u < \frac{\pi}{2}$	$\sec^{\varepsilon'} v$	$\tan^{\varepsilon'} v$	$-\frac{\pi}{2} < v < \frac{\pi}{2}$ * $\frac{\pi}{2} < v < \frac{3\pi}{2}$ **
Toroid	$\alpha+\cos^{\varepsilon} u$	$\sin^{\varepsilon} u$	$-\pi \le u < \pi$	$\cos^{\varepsilon'} v$	$\sin^{\varepsilon'} v$	$-\pi \le v < \pi$

* For the first sheet.
** For the second sheet.

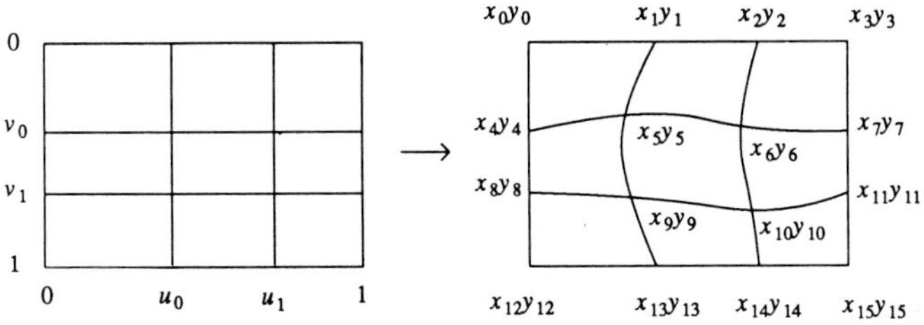

Figure 4. Bicubic frozen edge.

Table 2. 2-D Superquadric 2-Pass Horizontal Scanline Functions

Type	$f_{v_s}(u)$	A(v)	M(v)
Ellipsoid	$\frac{A(v_s)\cos^{\varepsilon} u + d}{M(v_s)\cos^{\varepsilon} u + p}$	$a\cos^{\varepsilon'} v + b\sin^{\varepsilon'} v$	$m\cos^{\varepsilon'} v + n\sin^{\varepsilon'} v$
1-Hyperboloid	$\frac{A(v_s)\sec^{\varepsilon} u + d}{M(v_s)\sec^{\varepsilon} u + p}$	$a\cos^{\varepsilon'} v + b\sin^{\varepsilon'} v$	$m\cos^{\varepsilon'} v + n\sin^{\varepsilon'} v$
2-Hyperboloid	$\frac{A(v_s)\sec^{\varepsilon} u + d}{M(v_s)\sec^{\varepsilon} u + p}$	$a\sec^{\varepsilon'} v + b\tan^{\varepsilon'} v$	$m\sec^{\varepsilon'} v + n\tan^{\varepsilon'} v$
Toroid	$\frac{A(v_s)(\alpha + \cos^{\varepsilon} u) + d}{M(v_s)(\alpha + \cos^{\varepsilon} u) + p}$	$a\cos^{\varepsilon'} v + b\sin^{\varepsilon'} v$	$m\cos^{\varepsilon'} v + n\sin^{\varepsilon'} v$

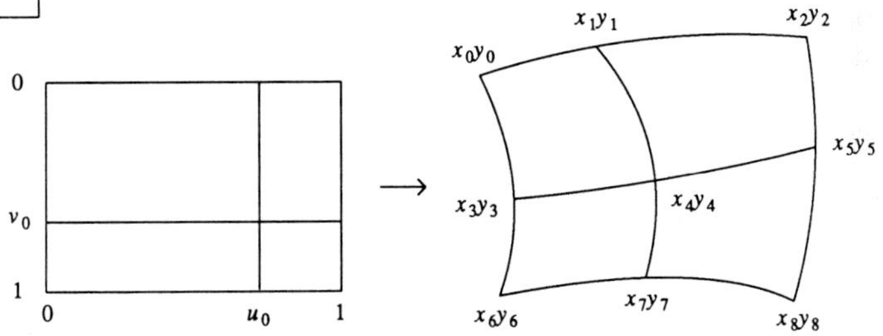

Figure 5. Biquadratic patch transformation.

Table 3. 2-D Superquadric 2-Pass Vertical Scanline Functions

Type	$g_{u_i}(v)$	E(u), F(u), G, H
Ellipsoid	$\frac{E(u_i)\cos^{\varepsilon'} v + F(u_i)\sin^{\varepsilon'} v}{G\cos^{\varepsilon'} v + H\sin^{\varepsilon'} v}$	$E(u) = \begin{vmatrix} m & p \\ e & h \end{vmatrix} u - \begin{vmatrix} a & d \\ e & h \end{vmatrix}$
1-Hyperboloid	$\frac{E(u_i)\cos^{\varepsilon'} v + F(u_i)\sin^{\varepsilon'} v}{G\cos^{\varepsilon'} v + H\sin^{\varepsilon'} v}$	$F(u) = \begin{vmatrix} n & p \\ f & h \end{vmatrix} u - \begin{vmatrix} b & d \\ f & h \end{vmatrix}$
2-Hyperboloid	$\frac{E(u_i)\sec^{\varepsilon'} v + F(u_i)\tan^{\varepsilon'} v}{G\sec^{\varepsilon'} v + H\tan^{\varepsilon'} v}$	$G = \begin{vmatrix} m & p \\ a & d \end{vmatrix}$
Toroid	$\frac{E(u_i)\cos^{\varepsilon'} v + F(u_i)\sin^{\varepsilon'} v}{G\cos^{\varepsilon'} v + H\sin^{\varepsilon'} v}$	$H = \begin{vmatrix} n & p \\ b & d \end{vmatrix}$

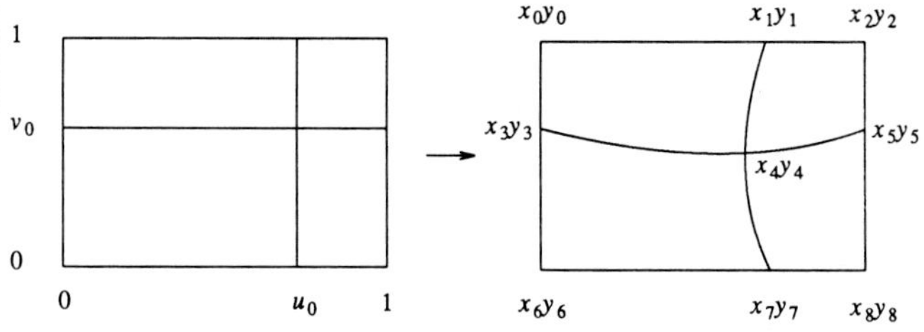

Figure 6. Biquadratic frozen edge.

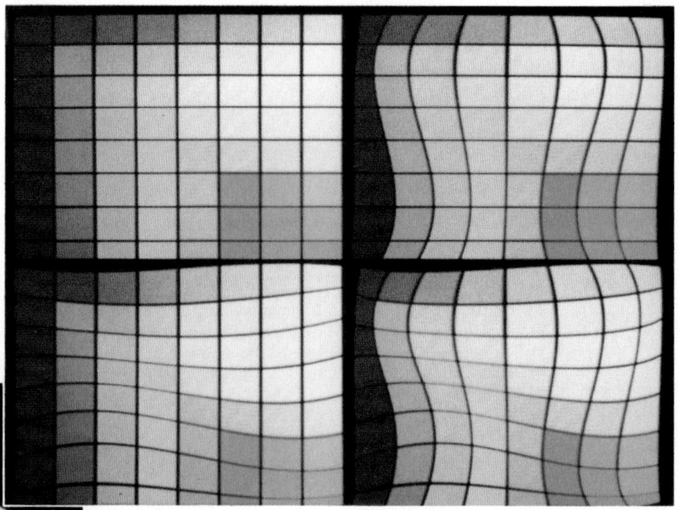

→
Figure 1. Planar nonfolded bicubic warp. Source at upper left. Target at lower right. Intermediate image at upper right is the horizontal pass for the horizontal pass first. Lower left is vertical pass for the vertical pass first.

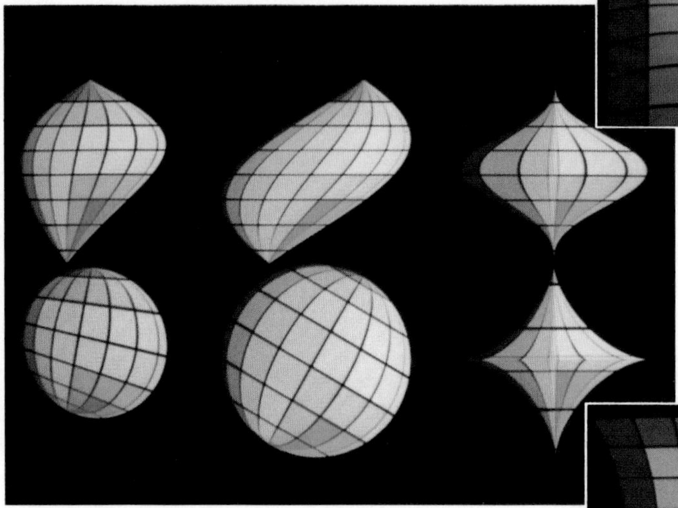

←
Figure 2. Superquadric texture mapping. Horizontal passes at the top, vertical at the bottom. Source is same as in Figure 1. Left mapping is onto a disk in perspective. Middle is a simple rotation. Right is superdisk with $\varepsilon = \varepsilon' = 3$.

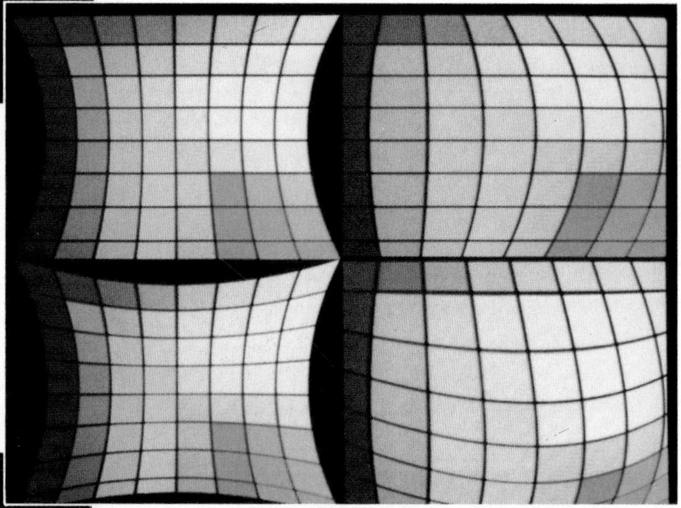

→
Figure 7. Biquadratic warps. Horizontal passes at the top, vertical at the bottom. Source is that of Figure 1. Left is a pincushion warp. Right is an assymmetric barrel warp.

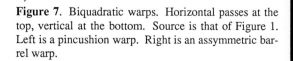

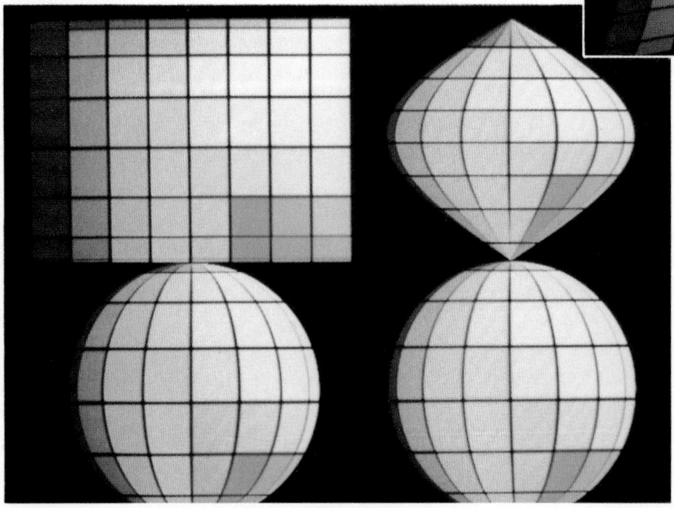

←
Figure 8. Antialiasing failure. Source is that of Figure 1. Left are the vertical and horizontal passes with the vertical pass first. Right are the horizontal and vertical passes with the horizontal pass first. The left disk is seriously aliased at the poles. Reversing order of the passes solves the problem.

Bidirectional Reflection Functions from Surface Bump Maps

BRIAN CABRAL, NELSON MAX, and REBECCA SPRINGMEYER
UC Davis/Lawrence Livermore National Laboratory

The Torrance-Sparrow model for calculating bidirectional reflection functions contains a geometrical attenuation factor to account for shadowing and occlusions in a hypothetical distribution of grooves on a rough surface. Using an efficient table-based method for determining the shadows and occlusions, we calculate the geometric attenuation factor for surfaces defined by a specific table of bump heights.

Diffuse and glossy specular reflection of the environment can be handled in a unified manner by using an integral of the bidirectional reflection function times the environmental illumination, over the hemisphere of solid angle above a surface. We present a method of estimating the integral, by expanding the bidirectional reflection coefficient in spherical harmonics, and show how the coefficients in this expansion can be determined efficiently by reorganizing our geometric attenuation calculation.

Categories and Subject Descriptors: I.3.7 [**Computer Graphics**]: Three-Dimensional Graphics and Realism — Color, shading, shadowing, and texture

General Terms: Computer graphics, image synthesis, reflectance, shading

Additional Key Words and Phrases: Bidirectional reflection function, lighting model, horizon mapping, spherical harmonics, environmental illumination

Introduction

It is possible to model the reflection properties of a rough surface with geometric optics, by assuming that at a small scale, which is still large with respect to the wavelength of light, the surface is actually continuous, smooth, and shiny, and reflects like a curved mirror, according to Fresnel's law. The shape of a patch of such a surface can be specified as a height function of two continuous parameters. If a two parameter family of parallel rays meets such a surface, they will be reflected with a certain density per solid angle, called the *bidirectional reflection density function*, or *bidirectional reflection function* for short. This function could be estimated stochastically, by tracing many parallel, randomly positioned rays.

Authors's address:
LLNL, P.O. Box 808, Livermore, CA 94550
(415) 423-0201 cabral@lll-crg.ARPA

In this paper, we approximate the bumpy surface by a collection of triangular facets, interpolating between the bump heights at a discrete array of points. The rays which hit a facet without being shadowed on the way in, and leave the surface directly without hitting another facet on the way out, define a parallel beam emerging from the non-obscured part of the facet. This reflected beam contributes a "delta function" peak to the bidirectional reflection, weighted by its cross-sectional area.

The bidirectional reflection function for the faceted approximation is the sum of these weighted delta functions, and is thus not continuous. We present two methods for capturing the information in the reflected beams. The first method divides the hemisphere of reflected directions into a number of bins, and assigns each reflected beam to one of the bins. This leads to a tabulated version of the bidirectional reflection function. The second method uses spherical harmonics to approximate the density per solid angle of the weighted delta functions. The result is a series of coefficients defining a continuous bidirectional reflection function as a linear combination of basis functions, effectively condensing the table into less data, and also smoothing it.

Section 1 gives several definitions from radiometry, leading up to a physical definition of the bidirectional reflection function. Section 2 summarizes previous models for rough surfaces and methods for finding their reflection properties. Section 3 summarizes previous work on using bidirection reflection functions to calculate the effects of environmental illumination. Section 4 describes horizon mapping, an efficient way for finding the non-obscured part of each facet. Section 5 shows how to assign the beams into bins corresponding to a collection of tabulated reflection directions, and section 6 argues that a bidirectional reflection function tabulated in this way should approximately satisfy Helmholtz's Law of Reciprocity. Section 7 shows how a spherical harmonic expansion of the bidirectional reflection function can be used to efficiently compute the effects of environmental illumination, and section 8 shows how to determine the coefficients in this expansion from the collection of beams reflected by the facets. Finally, section 9 explains the construction of the bump tables, and presents images rendered with the resulting reflection functions.

Our methods generate anisotropic reflection functions. However the anisotropy can be averaged out if desired for isotropic surfaces. For simplicity we consider only isotropic reflection functions in sections 7 and 8.

1. Radiometry

There are two methods of quantifying light measurements: 1) by radiant energy, which measures physical quantities, and 2) by luminous energy, which measures the response of the eye. In this paper we discuss only radiant energy, integrated over all wavelengths. However, the quantities defined below can also be considered as spectral quantities, which vary with wavelength. They can then be converted to luminous quantities by multiplying by the CIE luminous efficiency function and integrating over all wavelengths. They can similarly be multiplied by

Table of Notation

θ	polar angle in spherical coordinates
ϕ	azimuthal angle in spherical coordinates
Φ	radiant flux
D	radiant flux density
D_{in}	radiant flux density of incident beam
L	radiance
L_{in}	incident radiance
L_{ref}	reflected radiance
f_r	bidirectional reflection function
Q	unit sphere
H	unit hemisphere of directions above a surface
N	global normal to a surface
N'	local normal to bumps on a surface
W	incident direction (θ_{in}, ϕ_{in})
V	reflection and viewing direction $(\theta_{ref}, \phi_{ref})$
M	mirror reflection $(\theta_{mirror}, \phi_{mirror})$ of V
P	off specular peak direction $(\theta_{peak}, \phi_{peak})$
β	angle from surface normal to horizon
S_i	the ith facet
B_i	the non-obscured area of facet S_i
N_i	the normal to facet S_i
R_i	direction of the beam reflected from S_i
G_i	"fraction" of incident flux reflected from S_i
F	Fresnel's law
δ	Kronecker delta function
V_k	direction for bin k
Φ_k	flux in bin k
Y_{ln}	real spherical harmonics basis function
P_{ln}	associated Legendre function
M_{ln}	normalization factor
$\widehat{\cos}\theta$	$max(\cos\theta, 0)$
$D^l_{n'n}$	matrix element for rotating spherical harmonic basis functions
g_n	coefficients in Fourier series for L_{ref}

the CIE color matching functions, and integrated to get CIE x, y, and z color coordinates, which can be converted to the appropriate output colors for a specific device (See Hall [15] and Cook and Torrance [8].)

To measure solid angle, we use a spherical coordinate system with the Z axis at the surface normal N. A direction V has coordinates (θ, ϕ) where θ measures the polar angle of V from the Z axis, and ϕ measures the azimuthal angle between the X axis and the projection of V in the XY plane. The element of solid angle is then $d\omega = \sin\theta d\theta d\phi$. We now state several definitions taken from ANSI Z7.1-1967 [33].

The *radiant flux*, Φ, is the time rate of flow of energy traveling through a surface in the form of electromagnetic waves. It is usually measured in watts.

The *radiant flux density*, $D = d\Phi/dA$, at an element of a surface is the ratio of the radiant flux through that surface element, to the area of the element. It can be measured in watts per square meter. When referring to radiant flux incident on a surface, the density is called *irradiance*.

The *radiance*, $L = d^2\Phi/(d\omega \cos\theta dA)$, in a direction (θ, ϕ), at a point of a surface is the following ratio. The numerator is the radiant flux leaving, passing through, or arriving at an element of the surface surrounding the point, and propagated in directions within a cone containing the given direction. The denominator is the product of the solid angle of the cone and the area of the orthogonal projection of the element of the surface on a plane perpendicular to the given direction. Radiance can be measured in watts per square meter per steradian.

Consider a beam of incident light, with radiance L_{in}, coming from a solid angle $d\omega_{in}$ about an incident direction (θ_{in}, ϕ_{in}) and reflecting from a surface. Let dL_{ref} be the radiance reflected in the direction $(\theta_{ref}, \phi_{ref})$. Then the *bidirectional reflection function* f_r is the ratio:

$$f_r(\theta_{in}, \phi_{in}; \theta_{ref}, \phi_{ref}) = \frac{dL_{ref}}{L_{in} \cos\theta_{in} d\omega_{in}}$$

(See Snell [28].) In the limit when $d\omega_{in}$ approaches zero and the incident beam becomes parallel, the denominator becomes the irradiance onto the surface from the single direction (θ_{in}, ϕ_{in}). Since f_r is a radiance divided by a radiant flux density, the units of f_r are inverse steradians.

For a radiance function $L_{in}(\theta_{in}, \phi_{in})$ which varies continuously with the incident direction, we can get the total reflected radiance in the direction $(\theta_{ref}, \phi_{ref})$ by integrating dL_{ref} over the hemisphere H of possible incident directions above a surface. Thus

$$L_{ref} = \int_H dL_{ref} = \int_H f_r(\theta_{in}, \phi_{in}; \theta_{ref}, \phi_{ref}) L_{in} \cos\theta_{in} d\omega_{in}. \quad (1)$$

2. Bidirectional Reflection Models

Torrance and Sparrow [32] developed a geometric lighting model for specular reflection, which was applied to computer graphics by Blinn [1], and modified by Cook and Torrance [8], to take better account of colored light. It has been used to create spectacularly realistic shaded renderings of surfaces such as brushed metal.

The Torrance-Sparrow model assumes that an infinitely long, symmetrical, wedge-shaped groove has been cut into the surface. The normal N' to one of the two flat sides of this groove is used, together with the lighting direction and the viewing direction, to compute the fraction of the incoming light which is neither shadowed on the way in nor obscured on the way out by the opposite side of the groove. Random grooves, with some specific distribution of normals N' about the surface normal N, generate a distribution of reflected rays from each incoming direction. One can thus compute a bidirectional reflection coefficient. However on any real surface the grooves will interfere with each other, so they cannot be both randomly oriented and infinitely long.

A real surface can be more explicitly modeled by a bump table, which gives the surface height at a two dimensional array of sample points. Blinn [2] has shown how to perturb the surface normal for use in a lighting model which takes account of the bumps. The method has become known as "bump mapping." It gives realistic light reflections for a level of detail at which the bumps are visible, but need not be modeled in full 3-D perspective. Max [21] has shown how to account for the shadows from the bumps, by using a table of horizon angles. This might appropriately be called "horizon mapping." In the present paper, we divide the surface defined by the bump table into triangular facets. For each facet and each tabulated lighting direction, we compute the reflection direction and use the horizon table to find the reflected beam, that is, the portion of the beam potentially intercepted by the facet, which is neither shadowed on the way in nor obscured on the way out.

We accumulate this reflected flux into a tabulated bidirectional reflection function, using the tabulated reflection direction closest to the actual reflected beam. Because it is derived from the bump table, the resulting lighting model will be consistent with the area average of the light from an image rendered with bump mapping and horizon mapping. This should permit smooth transitions of detail between these two methods of representing surface roughness. This is the chief justification of our method: consistency with explicitly modeled surface structure, including anisotropic reflections. Kajiya [20] has proposed smooth transitions between three roughness representations: lighting models, bump mapping, and full 3-D visible-surface calculations which include the bumps in the data base. However his method uses the wave theory of light, and is not computationally practical. If bump mapped surfaces are rendered with horizon mapping, they should in addition allow smooth transitions to full 3-D renderings including cast shadows.

Perlin [24] has also proposed a smooth transition of surface roughness components, between lighting models and normal perturbations. However his normal perturbations do not come from an explicitly specified bump table, and therefore do not permit horizon mapping, or full 3-D modeling.

Ohira [23], Takagi [30], and Kajiya [20] have discussed bidirectional reflection functions which are anisotropic. These depend on all four parameters needed to define the lighting and viewing directions, with respect to a frame specifying the orientation of two surface tangents and the surface normal. Our calculations initially generate anisotropic reflections, since the two tangent vectors are needed to orient the bump tables on the surface. If isotropic reflection functions are desired, the anisotropic tables can be averaged over the possible orientations of the bump table on the surface, so that they depend on only three parameters. This will make more reflected rays contribute to each table entry, and improve the sampling statistics.

3. Environmental Illumination

Early illumination models handled only point light sources, but there have been many attempts to include the light coming from the whole environment, based on equation (1) above. Whitted and Cook [35] analyze various specific lighting models in terms of restrictions on the full generality of equation (1). For example, Blinn and Newell [3] created mirror reflections of a room in a teapot by assuming that L_{in} is independent of position, and that f_r is a delta function. If L_{in} instead is a delta function, we have the case of a point light source. Lambert's law for diffuse reflection results when f_r is constant. Phong [26], Blinn [1], and Cook and Torrance [8] have generated glossy highlights from point sources by using more general specular reflection functions f_r, concentrated near the mirror direction. Cook, Carpenter, and Porter [7] have used distributed ray tracing to model glossy reflections, with such a concentrated f_r and an arbitrary L_{in}. Because the integral is estimated by tracing sample rays near the mirror reflection, L_{in} can vary with position and multiple reflections can be rendered.

Kajiya [19] has demonstrated that by long calculation and a little pruning of the ray tree, it is possible to include diffuse as well as specular reflections in this scheme, allowing a completely general f_r. Immel, Cohen, and Greenberg [18] have also solved the same interreflection problem for general f_r, by dividing the surface into polygons, and solving a huge system of linear equations.

In this paper we apply our bidirectional reflection distribution function to the case that L_{in} is independent of position, as if the environment were painted on a sphere at infinity. In this case $L_{in}(\theta_{in}, \phi_{in})$ can be sampled into a texture table. Greene [13] has called techniques based on such a table "environment mapping", and surveyed methods for obtaining the integral for L_{ref} efficiently from the table. For example, if f_r is constant (diffuse reflection) L_{ref} depends only on the normal N, and Miller and Hoffman [22] suggest that it be precomputed and tabulated. In the Phong reflection model [26], f_r depends only on the mirror reflection $M = (\theta_{mirror}, \phi_{mirror})$ of the viewing direction $V = (\theta_{ref}, \phi_{ref})$, so L_{ref} can again be precomputed and tabulated as a function of $(\theta_{mirror}, \phi_{mirror})$ (See [22].)

Consider a somewhat more general f_r, which, as a function of (θ_{in}, ϕ_{in}) for fixed V and fixed normal N, has elliptical symmetry about some "off specular" peak direction $P = (\theta_{peak}, \phi_{peak})$ near M. (See [1] or [32].) That is, contours of constant f_r correspond to small concentric ellipses about P on the sphere of (θ_{in}, ϕ_{in}) directions. (See figure 1.) The shape of f_r is determined by the eccentricity, which is the same for all these ellipses, and by a curve on a cross section plane through N and P, specifying f_r as a function of the ellipse size. The shape of f_r usually varies with θ_{ref}, and the orientation of the ellipses varies with N, so the integrals cannot be precomputed as a function of $(\theta_{peak}, \phi_{peak})$ alone.

The elliptical weighted average filter of Greene and Heckbert [14] can take advantage of the elliptical symmetry of f_r to estimate the integral for L_{ref} from the tabulated values of $L_{in}(\theta_{in}, \phi_{in})$. Its computation time is proportional to the number of entries in the table which contribute to the integral, so this method is most efficient for shiny surfaces, with narrow specular peaks. Greene [13] has suggested using Williams' pyramidal parametrics [36] together with elliptical weighted averages, so that the number of entries in the selected table is bounded, independent of the width of specular peak. Glassner [12] has shown how to use summed area tables (See Crow [10]) to approximate the integral of L_{in} over larger ellipses. But his method requires that f_r be constant

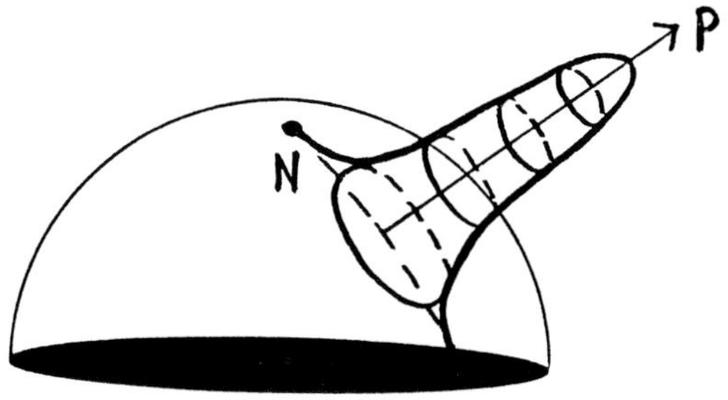

Figure 1.

inside the ellipse, and zero outside.

Perlin [25] has generalized summed area tables to higher order, and shown how to approximate an elliptical gaussian by piecewise quadratic polynomials, whose convolutions with L_{in} can be obtained using the second order tables, in time independent of the width of the gaussian. (See Heckbert [16] for a more detailed explanation.) The ellipses must be oriented with their major and minor axes horizontal or vertical in the texture table. This can be arranged in the following case. Suppose the view of the reflecting object is from far away, so that the viewing direction V can be assumed to be constant, and that L_{in} is tabulated in spherical coordinates, with V as the north pole. An isotropic bidirectional function will have mirror symmetry with respect to a plane through V and N, so its contour ellipses must also. This guarantees the required orientation, since a plane through the pole is a line of constant azimuthal angle in the texture table.

Greene [14] also considers the problem of antialiasing reflections in a curved, perfectly shiny mirror, to account for the fact that the ray from the eye reflects in directions which vary over the area of the pixel. He proposes elliptical weighted average filtering, using values of L_{in} tabulated on the six faces of an environment cube. A gaussian weighting about the pixel center, for slowly curving mirrors, will transform to an approximate elliptical gaussian in the environment map, in spherical coordinates as well as on an environment cube. To generalize this to the case of a glossy curved mirror, the appropriate filter is the convolution of the weighting function with the specular bidirectional reflection function f_r. If f_r can be approximated by an elliptical gaussian, the convolution of these two functions is again an elliptical gaussian, which may no longer be oriented consistently with the spherical axes. The method of Perlin [24] no longer applies, but the method of Greene and Heckbert [13,14] can still be used. Miller and Hoffman [22] also include antialiasing in their technique. Of course, in distributed ray tracing [2,7], the rays can be distributed simultaneously over both the subpixel positions and the glossy reflection directions.

The method of integration we propose in section 7 below works under restricting assumptions similar to those above: a) L_{in} is independent of position, b) V is constant, and c) f_r is isotropic. However, we can handle arbitrarily shaped f_r, which can combine specular and diffuse reflection. We expand both $\cos\theta_{in} f_r$ and L_{in} in spherical harmonics, with V as the north pole. The integral for L_{ref} can then be computed efficiently as the dot product of the coefficient vectors for $\cos\theta_{in} f_r$ and L_{in}. Because the computation time is proportional to the number of coefficients, our method works best for rougher surfaces, where f_r is wide and can be approximated by fewer terms. (This is in contrast to the methods of Greene and Heckbert [14] and Immel, Cohen, and Greenberg [18], which work better for narrow f_r.)

4. Horizon Mapping

Horizon tables were originally developed to create shadows on bump-mapped surfaces [21]. Imagine a bump height function, tabulated on an $m \times m$ grid, representing the altitude of a mountainous terrain, with $x = east$, $y = north$, and $z = up$. Suppose the sun sets to the west in a vertical plane, as it would at the equator on an equinox. Then a point on the terrain is in shadow whenever the sun is below the horizon, that is, whenever the angle θ from the Z axis to the sun is greater than the angle β from the Z axis to the western horizon. The angle to the western horizon can be computed at each tabulated position, by looking at the slopes of lines from that position to other tabulated positions to its west, and finding the maximum slope. The bump map is doubly periodic in x and y, so that the slope can be determined by the $m-1$ points to the west, even for a starting point near the western edge of the bump map. The angle of the horizon can be determined similarly for any sunset direction, that is, for any half plane through the Z axis. Max [21] proposed using only the eight principal compass directions, for which the slope to the horizon can be easily determined from the bump table. This resulted in a horizon table of size $m \times m \times 8$, and the horizon angle at other compass directions was determined by interpolation. Mountains which are missed by the sampled compass directions from a data point will fail to cast shadows on the point, so more compass directions will give more accurate results.

In this work, we have used 24 directions. Let PQ represent a ray from the data point P in one of these directions, shown intersecting the triangles in Figure 2. The bump heights at an intersection point with a triangle side are determined by interpolation from the tabulated vertices at endpoints of the side. Note that the interpolation factors, and the positions of the two endpoints relative to the start of the ray, depend only on the ray's direction. To speed up the calculation of the horizon table, this information is computed ahead of time for each ray direction [5].

Max [21] shows how to use the horizon table computed for a flat surface, to find the bump shadows when the flat surface is parametrized onto a curved surface patch. Here we will use it to estimate energy reflected from the bumpy surface.

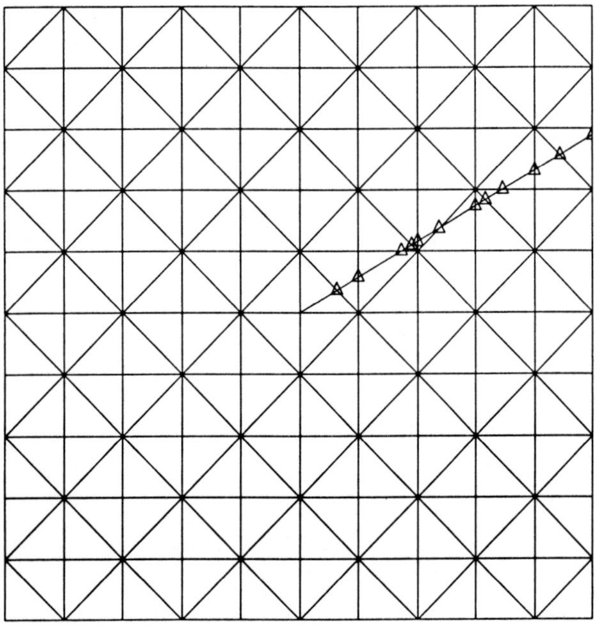

Figure 2. Ray PQ intersecting grid tessellations.

5. Reflection From Facets

Consider a collimated parallel beam of light coming to the surface S from the direction $W_{in} = (\theta_{in}, \phi_{in})$, with radiant flux density D_{in} measured per unit area normal to W_{in}. This is the limit for a source of radiance L_{in} and solid angle $d\omega_{in}$, as the source moves away to infinity, and $d\omega_{in}$ approaches zero, while the radiance increases to keep $L_{in}d\omega_{in}$ equal to D_{in}. Since W_{in} is tilted away from the normal N by an angle θ_{in}, the irrradiance incident on S is $D_{in}\cos\theta_{in} = D_{in}(W_{in}\cdot N)$.

We divide S into $2m^2$ triangular facets, as shown projected in figure 2. If U_i and V_i represent the vectors along the edges of facet S_i, which project to the horizontal and vertical edges in figure 2, then the area A_i of S_i is $|U_i \times V_i|/2$, and the normal N_i to S_i is $(U_i \times V_i)/|U_i \times V_i|$. Given N_i and W_{in} we can compute the reflected direction $R_i = 2(W_{in}\cdot N_i)N_i - W_{in}$ (See Whitted [34]).

The obscuring effects of other facets can be estimated from the horizon table. We can determine from the entries for the compass direction θ_{in}, the three horizon angles β_1, β_2, and β_3 for the three vertices of S_i. If the samples for θ_{in} for the tabulated bidirectional reflection function correspond to those in the horizon table, no interpolation is required. When β_1, β_2, and β_3 are all greater than θ_{in}, the facet S_i is completely lit, and when all are less than θ_{in}, the whole facet is in shadow. When some are greater and some are less, the partial shadowing is determined as follows. Along the two sides where $\beta_j - \theta_{in}$ changes sign, we interpolate to estimate two points where $\beta = \theta_{in}$. The line joining these two points separates the triangle into a quadrilateral and a smaller triangle, one of which is illuminated and the other, shadowed.

Shadowed light contributes its flux instead to the specular reflection from the facet which intercepted it. But, as in the Torrance-Sparrow model, reflected light which is obscured on the way out is lost from the specular energy computation, and assumed to contribute instead to diffuse reflection or absorption.

The illuminated portion of the facet sends out a reflected beam in the direction $R_i = (\theta_{ref}, \phi_{ref})$. The portion of this beam which is not obscured can be found similarly, using the convention of Duff [11], Figure 1, to treat the case where $\beta - \theta_{ref}$ changes sign along all four sides of a quadrilateral. Since ϕ_{ref} can be an arbitrary azimuthal angle, interpolation in the horizon table is now required, which introduces another approximation in our calculations.

Let B_i be the area of the facet S_i which reflects the non-obscured, non-shadowed portion of the beam. This area projects to an area $B_i(N_i, W_{in})$ normal to the incident beam, and therefore intercepts a flux of $D_{in}B_i(N_i, W_{in})$. We assume the facet is perfectly smooth, so that the reflected flux is this incident flux multiplied by the Fresnel factor $F(N_i, W_{in})$. (See Born and Wolf [4].)

Now take a collection $\{V_k | k = 1, n\}$ of sampled reflection directions, and let $Nearest(V)$ be the index k of the V_k nearest to the unit vector V. (Choose the lower index in case of a tie.) Then $C_k = \{V \in D | Nearest(V) = k\}$ represents the bin on the hemisphere H assigned to V_k. Let $d\omega_k$ be the solid angle measure of C_k.

To accumulate the reflected flux into the appropriate bins, we assign the flux from facet S_i to bin $k = Nearest(R_i)$. When all $2m^2$ facets have been considered the total flux $\Phi_k(\theta_{in}, \phi_{in})$ in bin k is

$$\Phi_k(\theta_{in}, \phi_{in}) = \sum_{i=1}^{2m^2} \delta(k - Nearest(R_i))F(N_i, W_{in})D_{in}B_i(W_{in}\cdot N_i) \quad (2).$$

We find the reflected radiance $L_{ref,k}$ in the direction V_k for bin k, by dividing the flux Φ_k by the area dB of S normal to the outgoing direction V_k, and by the solid angle $d\omega_k$ of the bin. The area dA of S is taken as the area of the flat lattice, shown in figure 2, on which the bumps are based. Then $dB = dA(V_k \cdot N)$. Thus

$$L_{ref,k} = \frac{\Phi(\theta_{in},\phi_{in})}{d\omega_k dA(V_k \cdot N)}$$

By definition, the bidirectional reflection function f_r is this reflected radiance, divided by the incoming irradiance. Since the incoming beam has a radiant flux density D_{in} measured normal to its direction W_{in}, its irradiance on the surface S is $D_{in}\cos\theta_{in} = D_{in}(W_{in} \cdot N)$, so

$$f_r(\theta_{in},\phi_{in};\theta_{ref},\phi_{ref}) = \frac{L_{ref,k}}{D_{in}(W_{in} \cdot N)}$$

Putting the above three equations together, we get

$$f_r(\theta_{in},\phi_{in};\theta_{ref},\phi_{ref}) = \frac{\sum_{i=1}^{2m^2} \delta(k - Nearest(R_i))F(N_i, W_{in})D_{in}B_i(W_{in} \cdot N_i)}{D_{in}(W_{in} \cdot N)d\omega_k dA(V_k \cdot N)}. \quad (3)$$

Note that D_{in} can be cancelled from both the numerator and denominator, so that $G_i = F(N_i, W_{in})B_i(W_{in} \cdot N_i)/(W_{in} \cdot N)dA$ represents the fraction of the incoming flux reflected by facet S_i, and

$$f_r(\theta_{in},\phi_{in};\theta_{ref},\phi_{ref}) = \frac{\sum_{i=1}^{2m^2} \delta(k - Nearest(R_i))G_i}{d\omega_k(V_k \cdot N)}. \quad (4)$$

If this computation is repeated for each of a finite collection of incident directions W_{in}, we can build up a bidirectional reflection table $f_r(\theta_{in},\phi_{in};\theta_{ref},\phi_{ref}) = f_r(W_j, V_k)$.

Torrance and Sparrow [32] consider a continuous distribution of hypothetical facets, all of the same projected area, with a density $\delta(N')$ per steradian having facet normal N'. They apply the formula $d\omega_{ref} = 4(W \cdot N')d\omega_{norm}$ from Rense [27], where $d\omega_{norm}$ is a small solid angle for normals about N', and $d\omega_{ref}$ is the solid angle of corresponding reflected directions for the incident ray from W. Because we are using an explicit collection of polygonal facets instead of a distribution, and accumulating the flux of the reflected beams into a predefined collection of bins, we do not need to include this solid angle spreading factor.

6. Reciprocity

Torrance and Sparrow also refer to the reciprocity law $f_r(V, W) = f_r(W, V)$ in Helmholtz [17], obtained by reversing the roles of the incident and reflected directions. Our calculated f_r should approximately satisfy this reciprocity law by the following reasoning.

Take the same collection of samples on the hemisphere H for both the viewing, V, and incident, W, direction indices in the tabulated bidirectional reflection. Assume that

$$C_k = \{V | Nearest(V) = k\} = \{V | Angle(V, V_k) < \gamma\}$$

for some small constant γ, so that C_k is a circular region on H, of radius γ. (This can never be exactly true, but is approximately true for a "hexagonally close packed" collection of directions based on icosahedral symmetry. The corresponding C_k's consist of 12 regular pentagonal regions and $30l^2 - 10$ regular or not-quite-regular hexagonal regions on the unit sphere. For example, a soccer ball is sewn from 12 black pentagonal and 20 white hexagonal pieces of leather, the case $l = 1$.)

Now consider a facet S_i of non-obscured area B_i, for incoming light direction W_j, and reflected beam direction R_i. Let $Nearest(R_i) = k$, so that $Angle(R_i, V_k) < \gamma$. Then the same facet will reflect V_k back to a ray within γ of W_j. The non-obscured area in the reverse situation will be close to B_i if γ is small, since all angles have changed by less than γ. Also, the angle between R_i and V_k is less than γ, so in equation (2) for incoming direction W_j, $W_j \cdot N_i = R_i \cdot N_i \approx V_k \cdot N_i$, and the Fresnel factors $F(N_i, W_j)$ and $F(N_i, V_k)$ are also close, since $F(N, W)$ depends only on the dot product of N and W. Thus the contributions of facet S_i to the sum $\Phi_k(W_j)$ in equation (2), and to the corresponding ray reversed sum $\Phi_j(V_k)$, are approximately equal. In the denominator of equation (3), we have assumed the solid angles $d\omega_k$ are all equal, and $V_k \cdot N$ and $W_j \cdot N$ both appear, so $f_r(W_j, V_k)$ and $f_r(V_k, W_j)$ are approximately equal also. We can thus decrease the size of the bidirectional reflection table by about half, and improve the sampling statistics, by setting both $f_r(W_j, V_k)$ and $f_r(V_k, W_j)$ to their average value, enforcing reciprocity.

Under the additional condition that the reflection is isotropic, $f_r(\theta_{in},\phi_{in};\theta_{ref},\phi_{ref})$ depends only on $\theta_{in}, \theta_{ref}$, and $|\phi_{in} - \phi_{ref}|$. Thus, the data for all bins with the same $|\phi_{in} - \phi_{ref}|$ can be averaged, reducing the table size and improving the statistics still further. In the following two sections, we assume f_r is isotropic.

7. Spherical Harmonics in Environment Mapping

The bidirectional reflection function can be used as a part of any shading algorithm. In this section, we discuss the use of spherical harmonics in shading computations based on environmental illumination. The spherical harmonic method can be used with any bidirectional reflection function. In section 8, however, we give a particularly efficient method of determining the spherical harmonic coefficients from the reflected beams.

For representing functions defined on the unit sphere, spherical harmonics functions are the analogues of the fourier series terms used on the unit circle. They are the products of associated Legendre functions with simple periodic functions in ϕ. When used to represent wave functions in physics, they are usually complex valued, but to represent images, we need real functions. The real spherical harmonics may be expressed in terms of $\cos n\phi$ and $\sin n\phi$:

$$Y_{ln}(\theta,\phi) = \begin{cases} M_{ln}P_{ln}(\cos\theta)\cos n\phi & n \geq 0; \\ M_{ln}P_{l|n|}(\cos\theta)\sin|n|\phi & n < 0; \end{cases}$$

where

$$M_{ln} = \begin{cases} \sqrt{\frac{(2l+1)}{2\pi}\frac{(l-|n|)!}{(l+|n|)!}}, & n \neq 0; \\ \sqrt{\frac{(2l+1)}{4\pi}}, & n = 0; \end{cases}$$

and $P_{ln}(\cos\theta)$ is the associated Legendre function. (See Courant and Hilbert [9].) The spherical harmonics form an orthonormal basis for the Hilbert space of functions on the unit sphere. Thus any real function $h(\theta,\phi)$ has an expansion

$$h(\theta,\phi) = \sum_{l=0}^{\infty}\sum_{n=-l}^{l} a_{ln}Y_{ln}(\theta,\phi).$$

We can speed up the calculation of the integral in equation (1) by approximating the factor $\cos\theta_{in} f_r(W, V)$ with spherical harmonics. We reorganize the spherical coordinates so that the pole is in the viewing direction V. The isotropic bidirectional reflection function $f_r(W, V)$ really depends on the three vectors W, V, and N. (For non-isotropic reflection functions, tangent vectors are also required.) In the previous section, N was assumed fixed, but now V is fixed. So we change notation, and let $f_{r_N}(\theta,\phi)$ denote the bidirectional reflection function of the illumination direction $W = (\theta,\phi)$, for V permanently fixed, and N temporarily fixed and indicated in the subscript. We have taken V along the Z axis, and will at first assume that N lies in the XZ plane, with spherical coordinates $(\alpha, 0)$. Since f_r is isotropic, $f_{r_N}(\theta,\phi)$ is symmetric with respect to the XZ plane, and $f_{r_N}(\theta,-\phi) = f_{r_N}(\theta,\phi)$. As a result, $\cos\theta_{in} f_{r_N}(\theta,\phi)$ can be expanded in spherical harmonics with terms in $\cos n\phi$ but none in $\sin n\phi$, that is, there are no a_{ln} terms for $n < 0$. This expansion is defined over the whole unit sphere Q, instead of just the hemisphere H, so we will replace $\cos\theta_{in}$ by $\widehat{\cos}\theta_{in} = max(\cos\theta_{in}, 0)$. Thus the expansion of $\widehat{\cos}\theta_{in} f_{r_N}(\theta,\phi)$ is:

$$\widehat{\cos}\theta_{in} f_{r_N}(\theta,\phi) = \sum_{l=0}^{\infty}\sum_{n=0}^{l} a_{ln}(\alpha)Y_{ln}(\theta,\phi).$$

The expansion is an infinite series, but if we replace the infinite upper bound in the first summation by a finite upper bound M, we get an approximation to $\widehat{\cos}\theta_{in} f_{r_N}(\theta,\phi)$. We will calculate the coefficients $a_{ln}(\alpha_j)$ for a finite sample $\{N_j | j = 1, J\}$ of normals in the XZ plane, with spherical coordinates $(\alpha_j, 0)$, and find $a_{ln}(\alpha)$ for other normals $N = (\alpha, 0)$ by interpolation.

Now let N be an unrestricted normal, with spherical coordinates (α, β). A rotation of $-\beta$ about the Z axis takes (α, β) to $N_0 = (\alpha, 0)$, and $W = (\theta, \phi)$ to $W_0 = (\theta, \phi - \beta)$. Since the reflection function is isotropic, and only depends on the relative angles between V, N, and W, $f_{r_N}(\theta,\phi) = f_{r_{N_0}}(\theta, \phi-\beta)$. Also, $\widehat{\cos}\theta_{in}$ depends only on the angle between W and N. Therefore

$$\widehat{\cos}\theta_{in} f_{r_N}(\theta,\phi) \approx \sum_{l=0}^{M}\sum_{n=0}^{l} a_{ln}(\alpha) M_{ln} P_{ln}(\cos\theta)\cos(n(\phi-\beta)).$$

But

$$\begin{aligned}\cos n(\phi-\beta) &= \cos(n\phi - n\beta)\\ &= \cos n\phi \cos n\beta + \sin n\phi \sin n\beta.\end{aligned}$$

Therefore

$$\widehat{\cos}\theta_{in} f_{r_N}(\theta,\phi) \approx \sum_{l=0}^{M}\sum_{n=-l}^{l} \tilde{a}_{ln} M_{ln} P_{l|n|}(\cos\theta) \begin{cases}\cos n\phi, & n \geq 0;\\ \sin |n|\phi, & n < 0;\end{cases}$$

where

$$\tilde{a}_{ln} = \begin{cases} a_{ln}(\alpha)\cos n\beta, & n \geq 0;\\ a_{l|n|}(\alpha)\sin |n|\beta, & n < 0.\end{cases}$$

We now have terms in $\sin n\phi$, so there are $\tilde{a}_{ln}$ for $n < 0$. The computation of the $a_{ln}(\alpha)$ is explained in section 4.

The radiance of the environment, $L_{in}(\theta,\phi)$, may also be expanded in real spherical harmonics:

$$L_{in}(\theta,\phi) = \sum_{l=0}^{\infty}\sum_{n=-l}^{l} b_{ln} Y_{ln}(\theta,\phi).$$

Since the Y_{ln} are an orthonormal basis, the coefficients b_{ln} are computed by integrating the product of the illumination function and the spherical harmonics over the unit sphere:

$$b_{ln} = \int_Q L_{in}(\theta,\phi) Y_{ln}(\theta,\phi) d\omega \qquad (5).$$

Having expanded both the reflection function and the environmental radiance function in spherical harmonics, we can now estimate the integral of equation (1):

$$\begin{aligned} L_{ref} &= \int_H \cos\theta_{in} f_r(V,W) L_{in}(\theta,\phi) d\omega\\ &= \int_Q \widehat{\cos}\theta_{in} f_r(V,W) L_{in}(\theta,\phi) d\omega\\ &\approx \int_Q \sum_{l=0}^{M}\sum_{n=-l}^{l} \tilde{a}_{ln} Y_{ln}(\theta,\phi) \sum_{l'=0}^{\infty}\sum_{n'=-l'}^{l'} b_{l'n'} Y_{l'n'}(\theta,\phi) d\omega\\ &= \sum_{l=0}^{M}\sum_{n=-l}^{l}\sum_{l'=0}^{\infty}\sum_{n'=-l'}^{l'} \tilde{a}_{ln} b_{l'n'} \int_Q Y_{ln}(\theta,\phi) Y_{l'n'}(\theta,\phi) d\omega\\ &= \sum_{l=0}^{M}\sum_{n=-l}^{l}\sum_{l'=0}^{\infty}\sum_{n'=-l'}^{l'} \tilde{a}_{ln} b_{l'n'} \quad \delta(l,l')\delta(n,n')\\ &= \sum_{l=0}^{M}\sum_{n=-l}^{l} \tilde{a}_{ln} b_{ln}. \end{aligned}$$

Thus L_{ref} becomes the inner product of these two coefficient vectors. If L_{in} has high spatial frequencies, but f_r does not, then f_r acts like a filter in the integral for L_{ref}, averaging out the high frequencies in L_{in}. Thus when the terms up to $l = M$ are sufficient to represent $\widehat{\cos}\theta_{in} f_{r_N}(\theta,\phi)$, the higher terms in L_{in} are eliminated from the integral by the orthogonality of the Y_{ln}.

For a curved or bump-mapped surface, the bidirectional reflection function should be further widened and frequency limited, to account for the variation of surface normals within a pixel, as mentioned in the introduction above. An inexpensive way to do this is to limit the range of l indices in the expansion for $\widehat{\cos}\theta f_{r_N}$ to some maximum M' less than M. The values of a_{ln} can be gradually decreased for large l, so that the expansion varies smoothly with the range of normals within a pixel. Decreasing the weight for terms with large l also helps eliminate the "ringing", or Gibbs phenomenon, at sharp edges or in $L_{in}(\theta,\phi)$.

The M-term approximation for $\widehat{\cos}\theta_{in} f_{r_N}(\theta,\phi)$ cannot be exactly zero in the hemisphere $Q - H$ behind the surface, where $\widehat{\cos}\theta_{in}$ is zero. This can cause slight reflections of objects behind the surface, but such artifacts do not appear disturbing in the images shown here.

If $L_{in}(\theta,\phi)$ is represented as a cube whose six faces are texture maps, as in Greene [13], the integral in equation (5) can be estimated by summation over the texture pixels. This integral must be computed only once, for the first viewing direction V. For each new viewing direction the set of coefficients b_{ln} may be transformed by taking a linear combination of the original coefficients:

$$\tilde{b}_{ln} = \sum_{n'=-l}^{l} b_{ln'} D^l_{n'n}(\alpha,\beta,\gamma)$$

where the matrices $D^l_{n'n}$ describe how the spherical harmonics transform under rotation through the Eulerian angles α, β, and γ. (See Tinkham [31].) Note that each D matrix will be of size $2l+1$, with the largest matrix requiring $(2M+1)\times(2M+1)$ elements. The use of these rotation matrices is clearly more efficient than recomputing the coefficients for each new viewing direction.

The expansion

$$L_{ref} \approx \sum_{l=0}^{M}\sum_{n=-l}^{l} \tilde{a}_{ln}(\alpha) b_{ln} \qquad (6)$$

has $(M+1)^2$ terms, each each requiring interpolation and rotation, and it must be computed once per pixel. This is better than doing an integral per pixel, but it can be simplified still further by precomputing some of the interpolation, as follows.

Once per surface texture, for $j = 1, ..., J$, for $l = 0, ..., M$, and for $n = 0, ..., l$, compute

$$a_{ln}(\alpha_j) = \int_Q \widehat{\cos}\theta_{in} f_{r_{N_j}}(\theta,\phi) Y_{ln}(\theta,\phi)\sin\theta d\theta d\phi \qquad (7)$$

for $N_j = (\alpha_j, 0)$. Once per viewing direction/surface-texture combination, and for $j = 1, ...J$, compute

$$g_n(\alpha_j) = \sum_{l=|n|}^{M} a_{l,n}(\alpha_j) b_{l,n}. \qquad (8)$$

There may be only one constant viewing direction, in the approximation of distant viewing discussed above. But suppose the scene contains several objects, each subtending a small angle of view, even if the whole image covers a large angle. Then there may be a separate viewing direction for each object. There may even be a separate environment for each object, if the hidden surface computation for the environment texture cube is recomputed from the point of view of each object. This allows one level of glossy interreflection between objects to be approximated. There may also be different viewing directions for different frames of an animation.

Now suppose we are at a specific pixel on a specific surface, where the normal N has spherical coordinates (α, β). For each $n = -M, ..., M$, we interpolate $g_n(\alpha)$ from the $g_n(\alpha_j)$ for the appropriate surface texture. In order not to introduce derivative discontinuities in the shading, which could be visible as Mach bands, some form of C^1 interpolation, such as Catmull-Rom splines [6], should be used. We can precompute ahead of time the coefficients of the interpolation polynomials for each interval $\alpha_j \leq \alpha \leq \alpha_j + 1$, for $n = 0, ...M$, and for each surface texture. Once the $g_n(\alpha)$ are found, the radiance L_{ref} becomes

$$L_{ref} = \sum_{n=0}^{M} (g_n(\alpha) \cos n\beta + g_{-n}(\alpha) \sin n\beta)$$

which results when equation (8) and the definitions for $\tilde{a}_{ln}$ are combined with equation (6). This equation represents L_{ref} as a Fourier series in β for fixed α, which is a useful way of approximating a smooth function on a circle. It is only necessary to evaluate $\cos\beta$ and $\sin\beta$, as $\cos n\beta$ and $\sin n\beta$ can be obtained from these inductively, with two multiplies and one add each. The cubic interpolations take three multiplies and three adds each. Therefore, the total cost per pixel is two trigonometric function evaluations, about 12M multiplies, and about 9M adds. On a vector computer like the Cray-1, it is easier to do 2M trig evaluations, 8M multiplies and 7M adds, because everything can then be vectorized.

8. Computing the coefficients $a_{ln}(\alpha_j)$

The bidirectional reflection function enters into the shading computations of the previous section, in the integral of equation (7) for the coefficients $a_{ln}(\alpha_j)$. We wish to apply the method of section 5 for the bidirectional reflection function from an explicit surface model. We could estimate this integral by assuming $f_{r_N}(\theta, \phi)$ was constant over each of the bins in the table. (Note that these bins are in spherical coordinates with N as axis, not V.) But it is possible to get a better estimate, taking advantage of the exact flux and direction of the beam reflected from each facet.

For each of the sampled normals $N_j = (\alpha_j, 0)$ in the XZ plane, place the bump texture in an orientation perpendicular to N_j. The texture can be rotated about N_j, and the calculations below can be summed over all the rotated positions, to get better statistics for an isotropic bidirectional reflection function. Neglecting the $\sin n\phi$ terms in the expansion automatically enforces averaging over the reflection of the texture in the XZ plane, by projecting onto the subspace of functions f_r with $f_r(\theta, \phi) = f_r(\theta, -\phi)$.

By reciprocity, we can trace the beams from the fixed viewing direction V, and accumulate the flux at the different lighting directions W. Recall from Section 2 that B_i represents the non-obscured area of the ith facet, N_i its normal, and $F(N_i, V)$ the Fresnel law, so that $G_i = B_i F(N_i, V)(N_i \cdot V)/(V \cdot N)dA$ is the fraction of the incoming flux reflected by the facet, in the direction $W_i = 2(V \cdot N_i)N_i - V$. Let $h_{W_i}(W)$ be a smoothing function of W which is maximum at W_i, zero far away from W_i and outside the hemisphere H, and has integral over the unit sphere equal to one. Then $G(W) = \sum_{i=1}^{2m^2} h_{W_i}(W) G_i$ is an approximation to the flux fraction per solid angle reflected from V to the unit sphere Q, by the faceted surface, smoothed so as to be integrable.

In Equation (4), we divided this flux fraction per solid angle by $V_k \cdot N$, which corresponds to $W_i \cdot N$ here, to get the bidirectional reflection function. We need not divide now by $W_i \cdot N = \cos\theta_{in} = \widehat{\cos}\theta_{in}$, since we want to estimate $\widehat{\cos}\theta_{in} f_{r_N}$ in the integral (7). Thus

$$\begin{aligned} a_{ln}(\alpha_j) &= \int_Q \widehat{\cos}\theta_{in} f_r(\theta, \phi) Y_{ln}(\theta, \phi) d\omega \\ &\approx \int_Q G(W) Y_{ln}(\theta, \phi) d\omega \\ &= \sum_{i=1}^{2m^2} G_i \int_Q h_{W_i}(W) Y_{ln}(\theta, \phi) d\omega \end{aligned}$$

Denote the spherical coordinates of W_i by (θ_i, ϕ_i), and take the limit as $h_{W_i}(W)$ approaches the delta function. We get

$$a_{ln}(\alpha_j) \approx \sum_{i=1}^{2m^2} G_i Y_{ln}(\theta_i, \phi_i)$$

Therefore we can estimate the $a_{ln}(\alpha_j)$ by computing G_i for each facet, and then for each l and n, adding $G_i Y_{ln}(\theta_i, \phi_i)$ to the appropriate sum. The resulting spherical harmonic expansion defines a smooth function which is a least squares approximation to the density distribution of the flux in the various reflected beams.

9. Bump Maps and Results

The bidirectional reflection algorithm presented in section 5 relies on precomputed height or bump maps. We generated several bidirectional reflection function tables based on several different 256 x 256 bump maps. These bump maps represented different types of surface micro geometries.

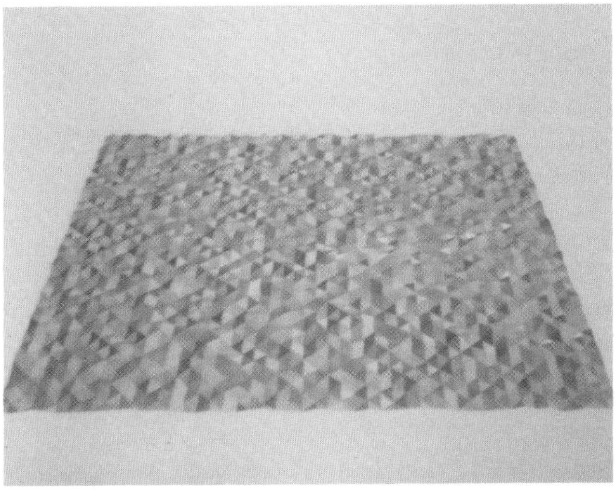

Figure 3a. Sample white noise surface.

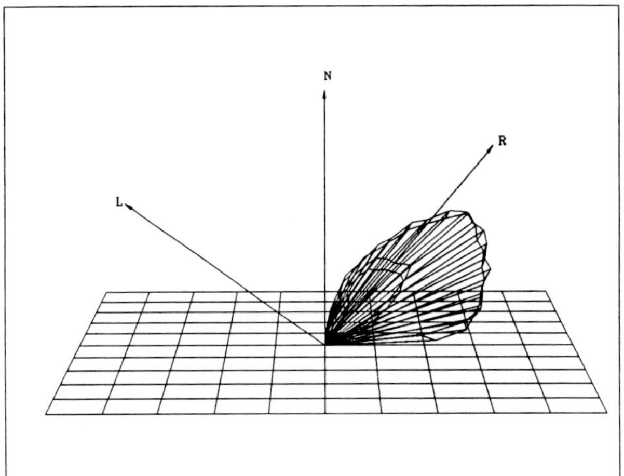

Figure 3b. BDRF with $\theta_{in} = 0.81$ and $\phi_{in} = 0.0$

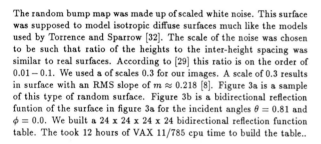

Figure 4a. Sphere reflecting environment map.

The random bump map was made up of scaled white noise. This surface was supposed to model isotropic diffuse surfaces much like the models used by Torrence and Sparrow [32]. The scale of the noise was chosen to be such that ratio of the heights to the inter-height spacing was similar to real surfaces. According to [29] this ratio is on the order of $0.01 - 0.1$. We used a of scales 0.3 for our images. A scale of 0.3 results in surface with an RMS slope of $m \approx 0.218$ [8]. Figure 3a is a sample of this type of random surface. Figure 3b is a bidirectional reflection funtion of the surface in figure 3a for the incident angles $\theta = 0.81$ and $\phi = 0.0$. We built a 24 x 24 x 24 x 24 bidirectional reflection function table. The took 12 hours of VAX 11/785 cpu time to build the table..

Figure 4a and 4b are front and back renderings of an environment map (from NYIT) as reflected off a sphere. The sphere surface's BDRF was generated with the method discussed in section 5. The BDRF was combined with the spherical harmonics with the method described in section 8.

Conclusion

Table generated bidirectional reflection functions based on bump mapped micro surfaces can be used with spherical harmonics to render environments reflected off of various surfaces. We presented methods to approximate the micro surfaces, light reflecting off the surfaces, and the environment-reflection integral (eq. 1).

There are a number of future directions that need to be explored. Much more study into the micro surface properties of real surfaces needs to be done in order to more accurately model various micro surfaces. A bidirectional reflection function algorithm based on ray tracing could produce a more accurate horizon approximation and model higher order reflections. This ray tracer could be designed to exploit the surface geometry and thus be made to run faster than an ordinary ray tracer. Lastly a technique could be developed for taking the bidirectional reflection tables and blending them into texture maps for specific viewing and lighting angles.

Acknowledgements

This work was performed under the auspices of the U.S. Department of Energy by Lawrence Livermore National Laboratory under contract number W-7405-ENG-48. We wish to thank Don Vickers, Ken Joy, Chuck Grant, Michael Gwilliam, Jeff Kallman, and Dave Temple for helpful discussions and suggestions, and Ned Greene and the New York Institute of Technology for the environment map from [19].

Disclaimer

References

1. Blinn, James. *Models of Light Reflection for Computer Synthesized Pictures.* Proceedings of SIGGRAPH '77 (San Jose, California, July 20-22, 1977). In Computer Graphics 11, 2, (July 1977), 192-198.

2. Blinn, James. *Simulation of Wrinkled Surfaces.* Proceedings of SIGGRAPH '78 (Atlanta, Georgia, August 23-25, 1978). In Computer Graphics 12, 3, (August 1978), 286-292.

3. Blinn, James, and Newell, Martin. *Texture and Reflection in Computer Synthesized Pictures.* Comm. ACM. Vol. 19, No. 10, pp. 542-547. 1976.

4. Born, Max, and Wolf, Emil. *Principles of Optics.* Pergamon Press. Oxford 1980

5. Bresenham, J. E. *Algorithm for computer control of a digital plotter.* IBM Systems Journal. Vol 4. pp. 25-30. 1965.

6. Catmull, Edwin, and Rom, Raphael. *A Class of Interpolating Splines,* in Computer Aided Geometric Design. Barnhill and Riesenfeld, Eds. Academic Press, pp. 317-326. New York.1974.

7. Cook, Robert, Porter, Thomas, and Carpenter, Loren. *Distributed Ray Tracing.* Proceedings of SIGGRAPH '84 (Minneapolis, Minnesota, July 23-27, 1984). In Computer Graphics 18, 3, (July 1984), 137-145.

8. Cook, Robert and Torrance, Kenneth. *A Reflectance Model for Computer Graphics.* Proceedings of SIGGRAPH '81 (Dallas, Texas, August 3-7, 1981). In Computer Graphics 15, 3, (August 1981), 307-316.

9. Courant, R., and Hilbert, D. *Methods of Mathematical Physics.* Interscience Publishers, Inc., p. 513. New York. 1953.

10. Crow, Franklin. *Summed-Area Tables for Texture Mapping.* Proceedings of SIGGRAPH '84 (Minneapolis, Minnesota, July 23-27, 1984). In Computer Graphics 18, 3, (July 1984), 207-212.

11. Duff, Tom. *Compositing 3-D Rendered Images.* Proceedings of SIGGRAPH '85 (San Francisco, California, July 22-26, 1985). In Computer Graphics 19, 3, (July 1985), 41-44.

12. Glassner, Andrew. *Adaptive Precision in Texture Mapping.* Proceedings of SIGGRAPH '86 (Dallas, Texas, August 18-22, 1986). In Computer Graphics 20, 4, (August 1986), 297-306.

13. Greene, Ned. *Applications of World Projections.* IEEE CG&A. Vol. 6, No. 11. pp. 21-29.1986.

14. Greene, Ned, and Heckbert, Paul. *Creating Raster Omnimax Images from Multiple Perspective Views using the Elliptical Weighted Average Filter.* IEEE CG&A. Vol. 6, No. 6, pp. 21-27. 1986.

15. Hall, Roy, and Greenberg, Donald. *A Testbed for Realistic Image Synthesis* IEEE Computer Graphics and Applications Volume 3, No. 8, pp. 10-20 1984

16. Heckbert, Paul. *Filtering by Repeated Integration* Proceedings of SIGGRAPH '86 (Dallas, Texas, August 18-22, 1986). In Computer Graphics 20, 4, (August 1986), 315-321.

17. Helmholtz, H.v. *Helmoltz's Treatise on Physiological Optics.* Optical Society Of America. Washington, D.C. 1924.

18. Immel, David, Cohen, Michael, and Greenberg, Donald. *A Radiosity Method for Non-Diffuse Environments.* Proceedings of SIGGRAPH '86 (Dallas, Texas, August 18-22, 1986). In Computer Graphics 20, 4, (August 1986), 133-142.

19. Kajiya, James. *The Rendering Equation.* Proceedings of SIGGRAPH '86 (Dallas, Texas, August 18-22, 1986). In Computer Graphics 20, 4, (August 1986), 143-150.

20. Kajiya, James, and Von Herzen, Brian. *Ray Tracing Volume Densities.* Proceedings of SIGGRAPH '84 (Minneapolis, Minnesota, July 23-27, 1984). In Computer Graphics 18, 3, (July 1984), 165-174.

21. Max, Nelson. *Shadows for Bump Mapped Surfaces.* Advanced Computer Graphics, T. L. Kunii, Ed. Springer Verlag, Tokyo. pp. 145-156. 1986.

22. Miller, Gene, and Hoffman, Robert. *Illumination and Reflection Maps: Simulated Objects in Simulated and Real Environments.* Advanced Image Synthesis Course Notes. Siggraph Conference. 1984.

23. Ohira, Tomohiro. *A Shading Model for Anisotropic Reflection.* Technical Report of The Institute of Electronics and Communication Engineers of Japan, in Japanese. Vol. 82, No. 235, pp. 47-54. 1983.

24. Perlin, Kenneth. Course Notes. Siggraph Conference. 1984.

25. Perlin, Kenneth. *Course Notes.* SIGGRAPH '85 State of the Art in Image Synthesis Seminar Notes. submitted to IEEE CG&A, and personal communication. 1986.

26. Phong, Bui-Tuong. *Illumination for Computer Generated Images.* Comm. ACM. Vol. 18, No. 6, pp. 311-17. 1975.

27. Rense, W. A. *Polarization Studies of Light Diffusely Reflected from Ground and Etched Glass Surfaces.* J. Opt. Soc. Am. Vol 40, No. 1. pp. 55-59. 1950.

28. Snell, Jay. *Radiometery and Photometery.* Handbook of Optics. Driscoll, W. G. and Vaughen. W., Eds. McGraw-Hill. 1978.

29. Spangenberg, D. B., Strang, A. G., and Chamberlin, J. L. *Surface Texture Measurments of Metal Surfaces* National Bureau Standards, Special Publication 300 Vol 7. Washington, D.C. 1971.

30. Takagi, J., Yokoi, S., and Tsurwoka, S. *Comment on the Anisotropic Reflection Model.* Bulletin of SIG. Graphics and CAD, Information Processing Society of Japan, in Japanese. Vol. 11. No. 1 pp. 1-9. 1983.

31. Tinkham, M. *Group Theory and Quantum Mechanics.* McGraw Hill pp.101-115. New York. 1964.

32. Torrance, Kenneth, and Sparrow, Ephraim. *Theory for Off-Specular Reflection from Roughened Surface.* Journal of the Optical Society of America. Volume 57 No. 9 1967.

33. *USA Standard Nomenclature and Definitions for Illuminating Engineering.* USAS Z7.1-1967. 1967.

34. Whitted, Turner. *An Improved Illumination Model for Shaded Display.* Comm. ACM. Vol. 23, No. 6, pp. 343-349. 1980.

35. Whitted, Turner, and Cook, Robert. *A Comprehensive Shading Model.* Image Rendering Tricks Course Notes. Siggraph Conference. 1985.

36. Williams, Lance. *Pyramidal Parametrics.* Proceedings of SIGGRAPH '83 (Detroit, Michigan, July 25-29, 1983). In Computer Graphics 17, 3, (July 1983), 1-11.

Rendering Antialiased Shadows with Depth Maps

William T. Reeves

David H. Salesin†

Robert L. Cook

Pixar
San Rafael, CA

ABSTRACT

We present a solution to the aliasing problem for shadow algorithms that use depth maps. The solution is based on a new filtering technique called percentage closer filtering. In addition to antialiasing, the improved algorithm provides soft shadow boundaries that resemble penumbrae. We describe the new algorithm in detail, demonstrate the effects of its parameters, and analyze its performance.

CR Categories and Subject Descriptors: I.3.3 [**Computer Graphics**]: Picture/Image Generation - Display algorithms; I.3.7 [**Computer Graphics**]: Three-Dimensional Graphics and Realism - Color, shading, shadowing, and texture

General Terms: Algorithms, Performance Analysis

Key Words: shadows, depth maps, antialiasing, percentage closer filtering

1. Introduction

Shadows enhance the images synthesized by computers. Although many algorithms for rendering shadows have been published, most have been either restricted to a limited class of modeling primitives or are computationally expensive. Max [Max86] has classified these shadow rendering techniques as ray tracing, preprocessing, shadow volumes, area subdivision, and z-buffer algorithms.

Ray tracing algorithms [Whi80] [Kay79] [CPC84] [HaG86] produce excellent shadows and are easy to implement, but they are expensive. In order to make ray tracing more tractable, many techniques have been developed for quickly determining which object a secondary ray hits [Ama84] [HeH84] [RuW80] [KaK86]. However, this does not completely solve the problem, since once the object is determined it must still be accessed from the database. As models become more complex, the need to access any part of the model at any stage becomes more expensive; model and texture paging can dominate the rendering time.

Non ray tracing algorithms produce shadows without tracing secondary rays. Because objects can be sorted into buckets or scan lines according to the part of the screen they affect, the model can be accessed efficiently. But these algorithms also have serious limitations. Shadow α maps [ReB85] [Coo84] provide only a 2½-D solution, not a general 3-D solution. Preprocessing algorithms [BoK70] are suitable mostly for static environments. Shadow volumes [Cro77] [Ber86] [Max86] [NON85] [BrB84] and area subdivision algorithms [AWG78] are restricted to polygonal data and are inefficient for complex environments.

The z-buffer shadow algorithm developed by Williams [Wil78] does not have these problems. It can support all types of primitives; it is not excessively expensive, even for complex environments; and it is easy to implement. Its most serious drawback is a severe aliasing problem; it also requires additional memory for the z-buffer.

The z-buffer algorithm's singular versatility, efficiency, and simplicity make it tempting to look for ways to overcome its drawbacks, particularly the more serious aliasing problem. Storing floating point values in the depth buffer instead of 16-bit integers (as Williams did) reduces but does not solve this problem. An approach proposed by Hourcade and Nicolas [HoN85] stores object tags instead of depth values, but a limitation is that surfaces may not cast shadows on themselves.

In this paper, we introduce percentage closer filtering, a new sampling technique that can be used to eliminate the aliasing problem in Williams's z-buffer shadow algorithm. In addition to providing antialiased shadows, our new technique can be used to render soft shadow edges that resemble penumbrae.

2. Percentage Closer Filtering

The z-buffer algorithm presented in [Wil78] operates in two passes, as illustrated for a simple scene in Figure 1. In the first pass, a view of the scene is computed from the light source's point of view, and the z values for objects nearest the light are stored in a z-buffer (also known as a *depth map*). In the second pass, the scene is rendered from the camera's position. At each pixel, a point on the surface is transformed to light source space, and its transformed z is compared against the z of the object nearest the light, as recorded in the depth map. If the transformed z is behind the stored z, the point is considered to be in shadow.

This algorithm has two aliasing problems: one in creating the depth maps, and the other in sampling them. The first aliasing problem can be solved by creating the depth maps with stochastic sampling [Coo86]. We solve the second problem by introducing a new technique called *percentage closer filtering*.

† Current address: Computer Science Dept., Stanford University, Stanford, CA 94305

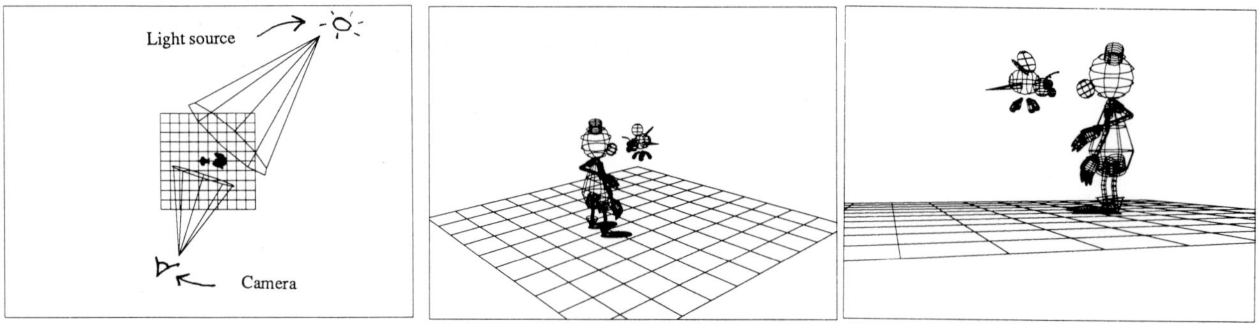

(a) View from high above the scene. (b) View from the light source. (c) View from the camera.

Figure 1. Points of view for a simple scene.

Ordinarily, texture maps are accessed by filtering the texture values over some region of the texture map. However, depth maps for shadow calculations cannot be accessed in this manner. The main problem is that the filtered depth value would be compared to the depth of the surface being rendered to determine whether or not the surface is in shadow at that point. The result of this comparison would be binary, making soft antialiased edges impossible. Another problem is that filtered depth values along the edges of objects would bear no relation to the geometry of the scene.

Our solution reverses the order of the filtering and comparison steps. The z values of the depth map across the entire region are first compared against the depth of the surface being rendered. This *sample transformation* converts the depth map under the region into a binary image, which is then filtered to give the proportion of the region in shadow. The resulting shadows have soft, antialiased edges.

The difference between ordinary texture map filtering and percentage closer filtering is shown schematically in Figure 2. In this example, the distance from the light source to the surface to be shadowed is $z = 49.8$. The region in the depth map that it maps onto (shown on the left in the figures) is a square measuring 3 pixels by 3 pixels.* Ordinary filtering would filter the depth map values to get 22.9 and then compare that to 49.8 to end up with a value of 1 meaning that 100% of the surface was in shadow. Percentage closer filtering compares each depth map value to 49.8 and then filters the array of binary values to arrive at a value of .55 meaning that 55% of the surface is in shadow.

* A square region and box filtering are used to simplify this example. The real algorithm, as described in subsequent sections, uses more sophisticated techniques.

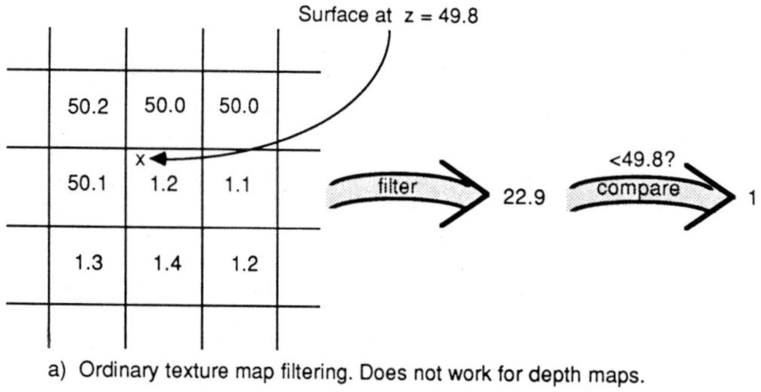

a) Ordinary texture map filtering. Does not work for depth maps.

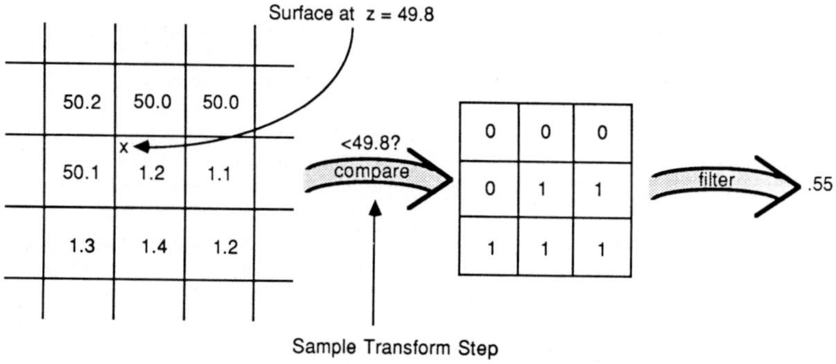

b) Percentage closer filtering.

Figure 2. Ordinary filtering versus percentage closer filtering.

In ordinary texture map applications, the cost of examining every pixel in a region can be avoided by saving the texture in some prefiltered format such as resolution pyramids [Wil83] or summed-area tables [Cro84]. Because our sample transformation depends on the *unfiltered* depth values, we cannot apply any such prefiltering technique here. But we can limit the number of texture pixel accesses in another way. By employing Monte Carlo techniques [Coo86], we can use a small, constant number of samples to approximate the result of transforming every sample in the region.

This can be done in one of several ways (Figure 3):

(a) choose samples randomly from a bounding box for the region;

(b) choose samples under some distribution, such as a Gaussian, from the same bounding box;

(c) partition the bounding box into subregions and sample each one with jitter;

(d) sample only positions inside the geometric boundary of the region.

Method (c), jitter sampling, approximates a Poisson disk distribution to produce shadows that are less noisy than those produced with either (a) or (b). All figures in this paper use (c), though (a) was used successfully in *Luxo Jr.* [Pix86]. Images made with (b) did not appear substantially different from those made with (a). We have not implemented (d), which is potentially more accurate, but also more complex and expensive.

Increasing the size of the sample region diffuses a shadow's edge over a larger area, resulting in a soft shadow edge resembling a penumbra. Although the shadow edges produced are not true penumbrae (in that their sizes do not depend on the relative distances between objects and light source), we have nevertheless found them convincing enough for many applications.

3. Implementation of the Algorithm

We now describe in detail how percentage closer filtering can be used with a depth buffer to create shadows. As in Williams's original z-buffer algorithm, we use two passes: one to create the depth map for each light source; and one to render the scene, using the depth maps to determine portions of objects in shadow.

3.1 First Pass: Creating the Depth Maps

The depth map for each light source is created by computing the depth values for all objects in the image from the light source's point of view. In the screen space of the light, the x- and y-coordinates correspond to pixel locations in the depth map, and the z-coordinate (in floating point) is the distance from the light in world space. We use the term *light space* to refer to these x, y, and z values.

In practice, we use regular sampling instead of stochastic sampling when creating the depth maps. This is because with one sample per pixel and low depth map resolutions, the slight aliasing of depth values with regular sampling is sometimes less objectionable than noise with stochastic sampling. We use a relatively course resolution for our depth maps in order to minimize the memory requirements.

The first pass can be implemented very easily. In our rendering system, we only needed to make one change: instead of computing and storing integer color values in a picture file, the closest z values (which are already being computed for hidden surface calculations) must be stored in floating point in a texture file.* This change amounted to about 40 lines of code out of over 30,000 for the rendering system as a whole.

A depth map can be computed faster than a shaded image for several reasons. First, none of the shading, texturing, and lighting calculations are needed. Second, objects (such as the ground plane) that never cast shadows on any other object can be ignored. Finally, depth maps require only one sample per pixel.

3.2 Second Pass: Rendering the Scene

In the second pass, the scene is rendered from the camera's point of view. Each shading calculation represents some region on a surface. Depending on the rendering system, these regions might represent anything from polygons covering large areas of pixels (e.g., for a painter's algorithm) to exact pixel regions (e.g., for scanline methods) to tiny subpixel regions (e.g., for micropolygons [CCC]). The shadow algorithm presented here is independent of the type of region used.

Each region to be shaded is first mapped into light space, giving a region in the depth map. Percentage closer filtering is used to determine the proportion of z values in the region of the depth map that are closer to the light than the surface. This gives the proportion of the surface in shadow over the region. This proportion is then used to attenuate the intensity of the light. If several lights in a scene cast shadows, this process is repeated for every light. The attenuated intensities are then used in the shading calculations.

One problem arises if the transformed region lies outside the extent of the depth map. Generally, we use the convention that regions outside the light source's field of view are *not* considered to be in shadow. For directed lights the distinction is not important, since objects outside a light's field of view are not illuminated by that light anyway. For lights that cast shadows in all directions, a more complex mapping scheme, such as spherical or cubical environment maps, should be used [Gre86].

* For pixels containing no visible surface, a very large constant is stored to denote an infinite depth.

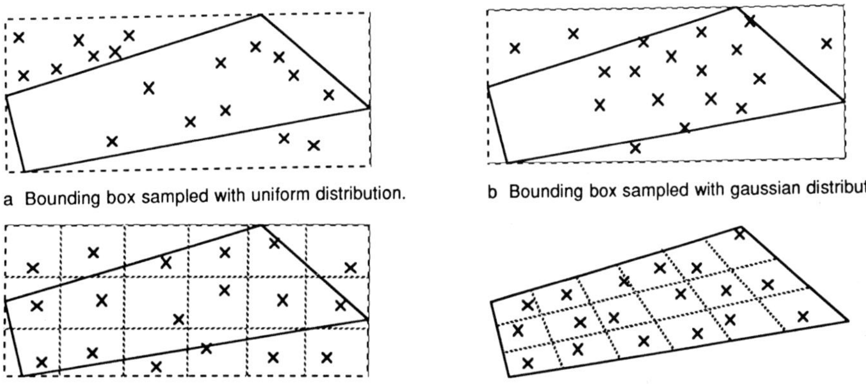

a Bounding box sampled with uniform distribution.

b Bounding box sampled with gaussian distribution.

c Bounding box sampled with jitter.

d Geometric boundary sampled with jitter.

Figure 3. Different methods for choosing samples.

Our implementation of the second pass is simplified by the use of light trees [Coo84]. Light trees are essentially small programs that describe the illumination calculations for individual light sources. They allow us to describe lights with different characteristics. For example, we can control the softness of shadow edges or distinguish lights that cast shadows from lights that do not. As each region is shaded, the light trees are called to determine the proportion of the region illuminated. Each light tree calls the percentage closer filtering routine, passing a pointer to the depth map and the region to be filtered, and uses the result (in conjunction, perhaps, with other parameters controlling the spatial distribution of the light) in computing its contribution to the illumination of the surface.

In our implementation, the second pass required about 370 lines of code. Most of this code served merely to integrate the heart of the percentage closer filtering algorithm, shown in Figure 4, with the rest of our renderer.

The code in Figure 4 provides a number of parameters that we can adjust in computing our shadows. The `NumSamples` parameter controls the number of sample points used per region. The `ResFactor` parameter artificially enlarges the size of the sampling region, allowing lights that cast softer shadows. The `Bias` parameter is used to offset the surface slightly when comparisons to the z values in the depth buffer are made. This prevents a surface from incorrectly shadowing itself if a z value for a point on the surface is compared to the depth map z from a nearby but different position on the same surface.* This incorrect self-shadowing can create Moiré patterns. The effects of these and other parameters are discussed later.

3.3 Storage Issues

Depth maps tend to be large. We store along with each depth map a bounding box of all pixels with finite depths, and pixels outside this box are not actually stored with the depth map. We have not found the working storage requirements of our algorithm to be too great. For a scanline rendering algorithm, locality in the screen space of the camera is correlated with locality in the screen space of the light source. Thus, a simple paging scheme works well for this application.

Still more memory could potentially be saved by dividing the depth map into rectangular tiles, which could be cached to take better advantage of the algorithm's two-dimensional locality. In addition, a tile scheme would allow us to store a maximum z value with each tile, thereby avoiding sampling the depth map altogether if a region were further away from the light than any object in the tile.

4. Examples

4.1 Effect of Stochastic Percentage Closer Filtering

Our first example, Figure 5, shows a simple scene. A light source off-screen to the left shines on a red sphere, which casts a shadow onto an upright green plane. Figure 6 is the result when the diffuse and specular shading components are removed, revealing only the shadow component of the shading. The image in Figure 6a was rendered with our algorithm but with its parameters set to simulate an ordinary z-buffer algorithm (i.e., the depth map is point sampled without jitter). The image in Figure 6b uses the same depth map as the other, but is rendered using our new technique of percentage closer filtering. This image has antialiased shadow edges.

* We actually specify a minimum and a maximum bias, and at every sample the actual bias is chosen stochastically from that range. This allows a surface to curve over to legitimately shadow itself without aliasing.

```
/* parameters setable in other parts of renderer */
float ResFactor = 3, MinSize = 0, Bias0 = .3, Bias1 = .4;
int NumSamples = 16, MinSamples = 1;

#define MAPRES 1024                 /* size of depth map */
float DepthMap[MAPRES][MAPRES];     /* actual depth map */

#define CLAMP(a, min, max) (a<min?min:(a>max?max:a))
float Rand();          /* returns random numbers in range [0.,1.) */
float ceil();          /* returns smallest integer no less than argument */
float floor();         /* returns largest integer no greater than argument */

typedef struct {
    int r_umin, r_umax;        /* min and max pixels in u dimension */
    int r_vmin, r_vmax;        /* min and max pixels in v dimension */
} TextureRect;

float SampleShadow(s, t, z, sres, tres, bbox)
    float s, t;                /* depth map indices. range [0.,1.) */
    float z;                   /* light space depth */
    float sres, tres;          /* size of sampling rectangle. range [0.,1.) */
    TextureRect *bbox;         /* bounding box on depth map in pixels */
{
    int i, j, inshadow, iu, iv, ns, nt, lu, hu, lv, hv;
    float bias, smin, tmin, ds, dt, js, jt;

    /* if point is behind light source, call it not in shadow */
    if (z < 0.)
        return(0.);

    /* convert to coordinates of depth map */
    sres = MAPRES * sres * ResFactor;
    tres = MAPRES * tres * ResFactor;
    if(sres < MinSize)
        sres = MinSize;
    if(tres < MinSize)
        tres = MinSize;
    s = s * MAPRES; t = t * MAPRES;

    /* cull if outside bounding box */
    lu = floor(s - sres); hu = ceil(s + sres);
    lv = floor(t - tres); hv = ceil(t + tres);
    if(lu>bbox->r_umax || hu<bbox->r_umin
                   || lv>bbox->r_vmax || hv<bbox->r_vmin)
        return(0.);

    /* calculate number of samples */
    if(sres*tres*4. < NumSamples) {
        ns = sres*2.+.5;
        ns = CLAMP(ns, MinSamples, NumSamples);
        nt = tres*2.+.5;
        nt = CLAMP(nt, MinSamples, NumSamples);
    } else {
        nt = sqrt(tres*NumSamples/sres)+.5;
        ns = CLAMP(ns, MinSamples, NumSamples);
        ns = ((float)NumSamples)/nt+.5;
        nt = CLAMP(nt, MinSamples, NumSamples);
    }

    /* setup jitter variables */
    ds = 2*sres/ns; dt = 2*tres/nt;
    js = ds*.5; jt = dt*.5;
    smin = s - sres + js; tmin = t - tres + jt;

    /* test the samples */
    inshadow = 0;
    for (i = 0, s = smin; i < ns; i = i+1, s = s+ds) {
        for (j = 0, t = tmin; j < nt; j = j+1, t = t+dt) {
              /* jitter s and t */
              iu = s + Rand() * js;
              iv = t + Rand() * jt;
              /* pick a random bias */
              bias = Rand()*(Bias1-Bias0)+Bias0;
              /* clip to bbox */
              if(iu>=bbox->r_umin && iu<=bbox->r_umax
                                  && iv>=bbox->r_vmin
                                  && iv<=bbox->r_vmax) {
                    /* compare z value to z from depth map plus bias */
                    if(z > DepthMap[iu][iv] + bias)
                          inshadow = inshadow+1;
              }
        }
    }
    return(((float) inshadow) / (ns*nt));
}
```

Figure 4. Percentage Closer Filtering Algorithm.

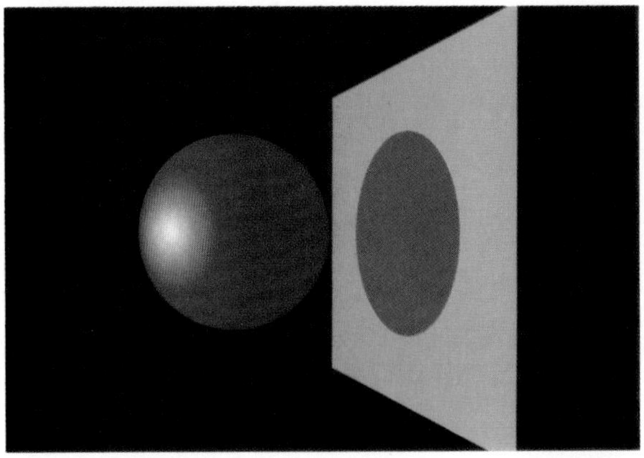

Figure 5. Sphere and plane example.

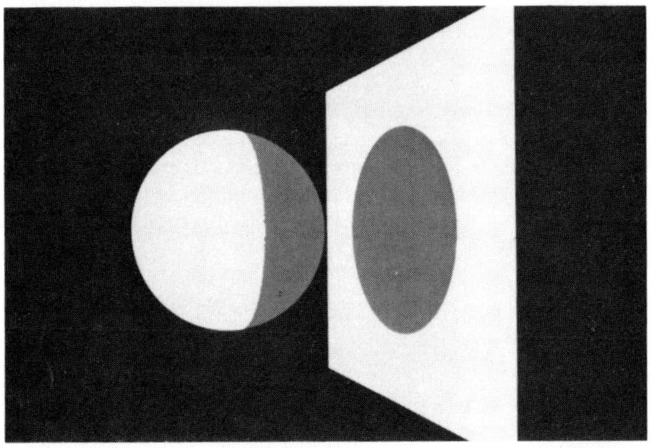

(a) Ordinary z-buffer algorithm.

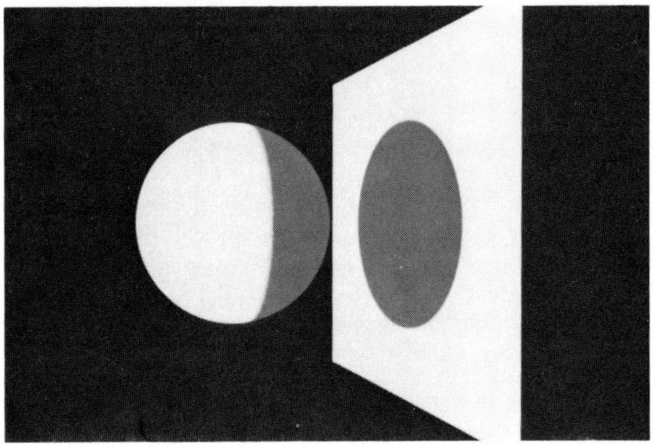

(b) Percentage closer filtering algorithm.

Figure 6. Shadow component.

4.2 Effect of Parameters

We now explore the effects of the shadow algorithm's parameters defined earlier. In most of the following figures, we have zoomed in by pixel replication on either the edge of the shadow cast onto the plane or on the boundary of the self-shadowing region on the sphere.

Figure 7 shows the effect of increasing the `NumSamples` parameter. Because the shadow intensity is the result of filtering `NumSamples` binary values, the number of bits in the shadow intensity is equal to the logarithm base 2 of this parameter's value. If `NumSamples` is too small, the shadow edges appear noisy; if it is larger, the filtering becomes better but more expensive. We normally use a `NumSamples` of 16.

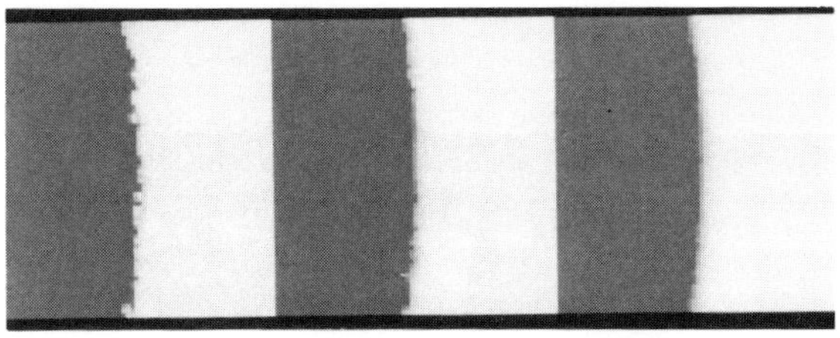

(a) `NumSamples` 1. (b) `NumSamples` 4. (c) `NumSamples` 16.

Figure 7. Effect of the `NumSamples` parameter.

Figure 8 shows the effect of increasing the `ResFactor` parameter. In general, increasing `ResFactor` produces softer shadow edges. Note that if `ResFactor` is large, the soft shadow edges are wider, making the quantization of the shadow intensity more apparent. This may become objectionable unless `NumSamples` is increased. `ResFactor` should never be less than one. If it is then any aliases or artifacts in the depth map are reproduced in the shadows. We normally use a `ResFactor` between 2 and 4.

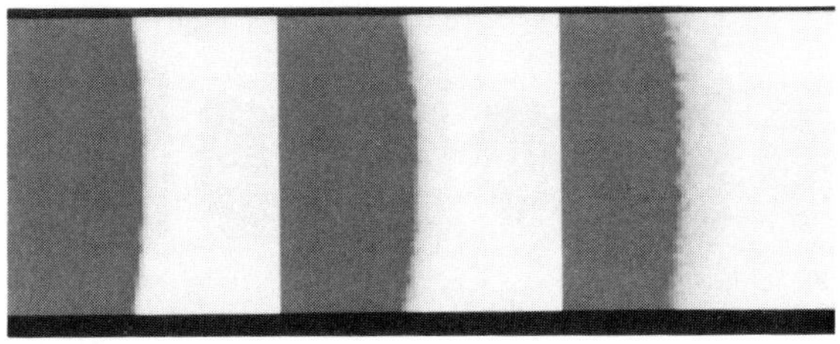

(a) `ResFactor` 1. (b) `ResFactor` 3. (c) `ResFactor` 8.

Figure 8. Effect of the `ResFactor` parameter.

Figure 9 shows the effect of increasing the `Bias` parameters. Increasing `Bias` eliminates the Moiré patterns due to incorrect self-shadowing, but moves the shadow boundary away from its true position. In practice, we have not found it difficult to select `Bias` values large enough to eliminate self-shadowing artifacts, yet small enough to avoid any noticeable problems from the offset boundary positions. Note that `Bias` values in our implementation depend on the world space metric of the object, since they are merely added to the z values of the depth map. In worlds measuring 100 by 100 by 100 units, typical bias values we use are (0.3, 0.4).

Figure 10 shows the effect of increasing the resolution of the depth map, relative to the resolution of the final image. When the resolution of the depth map is too small, the shadows are blurry and noisy because small detail is not represented in the depth map. When depth maps are too large, storage is wasted. We normally use depth maps whose resolutions are the same size or twice as large (in each dimension) as the resolution of the final image. Typically, we start with a depth map of the same size, make a few test images, and adjust if necessary.

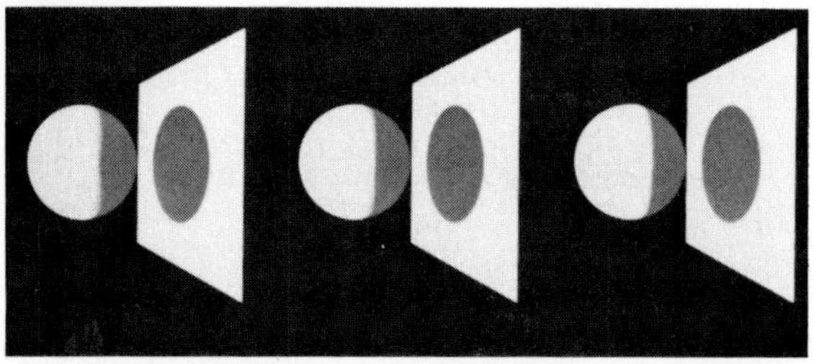

(a) (`Bias` (0.0, 0.0). (b) (`Bias` (0.2, 0.3). (c) (`Bias` (0.3, 0.4).

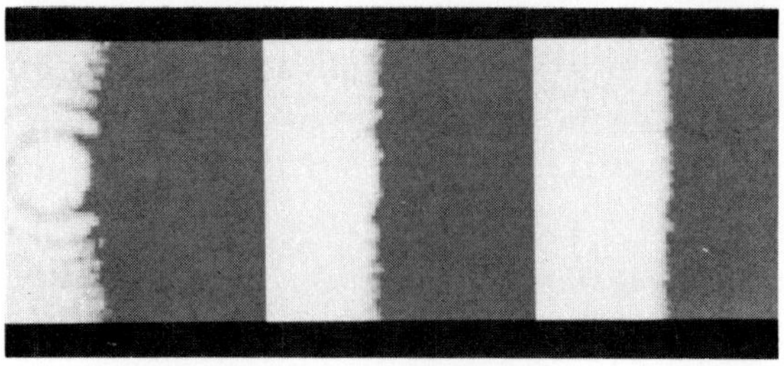

(d) (`Bias` (0.0, 0.0). (e) (`Bias` (0.2, 0.3). (f) (`Bias` (0.3, 0.4).

Figure 9. Effect of the `Bias` parameter.

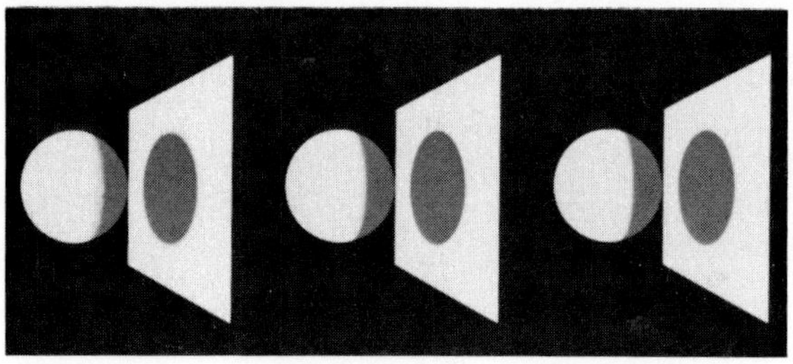

(a) Res 256x256. (b) Res 512x512. (c) Res 1024x1024.

Figure 10. Effect of depth map resolution.

Two other parameters that we have not illustrated are `MinSamples` and `MinSize`. These parameters supply absolute minimums for the number of samples taken along each of the region's x and y dimensions, and for the size in pixels of each dimension. As demonstrated in the sample code in Figure 4, they are used to control the effects of sampling oddly-shaped regions of the depth map. We typically set `MinSamples` to 2 or 3 to give us fair coverage in both dimensions of the depth map, and `MinSize` to 2 to give us samples from at least four pixels.

4.3 Colored Lights

The shadow algorithm presented can be used equally well for colored lights. Figure 11 shows a scene illuminated by three colored lights (red, green, and blue) at different positions off-screen to the left. They cast light onto a white sphere before a white plane. Because the light sources are at different positions, their shadows overlap partially, creating a multi-colored pattern on the plane.

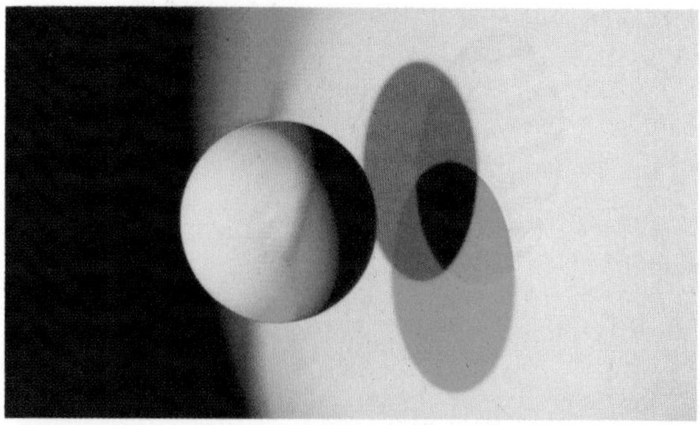

Figure 11. Colored lights example.

4.4 Animation

Our shadow algorithm was used in the computer animated film *Luxo Jr.* [Pix86]. Figure 12 is an example frame from the film. Figure 13 shows the three depth maps created for the three light sources (''Dad'', ''Junior'', and the ceiling light) that illuminate the scene. Here, levels of grey are used to represent the range of floating point z values of the depth map; objects closer to the light are darker in the image. Note that the ground plane does not appear in any of the depth maps. Since it never shadows other objects, it is made invisible, and its depths are never computed.

4.5 Complex Scenes

The shadow algorithm is currently being used in a new animated film called *Red's Dream* [Pix87]. Figure 14 is from a scene that takes place in a dimly lit bicycle store. The scene is illuminated by seven light sources, but only two of these lights actually cast shadows. While shadows are not the most prominent feature of this image, they add a subtlety that is important even in complex scenes.

5. Performance

The following measurements are for the shadow algorithm implemented as a part of the *reyes* rendering system [CCC] running on a CCI Power 6/32 computer under the Berkeley 4.3 UNIX† operating system. A CCI machine executes at about four to six times a VAX 11/780 on typical single precision floating point computations.

The computation time for each example is shown in Table 1. All of the images were computed at a horizontal resolution of 1024 pixels with 16 stochastic samples per pixel. The ''Without Shadows'' column gives the time to compute the image without shadows. The ''Number of Lights'' column gives the number of lights casting shadows, i.e., the number of depth maps used. The ''First Pass'' column gives the total time to compute the depth maps for all the light sources. The ''Second Pass'' column gives the time to compute the final image with shadows. The ''Total With Shadows'' column sums the times of the first and second passes. Finally, the ''% Increase'' column gives the percentage increase in time to compute the image with shadows over the time for the image without shadows.

On average, an image with shadows costs 40% to 50% more than the one without. We consider this increase in computation time to be reasonable. The cost grows as the number of light sources casting shadows grows, but it is significantly less than (1+*NumberOfLights*)×*CostWithoutShadows* which is what might be expected given that 1+*NumberOfLights* images were computed to make it.

† UNIX is a trademark of Bell Laboratories.

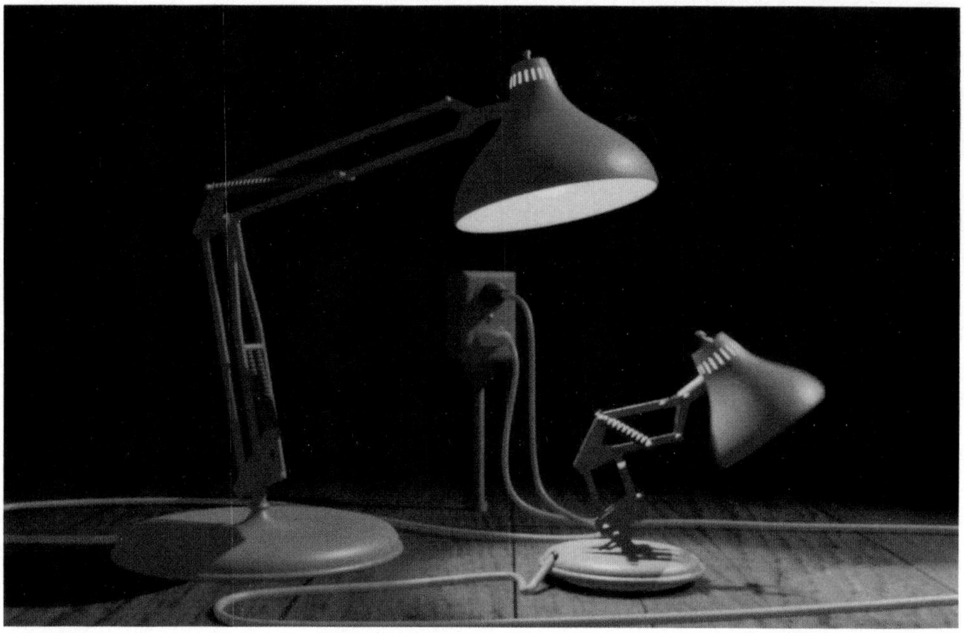

Figure 12. Frame from *Luxo Jr.*

Figure 13. Shadow maps from *Luxo Jr.*

Figure 14. Red's Dream

Computation Time (in minutes)						
Image	Without Shadows	Number of Lights	First pass	Second pass	Total With Shadows	% Increase
Sphere and plane	42.0	1	9.7	48.0	57.7	37.3
Colored lights	64.4	3	14.2	80.8	95.0	47.6
Luxo Jr.	58.8	3	14.6	74.2	88.8	50.9
Red's Dream	261.3	2	55.3	332.1	387.4	48.4

TABLE 1. Shadow Algorithm Performance

Depth Map Storage (in megabytes)				
Image	Resolutions	Raw Depth Maps	Bounding Box Scheme	Tile Scheme
Sphere and plane	1 at 1024^2	4.0	.4	.4
Colored lights	3 at 1024^2	12.0	2.6	2.9
Luxo Jr.	1 at 2048^2, 2 at 1024^2	24.0	13.0	3.7
Bike Store	2 at 1024^2	8.0	5.6	4.2

TABLE 2. Depth Map Storage

A breakdown of the extra time spent in computing our sample frame from *Luxo Jr.* gives an idea of where that extra time is spent. The first pass (creating the three depth maps) accounts for 50% of the extra time. Of the remaining half, the percentage closer filtering accounts for 28%, and the transformation of regions' coordinates into light space accounts for the remaining 22% of the extra time. This last transformation is performed by the light tree, which is implemented with an interpreted language. It could be sped up considerably if we wrote the transformation code in C.

Depth map storage statistics for the examples are shown in Table 2. The "Resolution" column lists the size of the depth maps used. The "Raw Depth Maps" column gives the total size of the depth maps if no storage compaction scheme is used. The "Bounding Box Scheme" column gives the size when only the parts of the depth map containing non-infinite depths are stored. The "Tile Scheme" column gives the size when 32×32-pixel tiles are used.

While the algorithm uses a lot of storage when the raw depth maps are stored, our bounding box scheme can give significant improvements. In some very complex images, such as Red's Dream, the bounding box scheme may not save much storage because objects that can potentially cast shadows are everywhere in the scene. In such images, a tile scheme may give better results.

6. Limitations and Future Work

Although the shadow algorithm described here provides an improvement to Williams's original depth buffer algorithm, it still has many limitations.

The algorithm does not handle motion blur nor compute exact penumbrae. We are currently investigating extensions of the algorithm that we believe will address these limitations. However, it is worth noting that for many situations the algorithm presented here is adequate. For instance, the shadows in *Luxo Jr.* did not have correct penumbrae, and while the lamps themselves were rendered with motion blur, the shadows were not. The algorithm presented here also does not address transparent or translucent objects that cast shadows.

Although the use of bounding boxes reduces the algorithm's storage requirements considerably, we would like to develop more sophisticated schemes for reducing this storage requirement further. The tile-based scheme outlined in this paper would be one approach. An adaptive scheme, where higher or lower resolution areas were used depending on the relative complexities of various regions of the scene, might also be appropriate.

We would like to develop better tools for automating the process of creating the depth maps and generating the light trees. We would also like to build a system that used more intuitive parameters that corresponded more closely with aspects of the appearance of shadows in the scene. This might obviate much of the trial-and-error we have relied upon in choosing parameter values for our scenes.

Finally, we hope to be able to generalize and formalize the sample transformation step in percentage closer filtering. We believe that this technique may have important implications to the use of texture maps for other purposes. For example, in bump mapping [Bli78], specular reflections could be computed before filtering, and the results could be filtered and sampled as ordinary textures. In this way, specular highlights from the microfacets of a bumpy surface would be maintained even as the surface were translated back into the far distance.

7. Conclusions

We have presented a solution to the aliasing problem for the depth buffer shadow algorithm. This solution is based on a new technique for using texture maps called percentage closer filtering. Other improvements to the algorithm include using floating point values in the depth map and including the shadow information as part of the shading calculations instead of as a postprocess. The new technique also provides a penumbra-like effect by providing control over the softness of shadow edges.

Our method is more expensive than the original, both in terms of time and space. Percentage closer filtering takes more time than evaluating a single sample, and floating point numbers typically consume more space than integers. However, because percentage closer filtering requires only a constant number of samples per region, the extra cost is bounded by a constant factor, and in practice this factor is small. We feel that the extra time and space are justified by the improved image quality. This improved image quality has proven robust in an animated sequence.

8. Acknowledgements

Eben Ostby, Loren Carpenter and Paul Heckbert provided many significant insights while the algorithm was being developed. Eben also found several bugs and optimized parts of the code. Eben and John Lasseter helped test the algorithm by designing animated sequences that depended on the shadows to work. Ricki Blau provided photographic assistance.

9. Bibliography

[Ama84] J. Amanatides, Ray Tracing with Cones, *Computer Graphics (SIGGRAPH '84 Proceedings) 18*, 3 (July 1984), 129-145.

[AWG78] P. R. Atherton, K. Weiler and D. P. Greenberg, Polygon Shadow Generation, *Computer Graphics (SIGGRAPH '78 Proceedings) 12*, 3 (August 1978), 275-281.

[Ber86] P. Bergeron, A General Version of Crow's Shadow Volumes, *IEEE Computer Graphics and Applications 6*, 9 (Sept. 1986), 17-28.

[Bli78] J. F. Blinn, Simulation of Wrinkled Surfaces, *Computer Graphics (SIGGRAPH '78 Proceedings) 12*, 3 (August 1978), 286-292.

[BoK70] J. Bouknight and K. Kelley, An Algorithm for Producing Halftone Computer Graphics Presentations with Shadows and Moving Light Sources, *SJCC, AFIPS 36* (1970), 1-10.

[BrB84] L. S. Brotman and N. I. Badler, Generating Soft Shadows with a Depth Buffer Algorithm, *IEEE CG&A*, October 1984.

[CPC84] R. L. Cook, T. Porter and L. Carpenter, Distributed Ray Tracing, *Computer Graphics (SIGGRAPH '84 Proceedings) 18*, 3 (July 1984), 137-145.

[Coo84] R. L. Cook, Shade Trees, *Computer Graphics (SIGGRAPH '84 Proceedings) 18*, 3 (July 1984), 223-231.

[Coo86] R. L. Cook, Stochastic Sampling in Computer Graphics, *ACM Transactions on Graphics 5*, 1 (January 1986), 51-72.

[CCC] R. L. Cook, L. Carpenter and E. Catmull, An Algorithm for Rendering Complex Scenes, submitted to SIGGRAPH '87.

[Cro77] F. C. Crow, Shadow Algorithms for Computer Graphics, *Computer Graphics (SIGGRAPH '77 Proceedings) 11*, 2 (1977).

[Cro84] F. C. Crow, Summed-Area Tables for Texture Mapping, *Computer Graphics (SIGGRAPH '84 Proceedings) 18*, 3 (July 1984), 207-212.

[Gre86] N. Greene, Applications of World Projections, *Graphics Interface '86*, May 1986, 108-114.

[HaG86] E. A. Haines and D. P. Greenberg, The Light Buffer: A Ray Tracer Shadow Testing Accelerator, *IEEE CG&A 6*, 9 (September 1986), 6-15.

[HeH84] P. S. Heckbert and P. Hanrahan, Beam Tracing Polygonal Objects, *Computer Graphics (SIGGRAPH '84 Proceedings) 18*, 3 (July 1984), 119-127.

[HoN85] J. C. Hourcade and A. Nicolas, Algorithms for Antialiased Cast Shadows, *Computers & Graphics 9*, 3 (1985), 259-265.

[Kay79] D. S. Kay, A Transparency Refraction and Ray Tracing for Computer Synthesized Images, master's thesis, Cornell University, Ithaca, New York, 1979.

[KaK86] T. L. Kay and J. T. Kajiya, Ray Tracing Complex Scenes, *Computer Graphics (SIGGRAPH '86 Proceedings) 20*, 4 (Aug. 1986), 269-278.

[Max86] N. L. Max, Atmospheric Illumination and Shadows, *Computer Graphics (SIGGRAPH '86 Proceedings) 20*, 4 (August 1986), 117-124.

[NON85] T. Nishita, I. Okamura and E. Nakamae, Shading Models for Point and Linear Sources, *ACM Trans. on Graphics 4*, 2 (April 1985), 124-146.

[Pix86] Pixar, Luxo Jr., July 1986.

[Pix87] Pixar, Red's Dream, July 1987.

[ReB85] W. T. Reeves and R. Blau, Approximate and Probabilistic Algorithms for Shading and Rendering Structured Particle Systems, *Computer Graphics (SIGGRAPH '85 Proceedings) 19*, 3 (July 1985), 313-322.

[RuW80] S. M. Rubin and T. Whitted, A 3-Dimensional Representation for Fast Rendering of Complex Scenes, *Computer Graphics (SIGGRAPH '80 Proceedings) 14*, 3 (July 1980), 110-116.

[Whi80] T. Whitted, An Improved Illumination Model for Shaded Display, *Communications of the ACM 23* (1980), 343-349.

[Wil78] L. Williams, Casting Curved Shadows on Curved Surfaces, *Computer Graphics 12*, 3 (August 1978), 270-274.

[Wil83] L. Williams, Pyramidal Parametrics, *Computer Graphics 17*, 3 (July 1983), 1-11.

THE ZONAL METHOD FOR CALCULATING LIGHT INTENSITIES IN THE PRESENCE OF A PARTICIPATING MEDIUM

Holly E. Rushmeier
Kenneth E. Torrance

Program of Computer Graphics and Sibley School of Mechanical and Aerospace Engineering
Rand Hall
Upson Hall

Cornell University
Ithaca, New York 14853

ABSTRACT

The zonal method for calculating radiative transfer in the presence of a participating medium is applied to the generation of realistic synthetic images. The method generalizes the radiosity method and allows for emission, scattering, and absorption by a participating medium. The zonal method accounts for volume/surface interactions which have not been previously included, as well as volume/volume and surface/surface interactions. In addition, new algorithms, based on the hemi-cube formulation, are introduced for calculating the geometric factors required by the zonal method.

Categories and Subject Descriptors: I.3.3 **[Computer Graphics]**: Picture/Image Generation -- display algorithms, viewing algorithms; I.3.7 **[Computer Graphics]**: Three-Dimensional Graphics and Realism -- color, shading, shadowing, and texture

General Terms: Algorithms

Additional Key Words and Phrases: Clouds, light scattering, participating media, radiative transport, radiosity, zonal method.

1. INTRODUCTION

The basic radiosity method applies when the lighting in an environment is controlled primarily by the ideal diffuse reflection and emission of light from opaque surfaces [2,4]. The method has been extended to allow for directional light sources [10], and directionally reflecting and transmitting surfaces [6,11]. This paper extends the radiosity method to include the emission, absorption, or scattering of light by radiatively-participating media. Such media might include flames as light emitters, soot clouds as absorbers, or dust, smoke or fog as light scatterers. A scene with a light scattering/absorbing medium is shown in Fig. 1.

Figure 1 - Light scattering/absorption by a participating medium using the zonal method.

In a participating medium, light is emitted, absorbed or scattered on a volumetric basis. Thus, light traveling from one opaque surface to another can be attenuated, augmented, or redirected by the participating medium. The result is a multiplicity of transfer paths for light as in Fig. 1.

Blinn was the first to apply radiative transfer theory to the generation of images of participating media [1]. Blinn presented results for one dimensional models of media with low scattering albedo (i.e., with low effective reflectance). Recently, Max [8] has introduced an approximation of Blinn's method to efficiently generate images of clouds of complex geometry illuminated by sunlight. Max [9] has also applied Crow's shadow volume algorithm to the shadowing of participating media by opaque solids. Impressive images of atmospheric haze can be generated. Volume/volume interactions and surface/volume reflections are not included.

Kajiya and Von Herzen [7] built on the ideas introduced by Blinn, and developed a more complete method for three dimensional models of media with unrestricted scattering properties. In a preprocessing step, the intensity in the participating medium is calculated by using the scattering equation of transfer. Direct input from a light source and from inter-volume scatter are included. In a second step, the intensity due to surface reflections is combined with the intensity of the participating medium by ray tracing. The method does not account for surface/volume interactions, nor for diffuse surface/surface reflections.

In this paper a general method is introduced which allows for all volume/volume, volume/surface, and surface/surface interactions. The method assumes isotropic, volumetric emission, absorption, and scattering by the participating medium, and ideal diffuse reflection from opaque surfaces. Directional (non-diffuse) lighting is allowed. The method is based on, and extends, the radiosity method. The method was developed for radiant heat transfer analysis by Hottel and Sarofim [5] and is known as the zonal method. The participating medium is discretized into small volumes (or zones), each with a uniform volume radiosity. Complex geometries with arbitrary reflecting surfaces are readily included.

In the following sections, the zonal method is described, extended, and applied to the calculation of light intensities in a scene.

2. BASIC CONCEPTS

In the zonal method, all surfaces are assumed to be opaque, ideal-diffuse emitters and/or reflectors of light. Scattering and emission within the participating medium is assumed to be isotropic (i.e. independent of direction). In this paper, it is further assumed that light absorbed in one wavelength band is not re-emitted in another. This leads to independent sets of equations for the light intensities within discrete wavelength bands.

2.1 Absorption - The intensity of light is defined as the radiant energy crossing an area per unit time, per unit area (projected on a plane perpendicular to the direction of travel), and per unit solid angle. When light travels through an absorbing medium, however, the intensity of light decreases along the path.

Consider a pencil of light of intensity I incident on a small volume of matter, dV, as in Fig. 2a. The energy absorbed by the volume per unit time is:

$$d^3P_{abs} = \kappa_a\, I\, d\omega\, dA \cos\Theta\, dx = \kappa_a\, I\, d\omega\, d^2V \quad (1)$$

where κ_a is the absorption coefficient (the fraction by which the intensity of the light is reduced by absorption as it passes through a unit distance in the volume), $d\omega$ is the solid angle of the pencil of light, $dA \cos\Theta$ is the illuminated surface area, Θ is the angle between the pencil of light and the normal to dA, and dx is the distance traveled through the volume. On the right side of Eq. (1), d^2V denotes the differential volume through which the light passes.

Next, consider a larger beam of light of uniform intensity I which has the same directional orientation as the original pencil but fully illuminates the volume dV, as shown in Fig. 2b. The energy absorbed per unit time is found by integrating Eq. (1) :

$$d^2P_{abs} = \kappa_a\, I\, d\omega\, dV \quad (2)$$

Finally, consider light of constant intensity I arriving uniformly from all directions, as shown in Fig. 2c. The energy absorbed per unit time is found by integrating Eq. (2) over 4π steradians to obtain:

$$dP_{abs} = 4\pi\kappa_a\, I dV \quad (3)$$

In this integration, all surfaces are presumed to be uniformly illuminated by light of intensity I. Equation (3) can also be written in terms of a directionally-uniform incident flux density H, which is equal to πI (or to πI_{ave} if the intensity is not directionally uniform) as

$$dP_{abs} = 4\, \kappa_a\, H\, dV \quad (4)$$

The units of H are energy per unit time per unit area.

2.2 Emission - Emitted energy leaving a surface is expressed by the energy flux density, E, in energy per unit time per unit area. The energy per unit time, P_{em}, emitted by a surface of area A is EA (watts). The analogous derivation of P_{em} for a volume with energy flux density E requires care, and the interested reader is referred to the first chapter of [5] for details. Basically, from the laws of thermodynamics it can be shown that the energy emitted per unit time, dP_{em}, from a volume

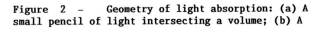

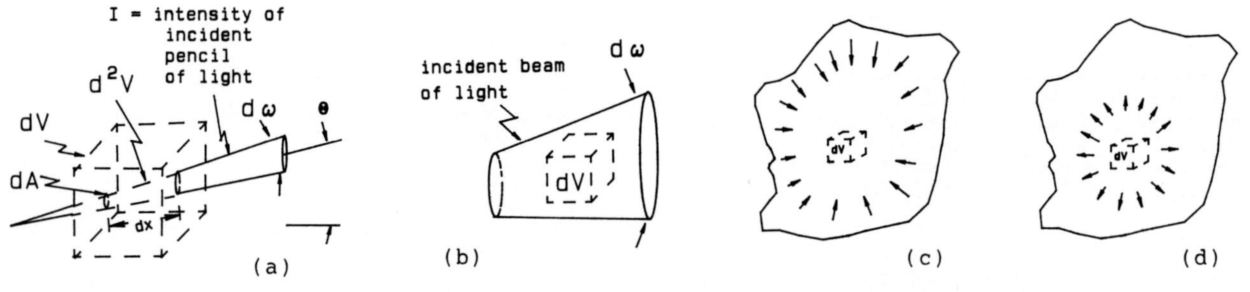

Figure 2 - Geometry of light absorption: (a) A small pencil of light intersecting a volume; (b) A beam of light encompassing a volume; (c) Uniform irradiation on a volume. (d) Geometry of light emission/scattering by a volume.

dV with emissive flux density E is:

$$dP_{em} = 4\ \kappa_a\ E\ dV \quad (5)$$

where κ_a is the absorption coefficient. Since κ_a is the fraction by which intensity is reduced by absorption per unit length, the product $\kappa_a E$ has units of energy per unit time per unit volume. For isotropic emission, κ_a and E are independent of direction. Thus, the emitted light goes out uniformly in all directions, as sketched in Fig. 2d.

2.3 Scattering - Scattering redirects energy within a volume. Similar to the definition for absorption, let κ_s be the fraction by which the intensity of a pencil of light in a particular direction is reduced by scattering as it travels a unit distance. The total energy scattered per unit time, dP_{sc}, is:

$$dP_{sc} = 4\ \kappa_s\ H\ dV \quad (6)$$

For isotropic scattering, the intensity of scattered light is uniform in all directions as sketched in Fig. 2d.

2.4 Volume Transmittance - The transmittance, τ, of a volume is a directional quantity which describes how much of the light on a given path will pass through the volume without being absorbed or scattered. For a pencil of light traveling a differential distance in a particular direction, the intensity is reduced by absorption and scattering by:

$$dI = -\kappa_t I\ dx, \quad \text{or,} \quad dI/dx = -\kappa_t I \quad (7a)$$

$$\text{where} \quad \kappa_t \equiv \kappa_a + \kappa_s \quad (7b)$$

Integration of Eq. (7) yields the intensity I(x) at a distance x into the medium:

$$I(x) = I_o \exp[-\textstyle\int_0^x \kappa_t\ dx^*] \quad (8a)$$

where I_o is the initial intensity, and * denotes a dummy variable. Thus, the transmittance is given by:

$$\tau(x) = \exp[-\textstyle\int_0^x \kappa_t\ dx^*] \quad (8b)$$

2.5 Volume Radiosity - The flux density leaving a volume element due to emission and scattering is defined as the volume radiosity B, given by:

$$4\ \kappa_t B = 4\ \kappa_a E + 4\ \kappa_s H \quad (9)$$

The radiosity of a volume includes only the energy which has been emitted or scattered by the volume. Energy that is transmitted directly through the volume is not included.

By introducing the isotropic scattering albedo, defined as $\Omega \equiv \kappa_s/\kappa_t$, Eq. (9) can be written in the alternate form:

$$B = (1 - \Omega)E + \Omega H \quad (10)$$

Equation (10) is similar to the defining equation for the radiosity of a surface. The isotropic scattering albedo Ω appears in place of the diffuse reflectance ρ of the surface.

2.6 Variation of Intensity along a Light Path - The intensity of light reaching the eye depends on the attenuation of intensity along the light path due to absorption and scattering, and on the enhancement due to emission and in-scattering. In-scattering refers to the scattering of incident light into the direction of interest. Equation (7) describes attenuation along a path. Similarly, the enhancement can be described by:

$$dI/dx = \kappa_t J(x) \quad (11)$$

where J(x) is the scattered and emitted intensity originating from an infinitesimal volume of thickness dx at x. For isotropic emission and scattering J(x) is related to the volume radiosity by $J(x) = B(x)/\pi$. Defining $t = \int_0^x \kappa_t(x^*)dx^*$, and summing Eqs. (7) and (11), the following relation between the local intensity and the scattered/emitted intensity results:

$$dI/dt = -I(t) + J(t) \quad (12)$$

Integration of Eq. (12) yields:

$$I(t) = \exp(-t)\{\ I_o + \textstyle\int_0^t J(t^*)\exp(t^*)\ dt^*\} \quad (13)$$

3. GEOMETRIC FACTORS

In the radiosity method [4], linear algebraic equations for the surface radiosities are constructed by using form factors which depend on geometry alone. In the zonal method the concept of form factors is extended to include volumes.

3.1 Surface to Surface (SiSj) Factors - The geometry of two surfaces interchanging energy is shown in Fig. 3a. In the absence of a participating medium, the fraction of energy leaving a differential element dA_i and reaching a differential element dA_j is:

$$F_{dAidAj} = \cos\Theta_i \cos\Theta_j dA_j/(\pi s_{ij}^2) \quad (14)$$

An absorbing/scattering medium will reduce the amount of energy traveling directly from dA_i to dA_j, and a transmittance τ (as given in Eq. (8b)) must be included:

$$F_{dAidAj} = \tau(s_{ij})\cos\Theta_i \cos\Theta_j dA_j/(\pi s_{ij}^2) \quad (15)$$

The fraction of energy leaving a finite surface A_i of uniform radiosity B_i that arrives at a second finite surface A_j is found by integrating over the two surfaces:

$$F_{ij} = (1/A_i) \int_{Ai} \int_{Aj} \tau(s_{ij})\cos\Theta_i \cos\Theta_j dA_j dA_i/(\pi s_{ij}^2) \quad (16)$$

This differs from a conventional form factor by the inclusion of the transmittance τ inside the

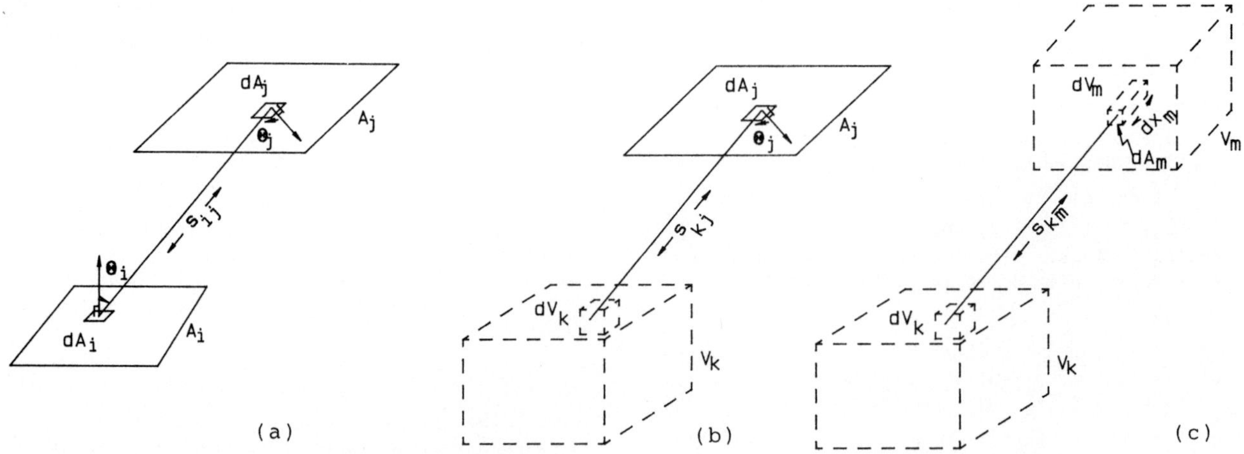

Figure 3 – Geometry of light interchange, (a) Between two surfaces; (b) Between a volume and a surface; and (c) Between two volumes.

integral. In the zonal method it is more convenient to use a factor SiSj given by $A_i F_{ij}$, or:

$$\underline{SiSj} = \int_{Ai} \int_{Aj} \tau(s_{ij}) \cos\Theta_i \cos\Theta_j dA_j dA_i / (\pi s_{ij}^2) \quad (17)$$

SiSj can be interpreted as the total energy reaching surface j from surface i, divided by the radiosity of surface i. Note that SiSj is equal to SjSi; this is consistent with the reciprocity requirements.

3.2 Volume to Surface (VkSj) Factors - The geometry of a volume exchanging energy with a surface is shown in Fig. 3b. The total energy scattered from and emitted by a volume is found by summing Eq. (5) and (6) and applying the definition given in Eq. (9). The fraction of energy emitted from or scattered by volume dV_k and reaching a surface dA_j, in the absence of any intervening medium, is the solid angle subtended by dA_j divided by 4π. The total energy d^2P_{kj} emitted or scattered by volume dV_k reaching dA_j is:

$$d^2P_{kj} = 4\kappa_t B_k dV_k \cos\Theta_j dA_j / (4\pi s_{kj}^2) \quad (18)$$

An intervening medium reduces the amount of energy reaching dA_j, and introduces the transmittance τ:

$$d^2P_{kj} = \tau(s_{jk}) \kappa_t B_k dV_k \cos\Theta_j dA_j / (\pi s_{kj}^2) \quad (19)$$

The total energy emitted from or scattered by a finite volume V_k and arriving at a finite surface A_j is found by integrating Eq. (19) over the entire volume and the entire receiving surface. If the radiosity of the volume is taken as spatially uniform, a purely geometric factor arises. Analogous to the factor SiSj, the factor VkSj is defined as the total energy emitted from or scattered by V_k that arrives at A_j, divided by the radiosity of volume V_k, or:

$$\underline{VkSj} = \int_{Vk} \int_{Aj} \tau(s_{jk}) \kappa_t dV_k \cos\Theta_j dA_j / (\pi s_{kj}2) \quad (20)$$

A factor SjVk can be defined which is the total energy leaving surface j (of uniform radiosity B_j), which is either scattered or absorbed by volume k, divided by the radiosity of surface j. The reciprocity relationship SjVk = VkSj holds.

3.3 Volume Volume (VkVm) Factors - The geometry of two volumes exchanging energy is shown in Fig. 3c. The energy d^2P_{km} emitted from or scattered by volume dV_k, and incident on volume dV_m, after attenuation by an intervening medium, is:

$$d^2P_{km} = \tau(s_{km}) \kappa_{t,k} B_k dV_k \cos\Theta_m dA_m / (\pi s_{km}^2) \quad (21)$$

The fraction of this energy absorbed or scattered by dV_m is $\kappa_{t,m} dx_m$. The energy scattered or emitted by dV_k, which is absorbed or scattered by dV_m, is given by:

$$d^2P_{km} = \tau(s_{km}) \kappa_{t,k} B_k dV_k \cos\Theta_m dA_m \kappa_{t,m} dx_m / (\pi s_{km}^2)$$
$$= \tau(s_{km}) \kappa_{t,m} \kappa_{t,k} B_k dV_k dV_m / (\pi s_{km}^2) \quad (22)$$

The product $\cos\Theta_m dA_m dx_m$ for the parallelepiped shown in Fig. 3c is equal to dV_m. Any arbitrary volume can be approximated by a set of such parallelepipeds. Thus, the amount of scattered or absorbed energy depends only on the volume of dV_m, and not on its orientation.

The total energy scattered by or emitted from a finite volume V_k of uniform volume radiosity B_k, which is absorbed or scattered by a finite volume V_m, is found by integrating over the two volumes. Similar to the factors SiSj and VkSj, a factor VkVj appears which represents the total scattered and emitted energy leaving V_k which is absorbed or scattered by volume V_j, divided by the radiosity B_k, or:

$$\underline{VkVm} = \int_{Vk} \int_{Vm} \tau(s_{km}) \kappa_{t,m} \kappa_{t,k} dV_k dV_m / (\pi s_{km}^2) \quad (23)$$

4. RADIOSITY EQUATIONS

A set of simultaneous linear algebraic equations for the zonal method is derived in this section. This set couples the radiosities of surfaces and volumes, and can be formed by expressing the energy scattered or absorbed by each surface and volume in terms of the radiosities of the other surfaces and volumes in the environment.

The total energy leaving a surface i is given by the product B_iA_i, where B_i is the radiosity of the surface. B_i consists of emitted and reflected energy. The energy emitted by the area is E_iA_i. Energy incident on the surface comes partially from other surfaces and partially from other volumes in the environment. The energy incident on surface i from surface j is $B_j\underline{SjSi}$. The energy incident on surface i from volume k is $B_k\underline{VkSi}$. Therefore, a complete equation for the radiosity B_i of a surface is:

$$B_iA_i = E_iA_i + \rho_i\{\Sigma B_j\underline{SjSi} + \Sigma B_k\underline{VkSi}\} \quad (24)$$

where the first term represents the emitted energy, the remaining terms represent reflected energy, and ρ_i is the surface reflectance.

The complete equation for the radiosity B_k of a volume is:

$$4\kappa_tB_kV_k = 4\kappa_aE_kV_k + \Omega_k\{\Sigma B_j\underline{SjVk} + \Sigma B_m\underline{VmVk}\} \quad (25)$$

On the left is the total energy emitted or scattered from a volume. The term $4\kappa_aE_kV_k$ is the emitted energy. The term $\Omega_kB_j\underline{SjVk}$ is the energy leaving a surface A_j which is scattered by the volume V_k. The energy emitted by or scattered from another volume m which is scattered by volume k is $\Omega_kB_m\underline{VmVk}$.

For a system of s surfaces and v volumes, equations of the form (24) for surfaces and (25) for volumes result in s+v simultaneous equations for the s+v radiosities in the environment. Both volume and surface radiosities appear. In general the equations are strongly coupled. The s+v equations represent an energy-conserving model of a lighting environment, and can be applied monochromatically or to discrete wavelength bands.

5. COMPUTATIONAL CONSIDERATIONS

5.1 Input Data - The geometry and properties of surfaces can be specified in the zonal method in the same way they are for the basic radiosity method. New data structures are required to store the attributes of volumes of participating media. A simple method is to define each volume containing a participating medium as a rectangular prism. Octree data structures used for accelerated ray tracing [3, 12] could also be used. For each volume of participating medium, E, κ_t, and Ω must be specified.

5.2 Finding Factors - The zonal method can be implemented by calculating the factors $\underline{SiSj}$, $\underline{VkSj}$ and $\underline{VkVm}$ using variations of the hemi-cube algorithm [2]. The algorithm calculates form factors by using a depth buffer to project surfaces onto a half cube. In the zonal method, reciprocity relations are used to reduce calculations.

Surface to Surface Form Factors - The factor $\underline{SiSj}$ is given by Eq. (17). This is approximated by:

$$\underline{SiSj} \simeq A_i \int_{Aj} \tau(s_{ij})\cos\Theta_i\cos\Theta_j dA_j/(\pi s_{ij}^2) \quad (26)$$

where it is assumed that the surfaces are sufficiently finely divided so that the integral is nearly constant over the surface A_i. Equation (26) is further approximated by :

$$\underline{SiSj} \simeq A_i\Sigma_p\ \tau(s_{ij}(p))\cos\Theta_i\cos\Theta_p dA_p/(\pi s_{ip}^2) \quad (27)$$

where the sum is over all of the hemi-cube grid cells p through which area A_j is visible, as shown in Fig. 4, and $s_{ij}(p)$ is the distance from surface A_i to the point on A_j which is visible through grid cell p. The terms in this summation, with the exception of the factor τ, are the same as for the basic hemi-cube algorithm. The value of τ needs to be approximated for each grid cell. For a medium completely filling the region between A_i and A_j, as shown in Fig. 4a, with spatially uniform properties, τ is given by:

$$\tau(s_{ij}(p)) = \exp\{-\kappa_t \sqrt{(x^2 + y^2 + z^2)}\} \quad (28)$$

where x, y, and z are the coordinates of a point on surface A_j as seen through grid cell p in a rectangular, undistorted, coordinate system based on surface A_i. A transformation is made to a perspective coordinate system in which:

$$x' = x/z \ ,\quad y' = y/z \ ,\quad z' = \alpha + \beta/z \quad (29)$$

where α and β are arbitrary constants. Equation (28) can be rewritten:

$$\tau(s_{ij}(p)) = \exp\{-(\kappa_t(\beta/(z'-\alpha))\sqrt{(x'^2+y'^2+1)}\} \quad (30)$$

Let $d_p = \sqrt{(x'^2 + y'^2 + 1)}$. Thus, Eq. (27) becomes:

$$\underline{SiSj} \simeq A_i\ \Sigma_p\ \exp\{-(\kappa_t\beta/(z'-\alpha))d_p\}\ [\cos\Theta_i\cos\Theta_p dA_p/(\pi s_{ip}^2)] \quad (31)$$

In Eq. (31) the quantity d_p and the quantity in square brackets are calculated once for each grid cell. As the factors for a particular surface A_j are calculated, the depth buffer is consulted to determine z' for A_j for each grid cell so that τ can be calculated. Pseudo-code for calculating factors after the depth buffer is filled is:

```
FOR each grid cell buffer location p BEGIN
    IF object[p] != null BEGIN
        z = β/(depth_buffer[p]-α);
        τ = exp(- Kt * z * d[p]);
```

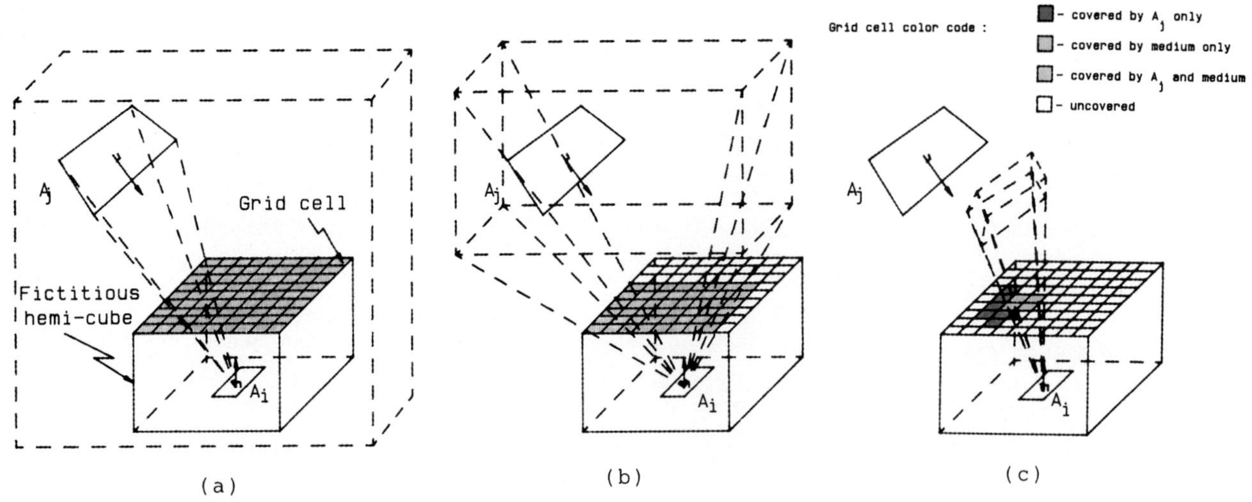

Figure 4 – Surface to surface form factor determination when the participating medium (a) surrounds both surfaces and the region in between; (b) surrounds one surface; and (c) lies between two surfaces.

```
            ss[i,object[p]) +=
                τ * bracketed_factor[p];
        END
    END
    FOR j = 1 to number of surfaces
        ss[i,j] *= A_i ;
```

When the medium occupies only part of the space, as shown in Figs. 4b and 4c, or if it is modeled as several small regions each of which has a different value for κ_t, a modification of the foregoing procedure is required. A value of τ is calculated for each region r, and the total value of τ is the product of these values. To determine each τ_r, before the factors are calculated but after the depth buffer is filled, the depths of the surfaces bounding each region r of a different κ_t at each grid cell must be determined. Two buffers are maintained for each region - a front buffer (fb) and a back buffer (bb). Using the values in fb and bb, an attenuation factor for each grid cell is calculated as follows:

```
Initialize atten_buffer to 0.;

FOR each region of medium r BEGIN
   fill front buffer fb;
   fill back  buffer bb;
   FOR each buffer location p  BEGIN
        IF ( fb[p] < depth_buffer[p]) THEN
           IF (fb[p] > 0) zfront = β/(fb[p]-α);
           ELSE zfront = 0;
           IF (bb[p] < depth_buffer[p])
                     zback = β/(bb[p]-α);
           ELSE zback =
                     β/(depth_buffer[p]-α);
           atten_buffer[p] +=
                κ_t * d[p] * (zback - zfront);
        END IF
   END FOR each p
END FOR each r

FOR each buffer location p BEGIN
     IF (atten_buffer[p] == 0.)
              atten_buffer[p] = 1.;
     ELSE atten_buffer[p] =
              exp ( - atten_buffer[p]);
END FOR
```

The pseudo-code for calculating factors after filling the depth buffer and the attenuation buffer becomes:

```
FOR each grid cell buffer location p
   IF (object[p] != null)
        ss[i,object[p]) += atten_buffer[p]
                    * bracketed_factor[p];
   FOR j = 1 to number of surfaces
        ss[i,j] *= A_i ;
```

Volume to Surface Factors VkSj - The factor VkSj given by Eq. (20) is approximated by:

$$\underline{VkSj} \approx V_k \kappa_t \, \Sigma_p \, \tau(s_{kj}(p))[\cos\Theta_p dA_p/(\pi s_{kp}^{\ 2})] \quad (32)$$

As before, τ is evaluated either for a single medium or for several media, and the quantity in brackets is calculated once for each grid cell. The factors VkSj are calculated similarly to the factors SiSj, except that a full-cube rather than a hemi-cube is used (see Fig. 5a).

Volume to Volume Factors VkVm - Volume to volume factors VkVm are given by Eq. (23). If the volumes are sufficiently subdivided the factor VkVm can be approximated by:

$$\underline{VkVm} \approx \tau(s_{km})\kappa_{t,k}\kappa_{t,m}V_k V_m/(\pi s_{km}^{\ 2}) \quad (33)$$

where the distance between two volumes is taken as the distance between their center points. The visibility of one volume to another is determined quickly by using the depth buffer previously filled in the determination of VkSj. For each volume V_m the grid cell on which the center of V_m will be projected is determined, as shown in Fig. 5b. Visibility is assessed by comparing the depth of

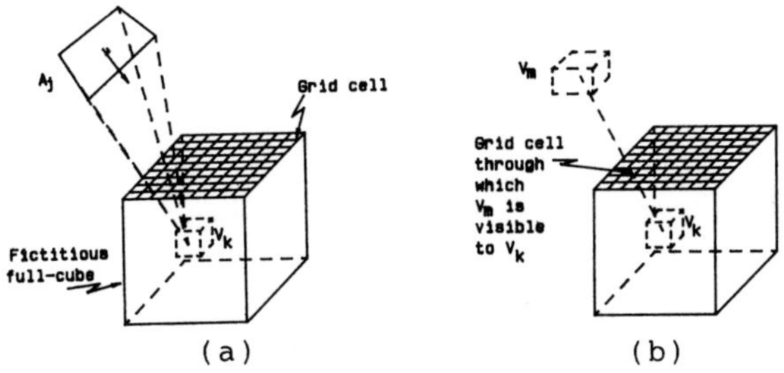

Figure 5 - Form factor determination (a) Volume to surface. (b) Volume to volume.

the volume center to the value stored in the depth buffer.

Once visibility is determined, the distance between the centers is calculated, both for use in the denominator in (33) and for calculating τ. (If many media are present the front buffer / back buffer method is repeatedly used to determine τ.)

5.3 Calculating Radiosities - After the geometric factors for an environment have been found, a system of equations for the radiosities of surfaces and volumes is formed using Eqs. (24) and (25). The equations are diagonally dominant, and the Gauss-Seidel iterative solution method can be used.

5.4 Rendering - The determination of the intensity of an individual pixel on the screen is diagrammed in Fig. 6. The intensity along the ray shown is determined by accounting for the attenuation, in-scattering and emission. It is assumed that there is no interference between light rays. The viewing intensity of each surface and volume along the path is determined separately and the results summed.

In an environment composed of opaque surfaces, there is only one visible surface along each ray. The visible surfaces are determined using the depth buffer algorithm. The intensity contribution of the visible surface is its intensity (equal to its radiosity divided by π) attenuated by the value of τ along the ray from the surface to the eye. The value of τ along the path is determined by the same front buffer/ back buffer method used to find τ in the determination of geometric factors.

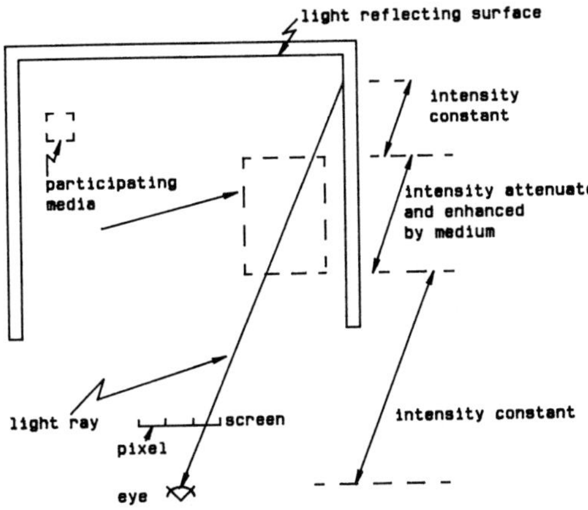

Figure 6 - Pixel intensity calculation.

For the intensity contributions of volumes, it is necessary only to find the intensity leaving the front face of the volume when the volume is isolated, and then attenuate that intensity by the appropriate value of τ. Consider a hypothetical light path through such an isolated volume V_k of radiosity B_k, for a particular screen pixel, as shown in Fig. 7. The points on the surface of the volume pierced by the rays passing through the centers of the pixels can be determined by finding the depths of the surfaces bounding the volume and storing the results in a front buffer and a back buffer.

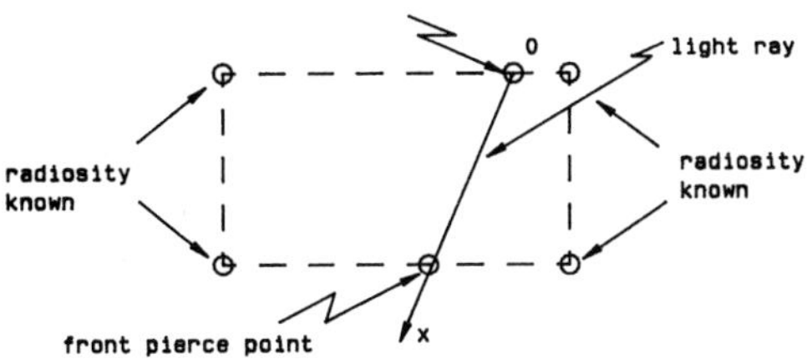

Figure 7 - Intensity calculation for an isolated volume.

Once the path through the volume has been found using the front buffer/back buffer, the intensity $I_k(x)$ is calculated using Eq. (13). For an isolated volume, I_0 is zero, $J(t)$ is the radiosity B_k divided by π, and t varies from 0 to $\kappa_t x$. Equation (13) yields:

$$I_k(x) = \exp(-\kappa_t x) \int_0^{\kappa x} (B_k(t)/\pi)\exp(t)\, dt \quad (34)$$

B_k is assumed to vary linearly along the path through the volume, and varies from some value B_{kb} at $t = 0$ to B_{kf} at $t = \kappa_t x$. The values at the front and back of the volume are found by bilinear interpolation between discrete points on the surface of V_k. The radiosities at the discrete points are found by averaging the radiosities of the surrounding volumes. The foregoing procedure reduces the visibility of spatial discretization of the participating medium.

6. ILLUSTRATIVE EXAMPLES

Several images will be presented to illustrate the zonal method. The images in Figs. 1, 8, 9, 10 and 11 were calculated using a Digital Equipment Corporation VAX 11/780, at a resolution of 400 x 400. Individual and composite images were displayed using 24 bit, 1280 x 1024 resolution frame buffers-- a Raster Technologies Model One/380 and a Hewlett Packard 98720A.

The images shown in Fig. 12 were calculated at a resolution of 1000 x 1000 using a VAX 8700 and were displayed using the HP 98720A frame buffer. The environment displayed in Fig. 12 was discretized into 1146 surfaces and 2744 volumes. Calculating geometric factors and solving for radiosities required approximately 3 cpu hours. Rendering each image required approximately 3 additional cpu hours.

6.1 Volume Interactions - Four images of a black-walled cubical enclosure are displayed in Fig. 8. The enclosure is filled with an absorbing/isotropically-scattering participating medium which is illuminated by a planar rectangular ideal diffuse white light source on the ceiling. A constant value of $\kappa_t = (1/L)$ was used, where L is the length of one side of the enclosure. The upper and lower rows of images were computed using scattering albedoes of $\Omega = 0.8$ and $\Omega = 0.3$ respectively.

The zonal method was used to calculate the images on the left, and a single scatter approximation was used to obtain the images on the right. For a high scattering albedo, top row, volume/volume interactions are absent in the image on the right. Either the zonal method or Kajiya and Von Herzen's method can be used to obtain the correct image of the high albedo medium in the upper left. For the lower row of images for a low scattering albedo, volume/volume interactions can be ignored without affecting the final image. The zonal method and single scatter models are in close agreement. Either Kajiya and von Herzen's method or Max's version of Blinn's single scatter model can be used for correct images.

6.2 Surface/Volume Interactions - The presence of opaque surfaces in a participating medium may either increase the illumination of the medium when light is reflected from a surface into the medium, or it may decrease the illumination of the medium when the opaque surface lies between the medium and light sources. In addition, a dense participating medium can cast shadows, and alter the illumination of opaque surfaces.

The effect of light reflected from an opaque surface is illustrated in Fig. 9, which shows the same enclosure displayed in Fig. 8, but with one of the walls given a non-zero reflectance. Values of $\kappa_t = (1/L)$ and $\Omega = 0.8$ were used for all four images. The upper and lower rows of images correspond to enclosures with a red and a cyan wall, respectively. In the left column of images, the colored wall is to the left. In the right column, the view is through the colored wall. Clearly the presence of the reflecting wall affects the illumination of the participating medium, and the wall color bleeds into the medium.

The shadowing effect of opaque objects in a participating medium is shown in Fig. 10. Two red blocks have been placed in the black walled enclosure. Values of $\kappa_t = (1/L)$ and $\Omega = 0.7$ were used. The blocks cast shadows on the medium.

The shadowing effect of a medium on an opaque object is shown in Fig. 11. A white planar rectangular light source illuminates a small dense cloud with high scattering albedo which casts a shadow (with penumbra) on an opaque green surface. The cloud was modeled by assigning values of of κ_t to each sub-volume. The κ_t values varied from (10/L) at the center of the cloud to zero at the outer edge, where L represents the length of one edge of the green surface. A uniform value of $\Omega = 0.8$ was used.

6.3 Combined Interactions - Figures 1 and 12 display images in which surface/surface, surface/volume, and volume/volume interactions are all present. Constant values of $\kappa_t = .7/L$ and $\Omega = 0.95$ were used to define the participating medium. The light source outside the windows simulate outdoor lighting, with a small intense distant light source and a distributed, weaker, hemispherical source. Figures 12a and 12b show the same environment (with the same illumination) from different viewing positions. Figure 12c shows the environment with the color and position of the source illumination changed. Figure 12d shows the environment with the light source embedded within the participating medium. Clearly the zonal method allows the subtle interactions between surfaces and volumes to be included, without restrictions on view point or the location of the light source.

7. CONCLUSIONS

The zonal method for radiant transfer in participating media [5] has been applied to the generation of synthetic computer images. The method allows all volume/volume, volume/surface, and surface/surface interactions to be included for the case of isotropic participating media and diffuse reflecting surfaces. The method requires extensions of the hemi-cube algorithm to calculate form factors.

The zonal method is the first method to correctly render images of participating media for all possible values of the scattering albedo. Surface/volume interactions such as color bleeding and shadowing are included. The method is more complicated than the basic radiosity method, but generalizes that method.

The zonal method is both view independent and view dependent. The view independence arises because for isotropic scattering radiosities can be calculated once. The view dependence arises because the total intensity leaving any point in the medium varies with direction. The total intensity must be calculated by path integration after the viewpoint is specified.

The zonal method is a potentially very powerful method which warrants further development. Possible extensions of the present study include adaptive subdivision and substructuring of volumes, directional volume and surface scattering, and the use of a hardware depth buffer.

8. ACKNOWLEDGMENTS

This study is part of a continuing effort in the Program of Computer Graphics at Cornell University to develop physically-based lighting models. We are grateful to Prof. Donald Greenberg, Prof. Michael Cohen, Gary Meyer and John Wallace for helpful discussions and encouragement during this study. We acknowledge the support of the National Science Foundation under Grants DCR 8203979 and MEA 8401489, and support from the Digital Equipment Corporation via a research grant in computer graphics. The raster images were photographed by Emil Ghinger.

REFERENCES

1. Blinn, James F. Light Reflection Functions for Simulation of Clouds and Dusty Surfaces. Proceedings of SIGGRAPH '82 (Boston, Massachusetts, July 26-30,1982). In Computer Graphics 16, 3 (July 1982), 21-29.

2. Cohen, Michael F. and Donald P. Greenberg. The Hemi-Cube: Radiosity Solution for Complex Environments. Proceedings of SIGGRAPH '85 (San Francisco, California, July 22-26, 1985). In Computer Graphics 19, 3 (July 1985), 31-40.

3. Glassner, Andrew S. Space Subdivision for Fast Ray Tracing. IEEE Computer Graphics and Applications 4, 10 (October 1984), 15-22.

4. Goral, Cindy M., Kenneth E. Torrance, Donald P. Greenberg, and Bennett Battaile. Modeling the Interaction of Light Between Diffuse Surfaces. Proceedings of SIGGRAPH '84 (Minneapolis, Minnesota, July 23-27, 1984). In Computer Graphics 18, 3 (July 1984), 213-222.

5. Hottel, Hoyt C., and Adel F. Sarofim, Radiative Transfer. McGraw-Hill, New York, New York, 1967.

6. Immel, David S., Michael F. Cohen and Donald P. Greenberg. A Radiosity Method for Non-Diffuse Environments. Proceedings of SIGGRAPH '86 (Dallas, Texas, August 18-22, 1986). In Computer Graphics 20, 4 (August 1986), 133-142.

7. Kajiya, James T. and Brian P. Von Herzen. Ray Tracing Volume Densities. Proceedings of SIGGRAPH '84 (Minneapolis, Minnesota, July 23-27, 1984). In Computer Graphics 18, 3 (July 1984), 165-174.

8. Max, Nelson L. Light Diffusion through Clouds and Haze. Computer Vision, Graphics, and Image Processing 33, 3 (March 1986), 280-292.

9. Max, Nelson L. Atmospheric Illumination and Shadows. Proceedings of SIGGRAPH '86 (Dallas, Texas, August 18-22, 1986). In Computer Graphics 20, 4 (August 1986), 117-124.

10. Meyer, Gary W., Holly E. Rushmeier, Michael F. Cohen, Donald P. Greenberg and Kenneth E. Torrance. An Experimental Evaluation of Computer Graphics Imagery. ACM Transactions on Graphics 5, 1 (January 1986) 30-50.

11. Rushmeier, Holly E. Extending the Radiosity Method to Transmitting and Specularly Reflecting Surfaces. Masters Thesis, Cornell University, 1986.

12. Wyvill, Geoff, Tosiyasu L. Kunii and Yasuto Shirai. Space Subdivision for Ray Tracing in CSG. IEEE Computer Graphics and Applications 6, 4 (April 1986) 28-34.

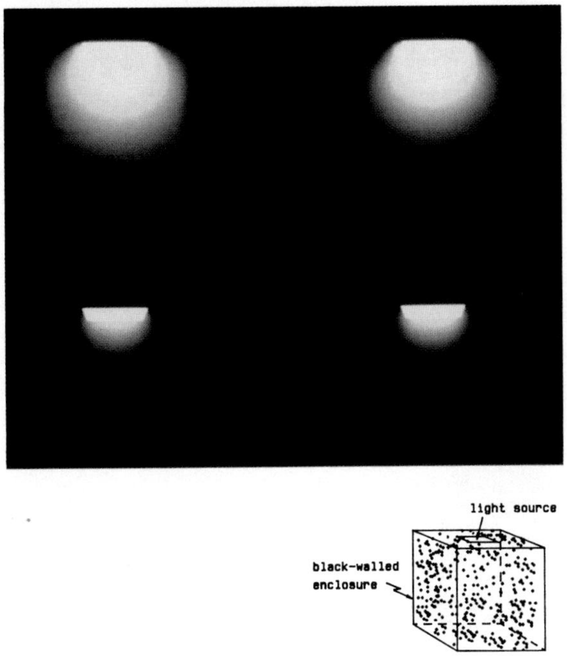

Figure 8 - Comparison of two solution techniques for a participating medium in a cubical enclosure. The top row corresponds to a high scattering albedo, the bottom row to a low scattering albedo. The left column shows the full solution, and the right column shows the single scatter solution.

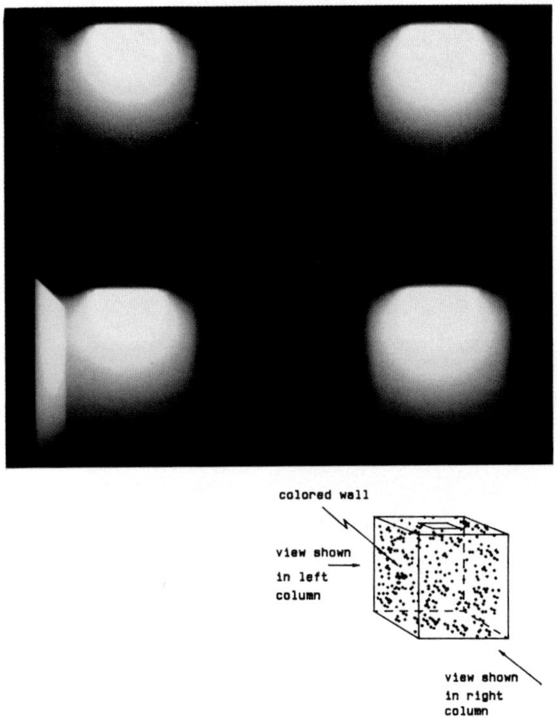

Figure 9 - Color bleeding from a wall to a participating medium in a cubical enclosure. The left column shows the colored wall to the left. The right column shows the view through the colored wall.

(12a)

(12b)

Figure 10 - Shadowing of a participating medium by opaque solids.

(12c)

Figure 11 - Shadowing of an opaque solid by a participating medium.

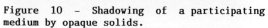

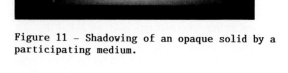

(12d)

Figure 12 - Light scattering/absorption in a smoky room using the zonal method -- (a) afternoon, (b) afternoon, second view, (c) sunset, (d) late at night.

A SHADING MODEL FOR ATMOSPHERIC SCATTERING CONSIDERING LUMINOUS INTENSITY DISTRIBUTION OF LIGHT SOURCES

Tomoyuki Nishita
Fukuyama University
Higashimura,Fukuyama
Hiroshima 729-02, Japan

Yasuhiro Miyawaki and Eihachiro Nakamae
Hiroshima University
Saijo, Higashi-Hiroshima
Hiroshima 724, Japan

Abstract

Studio spotlights produce dazzling shafts of light, while light scattered from fog illuminated by automobile headlights renders driving difficult. This is because the particles in the illuminated volume become visible by scattering light. A shading model for scattering and absorption of light caused by particles in the atmosphere is proposed in this paper. The method takes into account luminous intensity distribution of light sources, shadows due to obstacles, and density of particles. The intensity at a viewpoint is calculated by integration of light scattered by particles between the viewpoint and a given point on an object. The regions to be treated in this manner are localized by considering illumination volumes and shadow volumes caused by obstacles in the illumination volumes.

CR Categories and Subject Descriptions: I.3.7 [Computer Graphics]: Three-Dimensional Graphics and Realism: I.3.3 [Computer Graphics]: Picture/Image Generation

General Terms:Algorithm

Additional Key Words and Phrases: shading, atmospheric scattering, luminous intensity characteristic, shadow volumes

1. INTRODUCTION

Many papers have been published which enhance the realism of calculated images by considering properties of objects, such as reflection, refraction, and transparency, and properties of light sources such as point sources, linear sources, area sources, polyhedron sources [1-3], and sky light [4]. In order to produce realistic images, the phenomena in the space between light sources and objects must also be considered; that is, the effect of atmospheric particles along the path of the light. Light scattered from particles such as water and dust in the air causes illuminated volumes to glow. In particular, understanding this effect makes it possible to simulate such real-world phenomena as: 1) shafts of light caused by headlights of automobiles, street lamps, beacons, or searchlights at night (these effects are important for drivers), 2) light beams caused by spotlights in studios and on stages, 3) shafts of light pouring through windows, and 4) visibility reduction of traffic signals or traffic signs in fog or haze.

Representative of methods considering particles in the air is the fog effect in day time, commonly used in flight simulators. This method simply calculates attenuation as a function of depth from the viewpoint. Some light scattering models have been developed: Blinn first developed a method adapted to displaying Saturn's rings or cloud layers [5], but this method is limited to thin layers. Kajiya developed a method taking account of densities of particles [6]. Recently Max made it possible to display light beams passing through gaps of clouds or trees [7]. In all these methods, however, light sources are limited to a simple, single parallel or isotropic source, ignoring the distribution of luminous intensity of the light source. In order to display illumination effects in fog, we must take into account the luminous intensity characteristics of actual light sources, in particular spotlights and headlights, and also must consider effects due to multiple light sources. This paper presents a method considering these factors.

In this paper we use the following assumptions: 1) light sources treated here are point sources with variable angular intensity distributions, and a parallel source. 2) the light from multiple scattering and the illumination onto objects due to scattering can be neglected. 3) objects treated here are composed of convex polyhedra.

2. CALCULATION FOR LIGHT SCATTERING

Illuminated volumes in the air glow by light scattered from particles in the space, while light traversing the space is attenuated by absorption. These effects are modelled as follows: for scattering, particles are considered to be an infinite number of point sources; for attenuation, the atmosphere is supposed to be a semi-transparent object.

First, we discuss the effects of light scattering due to a point source whose angular range of illumination is limited (e.g. a spotlight).

As shown in Fig. 1, the intensity of light reaching a viewpoint P_v from a point P_i on an object can be obtained by summing the reflected intensity, attenuated by traversing P_iP_v through the absorbing medium, with the intensity scattered in the direction of the viewpoint from each point along P_iP_v. The attenuation varies exponentially with distance (e.g., from a point on P_iP_v to P_v), as described by Bouguer's law (e.g., [8]). The total contribution from scattering is obtained by integrating over all points along P_iP_v. For example, at any point P on P_iP_v at distance s from P_v, the intensity scattered in the direction of the viewpoint is $I_p(s)$, and will be attenuated by traversing distance s to the viewpoint. Thus, the intensity of light at the viewpoint is given by

$$I = I_i e^{-\tau(L)} + \int_0^L I_p(s) e^{-\tau(s)} \sigma ds \quad (1)$$

where $$\tau(s) = \int_0^s \sigma dt \quad (2)$$

σ is the extinction coefficient per unit length and depends on particle density (a function of position), $\tau(s)$ expresses the optical depth of PP_v, and $\tau(L)$ that of P_iP_v.

Consider the direct illumination due to a point light source with luminous intensity $I(\theta,\phi)$ (θ is the angle from illumination axis; ϕ is the revolution angle; see Appendix), and uniform ambient light I_a, which is due to interreflection of light from objects' surfaces and to multiple scattering. The intensity of light reaching the point P from the light source is also attenuated due to absorption by particles and subject to the inverse square law of distance. Then I_p is given by the following equation.

$$I_p(s) = \frac{I(\theta,\phi)}{r^2} w F(\alpha) e^{-\tau(r)} + I_a \quad (3)$$

Here w is the reflectance, r is the distance between the light source Q and the point P, $\tau(r)$ is the optical depth of PQ (see equation (2)), $F(\alpha)$ is the scattering phase function, and α is the angle between the forward scattering direction and the scattered ray (see Fig.1). The phase function is a function of particle radius, index of refraction, and wave length. The simplest example of the phase function is that for isotropic scattering, $F(\alpha)$ = constant. For extremely small particles such as molecules of the air, Rayleigh scattering theory is used; $F(\alpha) = K(1+\cos^2\alpha)$ (K is a constant). For relatively small particles such as fog, Mie scattering theory is used. Mie theory is very complicated, so this paper uses the following experimental approximation [9] for foggy atmosphere,

$$F(\alpha) = \begin{cases} K(1+ 9\cos^{16}(\alpha/2)) & \text{:hazy atmosphere} \\ K(1+50\cos^{64}(\alpha/2)) & \text{:murky atmosphere} \end{cases} \quad (4)$$

where K is a constant.

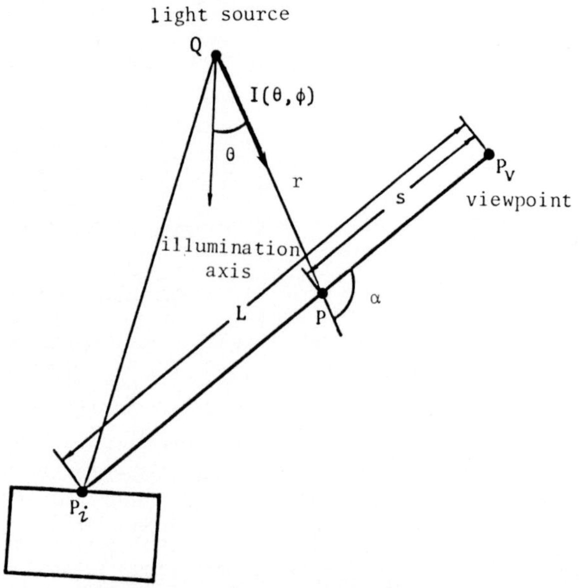

Fig. 1 Intensity of light reaching a viewpoint from a point P_i on an object.

In equation (1), I_i is the intensity of light arriving at point P_i on an object, and is also subject to attenuation due to the distance from the light source just as in equation (3) (i.e., I_i depends on $\exp(-\tau(r))/r^2$). Calculation of illuminance due to point sources with variable angular intensity distributions is performed by the method given in Reference [2]. If the density of particles is uniform, equation (1) can be expressed as follows

$$I=I_i e^{-\sigma L}+I_a(1-e^{-\sigma L})+\int_0^L wI(\theta,\phi)e^{-\sigma(r+s)}F(\alpha)/r^2\sigma ds \quad (5)$$

In applying this equation, the following properties should be noted:

a) The third term refers to the shaft of light. Thus, if the light ray doesn't pass through an illuminated volume, the intensity is given by the first two terms.
b) Even for uniform density, we may consider many types of luminous intensity distributions, therefore numerical integration is useful because of the difficulty of obtaining an analytical solution.
c) Outdoors, during the day, I_a corresponds to the intensity of the atmosphere at infinite distance, that is, the first two terms of equation (5) are equivalent to the equation for fog effect [10].
d) For multiple light sources, the total intensity is obtained by summing up the intensities yielded by equation (5) for each light source.
e) In the case of a parallel source, I_p of equation (3) becomes:

$$I_p(s) = wI_0F(\alpha)e^{-\tau(r)} + I_a \quad (6)$$

where I_0 is the intensity of light and $\tau(r)$ the optical depth from the reference plane (e.g., a

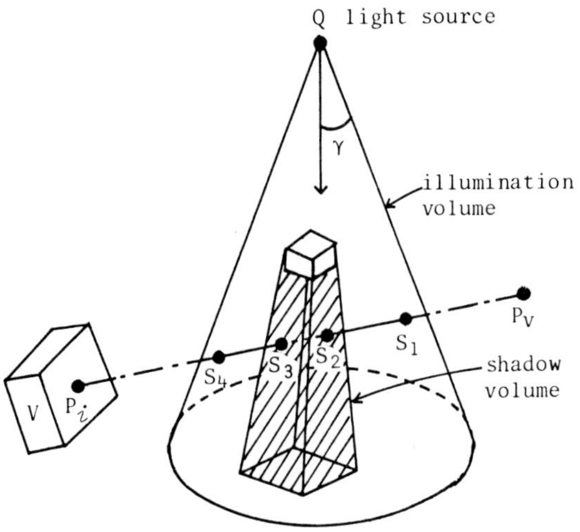

Fig. 2 Calculation of scattered light using illumination and shadow volumes.

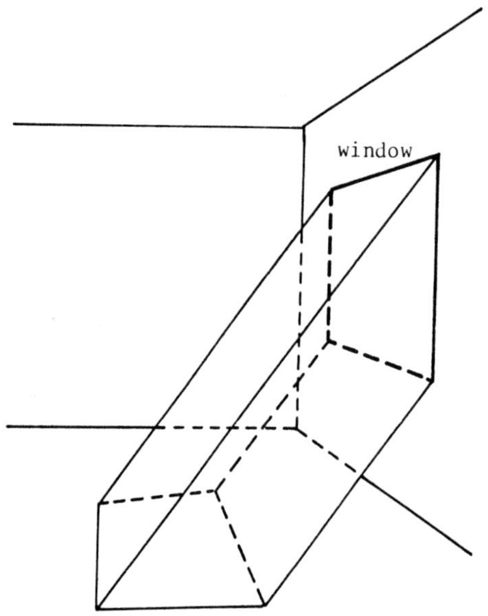

Fig. 3 Illumination volume for a parallel source.

window plane for a shaft of light pouring through a window).

3. ILLUMINATION VOLUMES AND INTEGRATION SEGMENTS

Light sources treated here are point sources with variable angular intensity distributions, and parallel sources. In order to minimize the application of equation (1) (requiring a lengthy calculation), illumination volumes are localized by the following principles: (1) For point sources, directions of radiation are limited by reflectors and lenses. (2) For axisymmetric luminous distributions, the illumination volume is defined as a circular cone whose vertex is the light center, and whose central axis coincides with the illumination axis (see Fig.2). (3) For non-axisymmetric luminous intensity distributions such as headlights, the illumination volume is an elliptical cone. (4) For a parallel light source entering through a window, the illumination volume is a prism of which the base is the window and the base is swept in the direction of light (see Fig. 3).

Shadows on particles in the atmosphere are as important as those on the surfaces of objects; when there are objects in an illumination volume, non-illuminated parts arise within it.

In order to detect shadows on objects, we use shadow volumes [11] defined by the light source and the contour lines of each polyhedron as viewed from the light source [2]. These shadow volumes are also used for detecting shadows in the atmosphere.

The shadows on each particle along the line between the viewpoint and a point on an object (hereafter called the ray) can be obtained by using the ray tracing algorithm (in this case, the ray tracing algorithm is applied for each sampling point on the ray). However, this is very time-consuming and gives rise to sampling errors. The following method is more efficient and accurate. The shadow segments on the ray are obtained by using intersection points between the ray and both illumination volumes and shadow volumes, which are pre-calculated before intensity calculation at each pixel. No aliasing problems caused by shadow calculation arise because shadow regions are accurately calculated.

The segments in which scattered light must be calculated (e.g., s_1s_2 and s_3s_4 in Fig.2) are extracted by the following processes.

The following preprocessing is executed:

i) Extract illumination volumes for each light source.

ii) Extract polyhedra intersecting illumination volumes.

iii) Extract shadow volumes formed by the light sources and those polyhedra.

Then the following steps are executed for each pixel on every scan line.

iv) Extract illumination volumes intersecting the ray, and calculate the intersection points. If there is no intersection, no calculation is required for scattered light.

v) Calculate the intersections between the ray and all shadow volumes within each illumination volume.

vi) Extract illuminated segments on the ray. (These segments are visible from the light source.)

vii) Integrate intensities of the scattered light on the illuminated segments of the ray.

In step ii), all polyhedra are given a spherical bounding volume, and the polyhedra intersecting illumination volumes are extracted using these bounding spheres. Steps i), ii) and iii) need not be recalculated if the viewpoint is changed, as they are independent of the viewpoint. They are also used for detection of shadows on faces.

For steps iv) and v), in order to calculate intersections between the ray and illumination and shadow volumes efficiently, the regions visible

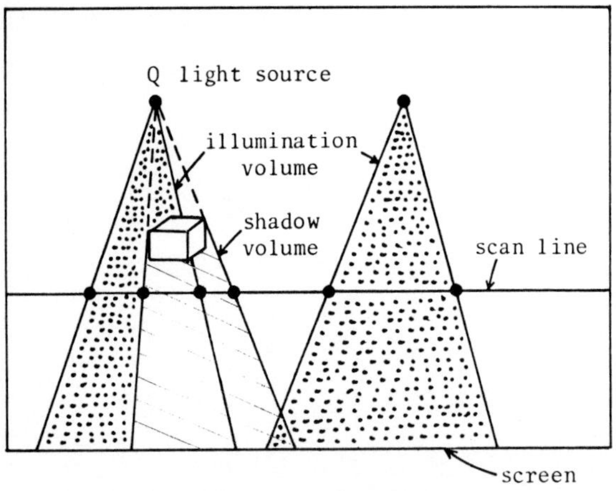

Fig. 4 Pre-calculation of intersections between the ray and shadow and illumination volumes on the screen.

from the screen are pre-calculated; the contour lines of shadow and illumination volumes viewed from the viewpoint are projected onto the screen as shown in Fig. 4. Since the projected contour lines are convex polygons, they can be extracted by means of polygon scan conversion. Then the illumination and shadow volumes intersecting with the ray are easily obtained. In this way, the regions in which scattered light is calculated are localized (see dotted parts in Fig. 4). When the light source is a point source, the illumination volume projects onto the screen as a triangle whose vertex is the projected light center. The projected shadow volume is a polygon (see shaded area in Fig. 4) bounded by a triangle with vertex at the projected light center. The shadow volumes intersecting the ray can be extracted efficiently by means of these bounding triangles. When an illumination volume includes the viewpoint, the illumination volume can't be projected onto the screen, and the intersection test must be executed in 3-D space, even though computation time increases.

The extraction of integration segments (i.e., the visible parts when viewed from a light source) in step vi) is perfomed by using the notion of quantitative invisibility, as in hidden line elimination [12]. For example, in Fig. 5, as we traverse the ray from P_v to P_i, the quantitative invisibility is incremented each time the ray enters a shadow volume (s_2, s_3, and s_6 in Fig.5), and decremented when it leaves (s_4 and s_5). Segments for which quantitative invisibility is zero are visible ($s_1 s_2$ and $s_5 s_6$ in Fig.5).

4. DENSITY DISTRIBUTION OF PARTICLES

In many cases, the effect of spotlights in studio or stage lighting is intensified by using dry ice. Dry ice, smoke, dust, and fog or haze exhibit non-uniform particle densities. We discuss calculation of scattered light under such conditions.

In a dense volume, the extinction of light increases due to the increased optical depths both from the light source to a particle and from the particle to the viewpoint. On the other hand, because the intensity of scattered light also increases, dense volumes in most cases are bright. In order to calculate the intensity at the viewpoint P_v due to scattered light from a point P on the ray, we must know the luminous intensity of light source Q in the direction of P, the particle density at P, and the optical depths of QP and PP_v. Therefore, to take into account the distribution of density, we establish a model for density distribution and a method for calculating optical depths:

1) Modelling of density distribution

In this paper, we do not consider arbitrary density distributions over the whole space, but rather the simpler case in which certain regions of the atmosphere are occupied by smoke or fog of uniform density. One researcher has represented volume density using a 3-D grid, with numerical densities for each element [6], but this method requires a great deal of memory. We use a model in which the boundaries of layers of different densities are represented by curved surfaces.

For a foggy medium due to dry ice, the difference of densities between the fog and the atmosphere is large, and because the fog is heavy,

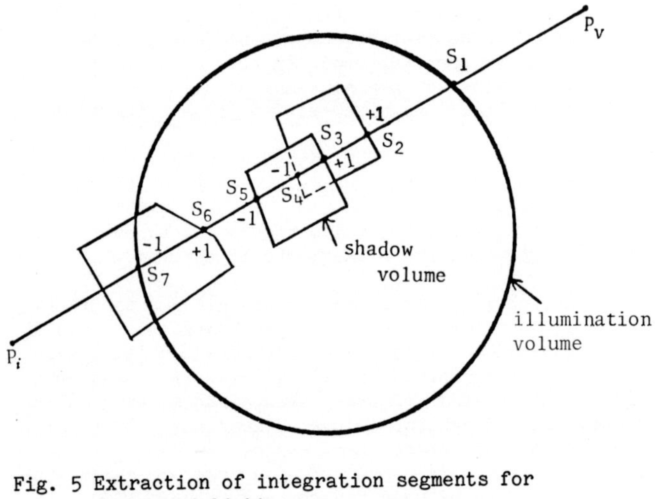

Fig. 5 Extraction of integration segments for scattered light.
(a view from the light source)

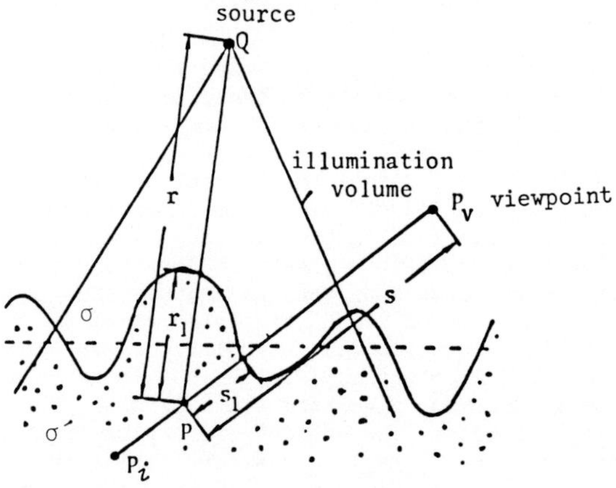

Fig. 6 Calculation of optical depths from the light source to a particle and from the particle to the viewpoint.

it lies below the atmosphere. The boundary surface between the layers can be expressed by mapping height functions onto a horizontal plane (see Fig. 6). Properly speaking, this boundary surface must be calculated by physical simulation, but here we use a Fourier series composed of a short sum of sine waves, as used to represent clouds in reference [13]. For smoke, we map thickness functions onto a number of ellipses.

2) Calculation of optical depth

As shown in equation (2), the optical depth can be obtained by integration of densities. We numerically integrate the density along the ray from the viewpoint to the object. By integrating in this direction, the optical depth of intermediate points is easily available for calculating attenuation of scattered light. When density is sampled only at uniform intervals along the ray, aliasing problems may occur. To overcome this problem, we pre-calculate the intersections between the ray and the boundary surface, detect the intervals in which sampling errors may occur, and add intermediate sampling points in those intervals.

For the case with upper and lower layers of different densities, as shown in Fig. 6, the ray can traverse at most one density boundary, so the calculation can be simplified as follows: we assume that the extinction coefficients for upper and lower layers are σ and σ', and the boundary surface of the layer is g(x,y). If the point P_i on an object exists above g, equation (5) can be used without any modification. If not, the optical depth, $\tau = \sigma(r+s)$, of equation (5) must be replaced by $\tau = \sigma(r+s)-(\sigma-\sigma')(r_1+s_1)$ (see Fig. 6 for r_1, s_1).

5. EXAMPLES

Fig. 7 shows examples of the proposed method. Pictures (a), (b) and (c) are examples for studio lighting: a scene of dancing pencils from the animation entitled "Feast of Light". Picture (a) shows the image illuminated by four spotlights and a special effects light that combines a daisy shape and polka dots. The front-left spotlight exhibits a soft edge, while the front-right exhibits a sharp edge. In picture (b), we see shadow effects due to obstacles; the shape of the shaft of light is clipped. Pictures (c) and (d) depict dry ice and smoke, respectively.

Pictures (e), (f) and (g) are examples of night scenes outdoors. Picture (e) shows a building illuminated by searchlights, street lamps and headlights; as analytical descriptions of the luminous intensities of street lamps and headlights are not available, actual numerical data are used (see Appendix). Note that due to the phase function, searchlights appear brighter when directed toward the observer than when directed away. Pictures (f) and (g) show the effect of the phase function (see equation (4)): the beams in (g) are more glaring than those in (f), where the phase function is neglected. Picture (h) shows a shaft of light pouring through a window.

As shown in these examples, the proposed method produces realistic images.

6. CONCLUSION

This paper describes a method of representing illumination effects considering particles in the atmosphere. The following conclusions can be stated from the results.

1) The proposed method could be used for lighting designs for selecting and arranging lights with consideration of atmospheric conditions, and for estimating illumination effects in studios or stages.

2) Shafts of light due to light sources such as spotlights and headlights, taking account of luminous intensity distributions, can be modelled by considering scattered light from particles in the atmosphere.

3) By considering illumination volumes for light sources, rendering efficiency can be increased by localizing regions in which light scattering is computed.

4) For shadows, intersections of rays with illumination volumes and with shadow volumes are

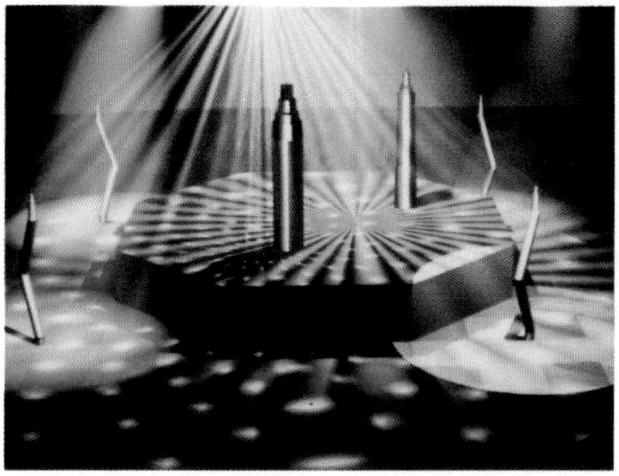

(a)

(b)

Fig. 7 Examples.

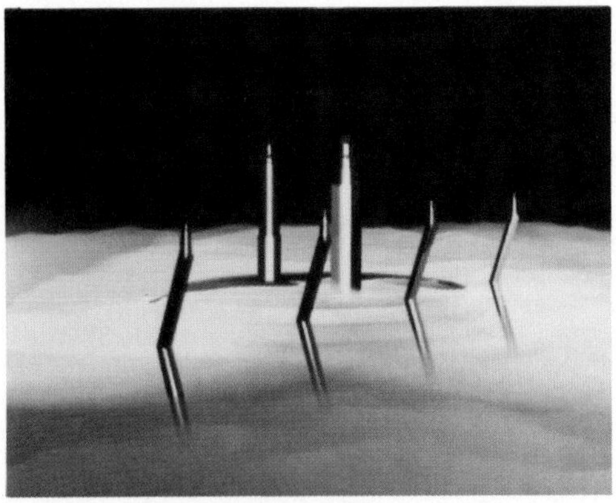

(c)

(d)

(e)

(f)

(g)

(h)

Fig.7 Examples (continued).

obtained efficiently by using their projected contour lines. The shadow segments on the ray are extracted using the hidden line technique, with the ray viewed from the light source.

Acknowledgements

The authors wish to thank Bonnie Sullivan for carefully reading and commenting on this paper.

REFERENCES

1) Warn, D.J.: Lighting Controls for Synthetic Images, Computer Graphics, Vol.17, No.3 (1983) pp.13-21.
2) Nishita, T., Okamura,I. and Nakamae,E.: Shading Models for Point and Linear Sources, ACM Trans. on Graphics, Vol.4, No.2 (1986) pp.124-146
3) Nishita, T. and Nakamae, E.: Half-Tone Representation of 3-D Objects Illuminated by Area Sources or Polyhedron Sources, IEEE, Proc. of COMPSAC (1983) pp.237-241.
4) Nishita, T. and Nakamae, E. : Continuous Tone Representation of Three-Dimensional Objects Illuminated by Sky Light, Computer Graphics, Vol.19, No. 3 (1986) pp.23-30.
5) Blinn, J. F.: Light Reflection Functions for Simulation of Clouds and Dusty Surfaces, Computer Graphics, Vol.16, No.3 (1982) pp.21-29.
6) Kajiya, J.T. and Von Herzen, B.P.: Ray Tracing Volume Densities, Computer Graphics, Vol.18, No.3 (1984) pp.165-174.
7) Max, N, L.: Atmospherical Illumination and Shadows, Computer Graphics, Vol.20, No.4 (1986) pp.117-124.
8) IES : IES Lighting Handbook Reference Volume, (1981) p.6-6.
9) Gibbons,M.G.: Radiation Received by Uncollimated Receiver from a 4π Source, J. Opt. Soc. of America, Vol.48, No.8 (1958) pp.550-555.
10) Nakamae, E., Harada,K., Ishizaki,T, Nishita,T.: A Montage; The Overlaying of the Computer Generated Images onto a Background Photograph, Computer Graphics, Vol.20, No.3 (1986) pp.207-214.
11) Crow, F. : Shadow Algorithms for Computer Graphics, Computer Graphics, Vol.11, No.3 (1977) pp.242-248.
12) Nakamae, E. and Nishita, T. : An Hidden Line Elimination of Polyhedra, Information Processing in Japan, Vol.12 (1972) pp.134-141.
13) Gardner, Y.G. : Visual Simulation of Clouds, Computer Graphics, Vol.19, No.3 (1985) pp.297-303.

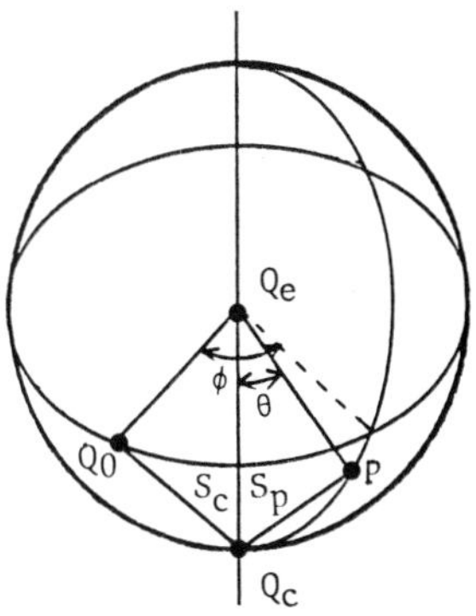

Fig. 8 Illustration of angles for non-axisymmetric luminous intensity.

APPENDIX

Calculation of Luminous Intensity Characteristics

1) Axisymmetric distribution of luminous intensity

In this case the intensity can be expressed by a function of angle θ from the illumination axis (see Fig. 8). In most cases the distribution curves of the intensity can be expressed as a polynominal of $\cos\theta$. Here we consider the sharpness of the illuminated edge. In order to control the illumination range, the expression $I(\theta) = Io(\cos\theta)^c$ has been proposed [1] (For this expression, the illumination range decreases as c increases). However, because sharp edges cannot be produced, and because of the computational expense of the exponent in the cosine term, this function is not well suited to modelling spotlights. Therefore we propose the following function for spotlights:

$$I(\theta) = I_0\{ (1-q)(\cos\theta-\cos\gamma)/(1-\cos\gamma) + q \}, \quad (7)$$

where I_0 is the luminous intensity at $\theta=0$, γ is the beam spread, and q is a parameter which controls the sharpness of the edge (q=1: very sharp, q=0: very soft) (see Fig. 2 for γ).

2) Non-axisymmetric distribution of luminous intensity

In this case the luminous intensity is expressed by $I(\theta,\phi)$, where ϕ is the revolution angle from the reference plane which includes the illumination axis (refer to Fig. 8). In the figure the light center is Q_e, the reference point is Q_0, Q_c is a point on the illumination axis, and P is an arbitrary point. Then $\cos\phi$ can be obtained by the inner product of the normal vectors of triangles, $Q_eQ_cQ_0$ and $Q_eP\,Q_c$.

First we discuss luminous intensity expressed by functions. For example, luminous intensities for the daisy shape and for polka dots like those produced by a mirror ball in a disco are calculated as follows. In these sources, the intensity $I(\theta,\phi)$

can be expressed as the product of $I(\theta)$ of equation (7) and the following function $k(\phi)$.

$$k(\phi) = \max\{\ p+(1-p)\left|2\mathrm{mod}(\phi,\Delta\phi)-\Delta\phi\right|/\Delta\phi,\ 0\ \} \quad (8)$$

where the symbol "mod" means modulo, $\Delta\phi$ and p ($p<1$) are the period of luminous intensity and the ratio of the minimum intensity to the maximum intensity, respectively: When p is small (including negative), the radius of the polka-dots becomes small. For the daisy shape, the distribution of luminous intensity is given by

$$I(\theta,\phi) = I(\theta)k(\phi)\ . \quad (9)$$

For the polka-dot pattern, the luminous intensity can be obtained by adding the variation in the θ direction to equation (9). That is,

$$I(\theta,\phi) = I(\theta)k(\phi)k(\theta)v \quad , \quad (10)$$

where $v=\mathrm{mod}([\phi/\Delta\phi]+[\theta/\Delta\theta],2)$ (i.e., v=0 or v=1): v is used to decrease the number of polka dots.

For arbitrary distributions, numerical luminous intensity data should be used, for example, every 5 degrees on θ and ϕ. Intervening luminous intensities are calculated by linear interpolation. For headlights, however, more detailed data, for example every 2 degrees, are necessary because of the radical change of intensities (see Fig. 9).

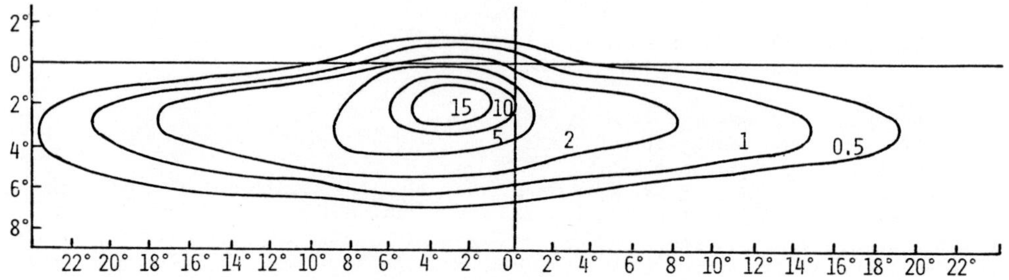

Fig. 9 Distribution curve of luminous intensity for a headlight.

A TWO-PASS SOLUTION TO THE RENDERING EQUATION: A SYNTHESIS OF RAY TRACING AND RADIOSITY METHODS

John R. Wallace, Michael F. Cohen,
Donald P. Greenberg
Cornell University
Ithaca, N. Y. 14853

ABSTRACT

View-independent and view-dependent image synthesis techniques, represented by radiosity and ray tracing, respectively, are discussed. View-dependent techniques are found to have advantages for calculating the specular component of illumination and view-independent techniques for the diffuse component. Based on these observations a methodology is presented for simulating global illumination within complex environments using a two-pass approach. The first pass is view-independent and is based on the hemi-cube radiosity algorithm, with extensions to include the effects of diffuse transmission, and specular to diffuse reflection and transmission. The second pass is view-dependent and is based on an alternative to distributed ray tracing in which a z-buffer algorithm is used to sample the intensities contributing to the specularly reflected or transmitted intensity.

CR Categories and Subject Descriptors: I.3.3 **[Computer Graphics]**: Picture/Image Generation; I.3.7 **[Computer Graphics]**: Three-Dimensional Graphics and Realism

General Terms: Algorithms

Additional Key Words and Phrases: radiosity, distributed ray tracing, z-buffer, global illumination, view-dependence, view-independence.

1.0 INTRODUCTION

The creation of realistic images for a raster display requires the calculation of the intensity of light leaving visible surfaces in the direction of the observer through each pixel of the image plane. Early methods for calculating this intensity accounted only for the direct illumination of surfaces by light sources [14][20]. The subsequent evolution of illumination models has provided increasingly sophisticated methods of accounting for global illumination, which includes the effect of all objects in the environment.

Algorithms to compute global illumination may be characterized by their approach to selecting the sample points within the environment and the directions for which the final intensity is calculated. For view-dependent algorithms these sample points and directions are determined by the view position and by the discretization of the image plane. View-independent algorithms, on the other hand, calculate the illumination of all surfaces for a set of discrete environment locations and directions determined by criteria that are independent of view. A two-pass method is presented in this paper that overcomes disadvantages of previous methods by computing the global diffuse component of illumination during a view-independent preprocess and the global specular component during a view-dependent postprocess.

Recently, in separate papers, Kajiya [18] and Immel et al [17] presented essentially the same equation to completely describe the intensity of light leaving a surface in a given direction in terms of the global illumination within an environment. However, each paper described radically different approaches to the equation's solution. Kajiya extended view-dependent ray tracing [24][8] to include global diffuse illumination, which ray tracing had previously not accounted for correctly. Immel extended the view-independent approach taken by the radiosity method [13][5][19] to include directional reflection, eliminating the restriction of purely diffuse environments. Although both approaches ultimately converge to the same solution, they illustrate the complementary advantages and disadvantages of solving the problem entirely on a view-dependent or view-independent basis.

Kajiya and Immel each described a complete illumination equation based on earlier work in radiative heat-transfer [22]:

$$I_{out}(\Theta_{out}) = E(\Theta_{out}) + \int_{\Omega} \rho''(\Theta_{out},\Theta_{in})\, I_{in}(\Theta_{in}) \cos(\theta)\, d\omega \quad (1)$$

where

I_{out} = the outgoing intensity for the surface

I_{in} = an intensity arriving at the surface from the rest of the environment
E = outgoing intensity due to emission by the surface
Θ_{out} = the outgoing direction
Θ_{in} = the incoming direction
Ω = the sphere of incoming directions
θ = the angle between the incoming direction Θ_{in} and the surface normal
$d\omega$ = the differential solid angle through which the incoming intensity arrives
ρ'' = the bidirectional reflectance/transmittance of the surface

The outgoing intensity, I_{out}, leaving a differential area of a surface in a given direction Θ_{out} is the sum of the light emitted by the surface in that direction, $E(\Theta_{out})$, plus any light arriving at the surface which is then reflected or transmitted in that direction. The reflected intensity depends on light arriving at the surface from all directions above the surface and the transmitted intensity depends on light arriving from all directions below the surface. Hence the integration is over the entire sphere of incoming directions. The bidirectional reflectance - transmittance $\rho''(\Theta_{out},\Theta_{in})$ represents the physical reflection properties of the surface and is expressed as the ratio of the reflected or transmitted intensity in the outgoing direction Θ_{out} to energy arriving from the incoming direction Θ_{in}. All quantities are also dependent on wavelength; assuming no energy exchange between wavelength bands, independent equations of the same form can be written for each wavelength band.

2.0 DIFFUSE RAY TRACING AND SPECULAR RADIOSITY

Kajiya describes an algorithm that solves equation (1) using an efficient approach to stochastic ray tracing [8] in which many rays are shot per pixel with each ray generating only one path through the environment. Since light sources seen by a surface typically make a very large contribution to the reflected intensity, one ray is also sent towards a light source for every ray shot stochastically at the rest of the environment. These modifications, along with other variance reduction techniques described in the same paper, allow sufficient incoming directions to be sampled by ray tracing to evaluate the outgoing intensity for diffuse reflection, thus successfully reproducing phenomena previously only modeled by radiosity methods.

Like its ray tracing antecedents, Kajiya's method is view-dependent, being restricted to those rays that ultimately reach the eye. This is enforced by tracing rays backwards from the eye, through the pixels of the image plane and into the environment. Thus, for a given point on a surface visible to the viewer, the intensity need only be determined for one outgoing direction. The directional nature of the bidirectional reflectivity function then provides an efficient basis for selecting the important directions in which to sample the incoming intensities. In other words, the incoming intensities may be sampled at a higher frequency in the direction of the specular peak (Fig. 1a).

For ideal diffuse reflection, however, the bidirectional reflectivity is independent of the outgoing direction; thus the view direction does not provide a basis for "importance sampling". To reduce the amount of sampling required, techniques may be used that take advantage of knowledge gained as sampling progresses. However a large number of directions may still have to be sampled, particularly when the assumption that lights are the most significant sources of illumination does not hold. Such cases may occur, for example, when a diffuse surface is entirely in shadow or when light reflected from a specular surface contributes significantly to the illumination of a diffuse surface (Fig. 1b). In addition, the pixel by pixel determination of intensity imposed by ray tracing from the eye may result in the performance of more work than necessary since the illumination of a diffuse surface as perceived by the viewer typically changes relatively slowly from one pixel to the next.

By contrast, in the radiosity approach all calculations are view-independent. The standard radiosity method treats only diffuse surfaces. The set of sample points for which the intensities are calculated depends on the discretization of the environment surfaces rather than the viewpoint and image resolution (Fig. 1d). This greatly reduces the number of sample points compared to the number of pixels in the final image. For surfaces with high intensity gradients, which occur at shadow boundaries, for example, a uniform surface discretization does not suffice. However, the distribution of these sample points for a given surface may be adaptively determined by the gradient of intensity over the surface [6].

Immel expanded the view-independent radiosity approach to include specular reflection. The relationship between a surface patch and all the other patches in the environment becomes, in Immel's approach, a relationship between a given outgoing reflection direction for a patch and all outgoing directions for all other patches. A simultaneous solution of the resulting system of equations gives an intensity in each direction for each patch.

Unfortunately, for specular surfaces the intensity as seen by the viewer typically changes very quickly from pixel to pixel. Therefore a view-independent solution may require that specular surfaces be subdivided to the point where each patch covers approximately one pixel in the final view. Although Immel's approach would eventually converge to an accurate solution as the discretization of the environment increased, the computation and space required to solve the resulting system of simultaneous equations precludes subdivision to the required level. As a result, artifacts appear when specular surfaces are rendered, since the correct intensity is known only at relatively widely spaced sample points (Fig. 1c).

2.1 A TWO COMPONENT MODEL OF THE TRANSFER OF LIGHT ENERGY

A reasonable approach to solving the global illumination problem is to divide it in a manner that allows the solution to take advantage of the strengths of both view-dependent and view-independent sampling.

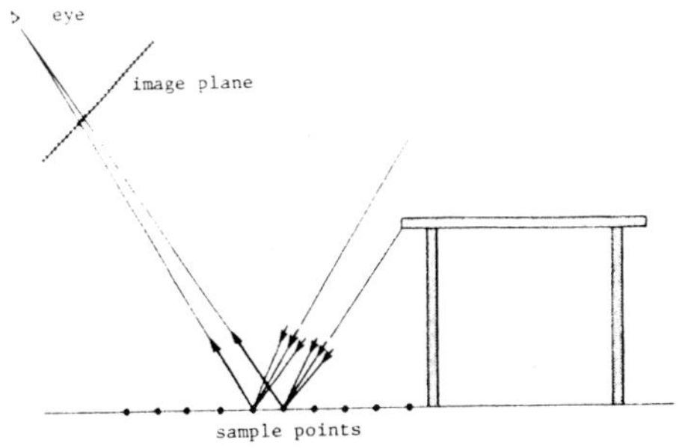

Figure 1a. View dependent calculation of specular component: The intensity calculation is limited to the outgoing directions that reach the eye. Incoming intensities may then be sampled at a higher frequency in the direction of the specular peak. The outgoing intensity on the floor will be calculated at points corresponding to each pixel, thus capturing the reflection of the table's edge to the accuracy required by the view.

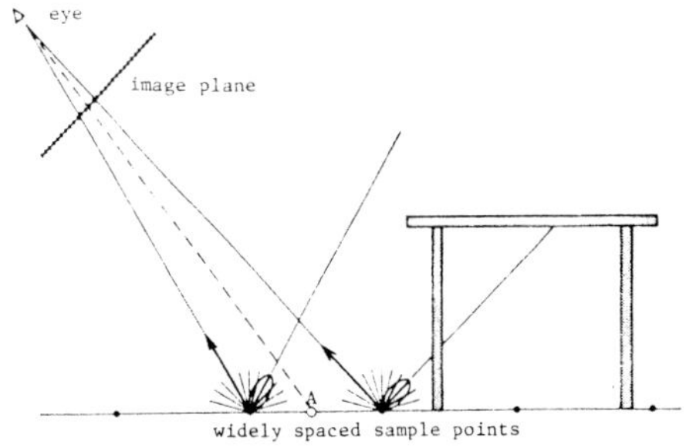

Figure 1c. View independent calculation of specular component: All outgoing directions must be accounted for, hence there is no preferred incoming direction. The outgoing intensity used when rendering from a specific view is the result of weighting the equally spaced incoming samples. The intensity at point A will be determined by interpolating from the widely spaced sample points. Thus the reflection of the edge of the table will not be accurately captured.

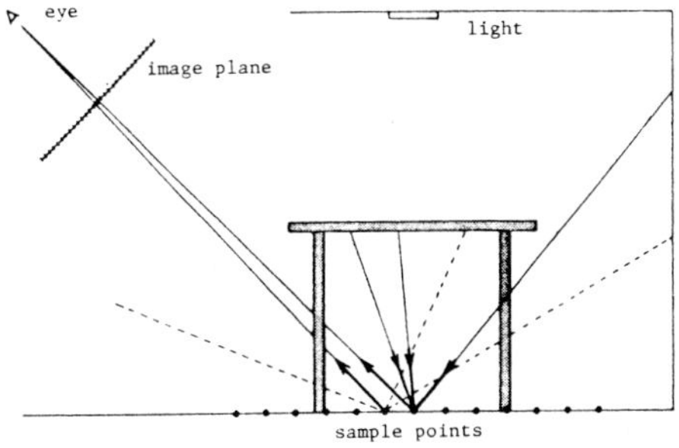

Figure 1b. View dependent calculation of diffuse component: For diffuse reflection the contribution of incoming intensities to the outgoing intensity is independent of the outgoing direction. If the light source is not visible to the sample point, many incoming directions may have to be sampled, since the significant sources of illumination may be difficult to find. This will be repeated for each pixel in which the floor is visible.

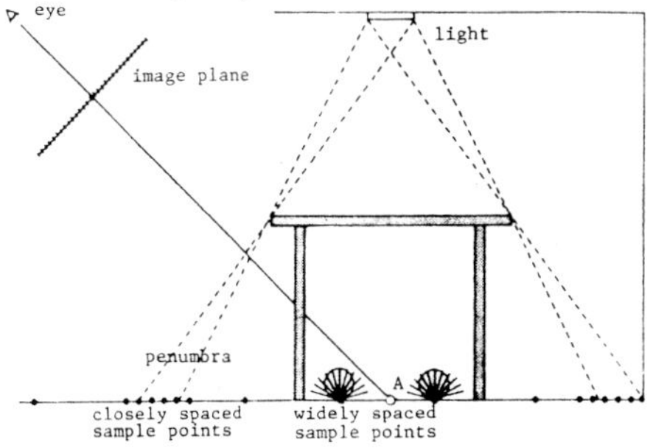

Figure 1d. View independent calculation of diffuse component: Many incoming directions are sampled for each sample point with their contributions weighted according to Lambert's cosine law. The sample points are spaced according to the gradient of illumination. The intensity at point A will be determined by interpolating from the surrounding sample points.

Local light reflection models for computer graphics traditionally separate the scattering of light from a surface into two components, a non-directional or diffuse term and a directional or specular term [20][4][7]. This corresponds to approximating the bidirectional reflectance function in equation (1) as the sum of a diffuse portion, ρ_d, which is independent of viewpoint, and a specular portion, ρ_s, which depends on the view direction. Thus,

$$\rho''(\Theta_{out},\Theta_{in}) = k_s \rho_s(\Theta_{out},\Theta_{in}) + k_d \rho_d$$

where

k_s = fraction of reflectance that is specular
k_d = fraction of reflectance that is diffuse
$k_s + k_d = 1$

Equation (1) can then be rewritten as

$$I_{out}(\Theta_{out}) = E(\Theta_{out}) + I_{d,out} + I_{s,out}(\Theta_{out}) \quad (2a)$$

where

$$I_{d,out} = k_d \rho_d \int I_{in}(\Theta_{in}) \cos(\theta)\, d\omega \quad (2b)$$

$$I_{s,out}(\Theta_{out}) = k_s \int \rho_s(\Theta_{out},\Theta_{in})\, I_{in}(\Theta_{in}) \cos(\theta)\, d\omega \quad (2c)$$

The outgoing diffuse and specular terms each depend on all incoming intensities I_{in}. Since these incoming intensities are, in fact, just outgoing intensities from other surfaces, they in turn contain both diffuse and specular components. Thus, it is not theoretically correct to solve for the diffuse and specular components independently, precluding a simple superposition of ray tracing and standard radiosity solutions, (although such an approach may be acceptable in many cases). Since the standard radiosity solution considers only diffuse inter-reflection, the illumination of a diffuse surface by light reflected specularly from another surface will not be accounted for and the subsequent effect of this light on the global illumination will be lost. The superposition of ray tracing will not recover it, since ray tracing

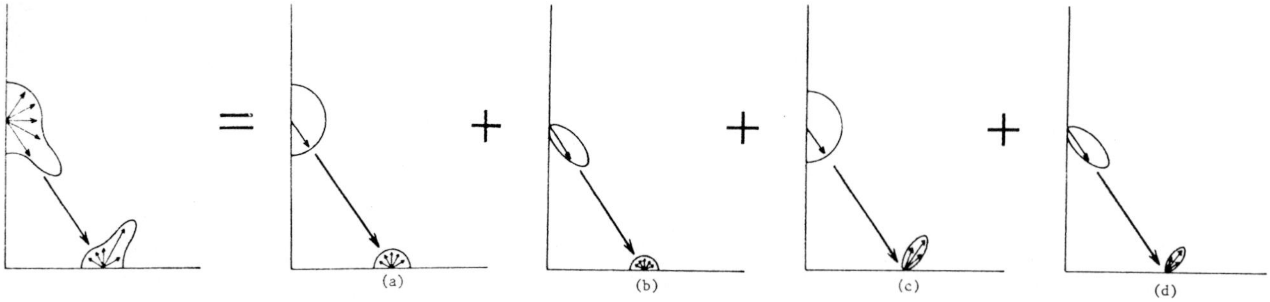

Figure 2. The four "mechanisms" of light transport: (a) diffuse to diffuse, (b) specular to diffuse, (c) diffuse to specular and (d) specular to specular.

does not consider the illumination of diffuse surfaces by other surfaces at all.

Given the separation of ρ" into ρ_d and ρ_s, the transfer of light from one surface to another can be thought of as occurring by way of four "mechanisms". These are illustrated in Figure 2. Light reflected diffusely by one surface may have arrived at that surface via diffuse reflection (Fig. 2a) or specular reflection (Fig. 2b) from another surface. Similarly, light reflected specularly may also have arrived via diffuse reflection (Fig. 2c) or specular reflection (Fig. 2d) from the other surface. The first two mechanisms are expressed by equation (2b) and the latter two by equation (2c). The diffuse to diffuse transfer is handled by the standard radiosity algorithms. Specular to specular and diffuse to specular transfer are handled by standard ray tracing algorithms, although the diffuse component is not correctly modeled. Neither approach in its conventional form has handled the specular to diffuse transfer, although other approaches, such as backwards ray tracing [2], beam tracing [16] and the methods of Kajiya and Immel described above, have been presented to account for this transfer mechanism. The backwards ray tracing method described by Arvo, in particular, anticipates the two-pass nature of the approach described below.

3.0 TWO-PASS IMAGE SYNTHESIS

The two-pass approach for computing global illumination described in the following sections accounts for all four mechanisms of light transfer. In a view-independent stage of the algorithm, called the preprocess, the complete global propagation of light is approximated in order to determine the diffuse component of intensity for all surfaces (Eq. 2b). All four transfer mechanisms are included in the preprocess. Thus specular reflection must be accounted for, but only to the extent necessary to accurately calculate the diffuse component. A view-dependent stage of the algorithm, called the postprocess, then uses the results of the preprocess as the basis for calculating the specular component (Eq. 2c) to the accuracy required by the view. The postprocess accounts for the specular to specular and diffuse to specular transfer mechanisms, in the latter case using the diffuse component calculated during the preprocess as the source. For each pixel in the final image, the resulting specular component is added to the diffuse component, interpolated from the preprocess sample points, providing a complete solution to equation (2a).

3.1 THE PREPROCESS

The standard radiosity solution using the hemi-cube algorithm provides the basis for the preprocess [5]. (Details of the radiosity method are not included here. The hemi-cube algorithm is a geometrically based numerical integration technique for calculating form-factors, which are purely geometric terms describing the transfer of energy from one surface to another.) Since the standard radiosity method accounts only for diffuse reflection, extensions to the hemi-cube algorithm must be made to add diffuse transmission and to approximate specular reflection and specular transmission in so far as it effects the diffuse component for all surfaces.

3.11 Translucency

Ideal diffuse transmission (translucency) is readily included by placing a hemi-cube on the back, as well as the front, of the transmitting surface and calculating backward in addition to the usual forward form-factors [11][21]. The backward form-factors represent the effect that light from surfaces seen by the back of the translucent surface has on the intensity of the front of the translucent surface.

3.12 Specular to Diffuse Transport

Specular reflection or transmission may also be accounted for in the standard radiosity solution by performing additional work during the calculation of form-factors [12]. The form-factor, it will be recalled, represents the fraction of the total energy leaving a given diffuse surface patch that arrives at a second diffuse surface patch. Specular surfaces are treated as additional routes by which light energy may reach one diffuse surface from others (Fig. 3). Thus, two diffuse surfaces that "see" each other via specular reflection or transmission by intermediate surfaces have an extra form-factor representing the additional fraction of energy that will be transfered over this route. The additional form-factors may be calculated by any method that can determine the path of specular reflection or transmission. The radiosity solution proceeds as before by solving the system of equations describing the interrelationships between

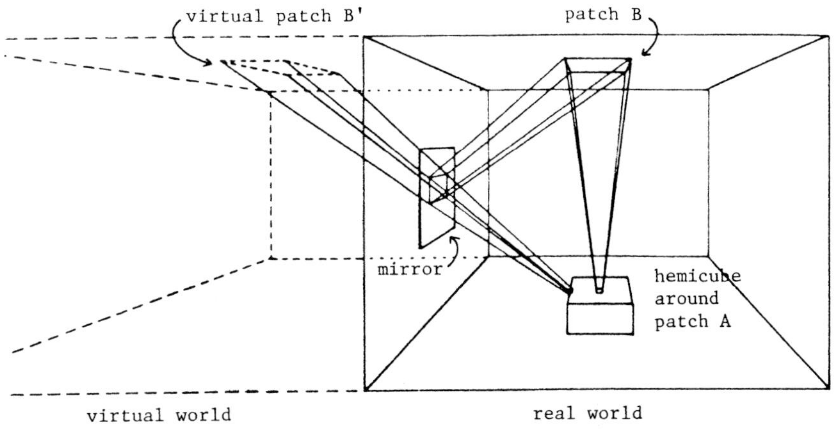

Figure 3. Calculation of extra form-factors to account for mirror reflection. Patch A receives light directly from patch B and indirectly through reflection by the mirror. The mirror is treated as a window into a virtual "mirror world." Projecting patch B′ onto the hemicube is then equivalent to following the actual path of reflection back to patch B.

diffuse surfaces, with specular reflection included implicitly to the extent that it affects these interrelationships. This accounts for the intensity of the diffuse component due to the diffuse to specular, specular to specular, and specular to diffuse transfer mechanisms without explicitly calculating the specular component for any surface.

In the current implementation, this technique is restricted to perfect, planar mirrors or filters. This allows the additional form-factors to be calculated with the current z-buffer hemi-cube algorithm by creating a "virtual world" which is seen through the mirror or filter [21] (Fig. 3). The approach may be generalized to handle curved surfaces and refraction by using ray tracing to determine the form-factors.

3.13 Result of the Preprocess

The final result of the preprocess is an accurate determination of the diffuse intensity at selected sample points (the element vertices) within the environment. Although some of these sample points may end up being hidden from a particular viewpoint, the number of sample points required is typically much less than the number that would have been imposed by a pixel to pixel calculation (although this would not necessarily be the case for environments with a very large number of surfaces). The hemi-cube algorithm, in effect, determines the incoming intensities at each sample point for a number of directions determined by the hemi-cube resolution. The effective number of directions is in the tens of thousands for typical hemi-cube resolutions. In a sense, the effort that would have been required to determine the diffuse component at every pixel in a view-dependent approach is applied instead to more accurately determining the illumination at a smaller number of points.

3.2 THE POSTPROCESS

The postprocess takes the results of the preprocess and, for a given view, completes the solution of the illumination equation for the surface visible at each pixel. The view-dependence of the postprocess permits the efficient calculation of the specular component $I_{s,out}(\Theta_{out})$ (Eq. 2b) by limiting the direction for which it must be calculated to the view direction. As in previous radiosity methods, the diffuse component $I_{d,out}$ is calculated by interpolation from the element vertex intensities determined during the preprocess. The sum $I_{d,out} + I_{s,out}(\Theta_{out})$ completes the solution to the integral in equation (1) and, with the addition of intensity due to emission, provides the final intensity at each pixel.

The specular component $I_{s,out}(\Theta_{out})$ depends on the intensities arriving at the surface from the entire hemisphere of directions, weighted by the specular bidirectional reflectance $\rho_s(\Theta_{in},\Theta_{out})$. Distributed ray tracing [8] and "cone tracing" [1] were the first algorithms for sampling these incoming intensities. The method presented in this section is based on the observation that in most specular reflection, the bidirectional reflectance is such that only a fraction of the incoming intensities over the hemisphere make a significant contribution to the outgoing intensity in a particular direction. Thus, with little loss of accuracy, the limits of integration may be reduced from the entire hemisphere to the smaller solid angle over which the weighted intensity is significant. The determination of the incoming intensities requires that the visible surfaces and intensities be found over the solid angle of interest, a problem that is precisely equivalent to that of computing an image from the surface intersection point with a view in the mirror direction.

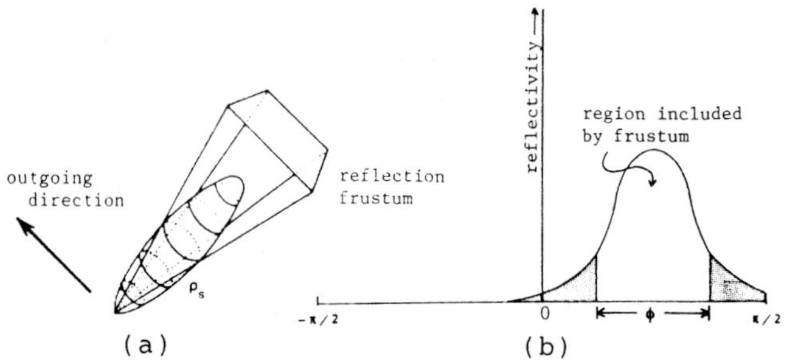

Figure 4. (a) A specular bidirectional reflectivity function for a particular outgoing direction showing the reflection frustum and the solid angle through which incoming intensities will be sampled.

(b) A two-dimensional slice through the reflectivity function of figure 4a plotted in rectangular coordinates with incoming angle on the x axis and reflectivity on the y axis. The weight that will be given to incoming intensities is proportional to the value of this function at the incoming angle.

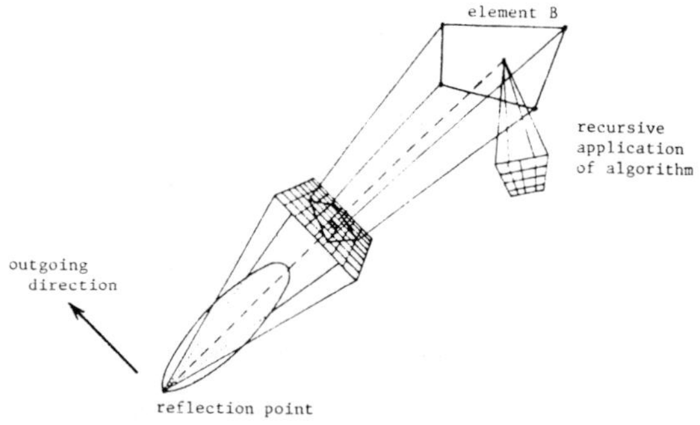

Figure 5. Sampling of the intensities arriving through the reflection frustum using the z-buffer algorithm. The incoming diffuse component due to element B at each "pixel" is obtained by interpolating from the diffuse intensities at the element vertices. The incoming specular component is obtained recursively.

3.21 The Reflection Frustum

A view frustum encompassing this solid angle is constructed (Fig. 4). The visible surfaces for this reflection frustum are determined using a standard low resolution z-buffer algorithm (typically on the order of 10 by 10 "pixels"). The incoming intensity "seen" through each "pixel" of this frustum is simply the intensity of the surface visible at that pixel (Fig. 5). This intensity may contain both diffuse and specular components. The incoming diffuse component at each reflection frustum pixel is determined during the z-buffer operation by Gouraud shading from the element vertex intensities calculated during the preprocess. Where a surface visible in a reflection frustum pixel has a specular component, its intensity is calculated by applying the entire postprocess algorithm recursively, analogously to the similar case in traditional ray-tracing. The work required for this recursive step may be reduced by adaptively limiting the depth of recursion [15] and by reducing the resolution of the frustum for successive bounces.

Once the incoming intensities have been determined, the integral in equation (2c) can be numerically evaluated. The subdivision of the reflection frustum into pixels acts as a discretization of the domain of integration. The integral thus becomes the summation:

$$I_{s,out} = k_s \sum_{i=0}^{n} \sum_{j=0}^{n} W_{i,j} \, I_{in}(\Theta_{i,j}) \cos(\theta_{i,j}) \, \Delta\omega_{i,j}$$

where the bidirectional reflectance function is represented by $W_{i,j}$, an array of weights, and n is the resolution of the reflection frustum. Each weight in the array corresponds to the incoming direction $\Theta_{i,j}$ determined by the "pixel" (i,j) of the reflection frustum and is proportional to the bidirectional reflectance for the view direction and the incoming direction determined by that "pixel".

The array of weights can be pre-computed as a look-up table for a simple Phong-like reflectance function at a given reflection frustum resolution, making the approximation that the variation of $\cos(\theta)\Delta\omega$ over the frustum is small and can be ignored. Various surface finishes can be simulated by simply varying the size of the frustum; the smaller the frustum, the more mirror-like the reflection. More complex physically based reflection models may require more elaborate look-up tables or require the weights to be computed on the fly based on reflection angle, frustum size and resolution.

3.22 Transparency

Specular transmission, including refraction, is accounted for analogously to reflection by defining a bidirectional transmittance and constructing a transmission frustum in the transmitted direction.

3.23 Antialiasing

Inevitably, a uniform point sampling method will produce aliasing in one form or another. Figure 6a provides an example of aliasing produced by the regular point sampling of the incoming intensities through the reflection frustum. The uniform sampling produces a striped or plaid effect due to an alignment of the sampling pattern with the projection of object edges in the environment. A small shift in the reflection frustum may result in a sudden jump in the number of reflection frustum "pixels" covered by the object. Selecting sample points stochastically rather than uniformly, as imposed by the regular grid of "pixels", may eliminate aliasing by converting it to noise [9][10]. However, this also eliminates the speed

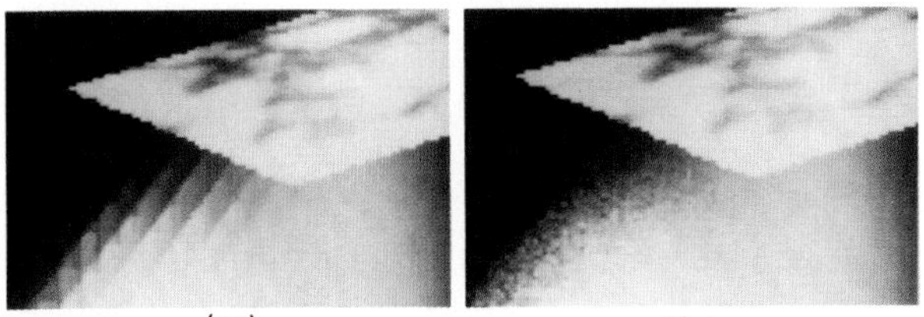

(a) (b)

Figure 6. (a) Aliasing due to uniform point sampling of the incoming intensities.

(b) Result of rotating the reflection frustum around its central axis by a random amount for each image pixel (enlargement of lower left corner of image in Figure 11b).

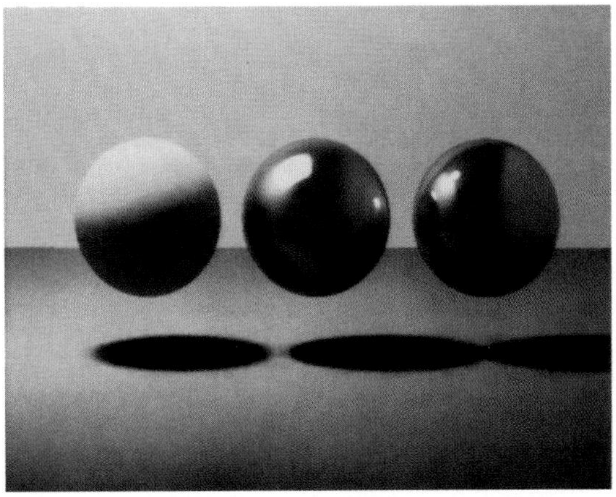

Figure 7. Stainless steel spheres with finishes ranging from completely diffuse to highly specular.

hemi-cube resolution = 50 by 50
reflection frustum resolution:
  first bounce = 15 by 15
  second bounce = 10 by 10
reflection frustum size:
  middle sphere = 0.79 radians
  right-hand sphere = 0.16 radians

advantages of an incremental algorithm like the z-buffer. To preserve this advantage, instead of randomly distributing the samples themselves, the reflection frustum used to calculate the specular component at each pixel in the final image is rotated around its central axis by a random amount before the z-buffering is performed. This rotation alters the alignment between the reflection frustum sampling pattern and the environment from pixel to pixel in the final image, thus reducing the aliasing artifacts considerably (Fig. 6b).

4.0 RESULTS

Figure 7 shows a series of spheres that range from completely diffuse to highly specular. The spheres were subdivided into 96 patches for the preprocess. Adaptive subdivision [6] was found to be particularly important for curved surfaces, because of the relatively rapid change in diffuse intensity produced as the surface normal turns away from a light source. The depth of recursion during the postprocess was limited to two by treating specular surfaces as entirely diffuse on the third bounce.

Figure 8 shows a series of thin glass sheets demonstrating a range from ideal diffuse to ideal specular transmission. The left hand glass panel acts as a purely diffuse transmitter (like opal glass), the center panel is more specular (like frosted glass), while the panel on the right is an almost ideal specular transmitter. The etched glass in Figure 9 was produced using a procedurally defined "translucency map" to determine the size of the transmission frustum at each point on the glass.

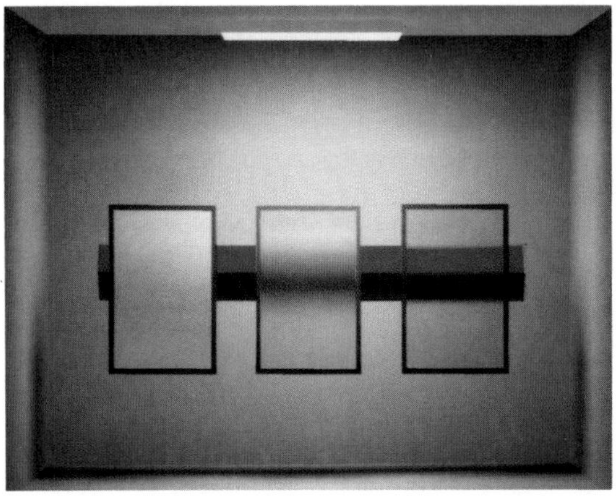

Figure 8. Three panes of translucent glass. The left-hand panel demonstrates ideal diffuse transmission.

hemi-cube resolution = 200 by 200
transmission frustum resolution = 15 by 15
transmission frustum size:
  middle panel = 0.79 radians
  right-hand panel = 0.16 radians

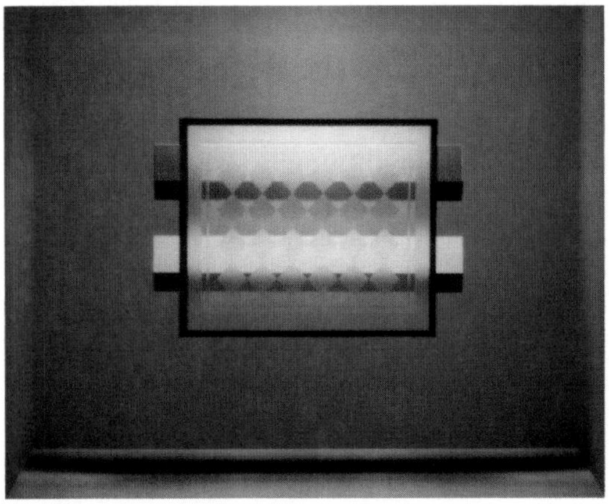

Figure 9. Etched glass.

Figures 10a, b and c show an environment for which the illumination of diffuse surfaces by specular reflection (via the specular to diffuse transfer mechanism) is significant. Several versions of the image have been calculated to emphasize the effects of various levels of sophistication provided by the preprocess. Overall illumination of the room is provided by a dim area source on the ceiling. The reflection in the mirror in each case was calculated during the postprocess. In Figure 10a only the direct illumination of surfaces by the light sources is accounted for, hence surfaces facing away from lights or in shadow are black. In Figure 10b the full radiosity solution has been applied but the effect of the specular reflection from the mirror on the illumination of diffuse surfaces has been ignored. In Figure 10c this specular to diffuse transfer has been accounted for using the mirror form-factor technique. The illumination of the top of the vanity along with the objects on it results primarily from light emitted by the lamp on the vanity and subsequently reflected by the mirror. The environment is subdivided into 4224 elements, providing only 5379 sample points for which the diffuse component was calculated. This is a significantly smaller number than the number of pixels at which an entirely view-dependent calculation would have calculated the diffuse component. The hemi-cube resolution during the preprocess was 150 by 150. The specular component of the mirror was calculated with a frustum of 0.032 radians.

Figure 11 shows an environment inspired by a well-known painting, "Lady and Gentleman at the Virginals", by the 17th century Dutch painter Jan Vermeer. Vermeer is particularly known for his use of light to define space, based, at least in part, on a sensitivity to the effects of what we would now call "global illumination", effects such as penumbra and "color bleeding", for example. For the image in Figure 11a the floor was treated as an ideal diffuse reflector. As far as is known, the floor of his studio never attained the high sheen demonstrated in Figure 11b. The hemi-cube resolution for the preprocess was 50 by 50 for both images. The resolution of the reflection frustum was 10 by 10 for the floor in Figure 11b, with a reflection frustum size of 0.079 radians.

All images were calculated on DEC VAX 11/750, 11/780, 8300 or 8700 computers and displayed using 1280 by 1024 24-bit frame buffers from Raster Technologies or Hewlett-Packard.

5.0 CONCLUSION AND FUTURE DIRECTIONS

A hybrid, two-pass methodology for simulating global illumination within general complex environments has been presented. The approach takes advantage of the complementary strengths of view-dependent and view-independent methods. The view independent preprocess, based on the radiosity method, provides an efficient computation of the diffuse component. The view-dependent postprocess, based on ray tracing, efficiently calculates the specular component. By taking advantage of the best features of each a complete simulation is achieved.

The standard radiosity algorithms are also extended to handle curved surfaces and diffuse transmission and to account for the contribution of specular reflection to the illumination of diffuse surfaces. An alternative to distributed ray tracing is described in which the specular component is determined by a regular sampling of intensities contributing to the reflected intensity using a z-buffer algorithm.

Both the preprocess and the postprocess require the performance of a very large number of independent visible surface calculations. These are necessary during the preprocess to calculate the form-factors and during the postprocess to determine incoming intensities contributing to the specular component. In fact, the total computation time in both processes is overwhelmingly dominated by these calculations. The choice of the standard z-buffer algorithm was motivated in part by recent advances in the implementation of such algorithms in special-purpose hardware [23]. The use of such hardware to perform the z-buffer portions of the hemi-cube algorithm and the distributed ray tracing algorithm described above promises dramatic increases in the speed of both the preprocess and the postprocess. In addition, with increased processing speed, aliasing problems may be reduced by increasing the resolution of the reflection frusta.

Future implementations should increase the generality of the preprocess by including ray tracing to calculate reflected and refracted form-factors where necessary. Future implementations should also provide for cases where the gradient of the diffuse intensity is extremely high, such as along sharp shadow boundaries. Just as with the specular component, the attempt to solve for these cases in an entirely view independent manner is inefficient. Regions of high diffuse gradient may instead be merely identified in the preprocess and solved for in the postprocess on a pixel by pixel basis.

The two-pass approach presented here is more general than the particular implementation described. Many alternative pre and post processes may be imagined. Conventional distributed ray tracing, for example, could be substituted for the z-buffer algorithm in the postprocess. Path tracing, as Kajiya named his approach, might use the approximate description of the propagation of light gained during the preprocess as a basis for importance sampling.

The two-pass approach also provides a framework for the progressive refinement of images, in the spirit of the approach described by Bergman, et al [3]. Using currently available hardware the pre-computed diffuse component provided by the preprocess may be rendered at interactive rates, enabling "walk-throughs" of static environments. When the viewer lingers at a certain view, refinement of the shading of visible surfaces by the postprocess may commence.

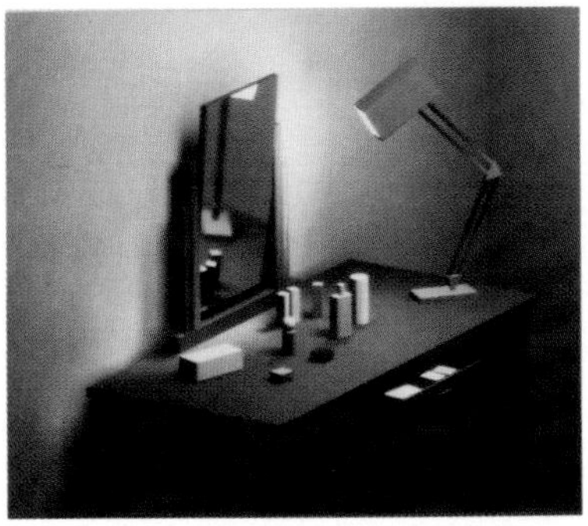

(a)

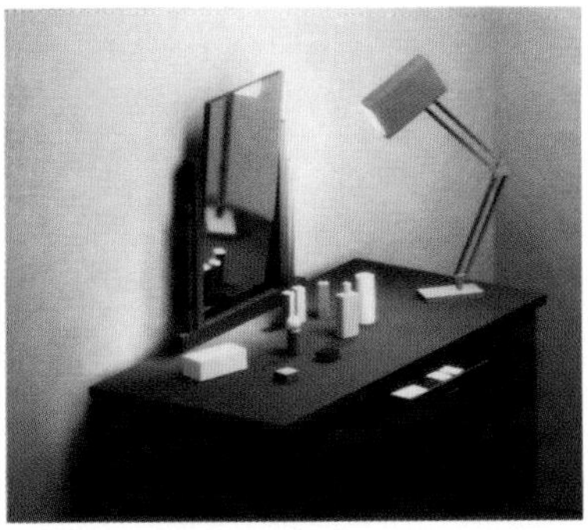

(b)

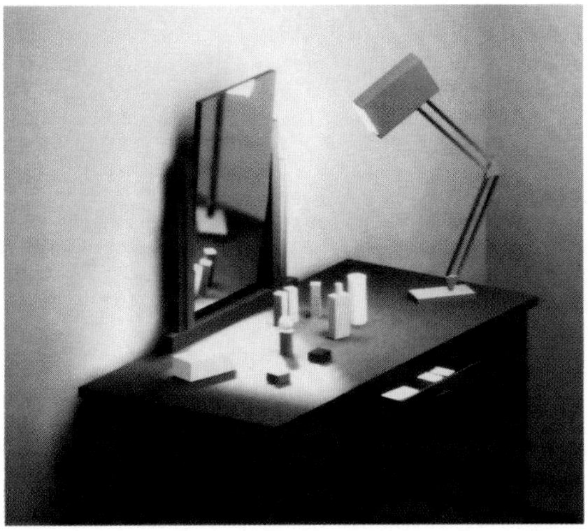

(c)

Figure 10. (a) Direct illumination by light sources only.

(b) Diffuse to diffuse transfer included. Specular to diffuse ignored.

(c) Full solution.

Figure 11a. A 17th-century Dutch interior.

Figure 11b. A 17th-century Dutch interior after polishing the floor.

ACKNOWLEDGMENTS

The z-buffer distributed ray tracing algorithm is based on ideas developed by Michael Cohen and Lisa Maynes. Particular thanks go to Holly Rushmeier for many valuable discussions, to Stewart Feldman and Wayne Lytle for the diagrams, to Emil Ghinger for photography, and to the reviewers for their helpful comments. This research was conducted under grant No. DCR-8203979 from the National Science Foundation and was supported by generous equipment grants from the Digital Equipment Corporation and Hewlett-Packard.

REFERENCES

1. Amanatides, John, "Ray Tracing with Cones," Proceedings of SIGGRAPH'84, In Computer Graphics, Vol. 18, No. 3, July 1984, pp. 129-136.

2. Arvo, James, "Backward Ray Tracing," Developments in Ray Tracing, SIGGRAPH Course Notes, Vol. 12, 1986.

3. Bergmann, Larry, Henry Fuchs, Eric Grant, Susan Spach, "Image Rendering by Adaptive Refinement," Proceedings of SIGGRAPH'86, In Computer Graphics, Vol. 20, No, 4, Aug. 1986, pp. 29-38.

4. Blinn, James F.,"Models of Light Reflection for Computer Synthesized pictures," Proceedings of SIGGRAPH'77, In Computer Graphics, Vol. 11, No. 2, 1977, pp. 192-198.

5. Cohen, Michael F. and Donald P. Greenberg, "A Radiosity Solution for Complex Environments," Proceedings of SIGGRAPH'85, In Computer Graphics, Vol. 19, No. 3, July 1985, pp. 31-40.

6. Cohen, Michael F., Donald P. Greenberg, David S. Immel, Philip J. Brock, "An Efficient Radiosity Approach for Realistic Image Synthesis," IEEE Computer Graphics and Applications, Vol. 6, No. 2, March 1986, pp. 26-35.

7. Cook, Robert L., and Kenneth E. Torrance, "A Reflection Model for Computer Graphics," ACM Transactions on Graphics, Vol. 1, No. 1, January 1982, pp. 7-24.

8. Cook, Robert L., Thomas Porter and Loren Carpenter, "Distributed Ray Tracing," Proceedings of SIGGRAPH'84, In Computer Graphics, Vol. 18, No. 3, July 1984, pp.137-145.

9. Cook, Robert L., "Stochastic Sampling in Computer Graphics," ACM Transactions on Graphics, Vol. 5, No. 1, January 1986, pp 51-72.

10. Dippe, Mark A. Z., Erling Henry Wold, "Antialiasing Through Stochastic Sampling," Proceedings of SIGGRAPH'85, In Computer Graphics, Vol 19, No. 3, July 1985, pp. 69-78.

11. Dunkle, R. V., "Radiant interchange in an enclosure with specular surfaces and enclosures with window or diathermanous walls.", in Heat Transfer, Thermodynamics and Education, edited by H. A. Johnson, Boelter Anniversary Volume, New York: McGraw-Hill, 1964.

12. Eckert, E. R. G., and Sparrow, E. M., "Radiative Heat Exchange Between Surfaces with Specular Reflection," International Journal of Heat and Mass Transfer, Vol. 3, pp. 42-54, 1961.

13. Goral, Cindy M., Kenneth E. Torrance, Donald P. Greenburg, Bennet Battaile, "Modeling the Interaction of Light Between Diffuse Surfaces," Proceedings of SIGGRAPH'84, In Computer Graphics, Vol. 18, No. 3, July 1984, pp. 213-222.

14. Gouraud, H., "Continuous Shading of Curved Surfaces," IEEE Transactions on Computers, Vol. 20, No. 6, June 1971, pp. 623-628.

15. Hall, Roy A. and Donald P. Greenberg, "A Testbed for Realistic Image Synthesis," IEEE Computer Graphics and Applications, Vol. 3, No. 10, Nov. 1983, pp. 10-20.

16. Heckbert, Paul S. and Pat Hanrahan, "Beam Tracing Polygonal Objects," Proceedings of SIGGRAPH'84, In Computer Graphics, Vol. 18, No. 3, July 1984, pp. 119-128.

17. Immel, David S., Michael F. Cohen, Donald P. Greenberg, "A Radiosity Method for Non-Diffuse Environments," Proceedings of SIGGRAPH'86, In Computer Graphics, Vol. 20, No. 4, Aug. 1986, pp. 133-142.

18. Kajiya, James T., "The Rendering Equation," Proceedings of SIGGRAPH'86, In Computer Graphics, Vol. 20, No. 4, Aug. 1986, pp. 143-150.

19. Nishita, Tomoyuki and Eihachiro Nakamae, "Continuous Tone Representation of Three-Dimensional Objects Taking Account of Shadows and Interreflection," Proceedings of SIGGRAPH'85, In Computer Graphics, Vol. 19, No.3, July 1985, pp. 22-30.

20. Phong, Bui Tuong, "Illumination for Computer Generated Pictures," Communications of the ACM, Vol. 18, No. 6, June 1975, pp. 311-317.

21. Rushmeier, Holly E., "Extending the Radiosity Method to Transmitting and Specularly Reflecting Surfaces," Master's thesis, Cornell Univ., Ithaca, 1986.

22. Siegel, Robert and John R. Howell, Thermal Radiation Heat Transfer, Hemisphere Publishing Corp., Washington DC., 1981.

23. Swanson, Roger W. and Larry J. Thayer, "A Fast Shaded-Polygon Renderer," Proceedings of SIGGRAPH'86, In Computer Graphics, Vol. 20, No. 4, Aug. 1986, pp. 95-102.

24. Whitted, Turner, "An Improved Illumination Model for Shaded Display," Communications of the ACM, Vol. 23, No. 6, June 1980, pp. 343-349.

Where Do User Interfaces Come From?

Chair: *Christopher F. Herot, Javelin Software Corporation*
Panelists: *Stuart Card, Xerox Corporation*
Bruce Tognazzini, Apple Computer, Inc.
Kent Norman, University of Maryland
Andrew Lippman, Massachusetts Institute of Technology

Introduction

Everyone who builds a graphics system has to build a user interface. In most cases, the design of such interfaces is based primarily on intuition. Proponents of this approach claim that attempts to codify principles of user interface design stifle innovation, human factors research is too narrow to prescribe solutions, and rigorous testing is too time consuming. Others claim that the fields of human factors and psychology have much to offer and need not be cumbersome or expensive.

The issue of the relative importance of intuitive design and empirical studies has been subject to debate since the early days of computer graphics. The members of this panel were chosen for their reputations of holding strong viewpoints on this subject, but as their statements below indicate, the discussion has now progressed to a more mature phase where there is an attempt to combine both approaches. There is a recognition that human factors and psychological research can be useful if they are directed towards discovering models of human cognition which apply to the application at hand. Interface designers have recognized the value of some form of evaluation of prototype designs short of acceptance or rejection in the marketplace. Researchers in empirical studies have begun to develop quick and inexpensive methods of doing these evaluations. Finally, the whole concept of interface design is evolving from the notion of grafting something onto a system to one of designing the entire system to fit a model of how a person uses a computer.

Statement from Stuart Card

If it can be said that many of the great breakthroughs of technology were the result of intuitive leaps, it can equally be said that many were not. The question of whether there can ever be anything better than intuitive design of human-computer interfaces is really just a version of the relative effectiveness of traditional "cut and try" engineering methods vs. science for advancing technology in this area. Unfortunately, in the history of different technologies one finds nearly all possible patterns: cases where science was of little or no importance in advancing the technology (e.g., the bicycle), cases where science was very important (e.g., the atomic bomb), and all manner of complex interactions in between. So we cannot argue for or against the primacy of intuitive design on general grounds, but must understand better the conditions under which cut-and-try methods or science are likely to be important contributors to technology progress. As a sort of intellectual first-aid until the historian arrives, let me suggest that science is most likely to be effective (1) when technology gets stuck, as it does from time to time, on problems that require more understanding than cut-and-try methods provide, (2) when science can identify the key constraints that underlie success for the technology, and (3) when science can provide tools for thought for the designer, especially helping the designer reconceptualize the design space.

It is important to distinguish in this discussion between the product development context, where the aim is making money, and the research context, where the aim is advancing the state of the art. Methods that are too time-consuming for product development, such as controlled experiments or theory building, can nonetheless be effective in the research context and, if sucessful, lead to commercial products. Few companies would attempt while developing a cryptographic product to derive a new method for factoring large numbers, but this task would make sense in an industrial research laboratory or a university department. Likewise, we have to distinguish between intuitive cut-and-try design (which usually means incremental improvements over existing designs), informal empirical observations (e.g., rapid prototyping), evaluation experiments, and theory building. The various methods for gaining empirical and analytical information about human interface design vary in the reliability of the information, the amount of insight it produces, and the generalization of the information. For example, informal observation of a rapid prototype may clearly demonstrate that users have difficulty with some part of the system without giving the designer the faintest clue as to why. Or comparison of two methods of doing some task may show that one is faster without showing why or whether the difference will hold up in practice or after system revision. Debate on cut-and-try design vs. empirical or analytical methods must therefore be grounded in whether the context is product development or research and just what sorts of methods are being discussed.

Two examples that illustrate the interaction of science and technology for human-computer interface designs are research on the mouse and the Rooms system. In the case of the mouse, numerous input devices had been constructed, but there was no way of deciding what constituted a good device other than empirically comparing every device to every other device for every program they were used in. Research showed that pointing speed with the mouse depended only on distance and target size (and not on what one was pointing at or the direction of pointing, for example). The research also showed that the speed of the mouse was limited by the human, not by the mechanics of the mouse itself. This research helped lead to the commercial introduction of the mouse, to proprietary ideas of how to make other devices, to key constraints that determine pointing, and to tools for conceptualizing design of the mouse (it helps to make the targets large or nearby).

In the case of the Rooms system (a window manager for switching among the use of many virtual workspaces) an analysis of window user overhead showed that the real problem is severe space contention because of small screens. This can be modeled in terms of working sets and helps suggest the design of the Rooms system by analogy with operating system memory preloading policies.

In both of the above cases, empirical and analytical science was used to augment cut-and-try engineering methods. In both cases, the issues were long-standing and the insight was of use in conceptual design. At PARC, we have found the coupling between science and design useful enough that we now try in research projects for the following quadruple (first suggested by John Seeley Brown): (1) a crisp statement of a problem, (2) a theory analyzing the problem, (3) an artifact in which the theory is embedded, and (4) an "entailment" of the theory, that is an application to a different problem showing that the theory has generality. Several projects in the cognitive sciences (with commercial or potentially commercial payoff) are now reasonable examples of this paradigm. Intuitions do not arise out of thin air, they come from experience, data, and knowledge of theory. In the case of the mouse and of Rooms, the intuitions of the designers are greatly improved by the understanding made possible through the research.

Nothing aids intuitive design like a good theory.

Statement from Bruce Tognazzini

Many of the great breakthroughs of science and invention were the result of intuitive leaps. The real power of western science comes from the extraction of what is important in new discovery, and in the building upon that extraction. A few decades ago, the Tomograph X-ray machine was invented, letting doctors view longitudinal "slices" of the human body. Like most intuitive inventions, how it works seems remarkably obvious once you see it work. Unfortunately, from the patient's point of view, it is rather terrifying to see it work, tearing down the length of the patient's body while its X-ray source, appearing to weigh several tons, careens around its axis over the patient's head.

Ungainly as it was, this mechanical contraption had within it a very important concept, one that was translated into the quiet sophistication of the next generation, the Computer Axial Tomograph, or CAT scan, a machine that has revolutionized diagnostic medicine. Western science performed that translation.

Computer science is too new not to depend on the creative talent of intuitive minds: The visual interfaces used by Apple, Xerox, and others when developed in the '50's and '60's, smashed every contemporary assumption of human interface design. It is unlikely that we have now reached such a doddering state of maturity that such leaps will no longer be an important factor in further evolution. On the other hand, we have reached a state of maturity where we need to look at what we have accomplished and learn from it, if only to prepare for the next leap.

Thus, I find myself (to my surprise) to be a moderate on the whole issue: I think that the tension between the intuitives and the empirical codifiers (for want of a better term) is the very stuff from which the future will be made. For without the intuitives we can only evolve into entropy; without the empirical codifiers, we can only have a disconnected series of fascinating starts.

Statement from Kent Norman

In the history of various sciences, empirical research has served either to "confirm the obvious" or to "dispel the myth." Either result contributes to our scientific knowledge base. In the same way, empirical research in computer graphics and human/computer interaction should serve the function of giving evidence that a particular design is either the right way to do it or the wrong way.

Critics of empirical research point out that more often than not system designers just don't have the time for iterative human-factors testing or even for a search of the relevant literature. The unfortunate result may be that down the road users just don't have the time for such untested systems. The consequence is that corporate research funds are in the end spent to analyze what went wrong rather than how to have designed it right in the first place. The point is that an empirical result will occur whether it has been experimentally planned or not. It is argued that the safest bet is to gather those data as early as possible.

Intuitive design is generally the result of intuitions based on anecdotal evidence, intuitions about the cognitive functions, and sheer creativity. Results in the psychology of intuitive statistics indicate that while people are generally good at making gross estimates, there are substantial and predictable errors. Consequently, we rely on calculators for statistics rather than on our heads. Results in the psychology of thinking and problem solving indicate that creativity is a function of divergent thinking rather than rote application. Consequently, we rely on our heads for new ideas rather than on calculators.

Designers are good at generating innovative alternatives. While they often make the right choices about software functionality, graphic layout, etc., they are nevertheless subject to biases such as the ethnocentric fallacy. Designers believe that users think like they do. One of our studies on the layout of menus reveals several discrepancies between how programmers would design menus versus how novice users would prefer them to be displayed. Usually designers make the right choices; however, discrepancies also exist between how programmers layout menus and performance data.

At present there is an uneasy relationship between system design and empirical research. Part of this stems from a conflict of interest. Planned empirical research is motivated by two different sources. Research may be theory driven in the sense that studies are motivated by a basic need for diagnostic information about a theoretical issue that may or may not impact on design questions. Basic research on theories, such as cognitive control and cognitive layout, help to provide ways of thinking about design as well as guidelines and design principles.

On the other hand, research may be design-driven in the sense that studies are motivated by a practical need for diagnostic information about whether Design A or Design B should be implemented. Such research is the mainstay of product testing in industry. The conflict arises due to the priority of theory versus product.

A more serious problem is the need for the development of research methods and experimental design specifically tailored to human/computer interaction. Off-the-shelf methods are ill-suited to the particular problems inherent in research on human/computer interaction. Instead researchers need to pursue efficient designs capable of studying multiple design factors while at the same time controlling nuisance variables such as individual differences and sporadic system variables. In addition, standardized performance measures and user evaluations are needed as a means of comparing different implementations. Finally, managers must decide to make a serious investment in qualified researchers in order to gain the edge on system design. It is no longer sufficient to produce an innovative product,;one has to provide empirical evidence that it is the right innovation.

Statement from Andrew Lippman

The notion that there is such a thing as a "user interface" is probably the most serious problem in the field today. The word interface carries with it the connotation that one designs a "system" to meet some performance criteria and then grafts an "interface" to it to make it useful. Whether the dictates of the interface come from human factors research or are intuitive is beside the point. The notion is akin to designing a user-friendly policeman who smiles as he hands you a speeding ticket. No interface can make that task a pleasure. The assumed separability of the interface and the task is basically incorrect. Only in the domain of computer systems, where functionality has historically had precedence over usability, has this simple predicate been violated.

A more direct approach is possible, and it is amenable to the incorporation of human factors research as well as intuition and design. There is certainly a place for all of these components. The important notion is that of "Systems Design." Perhaps the most productive approach one can take is to define a useful goal and then assume that technology can be bent to meet it. When the goal places constraints on computer technology, recent history has demonstrated that it is a mistake to underestimate the power of the next generation machine. Similarly, the next generation display hardware and input technology is not so far away nor as expensive as is often assumed.

One way to approach the design of useful systems is to consider models from existing media. For example, at the Architecture Machine Group, a personalized information retrieval system called Newspeek is modeled upon the style of presentation and interaction associated with a large format, daily newspaper. The screen is divided into columns, each of which contains a part of a "lead story" and a headline. Gestures on the screen scroll through these articles and highlight similar portions or neighboring ones. The editors and reporters associated with print newspaper production are computer programs in Newspeek, and they take their cues from the same gestures used to read any particular edition. Thus the newspaper is "programmed" as it is read; it evolves to reflect the interests of the individual reader.

Similarly, an electronic manual was designed based upon the styles of access associated with a printed book. It contained a table of contents, chapters, and pages; text was typeset on-the-fly as the book was read, and illustrations were interspersed throughout. The form of the book was extended by allowing the page to become a workspace rather than a primitive element. It could be queried for definitions of unfamiliar terms and for elaboration. The illustrations were sync-sound movies that could be coordinated with the text.

In both of these examples, an existing information resource was extended rather than replaced. Successful information resources were mapped into electronic forms, and the displays and database were built to accommodate successful styles of use.

Another approach involves modeling the mechanisms and language of interactions drawn from everyday life. In some cases, such as the book and the newspaper, this is not so difficult; in others, there is no well-understood history. While we know a little about how humans converse, we have yet to build a good computer conversationalist. However, Schmandt's Phone-Slave, which engages a telephone caller in a synthetic dialogue, goes quite far by exploiting the simple fact that most people will answer a question directly posed to them. Depending on how much the system knows about the caller, each dialogue can take one of several turns and twists that makes it somewhat individual.

A current challenge in this area is the notion of interactive movies. It is generally assumed that an interaction is better as the degrees of freedom and fidelity provided by the computer increase; movies are therefore a logical extension to graphically and aurally parsimonious, typewritten dialogues. However, we don't have either a technology or a language for interacting with moving images that approaches the simplicity and utility of those used for static printed material, and the movie itself may be "anti-interactive." For the most part, network television, the most ubiquitous example of moving images, has not made the leap to interactivity even though the television receivers and distribution systems contain many of the necessary components.

Bibliography

Gano, S. "Forms for Electronic Books." Masters thesis, Department of Architecture, Massachusetts Institute of Technology, Cambridge, MA, June 1983.

Lippman, A., and Backer, D.S. "Personalized Aides for Training: An Assault on Publishing." *Proceedings of the Fourth Annual Conference on Video Learning Systems.* Society of Applied Learning Technology, Arlington, Virginia, 1982.

Lippman, A., and Bender, W. "News and Movies in The 50 Megabit Living Room." *Globecom*, April 1987.

Lippman, A. "Computing with Television: Paperback Movies." Talk given at Images, Information & Interfaces Directions for the 1990s, symposium. New York, NY, November 19, 1986.

Lippman, A. "Optical Publishing." Computer Society International Conference (COMPCON), San Francisco, CA, February 1985.

Lippman, A. "Imaging and Interactivity." 15th Joint Conference on Image Technology, Tokyo, Japan, November 1984.

Lippman, A. "Video Instrument Control." Instrument Society of America (ISA), International Conference and Exhibit, Philadelphia, PA, October 1982.

Lippman, A, and Backer, D. "Future Interactive Graphics: Personal Video." National Computer Graphics Association Conference, Baltimore, MD, 1981.

Schmandt, C., and Arons, B. "Phone Slave: A Graphical Telecommunications Interface." *Proceedings, Society for Information Display*, San Francisco, CA, 1984.

SIGKIDS

Co-Chairs: *Creighton Helsley, Rockwell International*
Coco Conn, Homer & Associates
Panelists: *Scott Crow -12th grade, Grant High School, Sherman Oaks, CA*
Robert Holtz - 8th grade, Chaminade Prep, Northridge, CA
Joshua Horowitz - 4th grade, Open School, Hollywood, CA
Eddie Lew - 11th grade, Hollywood High School, Hollywood, CA
Ben Novida - 12th grade, Garfield High School, Los Angeles, CA
Joe Savella - 12th grade, Garfield High School, Los Angeles, CA
Discussant: *Margaret Minsky, MIT*

Summary

From a panel discussion and video display of the work of "kid" panel members, we consider the benefits of having access to computer graphics from a younger perspective. Each of the students on the panel has implemented programs involving computer graphics. Four of the panelists are semi-finalists in the 1987 Rockwell International Los Angeles Unified School District Computer Science Competition. The individual works are outlined below.

Scott Crow built "Star Creator" for the Rockwell International competition. "Star Creator" is both a program and an editor that enables a programmer to incorporate a scrolling or stationary star display onto a graphics screen. Scott did all his own work in creating star backgrounds which can be easily integrated with any other program.

Eddie Lew built "Super Slot," a combination hardware and software project, for the Rockwell International contest. It is designed to emulate a standard three reel, three pay line slot machine, similar to those used in casinos. It plays one to three quarters and has twelve stops per reel. This project is designed to work with an IBM Personal Computer equipped with the IBM Enhanced Graphics Adapter (with a 256k video buffer) and the Enhanced Color Display.

Robert Holtz worked on his first Apple at age 7. Now at 14 he has a software company, R J Software, that markets several programs that he has developed. Among these is the Artist program and screen dump for the Apple II GS. He has also set up a Bulletin Board. Robert focuses particularly on animation. He has put together several skits about Snappy, a character he created, on a video paint system that he manipulates to provide animation. Robert is currently working on a new game for Apple.

Joshua Horowitz uses LOGO and Video Works for his graphics and animation at the Open School in Hollywood. The Open School is the host site for the Apple Vivarium project, and Josh takes advantage of the Macintosh computers. As a result of his experience with LOGO, he recently held a guest speaker spot at the Los Angeles LOGO Conference. For SIGGRAPH '87, he will show his existing work with LOGO and perhaps a project on his new Apple II GS as well.

Ben Novida's project for the Rockwell International contest was "Mr. Egghead." Although "Mr. Egghead" is a program designed to entertain computer enthusiasts, it is also designed to introduce beginners to the concepts of using the computer. These concepts include: manipulating the keyboard, printing the screen contents to a printer, and saving and unloading files.

Joe Savella developed a program to compose music called "Compusynth" for the Rockwell contest. "Compusynth" involves animation, 3D graphics, page flipping, easy operation and sound manipulations. It offers a variety of commands, including two unique programmable operations. "Compusynth" comes with a tempo adjustment that can increase or decrease the relative speed of a composition, and six different sound effects like those recognized on Casio portable keyboards. To add visual effects, there is a piano keyboard that works exactly like a player piano and plays whatever music you compose.

Traditions and the Future of Character Animation

Chair: *John Lasseter, Pixar*
Panelists: *Brad Bird, Freelance Director*
Alex Carola, Director, Graphoui Studio, Brussels
John Musker, Director, Walt Disney Studios
Frank Thomas, Directing Animator, Walt Disney Studios

Introduction

Character animation using the computer is becoming more exciting and more accepted today. But this is not simply a new art form, it is another medium of animation with new and different potential. Other new mediums such as clay, sand, puppet, and cut-out animation have appeared in the past. Each of these has evolved into its own particular genre. But this evolution would have taken much longer if nothing had been learned from the many years spent in the development of traditional animation.

Hopefully, computer character animation will benefit from the history preceding it. As the basics of traditional character animation are understood and applied, new methods in computer animation will evolve. Then the computer as a medium of animation will be more solid because its roots will have already been proven in the Walt Disney Studios as well as other studios around the world.

The panelists will present their contributions to the field of traditional animation and show excerpts from their work. They will discuss their thoughts on the past, present, and future of traditional character animation. They will also contribute their thoughts on how computer character animation will fit into the future of traditional cel animation. Through their wide ranging experiences, from the Disney Studios past and present, high quality character animation for television, and character animation in Europe, we will get a better understanding of the state of the art of traditional animation today. Possibly, we will gain insight into the future of computer character animation.

Biographical Notes

John Lasseter joined the Pixar Computer Animation Group (formerly the Lucasfilm Computer Animation Group) in 1984 after five years as an animator at the Walt Disney Studios. At Disney, he worked on "The Fox and the Hound," "Mickey's Christmas Carol," "The Brave Little Toaster," and "The Wild Things Computer Animation Test," a combination of hand drawn Disney character animation with computer generated backgrounds. At Pixar, John most recently has written, directed and animated the computer animated short film "Luxo Jr," which received an Academy Award nomination for Best Animated Short Film for 1986. It has also won awards at the 1987 Berlin Film Festival, the 1986 Canadian International Animation Festival, the 1987 San Francisco Film Festival, NCGA's Computer Graphics '87, and Forum of New Images in Monte Carlo. John also has animated "The Adventures of Andre and Wally B." and the stained glass knight in "Young Sherlock Holmes." In March 1986, John was awarded the "Raoul Servais Animation Award" for his work in 3D computer generated character animation at the Genk International Animation Festival in Genk, Belgium. John received his BFA in Film from the California Institute of the Arts where he attended the Character Animation Program. He received two Student Academy Awards in Animation in 1979 and 1980 for his films "Lady and the Lamp" and "Nitemare."

Brad Bird is best known for writing and directing "Family Dog," the innovative animated episode of Steve Speilberg's Amazing Stories, which was aired in February of this year. Brad received his education at California Institute of the Arts, in the Character Animation Program. After CalArts, he worked as an animator at the Walt Disney Studio, working on "The Fox and The Hound" and "The Small One." As a freelance animator, he has worked on the feature films, "Animalympics" and "Plague Dogs." He has also directed the development of an animated feature film based on Wil Eisner's "The Spirit" comic book series. Brad's writing credits include "The Main Attraction," a live-action episode of Amazing Stories, and he has also co-written "Captain Eo" and the upcoming Spielberg feature film "Batteries Not Included." Brad is now working as a freelance writer and director.

Alex Carola graduated in 1978 from the animation school of La Cambre in Brussels, Belgium. He was a founding member of Collectif Shampoang Traitant, a group of experimental animation filmmakers. From 1979 to 1981, he worked in Rome, Italy on many short films including Pino Zac's film "Capricio Italino," "Ciel!," "Asteroide," and "Flashes Sante," a series of medical prevention films. From 1982 to 1986, Alex worked as an animator and director at the

Graphoui Studio in Brussels, where he worked on the TV series "Yakare." He directed several pilot films for TV series and he directed 260 one minute episodes of the popular Belgian TV series "Quick and Flupke." In 1986, Alex established his own production company, Flow S.C., specializing in 2D and 3D computer animation for television and advertising.

John Musker works as a director for the Walt Disney Studio. His latest film, "The Great Mouse Detective," was considered by many critics as one of Disney's best animated features in decades. He has worked at Disney since 1977. John animated the films "The Fox and the Hound" and "The Small One." He worked as a writer and director on "The Black Cauldron" before moving over to develop "The Great Mouse Detective." John is now co-writing and will co-direct the upcoming Disney animated feature "The Little Mermaid," based on Hans Christian Andersen's classic tale. John received a BA and an MA in English from Northwestern University and attended the Character Animation Program at CalArts.

One of Disney's famous Nine Old Men of animators, **Frank Thomas** has worked at the Disney Studio since the mid-1930's. His work on films such as "Snow White and the Seven Dwarfs," "Pinocchio," "Bambi," and "Peter Pan" has been important in the development of the art of animation. In 1978, Frank retired from Disney and authored with Ollie Johnston, "Disney Animation--The Illusion of Life," which has become the definitive book on Disney animation's history and technique. Also in 1978, Frank received the "Pioneer in Film" award from the University of Southern California chapter of Delta Kappa Alpha National Honorary Cinema Fraternity. He has also received honors from the American Film Institute. Frank lectures frequently on animation and the computer's application to character animation.

Bibliography

Adamson, J. *Tex Avery: King of Cartoons.* Da Capo Press, 1975.

Adamson, J. *The Walter Lantz Story.* Putnam, 1985.

Blair, P. *Animation.* Walter T. Foster, 1949.

Bocek, J. *Jiri Trnka: Artist and Puppet Master.* Artia, 1965.

Brasch, W. M. *Cartoon Monickers.* Bowling Green Univ. Press, 1983.

Canemaker, J. *The Raggedy Ann & Andy.* Bobbs-Merrill, 1977.

Carbaga, L. *The Fleischer Story.* Nostalgia Press, 1976.

Collins, M. *Norman McLaren.* Canadian Film Institute, 1976.

Crafton, D. *Before Mickey: The Animated Film 1898-1928.* MIT Press, 1982.

Culhane, J. *Walt Disney's Fantasia.* Abrams, 1983.

Culhane, S. *Talking Animals and Other People.* St. Martin's Press, 1986.

Edera, B. *Full Length Animated Feature Films.* Hastings House, 1977.

Feild, R. D. *The Art of Walt Disney.* Macmillan, 1942.

Finch, C. *The Art of Walt Disney.* Abrams, 1973.

Friedwald, W., and Beck, J. *The Warner Brothers Cartoon.* Scarecrow, 1981.

Halas, J. *Graphics in Motion.* Van Nostrand Reinhold, 1981.

Halas, J., and Manvell, R. *Art in Movement.* Hastings House, 1970.

Halas, J., and Manvell, R. *Design in Motion.* Studio, 1962.

Halas, J., and Manvell, R. *The Technique of Film Animation.* Hastings House, 1959.

Heath, B. *Animation in Twelve Hard Lessons.* R.P. Heath Productions, 1972.

Heraldson, D. *Creators of Life: A History of Animation.* Drake's, 1975.

Holloway, R. *Z is for Zagreb.* A.S. Barnes, 1972.

Kitson, C. *Fifty Years of American Animation.* American Film Institute, 1972.

Lasseter, J. "Principles of Traditional Animation Applied to Computer Animation." *Proceedings of SIGGRAPH '87. Computer Graphics,* July 1987.

Maltin, L. *Of Mice and Magic.* Plume, 1981.

Manvell, R. *The Animated Film.* Hastings House, 1954.

Manvell, R. *The Art of Animation.* Hastings House, 1980.

Peary, G., and Peary, D. *The American Animated Cartoon.* Dutton, 1981.

Richard, V. T. *Norman McLaren: Manipulator of Movement.* Univ. of Delaware Press, 1982.

Russett, R. *Experimental Animation.* Van Nostrand Reinhold, 1976.

Shale, R. *Donald Duck Joins Up.* UMI Research Press, 1982.

Snow, C. *Walt: Backstage Adventures with Walt Disney.* Windsong, 1980.

Thomas, B. *The Art of Animation.* Simon and Schuster, 1958.

Thomas, F. "Can Classic Disney Animation Be Duplicated on the Computer?" *Computer Pictures,* Vol.2, Issue 4, pp 20-26, July/August 1984.

Thomas, F., and Johnston, O. *Disney Animation--The Illusion of Life.* Abbeville Press, 1981.

Whitaker, H., and Halas, J. *Timing for Animation.* Focal Press, 1981.

White, T. *The Animator's Workbook.* Watson-Guptill, 1986.

Tool Kits: A Product of their Environments

Chair: *Ken Perlin, R/Greenberg Associates*
Panelists: *Jim Blinn, Jet Propulsion Laboratory*
Tom Duff, AT&T Bell Laboratories
Bill Lorensen, GE Corporate R&D Center
Craig Reynolds, Symbolics, Inc.

Summary

Are some environments inherently better than others for building tool kits? The panelists, all noted builders of tool kits who work in different software environments, have distinctly different and publicly stated views on this question.

Three dimensional computer graphics involves such diverse tasks as shape modeling, motion design, and rendering. Handling these tasks generally requires something more coordinated than an assortment of unrelated tricks and techniques. Also, something more flexible is required than a closed monolithic system with fixed capabilities.

A number of researchers have found it useful to create a semantically coherent environment, or "tool kit," within which new capabilities can be fitted to existing ones flexibly yet gracefully. The tool kit designer is trying to build a language that models a preferred way of working, or even of looking at the world. Thus there are as many different flavors of tool kit as there are research goals or methodologies. The advantages and disadvantages of the various environments available to build on have provoked marked disagreement among leading researchers in the field. This panel compares software environments within which different tool kits have been built.

Tom Duff believes that C and UNIX [1] provide an ideal environment in which to build a graphics tool kit. He notes that most environments suffer from over-integration, quickly becoming unmanageable, whereas: "The UNIX text processing tools avoid this syndrome by cutting the text processing problem into many small sub-problems with a small program to handle each piece. Because all the programs read and write a simple common data representation, they can be wired together for particular applications by a simple command language [2]."

Jim Blinn believes that this aspect of UNIX is vastly overrated, and maintains that most operating systems are ultimately equivalent, since the tool kit designer eventually builds his/her own preferred semantic layer anyway. He has said, "UNIX doesn't have a patent on that sort of philosophy, you know. Basically, just because you learn about something in some environment doesn't mean it was invented there. People who start off in UNIX find that it has some good ideas, and so they think, 'Ah, this must be the UNIX philosophy.' They never stop to think that maybe it's just a fundamentally good idea that works for any operating system. I can tell you I was using tools long before I had any contact with UNIX [3]." Dr. Blinn works in a FORTRAN/VMS environment.

The approach at Symbolics is to embed everything in the LISP programming language, taking particular advantage of LISP's generality and generic nature. The interesting thing here is that the properties of LISP are very different from those of UNIX. LISP users work in a unified programming language/operating system. Instead of many small interconnecting tools, the tool designer works with a single integrated runtime database. Compilation and loading of new procedures is possible at runtime, and interpreted and compiled commands can be intermixed within a common language.

Bill Lorensen represents the object-oriented approach. In this view, all data is viewed as procedural, with sets of procedural types forming a semantic entity. A tool kit is built from layers of such semantic entities. The philosophy is to allow for very rich semantics without losing the clarity of structure that a good toolkit needs.

Sometimes these views are combined effectively. For example, **Craig Reynolds** has written a modeling and animation system [4] in LISP that is distinctly object-oriented in structure.

A number of practical questions test these views. What types of tools are facilitated by having a particular environment? Are these tools really difficult or impossible to duplicate in other environments? For example, what important tools can you create in LISP or in an object-oriented environment that you cannot create in UNIX, or vice versa? Can all of these things be done in FORTRAN under VMS? If so, would this be very difficult? We will also touch on the relative efficiency, portability, and ease of learning of the various approaches.

Perhaps the preference for one's own environment arises because one's very goals become molded by one's environment; those things that are easier to accomplish seem more reasonable. The panel will try to determine to what extent the researchers' tool-building goals have themselves been influenced by what is easy or hard to do in their particular environment.

References

1. Kernighan, B., and Pike, R. *The UNIX Programming Environment.* Prentice Hall, Englewood Cliffs, 1984.
2. Duff, T. "Compositing 3-D Rendered Images." *Computer Graphics 19*, 3 (July 1985), 41-44.
3. Cook, R. "Interview with Jim Blinn." *UNIX Review* (September 1986).
4. Reynolds, C. "Computer Animation with Scripts and Actors." *Computer Graphics 16*, 3 (July 1982), 289-296.

Supercomputer Graphics

Chair: *Richard Weinberg, University of Southern California*
Panelists: *Donald P. Greenberg, Cornell University*
Michael Keeler, San Diego Supercomputing Center
Nelson Max, University of California Davis and Lawrence Livermore National Laboratory
Craig Upson, National Center for Supercomputing Applications
Larry Yaeger, Apple Computer (formerly of Omnibus Simulation)

Statement from Richard Weinberg

Supercomputers are proving to be an invaluable tool for science, engineering and computer animation. Although only a few years ago it was very difficult for researchers in the United States to gain access to supercomputers, the creation of five National Science Foundation supercomputer centers has made them widely available. Because of the enormous computing capacity of these systems, and their use in multi-dimensional, time-varying physical systems simulations, graphic capabilities are a major concern to their users. However, the most effective use of these systems requires high performance graphics systems coupled to the supercomputers over very high speed networks in integrated software environments. What lies on the horizon for users of these systems, and what remains to be done?

Statement from Donald P. Greenberg

Visualization is necessary in supercomputing for the problem-definition and result interpretation of temporal and spatial phenomena. To improve the potential for scientific discovery it is necessary to correlate multi-dimensional time-dependent parameters; the static display of data of reduced dimensionality can lead to misleading conclusions.

Today's advanced graphics workstations provide the most efficient and cost effective environments for the graphics display operations as contrasted to graphics processing on the supercomputer. By remotely computing these display operations, object data instead of image data can be transmitted, thus reducing the bandwidth requirements for the interactive steering of the computations. New workstation hardware provides hundreds of megaflops performance for the standard kernels of the display pipeline.

As computation power becomes more available, so will the complexity of the environments simulated. Standard, direct illumination models are not sufficiently accurate to represent complex spatial phenomena, particularly when color is used to abstractly depict scalar engineering parameters. Global illumination effects will have to be included to maintain the three-dimensional perception.

Using current software techniques, development time for the interactive graphics programming of scientific applications is excessive. There is a need to reduce attention to the input/output graphical operations by standardizing high level, user friendly modular graphics environments, thus allowing scientists to concentrate their efforts on science.

Statement from Michael Keeler

The primary focus of the San Diego Supercomputer Center is to provide a complete and balanced supercomputing environment for a very large number of research-oriented users. This environment extends over a large, high speed, nationwide communications network, and includes both the hardware and software resources at the central facility, as well as that at the remote user's terminal or workstation. We believe a systems approach based on network computing and distributed processing will provide the best way to use most of the available resources.

Graphics intensive applications will especially benefit from this approach. As an example, the ideal solution to many problems is to have multiple processes running concurrently on both a front-end workstation and the supercomputer, with interprocess communication via remote procedure calls. This is a highly complementary combination of technologies that permits each machine to do what it does best (interactive manipulation vs. intensive computation) and makes intelligent use of available bandwidth by reducing data traffic to small amounts of concentrated information. And most importantly, the user is presented a clean and efficient interface to the entire system.

We are keenly aware of the tremendous need for advanced graphics facilities that will serve a large number of people across a wide array of disciplines. Our approach is one of providing fundamental tools and general purpose utilities that take advantage of our unique resources and make it easier for users to tailor custom applications to the system. We continue to integrate more capabilities into the network, providing remote access to such things as high quality image generation software as well as film, video and laser disk recorders for animation.

We want to maximize the effectiveness and availability of expensive hardware and software development by sharing them throughout a large community of users. It is also essential to educate and train users and share expertise. The supercomputer center can serve as a focal point for this process by providing the new technologies and techniques in graphics to researchers who can apply them as analytical tools in their own endeavors.

Statement from Nelson Max

Our principal use for computer graphics at Lawrence Livermore National Laboratory (LLNL) is in the study of the results of large complex physics simulation codes. Research is also taking place in lighting and shadow effects for image realism. In order to develop and test new graphics algorithms, or to interactively study physics code output, rapid communication of color raster images from the supercomputer to the user's office is necessary. The MAGIC project at LLNL is a first step toward providing this high speed communication.

The architecture of a supercomputer like the Cray XMP puts certain constraints on programming style. Algorithms must be reorganized so that they can be vectorized for the pipelined arithmetic hardware, and storage must be limited due to timesharing and the lack of virtual memory. Examples will be given for these considerations and illustrated by computer animation. The working environment at LLNL will be compared to that at the Fujitsu Systems Laboratory in Tokyo, Japan.

Statement from Craig Upson

Use of computer graphics and animation falls into two major categories: entertainment-oriented and science-oriented. These two uses have distinctly different requirements in terms of hardware, software and people to accomplish the work. In scientific applications there are two major steps: (1) the simulation of the physical process, such as chemical bonding, the advection of a fluid, or the motion of gravity induced waves, and (2) the visual representation of simulated phenomena. There is little doubt that a supercomputer is the machine of choice for the first step. For entertainment applications, there is (currently) little need for the first step of physical simulation: a simplification that makes the supercomputer quite suitable for entertainment production. The only remaining question is that of economics, that is, can one charge enough to cover the cost of such a large machine? For the production of scientific films, there is a major I/O bottleneck if the simulation machine is not the visualization machine. This is further complicated by the fact that, in general, the supercomputer is a heavily shared resource and thus is difficult to use for interactive image computing and display. The approach of computing the physical simulation on the supercomputer and the visualization of the computation on another machine with less computing capacity, but perhaps with less system load, also has its advantages and disadvantages. The approach most promising is a network consisting of a supercomputer(s) connected to a near-supercomputer(s) dedicated to visualization. This approach is feasible if the bandwidth between machines is high enough, the near-supercomputer has a large enough compute capacity, and identical rendering software exists on both machines. This allows a distributed approach to visualization in the computational sciences.

Computer Graphics in Fashion

Chair: *Jane Nisselson, New York Institute of Technology*
Panelists: *Jerry Weil, AT&T Bell Laboratories*
Ronald Gordon, Microdynamics
Jim Charles, Esprit de Corp.

Introduction

Among the many design fields in which computer graphics is making its mark is the fashion industry. The crossover between these two fields is being stimulated by two key areas of development. The first is research efforts in computer graphics to create techniques for simulating the physical properties of flexible geometric objects, such as cloth. The second is the application of standard computer graphics techniques in systems in the fashion industry for design preview and pattern CAD/CAM (computer aided design and manufacturing).

This panel presents current research in techniques for representing clothing in computer animations, application of computer graphics in systems in the fashion industry, and the role of computer graphics in the work of a fashion designer.

The evolution of computer graphics techniques has rapidly expanded the scope of its visual realm from rigid geometrical objects to those which are naturalistic and organic. Naturally, as methods developed for simulating flexible surfaces such as that characterizing the human body, the problem of simulating clothing came into focus.

Garments are characterized by neither rigid surfaces nor simple geometrical construction. To accurately represent a garment requires techniques for modeling and animating flexible materials as well as accounting for the effects of physical forces such as gravity.

While such high-end simulations are being developed in the field of computer graphics, systems using less sophisticated methods for representing clothes are being used in the fashion industry. The purpose of these systems is to provide (1) an efficient means for visualizing garment designs and (2) an optimal way to create a design to be readily used in a CAM system. Such systems are faced with the aesthetic and technical challenges of how to simulate and improve upon traditional methods used in the fashion industry.

It is in the area of design that the question arises: can fashion benefit from computer graphics applications? Potential cost benefits from CAD/CAM systems alone may not be an adequate motive for a designer to make use of the technique.

It must be kept in mind that one shortcoming of a video image of a garment is that a person cannot touch the fabric and have direct exposure to its colors and its quality. To model a garment on the computer requires a method for generating a physically accurate model. But fashion is not merely a functional event whose conjunction of color, movement, and shape can be translated into an algorithm.

Computer graphics must be able to create visual effects that evoke the immediacy of a garment and capture the imagination in a way which is true to fashion. Whether for creating industrial systems, animations of figures, or fashion videos, as computer graphics continues to delve into the tools of the fashion trade, its imagery will be shaped by fashion's emphatic visual delivery.

Statement from Jerry Weil

Only recently has the computer graphics community addressed the need for modeling cloth which, in the past, was modeled as rigid surfaces. The rapid progress towards making realistic models will eventually have a great impact on the fashion industry.

Imagine a completely interactive, real-time system for designing garments. Such a system could be used to design, cut and manipulate fabric -- all on the computer screen. This fabric could be draped over other objects, such as a mannequin; thus a designer could interactively create clothes in a realistic, three-dimensional environment.

Although current computer hardware is not fast enough to actually allow real-time manipulation of realistic looking fabric, I will describe the model for such manipulation. In it, the fabric can be parameterized by factors such as its stiffness, elasticity and weight. By using simple physical equations, forces can be calculated over discrete points on the surface of the cloth. This will dictate the way in which each point will move. Furthermore, the movement of each point on the surface can be tested against collision with other solids which makes it possible to model fabric draped over other objects.

In the current implementation of such a system, instead of moving the cloth in real-time, a series of positions for selected points in the cloth's surface must be predetermined by the user. The movement of the remaining points is then determined according to the defined physical equations.

There is great potential for this work in the fashion industry. When this process takes place in real time, under the designer's control, he would be able to see how the clothing looks and moves before a single cut is made in the actual fabric.

Statement from Ron Gordon

Computer graphics may be used in the apparel industry to quickly evaluate new fashions. An initial place where computer graphics can be applied is in the design of new textiles. Prints, as well as woven or knit fabrics, may be simulated thread by thread and the resulting coloration evaluated on screen. An interface to numerically controlled knitting or weaving machines lets the designer obtain a sample swatch of the proposed fabric.

A paint or sketching package may be used to draw and edit new designs, supplementing the pen and paper traditionally used for illustrations. In this way, the proposed garment can be visualized without a stitch.

Once completed, the designer can obtain a hardcopy print of the creation with either a color calibrated thermal printer or film. Color accuracy, ease of use, and turn-around time are important parameters for this application.

Experience in using a color graphics design system to aid the development and evaluation of new fashions will be presented. Technical issues surrounding accurate color matching will be reviewed.

Statement from Jim Charles

The initial idea of using these ominous machines called computers for design struck fear into the hearts and pocketbooks of many people in the design room. Most of these fears were based on the presumption that computers would take away the designers' jobs or that they would be mercilessly tied to this ruthless machine with a mind of its own and never free to make creative decisions again.

Another response given by those considering themselves a bit up-to-date and open minded was the presumption that computers had arrived on the scene to assume a large part of their work and could quite possibly solve all their problems. Certainly the computers could boondoggle or dazzle management for at least a season or two.

In my first attempt to introduce CAD into the design room, I bought three Macintosh computers because of their reputation for flexible art oriented programs. We scheduled an orientation class for the textile artists and designers who were brave enough to attend. Being the arrogant leaders of California style and design, we were confronted by a teacher, who seemed to us to be the epitome of the computer nerd. He proceeded to confuse, confound and completely poison the sweet taste of even the most inoffensive little design oriented computer that we could begin with. Quelle disastre!

We were also introduced to some charming computer graphics done by a computer illustrator. But these gave CAD a definite aesthetic label. My boss now associated computer designed art with pixilated, jaggy lined images. We were to get those machines out of the design room; they were certainly not the right thing on which to base our future designs.

At about this same time, the head of our systems department had received the results of an intensive industry study on which CAD systems were best suited to the garment industry. From these I selected the one of my preference.

Now that I had discovered my dream machine, how could I resurrect the CAD subject in the proper light and convince management that it was a good idea, and could save hundreds of thousands of dollars a year. I arranged several demonstrations. One major consideration in making such a transition was how our decision fit into the big picture. We soon found out that other companies, such Levi Strauss & Co., were already receiving the systems that I wanted.

After my initial campaigning, my boss called me into her office and said, "I don't understand it but I can see that it's the way of the future. Okay, boys, go get us a computer!"

Once I started learning to operate the system, I found it easy and only sometimes frustrating. My experience using the Macintosh made it easier for me to learn a new system. But what are the benefits? The old way is still being used and is at hand for the deadline crunches with multicolor. As for the computer system, the first recognizable benefits are the ease of manipulation of color and the ability to make decisions on the production of fabrics and garment styles which can then be merchandised. I expect many more to come.

The Physical Simulation and Visual Representation of Natural Phenomena

Chair: *Craig Upson, National Center for Supercomputing Applications*
Panelists: *Alan Barr, California Institute of Technology*
Bill Reeves, Pixar
Robert Wolff, Jet Propulsion Laboratory
Steven Wolfram, Complex Systems Research Institute

Introduction

Within computer graphics and animation, two major sub-disciplines have developed: graphics for entertainment or artistic purposes, and graphics for scientific or technical purposes. Computer scientists working on entertainment applications have emphasized the correct visual representation of natural phenomena and have developed ad hoc physical simulations to accomplish this. Computational scientists working in the physical sciences have devoted their efforts to the underlying physics for simulating phenomena, with little emphasis on the visual representation.

In recent years these two approaches have begun to reach the limits of their ability to work without each other. The realism required in entertainment animation is beyond that obtainable without physically realistic models. Similarly, numerical simulations in the physical sciences are complex to the point of being incomprehensible without visual representations.

Statement from Alan Barr

Our research at Caltech centers on the goal of computed visual realism. We are developing fundamental mathematical and computational methods for synthesizing high fidelity complex images through:

1. new rendering methods which more accurately model the physical interaction of light with matter;
2. new geometric modeling techniques which simulate the shapes found in nature and manufacturing, and
3. methods for automatically setting up and solving stable equations of motion for constrained mechanical and biophysical systems.

While making films which visually simulate natural phenomena, we encountered an unexpected difficulty: a fundamental dichotomy between pure animation and pure simulation. In an animation project, the animator knows what he wants and controls the motion of the objects at a very detailed level to achieve the aesthetic goal. In a simulation project, an artificial universe is created with its own rules of physics. The objects within the universe act as if they had a mind of their own, and appear to choose what they wish to do rather than what you might want them to do. Even worse, you can't arbitrarily change their behavior, because it would not be simulation any more;--you have to get the objects to do what you want by suitably selecting the initial conditions that properly affect the behavioral equations of motion.

For instance, in the 1984 SIGGRAPH Omnimax film, we had difficulties with the swimming creatures. However, the problems were not due to the difficulties of setting up or deriving and solving the swimming equations. Problems resulted because the creatures were somewhat unmanageable and kept swimming off screen, away from the camera and away from each other. We had to aim and control them so they would arrive where and when we wanted them.

Statement from William T. Reeves

Typically, images of natural phenomena are expensive to generate with computer graphics. Two productions involving natural phenomena that we have done in the last several years are: the trees and grass background from "The Adventures of Andre and Wally B.," and the ocean waves from the film "Flags and Waves." The trees and grass models were pure ad hoc simulations. The waves were based on a simple model which ignored many parameters. In both, our purpose was to make an interesting film. The trees and grass required about 8 man-months to develop and the waves took about 6 man-months. The trees and grass averaged about two hours per frame on a VAX 11/750, and the waves averaged one hour per frame on a Computer Consoles Power 6/32 (about ten times faster than an 11/750).

I think it's obvious that the best means of making images of a natural phenomenon is to simulate it fully and then make pictures of the resulting data. If possible, this approach should be followed by both the entertainment and scientific disciplines. The problem is that quite often it's not possible. The computing resources necessary to do the simulation sometimes require supercomputers or beyond. Not many of us have access to this class of computing resource, and if we did there would still be a tradeoff between using it for simulating the phenomenon and for rendering the phenomenon. For some phenomena, an accurate physical model does not exist. For other phenomena, where an accurate physical model does exist, the problem is that the data it calculates is nothing you can render. And finally, sometimes you don't want an object to be physically accurate. Animation is full of "impossible" things like squash and stretch and exaggeration.

From the visual representation perspective where the sole goal is to make an image, I think it is perfectly acceptable to fake it for any of the reasons above. An important corollary is "don't get caught." Analyze what is important visually and what isn't. Spend most of the time making the important things accurate (perhaps by really simulating them) and cheat on the rest.

Statement from Robert S. Wolff

Most physical systems are described by many parameters (e.g., temperature, density, pressure, magnetic field, velocity, etc.). Depending upon the system, the actual value of each of these parameters can vary considerably over space and time. Moreover, knowledge of each parameter throughout a system is often severely limited by available data.

Based on these sparse data sets, one constructs "models," either numerical simulations with "best-guess" initial and boundary conditions, or "heuristic" models, which rely on the investigator's physical intuition to tie together bits and pieces of observational data with basic physical principles. Unfortunately, even the best physical intuition cannot provide a dynamical picture of a three-dimensional, time-dependent, multi-parameter physical system without some graphical aids.

Until a few years ago, such descriptions were confined to traditional artists' renderings of the physicists' concepts. Although these renderings are generally very visually appealing, they were based more on belief than on any sort of numerical simulation, and were as often misleading as informative. However, in the last several years advances in entertainment computer graphics have made possible the utilization of data, analytic and numerical simulations to produce near-realistic visualizations of astrophysical phenomena.

An example in point is "Jupiter's Magnetosphere: The Movie" (J. F. Blinn, R. S. Wolff, 1983) in which representations of spacecraft observations as well as analytic and numerical models of the plasma and magnetic fields in the Jovian system were employed to visualize the morphology and dynamical structure of Jupiter's magnetosphere. Using this same paradigm, computer graphic techniques developed for the entertainment industry (e.g., fractal representations, texture mapping, particle systems) could be used to model volcanic activity on Hawaii, dust storms on Mars, or accretion of matter into a black hole, among other things. Unfortunately, the scientific community as a whole has largely ignored the many significant advances in the field of computer graphics over the years, and as a result the general state of the art of science data analysis is not very much beyond that which was available 20-30 years ago.

Software Tools for User Interface Management

Chair: *Dan R. Olsen Jr., Brigham Young University*
Panelists: *David J. Kasik, Boeing Computer Services*
Peter Tanner, University of Waterloo
Brad Myers, University of Toronto
Jim Rhyne, IBM Watson Research Center

Background

The subject of User Interface Management Systems (UIMS) has been a topic of research and debate for the last several years. The goal of such systems has been to automate the production of user interface software. The problem of building quality user interfaces within available resources is a very important one as the demand for new interactive programs grows. Prototype UIMS have been built and some software packages are presently being marketed as such. Many papers have been published on the topic.

There still, however, remain a number of unanswered questions. Is a UIMS an effective tool for building high quality user interfaces or is the runtime cost of abstracting out the user interface too high? Why are there not more UIMS available and why are they not more frequently used? Is simple programmer productivity alone sufficient motivation for learning and adopting yet another programming tool? What is the difference, if any, between a "user interface toolbox," a windowing system and a UIMS? What are the differences between a UIMS and the screen generation languages found in fourth generation languages? In fact, exactly what is a UIMS?

In order to discuss these questions and to reassess the state of the UIMS art, SIGGRAPH sponsored a workshop on these issues [1]. The panelists represent the four workshop subgroups who have each addressed these questions from different points of view.

Goals and Objectives for User Interface Software (David Kasik)

In establishing the goals and objectives for user interface software, this group characterized UIMS. The definition looks at the UIMS as a tool that benefits two different audiences: the end user of an application and the team responsible for the design and implementation of the application. Both audiences levy different requirements on the UIMS and each benefits from the technology in terms of improved productivity.

As well as defining a UIMS, the group established a morphology that helps determine the applicability to a particular task of software labeled as a UIMS. The criteria listed are also useful for categorizing available UIMS to determine areas for future research. The criteria are aimed at the same two audiences.

While the early discussions focused on the UIMS as a technology, the participants in the group looked at the role of the UIMS in software development. In other words, the first audience affected by UIMS technology is composed of application programmers. The group examined how UIMS fits into or modifies "traditional" software engineering methodology. The principal effect lies in the ability to let the application development team focus on the user interface as one of the first components of a successful application.

This discussion lead to identification of some holes in the current UIMS technology, especially during the specification and testing/maintenance phases of application development. The effective implementation of UIMS technology also hinges on accommodation of other computing technologies such as artificial intelligence.

Reference Models, Window Systems and Concurrency (Peter Tanner)

Systems which support user interfaces must not only accommodate but take advantage of many factors that can enrich the human-computer interaction. Effective use of distributed systems, support for collaborative work, concurrent input, devices such as eye trackers or other head, body or foot mounted devices, and less common media such as voice, touch, and video must all be provided for. This group worked on defining a generalized expanded role for what are currently called "window systems." The result, the workstation agent (WA), is responsible for managing the hardware devices, including sharing devices among several applications and, through the use of virtual devices, changing the form of the input to better match the needs of its clients (the applications).

The WA position in the schema of an interactive system is best described as being one of several layers. The group identified four such layers: (1) hardware devices; (2) workstation agent; (3) dialogue managers; (4) applications, one or more of which will be the workstation manager(s).

The hardware devices provide the "raw" interface to the user and include both input and output devices. The workstation agent is responsible for managing those devices, presenting a device-independent but media-dependent interface to the clients. It also provides the basic support for multitasking; it must multiplex and demultiplex the devices between multiple clients. The multiplexing (or scheduling) "policy" is determined by the workstation manager. The dialogue managers are the implementation of the interaction techniques that convert the media-dependent interface to the media-independent interface required by the application. They provide for the invocation of application modules and for the handling of their responses.

The application layer is the set of modules that interact with the database specific to the application. Along with these modules, the layer contains one or more workstation agents responsible for setting the policy for sharing devices and allocating resources.

On the output side, many existing window systems do not provide any image retention possibilities, requiring clients to repaint windows in numerous situations such as when the screen is rearranged or a window is moved. There are a number of retention possibilities: (1) no retention (as is currently common); (2) device-dependent, such as a bitmap (as in the Teletype 5620); (3) partially structured, such as a text file; (4) complete, such as a PHIGS or Postscript display file (as in NeWS).

There are no obvious advantages to integrating the image retention into the workstation agent, but it must be done in a manner that can take advantage of whatever hardware rendering support is offered on a workstation. However, complete retention is inappropriately complex for many applications and may lead to too high a degree of graphical data structure redundancy for other applications.

With the recent advent of window systems, users are becoming accustomed to accessing several applications simultaneously. Accessing single applications through several windows and the use of several devices to control application parameters will become more common. Concurrent programming mechanisms supporting concurrent lightweight processes with rapid inter-process communication and synchronization will be necessary to fully implement the workstation agent and dialogue managers to provide the necessary level of concurrency.

Runtime Stucture of UIMS-Supported Applications (Brad Myers)

This group was responsible for generating a new model for the internal structure of Dialog Managers and how they interface to application programs. Traditionally, there has been an attempt to separate the Dialog Manager from application programs. The motivation was to provide appropriate modularization and the ability to change the user interface independent of the application. Unfortunately, this separation has made it difficult to provide semantic feedback and fine-grain control which are necessary in many modern user interfaces. Therefore, the group proposed the beginnings of a model which provides for tighter coupling of the application and the Dialog Manager through the "Semantic Support Component" (SSC). The group discussed a number of possible organizations but emphasized that this is an area for research.

The group also discussed two proposals for the internal architecture of the Dialog Manager: the traditional lexical-syntactic layering and a homogeneous object space. The lexical-syntactic division is based on language models and includes interaction modules such as menus, string input, etc., at the lexical level, and sequencing at the syntactic level. This division is often ad hoc. The homogeneous object model is based on object-oriented languages such as Smalltalk and is more flexible but provides less support. Which of these is the most appropriate internal architecture or whether something entirely different is better is an important research area.

Tools and Methodologies (Jim Rhyne)

For the past few years, UIMS research has concentrated on the tools and methodologies for implementing user interfaces. While many problems in this area remain unsolved, the Task Group on Tools and Methodologies felt that progress was also needed on tools to support requirements and design. There was consensus in the group that no single methodology would suit all interface designs and designers, and that tools to support design should be flexible and modular.

We treated design in two stages. Requirements Analysis and Conceptual Design (RA/CD) is a tight coupling of the tasks of gathering data about the intended use of the interface and of creating a design strategy well matched to the intended use. Design and Development encompasses the detailed design of the interface and choices about its implementation. Tools presently in use to support these activities include: drawing packages, rapid prototyping systems, user models, and interaction technique libraries. Tools needed, but not available include: design databases, design languages, consistency analyzers, and intelligent design assistants. Above all, these tools must be compatible with one another, so that designers at all stages can select tools appropriate to their needs.

Reference

1. "ACM SIGGRAPH Workshop on Software Tools for User Interface Management," *Computer Graphics 21*, 2 (April 1987), 71-147.

Managing a Computer Graphics Production Facility

Co-Chairs: *Wayne Carlson, Cranston/Csuri Productions*
Larry Elin, Abel Image Research
Moderator: *Larry Elin, Abel Image Research*
Panelists: *Wayne Carlson, Cranston/Csuri Productions*
Pete Fosselman, McDonnell Douglas Corp.
Ken Dozier, Interactive Machines, Inc.
Carl Rosendahl, Pacific Data Images

Introduction

The computer graphics industry, as no other, combines the disciplines of computer science, mathematics, art, engineering, and business, and presents graphic facilities managers with unique problems not faced by their counterparts in other industries. The growing proliferation of graphic facilities, for CAD/CAM and for other art and engineering uses, has created a new wave of managers who share the same fundamental problems: how to effectively manage the facility and personnel in order to succeed in the world of graphics.

This management distinctiveness is due to a number of reasons: the intricacies of the high-level software needed to produce top of the line graphics images, the dynamically changing hardware used in the graphics community, the creative personalities of the graphics personnel, the dynamics of the entertainment, engineering, and artistic community that the industry serves, and the lack of basic management training for supervisors that have come up the ladder from the production teams.

A good number of these management issues are directly related to the creative process itself, as well as to the kind of creative personality that is the life blood of our industry. A recent article [1] outlines the difference between managing creative people and employees in traditional work situations:

1. The employees are often better trained and more able than their managers.
2. The personality of the creative person is typically less self organized and more temperamental.
3. Creative people's motivations are usually different from those of other workers.

This same article quotes Bertolt Brecht: "The time needed for rehearsal is always one week more than the time available." This is particularly characteristic of the creative process in computer graphics production. Because of the nature of image or software design, testing, and creation, deadlines that can be adhered to in a traditional manufacturing environment are challenging to adhere to in the graphics industry.

The analysis of a recent management seminar listing [2] revealed that the course outlines for courses in facility personnel management, project management, and operations management differed significantly from the needs of the computer graphics supervisor. It is clear that the textbook examples of management techniques and philosophies do not always fit the environment in which we operate.

Summary of Panel Presentations

It is just these differences in management issues that this panel is trying to address. The panel consists of the general management of two of the premier commercial production houses, a special projects manager from a world renowned graphics software and production facility, a representative from an aerospace company utilizing graphics production techniques for in-house use, and a manager of a graphics hardware manufacturing firm. These panelists, with their diverse backgrounds and organizational structures, bring a wealth of experience to be shared with interested observers, many of whom will face similar issues at their respective facilities. The panelists concur with each other in certain areas of management, and widely disagree in others.

Each panelist will present an important issue that he faced in his management experience. He will try to focus on an issue which differs from the conventional management approach. The following topics suggest many of the critical issues in managing a computer graphics facility:

1. motivating creative employees
2. managing the finances of a graphics facility
3. keeping up with the changes in technology
4. the R & D issue: will it produce usable results?
5. coordinating sales/production personnel
6. managing job stress
7. dealing with the demanding client
8. training technical personnel
9. schedules and the creative process
10. budgets and the development process.

The creative and sometimes unexpected techniques used by these panelists in solving the management problems they encounter may provide insights for new CGI facility managers. Other managers may be pleased to find that they are not alone with their problems. This panel presents a stimulating and enlightening view of life in the commercial computer graphics production facility.

References

1. Fletcher, W. "How to Manage Creativity." *Management Today* (June 1983), 82-85.
2. *Course Catalog of the American Management Association*, January-October 1987.

A Comparison of VLSI Graphic Solutions

Chair: *Ed Rodriguez, National Semiconductor*
Panelists: *Brent Wientjes, Texas Instruments*
Tom Crawford, Advanced Micro Devices
Jack Grimes, Intel Corporation
John Blair, National Semiconductor
Discussant: *Jack Bresenham, Winthrop College*

Summary

Graphics capability, once required only by the high-end CAD applications, is now becoming standard equipment on new desktop systems which are used for a wide variety of applications. Recent developments in VLSI graphic devices are bringing sophisticated graphic techniques to more affordable levels.

In order to take advantage of the high level of functional integration achievable with today's technology, some architectural decisions must be made at the VLSI components level. These VLSI devices have become more than simple building blocks; they have become sub-system designs. Because of the many different graphics applications, architectural solutions which appear ideal for some applications are far from optimal for others. Unfortunately, because of the level of complexity, subtle features and/or limitations of a particular design are overlooked by quick evaluations. Careful scrutiny is required by the system's designer to select the appropriate device for his/her specific needs.

This panel brings together four of the major semiconductor companies which address bit-mapped graphic requirements, as well as a leading industry expert in rasterization. Each design has had to incorporate architectural trade-offs, reflecting different implementation philosophies. Only the system designer can adequately judge the significant impact each trade-off has to his/her particular application.

There are a few architectural differences immediately obvious among the four approaches. The following are a few of the main differences:

- planar vs. packed-pixel
- programmable vs. "hard-wired" functions
- open vs. closed frame buffer access
- hardware vs. software windowing
- partitioned vs. integrated architecture.

It is the intent of this panel session to provide the hardware and software designers with a comparison of these VLSI offerings, by clarifying the different architectural philosophies and trade-offs associated with each respective implementation.

Bibliography

Asal, M., Short, G., Preston, T., Simpson, R., Roskell, D., and Guttag, K. "The Texas Instruments 34010 Graphics System Processor." *IEEE Computer Graphics and Applications* (October 1986) 24-39.

Carasso, G., Goettsch, R., and Syrimis, N. "Controller Chip Puts Text and Graphics on the Same Bit Map." *Electronic Design* (June 27, 1985) 119-126.

Carinalli, C., and Blair, J. "National's Advanced Graphics Chip Set for High-Performance Graphics." *IEEE Computer Graphics and Applications* (October 1986) 40-48.

Greenberg, S., Peterson, M., and Witten, I. "Issues and Experience in the Design of a Window Management System." Research Report No. 86/240/14, Dept. of Computer Science, University of Calgary, Alberta, Canada, September 1, 1986.

Myers, B. "A Complete and Efficient Implementation of Covered Windows." *IEEE Computer* (September 1986) 55-67.

Shires, G. "A New VLSI Graphics Coprocessor--the Intel 82786." *IEEE Computer Graphics and Applications* (October 1986) 49-55.

Computer-Aided Industrial Design: The New Frontiers

Chair: *Del Coates, San Jose State University*
Panelists: *Bruce Claxton, Motorola Corporation*
Fred Polito, frogdesign
David Royer, Ford Motor Company

Introduction

Although industrial designers are relatively few in number, they affect product development and sales crucially because they determine aesthetic issues. If you wonder how crucial their role, ask yourself if you ever bought a car, furniture, or virtually any product without considering how good it looked? Probably not. Even military shoppers are known to insist on good looking hardware. Accordingly, industrial designers are indispensable to more than a third of all U.S. corporations, especially manufacturers of consumer goods. And their role is growing in importance as more manufacturers come to realize the dividends of good design. As Christopher Lorenz, Management Editor of *The Financial Times,* notes: "From Tokyo to Detroit, from Milan to London, companies have begun to realize that they must stop treating design as an afterthought, and cease organizing it as a low-level creature of marketing..... Instead, they have elevated it to fully-fledged membership of the corporate hierarchy, as it has been for decades in design-minded firms such as Olivetti and IBM. The design is being exploited more and more to create competitive distinctiveness, not only for premium products but also in the world of mass marketing."

Industrial designers are increasingly striving to apply computer technology. The members of this panel represent such pioneering efforts: at Ford Motor Company, the Motorola Company, and frogdesign, a trend-setting international consulting firm.

Inadequacies of Current Systems

As the CIM (computer-integrated manufacturing) revolution gains momentum, industrial designers will be forced to adopt computer technology. Yet, the means for doing so seems woefully inadequate to many industrial designers, including frogdesign's **Fred Polito**. Despite greater attention to their needs recently, no commerically available system (or combination of systems) adequately meets the needs of industrial designers. Polito shows the considerable extent to which frogdesign uses its turnkey CAD system, despite its limitations, and suggests how it could be improved.

Industrial designers belabor two shortcomings more than any others:

- *The sketching or conceptualization problem.* The designer cannot rapidly model and visualize concepts during the earliest, most creative phases of the design process, especially when they are as complex as an automobile. Normally, they are forced to work "off the tube" with conventional media while the computer idles uselessly. The computer seldom enters the process until after traditional sketches, drawings and, sometimes, even tangible three-dimensional models have been created.
- *The rendering problem.* CAD systems cannot produce "photographic" images that unambiguously simulate various materials and finishes. Shortcomings stem from the fact that realism requires simulation of two distinct kinds of reflection: diffuse reflection (also called "cosine" reflection); and specular (mirror-like) reflection which accounts for the appearance of gloss. Typical rendering software models only diffuse reflection. (Specular effects are approximated through modified diffuse reflection and by texture-mapping of hypothetical environmental reflections.) Despite claims to the contrary, no CAD system currently available models true specular reflection. And although specular reflection has been employed to a limited extent by animators, true specular reflection is not readily available in animation systems either.

Beneficial Side-Effects

In contrast to these objections, **Bruce Claxton** is decidedly upbeat about Motorola's CAD experiences. He is enthusiastic about benefits that more than make up for any inabilities at conceptualization and visualization. CAD has brought about a degree of consolidation and coordination of the diverse personnel and organization involved in product design and development that might not have been achieved otherwise. This is due simply to the fact that everyone working on a project now refers to the same database. Industrial design has become a more integral part of the design process, and the enhanced goodwill among departments whose objectives seem less disparate now is of inestimable value. The shortened development time and improved product quality that ensued are more important than how realistically the computer can simulate the appearance of a product or whether designers can do the whole project "on the tube."

Meeting the Computer Halfway

Rather than lamenting the lack of a perfect system, industrial design students working at San Jose University's CADRE Institute are exploring semiCAD techniques that combine the best capabilities of existing computer systems with their own special skills and traditional media. Results demonstrate that, although not yet optimal, computers have immense potential for increasing quality and productivity.

One student, for instance, designed wine bottles with a 3D modeling system ordinarily used for animation. She began on paper because the modeler was not spontaneous and interactive enough. But, once a concept was in digital form, she was able to create perspective views of it more quickly and accurately than she could on paper. She could design a label on a 2D paint system and "wrap" it onto the bottle's surface by transferring it to the 3D system. Renderings of such bottle/label combinations look very realistic in the label portion because the diffuse reflection algorithm simulates relatively non-glossy surfaces quite well. Because the system does not employ a ray-tracing algorithm, however, it merely suggests the glossy quality of glass and cannot show the refractive distortions of transparent material. However, a designer with reasonable rendering skills needn't be stymied. By transferring the image from the 3D system back to the paint sytem, it can be touched up with specular and refractive effects. Furthermore, the bottle's image can be combined with a real background image (a table setting, for instance) scanned in with a video camera to create a realistic rendering far beyond the capabilities of most designers or the practicalities of normal media.

Less Compliant Applications

Some industrial design applications, like those of the automobile industry addressed by Ford's **Dave Royer**, leave less room for compromise and are driving the technology toward the farthest frontier. The ability to sketch with the computer is important because subtle aesthetic nuances of form seldom can be captured by keystrokes or other relatively analytical methods of input. Although today's rendering algorithms simulate glossy surfaces well enough for animation, they give misleading impressions of actual surface geometry. This can be crucial in the case of an automobile's subtle surfaces. The specular reflection of the horizon on a car's surface, for instance, is a key design element as important aesthetically as the car's profile or any other line. Its proportions, even its apparent size, can change when specular reflection is missing. In the final analysis, a design cannot be properly judged aesthetically without specular reflection. Royer describes Ford's efforts to address these issues.

Pretty Pictures Aren't So Pretty Anymore: A Call for Better Theoretical Foundations

Chair: *Rae A. Earnshaw, University of Leeds, UK*
Panelists: *Jack E. Bresenham, Winthrop College*
David P. Dobkin, Princeton University
A. Robin Forrest, University of East Anglia, UK
Leo J. Guibas, Stanford University and DEC Systems Research Center

Analysis and exposition of the theoretical bases for computer graphics and CAD are becoming increasingly important. Software systems and display hardware are now so sophisticated that the deficiencies in the underlying models of displayed images can be more clearly seen. Consistency, accuracy, robustness and reliability are some key issues upon which the debate now focuses. Vendors and pragmatists feel satisfied if the results are "correct" most of the time. Theoreticians are horrified at the lack of rigor and formalism in many of the ad hoc approaches adopted by current work. This panel challenges the assumption that the pragmatic approach is adequate.

As parallel processing techniques bring the disciplines of computer graphics and image processing together, each can learn lessons from the other. In addition, it is becoming clear that interface modeling, expert system techniques, software engineering and VLSI design are all areas where a more formal and rigorous approach can produce significant benefits. All these impinge upon computer graphics to some extent. Computer graphics is rapidly moving from a discipline based on pragmatics to one based on formal methods. Vendors mut be prepared to subject their systems and software to validation criteria.

All the panel members are participants in the NATO Advanced Study Institute in Italy, July 4-17, 1987. The theme of this 1987 Institute is "Theoretical Foundations of Computer Graphics and CAD." Results arising from the Institute provide a basis for discussion.

Rae Earnshaw proposes the virtues of the industry/vendor position. The end justifies the means, and pragmatists need not be overly concerned with theory. **Jack Bresenham** outlines the industry position and the benefits and disadvantages of theory and practice. **David Dobkin** proposes the need for definition for computational geometry and rendering algorithms. **Robin Forrest** argues for consistency, accuracy, robustness, and reliability in graphical and geometric computations. **Leo Guibas** argues for the use of tools for the design and analysis of algorithms.

Integration of Computer Animation with Other Special Effects Techniques

Chair: *Christine Z. Chang, R/Greenberg Associates*
Panelists: *Tad Gielow, Walt Disney Studios*
Eben Ostby, Pixar
Randy Roberts, Abel/Omnibus
Drew Takahashi, Colossal Pictures

Introduction

Computer animation is used increasingly as a special effects technique in film and video production. Integrated with other imaging techniques such as motion control, stand animation, live action and optical printing, it can be a useful tool as well as a final element. Among other things, information can be shared with other computer-controlled cameras, or images can be generated for rotoscoping or for mattes. In fact, the final special effect may be largely dependent on computer imagery yet not contain a single computer-generated pixel.

Special Effects Via Integration of Computer Systems (Christine Chang)

Many principles of computer generated animation are shared with other computerized imaging techniques. The motion of the camera, aimpoint and/or subjects are manipulated in three dimensional space in CGI, motion control, animation stand and optical printer systems. By establishing a communications link between computer systems, motion information may be shared. Moreover, one system can create and preview a motion to be filmed on another. In addition, since each technique maintains repeatability, matte passes as well as "beauty" passes can be produced. CGI offers the additional capability of manipulating and processing mattes to create elements for new optical effects. All elements can then be combined via optical printer to yield the final special effect. Of course, it remains true that successful special effects rely on good design. Together with an integrated system, the potential of each technique is maximized and new capabilities realized.

Computer Graphics and Cel Animation (Tad Gielow)

Disney has been using computers and computer animation as a tool in special visual effects and in feature animation for several years. It is a unique approach and, as seen in the climax in "The Great Mouse Detective," can contribute to the drama of a scene. This presentation will provide an insight into the marriage of computer generated backgrounds with classic Disney animation.

Invisible Computer Graphics (Eben Ostby)

The desired goal of an effects shot is sometimes independent of the means of its production. In some of the effects we have produced for motion pictures, the goal is to produce images that look computer-generated; in others, the fact that a computer was used to produce the images should remain obscure. In the latter case, special care must be used to integrate the effect with the rest of the movie. Work done at Pixar and Lucasfilm to accomplish this has involved:

- proper anti-aliasing of rendered frames
- accurate motion-blur
- highly detailed models
- digital compositing
- laser frame recording.

Additional attention must be paid to these frames in the process of combining the computer-generated shots with the remainder of the film.

Integration of Computer Graphics with Live Action (Randy Roberts)

The integration of computer graphics and live action is attractive both economically and aesthetically. In the past, use of purely computer-generated imagery in film production has had problems in cost effectiveness. Mixing it with live action has made more economic sense. Whether using live backgrounds with CGI animation or shooting actors for rotoscoping CGI motion, the live action has made production more feasible. The live action offers images and motion which would be prohibitively expensive to generate or define on the computer, if possible at all. Aesthetically, the real world offers an infinite complexity of textures and fluid motion. The subtle combination of computer graphics with other techniques creates richer images. CGI should not constantly be calling attention to itself. In the future, art direction will emphasize images whose technical origins are not obvious.

Yes, Kids, Mixing and Matching Can Be Fun (Drew Takahashi)

For years I have been lamenting the fact that various special effects production tools each did marvelous things by themselves, but when you tried to combine them, their inability to talk to each other made the process rather cumbersome. While much has been done of late to address this problem, we at Colossal have found ourselves quite happy with a very different approach which we call Blendo. Blendo is not a style or technique but an attitude. It is an inclusive approach which seeks to combine techniques and styles to create a playful feel. Rather than striving to create a convincing reality, we instead celebrate complexity and contradiction.

This attitude was originally born from the limitations of the low-tech beginnings of our studio. Where others were using opticals to insert live people into animation, we shot black and white stills, tinted them and shot them combined with artwork under the animation stand. What we ended up with was very different from an optical solution. The stylized motion (by shooting the stills on 2's, 3's or even 6's) and the hand applied swimming color actually allowed the photographer's reality to participate in the animated reality without seeming "matted in." Aesthetically, it said something different.

As the studio's technical capabilities grew, we often chose techniques such as these, not out of necessity but by choice. This sensibility is not exclusive to low-tech solutions but can easily work with various high-tech approaches. While much of our work at Colossal is made up of more exclusive and invisible effects (actually, sometimes no effects at all), this attitude, Blendo, is perhaps the most appropriate contribution Colossal can make in the context of this discussion.

Notes

Notes

Index

(Pages marked with * are panel summaries.)

Credits for Cover Images

Cover: A Night in the Bike Store

Copyright © 1987 by Pixar
Artists: Eben Ostby and Bill Reeves
Insights: This image is a still from the short film, *Red's Dream*, produced by Pixar. The model description consists of 16,783 primitives which were rendered using the equivalent of 4.5 million polygons. Nineteen channels of texture information and two procedural textures were used in generating the image. The scene is lit by five light sources, two of which cast shadows. It was rendered on a CCI Power 6/32 at a resolution of 1024 by 788 48-bit pixels using the Reyes rendering system. All wheels were laced using a three-cross spoking pattern, and were tensioned using a Hozan tension gauge. The image was assembled and scanned using a Pixar Image Computer.
Production notes: Modeling, rendering, design, textures: Eben Ostby. Modeling, rendering, design, lighting: Bill Reeves. Design, modeling, textures: John Lasseter. Rendering software: Rob Cook. Laser output scanning: 'Big Don' Conway. Other *Red's Dream* team members: H. B. Siegel, Tony Apodaca, Bill Carson, Ralph Guggenheim, Craig Good, Susan Anderson.
References: *Rendering Antialiased Shadows with Depth Maps*, p 283, *The Reyes Image Rendering Architecture*, p 95

Title Page: Dutch Interior, after Vermeer

Copyright © 1987 by Cornell University, Program of Computer Graphics
Artist: John Wallace
Insights: This image was inspired by the work of the 17th century Dutch painter Jan Vermeer, whose sensitivity to the interplay of light and surfaces helped to give his paintings a dramatic feeling of depth. The radiosity method was used to compute the global diffuse illumination during a view-independent preprocess. After the view was determined, a z-buffer based algorithm similar to distributed ray tracing was used to compute the specular reflection on the marble floor.
Production notes: The image was rendered on a VAX 11/780. It was displayed at a resolution of 830 by 1024 using a Hewlett-Packard 9000 series 300 workstation and photographed directly from the monitor by Emil Ghinger.
References: *A Two-Pass Solution to the Rendering Equation: A Synthesis of Ray Tracing and Radiosity Methods*, p 311

Back cover, top left: Flock Gathering

Copyright © 1987 by Symbolics Graphics Division
Artist: Craig Reynolds
Insights: This image comes from a motion test of a flock of paper airplanes (pyramids) randomly scattered on the plane and flocking towards a goal. The image represents aligned, noncolliding aggregate motion, such as that of flocks, herds and schools. The model simulates the behavior of each individual element, named a 'boid,' that tries both to stick together and avoid collisions with one another and objects in the environment. The complex and dynamic flocking behavior is the result of the dense interaction of the relatively simple behaviors of the boids.
Production notes: The 'boids' software was written in Symbolics Common Lisp and ran on a Symbolics 3600 Lisp Machine. The skeleton scripts were animated by the S-Dyanmics animation system and geometrical modelling was done in the S-Geometry system.
Reference: *Flocks, Herds and Schools: A Distributed Behavioral Model*, p 25

Back cover, top right: Six Platonic Solids

Copyright © 1987 by Apollo Computer Inc.
Artists: James Arvo and David Kirk
Insights: The image was ray traced on an Apollo DN580 using "ray classification," an acceleration technique which employs 5D space subdivision. The marble was simulated using a solid texture formed by turbulent mixing of a stratified material. The fundamental solids depicted are the five originally identified by Plato, plus the recently discovered teapotahedron.
Reference: *Fast Ray Tracing by Ray Classification*, p 55

Back cover, middle left: Surprise

Copyright © 1987 by Middlesex Polytechnic
Artist: Keith Watters
Insights: The face, one of a series depicting emotions, was animated using a facial muscle process that incorporates a limited number of parameters to control the muscles, jaw rotations, eye focusing and eyelids.
Reference: *A Muscle Model for Animating Three Dimensional Facial Expression*, p 17

Back cover, middle right: Smoke in a shaft of light

Copyright © 1987 by Hiroshima University, Electric Machinery Lab.
Artists: Eihachiro Nakamae and Tomoyuki Nishita
Insights: This image was generated using a shading model for atmospheric scattering considering particle density.
Production notes: TOSBAC DS-600, color CRT, Graphica M508.
Reference: *A Shading Model for Atmospheric Scattering Considering Luminous Intensity Distribution of Light Sources*, p 303

Back cover, lower left: Smoky Room at Sunset

Copyright © 1987 by Cornell University, Program of Computer Graphics
Artist/Programmer: Holly E. Rushmeier
Insights: Light intensities for this image were calculated using the zonal method -- an extension of the radiosity method which includes radiatively participating media such as fog or smoke. The zonal method accounts for all surface/surface, surface/volume and volume/volume interactions. In this image note that portions of the smoke, as well as portions of the opaque surfaces, are in shadow. Also note that surfaces on the right wall which do not directly view the light source outside the window are indirectly illuminated -- partly by light reflected from other surfaces in the room, and partly by light scattered from the smoke.
Production notes: The image was rendered on a VAX 8700 at a resolution of 1000×1000 using software developed at the Program of Computer Graphics. The image was displayed using an HP 98720A frame buffer, and was photographed from the monitor.
Reference: *The Zonal Method for Calculating Light Intensities in the Presence of a Participating Medium*, p 293

Back cover, lower right: Flying Carpet 4

Copyright © 1987 by Schlumberger
Artist: Kurt Fleischer
Insights: This image is one frame from a simulation of a piece of cloth falling on some simple objects under the influence of gravity. It was generated by building computer models of the objects and then simulating the physics of their interactions. The cloth was described by specifying its size, stretchability, flexibility, and other properties, and then rendered with a texture map taken from a photograph of an oriental carpet.
Reference: *Elastically Deformable Models*, p 205